CENTRE FOR EDUCATIONAL RESEARCH
AND INNOVATION
INDICATORS OF EDUCATION SYSTEMS

EDUCATION
AT A GLANCE
OECD Indicators

1997

ORGANISATION FOR ECONOMIC CO-OPERATION AND DEVELOPMENT

Education at a Glance – OECD Indicators

The publication was prepared by the Statistics and Indicators Division of the OECD Directorate for Education, Employment, Labour and Social Affairs. This work was facilitated by the financial and material support of the four countries responsible for co-ordinating the INES Networks – the Netherlands, Sweden, the United Kingdom (Scotland) and the United States. In addition, work on the publication has been aided by a grant from the National Center for Education Statistics (NCES) in the United States. *Education at a Glance* is published on the responsibility of the Secretary-General of the OECD.

The OECD education indicators are published simultaneously with the volume *Education Policy Analysis*, which takes up selected themes of key importance for governments. The data underlying the OECD education indicators are accessible via the INTERNET [http://www.oecd.org/els/stats/els_stat.htm].

Organisation for Economic Co-operation and Development

Pursuant to Article 1 of the Convention signed in Paris on 14th December 1960, and which came into force on 30th September 1961, the Organisation for Economic Co-operation and Development (OECD) shall promote policies designed:

- to achieve the highest sustainable economic growth and employment and a rising standard of living in Member countries, while maintaining financial stability, and thus to contribute to the development of the world economy;
- to contribute to sound economic expansion in Member as well as non-member countries in the process of economic development; and
- to contribute to the expansion of world trade on a multilateral, non-discriminatory basis in accordance with international obligations.

The original Member countries of the OECD are Austria, Belgium, Canada, Denmark, France, Germany, Greece, Iceland, Ireland, Italy, Luxembourg, the Netherlands, Norway, Portugal, Spain, Sweden, Switzerland, Turkey, the United Kingdom and the United States. The following countries became Members subsequently through accession at the dates indicated hereafter: Japan (28th April 1964), Finland (28th January 1969), Australia (7th June 1971), New Zealand (29th May 1973), Mexico (18th May 1994), the Czech Republic (21st December 1995), Hungary (7th May 1996), Poland (22nd November 1996) and the Republic of Korea (12th December 1996). The Commission of the European Communities takes part in the work of the OECD (Article 13 of the OECD Convention).

The Centre for Educational Research and Innovation was created in June 1968 by the Council of the Organisation for Economic Co-operation and Development and all Member countries of the OECD are participants.

The main objectives of the Centre are as follows:

- *to promote and support the development of research activities in education and undertake such research activities where appropriate;*
- *to promote and support pilot experiments with a view to introducing and testing innovations in the educational system;*
- *to promote the development of co-operation between Member countries in the field of educational research and innovation.*

The Centre functions within the Organisation for Economic Co-operation and Development in accordance with the decisions of the Council of the Organisation, under the authority of the Secretary-General. It is supervised by a Governing Board composed of one national expert in its field of competence from each of the countries participating in its programme of work.

Publié en français sous le titre :

REGARDS SUR L'ÉDUCATION
Les indicateurs de l'OCDE 1997

TABLE OF CONTENTS

INTRODUCTION

Throughout OECD countries, governments are seeking effective policies for enhancing economic productivity through education, employing incentives to promote the efficiency of the administration of schooling, and searching for additional resources to meet increasing demands for education.

To inform the process of policy formation and to reinforce the public accountability of education systems, the OECD continually seeks to develop indicators that can provide an insight into the comparative functioning of education systems – focusing on human and financial resources invested in education and on returns to these investments.

A quantitative description of the functioning of education systems can enable countries to see themselves in the light of other countries' performances. Through international comparisons, countries may come to recognise weaknesses in their own systems, while also identifying strengths which may otherwise be overlooked in the heat of domestic debate. The OECD education indicators also show whether variations in educational experiences within a country are unique or if they mirror differences observed elsewhere.

The indicators presented here are the product of an ongoing process of conceptual development and data collection, the objective of which is to link a broad range of policy needs with the best data internationally available. Through extensive co-operation, Member countries and the OECD Secretariat are continually searching for a consensus in developing indicators that: *i)* express measures that are truly relevant to present policy debates, and thus give some genuine indication of performance relative to policy objectives and *ii)* use data that can validly be compared and feasibly be collected across countries.

The 1997 edition of *Education at a Glance – OECD Indicators* provides a richer and more comparable and up-to-date array of indicators than ever before. The 41 indicators that are included represent the consensus of professional thinking on how to measure the current state of education internationally.

The thematic organisation of the volume and the background information accompanying the tables and charts make this publication a valuable resource for anyone interested in analysing education systems across countries.

New developments

Education is an investment in human skills that can help foster economic growth and raise productivity, that can contribute to personal and social development and that has the potential to reduce social inequality. No equation can fully describe these relationships, but several of the new or enhanced indicators included in this edition allow for a better understanding of the cost and nature of the investment on the one hand and of the benefits or returns to education on the other.

On the investment side, the main expenditure indicator (B1) provides a more complete picture than previously of the structure of resources devoted to education. It is supplemented by two new indicators (B2 and B3) describing how governments differ in how they finance education, in how financial resources are targeted, and in the incentives they offer students and their families. Moreover, the indicator of spending per student (B4) has been expanded to show the total expenditure over the course of the typical student's studies, as well as annual expenditure per student. Investing in research and development activities is another way to try to improve aggregate productivity. A measure of the expenditure on research undertaken in non-instructional research centres and in private industry is included in Indicator B1.

To respond to increasing public and government concern with the outcomes of education, more than one-third of the indicators in this edition have been devoted to individual and labour market outcomes of education. There is a more detailed picture than in the past of the relationship between education and earnings (E4, E5), including an estimate of the relative rates of return across levels of education.

The effect of educational attainment on the labour force status of a typical person manifests itself not just at a single point in time, but over the entire life cycle. The number of years a person can expect to spend over the life cycle in employment, unemployment and out of the labour market (A3) now provides a long-term perspective on the relationship between educational attainment and labour force activity.

A comprehensive picture of mathematics and science achievement of primary and lower secondary students (F1 to F6) includes indicators of the relationship between students' achievement and their socio-economic background as well as their attitudes.

New indicators have been designed to help policy-makers to improve the foundations for lifelong learning.

As societies and economies have become more dependent on the production and use of knowledge, lifelong learning has become a central policy issue. This edition of *Education at a Glance* takes a first step towards reporting internationally comparable data on lifelong learning and its impact on society and the economy.

Indicators on participation in education (C1, C3 and C4) have been expanded to cover not just the young, but all age groups. Indicator C5 includes an estimate of the expected number of years of tertiary education over the lifecycle. Indicator C7 provides more detailed information on the percentage of employed and unemployed persons who have participated in job-related or career-related continuing education and training. For selected countries this indicator also provides, for the first time, comparative measures on the intensity of continued education and training, as well as information on the providers and financial supporters of job-related training.

Finally, the indicator on education and earnings (E4) has been expanded to reflect earnings not just at one point in time but also over the lifecycle.

The indicators give greater emphasis to tertiary education, which is now replacing secondary education as the focal point of access to rewarding careers.

A more dynamic picture is being built up of who participates in tertiary education. A new indicator (C4) estimates the percentage of today's school leavers who will enter university-level education during the course of their lives, given current conditions. It also gives information on the demographic composition of those entering tertiary education. Other indicators give a more comprehensive picture of the pattern of participation (C5) and look at international student mobility among OECD countries and between OECD and non-OECD countries (C6).

Rising demands for education require innovative strategies to mobilise resources, improve efficiency and stimulate education systems to be responsive. The relevant indicators on financing (B3, B4) have therefore been redesigned to provide new insights, including information on public subsidies to students and their families. Finally, student/teaching staff ratios have now also been calculated for the tertiary level of education (B8).

The coverage of the private sector has been improved.

Improved coverage throughout the volume of the private sector of education – with respect to both participation rates in institutions and sources of funds – provides a more complete picture of costs, resources and participation.

Enhanced indicators offer more insight into the learning environment and the organisation of schools.

Ongoing debates about teachers' salaries, professional status and time spent on instruction have sparked interest in comparative data on levels of teacher compensation, the amount of time teachers spend working, the number of classes they teach per day and the number of students in each class.

The indicator on teacher compensation (D1) has been expanded to the upper secondary level and now includes information on the criteria OECD countries use for salary increases. This indicator also offers insight into how structural characteristics of education systems, such as teachers' salary levels, class sizes and teaching hours, translate into teaching costs per student.

A new indicator (D2) has been introduced to describe the demographic composition and the years of teaching experience of mathematics teachers at the 8th-grade level. For the same group of teachers, there are also indicators on the way they spend their time outside the formal school day (D3) and on the size and organisation of their classes (D4, D5). Their students' out-of-school experiences are also shown, in terms of how much time they spend on homework or other out-of-school study (D8).

Trend data offer an insight into developments in the supply of and demand for learning opportunities.

The premise that current education and training systems must adapt to new conditions is based on an analysis of broad shifts in OECD economies and societies. That analysis, as well as a review of options and strategies for change, must be informed by an understanding of how education and training systems have evolved.

To this end, the 1997 edition of *Education at a Glance* complements its review of cross-sectional variation with a first set of trend indicators which examine how the demand for learning opportunities has evolved and who the main beneficiaries of public and private provision have been. Indicators show how the national resources invested in education (B1) and the supply of learning opportunities (C1) have evolved over time. But it is also possible to look ahead and calculate the future implications of today's education systems. Even without further expansion, the proportion of the adult population who have attained educational qualifications at upper-secondary or higher levels is set steadily to rise (A2).

Methodological advances have made the indicators more comparable.

In 1995, UNESCO, OECD and EUROSTAT introduced a new set of instruments through which they now jointly collect data on key aspects of education. The return on this collaboration, which was led by the OECD and carried out in close consultation with the OECD/INES Technical Group, has been substantial progress in the collection, organisation and quality of international education statistics as well as a reduction in the time taken to publish the indicators. The application of common definitions, the use of criteria for quality control, and improved data documentation have improved the international comparability of education statistics and led to an expansion of the knowledge base on which the OECD indicators on educational costs and resources, participation and graduation are based.

Furthermore, significant developments in methodology and new procedures for the treatment and reporting of data have enhanced the consistency and international comparability of the indicators.

Finally, for many indicators a significantly larger number of countries are now providing data.

Future priorities

The five editions of *Education at a Glance* have demonstrated that it is possib to produce a limited set of up-to-date and internationally comparable indic tors on education.

There are still deficiencies in the current management of comparative educ tional data, however, and the progress accomplished thus far has made cle how much further improvement is needed in terms of the coverage, validi comparability, accuracy and timeliness of the indicators.

More information is required on education and training beyond initial schooling.

As economies can no longer rely solely on a gradual expansion of init schooling to meet the demands for new and high-level skills, more and bet information is needed on education and training beyond initial schoolir and on their impact on society and the economy. This will require develo ment of data sources on enterprise-based training and continuing educati and training for adults, as well as information on other forms of learni outside school.

The knowledge base on student and school outcomes needs to be expanded.

Changing information needs also call for an expansion of the knowledge ba on outcomes of education, particularly student and school outcomes. Futu data collection will have to go beyond diagnostic assessments of relati country performance and seek to identify those factors of education pol that influence performance. Some schools achieve higher standards th others even though they may operate under similar socio-economic con tions. Such schools may be well equipped or have good teachers who excel their subject matter, know how to structure the material to be learne demand much from their students, obtain systematic feedback from stude on what objectives have been mastered, and give help to those who ë having particular problems. Some schools may be particularly well manag or have principals who stimulate teachers through enthusiastic and creati leadership in teaching methodology and foster an educational and soc climate conducive to learning. A significant expansion and analysis of t current knowledge base on student and school outcomes will be needed explore these questions.

Further methodological development is needed.

Finally, further methodological development is needed. The diversity of ec cation systems and differences in the structure of the governance of edu tion provide a challenge for international educational comparisons. Ev where data are reasonably accurate and adequate for the needs of natio information systems, they may, nevertheless, be inadequate for certain ty of international comparison. A number of significant comparability proble need to be resolved:

– One major constraint for the comparability of international educat indicators is the International Standard Classification of Educat (ISCED). ISCED, in its present form, is ill adapted to current needs ë imposes limitations on international comparisons of education sta tics as well as on the analytical use and interpretation of the indicato OECD is actively engaged in the development of a conceptually a quate and operational definition of the levels of education.

– Although substantial progress has been made in reducing doub counting, problems remain in particular with the indicators on r entrants and graduates. For the statistics on tertiary graduates a c sistent classification of tertiary qualifications will need to be de oped. It will also be important to develop better estimates of number of transfers between different levels and types of terti education.

– A consistent classification of types of educational programmes is yet available. The current distinction between general and vocatio programmes poses problems of validity, as it mainly draws on natio institutional structures and definitions, which differ significantly from country to country.

– Most countries report data covering participation in educational programmes outside the formal school sector only to a limited extent, even if the content of these programmes is similar to the content of ordinary school-based programmes.

– Many countries cover educational expenditure by households and other private entities only partially in their data submissions.

– Consistency has not been achieved in the coverage of expenditure for ancillary services, such as student lodgings, meals and transportation. There are also problems in comparing subsidies for students' living expenses between countries.

– Countries still differ in the extent to which they include research outlays by educational institutions in their expenditure figures. Countries also differ in the degree to which research takes place in educational institutions or independent research institutes.

– The methods for estimating full-time-equivalent participation have improved in recent years. However, the comparison of expenditure per tertiary student is still impaired by problems in defining and quantifying full-time-equivalent tertiary enrolment, particularly in countries which do not recognise the concept of part-time attendance.

	Financial and human resources invested in education											Participation in education			
	Expenditure for educational institutions as a percentage of GDP	Percentage of expenditure on educational institutions from private sources (initial sources of funds)	Annual expenditure per student in equivalent US dollars			Cumulative expenditure per tertiary student over the average duration of tertiary studies in equivalent US dollars	Teacher salaries in public lower secondary education after 15 years of experience		Ratio of students to teaching staff			Expected years of early childhood and primary education for children up to age 6	Years of school expectancy for a 5 year-old child (all levels of education)	Net entry rate for university-level education	Expec... yea... of tert... educa... for 17 yea...
			Primary level	Secondary level	Tertiary level		Annual statutory teacher salary in equivalent US dollars	Salary per statutory teaching hour in equivalent US dollars	Primary level	Secondary level	University level				
Australia	5.7	16.1	2 950	4 760	9 710	m	m	m	17.9	m	5.7	2.7	16.3	m	3.0
Austria	5.6	m	5 480	7 100	8 720	55 800	26 200	40	12.8	8.7	14.5	2.9	15.2	26	1.8
Belgium	m	m	3 350	5 780	6 390	m	28 360	39	m	m	m	4.4	17.6	m	2.5
Canada	7.2	6.8	m	m	11 300	21 260	m	m	17.0	19.4	17.3	2.4	16.0	48	3.7
Czech Rep.	m	m	1 810	2 690	5 320	m	6 810	10	19.6	11.4	10.9	3.4	14.1	m	1.
Denmark	7.0	6.0	4 930	6 310	8 500	35 610	28 990	39	11.3	9.8	m	3.1	16.3	31	2.
Finland	6.6	m	3 960	4 590	6 080	m	26 640	m	m	m	m	1.5	15.9	m	2.8
France	6.2	8.7	3 280	5 810	6 010	28 130	28 210	43	19.4	13.1	19.0	4.4	16.3	33	2.
Germany	5.8	22.3	3 350	6 160	8 380	46 170	37 060	52	20.7	15.0	m	2.8	16.2	27	1.8
Greece	2.4	m	m	1 490	2 680	16 270	16 420	29	m	m	m	2.4	14.0	16	1.9
Hungary	6.4	m	1 680	1 700	5 100	19 830	m	m	11.6	10.6	8.0	3.6	14.2	20	1.
Iceland	5.1	12.3	m	m	m	m	m	m	m	m	7.7	3.0	m	39	1.
Ireland	5.7	8.5	2 090	3 400	7 600	19 560	33 840	46	23.6	16.2	13.5	2.5	15.2	27	2.
Italy	4.7	m	4 430	5 220	4 850	20 150	23 360	38	10.6	9.9	29.1	1.0	m	m	n
Japan	4.9	22.7	4 110	4 580	8 880	m	m	m	19.5	16.1	8.5	3.5	14.8	m	2.6
Korea	6.2	40.6	1 890	2 170	4 560	15 640	33 580	m	31.7	23.7	m	1.7	14.1	m	2.6
Luxembourg	m	m	m	m	m	m	m	m	m	m	m	m	m	m	n
Mexico	5.6	m	1 050	1 960	5 750	19 680	m	m	28.8	18.1	9.6	2.5	11.7	m	0.8
Netherlands	4.9	3.0	3 010	4 060	8 540	33 290	35 340	37	m	m	m	3.0	16.9	34	2.
New Zealand	m	m	2 570	4 290	8 020	m	22 750	26	22.7	16.9	m	4.3	16.0	40	2.
Norway	m	m	m	m	m	m	21 120	35	9.5	8.7	10.1	2.8	16.2	25	2.
Poland	m	m	m	m	m	m	m	m	m	m	m	m	m	m	n
Portugal	5.3	m	m	m	m	m	24 560	36	m	m	m	2.8	15.7	m	1.
Spain	5.6	14.6	2 580	3 270	4 030	18 310	28 020	31	16.4	14.5	21.3	3.8	16.1	m	2.
Sweden	6.7	1.8	5 030	5 500	12 820	m	20 310	35	12.3	13.6	m	2.6	15.8	m	1.
Switzerland	m	m	5 860	7 250	15 850	57 460	50 400	48	15.7	m	21.5	2.1	15.4	15	1.
Turkey	3.4	2.2	710	510	3 460	m	m	m	27.9	23.7	21.5	1.0	9.3	16	1.
UK	m	m	3 360	4 430	7 600	25 840	m	m	21.9	14.9	a	3.4	15.3	43	2.
USA	6.6	25.5	5 300	6 680	15 510	m	30 460	32	17.2	16.5	14.4	3.0	15.8	52	3.
Country mean	5.6	12.7	3 310	4 340	7 740	28 870	27 496	36	18.2	14.4	14.4	2.8	15.2	31	2.
Indicator	B1	B2	B4	B4	B4	B4	D1	D1	B8	B8	B8	C2	C1	C4	C
Page	51	67	92	92	92	92	199	199	125	125	125	143	133	159	16

m = missing data.

Note: The student/teaching staff ratio is not the same as class size.

* Mostly short first university programmes.

** Mostly long first university programmes.

	Learning environment and organisation of schools		Individual and labour market outcomes of education											
	Percentage of 8th-grade students		Eighth-grade mathematics students' reports on the average hours per day of out-of-school study time	Educational attainment of the adult population and current graduation rates				Student achievement		Index of earnings differentials, university to upper secondary		Unemployment and education		
th matics hers more 0 years aching ience	in mathematics classes with 30 or fewer students			Upper secondary attainment or higher (25-64 year-olds)	Current upper secondary graduation rate	Tertiary attainment (25-64 year-olds)	First-time university graduation rate	IEA/TIMSS 4th-grade mathematics achievement score	Difference in 4th and 8th-grade IEA/TIMSS mathematics score	Men	Women	Unemployment rate of university graduates (25-64 year-olds)	Ratio of unemployment rates, university to upper secondary	
m	m	m		52.8	m	24.3	34.0*	546	127	162.9	144.3	3.3	0.5	Australia
m	m	m		69.5	m	7.9	9.6**	559	138	m	m	2.1	0.7	Austria
m	m	m		53.5	m	24.6	m	m	m	m	m	3.6	0.5	Belgium
.0	76.0	2.2		75.2	71.7	46.9	31.0*	532	130	149.6	166.5	4.6	0.5	Canada
.0	90.0	1.8		83.4	78.0	m	13.0**	567	164	153.5	153.6	0.7	0.3	Czech Rep.
m	m	m		62.0	81.3	20.4	28.3*	m	m	137.6	128.6	4.3	0.5	Denmark
m	m	m		65.4	102.3	20.5	20.7**	m	m	174.8	168.9	6.2	0.4	Finland
.0	97.0	2.7		68.4	87.3	18.6	m	m	m	180.0	169.6	7.0	0.8	France
m	m	m		83.7	88.0	22.6	15.7**	m	m	148.1	165.5	4.7	0.6	Germany
m	m	m		42.5	79.5	17.4	14.5**	492	161	m	m	7.1	0.8	Greece
.0	94.0	3.1		m	76.5	m	17.7*	548	175	m	m	m	m	Hungary
.0	100.0	2.4		m	m	m	17.4*	474	148	m	m	m	m	Iceland
.0	80.0	2.7		47.2	93.8	19.9	20.5*	550	149	m	m	3.4	0.5	Ireland
m	m	m		34.9	67.0	m	11.5**	m	m	138.8	120.0	7.3	0.9	Italy
.0	4.0	2.3		m	94.1	m	23.1*	597	140	m	m	m	m	Japan
.0	3.0	2.5		59.8	85.4	m	23.3*	611	105	m	m	2.0	1.2	Korea
m	m	m		29.3	m	m	m**	m	m	m	m	0.6	0.3	Luxembourg
m	m	m		m	25.7	m	11.1**	m	m	m	m	m	m	Mexico
m	m	m		61.2	80.0	m	19.0**	577	150	147.6	159.9	4.1	0.9	Netherlands
0	79.0	2.1		59.1	95.0	25.3	25.7*	499	147	163.0	146.2	2.6	0.8	New Zealand
.0	99.0	2.3		81.2	106.0	28.6	22.6*	502	150	153.3	146.8	1.7	0.4	Norway
m	m	m		73.7	m	13.1	m	m	m	m	m	2.8	0.2	Poland
.0	92.0	3.0		20.1	m	11.0	14.9**	475	165	176.3	174.5	3.3	0.5	Portugal
"0	61.0	3.6		28.0	72.9	16.1	24.0**	m	m	m	m	13.8	0.7	Spain
0	97.0	2.3		74.7	63.8	28.3	15.7*	m	m	151.5	138.0	4.2	0.5	Sweden
.0	100.0	2.7		82.2	79.4	21.1	9.1**	m	m	131.8	161.4	2.6	0.9	Switzerland
m	m	m		23.0	37.1	m	7.7*	m	m	m	m	3.3	0.5	Turkey
m	m	m		75.9	m	21.5	30.9*	m	m	162.1	209.6	3.5	0.5	UK
.0	83.0	2.3		85.8	75.8	33.3	32.0*	545	113	169.8	186.1	2.5	0.5	USA
.9	82.3	2.5		59.7	79.6	21.9	20.3	537	144	157.0	161.0	4.0	0.6	**Country mean**

2	D4	D7	A2	G1	A2	G2	F1	F4	E4	E4	E2	E2
3	222	234	33	319	33	326	279	303	257	257	247	247

A GUIDE TO THE 1997 INDICATORS

This guide summarises key results and guides the reader through the 19▪ edition of *Education at a Glance - OECD Indicators*. The 41 indicators in th volume are organised in 7 chapters:
- Chapter A: Demographic, social and economic context of education
- Chapter B: Financial and human resources invested in education
- Chapter C: Access to education, participation and progression
- Chapter D: The learning environment and the organisation of schoo▪
- Chapter E: Social and labour market outcomes of education
- Chapter F: Student achievement
- Chapter G: Graduate output of educational institutions

Three annexes provide basic demographic and financial statistics that c▪ help the reader to set the indicators in their national contexts, as well information on the coverage of the indicators and on methods, sources ar the interpretation of national data.

Chapter A: Demographic, social and economic context of education

In order to interpret differences in educational structures, processes ar outcomes between countries, the conditions under which education syster operate need to be taken into account. Such conditions include the dema▪ for education at the different levels and in the various sectors of education, well as the structures of governance of education systems and the attainme▪ profiles of different sections of the population.

On average, 60 per cent of adults in OECD countries have completed upper secondary education...

OECD countries differ widely in the levels of educational attainment of th▪ populations. In some OECD countries, more than 80 per cent of the popu▪ tion aged 25 to 64 have completed at least upper secondary education, b▪ that proportion is less than 50 per cent in Greece, Ireland, Italy, Luxembou▪ Portugal, Spain and Turkey (see Table A2.2a). With the increasing sk▪ requirements of today's economies, persons with low levels of attainme▪ find themselves at a distinct disadvantage in the labour market (see Indic▪ tors E2, E3, E4 and E5).

... but upper secondary education is now becoming the norm and the attainment gap between countries is closing.

A comparison of the attainment of the population aged 25 to 34 years w▪ that of those aged 55 to 64 years shows that the proportion of people co▪ pleting less than upper secondary education has been shrinking (s▪ Table A2.2a). However, changes are uneven across OECD countries, and su▪ stantial differences in attainment persist.

The proportion of the population aged 25 to 64 who have completed tertiary education ranges between 8 and 47 per cent across countries.

Differences between countries in tertiary attainment are even more p▪ nounced. In Canada, Norway, Sweden and the United States, more th▪ 25 per cent of the population aged 25 to 64 have attained tertiary educatic▪ while in Austria, Italy and Turkey this figure is only 8 per cent (s▪ Table A2.1).

Among older age groups women have lower levels of education than men...

The pattern of educational attainment among men and women in the adult population is uneven in most OECD countries, suggesting that historically women have not had sufficient opportunities and/or incentives to reach the same level as men. Women are generally over-represented among those who did not proceed to upper secondary education and under-represented at the higher levels of education.

. but for younger persons the pattern is now reversing...

However, these differences are mostly attributable to the large gender differences in the attainment of older age groups and have been significantly reduced or reversed among younger age groups (see Table A2.3). Today, graduation rates no longer show significant differences between men and women (see Indicators G1 and G3).

... and yet, women still earn less than men with similar levels of education.

However, despite these gains in educational attainment, young women still earn less than young men with similar levels of education. In all countries and at all attainment levels, the earnings of women are on average approximately one-half to three-quarters of the earnings of men (see Table E4.2). In addition, there is only a relatively weak tendency for earnings differences between men and women to decrease with the level of educational attainment. Differences in progression rates, types of course and fields of study, and the relative incidence of part-time work, may all affect the labour market opportunities of women relative to men.

Projections of future educational attainment suggest a narrowing of the attainment gap between countries.

What patterns of educational attainment will prevail if current graduation rates are sustained into the future? The projections of educational attainment shown in Table A2.2a show how slowly the average educational attainment level of the population would change over the next two decades if current graduation rates presisted. However, given current graduation and "second-chance" education, many countries with low levels of attainment at present in the adult population (Greece, Ireland, Italy, Portugal and Spain) would move nearer to countries with high attainment levels such as the United States (see Table A2.2a).

In OECD countries, persons with tertiary attainment can expect to spend more years in unployment than persons with lower levels of education.

Expected years in employment tend to rise with the level of educational attainment (see Table A3.1). However, the number of years in unemployment appears to be less affected by educational attainment, the main difference lying in the amount of time people spend out of the labour force.

Chapter B:

Financial and human resources invested in education

Education can help to foster economic growth, productivity, personal and social development, and a reduction in social equality. But as with any investment, there are costs. Chapter B provides a comparative examination of cost patterns across OECD countries.

Educational services are a major factor in national economies.

Taking both public and private sources of funds into account, OECD countries as a whole spend 5.9 per cent of their collective GDP on educational institutions, and in only 5 of 21 reporting countries is this figure less than 5 per cent of GDP. Under current conditions of tight public budget constraints, such a large spending item is subject to close scrutiny by governments looking for ways to trim or limit the growth of expenditure.

Government spending remains the main source of educational funding...

Most of this amount, 4.7 per cent of the collective GDP of OECD countries, is accounted for by direct public expenditure on educational institutions. Inclusion of public subsidies to households and other private entities for educational institutions (*e.g.*, scholarships and loans to students for tuition and fees) adds another 0.08 per cent of the collective GDP (see Table B1.1a). Government financial aid to students for living expenses can also be significant, ranging from below .05 per cent of GDP in Korea, Greece and the

United States to over 1 per cent of GDP in Denmark, Norway and Sweden (se Table B1.1a).

... but contributions by households and enterprises are significant.

However, public funding is increasingly seen as providing only a part of tot educational investment. Particularly at the tertiary level of education, fina cial mechanisms are being used to leverage the participation of the learne and third-party payers in the funding of tertiary education. In many countrie households, enterprises, and other private entities contribute significantly the funding of education. On average, private payments to educational ins tutions account for 1.2 per cent of the collective GDP of OECD countries (se Table B1.1a).

Among the 15 countries reporting data, the proportion of funding for educ tional institutions that comes from the private sector ranges from 2 per cent below in Portugal, Sweden and Turkey to over 22 per cent in Germany, Japa Korea and the United States. Differences between countries are largest at t tertiary level of education, with over half of tertiary expenditure on educ tional institutions coming from private sources in Japan, Korea and the Unit States and 2 per cent or less in Denmark, the Netherlands, Portugal and t United Kingdom (see Table B2.3).

On average, OECD countries devote 13 per cent of total government outlays to education.

Government funding of educational services ensures that education is n beyond the reach of all members of society. Education, however, does co pete for public financial support against a wide range of other areas cover in government budgets. On average, OECD countries devote 13 per cent total government outlays to education; Germany, Greece, Italy and t Netherlands spend less than 10 per cent, and Hungary, Korea, Mexi New Zealand, Norway and Switzerland more than 15 per cent (s Table B2.1).

Public funding of education is a social priority, even in countries with little public involvement in other areas.

In many countries where public spending is low relative to overall GDP, su as Korea and Mexico, the proportion of public expenditure dedicated education is relatively high (see Table B2.1). Likewise, in countries such Italy or the Netherlands, where education accounts for a relatively low prop tion of total public spending, total public spending relative to GDP is hi This is evidence that public funding of education is a social priority all countries, even those with little public involvement in other areas.

Public funds are largely spent on educational institutions but some countries provide sizeable subsidies for education to the private sector.

At the primary and secondary levels of education most public money is spe either directly by governments or transferred to educational institutions acquire resources. More variation in spending patterns can be observed the tertiary level: in 11 out of 24 countries, more than 20 per cent of pub spending at the tertiary level is transferred to households (through scho ships, grants and loans) or is transferred to other recipients which are educational institutions (such as enterprises or labour unions) (s Table B2.2).

The range of subsidies offered, largely at the upper secondary and terti levels, includes tax concessions, grants, loans and reduced charges for put services contingent on student status (see Table B3.2). In the majority reporting countries, the receipt of subsidies and the amount awarded depe on family income and satisfactory progress in studies (see Table B3.3).

General public spending restraints have created pressure to reduce spending, but other factors have pushed spending higher.

In the early 1970s, the dominant position of education in publicly func social programmes began to change as a consequence of two factors: slow economic growth and decreasing enrolments, with the drop in birth ra beginning to influence the size of the school-age population.

At the same time a number of factors, such as rising participation rates higher levels (see Indicators C1 and C6) and changes in teachers' pay, beg to exert upward pressure on education spending. Overall, as a proportior GDP, public educational expenditure has roughly held its ground, but data suggest a trend towards convergence of public educational expendit among OECD countries (see Table B1.t).

Expenditure per student varies widely from one country to another.

Policy-makers must balance the need to improve the quality of educational services for each student with the need to expand access to educational opportunities. While the optimal level of resources that will prepare each student for life and work in the modern economy is not known, international comparisons of per-student investment in education can provide a starting point for evaluating the effectiveness of different models of educational provision.

As a whole, OECD countries spend about US$4 880 per student each year but this average masks wide variation both between countries and between levels of education.

The range in expenditure per student is wide: from US$1 700 or less per primary student to US$5 300 or more; from US$1 700 or less at the secondary level to US$6 500 or more; and from less than US$4 100 at the tertiary level to between US$11 000 and US$16 000 in Canada, Sweden, Switzerland and the United States (see Table B4.1). It would, however, be erroneous to equate lower expenditure with lower quality since high levels of student performance (see Indicator F1) are achieved in countries which spend relatively little.

"Poorer" countries tend to spend relatively less per student, but there are exceptions.

Measuring spending per student relative to GDP per capita shows that among poorer countries, Turkey spends about half of what Hungary spends in terms of GDP per capita on the average primary student, while among the richer countries, Switzerland spends 25 per cent of per capita GDP on each primary student, and the United States 21 per cent. Spending at tertiary level shows even greater variation.

Expenditure per student rises sharply with the level of ucation, is dominated by staff costs and has a built-in tendency to rise over time.

Despite wide differences in absolute amounts, expenditure per student exhibits a common pattern throughout the OECD: in each country it rises sharply with the level of education, it is dominated by staff costs (see Table B5.1), and it has a built-in tendency to rise over time. This pattern can be understood by looking at the determinants of expenditure, particularly the place and mode of educational provision. Education still takes place predominantly in traditional school and university settings with, despite some differences, similar organisation, curriculum, teaching style and management. The labour intensiveness of traditional education accounts for the predominance of teachers' salaries in overall costs. Differences in student/ teaching staff ratios and staffing patterns (Indicator B8), teachers' salaries (Indicator D1), and teaching materials and facilities largely account for the cost differences among levels of education, types of programme, and types of school. Pay-scales based on qualifications, years of service, and automatic promotion make staff costs rise over time.

The higher the level of education, the more countries differ in expenditure per student.

Not only does expenditure per student differ between countries in absolute terms, but relative spending per student also varies markedly across levels of education. For example, at the secondary level, the variation ranges from 72 per cent of expenditure per primary student in Turkey to more than 180 per cent in Germany and Mexico. The most significant differences occur at the tertiary level: whereas Italy only spends 10 per cent more on a tertiary student than on a primary student, Mexico and Turkey spend between 4.9 and 5.5 times as much.

ow annual expenditure may nslate into high overall costs of tertiary education if the duration of tertiary studies is long.

Comparatively low annual expenditure per student may result in comparatively high overall costs of tertiary education if students study over a long time. For example, annual spending per university student in Canada is about a third higher than in Germany (US$11 700 in Canada as compared to US$8 400 in Germany) (see Table B4.1). However, due to differences in the degree structure at the tertiary level (see Indicator G2), the average duration of tertiary studies is almost twice as long in Germany as in Canada (5.5 years in Germany, which provides only "long university programmes" compared with 1.9 years in Canada which provides mostly "short" university and non-university-level tertiary programmes). As a consequence of this, the aggregate expenditure for each tertiary student is more than twice as high in Germany as in Canada.

Responsibility for funding tertiary education is largely centralised.

The level of government that has responsibility for, and control over, th funding of education, is likely to have control over decisions regarding hc those funds are spent. An important factor in educational policy is, therefor the division of responsibility for educational funding between nation; regional and local authorities. At tertiary level, over 85 per cent of final pub funds originate with the central government in 19 out of 25 OECD countri (see Table B6.1c).

At primary and secondary level, countries differ in the division of responsibility for educational funding.

At the primary and secondary level, however, countries differ significantly whether funds come from central, regional or local government. Four ba: patterns are observed (see Table B6.1b): *i*) the central government is both th main initial source of funds and the main final spender on education (e Ireland, New Zealand and Turkey); *ii*) the central government is the ma initial source but funds are transferred to regional or local authorities (e Finland, Korea and Mexico); *iii*) regional authorities are both main init sources and the main final spenders (*e.g.* Belgium, Germany and Switzerlan and *iv*) funding responsibility is shared between regional and local authorit (*e.g.* Canada and the United States).

An alternative is the transfer of public money to private institutions.

In some countries, final funding is transferred to government-dependent p vate institutions (see Table B6.2). In Belgium and the Netherlands, arou half or more of public money for primary, secondary and tertiary educatior institutions is transferred from government to private government-depende institutions.

The education sector occupies a significant place in OECD labour markets.

The number of teachers employed either full-time or part-time in primary a secondary education combined varies from less than 1.8 per cent of t employed national labour force in Japan and Korea to over 3.5 per cent in t Flemish Community of Belgium, Hungary, Italy and Spain (see Table B7.1). the tertiary level, the proportion ranges from 0.4 to more than 1.3 per ce This variation is explained not only by the size of the school-age populati but also by class sizes, teachers' working time, etc.

In all countries except Turkey, women outnumber men at the lower levels of education...

In all countries except Turkey, women outnumber men at the primary a lower secondary levels of education (see Table B7.2). Among teachers of ea childhood programmes, the percentage of female teachers exceeds 90 p cent in nearly all OECD countries.

... but women are generally under-represented in the better paid teaching jobs at the higher levels of education.

At the upper secondary level, the percentage of full-time teachers who ; female ranges from less than 25 per cent in Germany, Japan and Korea between 50 and 65 per cent in Canada, Hungary, Italy and the United Stat At the tertiary level, male teachers make up the majority in all countries which such data are available.

Student access to teachers improves from the primary to the secondary level of education.

Student/teacher ratios vary widely between countries. On average acr OECD countries, the number of students per teacher falls as the level education rises, from 18:1 at the primary level to 16:1 at lower secondary ; 14:1 at upper secondary (see Table B8.1).

At university level, estimates of student/staff ratios vary from below 10:1 Australia, Hungary and Mexico to over 20:1 in Italy, Spain, Switzerland ; Turkey (see Table B8.1), although better counts of full-time equivalent s dents and teachers would be required to produce fully comparable ratio

Chapter C: **Access to education, participation and progression**

Societies have an interest in both providing a wide range of educatic opportunities for children and adults and ensuring broad access to th opportunities. Early childhood programmes prepare young children soci; and academically for entry into primary education; primary and second education provide a foundation of basic skills that prepare young peopl become productive members of society; and tertiary education provides a range of opportunities for individuals to gain advanced knowledge and skills, either immediately after initial schooling or later in life. In addition, many employers either encourage, or even assist, workers to upgrade or reorient their skills in order to meet the demands of changing technologies.

In nearly half of OECD countries, over 60 per cent of the population aged 5 to 29 is enrolled in education.

Virtually everyone participates in formal education at some stage of his or her life. In more than half of the OECD countries, the number of persons enrolled in formal education who are aged 5 years or above exceeds 60 per cent of the population aged 5 to 29 years (see Table C1.1a). The variation between countries is largely explained by the uneven weight of tertiary enrolment: from 3 tertiary education students per 100 persons in the population aged 5 to 29 in Mexico to more than 15 in Canada and the United States. In the majority of OECD countries, universal enrolment starts between the ages of 5 and 6 years, although in Belgium, France, the Netherlands, New Zealand and Spain 97 per cent or more of 4 year-olds are already enrolled in either early childhood or primary education programmes (see Table C2.1).

In most countries, public schools compete with private providers...

In most countries, public schools compete with private providers of educational services. Private school participation rates range from around 1 per cent of all students in Ireland, the Russian Federation and Turkey to 35 per cent or more in Belgium, Korea and the United Kingdom, and about 75 per cent in the Netherlands (see Table C1.1a).

... but private schools depend on governments for funding in most countries.

However, only in Korea, Portugal and the United States is the independent private sector (in which less than 50 per cent of funding is from government sources) a fairly important provider (see Table C1.1a).

Compulsory education ends around the age of 15-16 in many countries with the transition to upper secondary education.

Compulsory schooling ends in OECD countries between the ages of 14 and 18, beyond which enrolment remains universal in half of the countries (although in Mexico and Turkey the enrolment rate has already sunk to around 50 per cent during compulsory education) (see Table C3.1). The sharpest drop in enrolments occurs at the end of upper secondary education in two-thirds of the countries. In more than half of OECD countries, the majority of upper secondary students are attending vocational or apprenticeship programmes (see Table C3.2), although women are less likely than men to pursue vocational courses.

The transition from upper secondary to tertiary education is less clear-cut.

By age 19, no country has an enrolment rate exceeding 75 per cent, and by age 21 only one is over 50 per cent (see Table C3.1). Only the Nordic countries report enrolment rates of more than 25 per cent for 24 year-olds. However, the age of transition from upper secondary to tertiary education varies. In some countries, a significant proportion of young people opt for a second upper secondary programme rather than tertiary education (see Table C3.2).

First-time entry rates to university-level education vary widely between countries. In 5 OECD countries they are 39 per cent or more.

In Canada, Iceland, New Zealand and the United Kingdom, 39 per cent or more of today's school-leavers can expect to enter university-level education at some time in their lives, and in the United States, more than 50 per cent, while the rate is only 15 per cent in Switzerland, where non-university programmes to some extent redress the balance, as may be the case in other countries too (see Table C4.1). These differences reflect variations both in the accessibility of tertiary education and the perceived value of attending tertiary programmes.

In some countries university-level education tends to immediately follow the completion of upper secondary schooling...

Traditionally, university-level education has tended to immediately follow the completion of upper-secondary schooling. In a number of countries this is still the case. In France and Ireland, for example, more than 80 per cent of all first-time entrants are aged 20 years or younger (see Chart C4.3). A similar age profile can be observed in Greece, New Zealand and the United States.

... whereas in others a prolonged transition has involved more flexible

In other countries, the transition has been prolonged by more flexible interspersion of study and work, often combining part-time study, distance learning or "sandwich" courses. In these countries, first time entrants to the univer-

interspersion of study and work and a delayed entry to university.

A growing minority participates in tertiary education: On average, a 17 year-old can now expect about two years of tertiary education.

Higher participation in post-compulsory education outweighs lower birth rates – in some countries, enrolment rates in tertiary education have doubled over the last decade.

Tertiary education is increasingly international.

Differences in educational attainment are amplified by subsequent training decisions by employers and employees.

sity level are typically older and show a much wider range of entry ages. Denmark, Norway and Sweden, for example, more than half of students en university-level education for the first time after the age of 22, and less th 20 per cent of first-time entrants are younger than 20 years of age (s Table C4.1).

Today, a 17 year-old in Australia, Canada and the United States can expect participate for three years or more in tertiary education, and in the majority other countries for at least two years (see Table C5.1). Demand has grown only in countries that have recently started expanding but also in those w longer experience of high-level participation. In many countries, tertiary ec cation is replacing secondary as the criterion for entry to rewarding caree

Despite decreasing birth rates in many countries, increasing full-time enr ment rates among 5 to 29 year-olds has kept total enrolment from falling. Fu time enrolment rates among 5 to 29 year-olds have increased, on avera from 51 to 55 per cent over the last decade, and the proportion of this a group in full-time tertiary education has doubled over the last 20 years (s Table C1.t). The general expansion in tertiary enrolments has been driven demand from wider and more diverse groups of secondary completers than the past.

The international, cross-cultural dimension of tertiary education is receiv increased attention. However, a relatively small number of countries enrol vast majority of foreign students (see Chart C6.1). The United States 34 per cent of the total, followed by France, Germany and United Kingdom, with around 12 per cent each, Australia (7 per cent), Cana and Japan (4 per cent each). Among all foreign students studying OECD countries, Japanese and Koreans (about 5 per cent each) comprise largest proportion from OECD countries (see Chart C6.2); the major prop tions from non-OECD countries come from China (11.1 per cent), India (3.5 cent) and other Southeast Asian countries (9 per cent). A broad measure the flow of students from and to OECD countries shows that the OECD co tries with the largest number of students studying abroad are Greece, Icela and Ireland (see Table C6.2): in some cases, insufficient provision of univ sity places at home explains some of the outflow.

In job-related continuing education and training (CET), participation amc employed adults over a 12-month period ranges from 28 per cent in Cana to 45 per cent in Finland (see Table C7.1a). Sweden has a relatively high r (42 per cent), even over a 6-month period. The degree of participation amc the unemployed appears in general to be lower, and it rises with the leve educational attainment, those with university degrees being at least twice likely to participate as those with primary or lower secondary qualificatic Skill differences are thus being amplified.

Chapter D: The learning environment and the organisation of schools

Ongoing debates over the level of teachers' salaries, professional status time spent on instruction have increased interest in the working condition teachers.

Ensuring that there will be enough skilled teachers to educate all childre an important policy concern in all OECD countries. Key determinants of supply of teachers are the salaries and working conditions of teachers and costs incurred by individuals in becoming teachers.

Salaries and working conditions are key determinants of the supply of teachers – and they differ considerably between countries.

Annual statutory starting salaries of public school teachers at primary l range from US$5400 to US$15000 in the Czech Republic, Gree

New Zealand and Sweden, and reach US$27 000 in Germany and US$31 000 in Switzerland (see Table D1.1a). Significant differences between countries with comparable standards of economic development raise questions about recruitment and retention policy, and the status of the teaching profession.

Comparing teachers' salaries with per capita GDP provides some indication of the economic status of the teaching profession in a country (see Table D1.1). In Korea and Spain the starting salary of primary and secondary teachers is more than 1.7 times the per capita GDP, which suggests that the teaching profession in those countries has a comparatively high standing. Starting salaries are lowest relative to per capita GDP in the Czech Republic and Norway. After 15 years of experience, statutory salaries are above per capita GDP in most countries.

Seniority is a universal criterion for salary increments. Performance, training and qualifications are other criteria that some countries apply.

Almost all countries report "seniority" as a criterion that is universally applied for salary increments (see Chart D1.3). In France, New Zealand and in Portugal at the primary level, "performance" is a second criterion. "In-service training" (*e.g.* in Spain) and "qualifications" (*e.g.* in Greece and the United States) are also criteria for salary increments.

Salaries are not the only factor educational budget decisions.

Decisions on education budgets represent trade-offs between factors such as salaries, class sizes, numbers of teaching hours and planned instruction time for students. Table D1.2 sheds some light on this relationship through a decomposition of statutory teachers' salary costs per student at lower secondary level into some of these factors. In countries such as Austria, Italy and Norway, annual teaching hours are relatively low and classes are small, resulting in higher costs per student. In Germany, Ireland and the Netherlands, statutory salaries are relatively high, but class sizes larger. The additional salary costs are generally more than offset by lower costs per student.

In 20 out of 25 countries the majority of 8th-grade students are taught by mathematics teachers aged 40 years or older.

Teacher demography is becoming a major concern in many OECD countries, particularly in the context of recent and future trends in student numbers (see Indicator A1). The recruitment of new teachers will therefore be an important issue for many OECD countries over the coming decade, particularly in mathematics and the sciences. On the other hand, years of teaching experience can be considered one aspect of the quality of teaching. Table D2.1 shows that most 8th-grade students are taught by teachers aged 40 years and above. In Germany, mathematics teachers of more than half of the students reported their age as 50 years or older. Professionals in other related fields are usually much younger.

The average time 8th-grade mathematics teachers spend on school-related activities outside the formal school day ranges from 9.8 hours a week in Ireland to 17.1 hours in Hungary.

A teacher's working day does not end when classes are over. Time for school-related activities outside the formal school day can contribute substantially to the workload of teachers. Eighth-grade mathematics teachers spend an average of 13 hours a week on school-related activities outside the formal school day on planning lessons, preparing and grading tests and other student work, professional development, meetings and record-keeping (see Table D3.1).

Eighth grade mathematics classes generally number 21-30 students, and whole-class teaching is one of the most common forms of classroom organisation.

In most OECD countries, the majority of 8th-grade students are in classes of between 21 and 30 students (Indicator D5). Sizes in the 4th grade are similar. Only in Japan and Korea are classes significantly larger: in 8th grade, 93 per cent of students in Korea are in mathematics classes with more than 40 students and 96 per cent of students in Japan are in classes with more than 30 students. Whole-class teaching is one of the most common forms of classroom organisation in 8th-grade mathematics: in most countries, around 50 per cent or more of 8th-grade students are taught in this way during most lessons or every lesson (see Table D5.1). Individual work with assistance from the teacher is equally popular, but students working together as a class and responding to each other, and group work, are in general less common.

Homework is an important tool, particularly at the secondary level.

The average time spent each day by 8th-grade students on mathematics homework ranges from half an hour in Denmark to 70 minutes in Greece and Spain (see Table D7.1). On average, students report spending slightly less time on science homework, while other subjects occupy between half an hour in Denmark and 2 hours in Greece. With the exception of Ireland, studying mathematics and science takes up more than half of homework time. The highest achievement in mathematics appears to be associated with a moderate amount of homework each day (between 1 and 3 hours).

Chapter E: Social and labour market outcomes of education

Education has many benefits, some of them unquantifiable. Social cohesion rather than narrow economic gain is the greatest prize for societies in which citizens use learning to become more effective participants in democratic civil and economic processes. No equation can fully describe this relationship. But the indicators can aid an understanding of some of the contributing factors.

There is a strong link between education and employment – whatever the unemployment rate or the rate of job creation.

Higher levels of educational attainment are clearly associated, for individuals with higher earnings, a lower chance of unemployment and more skills that yield social advantage. In all countries except Spain, where the unemployment rate for persons with tertiary attainment is particularly high (13.8 per cent) and France, Greece and Italy (around 7 per cent), unemployment rates for persons aged 25-64 with tertiary attainment are under 5 per cent, while the rates for those with less than upper secondary attainment range from 1 per cent in Korea to over 20 per cent in Finland and Spain (see Table E2.1).

With increasing unemployment and continuing upskilling of jobs, the position of those with low educational attainment has become increasingly vulnerable.

Since persons with less than upper secondary education still comprise a substantial proportion of the working-age population and of the labour force in most countries (see Indicator A2), an economy's ability to provide jobs adult persons at this level has a significant effect on the overall unemployment rate. Over the 1989 to 1994 period, in a climate of generally increasing unemployment and continuing upskilling of jobs, the position of this group relative to that of the rest of the labour force has, with some exceptions (Germany, Ireland, the Netherlands and Norway), deteriorated in many reporting countries, and most notably in Canada, Denmark, Finland, Spain, Sweden, the United Kingdom and the United States.

Unemployment rates of young people are substantially higher than those of workers in older age groups in all OECD countries.

Across OECD countries, unemployment rates among 20 to 24 year-olds with less than upper secondary education are, on average, about 22 per cent. Unemployment rates for this age group are under 10 per cent only in Austria, Korea and Luxembourg and are 30 per cent or above in Poland, Spain, Sweden and the United Kingdom and even above 40 per cent in Finland and France (see Table E3.1).

The situation for those with an upper secondary qualification is somewhat better: unemployment rates average 16 per cent for 20-24 year-olds and 10 per cent for 25-29 year-olds (but this rate is over 15 per cent in Finland, France, Greece, Italy and Spain). In contrast, job prospects for 25-29 year-olds with university qualifications are much more favourable in most countries, with unemployment rates under 8 per cent in 19 out of 25 OECD countries.

Education and earnings are positively linked, whatever the type of socio-economic system or the level of economic development.

The economic benefit of tertiary education can be seen by comparing ratio of the mean annual earnings of tertiary graduates with those of persons with upper secondary and less than upper secondary attainment (Indicator E4).

Among countries reporting gross earnings, the earnings premium for university-level education ranges from about 40 per cent for men aged 25-64 in Denmark and Switzerland to 80 per cent or more in Finland, France and

Portugal. For women in the same age range, the premium ranges from 20 per cent in Italy to 95 per cent in the United Kingdom. Upper secondary education is a break-point for many countries beyond which additional education attracts a particularly high premium.

The earnings advantage of increased education outweighs the costs of acquiring it.

From an investment standpoint, it is also necessary to consider the costs involved in completing a particular level of education. Social costs include both the direct costs incurred by public authorities and individual students' costs of tuition, materials, living costs and foregone earnings. A rate of return to this total social cost of an additional 10 per cent on individual lifetime earnings may be seen as "profitable". By this measure, both upper secondary and tertiary education prove worthwhile (see Table E5.1).

Chapter F: Student achievement

There is growing demand for indicators on student performance in order to make education accountable, to provide tools for school improvement, and to allow standards to be monitored. Indicators F1 to F6 focus on student performance in mathematics and science.

Variation in achievement between countries is substantial, with the average Japanese and Korean 4th-graders outperforming the average Portuguese 8th-graders in mathematics.

In mathematics, Japanese and Korean 4th-grade pupils score significantly better than those in all other countries (see Table F1.1). Korea also scores significantly better in science than all other participating countries (see Table F1.2). Achievement differences between countries remain substantial when compared with the average gap between children a year apart in age.

Some countries differ in their relative standing in mathematics and science, which suggests that variation can in part be explained by differences in curriculum and instruction.

Most countries that perform well in mathematics at the 4th-grade level also perform well at the 8th-grade level, which underlines the importance of primary education for later success (see Table F1.3).

The fact that there appears to be neither a strong nor a consistent relationship at the national level between the level of resources (see Indicators B1, B4 and B7) and student outcomes provides further evidence that variation between countries cannot be explained alone in terms of financial or staff resource levels and that the search for improvement in school performance must extend to factors that lie beyond material inputs.

Countries vary considerably in the achievement of their low-performing students.

Mean achievement scores are typically used to assess the quality of schools and education systems. However, mean achievement does not provide a full picture and can mask significant variation within an individual classroom, school or education system. In many countries, a sizeable number of students fall behind in performance and may face difficulties in following the programmes of study set out in the curriculum. Less than 5 per cent of 4th-graders in Iceland and Portugal reach the average level of mathematics performance in Korea (see Table F2.3).

There is also substantial achievement variation within each country.

The interquartile range – the difference between scores at the 75th and 25th percentiles – varies between countries in both mathematics and science, although the variation is wider in science (see Tables F2.1 and F2.2). In many countries the interquartile range of achievement is twice as wide as the average gap between children one year apart.

Some countries with similar levels of average performance show different spreads of disparities in achievement...

It is notable that some countries with similar levels of average performance show a considerable variation in disparities of student achievement. For example, Norway and New Zealand show the same average level of mathematics performance, but the 25th percentile in New Zealand is 14 score points below the 25th percentile in Norway, indicating that the weaker performers in

New Zealand have markedly lower scores than their counterparts in Norw (see Table F2.1).

... which indicates that a wide range of achievement is not a necessary condition for a system to attain a high level of overall performance.

At the other end of the scale, the stronger performers in New Zealand sco more highly than the stronger performers in Norway.

Some countries with comparatively low disparities in mathematics achiev ment at the 4th-grade level show wide disparities at the 8th-grade lev whereas other countries contain the growth in disparities better.

Some countries catch up at the 8th grade whereas others fall behind.

It is important to measure not only absolute performance but also progre from grade to grade. Iceland, New Zealand and Norway, whose 4th-gra pupils perform particularly poorly in mathematics, are among the countri with the highest gains over the four years (see Table F4.1). At the same tim there are some high-performing countries which even extend their advantag And there are countries that perform well at the 4th-grade level but f behind at the 8th grade.

Higher levels of parental education are associated with higher student achievement, and linguistic disadvantage may play a part in low achievement...

Children come from a variety of family, socio-economic and cultural ba grounds. As a result, schools are faced with a multiplicity of challenges as th strive to provide equal opportunities to all students. Parental educati continues to be an important source of disparities in student achieveme On average, the gap in mathematics achievement between students w report that their parents have not completed upper secondary education a those at least one of whose parents has, amounts to 28 score points, abc the same level as the average difference in performance between the 7th a 8th grades (see Table F5.1). The gap between those whose parents ha completed university level and those whose parents have less than upp secondary education is more than twice as large.

... but substantial differences between countries in this measure indicate that such disparities may not be inevitable.

However, there are substantial differences between countries in this measu indicating that such disparities may not be inevitable. An additional facto language: on average across countries, 28 per cent of all students from linguistic background different from the language of instruction are in t bottom 15 per cent in mathematics (see Table F5.1).

High mathematics and science achievement is associated with a positive attitude towards the subject.

Students who do well in mathematics and science generally have more po tive attitudes towards those disciplines (see Table F6.1). On the whole higher percentage of students have positive attitudes towards mathematics the 4th grade than at the 8th.

Chapter G: **Graduate output of educational institutions**

The award of a degree or other type of qualification marks the formal culmi tion of an investment in education or training activities. The level, type a field of a particular educational qualification earned can serve as use information to employers, signalling that the recipient has gained occupati ally relevant skills and knowledge.

Upper secondary completion rates range from below 40 per cent in two countries to above 85 per cent in eight, but they do not guarantee adequate literacy.

In all but two countries, the upper secondary graduation rate exceeds 64 cent. In 6 out of 23 countries, it exceeds 90 (see Table G1.1). The lowest ra are in Mexico (26 per cent) and Turkey (37 per cent). Gender disparities upper secondary graduation rates have been successfully eliminated almost all countries (see Table G1.1). However, Chart G1.2 shows that e among upper secondary completers in 7 countries, a significant propor have inadequate levels of literacy.

Increasing upper secondary completion rates appear to be pushing the expansion of tertiary education.

On average across OECD countries, 12 per cent of a typical age cohort c plete a short university-level programme (4 years or less); in Austra Canada, the United Kingdom and the United States, the figure is more t 30 per cent (see Table G2.1). The rate averages 8 per cent for long university programmes, 4 per cent for second university-level programr (from less than 1 per cent in Greece and Turkey to 12 per cent in Australia and the United States), and 1 per cent for programmes leading to an advanced research degree. Although first degree graduation rates for women equal or exceed those for men in most OECD countries, men are still more likely than women to attain more advanced degrees. Graduation rates for non-university tertiary programmes range from above 20 per cent in the Flemish Community of Belgium, Finland, Japan, Norway, Switzerland, the Russian Federation and the United States to below 3 per cent in Spain and Turkey.

The structure of upper secondary and tertiary education affects graduation rates.

The level or age group at which vocational and technical programmes are targeted in a particular country will affect that country's non-university tertiary graduation rate. University-level graduation rates are affected by the typical duration, graduation requirements, and variety of credentials offered at the tertiary level. In general, countries which do not offer short first university-level programmes have lower first university degree graduation rates than those which offer such programmes as well.

READER'S GUIDE

Coverage of the statistics

Although a lack of data still limits the scope of the indicators in many cou
tries, the coverage extends, in principle, to the entire national educati
system regardless of the ownership or sponsorship of the institutions cc
cerned and regardless of the education delivery mechanisms. With o
exception described below, all types of students and all age groups a
meant to be included: children (including those classified as exceptiona
adults, nationals, foreigners, as well as students in open distance learning,
special education programmes or in educational programmes organised
ministries other than the Ministry of Education, provided the main aim of t
programme is the educational development of the individual. However, vo
tional and technical training in the work place, with the exception of co
bined school and work-based programmes that are explicitly deemed to
parts of the education system, is not included.

Educational activities classified as "adult" or "non-regular" are covered, p
vided that the activities involve studies or have a subject-matter conte
similar to "regular" education studies or that the underlying programmes le
to potential qualifications similar to corresponding regular educational p
grammes. Courses for adults that are primarily for general interest, perso
enrichment, leisure or recreation are excluded.

**Regional groups
of countries**

The categories "OECD" and "European Union" in the tables refer to t
respective membership as of 1 October 1997 when this publication went
press.

**Calculation of
international means**

For many indicators a country mean is presented and for some an OECD to

The *country mean* is calculated as the unweighted mean of the data values
all countries for which data are available or can be estimated. The coun
mean therefore refers to an average of data values at the level of the natio
systems and can be used to answer the question of how an indicator value
a given country compares with the value for a typical or average country
does not take into account the absolute size of the education system in ea
country.

The OECD *total* is calculated as a weighted mean of the data values
all countries for which data are available or can be estimated. It reflects
value for a given indicator when the OECD area is considered as a whole. T
approach is taken for the purpose of comparing, for example, expendit
figures for individual countries with those of the entire OECD area for wh
valid data are available, with this area considered as a single entity.

Note that both the country mean and the OECD total can be significar
biased by missing data. Given the relatively small number of countries,
statistical methods are used to compensate for this. In cases where a categ
is not applicable in a country or where the data value is negligible for
corresponding calculation, the value zero is imputed for the purpose of ca
lating means. In cases where a data value represents the ratio of two valu

which are both not applicable, the countries are not taken into account for the mean.

ISCED levels of education

The classification of the levels of education is based on the International Standard Classification of Education (ISCED). ISCED is an instrument for compiling statistics on education internationally and distinguishes among seven levels of education. The *Glossary* describes the ISCED levels of education and Annex I shows corresponding theoretical durations and the typical starting and ending ages of the main educational programmes by ISCED level.

Country abbreviations

Australia	AUS
Austria	AUT
Belgium	BEL
Canada	CAN
Czech Republic	CZE
Denmark	DNK
Finland	FIN
France	FRA
Germany	DEU
Greece	GRC
Hungary	HUN
Iceland	ISL
Ireland	IRL
Italy	ITA
Japan	JPN
Korea	KOR
Luxembourg	LUX
Mexico	MEX
Netherlands	NLD
New Zealand	NZL
Norway	NOR
Poland	POL
Portugal	PRT
Russian Federation	RUS
Spain	ESP
Sweden	SWE
Switzerland	CHE
Turkey	TUR
United Kingdom	GBR
United States	USA

Missing data

Four symbols are employed in the tables and graphs to denote missing data:

a   Data not applicable because the category does not apply.
m   Data not available.
n   Magnitude is either negligible or zero.
x   Data included in another category / column of the table.

Rounding of data

Data may not always add up to the totals indicated because of rounding.

Chapter A

DEMOGRAPHIC, SOCIAL AND ECONOMIC CONTEXT OF EDUCATION

In order to interpret differences in educational structures, processes and outcomes between countries, e conditions under which education systems operate need to be taken into account. Such conditions clude the demand for education at the different levels and in the various sectors of education, as well as e attainment profiles of different subgroups of the population. Projections of educational attainment rates, sed on the current institutional set-up of the education system and current completion rates, provide a oad indication of skill supplies in the years to come.

This chapter shows demographic trends in the size of the youth population, rates and projections of lucational attainment and the impact of education on labour force participation and employment over the e cycle.

Demographic characteristics are an important factor in the design and implementation of education olicies. The number of children and young people in a population (see **Indicator A1**) is the primary eterminant of the demand for schooling and thus influences the demand for teachers, educational supplies d facilities, as well as other educational resources.

Similarly, educational attainment levels – and, by extension, the average level of qualification of the our force – is an important factor shaping economic outcomes and the quality of life for both individuals d society. **Indicator A2**, which compares populations on the basis of completed levels of education, ovides a broad and indirect measure of the stock of human capital in a country and of its evolution over ne (through an examination of differences between younger and older persons).

What patterns of educational attainment would prevail if current graduation rates were sustained into e future? Projections of educational attainment levels based on existing rates of upper secondary comple-on can provide an indication of this. **Indicator A2** shows such projections, which have been derived by acking existing cohorts of persons in various age-bands over time while assuming that they do not acquire dditional educational qualifications, apart from what could be expected from present rates of "second ance" participation by older adults. One outcome of this analysis is a clear depiction of how even relatively gh upper secondary completion rates in many countries (Indicator G1) will only have a gradual effect on the erage educational level of the population. Countries interested in more rapid improvement in the average ill level of the population will have to actively encourage, and finance, adult education and training ogrammes (see Indicator C7).

The effect of educational attainment on the labour force situation of an average person manifests itself t just at a particular point in time, but over the entire life cycle. In particular, people's level of education n affect the total number of years spent over the lifetime in employment, in unemployment and outside e labour force. While social and labour market policies are often designed to deal with the immediate our force status of an individual, the effects of educational attainment on labour force activity are mulative and thus educational effects are likely to have a larger long-term impact. The expected number of ars employed, unemployed and out of the labour market between the ages 25 and 64 by level of ucational attainment shown in **Indicator A3** provide a long-term perspective on the relationship between ucational attainment and labour force activity.

Since the values of the indicators shown in this chapter are largely a reflection of the history of rticipation in education, it is instructive to look at them alongside the indicators on the current output of ucational institutions (particularly Indicators G1 and G2). Such a comparison reveals the progress that tually all countries have made in recent decades in raising the educational attainment of their populations d in reducing gender inequality.

Indicator A1: The relative size of the young population

Policy context

This indicator shows the relative size of the traditional school-age population and forecasts the proportion of the population aged 5 to 14 up to the year 2010.

The number of young people in a population influences both the rate renewal of labour force qualifications and the amount of resources a organisational effort a country must invest in its education system. Oth things being equal, countries with a larger proportion of young people in t population must allocate a greater proportion of their national income initial education and training than countries with smaller young populatio but similar participation rates.

Evidence and explanations

Differences between countries in the relative size of the youth population have diminished since 1975, but the proportion of people aged 5 to 14 years still varies widely.

The proportion of 5 to 14 year-olds in the total population varies betwe 11 and 16 per cent in most OECD countries; the proportion of 15 to 24 ye olds is slightly larger (see Table A1.1). Although differences between cou tries in the relative size of the youth population have diminished since 19 there are still notable contrasts (see Chart A1.1). In Mexico and Turkey, mo than 20 per cent of the population are between 5 and 14 years old. Thus, t of the least prosperous countries in the OECD have both fewer resources allocate to education and more children over whom to distribute the resources (see also Indicators B1 and B4). Mexico and Turkey are clos followed by Iceland, Ireland, Korea and Poland, in which between 16 a 18 per cent of the population are aged 5 to 14. At the other end of t spectrum are Denmark and Italy, where the proportion of 5 to 14 year-olds between 10 and 11 per cent.

The proportion of young people aged 5 to 14 has gone through a cycle of modest increase and decline in all OECD regions.

In almost all countries, the proportion of young people aged 5 to 14 years the total population declined between 1975 and 1995 – in Canada, Ita Korea, the Netherlands, New Zealand, Portugal and Spain by 5 percenta points or more. The decline in the relative number of young people h somewhat eased the pressure on expanding school systems at the lov levels of education. However, the long-term decline in birth rates has sign cant implications for the rate of renewal of labour force qualifications, wh will reveal their full impact in the years to come. It should also be noted tl in most countries higher participation in post-compulsory schooling has o weighed lower birth rates (see Indicators C3 and C5).

Population forecasts suggest that over the next decade the proportion of 5-14 year-olds will stabilise in most countries and differences between countries in the relative size of the youth population will diminish.

During the last ten years the decline in the proportion of young people h slowed down in many countries – Italy, Japan, Mexico and Spain are t exceptions – and population forecasts suggest that over the next decade t proportion of 5 to 14 year-olds will stabilise in most countries (s Table A1.1). The exceptions are Ireland, Mexico, Poland, the Russian Fede tion and Turkey where this proportion is expected to decrease by 3 perce age points or more, and on the other hand Denmark, where it is expected increase by 2 percentage points. The forecasts also indicate that over differences between countries in the relative size of the youth population will continue to diminish.

Definitions

Data are derived from the 1996 OECD Demographic database. Projections are based on the UN Population database.

Table A1.1 shows the percentage of persons in different age groups in the total population. Chart A1.1 shows, for each country, the sizes of the populations 5 to 14, 15 to 24 and 25 to 34 years of age at different points in time. It thus provides an indication of the increase/decrease in the respective school age populations (in percentages). For a definition of the typical entry ages see Annex 1. The statistics cover all persons residing in the country, regardless of citizenship and of educational or labour market status.

◆ Chart A1.1. **Number of persons in selected age groups as a percentage of the total population (1980-2010)**

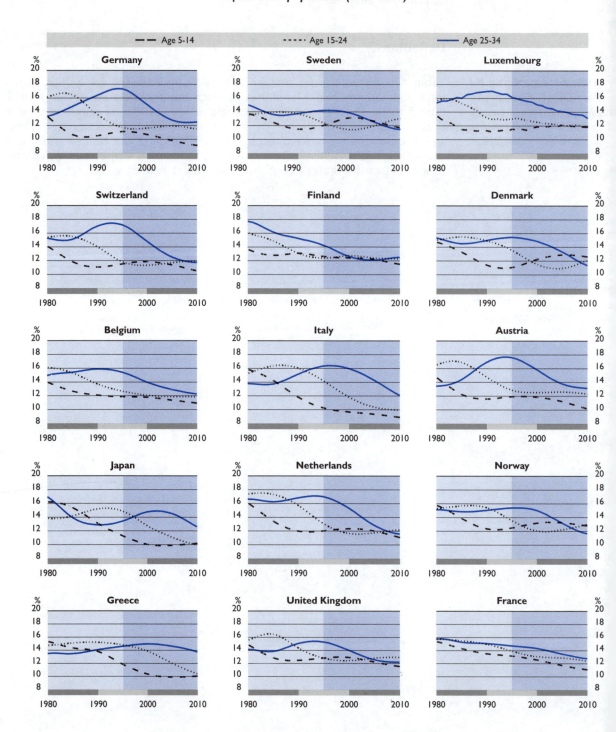

Countries are ranked in ascending order of the percentage of persons in the age group 5-29 (1995).

Source: OECD.

◆   Chart A1.1. *(cont.)* **Number of persons in selected age groups as a percentage of the total population (1980-2010)**

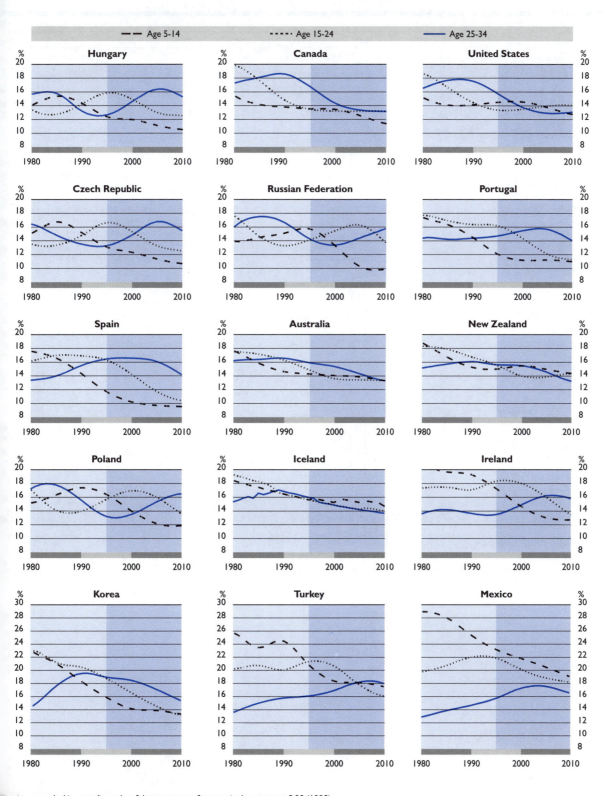

Countries are ranked in ascending order of the percentage of persons in the age group 5-29 (1995).

Source: OECD.

Table A1.1 **Number of persons in selected age groups as a percentage of the total population
(1975, 1985, 1995, 2005 and 2010)**

	Age 5-29	Age 5-14					Age 15-24	Age 25
	1995	1975	1985	1995	2005	2010	1995	1995
North America								
Canada	35.2	18.5	14.1	13.5	12.5	11.4	13.7	7.9
Mexico	54.1	28.2	28.0	23.9	20.5	19.1	21.4	8.8
United States	35.6	17.6	14.2	14.4	13.8	12.8	13.8	7.3
Pacific Area								
Australia	37.2	18.4	15.8	14.3	13.8	13.3	15.3	7.6
Japan	33.5	15.4	15.3	11.5	9.9	10.2	15.1	6.9
Korea	44.7	25.1	20.9	16.4	13.9	13.3	19.0	9.3
New Zealand	37.7	20.2	16.7	14.9	15.0	14.4	15.2	7.6
European Union								
Austria	33.4	16.7	12.2	11.7	11.2	10.2	12.8	8.8
Belgium	32.3	15.5	12.7	12.0	11.4	10.9	12.8	7.5
Denmark	32.1	15.5	13.3	10.8	12.9	12.6	13.5	7.8
Finland	32.0	15.6	12.8	12.6	12.2	11.5	12.4	7.0
France	34.7	16.1	14.3	13.4	11.8	11.1	13.9	7.4
Germany	31.1	16.0	10.7	11.2	9.8	9.1	11.4	8.5
Greece	34.7	16.2	14.4	12.1	9.9	10.1	14.9	7.6
Ireland	41.8	20.3	19.7	17.5	13.1	12.8	17.4	6.9
Italy	32.6	16.4	14.2	10.2	9.3	8.9	14.2	8.2
Luxembourg	31.7	15.2	11.4	11.6	12.1	11.8	11.8	8.2
Netherlands	33.8	17.8	13.4	12.0	12.0	11.1	13.4	8.4
Portugal	36.4	18.9	16.3	12.4	11.2	11.0	16.5	7.6
Spain	36.8	18.3	16.6	11.9	9.7	9.5	16.6	8.2
Sweden	31.7	14.0	12.4	12.0	12.6	11.7	12.4	7.2
United Kingdom	34.7	16.3	12.9	13.2	12.2	11.6	13.3	8.2
Other OECD countries								
Czech Republic	36.2	13.8	16.7	13.0	11.3	10.7	16.5	6.6
Hungary	34.8	12.8	15.3	12.4	11.1	10.5	15.8	6.6
Iceland	39.3	20.2	17.4	16.0	15.3	14.7	15.6	7.8
Norway	34.1	16.1	13.9	12.4	13.3	12.8	13.7	7.9
Poland	38.3	15.6	16.3	16.5	12.1	11.8	15.5	6.2
Switzerland	31.8	15.7	11.8	11.6	11.3	10.5	12.2	8.
Turkey	50.6	25.3	23.5	21.9	18.1	17.5	20.3	8.4
Country mean	**36.3**	**17.6**	**15.4**	**13.7**	**12.5**	**12.0**	**14.8**	**7.8**
Other non-OECD countries								
Russian Federation	36.3	15.8	14.5	15.9	10.3	9.9	13.9	6.

Source: OECD Database.

Indicator A2: Educational attainment of the adult population

Policy context

This indicator shows a profile of the educational attainment of the adult population and the labour force, providing a proxy for assessing the average level of skill of the labour force.

A well-educated and well-trained population is important for the social and economic well-being of countries. Education plays a role in expanding scientific knowledge and transforming it into productivity-enhancing technology. Education can also raise the skills and competencies of the general population, thereby broadening both economic and social opportunities.

On the basis of current graduation rates, the indicator also projects levels of upper secondary attainment in the population for the years 1995, 2005 and 2015.

Educational attainment – and, by extension, labour force qualifications – are important factors in determining economic outcomes and the quality of life for individuals and society as a whole. Educational attainment is not only an indirect measure of how much subject matter students may have learned but also of how much competency students have potentially acquired in learning civic responsibilities, social skills, work ethics and life skills.

Evidence and explanations

Educational attainment provides a convenient way of measuring skill levels in the labour force.

Educational attainment is often used as a proxy for measuring the quality or average level of skill of the labour force (*i.e.*, as a measure of human capital), even if many of the skills are acquired independently of initial education. Educational attainment is an indirect measure, largely based on formal educational qualifications, and only partially captures the skills and competencies that are acquired through continuing education and training or other non-traditional forms of learning. Furthermore, there is not always a close correspondence between educational attainment and the skill requirements of jobs, which are more difficult to identify and measure.

Overall levels of educational attainment

The proportion of the population aged 25 to 64 who have completed at least upper secondary education ranges from 20 to 86 per cent across OECD countries.

OECD countries differ widely in the average levels of educational attainment of their populations (see Chart A2.1). In most OECD countries more than 60 per cent of the population aged 25 to 64 have completed at least upper secondary education and in five countries – the Czech Republic, Germany, Norway, Switzerland and the United States – this proportion exceeds 80 per cent. In other countries, especially in Southern Europe, the educational structure of the adult population shows a different profile. In Greece, Ireland, Italy, Luxembourg, Portugal, Spain and Turkey, more than half of the population aged 25-64 years have not completed upper secondary education, with a figure as high as 80 per cent for Portugal.

Persons with low attainment levels are at a distinct disadvantage in the labour market.

With the increasing skill requirements of jobs in today's economies, persons with low levels of educational attainment may find themselves at a distinct disadvantage in the labour market (see also Indicators E2, E3 and E4). Similarly, countries with a relatively high proportion of persons with low

◆ Chart A2.1. *Distribution of the population by the highest completed level of education (1995)*

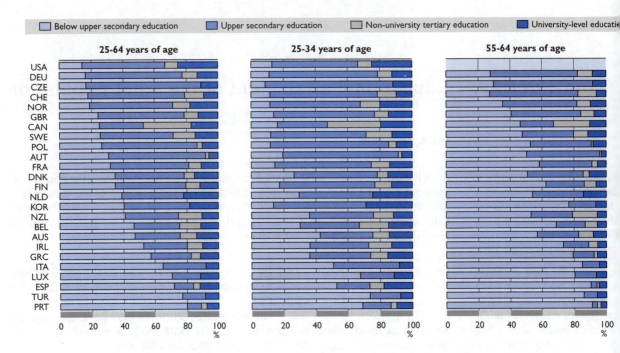

☐ Below upper secondary education ☐ Upper secondary education ☐ Non-university tertiary education ■ University-level education

Countries are ranked in descending order of the percentage of the population attaining educational levels below upper secondary education.
Source: OECD.

attainment may find themselves disadvantaged internationally in attract investment in high-technology sectors.

Educational attainment by age cohort

Changes in educational attainment over time reflect changes in the demand for skills and knowledge in the workforce.

Of key interest is the flexibility with which education systems have adapt to changes in labour markets and socio-economic conditions. Changes educational attainment over time reflect changes in the demand for skills a knowledge in the workforce. Changes in educational attainment can a follow the increasing emphasis which society places on graduating from s ondary and tertiary education. One way of looking at differences in edu tional attainment over time is to examine the attainment levels of differ age cohorts.

The proportion of persons not reaching upper secondary education has been shrinking in all OECD countries, but substantial differences in attainment remain.

A comparison of the attainment of the population aged 25 to 34 years with attainment of the population aged 55 to 64 years (see Chart A2.1) shows t the proportion of persons completing less than upper secondary educat has been shrinking in all OECD countries. The attainment gap within count is becoming smaller, with younger generations obtaining more education t their elders. The difference in attainment of at least upper secondary edu tion between 25-34 year-olds and 55-64 year-olds is 44 percentage point: more in Finland and France and it is as high as 63 percentage points in Ko In Austria, Belgium, Greece, Ireland, Italy, Poland, Spain and Sweden difference between generations still exceeds 30 percentage points. Howe the changes in educational attainment have been uneven in OECD count and substantial differences in educational attainment still remain. O persons may increasingly find their comparatively low levels of skills competencies overtaken by rising qualification requirements, and may find their limited basic educational competencies a hindrance in updating their qualifications through retraining.

The proportion of 25-64 year olds who have completed tertiary education ranges between 8 and 47 per cent across countries.

Differences between countries in educational attainment at the tertiary level are even more pronounced (see Table A2.1). In Canada 47 per cent of the population aged 25 to 64 years have attained a tertiary level of education – with the greater part at the non-university level. In Norway, Sweden and the United States this figure is more than 25 per cent, whereas in Austria, Italy and Turkey it is only 8 per cent. However, it should be noted that countries such as Austria, Denmark, Germany, the Netherlands and Switzerland classify many advanced vocational programmes at the upper secondary level. These programmes may be similar in content, orientation and qualifications to programmes that are classified at the tertiary level in, for example, Canada and the United States.

There has been a marked increase in the proportion of young people who have attained a qualification at the tertiary level of education.

Rising skill requirements of labour markets, an increase in unemployment during recent years and higher expectations of individuals and society have led to a marked increase in the proportion of young people who have attained a qualification at the tertiary level of education. In Belgium, Canada, Korea and Spain the proportion of persons who have attained a tertiary qualification is 20 to 22 percentage points higher among 25-34 year-olds than among 55-64 year-olds (see also Indicator C5 on enrolment in tertiary educational programmes). In Austria, the Czech Republic, Germany, Italy, New Zealand, Switzerland and Turkey this difference is below 5 percentage points (see Table A2.2b). The smaller increase in tertiary attainment between 25-34 and 55-64 year-olds in Austria, Germany, Italy and Switzerland may, in part, be due to the relatively late completion of the tertiary level of education in these countries (see Annex 1).

Gender differences in educational attainment

Women form the majority of those who have completed only primary or lower secondary education, and are over-represented at the non-university tertiary level...

Women are generally over-represented among those who ended their education at a level below upper secondary. There is also a prevalence of young women among completers of tertiary programmes that do not lead to a university degree or equivalent. Programmes at this level are often of shorter duration than university courses, and often lead to occupations with a traditionally strong female presence.

but the under-representation of women at the university level is mostly attributable to large gender differences in the attainment of older age groups.

However, the data suggest a trend towards greater equality in the attainment of men and women in most OECD countries. Differences in attainment between men and women are much more pronounced among older age groups; specifically, the proportion of women having attained only primary or lower secondary education is much greater among 55 to 64 year-olds than among 25 to 34 year-olds (see Table A2.3). It should also be noted that upper secondary graduation rates no longer show significant differences between men and women (see Indicator G1).

Educational attainment levels of the labour force

In the labour force aged 25 to 64, educational attainment is generally higher compared with the total population of the same age group.

A comparison of the distribution of educational attainment levels of the labour force aged between 25 and 64 (Table A2.4) with the distribution of educational attainment levels of the total population in the same age range (Table A2.1) shows a relatively higher percentage of people in the labour force with upper secondary and tertiary-level educational qualifications. While across countries, on average, the percentage of the adult population with at least upper secondary attainment is 60 per cent, it is 65 per cent in the adult labour force. The level of educational attainment in the labour force is higher than in the general population because adults with more education are generally more likely to participate in the labour force (see Indicator E1).

Projections of educational attainment levels

Projections of educational attainment levels show the patterns of attainment which will prevail if current graduation rates are sustained into the future.

What patterns of educational attainment will prevail if current graduat rates are sustained into the future? The projections of educational attainm levels up to the year 2015 presented in Table A2.2a provide a means answering this question.

Many countries with low levels of attainment in the adult population at present will move closer to countries with higher attainment levels in the future.

Projected attainment at ten-year intervals shows that on the basis of curr graduation and "second-chance" education, many countries with low level: attainment at present in the adult population (Greece, Ireland, Italy, Portu and Spain) would move nearer to countries with high attainment levels s as the United States (see Table A2.2a). Moreover, between 1995 and 2 some countries would overtake others in a ranking of countries by up secondary attainment.

However, these outcomes are based on the assumption of no change in current graduation rates across countries...

However, these outcomes are based on the assumption of no change current graduation rates across countries. The projected ranking of counti in 2005 and 2015 will remain fairly similar to what existed in 1995. This i: spite of the fact that many countries (such as Greece, Italy and Spain) likely to make large strides in the attainment of their adult populations, v increases of over 20 percentage points in the proportion of the adult pop tion gaining at least upper secondary education.

... while these are likely to continue rising into the next decade.

If current graduation rates are maintained, it will take more than 20 years some of the countries with low attainment to move close to the position r occupied by countries with high attainment levels. In practice, things will stand still – second-chance education will continue to increase as well graduation rates from initial education in most OECD countries. Howe these trends are likely to be more pronounced in countries which curre

◆ Chart A2.2. ***Percentage of the population 25 to 64 years of age who have completed at least upper secondary education (1995, 2005 and 2015)***

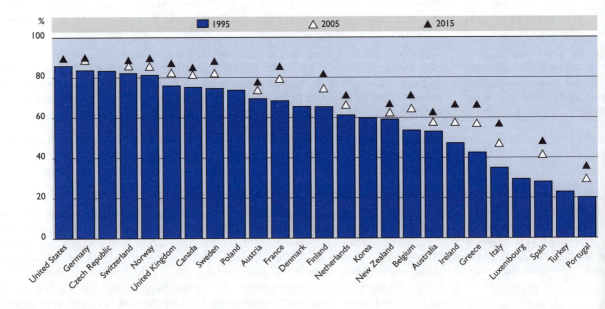

Countries are ranked in descending order of the percentage of the population who have reached at least upper secondary (1995).

Source: OECD.

experience lower levels of educational attainment in the adult population. If this is the case, countries such as Greece, Ireland, Italy and Spain will move closer to attainment levels currently observed in North America and other parts of Europe. In countries with already high upper secondary completion rates, the average educational attainment level of the population is likely to be driven up by further expansion of the tertiary level of education.

Age differences in levels of educational attainment are likely to be reduced over time.

These projections, based on current completion rates, show a narrowing of the attainment differences between younger and older age groups. This narrowing is simply a function of the "static attainment profile" used in the projections model (*i.e.*, as the incoming cohort ages 20 years, the educational attainment of 25 to 29 year-olds will be carried through to older age groups). For many countries with already high attainment levels for their young populations, the scope for increasing graduation rates from initial education appears to be limited. The option for these countries may be to try to accelerate adult education and training in order to enhance human capital at the older end of the age distribution.

Definitions

...ata are derived from National Labour Force Surveys (for details see Annex 3). Projections are based on the UN Population database and the UN World Population Prospects (1950-2050).

The attainment profiles shown here are based on the percentage of the population aged 25 to 64 years who have completed a specified highest level of education, defined according to the International Standard Classification of Education (ISCED 1976).

However, the education systems of many countries have changed considerably since the ISCED classification was adopted. As a result, many educational programmes now in existence cannot be easily classified and the contents of a specific ISCED level may differ between countries. Countries may not always classify diplomas and qualifications at the same ISCED levels, even if they are received at roughly the same age or after a similar number of years of study. Annex 1, which shows the average number of years of schooling corresponding to each completed level of education in each country, sheds some light on this question. For details on the methodology see Annex 3.

Table A2.1   **Percentage of the population 25 to 64 years of age by the highest completed level of education (1995)**

	Early childhood, primary and lower secondary education	Upper secondary education	Non-university tertiary education	University-level education	Total
North America					
Canada	25	28	30	17	100
United States	14	53	8	25	100
Pacific Area					
Australia	47	29	10	14	100
Korea	40	42	x	18	100
New Zealand	41	34	15	10	100
European Union					
Austria	31	62	2	6	100
Belgium	47	29	14	11	100
Denmark	38	42	6	14	100
Finland	35	45	9	12	100
France	32	50	8	11	100
Germany	16	61	10	13	100
Greece	57	25	6	11	100
Ireland	53	27	10	10	100
Italy	65	27	x	8	100
Luxembourg	71	18	x	11	100
Netherlands	39	39	a	22	100
Portugal	80	9	4	7	100
Spain	72	12	4	12	100
Sweden	25	46	14	14	100
United Kingdom	24	54	9	12	100
Other OECD countries					
Czech Republic	17	73	x	11	100
Norway	19	53	11	18	100
Poland	26	61	3	10	100
Switzerland	18	61	12	9	100
Turkey	77	15	x	8	100
Country mean	**40**	**40**	**9**	**13**	**100**

Source: OECD Database. See Annex 3 for notes.

Table A2.2a **Percentage of the population who have completed at least upper secondary education, by age group (1995, 2005 and 2015)**

	1995					2005	2015
	Age 25-34	Age 35-44	Age 45-54	Age 55-64	Age 25-64	Age 25-64	Age 25-64
North America							
Canada	84	80	71	54	75	81	84
United States	87	m	m	m	86	88	88
Pacific Area							
Australia	57	54	51	43	53	58	62
Korea	86	61	39	23	60	m	m
New Zealand	64	64	55	47	59	64	68
European Union							
Austria	81	73	66	50	69	76	79
Belgium	70	58	47	31	53	64	70
Denmark	69	65	61	47	62	66	69
Finland	83	74	59	37	65	74	81
France	86	74	62	42	68	79	84
Germany	89	88	84	72	84	88	89
Greece	64	50	34	21	43	57	66
Ireland	64	51	36	27	47	58	66
Italy	49	43	28	15	35	48	57
Luxembourg	32	33	28	20	29	m	m
Netherlands	70	65	56	46	61	66	70
Portugal	31	24	16	9	20	30	36
Spain	47	32	18	10	28	41	49
Sweden	88	81	69	52	75	82	87
United Kingdom	86	80	72	59	76	82	86
Other OECD countries							
Czech Republic	91	86	83	70	83	m	m
Norway	88	86	79	65	81	86	89
Poland	88	82	68	47	74	m	m
Switzerland	88	85	79	73	82	86	88
Turkey	26	23	20	14	23	m	m
Country mean	**71**	**63**	**53**	**41**	**60**	**69**	**73**

Source: OECD Database. See Annex 3 for notes.

Table A2.2*b*   **Percentage of the population who have completed tertiary education, by age group (1995)**

	25-34	35-44	45-54	55-64
North America				
Canada	53	49	46	33
United States	34	m	m	m
Pacific Area				
Australia	25	28	24	17
Korea	29	16	11	7
New Zealand	24	28	26	21
European Union				
Austria	9	11	7	4
Belgium	33	27	22	13
Denmark	20	25	21	14
Finland	23	23	20	14
France	25	20	17	9
Germany	21	27	24	18
Greece	26	21	14	8
Ireland	27	21	16	11
Italy	8	11	8	4
Luxembourg	11	14	12	6
Netherlands	25	25	21	14
Portugal	14	14	10	6
Spain	27	18	11	6
Sweden	29	32	29	20
United Kingdom	23	24	21	16
Other OECD countries				
Czech Republic	12	11	11	8
Norway	32	33	27	18
Poland	15	13	14	9
Switzerland	22	23	21	17
Turkey	8	9	10	6
Country mean	**23**	**22**	**18**	**12**

Source: OECD Database. See Annex 3 for notes.

Table A2.3 **Percentage of women in the population 25 to 34 and 55 to 64 years of age by the highest completed level of education (1995)**

	Age group	Early childhood, primary and lower secondary education	Upper secondary education	Non-university tertiary education	University-level education	Total
North America						
Canada	Age 25-34	45	51	51	50	50
	Age 55-64	53	56	48	35	51
United States	Age 25-34	46	50	57	50	50
	Age 55-64	53	57	56	38	52
Pacific Area						
Australia	Age 25-34	61	35	52	51	51
	Age 55-64	60	35	44	37	50
Korea	Age 25-34	59	51	x	40	49
	Age 55-64	63	24	x	13	53
New Zealand	Age 25-34	56	45	66	43	51
	Age 55-64	58	27	63	39	50
European Union						
Austria	Age 25-34	60	45	74	42	49
	Age 55-64	63	41	39	26	52
Belgium	Age 25-34	45	48	62	46	49
	Age 55-64	54	48	55	23	51
Denmark	Age 25-34	48	47	57	51	49
	Age 55-64	59	42	47	43	51
Finland	Age 25-34	44	50	58	46	49
	Age 55-64	53	56	46	36	52
France	Age 25-34	56	47	57	51	50
	Age 55-64	57	45	62	34	52
Germany	Age 25-34	58	49	44	44	49
	Age 55-64	73	47	26	25	50
Greece	Age 25-34	51	52	52	57	52
	Age 55-64	56	47	28	26	52
Ireland	Age 25-34	43	57	53	50	50
	Age 55-64	49	59	58	34	50
Italy	Age 25-34	48	52	x	53	50
	Age 55-64	54	44	x	32	52
Luxembourg	Age 25-34	49	52	x	42	49
	Age 55-64	55	38	x	22	51
Netherlands	Age 25-34	48	50	a	48	49
	Age 55-64	62	38	a	35	50
Portugal	Age 25-34	49	54	72	58	52
	Age 55-64	53	35	74	33	53
Spain	Age 25-34	48	49	44	57	50
	Age 55-64	54	42	23	37	52
Sweden	Age 25-34	44	49	53	49	49
	Age 55-64	49	51	51	46	50
United Kingdom	Age 25-34	54	49	52	44	49
	Age 55-64	63	43	61	31	52
Other OECD countries						
Czech Republic	Age 25-34	56	49	x	42	49
	Age 55-64	76	45	x	31	53
Norway	Age 25-34	43	47	52	55	49
	Age 55-64	56	50	48	35	51
Poland	Age 25-34	45	48	80	54	49
	Age 55-64	61	46	77	44	54
Switzerland	Age 25-34	62	53	25	38	49
	Age 55-64	73	52	18	26	52
Turkey	Age 25-34	52	41	a	44	49
	Age 55-64	m	38	a	25	m
Country mean	**Age 25-34**	**51**	**49**	**56**	**48**	**50**
	Age 55-64	**59**	**44**	**49**	**32**	**52**

Source: OECD Database. See Annex 3 for notes.

Table A2.4 **Percentage of the labour force 25 to 64 years of age by the highest completed level of education (1995)**

	Early childhood, primary and lower secondary education	Upper secondary education	Non-university tertiary education	University-level education	Total
North America					
Canada	19	29	32	19	100
United States	11	52	9	28	100
Pacific Area					
Australia	42	31	12	16	100
Korea	39	41	x	20	100
New Zealand	36	37	16	12	100
European Union					
Austria	24	66	2	7	100
Belgium	37	32	17	14	100
Denmark	33	44	7	16	100
Finland	30	47	10	13	100
France	25	54	9	12	100
Germany	12	62	11	15	100
Greece	52	26	8	15	100
Ireland	45	29	12	13	100
Italy	56	33	x	11	100
Luxembourg	63	21	x	16	100
Netherlands	31	43	a	27	100
Portugal	76	10	4	9	100
Spain	64	15	6	16	100
Sweden	24	47	14	15	100
United Kingdom	19	57	10	14	100
Other OECD countries					
Czech Republic	12	76	x	12	100
Norway	15	53	12	20	100
Poland	21	64	4	12	100
Switzerland	15	61	14	10	100
Turkey	76	15	a	9	100
Country mean	**35**	**42**	**10**	**15**	**100**

Source: OECD Database. See Annex 3 for notes.

Indicator A3: Expected years in employment, unemployment and outside the labour market between ages 25 and 64 by level of educational attainment

Policy context

This indicator shows how the years between the ages 25 and 64 are divided between employment, unemployment and time outside the labour market for individuals at each level of educational attainment.

The effect of educational attainment on the labour force status of a typical person manifests itself not just at a single point in time, but over the entire life cycle. In particular, it affects the total number of years over a lifetime which are spent in employment, in unemployment and outside the labour force. While social and labour market policies are often designed to deal with the immediate labour force status of an individual, the effects of educational attainment on labour force activity are cumulative and likely to have a larger long-term impact. The expected number of years employed, unemployed and out of the labour market between the ages 25 and 64 by level of educational attainment can provide a long-term perspective on the relationship between educational attainment and labour force activity.

Evidence and explanations

Persons with tertiary attainment can expect to spend more years employed than persons with upper secondary education or less.

Expected years in employment tend to rise with the level of educational attainment, except in Greece and Turkey and for females in Korea. Over the period between the ages of 25 and 64, persons with tertiary attainment in OECD countries can expect to spend on average more years in employment and fewer years in unemployment or out of the labour force than can persons with upper secondary education or less. For women, the differences in expected years in employment between tertiary graduates and women with lower levels of education are substantial. Over the life cycle, the trade-off seems to be more between employment and time outside the labour force than between employment and unemployment – that is, lower expected years in employment tend to be mirrored more by higher expected years outside the labour force than by years in unemployment. This reflects both lower participation rates and a higher incidence of early retirement among those with lower levels of education.

But estimates of expected time in employment, unemployment and inactivity assume that current labour market conditions will continue into the future.

The estimates shown here of expected time in employment, in unemployment and outside the labour force over the period from 25 to 64 years of age need to be treated with some caution. They are based on the observed labour force situation of persons presently 25 to 64 years of age and assume that current labour market conditions will continue into the future, both in general and for each attainment level and age group. Older persons with low attainment levels (particularly less than upper secondary) who are currently in the labour force started work at a time in the past when low educational levels were less of a handicap.

◆ Chart A3.1. **Expected years in employment, out of the labour force and in unemployment for persons aged 25-64, men and women (1995)**

Countries are ranked in descending order of the years in employment for men with upper secondary education.

Source: OECD.

On average across countries, women are expected to spend about 9 years more outside the labour force than men between the ages of 25 and 65.

On average across OECD countries for all levels of educational attainment, males between the ages of 25 and 64 spend 6 years outside the labour force and 2 years unemployed. Expected years of employment vary between 27 in Finland and 37 in Switzerland, years outside the labour force range from 2 and a half in Switzerland to 9 in Belgium and Poland, and years of unemployment from one-half in the Czech Republic, Korea and Luxembourg to about 5 in Finland and Spain. Women have, on average across countries, about 9 years less of expected employment and 9 years more of expected time outside the labour force than have men. The greatest differences in the numbers of years for which men and women can expect to be employed – around 14 years or more – are found in Greece, Ireland, Italy, Korea, Luxembourg, Spain and Turkey. Expected years of unemployment are roughly equal for men and women.

Variation between countries is much greater for women than for men.

Variation between countries in labour force activity is much greater for women than for men. Expected years of employment for women vary between 11 in Turkey and 33 in Sweden, years out of the labour force between 5 in Sweden and 28 in Turkey, and years of unemployment between a few months in Korea and 5 years in Finland and Spain.

Differences in expected years in employment between tertiary graduates and those with lower levels of education are larger for women than for men.

The average 25 year-old man with tertiary-level attainment in OECD countries can expect to spend, over the period between his 25th and 65th birthdays, over 34 years in employment, about a year and a half in unemployment and over 4 years outside the labour force. The corresponding figures for a female tertiary graduate are 29 years in employment, 1.3 years in unemployment and about 10 years outside the labour force. By contrast, a man with upper secondary attainment can expect to spend about 32 years in employment, 2 years in unemployment and 6 years outside the labour force, the estimates for women being about 23 years in employment, 2 years in unemployment and 15 years outside the labour force. Thus, on average across all countries and between the ages of 25 and 65, tertiary attainment results in only two and a half more years of employment among male tertiary graduates but six more years of employment for female tertiary graduates relative to upper secondary completers of the same gender. Differences between the genders are therefore less marked for those with higher educational attainment levels.

Differences in expected years of unemployment across educational levels are small.

Over the life cycle, educational attainment appears to have a larger impact on the extent of employment and of time outside the labour force than on the extent of unemployment. Unemployment, although it can be prolonged in some countries, is generally sporadic, whereas years outside the labour force can accumulate rapidly as a result of more or less permanent withdrawal from the labour force, for example because of caring for children, inadequate skill levels or early retirement.

Definitions

Data are derived from National Labour Force Surveys (for details see Annex 3).

This indicator shows expected years in employment, outside the labour force and in unemployment for men and women aged 25 to 64 with different levels of educational attainment. These estimates are calculated by summing, over all age groups, the product of age-specific ratios of employment, unemployment and inactivity to population ratios and the number of years in each corresponding age group (see Annex 3 for a description of the methodology). The total number of years spent in the three statuses, that is, employed, unemployed and not in the labour force, is 40 – the number of years from 25 to 64 years. The labour force statuses are defined according to the guidelines specified by the International Labour Office.

Table A3.1a **Expected years in employment, out of the labour force and in unemployment for men aged 25-64 (1995)**

	Expected years in employment				Expected years out of the labour market				Expected years in unemployment			
	Below upper secondary education	Upper secondary education	Tertiary education	All levels of education	Below upper secondary education	Upper secondary education	Tertiary education	All levels of education	Below upper secondary education	Upper secondary education	Tertiary education	All levels of education
North America												
Canada	25.8	30.8	32.7	30.3	10.1	6.4	5.1	6.9	4.1	2.8	2.3	2
United States	25.4	32.2	35.4	32.3	11.6	6.1	3.5	6.1	3.0	1.7	1.1	1
Pacific Area												
Australia	28.9	32.3	34.4	31.5	7.6	5.5	4.0	6.0	3.5	2.2	1.6	2
Korea	35.2	35.7	36.7	35.7	4.2	3.7	2.7	3.7	0.6	0.6	0.6	0
New Zealand	29.5	34.5	35.2	32.6	8.2	4.4	3.6	5.9	2.3	1.1	1.2	
European Union												
Austria	28.9	31.8	35.8	31.4	9.5	7.3	3.6	7.6	1.6	0.9	0.6	
Belgium	25.8	31.3	33.7	29.0	11.2	7.3	5.4	9.0	3.0	1.4	0.9	2
Denmark	27.7	32.2	35.2	30.8	8.4	4.9	2.9	6.1	4.0	2.8	2.0	3
Finland	23.3	26.8	31.7	26.6	9.9	7.4	5.2	8.1	6.8	5.8	3.1	
France	26.3	30.8	33.2	29.8	9.3	6.7	4.6	7.4	4.4	2.5	2.1	2
Germany	26.9	31.5	34.8	31.9	8.6	6.2	3.6	5.7	4.5	2.3	1.6	2
Greece	33.0	31.5	32.9	32.8	5.2	6.9	5.2	5.4	1.8	1.7	1.9	
Ireland	27.2	32.9	35.4	30.0	7.8	4.7	3.2	6.5	5.0	2.3	1.4	3
Italy	28.8	31.8	34.0	29.7	9.0	6.9	4.2	8.4	2.2	1.4	1.8	
Luxembourg	29.8	33.1	36.0	31.1	9.5	6.3	3.9	8.3	0.7	0.6	0.1	
Netherlands	27.8	31.7	33.1	30.7	10.3	7.2	5.8	8.0	1.9	1.1	1.1	
Portugal	32.1	31.4	35.2	32.3	6.0	6.9	3.5	6.0	1.9	1.6	1.4	
Spain	27.3	30.6	32.8	28.4	7.2	5.5	4.2	6.8	5.6	3.9	2.9	
Sweden	32.2	33.6	35.1	33.6	3.5	3.0	2.9	3.2	4.3	3.3	2.0	
United Kingdom	24.6	31.8	34.2	31.0	10.0	5.3	4.2	6.0	5.4	2.9	1.6	
Other OECD countries												
Czech Republic	27.1	33.4	36.5	33.2	10.1	6.0	3.4	6.1	2.8	0.6	0.2	
Norway	28.6	33.6	36.3	33.2	9.3	5.0	2.8	5.4	2.2	1.4	0.9	
Poland	24.8	27.9	33.6	28.1	10.6	9.2	5.1	8.9	4.6	2.9	1.3	
Switzerland	33.7	36.7	37.3	36.5	4.0	2.5	2.0	2.5	2.3	0.9	0.7	
Turkey	35.3	28.4	29.9	34.0	3.0	9.9	9.2	4.4	1.7	1.6	1.0	
Country mean	**28.6**	**31.9**	**34.4**	**31.5**	**8.2**	**6.0**	**4.2**	**6.3**	**3.2**	**2.0**	**1.4**	

Source: OECD Database. See Annex 3 for notes.

Table A3.1*b*   **Expected years in employment, out of the labour force and in unemployment for women aged 25-64 (1995)**

	Expected years in employment				Expected years out of the labour market				Expected years in unemployment			
	Below upper secondary education	Upper secondary education	Tertiary education	All levels of education	Below upper secondary education	Upper secondary education	Tertiary education	All levels of education	Below upper secondary education	Upper secondary education	Tertiary education	All levels of education
North America												
Canada	16.9	24.4	28.3	24.2	20.5	13.4	9.8	13.7	2.6	2.2	1.8	2.1
United States	17.4	26.4	30.9	26.4	21.0	12.3	8.3	12.4	1.6	1.3	0.8	1.2
Pacific Area												
Australia	20.3	22.1	28.7	22.5	18.4	16.4	10.2	16.2	1.3	1.4	1.1	1.3
Korea	23.3	17.4	19.2	21.9	16.6	22.4	20.7	18.0	0.1	0.2	0.1	0.2
New Zealand	21.3	27.2	28.9	24.5	17.4	11.8	10.3	14.4	1.3	0.9	0.8	1.0
European Union												
Austria	19.9	23.6	30.1	22.7	18.7	15.5	9.2	16.3	1.3	0.8	0.7	1.0
Belgium	14.0	20.6	27.1	19.3	22.5	17.0	11.9	18.3	3.5	2.5	1.1	2.4
Denmark	22.6	29.3	33.6	26.8	12.8	7.4	4.9	9.7	4.6	3.3	1.5	3.4
Finland	21.1	25.7	30.6	25.1	12.6	9.4	7.2	10.2	6.3	4.9	2.2	4.7
France	18.3	24.2	28.9	23.1	17.8	12.5	9.3	13.8	3.9	3.3	1.8	3.1
Germany	15.7	24.3	30.5	23.4	21.9	13.0	7.5	14.1	2.4	2.7	2.1	2.5
Greece	14.8	14.2	24.1	17.0	23.4	23.7	13.6	20.9	1.8	2.1	2.3	2.1
Ireland	10.6	18.0	27.8	16.2	26.8	20.4	11.1	21.8	2.6	1.6	1.2	1.9
Italy	12.0	21.3	27.8	15.4	26.1	16.8	9.7	22.6	2.0	1.9	2.5	2.0
Luxembourg	14.2	22.5	29.7	16.7	24.9	17.1	10.0	22.5	0.9	0.5	0.3	0.8
Netherlands	15.2	22.2	27.5	20.1	23.1	16.3	11.2	18.4	1.6	1.5	1.2	1.5
Portugal	22.6	24.8	33.2	24.0	15.6	13.2	6.0	14.3	1.8	2.0	0.9	1.7
Spain	11.1	18.3	26.6	13.7	24.2	16.5	9.3	21.6	4.7	5.2	4.1	4.7
Sweden	28.2	32.9	35.4	32.5	8.3	4.6	3.3	5.2	3.5	2.6	1.3	2.4
United Kingdom	19.7	27.6	31.6	26.2	18.3	10.7	7.3	12.2	2.0	1.7	1.0	1.6
Other OECD countries												
Czech Republic	22.4	28.4	33.5	27.4	15.7	10.8	6.2	11.7	1.9	0.8	0.3	1.0
Norway	21.0	29.5	34.6	28.9	17.3	9.5	4.9	10.1	1.7	1.0	0.6	1.0
Poland	18.2	22.2	29.3	22.6	17.8	14.5	9.3	14.4	3.9	3.3	1.3	3.0
Switzerland	24.2	26.6	30.7	26.3	14.2	12.6	8.6	12.8	1.6	0.9	0.7	1.0
Turkey	10.7	8.2	19.8	11.1	28.9	30.7	19.6	28.4	0.4	1.1	0.6	0.5
Country mean	**18.2**	**23.3**	**29.1**	**22.3**	**19.4**	**14.7**	**9.6**	**15.8**	**2.4**	**2.0**	**1.3**	**1.9**

Source: OECD Database. See Annex 3 for notes.

Chapter B

FINANCIAL AND HUMAN RESOURCES INVESTED IN EDUCATION

Education is an investment in human skills that can help foster economic growth and enhance productiv-
, that can contribute to personal and social development, and that can reduce social inequality. Like any
vestment, it involves both costs and returns. This chapter provides a comparative examination of cost
tterns in OECD countries, whereas monetary and labour market returns to education are examined in
apter E.

The 1997 edition of *Education at a Glance* examines four aspects of education spending patterns:

- How investments in education compare with the levels of national resources in countries.
- Who pays for education – through an analysis of the sources of funding.
- How the resources that countries invest are used – through an examination of educational expenditure
  by resource, or functional, category and a comparison of student/teaching staff ratios.
- Unit costs.

The indicators presented in this chapter can assist in the comparative analysis of cost patterns and
ource utilisation.

Indicator B1 examines the proportion of national resources devoted to educational institutions, the
urces of these funds and the levels of education to which they are directed. The nature of the expenditure,
particular the proportion of current expenditure that is accounted for by the compensation of staff
cluding both salary and non-salary compensation), is shown in **Indicator B5**.

Indicator B2 provides another way of comparing the national resources invested in education, by
amining the share of total national public expenditure that is spent on education.

While Indicators B1 and B2 provide a broad picture of the resources devoted to education, they need to
interpreted in the light of a number of inter-related supply and demand factors, such as the demographic
ucture of the population (Indicator A1), enrolment rates (Indicator C1), the level of income per capita and
ional price levels for educational resources. The relative size of the youth population, for example, shapes
 potential demand for initial education and training in a country. The greater this proportion, the more
ources need to be devoted to education, other things being equal. Similarly, participation rates affect
penditure on education: the higher the enrolment rates, the more financial resources will be required,
in other things being equal.

The data for Indicator B2 are also affected by various patterns of public spending. The proportion of total
lic expenditure devoted to education is affected by the relative size of public budgets (in relation to
P), and by the degree to which the private sector is involved in the financing of education. For example,
ntries that require students to pay tuition fees and/or to fund most or all of their living expenses are likely
levote a smaller percentage of public funds to tertiary education, other things being equal, than countries
t provide "free" tertiary education and/or generous public subsidies to tertiary students. Similarly,
ntries in which private enterprises contribute significantly to the education of students (such as those
ch have adopted the dual system) can be expected to devote a comparatively lower share of public
penditure to education.

Indicator B3, which is still at the development stage, provides a tentative breakdown of what arrange-
nts governments make for the distribution of subsidies to households to cover educational expenses.
le Indicators B1 and B2 focus on expenditure on educational institutions, B3 broadens the perspective by

taking into account all public transfers to households, not just those that will be used to pay tuition and oth fees in educational institutions.

The various financial resources spent on education taken together translate eventually into a mo amenable statistic, the amount of funds ultimately spent per student (**Indicator B4**). Policy-makers m balance the need to improve the quality of educational services against the need to expand access educational opportunities. They must also decide how to apportion expenditure per student among t different levels of education – including continuing education and training – and among different types education programmes. For example, some countries emphasise broad access to higher education wh others invest in near-universal education for children as young as two or three. Since there are no absol standards for the resources per student needed to ensure optimal returns for both the participant a society as a whole, international comparisons of national investment in education provide an import insight. Spending per student is examined in this chapter both in absolute terms and in the light of natio levels of GDP per capita.

As both the typical duration and the typical intensity of tertiary study varies between countries (s Indicator G2), variations between countries in annual expenditure per student on educational services do accurately reflect the variability in the total cost of educating the typical student at the tertiary level. Too students can choose from a range of types of institution and enrolment options to find the best fit betwe their degree objectives, abilities, personal interests and social and economic circumstances. Many stude attend part-time, work while enrolled, attend sporadically, and attend more than one institution bef graduating. These varying enrolment patterns can affect the interpretability of expenditure per stude Some countries count every participant at the tertiary level as a full-time student while others determin student's intensity of participation by the credits he or she obtains for successful completion of spec course units during a certain reference period. Moreover, comparatively low annual expenditure per stud may actually translate into comparatively high overall costs of tertiary education if the typical duratior tertiary studies is very long. To shed light on this, Indicator B4 compares countries with respect to average expenditure that is incurred per student throughout the course of studies.

In addition to financial resources, the intangible qualities of dedicated teachers are of utmost imp tance. **Indicator B7** shows the percentage of the labour force employed in education and **Indicator B8** sh the ratio of students enrolled to teaching staff by level of education. The percentage of the total emplo population that is employed in education is an indicator of the proportion of a country's human resour that are devoted to educating the population. The ratio of students to teaching staff is an important indica of how financial resources for education translate into human resources for students.

Indicator B1: Educational expenditure relative to Gross Domestic Product

Policy context

This indicator examines the proportion of national resources devoted to educational institutions, the sources from which this expenditure originates and the levels of education to which it is directed.

Expenditure on education is an investment that can help foster economic growth, enhance productivity, contribute to personal and social development and reduce social inequality. So long as the private and social returns on that investment are sufficiently greater than the relevant costs, there is encouragement for enrolment to expand and overall investment to increase.

This indicator measures the relative share of a nation's wealth that is invested in education. The share of total financial resources devoted to education is one of the key choices made in each country, a choice made aggregately by governments, heads of enterprises, and individual students and their families. Rising demands for education require innovative strategies to mobilise new resources, improve efficiency and stimulate education systems to be responsive. Governments are forging new partnerships in which different actors and stakeholders can participate more fully and share the costs and benefits more equitably. In particular, public funding is now increasingly seen as providing only a part, albeit a very significant part, of the investment in education and private sources of funds are playing an increasingly important role. Here the debate focuses in many countries on the question to what extent the costs of education should be shared by the individuals who benefit from education and by society as a whole. This has led to debate over the questions of access to different educational opportunities, as well as the allocation of available resources among the various levels of education and types of education and training.

In reappraising the amount that they spend on education, governments need to take a view both on how much education should be provided and on how effectively existing resources are being used. While this indicator cannot answer these questions directly, it provides a point of reference with respect to the structure of educational expenditure in countries with comparable levels of economic development.

Evidence and explanations

Overall levels of investment in relation to GDP

As a whole, OECD countries spend 5.9 per cent of GDP in support of their educational institutions.

In all OECD countries, education consumes a significant proportion of national resources. Taking into account both public and private sources of funds, OECD countries as a whole spend 5.9 per cent of their collective GDP in support of their educational institutions and in only 5 of 21 reporting countries is it less than 5 per cent of GDP. Under current conditions of tight public budget constraints, such a large spending item is subject to close scrutiny by governments looking for ways to trim or limit the growth of expenditure.

◆   Chart B1.1.   ***Expenditure on educational institutions as a percentage of GDP, by source of funds (1994)***

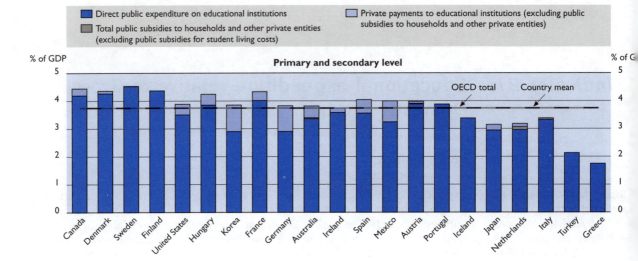

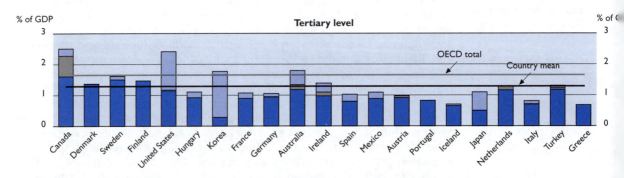

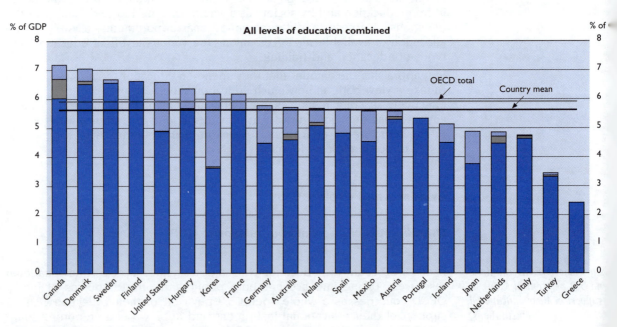

Countries are ranked in descending order of total expenditure from both public and private sources on educational institutions for all levels of education combined.

Source: OECD.

Most of this amount, 4.7 per cent, is accounted for by direct public expenditure on educational institutions.

Most of this amount, 4.7 per cent of the collective GDP, is accounted for by direct public expenditure on educational institutions. The next largest share consists of private payments to educational institutions (accounting for 1.2 per cent of the overall GDP of OECD countries). Public subsidies to households and other private entities for educational institutions comprise another 0.08 per cent of GDP.

In some countries, private payments other than to educational institutions (*e.g.* expenditure by households on student living expenses, books, and other supplies) are substantial, exceeding 0.5 per cent of GDP in Finland, the Netherlands, Norway, Spain, Sweden and Turkey. Government financial aid to students for living expenses is also substantial in many countries, ranging from below 0.05 per cent of GDP in Korea, Greece, and the United States to over 1 per cent of GDP in Denmark, Norway and Sweden (see Table B1.1a).

There is considerable variation between countries in the percentage of GDP spent by both public and private sources on educational institutions. This ranges from below 3.5 per cent in Greece and Turkey to 7 per cent or more in Canada and Denmark. Many factors influence the relative position of countries on such an indicator: high expenditure countries may be enrolling larger numbers of students while low expenditure countries may either be very efficient in delivering education or may be limiting access to higher levels of education; the distribution of enrolments between sectors and fields of study may differ as may the duration of studies; the scale and organisation of linked research activities may vary; and so on.

Expenditure on education by source of funds

Although government spending is the main source of educational funding, contributions by households and enterprises are significant.

Government spending continues to be the main source of educational funding in OECD countries. The percentage of GDP spent by governments on educational institutions varies by more than a factor of two across OECD countries, ranging from 3.8 per cent or less in Greece, Japan, Korea and Turkey to over 6.5 per cent in the Nordic countries (Denmark, Finland, Norway and Sweden) (see Table B1.1a). Inclusion of public subsidies to households (*e.g.* scholarships and loans to students for tuition and fees) and other private entities for education (*e.g.* subsidies to firms or labour organisations that operate apprenticeship programmes) increases the percentage by more than 0.4 per cent in Canada and New Zealand.

Although the primary concern of governments generally relates to expenditure of public origin, a broader understanding of how the private sector can be mobilised to fund educational activities is also important for policy-makers. More and more, public funding is seen as providing only a part, albeit a very significant part, of total educational investment. Particularly at the tertiary level of education, financial mechanisms are being used to leverage the participation of the learners and third-party payers in the funding of tertiary education (see Box).

In many countries, households, enterprises and other private entities contribute significantly to the funding of education. For example, among the 19 countries supplying data on non-governmental payments to educational institutions, in seven countries private contributions account for about 15 per cent or more of total expenditure on educational institutions.

Ideally, this indicator should cover both direct private costs (such as tuition and other education-related fees and the costs of textbooks, uniforms and transportation) as well as indirect private costs (lost output when employees participate in on-the-job training). However, many of these private costs are difficult to measure and to compare internationally. The indicator therefore focuses on public and private expenditure on educational institutions. Although the relative share of private expenditure on educational institutions in many countries may appear comparatively low, it should be remembered that the total costs which families incur for the education of their children can far exceed the private payments to educational institutions captured in this indicator. It should also be noted that the coverage of private sources funds in this indicator is not complete in many countries.

Funds generated by the private sector amount, for the reporting countries taken as a whole, to 1.2 per cent of GDP but there are wide differences between countries.

If the 19 OECD countries providing private expenditure data are taken as whole, the private sector is the source of 20 per cent of aggregate expenditure on educational institutions, amounting to 1.2 per cent of aggregate GDP 1994. These countries differ significantly, however, in the degree to which expenditure on educational institutions is shared by the beneficiaries education and society as a whole. For example, private payments to educational institutions (net of public subsidies) exceed 1.0 per cent of GDP Germany, Japan, Korea, Mexico and the United States. In Germany, Japan, Korea and the United States more than 22 per cent of initial funds for educational institutions originate in the private sector (see also Chart B2. Whereas in Korea and the United States most of this expenditure comes from households, in Germany funds from business enterprises provide and support the work-based component of the dual apprenticeship system. Australia, Canada, Denmark, France, Hungary, Iceland, Ireland and Spain, the private share of expenditure still lies between 0.42 and 0.92 per cent of GDP which corresponds to a relative share of private funds for educational institutions of between 6.0 and 16.1 per cent. The proportion of expenditure educational institutions that is funded by the private sector is 3 per cent less in Italy, the Netherlands, Sweden and Turkey.

If the indicator is broadened to include funds from international sources well as all public subsidies to students and households as far as these attributable to household payments to educational institutions, then proportion of educational expenditure rises to more than 7.2 per cent of GDP in Canada and the Nordic countries (except for Norway, where no data were available), and to between 6 and 7 per cent in Australia, France, Germany Hungary, Ireland, Korea and the United States, while it remains below 5 per cent in Greece, Italy, Japan and Turkey. However, the coverage of public subsidies to households in these data is still uneven across countries.

Options for the funding of tertiary institutions

While at lower levels of education funding is largely provided by governments, more variation can be observed at the higher levels of education, where participants are often considered the primary beneficiaries. Countries have found different ways of securing funding for tertiary education:

One option has been for government authorities to define an "appropriate" level of tuition fees, financed in different ways (see also Indicator B3). For example, the Higher Education Contribution Scheme in Australia obliges every student to repay about one-fourth of the costs of instruction for each year of study leading to the first degree. In New Zealand, the formula for core funding provides about 80 per cent of the 'fully budgeted' level of support per student, leaving to each institution the decision to establish a schedule of tuition fees. Students can finance the tuition fees through student loans, to be repaid in instalments in periods when incomes exceed a threshold.

A second option has been to shift all or part of the responsibility for financing student maintenance costs from the public education budget to either the student and his or her family or to other government departments, such as unemployment or training funds. In Germany and Sweden, student financial support is provided partly in the form of a grant and partly in the form of a subsidised loan. The debate continues in both countries on the appropriate balance between the two components, although the principle of some level of student repayment obligation is not in question. In France, proposals to rationalise further indirect support for students

(continued on next page)

(continued)

have figured in the public debate on financing and reform. Recent changes in social insurance eligibility criteria in Denmark have already brought otherwise inactive beneficiaries into tertiary education; for these new tertiary education learners, social insurance budgets will bear at least some share of the maintenance costs.

A third option has been to strengthen the external earnings capacity of educational institutions, both in teaching and training services and in a range of other activities. Such activities increase the scope for subsidising traditional education programmes. For example, contract teaching, international programmes and research – funded from other sources – can help to underwrite administrative overheads, as well as to support teaching and learning.

A fourth option, related to the previous one, has been to promote the development of new forms of teaching and learning in partnership with business and industry, as in the Enterprise in Higher Education initiative in the United Kingdom. These initiatives not only build on the expertise and contexts for learning residing in the partner organisations, but draw on financial, human and material resources provided by the partners (both private and public, in the latter case from other budget functions and regional and local authorities). This is one means of drawing financial resources from business and industry into tertiary institutions.

A fifth option has been to draw systematically on full or part-time student earnings, in part building on changes in study programmes which cater for alternate periods of work and study. While earnings generated through concurrent or consecutive work both permit learners to shoulder a larger share of the investment in tertiary education and give them an introduction to the world of work, they also may delay their studies and transition to full-time employment.

Source: OECD, *Thematic Review of the First Years of Tertiary Education (forthcoming).*

Expenditure on educational institutions by level of education

The percentage of GDP devoted to the primary and secondary levels follows by and large the overall spending pattern...

The percentage of GDP devoted to the primary and secondary levels across countries follows, by and large, the overall spending pattern described above. Total public expenditure on primary and secondary education institutions ranges from 3 per cent or below in Germany, Greece, Japan, Korea, the Netherlands and Turkey to 4 per cent or above in Canada, the Czech Republic, Denmark, Finland, France, New Zealand, Norway, Sweden and Switzerland. Deviations from this overall pattern can be explained largely by differences in primary and secondary enrolment rates and in institutional structures (*e.g.* pupil-teacher ratios and teachers' salaries) and by demographic factors. The vast majority of the funding for these levels comes from public sources – about 90 per cent of expenditure on educational institutions across the 18 countries able to provide data by source (see Table B1.1b). In several countries, however, the private sector (*e.g.* households and business enterprises) funds a significant portion of the expenditure on educational institutions – almost 20 per cent or more in Germany, Korea and Mexico. There were virtually no private sector transfers to educational institutions in Italy, Portugal, Sweden and Turkey. Many countries remain unable to report private sector transfers at this level, however.

whereas at the tertiary level there are marked differences between countries.

At the tertiary level, there are significant differences in investment patterns between countries (see Table B1.1c). While the OECD as a whole devotes 1.6 per cent of its GDP to the funding of tertiary education, Canada and the United States spend significantly larger fractions of their GDP on this level (2.4 per cent of GDP or more). At the other end of the scale are Greece, Iceland, Italy, Portugal and the United Kingdom, which devote less than 1 per cent of their GDP to the funding of tertiary institutions. Differences depend to some extent, however, on the amount of research expenditure included. In theory, expenditure should include all expenditure on research performed within tertiary-level institutions, regardless of whether the research is financed from general institutional funds or through separate grants or contacts from public and private sponsors. As a result, even if countries c accurately report expenditure on research according to these instructions, t level of expenditure can vary according to the extent to which research carried out within tertiary institutions.

The degree to which tertiary institutions rely on non-governmental funding varies widely.

In many countries, selective user fees (*e.g.* tuition) are charged at the terti level and subsidies are often reduced for educational programmes that a deemed to have higher private returns. The degree to which tertiary insti tions rely on non-governmental funding varies widely, however. For examp the proportion of spending on tertiary institutions that originates in the p vate sector ranges from 0.08 per cent of GDP or less in Austria, Denma Iceland, the Netherlands, Turkey and the United Kingdom to more th 1.2 per cent in Korea and the United States (see Table B1.1c). In fact, in Jap Korea and the United States more than half of the expenditure on terti institutions is funded through non-governmental funds (54, 84 and 52 per ce respectively). In most OECD countries, however, public expenditure, bc direct and indirect, continues to be the principal source of funding for types of tertiary education.

Additional expenditure on research and development

Expenditure on research and development activities outside higher education institutions is considerable in many countries.

Investing in research and development activities is another way to try improve aggregate productivity. Although some research and developme work is carried out in higher education institutions, another important comp nent is the research undertaken in non-instructional research centres and private industry. Across the 18 countries for which research and developme data are available, expenditure as a percentage of GDP (excluding the hig education sector) ranges from 0.2 per cent or below in Mexico and Turkey 1.9 per cent or above in Finland, France, Germany, Japan and t

◆ Chart B1.2. **Gross domestic expenditure on research and development (excluding expenditure on higher education) as a percentage of GDP (1994)**

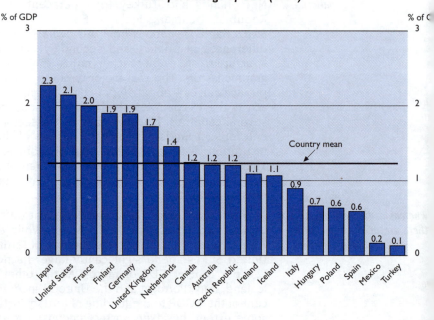

Source: OECD.

United States. While relative expenditure on research and development (see Chart B1.2) appears to follow a similar pattern to total tertiary expenditure from both public and private sources on educational institutions (Table B1.1c), there are some notable exceptions. For example, while France and Japan both spend less than half as much of their GDP on tertiary educational institutions (1.1 per cent in both countries) as does the United States (2.4 per cent), they spend about the same proportion of their GDP or more on research and development activities outside the higher education sector (2.3 and 2.0 per cent respectively, compared with the United States' 2.1 per cent). These differences are likely to reflect value placed on research and development relative to investment in tertiary institutions, as well as the degree to which R&D activities take place in independent research centres and private industry, rather than in higher education institutions.

Important factors influencing national expenditure on education

The national resources devoted to education depend on a number of inter-related supply and demand factors.

The national resources devoted to education depend on a number of inter-related supply and demand factors, such as the demographic structure of the population, enrolment rates, the level of income per capita, national price levels for educational resources and the organisation and delivery of instruction. Teacher costs do not appear to be proportionately lower in poorer countries. In these countries, teachers' pay tends to be relatively high as a percentage of GDP, most likely because teachers are members of a comparatively small cadre of well-educated professionals.

Educational participation, often combined with a smaller youth population, tends to be higher in richer countries. To demonstrate how national resources devoted to education (expressed by Indicator B1) translate into the resources that are ultimately available per student (shown in Indicator B4), the following illustration examines the extent to which deviations from the OECD average in educational expenditure relative to GDP are related to two key indicators in this publication: the age structure of the population (Indicator A1) and the rate of enrolment of the youth population (Indicator C1).

The overall wealth of a country determines the resources that can be devoted to education.

The overall wealth of a country, as measured by GDP per capita, obviously has a significant influence over the resources that can be devoted to education. National GDP levels are taken as the benchmark against which education expenditure is compared in Indicator B1.

Comparisons of educational expenditure depend also on who is eligible to attend school and who actually participates.

The size of the youth population in a particular country shapes the potential demand for initial education and training. The larger the number of young people, the greater the potential demand for educational services. Among countries of comparable wealth, a country with a relatively large youth population would have to spend a greater percentage of its GDP on education for each young person to have the opportunity to receive the same quantity of education as young people in other countries. Conversely, if the relative size of the youth population is smaller, the same country would need to spend less of its wealth on education to achieve similar results. Across OECD countries, the proportion of the total population that is between the ages of 5 and 29 varies from less than 32 per cent in Germany, Luxembourg, Sweden and Switzerland to over 50 per cent in Turkey and Mexico, with an average of a little under 37 per cent (see Indicator A1).

The larger the number of young people, the greater the potential demand for educational services.

Chart B1.3A shows the changes in expenditure on educational institutions as a percentage of GDP that would be expected if the proportion of the population aged 5-29 were equal in OECD countries, other factors remaining the same. In Germany and Sweden, two countries with relatively small youth populations, educational expenditure as a percentage of GDP would be expected to rise by 1 per cent if the relative size of the youth population in these countries were to be at the level of the OECD average.

◆ Chart B1.3. *Impact of demography and enrolment on expenditure on educational institutions as a percentage of GDP (1994)*

A. Estimated increase/decrease in expenditure on educational institutions as a percentage of GDP if the proportion of the population 5 to 29 years of age in each country were at the OECD average level

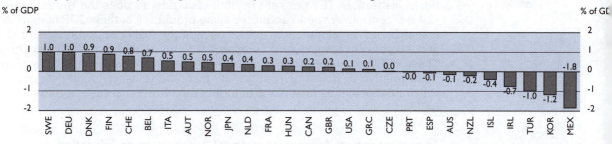

B. Estimated increase/decrease in expenditure on educational institutions as a percentage of GDP if enrolment patterns in each country (all levels combined) were at the OECD average level

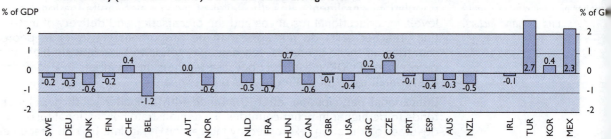

C. Estimated increase/decrease in expenditure on educational institutions as a percentage of GDP if enrolment patterns at levels up to upper secondary education in each country were at the OECD average level

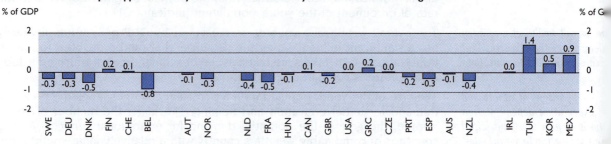

D. Estimated increase/decrease in expenditure on educational institutions as a percentage of GDP if enrolment patterns at the tertiary level in each country were at the OECD average level

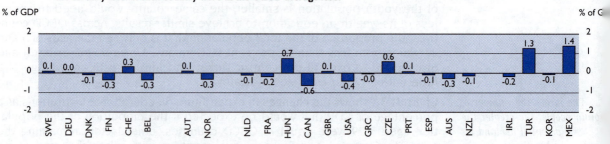

Countries are ranked in descending order of the values in Chart B1.3A.

Source: OECD.

In contrast, in Korea, Mexico and Turkey, expenditure on education could be expected to be lower (by 1.8 per cent of GDP in Mexico, and by around 1 per cent of GDP in Korea and Turkey) if the proportion of the youth population in these two countries were at the OECD average. Although the difference in the size of the young population in comparison with the OECD-average is smaller for Korea than for Turkey, the difference in spending would be larger for Korea (1.2 per cent), because of the higher level of costs per student.

The higher the enrolment rate, the more financial resources will be required.

While countries have little control over the size of their youth populations, the proportion who participate at various levels of education is a central policy issue. Variations in enrolment rates between countries reflect differences in the demand for education, from pre-primary schooling through higher education, as well as the supply of programmes at all levels. Indicator C1 (Table C1.2) shows that the years in education a five year-old child can expect range from less than 12 years up to 18 years. The variation in expected years in tertiary education is even wider, from less than 1 year to more than 3.5 years (see Indicator C5, Table C5.1).

Differences in the length of schooling translate into differences in enrolment rates which, in turn, influence educational expenditure. Chart B1.3B shows the change in expenditure on educational institutions as a percentage of GDP that would be expected if enrolment profiles were equal across OECD countries, other factors remaining the same. Generally, countries such as Denmark, Finland and Sweden that have higher than average enrolment rates also spend more of their GDP on education whereas low spending countries such as Greece, Mexico and Turkey have below average enrolment rates. Exceptions to this pattern are Norway, which is relatively high spending even with an average enrolment rate, and the United Kingdom, which is relatively low spending even though it has an above-average enrolment rate.

If enrolment patterns were equal across OECD countries, then expenditure as a percentage of GDP would be expected to rise by 2.3 per cent of GDP or more in Mexico and Turkey (see Chart B1.3B) while it would fall by more than 1 per cent of GDP in Belgium and still by more than half a per cent in Canada, Denmark, France and Norway, other things being equal.

It is important not to look at the different factors that affect spending on education in isolation. Chart B1.3 indicates that in several cases where demography has the greatest potential impact on educational costs, its impact is often counterbalanced by participation rates in the opposite direction. Belgium, Denmark, Germany and Norway, for example, are countries in which a smaller share of the youth population is, in part, balanced by comparatively high participation rates. Similarly, in Korea, Mexico and Turkey a proportionately large youth population is counterbalanced by below-average enrolment rates. Hungary and Switzerland, on the other hand, are countries with both comparatively small youth populations and comparatively low enrolment rates, which enables them to spend relatively more per student.

Such effects are most clearly visible at the tertiary level (see Chart B1.3D) where both enrolment rates (Indicator C1) and costs per student (Indicator B4) differ widely between countries. If tertiary enrolment patterns in Canada and the United States were at the level of the OECD average, expenditure on tertiary education as a percentage of GDP in these countries would be expected to fall by more than 0.4 per cent of GDP. Belgium shows similarly high expected years of tertiary education, but lower costs per student make the expected decline in expenditure as a percentage of GDP less pronounced.

At the other end of the scale are Mexico and Turkey, whose expenditure on tertiary education would be expected to increase by more than 1.3 per cent of GDP, if the enrolment patterns were at the OECD average level.

Trends in public expenditure on education

Since the mid-1970s, the proportion of GDP spent by the public sector on education has stabilised or fallen slightly in most countries.

Table B1.t shows changes over time in public educational expenditure a percentage of GDP for selected countries. These changes are influenced b by changes in supply factors (such as the growth rate of the national econc or competing demands of other public services) as well as by change: demand, particularly changing demographic conditions.

In 1970, public expenditure on education as a percentage of GDP ranged f 2.4 per cent in Mexico to 10.2 per cent in Canada. In half of the count public expenditure was 6 per cent of GDP or more.

General public spending restraints have created pressure to reduce spending, but other factors have pushed spending higher.

In the early 1970s, the dominant position of education in publicly func social programmes began to change as a consequence of two factors: slow economic growth and decreasing enrolments, with the drop in birth ra beginning to influence the size of the school-age population. At the sa time a number of factors, such as rising participation rates at higher levels i changes in teachers' pay, began to exert an upward pressure on educat spending.

There is a trend towards convergence of public educational expenditure.

Overall, as a proportion of GDP, public educational expenditure roughly h its ground, but the data suggest a trend towards convergence of public edu tional expenditure among OECD countries.

Table B1.t would ideally show trends in the proportion of GDP devotec education from both public and private sources. However, comparable tre data for expenditure on education from private sources are not availal Note that, unlike the data shown in Table B1.1, the expenditure showr Table B1.t includes not only public expenditure on educational instituti but, to a varying extent, public subsidies for student living expenses should also be noted that the broadened statistical coverage of educatic spending in recent years for some countries is likely to have contributed rise over time in the figures on educational expenditure as a percentage GDP (irrespective of any real change).

Definitions

Data refer to the financial year 1994 and are based on the UOE data collection on education statistics, administered in 1996 (for details see Annex 3).

In this indicator, expenditure on education is expressed as a percentage GDP and presented by source of funds and by level of education. The dist tion by source of funds is based on the initial source of funds and does reflect subsequent public-to-private or private-to-public transfers.

Direct public expenditure on educational institutions (see column 1 of Tak B1.1a, b and c) can take the form either of purchases by the governm agency itself of educational resources to be used by educational institutic or of payments by the government agency to educational institutions t have responsibility for purchasing educational resources.

Public subsidies to households and other private entities for educatic institutions (see column 2 of Tables B1.1a, b and c) are composed of gove ment transfers and certain other payments to students/households, in so as these translate into payments to educational institutions for educatic services (*e.g.* fellowships, financial aid awards or student loans for tuiti They also include government transfers and certain other payments (ma subsidies) to other private entities, for example subsidies to firms or lab organisations that operate apprenticeship programmes and interest subsic to private financial institutions that provide student loans, etc.

Payments from households and other private entities to educational inst tions (see column 3 of Tables B1.1a, b and c) include tuition fees and oth fees, net of offsetting public subsidies.

Public subsidies to households that are not attributable to payments to educational institutions (see column 7 of Tables B1.1a, b and c) include subsidies for student living expenditure or the value of special subsidies provided to students, either in cash or in kind, such as free or reduced-price travel on public transport or family allowances that are contingent on student status. (Those subsidies are also included in column 5 of Tables B1.1a, b and c.)

Private payments other than to educational institutions (see column 6 of Tables B1.1a, b and c) include direct purchases of personal items used in education or subsidised expenditure on student living expenses.

The data do not include benefits provided to students or households in the form of tax reductions, tax subsidies or other special tax provisions. Note also that the coverage of expenditure from private sources is still uneven across countries.

The methodology that was used for the calculation of the estimates in Chart B1.3 is described in Annex 3.

The country mean is calculated as the simple average over all OECD countries for which data are available. The OECD total reflects the value of the indicator when the OECD region is considered as a whole (for details see Reader's Guide).

Table B1.1a **Educational expenditure as a percentage of GDP for all levels of education combined, by source of funds (1994)**

	Expenditure on educational institutions						
	Direct public expenditure on educational institutions	Total public subsidies to households and other private entities excluding public subsidies for student living costs	Private payments to educational institutions excluding public subsidies to households and other private entities	Total expenditure from both public and private sources on educational institutions	Total expenditure from public, private and international sources on educational institutions **plus** public subsidies to households	Private payments other than to educational institutions	Financial aid to students *not* attributable to household payments to educational institutions
North America							
Canada	6.0	0.67	0.49	7.2	7.2	m	0.06
Mexico	4.5	x	1.05	5.6	5.6	0.25	x
United States	4.9	0.02	1.68	6.6	6.6	0.15	0.02
Pacific Area							
Australia	4.6	0.19	0.92	5.7	6.2	m	0.51
Japan	3.8	m	1.11	4.9	4.9	m	m
Korea	3.6	0.05	2.51	6.2	6.2	m	0.01
New Zealand	5.6	0.43	m	m	m	m	0.43
European Union							
Austria	5.3	0.08	0.20	5.6	5.6	m	a
Belgium	5.5	n	m	m	m	m	0.20
Denmark	6.5	0.11	0.42	7.0	8.4	m	1.37
Finland	6.6	m	x	6.6	7.3	0.65	0.65
France	5.6	n	0.53	6.2	6.4	0.26	0.26
Germany	4.5	0.01	1.29	5.8	6.0	m	0.19
Greece	2.4	n	m	2.4	2.4	m	0.01
Ireland	5.1	0.11	0.48	5.7	6.0	m	0.30
Italy	4.6	0.08	0.03	4.7	4.8	m	0.08
Luxembourg	m	m	m	m	m	m	m
Netherlands	4.5	0.24	0.14	4.9	5.4	0.62	0.53
Portugal	5.3	n	a	5.3	5.5	0.16	0.16
Spain	4.8	n	0.83	5.6	5.8	0.57	0.11
Sweden	6.6	a	0.12	6.7	7.8	1.23	1.10
United Kingdom	4.6	0.30	m	m	m	0.30	0.30
Other OECD countries							
Czech Republic	5.7	n	m	m	m	m	0.43
Hungary	5.7	n	0.68	6.4	6.5	m	0.17
Iceland	4.5	m	0.63	5.1	5.5	0.21	0.39
Norway	6.8	n	m	m	m	1.56	1.24
Poland	m	m	m	m	m	m	m
Switzerland	5.5	0.07	m	m	m	m	0.12
Turkey	3.3	0.06	0.08	3.4	3.5	0.66	0.06
Country mean	**5.1**	**0.11**	**0.69**	**5.6**	**5.9**	**0.55**	**0.35**
OECD total	4.7	0.08	1.17	5.9	6.0	0.26	0.14

Source: OECD Database. See Annex 3 for notes.

Table B1.1*b* **Educational expenditure as a percentage of GDP for primary and secondary education, by source of funds (1994)**

	Expenditure on educational institutions					Private payments other than to educational institutions	Financial aid to students *not* attributable to household payments to educational institutions for educational services
	Direct public expenditure on educational institutions	Total public subsidies to households and other private entities excluding public subsidies for student living costs	Private payments to educational institutions excluding public subsidies to households and other private entities	Total expenditure from both public and private sources on educational institutions	Total expenditure from public, private and international sources on educational institutions **plus** public subsidies to households		
North America							
Canada	4.2	n	0.25	4.4	4.4	m	n
Mexico	3.2	x	0.76	4.0	4.0	0.21	m
United States	3.5	x	0.39	3.9	3.9	0.02	m
Pacific Area							
Australia	3.4	0.03	0.43	3.8	4.1	m	0.32
Japan	2.9	m	0.20	3.1	3.1	m	m
Korea	2.9	n	0.96	3.9	3.9	m	m
New Zealand	4.1	0.11	m	m	m	m	0.11
European Union							
Austria	3.9	0.02	0.07	4.0	4.0	m	a
Belgium	3.9	n	m	m	m	m	0.01
Denmark	4.3	n	0.09	4.4	4.8	m	0.39
Finland	4.4	m	x	4.4	4.6	0.25	0.25
France	4.0	n	0.32	4.3	4.5	0.16	0.17
Germany	2.9	n	0.93	3.8	3.9	m	0.11
Greece	1.7	n	m	1.7	1.7	m	n
Ireland	3.6	n	0.16	3.7	3.8	m	0.11
Italy	3.3	0.06	n	3.4	m	m	n
Luxembourg	m	m	m	m	m	m	m
Netherlands	3.0	0.10	0.11	3.2	3.4	0.26	0.20
Portugal	3.9	a	a	3.9	4.0	0.07	0.07
Spain	3.6	n	0.49	4.0	4.1	0.32	0.05
Sweden	4.5	a	0.01	4.5	5.1	0.56	0.56
United Kingdom	3.8	0.03	m	m	m	0.04	0.03
Other OECD countries							
Czech Republic	4.0	n	m	m	m	m	0.33
Hungary	3.9	n	0.39	4.2	4.3	m	0.01
Iceland	3.4	m	m	m	m	m	m
Norway	4.1	n	m	m	m	0.33	0.33
Poland	m	m	m	m	m	m	m
Switzerland	4.1	0.05	m	m	m	m	0.07
Turkey	2.1	a	n	2.1	2.2	m	0.05
Country mean	**3.6**	**0.02**	**0.31**	**3.7**	**3.9**	**0.22**	**0.14**
OECD total	3.4	0.02	0.39	3.7	3.8	0.08	0.10

Source: OECD Database. See Annex 3 for notes.

Table B1.1c **Educational expenditure as a percentage of GDP for tertiary education, by source of funds (1994)**

	Expenditure on educational institutions						
	Direct public expenditure on educational institutions	Total public subsidies to households and other private entities excluding public subsidies for student living costs	Private payments to educational institutions excluding public subsidies to households and other private entities	Total expenditure from both public and private sources on educational institutions	Total expenditure from public, private and international sources on educational institutions **plus** public subsidies to households	Private payments other than to educational institutions	Financial aid to students *not* attributable to household payments to educational institutions
North America							
Canada	1.6	0.67	0.23	2.5	2.6	0.42	0.06
Mexico	0.9	x	0.21	1.1	1.1	0.02	m
United States	1.1	0.02	1.24	2.4	2.4	0.12	0.02
Pacific Area							
Australia	1.2	0.16	0.45	1.8	2.0	m	0.19
Japan	0.5	m	0.59	1.1	1.1	m	m
Korea	0.3	n	1.48	1.8	1.8	m	0.01
New Zealand	1.1	0.29	m	m	m	m	0.29
European Union							
Austria	0.9	0.06	0.01	1.0	1.0	m	a
Belgium	1.0	n	m	m	m	m	0.19
Denmark	1.4	n	0.01	1.4	2.1	m	0.71
Finland	1.5	m	x	1.5	1.9	0.40	0.40
France	0.9	n	0.18	1.1	1.2	0.09	0.09
Germany	0.9	0.01	0.10	1.1	1.1	m	0.09
Greece	0.7	n	m	0.7	0.7	m	0.01
Ireland	1.0	0.12	0.29	1.4	1.6	m	0.16
Italy	0.7	0.02	0.09	0.8	0.9	0.06	0.05
Luxembourg	m	m	m	m	m	m	m
Netherlands	1.2	0.13	0.03	1.3	1.7	0.36	0.33
Portugal	0.8	a	a	0.8	0.9	0.08	0.08
Spain	0.8	n	0.23	1.0	1.1	0.11	0.06
Sweden	1.5	a	0.11	1.6	2.2	0.68	0.54
United Kingdom	0.7	0.27	0.005	0.9	1.2	0.26	0.27
Other OECD countries							
Czech Republic	0.8	n	m	m	m	m	0.09
Hungary	0.9	n	0.19	1.1	1.3	m	0.15
Iceland	0.7	m	0.05	0.7	1.0	m	0.32
Norway	1.4	n	m	m	m	0.75	0.75
Poland	m	m	m	m	m	m	m
Switzerland	1.1	0.01	m	m	m	m	0.05
Turkey	1.2	0.05	0.08	1.3	1.3	0.66	0.01
Country mean	**1.0**	**0.08**	**0.28**	**1.3**	**1.5**	**0.31**	**0.20**
OECD total	0.9	0.06	0.64	1.6	1.7	0.16	0.08

Source: OECD Database. See Annex 3 for notes.

Table B1.1d **Educational expenditure from public and private sources on educational institutions as a percentage of GDP by level of education (1994)**

	Primary and secondary education			Tertiary education			All levels of education combined (including pre-primary and undistributed)
	Primary and secondary	Primary	Secondary	All tertiary	Non-university	University-level	
North America							
Canada	4.4	x	x	2.5	0.9	1.6	7.2
Mexico	4.0	2.1	1.9	1.1	x	1.1	5.6
United States	3.9	x	x	2.4	x	x	6.6
Pacific Area							
Australia	3.8	1.6	2.2	1.8	0.3	1.5	5.7
Japan	3.1	1.4	1.8	1.1	0.1	1.0	4.9
Korea	3.9	1.7	2.2	1.8	0.3	1.5	6.2
New Zealand	m	m	m	m	m	m	m
European Union							
Austria	4.0	1.2	2.8	1.0	0.1	0.9	5.6
Belgium	m	m	m	m	m	m	m
Denmark	4.4	1.5	2.8	1.4	x	x	7.0
Finland	4.4	1.9	2.5	1.5	0.2	1.2	6.6
France	4.3	1.2	3.1	1.1	x	x	6.2
Germany	3.8	x	x	1.1	n	1.0	5.8
Greece	1.7	0.8	1.0	0.7	0.1	0.5	2.4
Ireland	3.7	1.4	2.3	1.4	x	x	5.7
Italy	3.4	1.1	2.4	0.8	0.1	0.8	4.7
Luxembourg	m	m	m	m	m	m	m
Netherlands	3.2	1.2	2.0	1.3	a	1.3	4.9
Portugal	3.9	1.8	2.1	m	m	0.8	5.3
Spain	4.0	1.2	2.8	1.0	x	x	5.6
Sweden	4.5	2.0	2.5	1.6	x	x	6.7
United Kingdom	m	m	m	0.9	x	x	m
Other OECD countries							
Czech Republic	m	m	m	m	m	m	m
Hungary	4.2	1.3	2.9	1.1	n	1.1	6.4
Iceland	m	m	m	0.7	x	m	5.1
Norway	m	m	m	m	m	m	m
Poland	m	m	m	m	m	m	m
Switzerland	m	m	m	m	m	m	m
Turkey	2.1	1.4	0.7	1.3	x	x	3.4
Country mean	**3.7**	**1.5**	**2.2**	**1.3**	**0.2**	**1.1**	**5.6**
OECD total	3.7	1.4	2.2	1.6	0.2	1.1	5.9

Source: OECD Database. See Annex 3 for notes.

Table B1.t **Public expenditure on education as a percentage of GDP, including public subsidies to households (1970-1994)**

	1970	1975	1980	1985	1990	1994
North America						
Canada	10.2	8.5	7.7	6.9	6.2	6.7
Mexico	2.4	3.9	4.6	3.8	4.0	4.6
United States	6.0	5.7	4.9	4.6	5.2	4.9
Pacific Area						
Australia	4.6	6.2	5.6	5.4	4.6	5.3
Japan	m	m	m	m	3.6	3.8
New Zealand	m	6.5	6.7	5.1	m	6.4
European Union						
Austria	4.6	5.7	5.7	5.8	5.4	5.4
Denmark	m	6.9	7.4	6.2	6.3	8.0
Finland	m	m	5.8	5.7	6.0	7.3
France	m	5.6	5.1	5.7	5.1	5.9
Germany	3.7	5.1	4.8	4.6	4.1	4.7
Greece	2.8	3.4	3.2	4.0	m	2.4
Ireland	6.2	6.5	6.4	6.0	5.0	5.5
Italy	m	4.8	4.5	5.0	5.2	4.8
Netherlands	7.5	7.4	7.1	6.6	5.7	5.2
Portugal	m	3.3	3.7	4.0	4.3	5.5
Spain	m	m	m	3.6	4.4	4.9
Sweden	7.9	7.1	8.5	7.0	5.6	7.7
United Kingdom	6.2	6.8	5.7	4.9	4.9	5.2
Other OECD countries						
Czech Republic	m	m	m	m	4.2	6.2
Norway	m	6.4	5.8	5.6	m	8.1
Switzerland	3.9	5.3	5.2	5.1	5.2	5.7

Vertical bars indicate a break in the series.
Source: OECD Database. See Annex 3 for notes.

Indicator B2: Public expenditure on education

Policy context

This indicator shows direct public expenditure on educational services, public subsidies to the private sector and total educational expenditure as a percentage of total public expenditure.

Governments become involved in providing services to the public for different reasons. If the public benefits from a particular service are greater than the private benefits, then markets alone may fail to provide those services adequately. Education is one area where all governments intervene to fund or direct the provision of services. As there is no guarantee that markets would provide equal access to educational opportunities, government funding of educational services ensures that education is not beyond the reach of some members of society. Education, however, does compete for public financial support against a wide range of other areas covered in government budgets.

The indicator also shows the relative size of different types of direct and indirect transfers to educational institutions.

The share of a government's budget that is devoted to education is a function of the perceived value of education relative to the perceived value of other public investments, including defence and security, health care, social security for the unemployed and elderly, and other social programmes. Government funding of education can be primarily through direct transfers to educational institutions or through public subsidies to households and other private entities. The level of public spending on education is also influenced by the level of private funding directed at education.

Evidence and explanations

Overall level of public resources invested in education

On average, OECD countries devote 13 per cent of total government outlays to support for educational institutions.

On average, OECD countries devote 13 per cent of total government outlays to support for educational institutions, with the values for individual countries ranging between 7 and 26 per cent. The educational share of the public sector budget is lowest (below 10 per cent) in Germany, Greece, Italy and the Netherlands. These countries also devote the smallest share of the public budget to primary and secondary education. By contrast, the highest percentages of total public spending allocated to education (15 per cent or more) are in Korea, Mexico, New Zealand, Norway and Switzerland.

Public investment by level of education

Between 5.0 and 18.5 per cent of total public expenditure is allocated to primary and secondary education and between 1.4 and 5.3 per cent to tertiary education.

Countries differ widely with respect to the involvement of the public sector in the funding of education at the different levels of education. Between 5.0 and 18.5 per cent of total public expenditure is allocated to primary and secondary education and between 1.4 and 5.3 per cent to tertiary education. Korea, Mexico, New Zealand and Switzerland all spend more than 10 per cent of total government expenditure on primary and secondary education. Mexico and Turkey devote the largest fraction of public spending to tertiary education (5.2 and 5.3 per cent respectively). A heavy reliance on private funding of

◆ Chart B2.1. *Public expenditure on education as a percentage of total public expenditure (1994)*

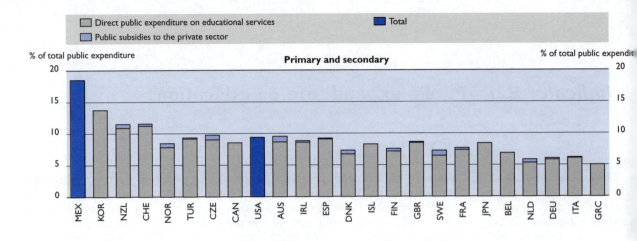

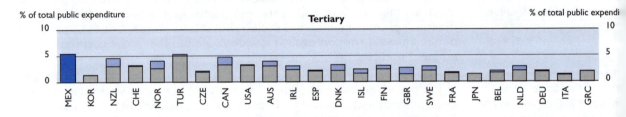

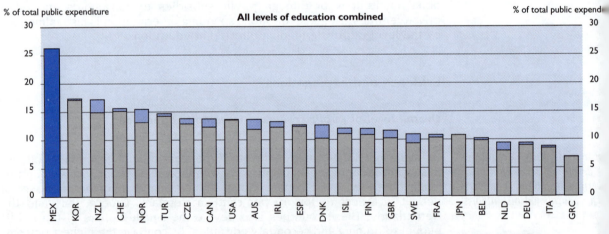

Estimated increase/decrease in public expenditure on education as a percentage of total public expenditure if the proportion of the population 5 to 29 years of age in each country were at the OECD average level

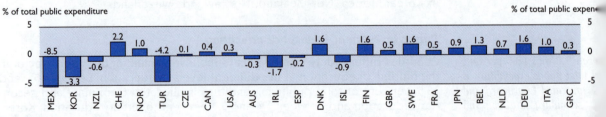

Countries are ranked in descending order of the proportion of public expenditure on education for all levels of education combined.
Source: OECD.

tertiary education may contribute to Japan's low public spending on tertiary education (1.5 per cent of total public spending). Other countries that spend relatively small proportions of public funds on tertiary education (1.8 per cent or less) are France, Italy and Korea.

In Canada, the Netherlands and Turkey the proportion of public expenditure on education that is devoted to the tertiary level exceeds 30 per cent and the respective total enrolment shares at the tertiary level are 26 per cent, 15 per cent and 9 per cent. In Japan and Korea the vast majority of public educational expenditure is invested in the primary and secondary levels of education, with the tertiary sector receiving 14 per cent or less of total public expenditure on education.

Public expenditure relative to the size of public budgets

...lic funding of education is a ...al priority, even in countries ...i little public involvement in other areas.

The relative size of public budgets (as measured by public spending in relation to GDP) appears to be associated with the relative proportion of public expenditure devoted to education. For example, in countries where public spending is low relative to overall GDP, such as Korea and Mexico, the proportion of public expenditure dedicated to education is relatively high. Likewise, countries such as Italy or the Netherlands, where education accounts for a relatively low proportion of total public spending, total public spending relative to GDP is high. This is evidence that public funding of education is a social priority in all countries, even those with little public involvement in other areas.

◆   Chart B2.2.   **Total public expenditure as a percentage of GDP (1994)**

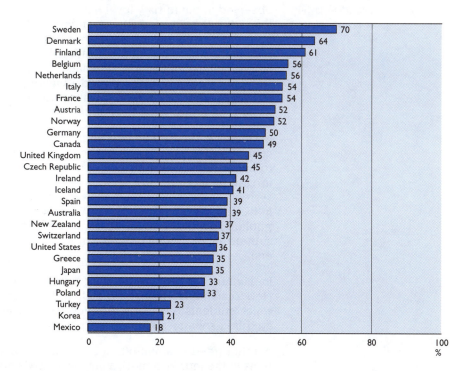

Public investment compared with private investment in education

The involvement of the private sector in the funding of education influences public sector spending.

Another factor that appears to contribute to the variation between count in the proportion of total public spending devoted to education is the lev involvement of the private sector in the funding of education. For exam countries that require students to pay tuition fees and/or to fund most o of their living expenses appear to devote a smaller percentage of total pu funds to tertiary education, other things being equal, than countries provide "free" education and/or generous public subsidies to students. S larly, countries in which private enterprises contribute significantly to education of students (as is the case in countries with the dual system) devote a comparatively smaller proportion of public expenditure to ed tion.

Chart B2.3 shows the relative proportions of funds for educational institut that come from public and private sources (taken before transfers betw levels of government and before transfers from the public to the pri sector). Among the 15 countries reporting data, the proportion of funding educational institutions that comes from the private sector ranges f around 2 per cent or below in Portugal, Sweden and Turkey to over 22 cent in Germany, Japan, Korea and the United States. Differences betw countries are largest at the tertiary level of education, with over half of tert expenditure on educational institutions coming from private sources in Jaj Korea, and the United States and 2 per cent or less in Denmark, Netherlands, Portugal and the United Kingdom.

Public transfers to the private sector for education

Public funds are largely spent on educational institutions but some countries provide sizeable subsidies for education to the private sector.

While at the primary and secondary levels of education most public mone spent either directly by governments or transferred to educational ins tions to acquire resources, more variation in spending patterns can observed at the tertiary level (see Table B2.2). In 11 out of 24 countries, n than 20 per cent of public spending at the tertiary level is transferre households (through scholarships, grants and loans) or is transferred to o recipients which are not educational institutions (such as enterprise labour unions). In Canada, Denmark, Iceland, the Netherlands, New Zeal Norway, Sweden and the United Kingdom more than 25 per cent of pu resources are transferred to private entities which in turn spend them, at I in part, on educational institutions.

In Denmark, the Netherlands and the United Kingdom between 25 and 40 cent of public expenditure at the tertiary level is for scholarships and gr to households, which include special subsidies provided to students, ei in cash or in kind, such as free or reduced-price travel on public trans systems and family or child allowances that are contingent on student st In Iceland, New Zealand, Norway and Sweden between 16 and 33 per cer public expenditure is for student loans (reported on a gross basis, with subtracting or netting out repayments or interest payments from the bor ers).

In countries where tertiary education is expanding, including Austr New Zealand, Norway and the United Kingdom, and particularly in thos which students are charged tuition fees, public to private transfers of fu are often seen as a means to expand access for lower income students.

Another trend in a number of countries has been to provide funds to ins tions in the form of a block grant, which gives institutions greater discretic spending.

◆   Chart B2.3.   *Distribution of public and private sources of initial funds for educational institutions (1994)*

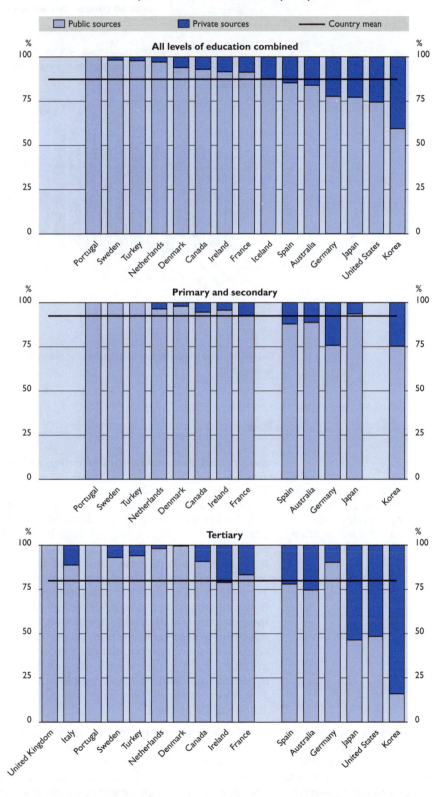

Countries are ranked in descending order of the percentage of public sources of initial funds for all levels of education combined.

Source: OECD.

◆ Chart B2.4. ***Direct public expenditure on tertiary educational institutions and transfers to the private sector as a percentage of total government expenditure (1994)***

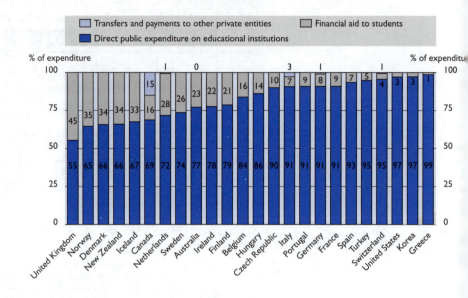

Countries are ranked in ascending order of the proportion of direct public expenditure on educational institutions.

Source: OECD.

Supply and demand factors affecting public expenditure

The relative size of the youth population and corresponding enrolment rates shape the potential demand for initial education and training.

The relative size of the youth population shapes the potential demand initial education and training in a country. The greater this proportion, more resources need to be devoted to education. Conversely, the few people that are at the age relevant for initial education, the less a cou needs to spend on education. Chart B2.1 indicates the changes in the prop tions of educational expenditure for a given total government outlay t would be expected if the size of the population aged 5-29 were at the OE average in each country, other things being equal. In countries such Belgium, Denmark, Finland, Germany, Italy, Sweden and Switzerland, wh the proportion of the youth population is relatively small, public spending education would be more than 10 per cent higher if the proportion of you people in the total population were increased to the level of the OE average. On the other hand, the relative expenditure of Korea would expected to be almost 20 per cent lower, and that of Mexico and Turkey ab 30 per cent lower, if the proportion of young people in these countries w at the OECD average.

Variations in the proportion of total public spending on education can also reflect differences in the scope of the education sector between countries.

Finally, variations in the proportion of total public spending on edu tion tend to reflect differences in the scope of the education sector betwe countries, as well as differences in the breadth and depth of the pu sector's involvement in areas outside education. For example, countries t spend relatively large amounts on their social security and national he care systems (such as Austria, Denmark, France, Germany and Sweden) r appear to be spending relatively small proportions of their public budget education, even though educational institutions and participants in education may still benefit directly or indirectly from other public expenditure. Furthermore, some countries provide benefits to students or households in the form of tax reductions, tax subsidies or other special tax provisions which are not accounted for in the educational expenditure shown in this indicator.

Trends in the proportion of public expenditure on education

Over the last decade, the proportion of public expenditure spent on education has been fairly stable in most countries, the notable exceptions being Mexico and Spain where it has risen by 13 and 4 per cent respectively (see Table B2.t). In Korea, the expansion of public expenditure has been smaller in the education sector than in other sectors, which has led to a decrease in the proportion of public sector spending on education by almost 3 per cent. However, at 17 per cent, the proportion spent on education in Korea is still one of the largest in the OECD.

Definitions

ta refer to the financial year 1994 and are based on the UOE *data collection on education statistics, administered in* 1996 (*for details see* Annex 3).

In this indicator each of the following three expenditure variables is expressed as a percentage of a country's total public sector expenditure: *i*) direct public expenditure on educational services; *ii*) public subsidies for educational services; and *iii*) total educational expenditure. The percentages are calculated separately for primary-secondary education, tertiary education, and all levels combined.

Direct public expenditure on educational services includes both amounts spent directly by governments to hire educational personnel and to procure other resources, and amounts provided by governments to public or private institutions for use by the institutions themselves to acquire educational resources. Public subsidies include scholarships and other financial aid to students plus certain subsidies to other private entities, although subsidies which eventually end up as payments to institutions have been netted out to prevent double counting. The data on total public expenditure for all purposes (the denominator in all percentage calculations) have been taken from the OECD National Accounts Database (see Annex 2).

The methodology that was used for the calculation of the estimates in Chart B2.1 is explained in Annex 3.

The country mean is calculated as the simple average across all countries for which data are available. The OECD total reflects the value of the indicator when the OECD region is considered as a whole (for details see Reader's Guide).

Table B2.2 shows direct public educational expenditure on institutions and transfers to the private sector for education as a percentage of total public educational expenditure for the tertiary level of education. It also shows different types of transfers to the private sector as a percentage of total public educational expenditure at the tertiary level.

Scholarships and grants include special subsidies provided to students, either in cash or in kind, such as free or reduced-price travel on public transport systems, and family or child allowances that are contingent on student status. Student loans are reported on a gross basis, without subtracting or netting out repayments or interest payments from the borrowers. Financial aid to students attributable to household payments to educational institutions is the amount of the subsidies to students or households which is further transferred to educational institutions, *i.e.* indirect public payments to educational institutions. Payments to other private entities include such payments to private entities which are not defined as educational institution. These include transfers to business or labour associations that provide ad education, subsidies to firms or labour associations that operate apprentic ship programmes, subsidies to non-profit organisations that provide stude housing or student meals and interest rate subsidies to private financ institutions that make student loans.

Table B2.1 **Public expenditure on education as a percentage of total public expenditure by level of education (1994)**

	Total: direct expenditure plus public subsidies to the private sector			Direct public expenditure on educational services			Public subsidies to the private sector		
	Primary and secondary education	Tertiary education	All levels of education combined	Primary and secondary education	Tertiary education	All levels of education combined	Primary and secondary education	Tertiary education	All levels of education combined
North America									
Canada	8.6	4.8	13.8	8.6	3.3	12.3	n	1.5	1.5
Mexico	18.5	5.2	26.0	18.4	5.0	25.8	x	x	x
United States	9.4	3.3	13.6	9.4	3.2	13.5	x	0.1	0.1
Pacific Area									
Australia	9.5	3.9	13.6	8.6	3.0	11.8	0.9	0.9	1.8
Japan	8.4	1.5	10.8	8.4	1.5	10.8	m	m	m
Korea	13.7	1.4	17.4	13.7	1.3	17.1	n	n	0.3
New Zealand	11.5	4.6	17.2	10.9	3.0	14.9	0.6	1.6	2.3
European Union									
Austria	m	m	m	m	m	m	m	m	m
Belgium	6.9	2.1	10.2	6.9	1.7	9.9	n	0.3	0.4
Denmark	7.3	3.3	12.6	6.7	2.1	10.2	0.6	1.1	2.3
Finland	7.6	3.1	11.9	7.2	2.4	10.9	0.4	0.7	1.1
France	7.7	1.8	10.8	7.4	1.6	10.4	0.3	0.2	0.5
Germany	6.1	2.1	9.4	5.8	1.9	9.0	0.2	0.2	0.4
Greece	5.0	2.0	7.0	5.0	1.9	6.9	n	n	n
Ireland	8.9	3.0	13.2	8.6	2.4	12.2	0.3	0.7	1.0
Italy	6.2	1.4	8.8	6.1	1.3	8.5	0.1	0.1	0.3
Luxembourg	m	m	m	m	m	m	m	m	m
Netherlands	5.9	2.9	9.4	5.3	2.1	8.0	0.5	0.8	1.4
Portugal	m	m	m	m	m	m	m	m	m
Spain	9.2	2.2	12.6	9.1	2.1	12.3	0.1	0.1	0.3
Sweden	7.3	2.9	11.0	6.5	2.2	9.4	0.8	0.8	1.6
United Kingdom	8.7	2.7	11.6	8.5	1.5	10.3	0.2	1.2	1.3
Other OECD countries									
Czech Republic	9.8	2.1	13.8	9.0	1.9	12.9	0.7	0.2	1.0
Hungary	m	3.3	m	m	2.8	m	n	0.5	0.5
Iceland	m	2.4	12.0	8.3	1.6	11.0	m	0.8	1.0
Norway	8.5	4.0	15.5	7.8	2.6	13.1	0.6	1.4	2.4
Poland	m	m	m	m	m	m	m	m	m
Switzerland	11.6	3.2	15.6	11.2	3.1	15.1	0.3	0.1	0.5
Turkey	9.4	5.3	14.7	9.2	5.1	14.3	0.2	0.3	0.5
Country mean	**8.7**	**3.0**	**13.0**	**8.4**	**2.4**	**12.1**	**0.3**	**0.6**	**1.0**

Source: OECD Database. See Annex 3 for notes.

Table B2.2 **Direct expenditure on educational institutions and transfers to the private sector for educational purposes as a percentage of total educational expenditure, tertiary education (1994)**

	Direct expenditure on institutions	Transfers to the private sector for educational purposes					Total
		Financial aid to students			Transfers and payments to other private entities	Total	
		Scholarships/ other grants to households	Student loans	Total			
North America							
Canada	68.7	15.6	n	16.1	15.11	31.3	100.0
Mexico	m	m	m	m	m	m	m
United States	96.9	x	x	3.1	x	3.1	100.0
Pacific Area							
Australia	77.1	12.6	10.3	22.9	n	22.9	100.0
Japan	m	a	m	m	n	m	m
Korea	97.1	2.6	n	2.9	n	2.9	100.0
New Zealand	66.0	14.3	19.7	34.0	a	34.0	100.0
European Union							
Austria	m	m	m	m	m	m	m
Belgium	83.7	16.3	a	16.3	x	16.3	100.0
Denmark	65.7	29.3	5.0	34.3	n	34.3	100.0
Finland	78.6	21.4	n	21.4	m	21.4	100.0
France	90.8	9.2	m	9.2	n	9.2	100.0
Germany	90.8	4.7	3.5	8.2	1.02	9.2	100.0
Greece	98.6	1.4	n	1.4	n	1.4	100.0
Ireland	77.5	22.5	n	22.5	n	22.5	100.0
Italy	90.6	6.6	a	6.6	2.80	9.4	100.0
Luxembourg	m	m	m	m	m	m	m
Netherlands	71.7	25.0	2.6	27.6	0.69	28.3	100.0
Portugal	90.7	9.3	a	9.3	a	9.3	100.0
Spain	93.3	6.7	n	6.7	n	6.7	100.0
Sweden	73.5	10.0	16.5	26.5	a	26.5	100.0
United Kingdom	55.4	40.2	4.4	44.6	n	44.6	100.0
Other OECD countries							
Czech Republic	89.9	10.1	a	10.1	n	10.1	100.0
Hungary	86.0	14.0	a	14.0	n	14.0	100.0
Iceland	67.5	m	32.5	32.5	m	32.5	100.0
Norway	64.5	8.2	27.3	35.5	n	35.5	100.0
Poland	m	m	m	m	m	m	m
Switzerland	95.4	3.6	n	3.9	0.69	4.6	100.0
Turkey	94.7	a	5.3	5.3	a	5.3	100.0
Country mean	**81.9**	**12.3**	**5.8**	**17.3**	**0.97**	**18.1**	**100.0**

Source: OECD Database. See Annex 3 for notes.

Table B2.3 **Distribution of public and private sources of initial funds for educational institutions (1994)**

	Primary and secondary education		Tertiary education		All levels of education combined	
	Public sources	Private sources	Public sources	Private sources	Public sources	Private sources
North America						
Canada	94.4	5.6	90.8	9.2	93.2	6.8
Mexico	m	m	m	m	m	m
United States	m	m	48.4	51.5	74.5	25.5
Pacific Area						
Australia	88.7	11.3	74.7	25.3	83.9	16.1
Japan	93.6	6.3	46.4	53.5	77.2	22.7
Korea	75.2	24.8	16.0	84.0	59.4	40.6
New Zealand	m	m	m	m	m	m
European Union						
Austria	m	m	m	m	m	m
Belgium	m	m	m	m	m	m
Denmark	97.9	2.1	99.5	n	94.0	6.0
Finland	m	m	m	m	m	m
France	92.6	7.4	83.4	16.6	91.3	8.7
Germany	75.7	24.3	90.4	9.6	77.7	22.3
Greece	m	m	m	m	m	m
Ireland	95.6	4.4	79.0	21.0	91.5	8.5
Italy	m	m	88.8	11.2	m	m
Luxembourg	m	m	m	m	m	m
Netherlands	96.4	3.6	98.0	2.0	97.0	3.0
Portugal	100.0	n	100.0	n	100.0	n
Spain	87.8	12.2	78.1	21.9	85.4	14.6
Sweden	99.8	n	93.1	6.9	98.2	1.8
United Kingdom	m	m	100.0	n	m	m
Other OECD countries						
Czech Republic	m	m	m	m	m	m
Hungary	m	m	m	m	m	m
Iceland	m	m	m	m	87.7	12.3
Norway	m	m	m	m	m	m
Poland	m	m	m	m	m	m
Switzerland	m	m	m	m	m	m
Turkey	100.0	n	94.1	5.9	97.8	2.2
Country mean	**92.1**	**7.9**	**80.0**	**19.9**	**87.3**	**12.7**

Source: OECD Database. See Annex 3 for notes.

Table B2.t **Public expenditure on education as a percentage of total public expenditure (1985-1994)**

	1985	1990	1994
North America			
Canada	13.7	13.6	13.8
Mexico	12.8	15.7	26.0
United States	13.1	14.3	13.6
Pacific Area			
Australia	15.5	12.2	13.6
Korea	20.3	22.3	17.4
Japan	m	11.3	10.8
European Union			
Austria	11.0	10.6	m
Belgium	10.3	9.5	10.2
Denmark	11.6	10.6	12.6
Finland	12.9	12.9	11.9
France	m	10.3	10.8
Germany	9.6	m	9.4
Ireland	m	12.2	13.2
Italy	9.1	9.6	8.8
Netherlands	10.2	9.9	9.4
Portugal	m	m	m
Spain	8.6	10.1	12.6
Sweden	m	9.3	11.0
United Kingdom	11.1	11.9	11.6
Other OECD countries			
Norway	13.2	m	15.5
Switzerland	15.0	15.4	15.6

Vertical bars indicate a break in the series.
Source: OECD Database. See Annex 3 for notes.

Indicator B3:   Public subsidies to households

Policy context

Through subsidies to students and their families, governments can help to cover the costs of education and related expenditure and increase access to education. These subsidies are particularly important in systems where students are expected to pay at least a share of the cost of their education and living expenses. Public subsidies come in many forms, including academic scholarships, need-based aid, guaranteed or subsidised student loans, education-related tax breaks or other household transfers. Subsidies to households can provide access to educational opportunities, particularly at the post-compulsory level, for students who do not have the financial resources to attend on their own. As aid can also serve as a substitute for work as a financial resource, public subsidies may facilitate persistence and attainment by enabling students to attend full-time and work fewer hours or not at all.

While the preceding indicators focus on expenditure on educational institutions, this indicator broadens the perspective by taking into account all public transfers to households, not just those that will be used to pay tuition and other fees in educational institutions.

Evidence and explanations

In all OECD countries, governments provide the largest share of the financial resources for education. Governments differ widely, however, in the way in which they finance education, in how they target financial resources and in the effect that their funding strategies have on the incentive structure for students. While some countries finance education largely through direct payments to educational institutions, without requiring students to pay for tuition, other countries channel significant resources to institutions through subsidies to students and their families. These household subsidies are then used to cover tuition fees, as well as all or part of their living costs. Across countries, many different funding strategies are used, often combined in different ways, including:

- direct payments to institutions to cover the cost of educational provision;
- unconditional payments to all students in the form of grants, which can be used to pay tuition and fees or to cover student living costs;
- payments to selected students, in the form of scholarships, grants, or bursaries, awarded on the basis of academic ability;
- payments to selected students, in the form of means-tested grants or scholarships, awarded on the grounds of financial need;
- repayable loans, provided to students from public funds on favourable terms, or government guarantees and interest subsidies for loans provided by the private sector;

– provision of meals, housing, books, health care or travel at pri
below market rates, either to educational institutions or to student
– tax concessions to students or their families to cover educational cos

The data presented in this indicator are still developmental and compariso
between countries need to interpreted with great caution. These data c
however, provide a broad overview of the various arrangements that e
within OECD Member countries for providing financial aid to households
education.

Public subsidies to households
need to be considered jointly
with the way in which
educational institutions are
structured and funded.

Chart B3.1 shows the percentage of total expenditure on tertiary-level edu
tional institutions that is paid by households. Unlike the data presented
private sources in Table B2.3, the data presented here are after transfers
they include public subsidies to households) and focus on household ex
diture, as opposed to other private expenditure (*e.g.* from business ent
prises). The data presented in this chart give some indication of the degree
which tertiary institutions are funded through tuition and other fees paid
households.

For example, at the tertiary level in the United States there are both pu
and private institutions. Both types of institution typically charge tuition
fees (public fees being typically lower than private), which are paid by hou
holds. In 1994, 39 per cent of total expenditure in US tertiary educatio
institutions was funded by households (See Chart B3.1). Japan and Korea f
an even larger share of expenditure by educational institutions thro
charges to households (51 and 62 per cent, respectively). As a result, pu
financial aid to students in these countries, whether in the form of loans

◆   Chart B3.1.   ***Percentage of total expenditure on tertiary-level educational instituti***
from both public and private sources that is paid by households (1994)

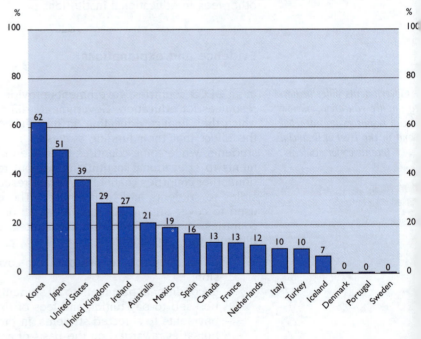

Note: Household expenditures are "after transfers", that is, they include public subsidies to households. These da
differ from those presented in Table B2.3 in that other private expenditure (e.g., from business enterpri
excluded from this chart.

Source: OECD.

grants, is particularly important for paying for tuition and fees. The percentage of total expenditure by educational institutions that is funded by households is between 20 and 30 per cent in Australia, Ireland and the United Kingdom and between 10 and 20 per cent in Canada, France, Hungary, Italy, Mexico, the Netherlands, Spain and Turkey. In Denmark, Portugal and Sweden there are no reported household payments for educational services at the tertiary level and the percentage for Iceland is small (7 per cent). Public subsidies to households in the latter countries are primarily for funding student living expenses.

While some argue that tuition fees impose a potential barrier to student participation and equity, there is little comparative evidence of the effects of tuition fees on the patterns of participation. In fact, those countries which charge tuition fees generally show much higher rates of participation than countries with mainly public sources of funds (see Indicator C5).

An additional complicating factor is that educational institutions can also provide auxiliary services such as housing and meals. In some countries these services are primarily funded by the government, while in other countries they are paid for through fees and other charges to households. To the extent that these services are funded by direct government transfers to institutions, the living expenses of students will be reduced, as will the need for public subsidies to households.

A special survey provides preliminary data on the scope and significance of the various subsidy categories.

To gain a better understanding of the importance of public subsidies to households a special survey was conducted. The response of 20 OECD countries allows for an interesting insight into the application of public subsidies as an instrument to enhance educational participation. Although the results of this survey should be regarded as experimental, its outcomes, if cautiously interpreted, can convey valuable impressions of the similarities and differences between countries.

In all countries, public subsidies to households are focused on students who attend either upper secondary or tertiary education, with the vast majority of funds in most countries targeted at the tertiary level. Only in Sweden and Switzerland are public subsidies for households greater at the upper secondary than at the tertiary level (see Table B3.2). Data on public subsidies to households for the lower levels of education are therefore not shown in this indicator.

Mechanisms for providing public subsidies to households

untries use different mixes of grants and loans to subsidise students' educational costs.

A central question in many countries is whether financial subsidies for households should primarily be provided in the form of grants or loans (see Tables B3.1a and B3.1b). Governments choose to subsidise students' educational costs through different mixes of grants and loans for several reasons: differences in the costs of grants versus loans over the short term and the long term; the relative equity of different forms of student subsidy; and the effects of different forms of subsidy on student persistence and completion. Advocates of student loans argue that loans impose less of a burden on the pubic budget than grants and scholarships. They also argue that money spent on loans goes farther, that is, if the amount spent on grants were instead used to guarantee or subsidise loans, more total aid would be available to students and overall access would be increased. Loans also shift some of the cost of education to those who benefit most from the educational investment – which involves less transfer of income from less wealthy taxpayers to students who will, on average, have higher incomes. Opponents of loans argue that student loans will be less effective than grants in encouraging low-income students to pursue their education.

Most countries provide both scholarships/grants and loans to students. Whi
at the upper secondary level student loans play only a very minor role, at tl
tertiary level the relative weight of grants and scholarships on the one har
and student loans on the other, varies considerably between countries (se
Table B3.1b).

Loans can be an important component of financial aid to students.

In some countries, student loans are an important component of financial a
to students, provided along with, as part of, or instead of grants. The major
of such student loan programmes provide long-term low-interest loans
students to enable them to cover tuition fees and/or living expenses. Loa
are typically provided from public funds, although it is also common
governments to guarantee the repayment of loans to students made
private lenders. In Canada, for example, the student loan application p
gramme is government-run and the government provides loan guarante
Once the loan eligibility and amount are established, however, the act
lending and repayment become a private matter between the applicant a
their preferred bank.

The optimal mix of grants and loans continues to be a point of debate
many countries. At the tertiary level of education, Austria, the Flemish Co
munity of Belgium, the Czech Republic, France, Ireland and Spain provi
student aid largely in the form of grants. The proportion of loan-related pul
subsidies ranges from below 10 per cent (Canada, France, Greece a
Switzerland) to a loan-share of above 60 per cent (Mexico, New Zeala
Norway and Sweden) (see Table B3.1b).

Family and child allowances contingent on student status, tax reductions and living allowances are other important forms of subsidy.

Family and child allowances that are contingent on student status, tax red
tions and subsidies specifically for housing, meals, transport, med
expenses, books and supplies, etc., are other important forms of pul
subsidies. In the Czech Republic and France tax reductions and special sul
dies account for over half of the amount of public subsidies to househol
For example, at the tertiary level in France, scholarships and loans
approximately 1.5 per cent to total public expenditure for education, while
reductions and other specific subsidies for tertiary students add 2.2
2.6 per cent, respectively (see Table B3.2). These forms of subsidy
represent a sizeable element in Australia, Germany and Sweden.

Criteria for receiving public subsidies

Countries apply different criteria for the eligibility of students for public subsidies.

Another aspect in which countries differ pertains to the criteria by wl
students become eligible for public subsidies (see Table B3.3). In m
countries, eligibility for public subsidies is restricted.

In a majority of the countries included in this indicator, both the receip
subsidies and the amount awarded are contingent on the student's far
income. The level of restriction has a large effect on the proportion of
dents eligible. Countries roughly fall into three groups: the United Kingc
and the United States with eligibility rates of nearly 70 per cent form
group, another group includes a number of Western European count
whose rates reach from about 15 per cent (Switzerland) and 20 per c
(France) to some 25 per cent (Germany and Ireland), and a third group
below 10 per cent rates includes several Southern European countries.

In some loan schemes the level of repayment is contingent on the later income of the beneficiaries.

Some countries have introduced loan schemes in which the level of re
ment is contingent on the later income of the beneficiaries. In these
systems, students pay a fixed proportion of their income each year
graduation until their dept is repaid. For example, the Higher Educa
Contribution Scheme (HECS), introduced in Australia in 1989, obliges e
student to repay about one-fourth of the average cost of instruction for
year of study leading to the first university-level degree. These payments
either be made up-front for a discount or, more typically, once the stud

earnings exceed a specified amount. In this scheme, the real interest rate on deferred repayments is zero (OECD *Economic Surveys: Australia* 1997). This form of repayment structure allows students more flexibility for repaying their debt upon graduation; students who take lower-paid jobs will make lower loan repayments, but they will be making payments for a longer period of time.

The majority of countries reporting data on public subsidies require that at least a portion of these subsidies be paid back. The loan-related proportions of these transfers ranges from 3 per cent in Canada to some 70 per cent in Norway and Sweden.

Evidence of progress in studies is another important criterion for eligibility in many countries.

Evidence of progress in studies, especially at the tertiary level of education, is a condition for obtaining scholarships/grants and loans in the majority of the OECD countries (see Table B3.3). For example, Denmark has encouraged students to progress more rapidly through its "taximeter" funding mechanism. Two features of the "taximeter" provide added incentive for progress towards a degree: eligibility for payments to students for living expenses is limited to twelve semesters of enrolment and institutions receive appropriations on the basis of the number of "passes" in examinations. Similar performance criteria are applied in Finland and Sweden, in which part of the public funding provided to institutions is based on the volume of completed degrees (especially advanced degrees).

◆ Chart B3.2. **Public subsidies to households for tertiary education as a percentage of public expenditure on education (net of subsidies) (1994-1995)**

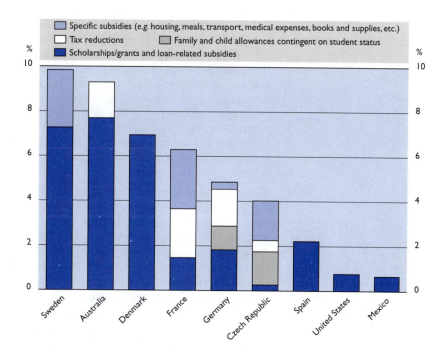

No data available on loans for the United States, and on family and child allowances contingent on student status for France.

Source: OECD.

In Germany also, the number of semesters for which public subsidies a available is limited to 8-10 semesters in universities and 6-8 semesters *Fachhochschulen.*

There remain a number of countries (Australia, the Czech Republic, t United Kingdom and the United States – and with regard to certain areas al France and Switzerland) that do not link public subsidies to student progre:

In most countries the use made of public payments to households for education is determined by the beneficiaries.

In most countries the bulk of public payments to households for educati are not earmarked, that is, their use is determined by the direct beneficiarie the students and their families. In some countries, however, public subsidi are earmarked for payments to educational institutions. Ireland, Spain a the United Kingdom, for example, earmark public subsidies for tuition. In t Netherlands, Norway and Spain certain proportions of scholarships/grar provided for general purposes are used for the payment of tuition fees. Sor countries also earmark other types of subsidies. Mexico's scholarship/gr: system includes, for example, special payments (partly) to cover the costs housing, meals etc. In countries where tuition costs are relatively high (*e.g.* t United States), a large proportion of the public subsidy to households effectively earmarked for payments to educational institutions, even witho an official policy.

Another form of public subsidies is family and child allowances contingent student status. At the upper secondary level, these allowances would a 2 per cent or more to total public expenditure on education in the Cz Republic and Sweden (see Table B3.2). A further transfer channel, namely tax incentives, is used by other countries, of which four are able to report st data.

Relative size of public subsidies to households for education

The size of subsidies as a proportion of GDP varies widely between countries.

For nine out of the 20 countries reporting data on public subsidies to hou holds, the coverage of the data is sufficiently comprehensive to allow comp isons of the relative size of these subsidies (see Chart B3.2) . When the siz all public subsidies to households (including scholarships/grants, loans, f: ily allowances, tax reductions and other specific subsidies) for all level: education are compared with total public expenditure on education (ne subsidies), wide differences between countries become visible. There wide gap between Mexico and the United States (with public subsic equivalent to 1 per cent or less of public expenditure) and Austr: Denmark, France and Sweden (with subsidies equivalent to over 6 per cen total public expenditure). The Czech Republic, Germany and Spain between the two groups.

It is important to remember, as noted above, that public subsidies to hor holds need to be considered jointly with the way in which educational inst tions are structured and funded. Although more information is needed cerning the degree to which similar services are provided by educatic institutions (*e.g.* room and board) and/or funded through direct public su dies to educational institutions, some tentative conclusions can be draw

Governments which spend much on educational institutions also provide high levels of subsidies.

Generally, those countries with relatively high levels of direct public expe ture on educational institutions also provide relatively large amounts of p lic subsidies to households for education.

The size of the resources that are invested in education needs, of course be seen in the context of the number of persons who participate in educa and, as far as public subsidies to households are concerned, in the conte: the beneficiaries of these subsidies. Dividing the total amount of pt subsidies to households by the number of students enrolled reveals cor erable variation between countries, ranging from an annual equiva US$155 per tertiary student in Mexico to some US$2 800 in Denmark

◆ Chart B3.3. *Average annual household subsidies per student at the tertiary level*
(1994-1995)

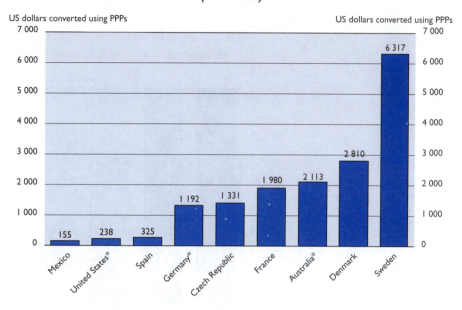

* Values for certain sub-categories of specific subsidies missing.
Subsidies to cover interest on private loans are included.
Source: OECD.

US$6 300 in Sweden (See Chart B3.3). At the upper secondary level the amounts per student are much lower, though not negligible in most countries (see Table B3.1a). A few countries report considerable amounts for subsidies even for pupils at lower secondary and pre-primary/primary levels of education. Because of coverage problems in the data it should be noted that the actual amounts transferred to households are likely to be higher – and in countries with low eligibility rates for certain subsidy categories, much higher.

The incentive for individuals to participate in education can also be increased through the provision of tax incentives and family and child allowances for students. In countries that arrange substantial proportions of their transfers to households in ways other than through scholarships/grants and loans – such as the Czech Republic, France and Germany – the full measure of their support is not as visible as in countries that mainly rely on direct financial subsidies to students, such as Denmark, the Netherlands, Spain, Sweden and the United Kingdom.

Definitions

Data are based on a special survey carried out among OECD Member countries in 1997.

In this survey, countries provided, for each level of education, information on public educational subsidies to households in 1993, 1994 or 1995. The following categories of public subsidies were included: *i*) scholarships/grants (with a distinction between public subsidies for household payments to educational institutions and those for general purposes); *ii*) loan-related subsidies (with a distinction between student loans and interest-related subsidies for private loans); *iii*) family or child allowances contingent on pupil/student status; *iv*) tax

◆ Chart B3.4. ***Distribution of public subsidies to households by type of subsidy for upper secondary and tertiary education (1994-1995)***

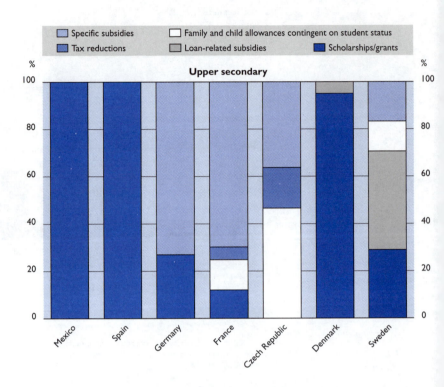

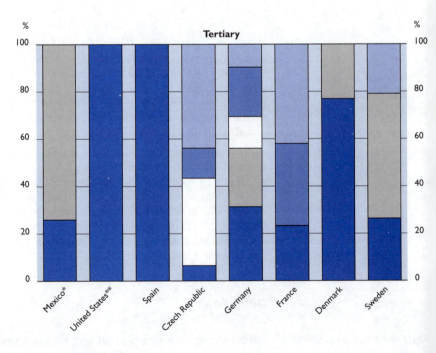

* Including family and child allowances as well as specific subsidies.
** Including loan-related subsidies.

Countries are ranked in ascending order of total subsidies.

Source: OECD.

reductions and *v*) public subsidies specifically for housing, meals, transport, medical expenses, books and supplies, social, recreational and other purposes. The indicative nature of the data should be emphasised. The survey also collected descriptive information on the types of funding systems in the different countries.

Public subsidies reported in this indicator have been included in Indicator B1 only to the extent that they are destined for educational institutions. Values in Indicator B1 are therefore usually smaller than in this indicator.

Subsidies include the value of special subsidies provided to students, either in cash or in kind. Expenditure on student loans has been reported on a gross basis – that is, without subtracting or netting out repayments or interest payments from the borrowers (students or households). The reason is that the gross amount of loans including scholarships and grants, is the relevant variable for measuring financial aid to current participants in education. Although interest payments and repayments by the borrowers would have to be taken into account to assess the net cost of student loans to public and private lenders, such payments are not usually made by current students but rather by former students. (In most countries, moreover, loan repayments do not flow to the education authorities, and thus the money is not available to them to cover other educational expenditure.)

Table B3.1a **Average annual public subsidies to households for education as a percentage of GDP and per student enrolled (US dollars converted using PPPs) by subsidy category (1994-1995), upper secondary education**

	Scholarships/ grants and loan-related subsidies		of which loan-related subsidies (%)	Scholarships/ grants net of fees and loan related subsidies		Family and child allowances contingent on student status		Tax reductions contingent on student status		Specific subsidies	
	as % GDP	per student enrolled		as % GDP	per student enrolled	as % GDP	per student enrolled	as % GDP	per student enrolled	as % GDP	per student enrolled
North America											
Canada	m	m	a	m	m	a	a	m	m	m	m
Mexico	0.01	19	a	0.01	19	a	a	a	a	a	a
United States	a	a	a	a	a	a	a	a	a	a	a
Pacific Area											
Australia	0.17	1 000	a	0.17	1 000	0.001	3	x	x	0.01	79
New Zealand	0.24	874	33.9	0.16	577	a	a	m	m	*0.002*	*9*
European Union											
Austria	0.01	80	a	0.01	80	m	m	m	m	*0.04*	*236*
Belgium (Flemish Community)	0.01	15	a	0.01	15	m	a	m	m	m	m
Denmark	0.26	1 182	5.0	0.25	1 123	a	a	m	m	a	a
Finland	0.24	783	14.1	0.21	673	a	a	m	m	*0.04*	*142*
France	0.04	102	a	0.04	102	0.02	109	0.02	45	0.14	*593*
Germany	0.02	45	a	0.02	45	x	x	x	x	*0.09*	*122*
Greece	0.001	2	m	0.001	2	a	a	a	a	m	m
Ireland	a	a	a	a	a	0.06	201	a	a	0.02	80
Netherlands	0.32	1 014	2.2	0.11	509	m	m	m	m	0.05	248
Spain	0.04	87	a	0.04	87	a	a	a	a	a	a
Sweden	0.83	3 269	59.0	0.34	1 339	0.15	588	a	a	0.20	772
United Kingdom	0.07	120	2.7	0.03	64	m	m	a	a	m	m
Other OECD countries											
Czech Republic	0.0005	1	a	0.0005	1	0.32	483	0.12	177	0.25	376
Switzerland	0.06	360	3.1	0.05	349	m	m	m	m	m	m
Norway	0.29	1 309	45.2	0.16	717	m	m	m	m	m	m

Figures in italics indicate that values for certain sub-categories of specific subsidies are missing.
Source: Special survey conducted by OECD, 1997. See Annex 3 for notes.

(US dollars converted using PPPs) by subsidy category (1994-1995), tertiary education

	Scholarships/grants and loan-related subsidies		of which loan-related subsidies (%)	Scholarships/grants net of fees and loan related subsidies		Family and child allowances contingent on student status		Tax reductions contingent on student status		Specific subsidies	
	as % GDP	per student enrolled		as % GDP	per student enrolled	as % GDP	per student enrolled	as % GDP	per student enrolled	as % GDP	per student enrolled
North America											
Canada	0.38	1 693	3.1	0.36	1 641	a	a	m	m	m	m
Mexico	0.03	155	74.1	0.01	40	a	a	a	a	a	a
United States	0.04	238	m	0.04	238	a	a	a	a	m	m
Pays du Pacifique											
Australia	0.35	1 903	45.6	0.19	1 035	a	a	0.07	210	m	m
New Zealand	0.65	3 019	61.1	0.25	1 175	a	a	m	m	m	m
Union européenne											
Austria	0.06	445	a	0.06	445	0.12	836	m	m	0.01	95
Belgium (Flemish Community)											
Denmark	0.45	2 810	23.0	0.35	2 162	m	m	a	a	m	m
Finland	0.39	1 595	14.2	0.33	1 370	a	a	m	a	a	a
France	0.08	462	0.3	0.08	457	m	m	0.12	686	0.07	290
Germany	0.08	668	44.2	0.05	373	0.05	160	0.07	249	0.15	831
Greece	0.01	44	4.7	0.01	42	a	a	a	a	0.01	115
Ireland	0.28	1 502	a	0.13	712	x	x	m	m	m	m
Netherlands	0.51	2 469	12.7	0.22	1 374	m	m	m	m	0.07	470
Spain	0.11	325	a	0.06	241	a	a	a	a	a	a
Sweden	0.64	4 995	66.7	0.21	1 663	a	a	a	a	0.17	1 322
United Kingdom	0.49	3 981	16.8	0.21	1 714	m	m	a	a	m	m
Autres pays OCDE											
Czech Republic	0.01	86	a	0.01	86	0.09	493	0.03	168	0.10	584
Switzerland	0.05	579	7.8	0.04	534	m	m	m	m	m	m
Norway	0.86	4 578	70.1	0.22	1 233	m	m	m	m	0.03	155

Figures in italics indicate that values for certain sub-categories of specific subsidies are missing.
Source: Special survey conducted by OECD, 1997. See Annex 3 for notes.

Table B3.2 **Average annual public subsidies to households for education by subsidy category as a percentage of total public expenditure on education (net of subsidies) (1994-1995), upper secondary and tertiary education**

	Upper secondary education					Tertiary education				
	Scholarships/grants and loan-related subsidies	Scholarships/grants net of fees and loan-related subsidies	Family and child allowances contingent on student status	Tax reductions contingent on student status	Specific subsidies	Scholarships/grants and loan-related subsidies	Scholarships/grants net of fees and loan-related subsidies	Family and child allowances contingent on student status	Tax reductions contingent on student status	Specific subsidies
North America										
Canada	m	m	a	m	m	6.3	6.1	a	m	m
Mexico	0.1	0.1	a	a	a	0.7	0.2	a	a	a
United States	a	a	a	a	a	0.8	0.8	a	a	m
Pacific Area										
Australia	3.8	3.8	0.01	x	0.3	7.7	4.2	a	1.6	m
New Zealand	4.3	2.9	a	m	0.05	11.7	4.6	a	m	m
European Union										
Austria	0.3	0.3	m	m	0.8	1.3	1.3	2.4	m	0.3
Belgium (Flemish Community)	0.1	0.1	a	m	m	0.4	0.4	m	m	m
Denmark	4.0	3.8	a	a	a	6.9	5.3	a	a	a
Finland	3.6	3.1	a	m	0.7	5.8	5.0	a	m	1.1
France	0.8	0.8	0.3	0.3	2.5	1.5	1.5	m	2.2	2.6
Germany	0.5	0.5	x	x	1.9	1.8	1.0	1.1	1.6	0.3
Greece	0.03	0.03	a	a	m	0.5	0.4	a	a	m
Ireland	a	a	1.2	m	0.5	5.6	2.6	x	m	m
Netherlands	7.2	2.5	m	m	1.2	11.3	4.8	m	m	1.6
Spain	0.9	0.9	a	a	a	2.2	1.3	a	a	a
Sweden	12.7	5.2	2.3	a	3.0	7.3	3.2	a	a	2.6
United Kingdom	1.4	0.8	m	a	m	10.8	4.7	m	a	m
Other OECD countries										
Czech Republic	0.01	0.01	5.5	2.0	4.3	0.3	0.3	1.5	0.5	1.8
Norway	4.3	2.4	m	m	m	12.5	3.3	m	m	0.4
Switzerland	1.0	1.0	m	m	m	0.8	0.8	m	m	m

Figures in italics indicate that values for certain sub-categoires of specific subsidies are missing.
Source: Special survey conducted by OECD, 1997. See Annex 3 for notes.

| | Scholarships/ grants related to progress | Eligibility dependent on: | | | |
		student's income	parents' income	partner's income	
North America					
Canada	yes	yes	yes	yes	No tuition fees for public primary and secondary institutions.
Mexico	yes	yes	yes	yes	At the upper secondary level of education, criteria for eligibility do not apply.
United States	no	yes	yes	yes	Eligibility not specifically dependent on progress, but if students fail or do not maintain a certain grade point average, they could lose their scholarship. No tuition fees up to upper secondary education, except private schools.
Pacific Area					
Australia	no	yes	yes	yes	Eligibility for student grants depends on parents' income if student is under 25 and single. Grants are also related to progress. Eligibility and relation to progress for scholarships vary according to scholarship under consideration.
New Zealand	yes	yes	yes	yes	
European Union					
Austria	yes	yes	yes	yes	Related to progress only for scholarships at the secondary level when the student is no longer of school age, and at the tertiary level.
Belgium (Flemish)	yes	yes	yes	yes	Tuition fee at tertiary level in public and government-dependent institutions depends on the institution. Only minimum and maximum are fixed by decree.
Denmark	yes	yes	yes	no	No tuition fees for public institutions; eligibility based on parents' income for students aged 18-19.
Finland	yes	yes/no	yes/no	no	No tuition fees for public institutions. If student works outside the academic year, income has no effect on scholarship; parents' income has effect at age 17-19.
France	yes	yes	yes	yes	Related to progress only for scholarships at the tertiary level.
Germany	yes	yes	yes	yes	No tuition fees for public institutions; within tertiary education, eligibility related to certified progress. Maximum duration of scholarships/grants limited to the theoretical duration of study.
Greece	yes	no	yes	no	No tuition fees for public institutions.
Ireland	yes	yes	yes	yes	Eligibility depends on student's and partner's income only if student is over 23. In upper secondary only, a few institutions charge fees.
Netherlands	yes	no	yes	no	Related to progress in tertiary education.
Spain	yes	yes	yes	yes	
Sweden	yes	yes	no	yes	No tuition fees.
United Kingdom	no	yes	yes	yes	Eligibility mainly dependent on parental income. Students aged over 25 have their own income taken into account.
Other OECD countries					
Czech Republic	no	yes	yes	yes	No tuition fees for public institutions; eligibility depends on total income of student's family.
Norway	yes	yes	yes	no	Eligibility depends on parents' income only for students under 19 in upper secondary education. In public higher education, institutions may ask a small term fee for running of student welfare activities.

Loans include subsidies to cover interest on private loans.
Specific subsidies: for housing, meals, transport, medical expenses, books and supplies, social and recreational purposes, etc.
Source: Special survey conducted by OECD, 1997. See Annex 3 for notes.

Indicator B4: **Educational expenditure per student**

Policy context

This indicator shows annual expenditure per student in absolute terms (in equivalent US dollars) as well as the cumulative expenditure over the average duration of tertiary studies.

Effective schools require the right combination of talented personnel, adquate facilities, state-of-the-art equipment, and motivated students ready learn. Across OECD countries, the demand for high-quality education is banced against the need to avoid undue burden on taxpayers. As a result, question of whether the resources devoted to education are yielding aquate value for the cost figures prominently in public debate. Even smgains in efficiency, on the order of 1 or 2 per cent, could release prodigiresources that could be used to reduce educational costs or to increaaccess.

It also compares per-student expenditure in relative terms – with per capita GDP, as a broad measure of a country's standard of living, taken as the basis for comparisons.

Policy-makers must balance the need to improve the quality of educatioservices with the need to expand access to educational opportunities. Thmust also decide how to allocate funding over the different levels of edution – including continuing education and training – and over different typof educational programmes. For example, some countries emphasise braccess to higher education while others invest in near-universal education children as young as two or three.

While the optimal level of resources that will prepare each student for life work in the modern economy is not known, international comparisons of pstudent investment in education can provide a starting point for evaluatthe effectiveness of different models of educational provision.

Evidence and explanations

Expenditure per student in equivalent US dollars

As a whole, OECD countries spend about US$4 880 per student each year – US$3 310 per primary student, US$4 670 per secondary student and US$9 820 per tertiary student...

OECD countries as a whole spend about US$4 880 per student each year levels of education combined). US$3 310 are spent per student at the prinlevel, US$4 670 per student at the secondary level and US$9 820 per stucat the tertiary level. However, these OECD-wide totals are heavily influenby the high expenditure levels in the United States. The levels per studerthe "typical" OECD country, as represented by the simple mean acrosscountries, are US$3 310 at the primary level, US$4 340 at the secondary land US$7 740 at the tertiary level of education.

... but these averages mask a broad range of expenditure per student across countries.

These averages mask a broad range of expenditure per student across cotries. Even excluding the two countries with the highest and the two with lowest expenditure, the range in expenditure per student is wide: from abUS$1 700 to US$5 300 at the primary level, from US$1 700 to more US$6 500 at the secondary level, and from less than US$4 100 to more US$12 800 at the tertiary level.

◆ Chart B4.1. ***Annual expenditure per student (US dollars converted using PPPs)***
in public and private institutions by level of education (1994)

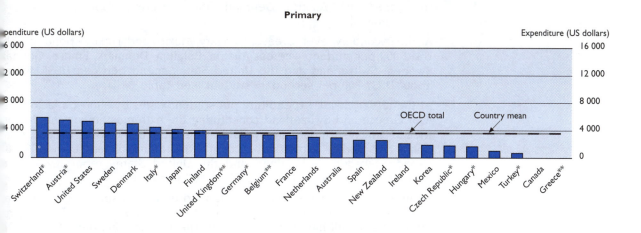

Primary

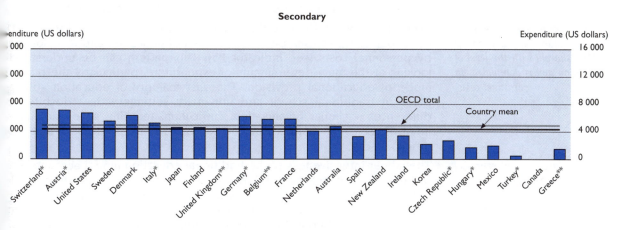

Secondary

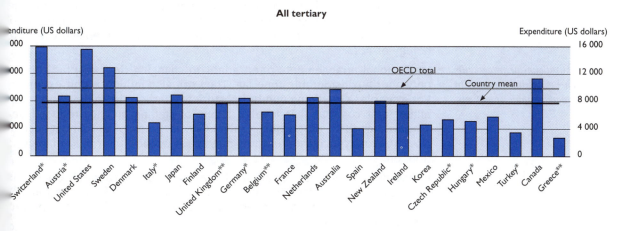

All tertiary

ublic institutions.

ublic and government-dependent private institutions.

tries and ranked in descending order of expenditure per student at the primary level of education.

e: OECD.

Of the 22 countries for which data on expenditure per primary student a available, five spend about US$1 900 or less per primary student (the Cze Republic, Hungary, Korea, Mexico and Turkey) and six countries spend mc than US$4 400 (Austria, Denmark, Italy, Sweden, Switzerland and t United States).

At the secondary level, Greece, Hungary, Mexico and Turkey spend less th US$2 000 per student, whereas Austria, Belgium, Denmark, France, Germal Sweden, Switzerland and the United States spend between US$5 400 a about US$7 300 per secondary student (see Table B4.1).

At the tertiary level, expenditure per student varies by almost a factor of s with Greece and Switzerland constituting the extremes among the 24 cou tries for which such data are available (see Table B4.1). While Greece, Kor Spain and Turkey report per-student expenditure of less than US$4 6 Canada, Sweden, Switzerland and the United States report expenditu between US$11 000 and almost US$16 000 per year.

To interpret the figures on early childhood education spending per stude one must consider the differences between the Nordic countries and m others. Early childhood institutions in the Nordic countries often prov extended day and evening care for young children, the costs of which included in the spending per student reported for Finland and Norway.

There is a common pattern: expenditure per student rises sharply with the level of education and is dominated by personnel costs.

Expenditure per student exhibits a common pattern throughout the OECD each country it rises sharply with the level of education and it is dominat by personnel costs (see Indicator B5). This pattern can be understood looking at the main determinants of expenditure, particularly the place a mode of educational provision. The vast majority of education still tal place in traditional school and university settings with – despite so differences – similar organisation, curriculum, teaching style and mana ment. These commonalties are likely to lead to similar patterns of unit exp diture.

The labour intensiveness of education accounts for the predominance of teachers' salaries in overall costs.

The labour intensiveness of the traditional education model accounts for predominance of teachers' salaries in overall costs. Differences in stude teaching staff ratios (see Indicator B8), staffing patterns, teachers' sala (see Indicator D1), teaching materials and facilities influence cost differen between levels of education, types of programmes and types of schools.

Technology may allow some savings to be made.

Future gains in efficiency may be achieved through the use of new infor tion technologies, both to hold down unit costs and to maintain, if improve, learning outcomes. Unit cost savings may also be available thro the expansion of distance education, whether making intensive use of te nology or not.

Institutional arrangements often lag behind changes in demographic conditions.

Institutional arrangements often adapt to changing demographic conditi only after a considerable time lag. They can also influence unit expendit For example, a declining number of students at the primary level may lea higher unit costs at that level if levels of staffing are not reduced an schools closed in proportion. Conversely, in times of enrolment increa class sizes may increase, teachers may teach outside their field of special tion, etc.

In addition, differences in national price levels for educational services, i far as they deviate from overall price levels accounted for in the purcha: power parities, have an impact on the differences in unit expendi between countries.

Lower unit expenditure cannot simply be equated with lower quality of educational services.

It would be misleading to equate lower unit expenditure generally wit lower quality of educational services. The Czech Republic, the Netherla Japan and Korea, for example, which report comparatively moderate expe ture per student, are the countries with the highest level of performance students in mathematics (see Indicator F1).

Chart B4.2. **Annual educational expenditure per student in relation to GDP per capita, by level of education (1994)**

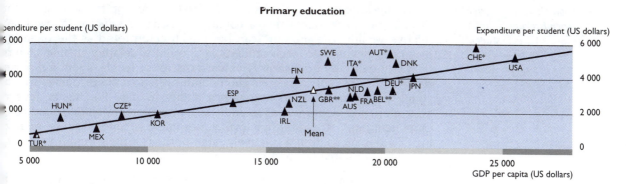

Primary education

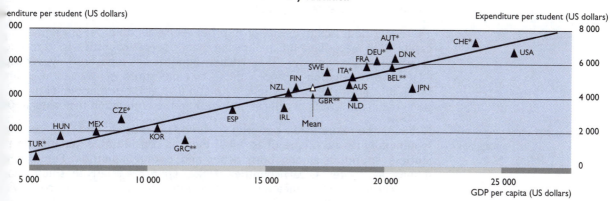

Secondary education

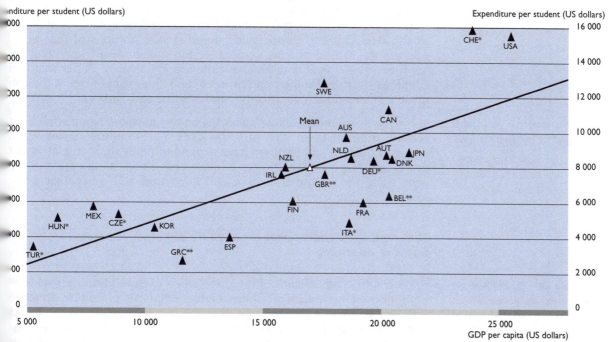

Tertiary education

blic institutions.

blic and government-dependent private institutions.

: OECD.

Educational expenditure per student in relation to national GDP levels

"Poorer" countries tend to spend relatively less per student...

Measuring spending per student relative to GDP per capita takes into accou the number of students that a country is trying to educate, as well as relative wealth. The measure can be roughly interpreted as the quantity resources devoted to each student in a country, relative to that countr relative wealth. As education is universal at lower levels, spending per s dent relative to GDP per capita can be interpreted as the resources spent young people relative to a country's ability to pay. For higher levels education, this measure is affected by a combination of wealth, spending a enrolment rates. At the tertiary level, for example, countries can be relativ high on this measure if a relatively large portion of their wealth is spent educating a relatively small number of students.

For the OECD as a whole, expenditure per student averages 18 per cent GDP per capita at the primary level, 25 per cent at the secondary level a 50 per cent at the tertiary level.

There is a clear positive relationship between spending per student and capita GDP (see Chart B4.2), showing that "poorer" countries tend to spe relatively less per student than "richer" countries as measured by per cap GDP. The correlation between these two measures is 0.82 at the prim level, 0.74 at the secondary level and still 0.70 at the tertiary level of edu tion. Taking all levels of education together, the correlation increases to 0

... but there are many exceptions.

Although the relationship between spending per student and GDP per ca is generally positive (see Chart B4.2) there is considerable variation in student spending among both richer and poorer countries. For examp among the poorest OECD countries, Turkey spends a relatively small amo of per capita GDP to educate the average primary student (13 per cent), w Hungary spends twice as much (27 per cent). Among the wealthiest OE countries, Switzerland spends 25 per cent of per capita GDP to educate average primary student, while the United States spends slightly less (21 cent). On this measure, two countries with vastly different levels of per ca wealth (Hungary and Switzerland) spend similar portions of that wealth educate the typical primary student. At the primary level, spending on measure is 7 per cent or more above the country mean of 20 per cent in th countries (Austria, Hungary and Sweden) and 7 per cent or below the cou mean in three other countries (Ireland, Mexico and Turkey).

The range in variation is largest at the tertiary level.

The range in spending across countries on this measure is much wider at tertiary level than at the primary level. For example, three count (Hungary, Mexico and Sweden) have expenditure per student relative to C per capita 24 percentage points or more above the country mean of 49 cent, while two countries (Greece and Italy) spend 23 percentage point more below the country mean.

Differentials in educational expenditure per student across levels of education

Not only does expenditure per student differ between countries in absolute terms, but relative spending per student across levels of education also varies markedly.

Cross-country comparisons of the distribution of expenditure across leve education are an indication of the relative emphasis placed on educatic different levels in a country, as well as the relative costs of providing ed tion at those levels. Chart B4.3 presents expenditure per student at the primary, secondary and tertiary levels of education relative to expend per student at the primary level of education. Although in almost all coun expenditure per student rises with the level of education, the relative si: the differences varies markedly across countries.

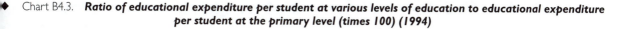

◆ Chart B4.3. *Ratio of educational expenditure per student at various levels of education to educational expenditure per student at the primary level (times 100) (1994)*

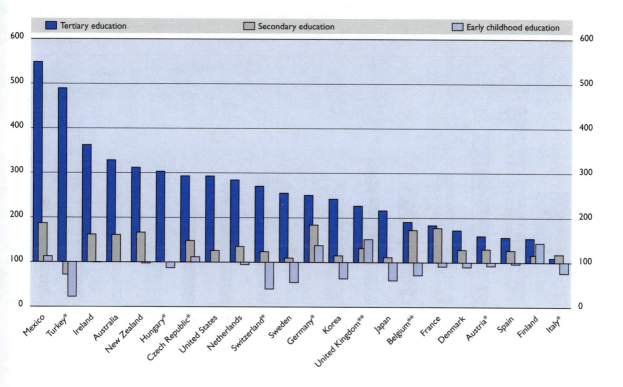

w to read this chart: for example, the ratio of 548 for tertiary education in Mexico means that expenditure per student at the tertiary level is 5.5 times the expenditure
student at the primary level. The ratio of 23 for early childhood education in Turkey means that the expenditure per student at the early childhood level is 77 per
t less than at the primary level, *i.e.* one quarter of the expenditure at the primary level.

Public institutions.

Public and government-dependent private institutions.

ntries are ranked in descending order of expenditure per student in tertiary education relative to educational expenditure per student at primary level.

ce: OECD.

At the secondary level, expenditure per student is, on average, 1.37 times higher than expenditure per student at the primary level, although the variation here ranges from 0.72 times the expenditure per primary student in Turkey to more than 1.75 times in France, Germany and Mexico. Nearly three-quarters of the countries have expenditure per secondary student which is between 1.05 and 1.70 times the expenditure per student at the primary level.

The most significant differentials occur at the tertiary level.

While, on average, OECD countries spent 2.6 times more per student at the tertiary level than at the primary level, spending patterns vary widely between countries. For example, whereas Italy only spends 1.1 times more for a tertiary student than for a primary student, Mexico and Turkey spend between 4.9 and 5.5 times more for a tertiary student than for a primary student. These differentials may even underestimate real cost differences, as in some countries funding provided for tertiary education by private sources has not been adequately taken into account.

◆ Chart B4.4. *Average duration and cumulative expenditure per student for tertiary education (1994)*

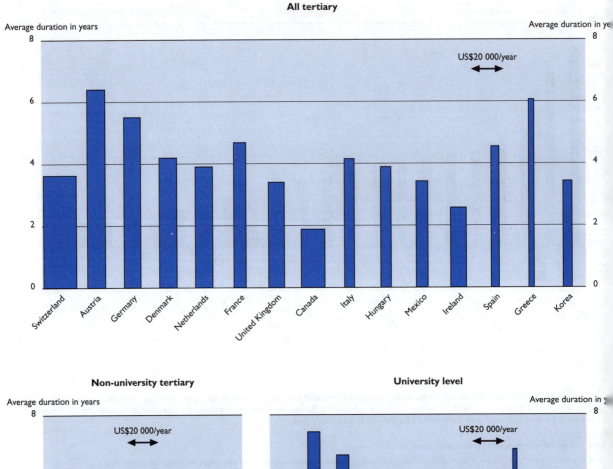

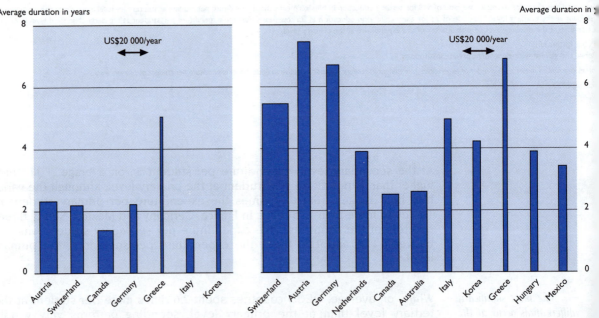

The height of the bar indicates the average duration of studies. The width of the bar indicates the average expenditure per student and year. The area of the bar represents the cumulative expenditure per student over the average duration of studies.

Countries are ranked in each chart in descending order of cumulative expenditure per student at the corresponding level.

Source: OECD.

Educational expenditure per student over the average duration of tertiary studies

nnual expenditure per student reflects the costs incurred during tertiary studies to varying degrees.

As both the typical duration and the typical intensity of tertiary study vary between countries (see Indicator G2), cross-country variation in annual expenditure per student on educational services shown in Tables B4.1 and B4.2 does not accurately reflect the variability in the total cost of educating the typical student at the tertiary level.

Students can choose from a range of institutions and enrolment options.

Today, students can choose from a range of types of institutions and enrolment options to find the best fit between their degree objectives, abilities, personal interests and social and economic circumstances. Many students attend part-time, work while enrolled, attend sporadically and attend more than one institution before graduating. These varying enrolment patterns can affect the interpretability of expenditure per student.

Part-time attendance may xplain some of the differences between countries.

The ranking of countries by annual expenditure per student on educational services is strongly affected by differences in how countries define full-time, part-time and full-time-equivalent enrolment. Some countries count every participant at the tertiary level as a full-time student while others determine a student's intensity of participation by the credits he or she obtains for successful completion of specific course units during a specified reference period. Countries that can accurately account for part-time enrolment will have higher expenditure per full-time equivalent student than countries that cannot differentiate between different modes of student attendance.

ow annual expenditure may nslate into high overall costs of tertiary education if the uration of tertiary studies is long.

Similarly, comparatively low annual expenditure per student may result in comparatively high overall costs of tertiary education if the typical duration of tertiary studies is relatively long. Chart B4.4 shows the average expenditure that is incurred per student throughout the course of tertiary studies for 15 countries. The figures account for all students for whom expenditure is incurred, including those who do not finish their studies. Although the calculations are based on a number of simplifying assumptions and therefore need to be treated with some caution (see Annex 3), significant shifts in the rank order of countries across the annual and the aggregate expenditure measures can be noted.

For example, annual spending per university (or equivalent) student in Canada is about a third higher than in Germany (US$11 700 in Canada against US$8 600 in Germany). However, because of differences in the degree structure at the tertiary level (see Indicator G2), the average duration of university-equivalent studies is more than twice as long in Germany as in Canada (6.7 years in Germany which provides only "long university or equivalent programmes" compared with 2.5 years in Canada which provides mostly "short" university-equivalent programmes). As a consequence of this, the aggregate expenditure for each university-equivalent student is almost twice as high in Germany as in Canada.

Austria and the Netherlands spend similar amounts per tertiary student each year but a duration of tertiary studies of 6.4 years in Austria as against 3.9 years in the Netherlands means that total spending in Austria is US$55 800 compared with only US$33 300 in the Netherlands. In Canada, a low duration of tertiary studies translates an above-average annual cost into a below-average total cost.

Important notes on interpretation

When differences between countries in expenditure per student are interpreted, the following factors should be taken into account:

The data include only direct public and private expenditure on institutions.

- The data used in calculating expenditure per student include only direct public and private expenditure on educational institutions. Public subsidies for students' living expenses have been excluded to ensure the international comparability of the data.
- For some countries, expenditure data for students in private educational institutions were not available (indicated by one or two asterisks in the table). However, many of the countries that do not have data on independent private institutions have a very small number of those institutions. In such cases, only the expenditure on public and government-dependent private institutions are accounted for.

Variation in expenditure does not always reflect variation in real resources.

- The variation in expenditure per student does not always reflect variation in real resources provided to students (*e.g.* variations in student-teaching staff ratios). In some cases, it reflects variation in relative prices. For example, a country may appear to spend an above-average amount because the salaries of its teachers are high relative to the country's general price level.

Definitions

Data refer to the financial year 1994 and are based on the UOE data collection on education statistics, administered in 1996 (for details see Annex 3).

Expenditure per student on a particular level of education is calculated by dividing the total expenditure at that level by the corresponding full-time equivalent enrolment. Only those types of educational institutions and programmes are taken into account for which both enrolment and expenditure data are available. The enrolment data are adjusted by interpolation so as to match either the financial year or the calendar year of each country (for details see Annex 3). The result in national currency is then converted into equivalent US dollars by dividing by the purchasing power parity (PPP) exchange rate between the national currency and the US dollar. The PPP exchange rates used pertain to GDP and were derived from the OECD National Accounts Database (see Annex 2). The PPP exchange rate gives the amount of a national currency that will buy the same basket of goods and services in a country as the US dollar will in the United States. The PPP exchange rate is used because the market exchange rate is affected by many factors (interest rates, trade policies, expectations of economic growth, etc.) that have little to do with current, relative domestic purchasing power in different countries.

The country mean is calculated as the simple average over all OECD countries for which data are available. The OECD total reflects the value of the indicator when the OECD region is considered as a whole (for details see Reader's Guide).

Expenditure per student relative to GDP per capita is calculated by expressing expenditure per student in units of national currency as a percentage of GDP per capita, also in national currency. In cases where the educational expenditure data and the GDP data pertain to different reference periods, the expenditure data are adjusted to the same reference period as the GDP data, using inflation rates for the country in question (see Annex 2).

For the estimation of the duration of tertiary education, data are based on a special survey carried out among OECD Member countries in 1997.

Expected expenditure over the average duration of tertiary studies (see table B4.4) is calculated by multiplying current annual expenditure by the typical duration of tertiary studies. The methodology used for the estimation of the typical duration of tertiary studies is described in Annex 3.

Table B4.1 **Expenditure per student (US dollars converted using PPPs) on public and private institutions by level of education (1994)**

	Early childhood	Primary	Secondary	Tertiary			All levels of education combined
				All	Non-university	University	
North America							
Canada	5 410	x	x	11 300	10 720	11 680	6 640
Mexico	1 190	1 050	1 960	5 750	x	5 750	1 560
United States	m	5 300	6 680	15 510	x	x	7 790
Pacific Area							
Australia	m	2 950	4 760	9 710	6 320	11 030	4 690
Japan	2 450	4 110	4 580	8 880	5 760	9 600	5 070
Korea	1 200	1 890	2 170	4 560	2 830	5 240	2 580
New Zealand	2 510	2 570	4 290	8 020	8 200	7 970	4 100
European Union							
Austria*	5 050	5 480	7 100	8 720	12 040	8 530	6 890
Belgium**	2 390	3 350	5 780	6 390	x	x	4 690
Denmark	4 420	4 930	6 310	8 500	x	x	6 070
Finland	5 680	3 960	4 590	6 080	x	x	4 820
France	2 980	3 280	5 810	6 010	x	x	4 700
Germany*	4 600	3 350	6 160	8 380	4 960	8 560	5 850
Greece**	x	x	1 490	2 680	1 870	3 030	1 540
Ireland	2 080	2 090	3 400	7 600	x	x	3 240
Italy*	3 370	4 430	5 220	4 850	5 350	4 820	5 030
Luxembourg	m	m	m	m	m	m	m
Netherlands	2 840	3 010	4 060	8 540	a	8 540	4 160
Portugal*	m	m	m	m	m	m	m
Spain	2 490	2 580	3 270	4 030	x	x	3 170
Sweden	2 750	5 030	5 500	12 820	x	x	5 680
United Kingdom**	5 080	3 360	4 430	7 600	x	x	4 340
Other OECD countries							
Czech Republic*	2 030	1 810	2 690	5 320	2 630	5 660	2 650
Hungary*	1 460	1 680	1 700	5 100	a	5 100	1 900
Iceland	m	m	m	m	m	m	m
Norway*	x	x	x	x	x	x	6 380
Poland	m	m	m	m	m	m	m
Switzerland*	2 360	5 860	7 250	15 850	8 850	18 020	7 110
Turkey*	160	710	510	3 460	x	x	880
Country mean	**2 980**	**3 310**	**4 340**	**7 740**	**x**	**x**	**4 460**
OECD total	**2 590**	**3 310**	**4 670**	**9 820**	**x**	**x**	**4 880**

* Public institutions.

** Public and government-dependent private institutions.

Source: OECD Database. See Annex 3 for notes.

Table B4.2 **Expenditure per student relative to GDP per capita on public and private institutions by level of education (1994)**

| | Early childhood | Primary | Secondary | Tertiary | | | All levels of education combined |
				All	Non-university	University	
North America							
Canada	27	x	x	56	53	58	33
Mexico	15	13	25	74	x	74	20
United States	m	21	26	61	x	x	31
Pacific Area							
Australia	m	16	26	52	34	60	25
Japan	12	19	22	42	27	45	24
Korea	12	18	21	44	27	50	25
New Zealand	16	16	27	50	51	50	26
European Union							
Austria*	25	27	35	43	60	42	34
Belgium**	12	16	28	31	x	x	23
Denmark	22	24	31	42	x	x	30
Finland	35	24	28	37	x	x	30
France	15	17	30	31	x	x	24
Germany*	23	17	31	43	25	44	30
Greece**	x	x	13	23	16	26	13
Ireland	13	13	22	48	x	x	21
Italy*	18	24	28	26	29	26	27
Luxembourg	m	m	m	m	m	m	m
Netherlands	15	16	22	46	a	46	22
Portugal*	m	m	m	m	m	m	m
Spain	18	19	24	30	x	x	23
Sweden	16	29	31	73	x	x	32
United Kingdom**	29	19	25	43	x	x	25
Other OECD countries							
Czech Republic*	23	20	30	60	30	64	30
Hungary*	23	27	27	81	a	81	30
Iceland	m	m	m	m	m	m	m
Norway*	x	x	x	x	x	x	29
Poland	m	m	m	m	m	m	m
Switzerland*	10	25	30	66	37	76	30
Turkey*	3	13	10	66	x	x	17
Country mean	**18**	**20**	**26**	**49**	**x**	**x**	**26**
OECD total	17	18	25	50	x	x	26

*   Public institutions.
** Public and government-dependent private institutions.
Source: OECD Database. See Annex 3 for notes.

Table B4.3 **Educational expenditure per student by level of education relative to educational expenditure per student at the primary level (1994)**

	Early childhood education	Primary education	Secondary education	Tertiary education
North America				
Canada	m	m	m	m
Mexico	113	100	187	548
United States	m	100	126	293
Pacific Area				
Australia	m	100	161	329
Japan	60	100	112	216
Korea	64	100	115	242
New Zealand	98	100	167	312
European Union				
Austria*	92	100	130	159
Belgium**	71	100	173	191
Denmark	90	100	128	172
Finland	144	100	116	154
France	91	100	177	183
Germany*	137	100	184	250
Greece**	m	m	m	m
Ireland	99	100	162	363
Italy*	76	100	118	110
Luxembourg	m	m	m	m
Netherlands	95	100	135	284
Portugal*	m	m	m	m
Spain	97	100	127	156
Sweden	55	100	109	255
United Kingdom**	152	100	132	226
Other OECD countries				
Czech Republic*	112	100	148	293
Hungary*	87	100	101	303
Iceland	m	m	m	m
Norway*	m	m	m	m
Poland	m	m	m	m
Switzerland*	40	100	124	270
Turkey*	23	100	72	490
Country mean	**90**	**100**	**137**	**264**
OECD total	78	100	141	297

* Public institutions.
** Public and government-dependent private institutions.
Source: OECD Database. See Annex 3 for notes.

Table B4.4 **Expenditure per student over the average duration of tertiary studies (1994)**

	Method	Average duration of tertiary studies (in years)			Cumulative expenditure per student over the average duration of tertiary studies		
		All	Non-university	University	All	Non-university	University
North America							
Canada	CM	1.9	1.4	2.5	21 260	14 850	29 340
Mexico	AF	3.4	x	3.4	19 680	x	19 670
Pacific Area							
Australia	CM	m	m	2.6	m	m	28 680
Korea	CM	3.4	2.1	4.2	15 640	5 860	22 110
European Union							
Austria	AF	6.4	2.3	7.4	55 800	27 990	63 550
Denmark	AF	4.2	2.1	4.4	35 610	x	x
France	AF	4.7	2.8	5.3	28 130	x	x
Germany	CM	5.5	2.2	6.7	46 170	10 990	57 330
Greece	CM	6.1	5.0	6.9	16 270	9 400	20 870
Ireland	CM	2.6	2.0	3.0	19 560	x	x
Italy	CM	4.2	1.1	4.9	20 150	5 930	23 770
Netherlands	CM	3.9	a	3.9	33 290	a	33 290
Spain	AF	4.6	1.5	4.7	18 310	x	x
United Kingdom	CM	3.4	1.8	3.5	25 840	x	x
Other OECD countries							
Hungary	CM	3.9	a	3.9	19 830	a	19 830
Norway	AF	3.3	2.5	4.0	m	m	m
Switzerland	CM	3.6	2.2	5.5	57 460	19 340	98 290
Country mean		**4.1**	**1.9**	**4.5**	**28 870**	x	
OECD total		4.2	1.8	4.4	26 120	x	
Other non-OECD countries							
Russian Federation	CM	4.9	6.9	4.2	m	m	m

Either the Chain Method (CM) or an Approximation Formula (AF) was used to estimate the duration of tertiary studies.
See Annex 3 for explanations.
Source: OECD Database. See Annex 3 for notes.

Indicator B5: Educational expenditure by resource category

Policy context

This indicator compares countries with respect to the division of spending between rent and capital outlays and the distribution of current expenditure by resource category.

How educational funding is spent can have an important impact on educational outcomes. How spending is allocated between different functional categories can affect the quality of instruction (*e.g.* through teachers' salaries), the condition of educational facilities (*e.g.* expenditure on school maintenance) and the ability of the education system to adjust to changing demographic and enrolment trends (*e.g.* construction of new schools). Since it is not obvious how resources should be allocated to best effect between functional categories, comparisons of how different countries do distribute educational expenditure between them can provide some insight into variations in the organisation and operation of educational institutions. Allocation decisions made at the system level, both budgetary and structural, eventually feed through to the classroom and affect the nature of instruction and the conditions under which it is provided.

Educational expenditure can first be divided into current and capital expenditure. Current expenditure includes financial outlays for school resources used each year for the operation of schools. Current expenditure can be further subdivided into three broad functional categories: compensation of teachers, compensation of other staff and current expenditure other than on compensation of personnel (*e.g.* teaching materials and supplies, maintenance of school buildings, preparation of student meals, rent of school facilities). Capital expenditure includes outlays for assets that last longer than one year and includes spending on the construction, renovation and major repair of buildings. The amount allocated to each of these functional categories will depend in part on current and projected changes in enrolment, in the salary levels of educational personnel and in costs for the maintenance and construction of educational facilities.

Evidence and explanations

At the combined primary and secondary level, current expenditure accounts, on average, for 93 per cent of total outlays on educational institutions.

Education takes place mostly in school and university settings. The labour-intensive technology of education explains the large proportion of current spending in total educational expenditure. At the combined primary and secondary levels of education, current expenditure accounts, on average, for 93 per cent of total outlays. In terms of expenditure per student, this amounts to an average of US$3 571, converted using purchasing power parity indices.

Nevertheless, there is still wide variation between countries with respect to the relative split between current and capital spending: at the primary-secondary level, the capital proportion ranges from less than 5 per cent in Belgium, Canada, Ireland, Italy, Mexico, the Netherlands and the United Kingdom to more than 10 per cent in Greece, Japan, Korea and Switzerland (see Chart B5.1).

◆ Chart B5.1. *Distribution of total expenditure and distribution of current expenditure by resource category,*
by level of education (1994)

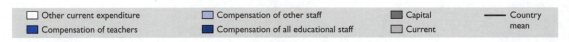

Primary and secondary education

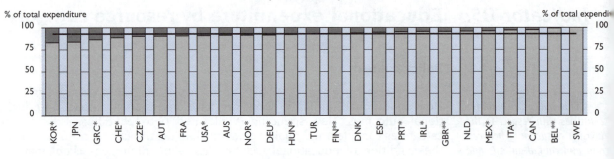

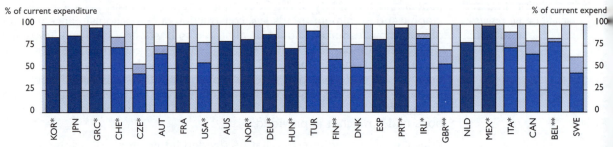

Tertiary education

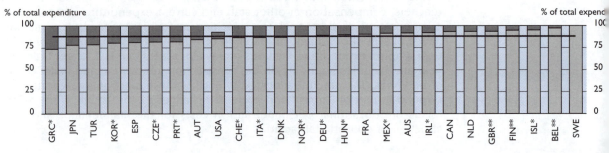

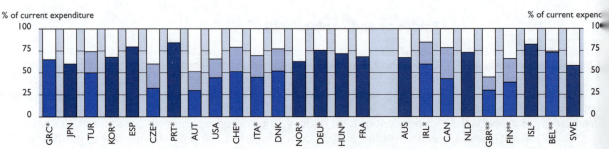

* Public institutions.
** Public and government-dependent private institutions.

Countries are ranked in ascending order of current expenditure.

Source: OECD.

n most countries, over 80 per cent of current expenditure at the primary and secondary levels is devoted to the compensation of staff.

The salaries of teachers and other staff employed in education comprise the largest share of current expenditure in all OECD countries. On average, expenditure on the compensation of educational personnel accounts for 81 per cent of current expenditure at the combined primary and secondary levels of education (which is equivalent to an expenditure of US$2 860 spent per student). While in the Czech Republic and Sweden 63 per cent of expenditure or less is devoted to the compensation of educational personnel, the proportion is larger than 90 per cent in Greece, Italy, Mexico and Portugal.

Countries with smaller relative education budgets (*e.g.* Greece, Mexico and Portugal) tend to devote a larger share of current educational expenditure to the compensation of personnel and less to other contracted and purchased services such as support services (*e.g.* for the maintenance of school buildings), ancillary services (*e.g.* for the preparation of meals for students) and rents paid for school buildings and other facilities. Notable exceptions to this pattern are the Czech Republic and Hungary, which spend less than the OECD average (81 per cent of current expenditure) on the compensation of staff (55 and 72 per cent, respectively).

The distribution of expenditure by resource category and, in particular, the proportion of expenditure accounted for by the compensation of educational personnel depends among other things on the ratio of students to teaching staff (see Indicator B8), the level of teachers' salaries (see Indicator D1), the number of instructional hours for teachers and the division of teachers' time between teaching and other duties.

Countries vary with regard to the proportions of current expenditure allocated to the compensation of teachers and e compensation of other staff.

In Denmark, Sweden and the United States around 30 per cent or more of staff expenditure goes towards compensation of personnel other than teachers, while in Belgium and Ireland the percentage is 6 per cent or below (primary and secondary levels combined). These differences are likely to reflect the degree to which educational personnel specialise in non-teaching fields in a particular country (*e.g.* principals who do not teach, guidance counsellors, bus drivers, school nurses, janitors and maintenance workers), as well as the relative salaries of teaching and non-teaching personnel (Indicator B7 provides some insight into differences between countries in the definition of teachers).

In practice, the allocation of staff compensation expenditure between teaching and non-teaching personnel is not clear-cut. Some countries define "teachers" narrowly as persons who teach students in the classroom while others include heads of schools and other professional personnel. Because of these (and other) definitional differences, as well as differences between countries in the coverage of non-teaching staff, the variation observed in the reported percentages of expenditure on non-teaching staff should be viewed with caution.

Two alternative measures for comparing relative expenditure on teachers are shown in columns 7 and 8 of Table B5.1a. Here the expenditure on the compensation of teachers is first divided by the number of students enrolled (column 7), and then this measure is divided by the intended number of instructional hours at the lower secondary level (column 8). The former is a measure of the expenditure per student devoted to the human resource most closely associated with the transmission of education; the latter is a measure of the amount of these teaching resources that is invested per hour of instruction per student. Among the 12 countries for which data are available, the average amount of teacher compensation per student ranges from below US$1 000 in the Czech Republic and Turkey to over US$4 000 in Switzerland. Although data are available only for a few countries on average teacher compensation per student hour, those figures show considerable differences among countries.

At the tertiary level, the proportion of capital expenditure is generally larger, because of more differentiated and advanced teaching facilities.

At the tertiary level, the proportion of total expenditure spent on capi outlays is greater than at the primary/secondary level. In 13 out of 25 cou tries, the proportion spent on capital is above 10 per cent, and in Gree Japan, Korea and Turkey, it lies between 20 and 26 per cent (see Chart B5. This difference can also be seen in comparisons of the average capital out per student, although the distribution of outlays is wide at both levels education. At the primary and secondary level, average capital outlays student range from US$50 or less in Belgium, Mexico and Turkey to o US$700 in Japan and Switzerland. At the tertiary level, capital outlays student range from US$185 in Belgium to US$2 160 in Switzerland. These wi differences are likely to reflect differences in how tertiary education organised in each country, as well as the degree to which expansion enrolments is being accommodated by new construction.

Countries devote a smaller amount of current expenditure to the compensation of staff at the tertiary level.

At the same time, the proportion of current expenditure spent on staff significantly lower at the tertiary level than at the primary/secondary level: countries for which data are available spend 15 per cent or more of curre expenditure on purposes other than the compensation of educational pers nel, and in more than half of the countries the proportion is above 30 cent.

Definitions

Data refer to the financial year 1994 and are based on the UOE data collection on education statistics, administered in 1996 (for details see Annex 3).

The current and capital portions of expenditure are the percentages of t expenditure reported as current expenditure and capital expenditu respectively. Only expenditure on educational institutions is consider Subsidies for students' living expenses are excluded. Calculations co expenditure by public institutions or, where available, those of public private institutions combined. The proportions of current expenditure a cated to compensation of teachers, compensation of other staff, total s compensation, and other (non-personnel) current outlays are calculated expressing the respective amounts as percentages of total current exper ture. In some cases, compensation of teaching staff means compensatio classroom teachers only, but in others it includes that of heads of schools other professional educators. Capital expenditure does not include d servicing.

The average expenditure per student by resource category is calculated multiplying expenditure per student in purchasing power parities as show Indicator B4, by the respective proportions of teacher and staff compensa in total expenditure for educational institutions. Current expenditure ot than for the compensation of personnel includes expenditure on contrac and purchased services such as expenditure on support services (*e.g.* for maintenance of school buildings), ancillary services (*e.g.* for the preparatio meals for students) and rent paid for school buildings and other facilit These services are obtained from outside providers as opposed to the vices produced by the education authorities or educational institutions th selves using their own personnel.

The country mean is calculated as the simple average over all OECD count for which data are available. The OECD total reflects the value of the indic when the OECD region is considered as a whole (for details see Read Guide).

Table B5.1a **Educational expenditure on primary and secondary education by resource category for public and private institutions (1994)**

	Percentage of total expenditure		Percentage of current expenditure				Average compensation per student (in equivalent US dollars)				
	Current	Capital	Compensation of teachers	Compensation of other staff	Compensation of all staff	Other current expenditure	Teachers	Teacher compensation per student divided by the number of intended instructional hours (ISCED 2)	All staff	Current	Capital
North America											
Canada	97	3	66	15	81	19	3 485	m	4 283	5 295	143
Mexico*	96	4	x	x	98	2	x	m	1 133	1 155	48
United States*	91	9	56	23	79	21	3 125	m	4 415	5 557	555
Pacific Area											
Australia	91	9	x	x	81	19	x	m	2 774	3 441	330
Japan	84	16	x	x	87	13	x	m	3 177	3 652	709
Korea*	83	17	x	x	85	15	x	m	1 476	1 731	352
New Zealand	m	m	m	m	m	m	m	m	m	m	m
European Union											
Austria	90	10	67	9	76	24	m	m	m	m	m
Belgium**	99	1	80	4	84	16	3 741	m	3 914	4 683	33
Denmark	94	6	51	26	77	23	2 757	3.4	4 147	5 391	361
Finland**	93	7	60	12	72	28	2 407	2.7	2 884	4 005	291
France	91	9	x	x	79	21	x	m	3 417	4 332	449
Germany*	91	9	x	x	88	12	x	m	3 151	3 571	337
Greece*	86	14	x	x	96	4	x	m	1 209	1 257	180
Ireland*	96	4	84	5	89	11	2 195	2.8	2 331	2 619	123
Italy*	97	3	73	18	91	9	3 495	4.1	4 347	4 783	150
Luxembourg	m	m	m	m	m	m	m	m	m	m	m
Netherlands	96	4	x	x	79	21	x	m	2 696	3 428	147
Portugal*	95	5	x	x	96	4	m	m	m	m	m
Spain	95	5	x	x	83	17	x	m	2 372	2 868	163
Sweden	100	x	44	19	63	37	2 328	3.0	3 305	5 278	x
United Kingdom**	96	4	55	16	71	29	2 047	m	2 646	3 739	175
Other OECD countries											
Czech Republic*	90	10	44	11	55	45	950	m	1 198	2 174	237
Hungary*	92	8	x	x	72	28	x	m	1 127	1 557	135
Iceland	m	m	m	m	m	m	m	m	m	m	m
Norway*	91	9	x	x	83	17	x	m	4 250	5 143	487
Poland	m	m	m	m	m	m	m	m	m	m	m
Switzerland*	89	11	74	12	86	14	4 315	m	5 016	5 865	752
Turkey	92	8	92	x	x	8	561	m	565	607	50
Country mean	**93**	**8**	**65**	**14**	**81**	**18**	**2 617**	**3.2**	**2 862**	**3 571**	**282**
OECD total	91	9	60	20	82	18	2 642	3.7	2 964	3 618	346

ublic institutions.
ublic and government-dependent private institutions.
ce: OECD Database. See Annex 3 for notes.

Table B5.1*b* **Educational expenditure on tertiary education by resource category for public and private institutions (1994)**

	Percentage of total expenditure		Percentage of current expenditure				Average compensation per student (in equivalent U.S. dollars)			
	Current	Capital	Compensation of teachers	Compensation of other staff	Compensation of all staff	Other current expenditure	Teachers	All staff	Current	Capital
North America										
Canada	93	7	43	35	79	21	x	8 270	10 524	77
Mexico*	91	9	m	m	m	m	x	5 285	5 443	52
United States	85	8	44	21	66	34	5 847	8 684	13 221	1 17
Pacific Area										
Australia	92	8	x	x	67	33	x	5 979	8 899	81
Japan	78	22	x	x	60	40	x	4 175	6 939	1 94
Korea*	80	20	x	x	68	32	x	2 634	3 894	94
New Zealand	m	m	m	m	m	m	m	m	m	
European Union										
Austria	84	16	30	22	51	49	m	m	m	
Belgium**	97	3	73	2	74	26	4 515	4 609	6 205	18
Denmark	87	13	52	25	77	23	3 826	5 684	7 374	1 1?
Finland**	95	5	39	27	66	34	2 239	3 790	5 758	3?
France	90	10	x	x	68	32	x	3 693	5 421	58
Germany*	89	11	x	x	75	25	x	5 622	7 460	9?
Greece*	74	26	65	n	65	35	1 286	1 286	1 974	7?
Ireland*	92	8	60	25	85	15	4 262	6 035	7 137	6?
Italy*	86	14	45	25	70	30	1 875	2 918	4 196	6*
Luxembourg	m	m	m	m	m	m	m	m	m	
Netherlands	93	7	x	x	73	27	x	5 814	7 966	5?
Portugal*	82	18	x	x	84	16	m	m	m	
Spain	81	19	x	x	80	20	x	2 598	3 267	7?
Sweden	100	x	x	x	58	42	x	7 434	12 818	
United Kingdom**	93	7	30	15	45	55	2 120	3 182	7 100	5?
Other OECD countries										
Czech Republic*	82	18	32	28	60	40	1 407	2 611	4 342	9
Hungary*	90	10	x	x	72	28	x	3 268	4 569	5
Iceland*	95	5	x	x	82	18	m	m	m	
Norway*	88	12	x	x	63	37	x	4 347	6 946	9?
Poland	m	m	m	m	m	m	m	m	m	
Switzerland*	86	14	51	28	79	21	7 023	10 808	13 694	2 1?
Turkey	79	21	50	24	74	26	1 500	2 233	3 003	8?
Country mean	**88**	**12**	**47**	**21**	**70**	**30**	**3 264**	**4 824**	**6 876**	**8?**
OECD total	86	10	44	22	67	33	4 575	5 883	8 736	1 0?

*   Public institutions.
** Public and government-dependent private institutions.
Source: OECD Database. See Annex 3 for notes.

Indicator B6:   Public funds by level of government

Policy context

This indicator shows the sources of public funds by level of government.

The level of government that has responsibility for, and control over, the funding of education is likely to have control over decisions regarding how those funds are spent. An important factor in educational policy is, therefore, the division of responsibility for educational funding between national, regional and local authorities. Important decisions regarding educational funding are made both at the level of government where the funds originate and at the level of government in which they are finally spent or distributed. At the initial source of educational funding, decisions are made concerning the level of resources allocated, and any restrictions on how that money can be spent. At the final governmental source of educational funding, additional restrictions may be attached to the funds, or this level of government may even pay directly for educational resources (*e.g.* by paying teachers' salaries).

Complete centralisation can cause delays in decision-making and decisions that are far removed from those affected can fail to take proper account of changes in local needs and desired practices. Under complete decentralisation, however, units of government may differ in the level of educational resources they spend on students, either because of differences in priorities related to education or differences in the ability to raise education funds. Wide variability in educational standards and resources can also lead to inequality of educational opportunity and insufficient attention to long-term national needs.

Although the source of educational funds is typically the public sector, the provision of education can be organised by private institutions. This way of organising, or subcontracting, education is seen in many countries as a cost-effective strategy for providing education.

Evidence and explanations

With some notable exceptions, responsibility for funding tertiary education is more than 85 per cent centralised.

The way responsibility for funding education is divided between levels of government differs between the primary/secondary levels and the tertiary level of education. Whereas countries differ significantly in the origin of financial sources for primary and secondary education, the pattern is quite similar for most countries at the tertiary level. At this level of education, the vast majority of public funds originate at the central level of government. In 19 out of 25 countries, the central government is the initial source of more than 85 per cent of public education funds. On average, the central government is also the final source of 75 per cent of all public education funds in OECD countries (after transfers between levels of government). In fact, in all except six of the OECD countries considered, more than 50 per cent of the final funds come from the central government, and in 17 countries it is 85 per cent or more.

◆ Chart B6.1*a.* ***Educational resources by level of government for tertiary education (1994)***

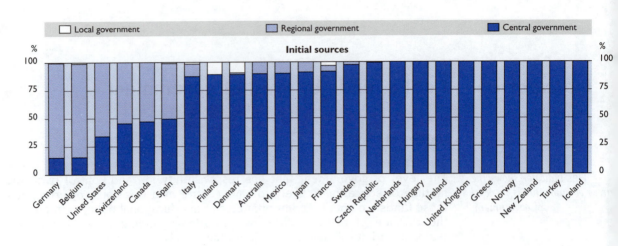

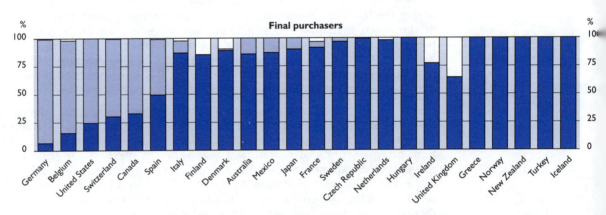

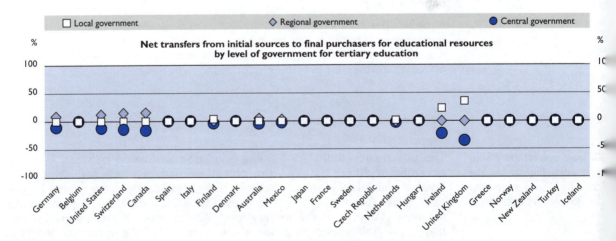

Example: Net transfers from initial to final sources in the United Kingdom are transfers from the central to the local government. The proportion of funds from government sources decreases by 35 percentage points after intergovernmental transfers, the proportion of funds from local governmental sources increases 35 percentage points, and regional government sources remain unchanged.

Countries are ranked in ascending order of the percentage of initial funds from the central government.

Source: OECD.

◆   Chart B6.1b.   *Educational resources by level of government for primary and secondary education (1994)*

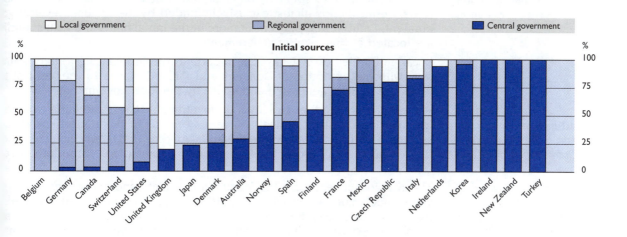

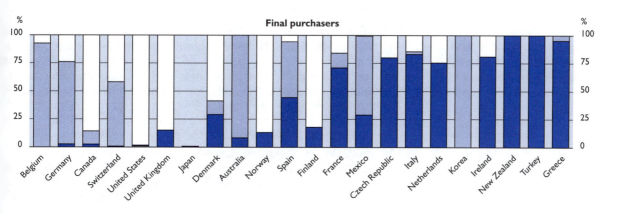

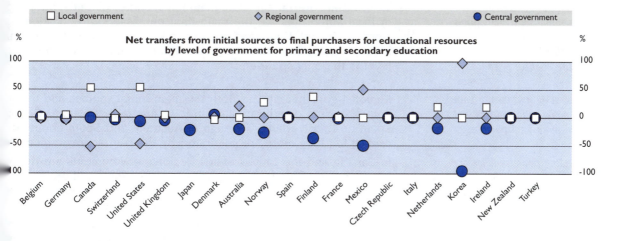

ple: Net transfers from initial to final sources in Mexico are transfers from the central to the regional government. The proportion of funds from central government
es decreases by 50 percentage points after intergovernmental transfers, the proportion of funds from regional governmental sources increases by 50 percentage
s, and local government sources remain unchanged.

tries are ranked in ascending order of the percentage of initial funds from the central government.

e: OECD.

In six countries regional governments play an important role in funding tertiary education.

In Canada, Spain, Switzerland and the United States around half of the init funds for tertiary education are generated by regional governments, and 50 75 per cent are also spent by regional authorities. In Belgium and Germa tertiary education is almost exclusively funded by the regional level of go ernment. Eighty-three per cent or more of the initial funds and final spendi are located at this level of government.

Local authorities do not have an important role in financing tertiary edu tion, with the exception of Denmark and Finland, where 10 per cent of t funds are initially generated and spent by the local government.

In Ireland and the United Kingdom resources are generated centrally but a significant proportion is spent locally.

While in most countries the level of government that is the initial source tertiary funds is also the final source, exceptions to this pattern are Irela and the United Kingdom, where the initial funding is 100 per cent centralise but a quarter to a third of the final spending takes place at the local leve

At the primary and secondary levels of education countries differ in the division of responsibility for funding education between levels of government.

The division of responsibility for funding primary and secondary educati varies much more across OECD countries than it does at the tertiary level. many countries, decentralisation is much more prominent for primary a secondary education than for tertiary education. Countries can be group according to the percentage of public funds generated and spent by cent regional and local governments.

Four basic patterns can be observed:

The central government is both the main initial source of funds and the main final spender on education.

- In New Zealand and Turkey the funding of elementary and second education is completely centralised. Here the central governmen the only main initial source of funds and the only final purchaser Ireland 100 per cent of the initial funds and over 80 per cent of the fi spending comes from the central level. In the Czech Republic, Fran Italy and the Netherlands, the central government is still the source the majority of initial funds and the main final spender.

  In contrast, in Belgium, Canada, Germany, Switzerland and United States, the central government generates less than 10 per c of educational funds. In these five countries, as well as in Japan a Korea, less than 5 per cent of final educational funds are spent by central government.

The central government is the main initial source but funds are transferred to regional or local authorities, which are the main direct source of education funds.

- The central government is the main initial source of funds, but regic or local authorities are the main final purchasers of educational vices in Finland, Korea and Mexico. In Korea 96 per cent of the in funds originate from the central level of government and the regic level is the only spender.

Regional authorities are both the main initial sources and the main final purchasers.

- Regional governments are both the main initial sources and the n final spenders of educational funds in Australia, Belgium, Germa Spain and Switzerland, although in Australia and Spain about 30 cent of funds or more are generated by the central government.

Funding responsibilities are shared between regional and local authorities.

- In Canada and the United States, regional governments are the n initial source of funds, but in these countries local authorities are main final purchasers of educational services, with the regional gov ments spending 12 and 1 per cent of funds respectively.

  In Denmark, Norway and the United Kingdom, local authorities both the main initial source of funds and the main final purchase educational services.

An alternative form of final spending is the transfer of public money to private institutions.

While in the majority of OECD countries education that is funded from pu sources is also organised and delivered by public institutions, in some c tries, the final funding is transferred to government-dependent private i tutions. In other words, the final spending and delivery of education is contracted to non-governmental institutions (see Table B6.2). In the O countries, overall, 10 per cent of the public funds designated for educational institutions are spent in institutions that are privately managed. In the Netherlands, where the central government is the major final source of funds, 78 per cent of public money for primary and secondary educational institutions and 44 per cent of public money for tertiary institutions are transferred from the central government to government-dependent private institutions. In Belgium more than half of the funds for educational institutions are transferred to government-dependent private institutions. In the United Kingdom 100 per cent of public funding at the tertiary level is spent by government-dependent private institutions. While these funds are spent in privately managed institutions, they can also come with restrictions attached. For example, teachers may be required to meet some minimum level of qualification and students may be required to pass a government-regulated examination in order to graduate. Government-dependent private institutions are commonly subject to a range of government legislation and oversight (*e.g.* inspection).

At the primary and secondary levels of education, government funding of independent private institutions (defined as institutions receiving less than 50 per cent of their core funding from public sources) is negligible (only in Japan and Germany are public funds used for independent institutions at that level – 3 and 2 per cent, respectively). It is more usual for independent institutions at the tertiary level to receive public funding. Fifteen per cent or more of the funds designated for tertiary education institutions in both Japan and the United States, and 11 per cent in Korea, are spent in independent private institutions.

Definitions

a refer to the financial year 1994 and are based on the UOE data collection on education statistics, administered in 1996 (for details see Annex 3).

The initial educational expenditure of each level of government – also referred to as the expenditure originating at that level – is the total educational expenditure of all public authorities at the level in question (direct expenditure plus transfers to other levels of government and to the private sector), less the transfers received from governments at other levels. The share of initial expenditure by a particular level of government is calculated as a percentage of the total, consolidated expenditure of all three levels. Funds received from international sources have been excluded. Only expenditure specifically designated for education is taken into account in determining the share of initial expenditure borne by a particular level. General-purpose transfers between levels of government, which provide much of the revenue of regional and local governments in some countries, have been excluded from the calculations.

The final expenditure of each level of government is the amount spent directly on educational services by all public authorities at that level. It does not include transfers to other levels of government or to households or other private entities. The share of final expenditure by a particular level of government is calculated as a percentage of the total direct expenditure on educational services of all levels of government combined. For the public sector as a whole, final expenditure is less than initial expenditure because some funds generated in the public sector are transferred to, and ultimately used by, households and other private parties.

The country mean is calculated as the simple average over all OECD countries for which data are available. The OECD total reflects the value of the indicator when the OECD region is considered as a whole (for details see Reader's Guide).

Table B6.1a **Distribution of initial sources of public educational funds and final purchasers of educational resources by level government for primary and secondary education (1994)**

	Initial funds (before transfers between levels of government)				Final funds (after transfers between levels of government)			
	Central	Regional	Local	Total	Central	Regional	Local	Total
North America								
Canada	3	64	32	100	3	12	86	100
Mexico	79	21	1	100	29	71	1	100
United States	8	48	44	100	1	1	98	100
Pacific Area								
Australia	29	71	n	100	8	92	n	100
Japan	23	x	x	100	1	x	x	100
Korea	96	4	a	100	n	100	a	100
New Zealand	100	a	a	100	100	a	a	100
European Union								
Austria	m	m	m	m	m	m	m	m
Belgium	a	94	6	100	a	93	7	100
Denmark	25	12	63	100	29	12	59	100
Finland	55	a	45	100	18	a	82	100
France	72	12	16	100	71	13	16	100
Germany	3	77	19	100	3	73	24	100
Greece	m	m	m	m	96	5	n	100
Ireland	100	a	n	100	81	a	19	100
Italy	83	3	14	100	83	2	15	100
Luxembourg	m	m	m	m	m	m	m	m
Netherlands	94	n	6	100	75	n	24	100
Portugal	m	m	m	m	m	m	m	m
Spain	44	50	6	100	44	50	6	100
Sweden	m	m	m	m	m	m	m	m
United Kingdom	20	a	80	100	15	a	85	100
Other OECD countries								
Czech Republic	80	a	20	100	80	a	20	100
Hungary	m	m	m	100	m	m	m	100
Iceland	m	m	m	m	m	m	m	m
Norway	40	a	60	100	13	a	87	100
Poland	m	m	m	m	m	m	m	m
Switzerland	4	53	43	100	1	57	42	100
Turkey	100	a	a	100	100	a	a	100
Country mean	**50**	**25**	**23**	**100**	**39**	**28**	**32**	**100**

Source: OECD Database. See Annex 3 for notes.

Table B6.1*b* **Distribution of initial sources of public educational funds and final purchasers of educational resources by level of government for tertiary education (1994)**

	Initial funds (before transfers between levels of government)				Final funds (after transfers between levels of government)			
	Central	Regional	Local	Total	Central	Regional	Local	Total
North America								
Canada	47	53	n	100	33	67	n	100
Mexico	90	10	n	100	87	13	n	100
United States	34	66	x	100	25	75	x	100
Pacific Area								
Australia	90	10	n	100	86	14	n	100
Japan	91	x	x	100	90	x	x	100
Korea	100	a	a	100	100	a	a	100
New Zealand	100	a	a	100	100	a	a	100
European Union								
Austria	m	m	m	m	m	m	m	m
Belgium	16	83	1	100	16	83	2	100
Denmark	89	1	10	100	89	1	10	100
Finland	89	a	11	100	85	a	15	100
France	92	5	3	100	92	5	3	100
Germany	15	84	1	100	7	93	1	100
Greece	100	n	a	100	100	n	n	100
Ireland	100	a	n	100	77	a	23	100
Italy	87	11	2	100	87	11	2	100
Luxembourg	m	m	m	m	m	m	m	m
Netherlands	100	n	n	100	98	n	2	100
Portugal	m	m	m	m	m	m	m	m
Spain	49	50	1	100	49	50	1	100
Sweden	97	3	a	100	97	3	a	100
United Kingdom	100	a	n	100	65	a	35	100
Other OECD countries								
Czech Republic	99	a	1	100	99	a	1	100
Hungary	100	n	n	100	100	n	n	100
Iceland	100	n	n	100	100	n	n	100
Norway	100	a	a	100	100	a	a	100
Poland	m	m	m	m	m	m	m	m
Switzerland	45	54	n	100	30	69	1	100
Turkey	100	a	a	100	100	a	a	100
Country mean	**80**	**19**	**1**	**100**	**75**	**21**	**4**	**100**

Source: OECD Database. See Annex 3 for notes.

Table B6.2 **Proportion of public expenditure on public and private educational institutions (1994)**

	Primary and secondary				Tertiary			
	Public institutions	Government-dependent institutions	Independent private institutions	All private institutions	Public institutions	Government-dependent institutions	Independent private institutions	All private institutions
North America								
Canada	98	1	1	2	100	n	n	r
Mexico	100	a	a	a	100	a	a	a
United States	100	a	n	n	83	a	17	1
Pacific Area								
Australia	84	16	n	16	100	n	n	r
Japan	97	a	3	3	85	a	15	1
Korea	88	12	n	12	89	a	11	1
New Zealand	100	a	n	n	100	a	a	a
European Union								
Austria	m	m	a	m	m	m	a	n
Belgium	48	52	a	52	39	61	a	6
Denmark	93	7	n	7	100	a	n	r
Finland	95	5	a	5	95	5	a	
France	87	13	n	13	96	4	n	
Germany	93	4	2	7	98	2	n	
Greece	100	n	n	n	100	n	n	r
Ireland	100	x	n	n	100	x	n	
Italy	100	a	n	n	99	a	1	
Luxembourg	m	m	m	m	m	m	m	n
Netherlands	22	78	n	78	56	44	n	4
Portugal	96	4	n	4	100	a	n	
Spain	87	13	n	13	100	n	n	
Sweden	99	1	n	1	100	n	n	
United Kingdom	85	15	n	15	a	100	n	10
Other OECD countries								
Czech Republic	96	4	a	4	99	1	a	
Hungary	m	m	a	m	95	4	a	
Iceland	100	x	n	n	100	n	n	
Norway	95	x	x	5	95	x	x	
Poland	m	m	m	m	m	m	m	r
Switzerland	91	x	x	9	96	x	x	
Turkey	100	a	a	a	99	a	1	
Country mean	**90**	**10**	**n**	**9**	**89**	**9**	**2**	**1**

Source: OECD Database. See Annex 3 for notes.

Indicator B7: Staff employed in education

Policy context

This indicator shows the persons employed in education as a percentage of the total employed population, and the percentage of teaching staff who work part-time.

The percentage of the total employed population that is employed in education is an indicator of the proportion of a country's human resources that are devoted to educating the population. The number of persons employed as either teachers or educational support personnel is one of the two main factors – the other being the level of compensation for educational staff (see Indicator D1) – that determine the financial resources that countries must commit to education.

Evidence and explanations

The education sector occupies a significant place in OECD labour markets, comprising, on average, 5.4 per cent of the employed population.

The education sector is a significant proportion of the labour market in all OECD countries. On average, 5.4 per cent of the employed labour force work in education, including teaching, educational and administrative personnel, and other support staff.

The largest group is teachers, who represent an average of 3.9 per cent of the employed population.

The vast majority of educational personnel are teachers. For all levels of education combined, teaching personnel accounts, on average, for 3.9 per cent of the labour force. At the combined primary and secondary level of education it accounts for 2.9 per cent of the employed labour force, and at the tertiary level for 0.6 per cent. However, there is substantial variation between countries in the proportion of the labour force who are teachers. The number of teachers employed either full or part-time in primary and secondary education combined ranges from 1.8 per cent or less of the employed labour force in Japan and Korea to over 3.5 per cent in the Flemish Community of Belgium, Hungary, Italy and Spain. At the tertiary level this percentage ranges from 0.4 per cent or less in Denmark, Greece, Italy, Turkey and the United Kingdom to 1.3 per cent in Canada.

Variation between countries is influenced by factors such as the size of the school-age population, average class sizes, total instruction time and teacher working time.

The variation between countries in the relative size of the teaching workforce cannot be accounted for solely by differences in the size of the school-age population, but is also affected by the average size of classes, the total instruction time of students, teachers' average working time, and the division of teachers' time between teaching and other duties.

The relative proportions of teachers and other educational personnel differ widely between countries – reflecting differences in the organisation and management of schooling.

There are significant differences across the OECD countries in the distribution of educational staff between teaching and other categories, reflecting differences between countries in the organisation and management of schooling. In almost half of the countries, administrative and support staff represent between 20 and 35 per cent of persons employed in education, with a high of more than 50 per cent in the United States and a low of 5 per cent in Greece. These differences reflect, to some extent, the degree to which

◆ Chart B7.1. ***Percentage of women among teaching staff by level of education (1995)***

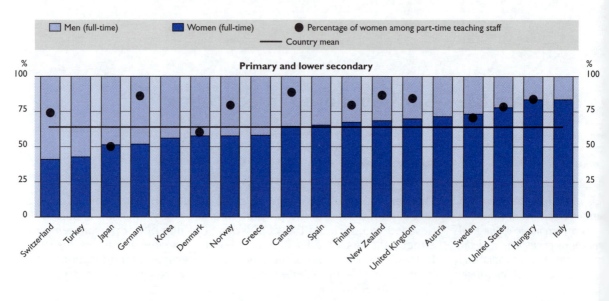

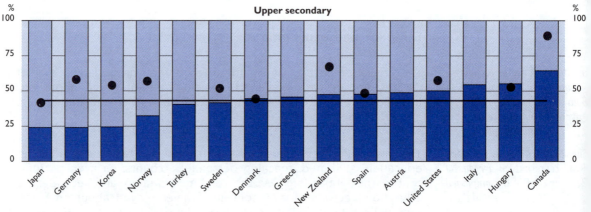

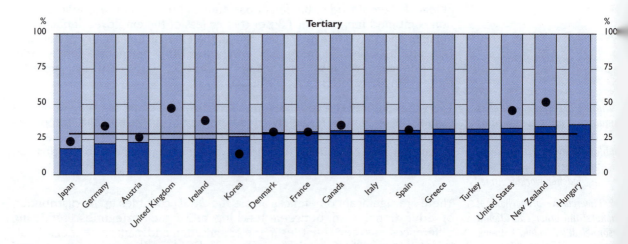

Countries are ranked in ascending order of the percentage of women among teaching staff at each level specified.

Source: OECD.

educational personnel specialise in non-teaching fields in a particular country (*e.g.* principals without instructional responsibilities, guidance counsellors, bus drivers, school nurses, librarians, researchers without instructional responsibilities, janitors and maintenance workers).

In Denmark, Hungary, New Zealand and the United States, educational and administrative personnel and other support staff in the education sector represent between 2.4 and 4.0 per cent of the employed labour force. In these countries the percentage of all educational staff in the employed labour force ranges from 5.9 to 8.6 per cent.

On average, 82.5 per cent of teachers are under full-time contracts.

The extent to which teachers work on a part-time basis can be an indication of the relative flexibility of the specialised education labour market, which is largely within the public sector. In all countries for which such a distinction is available, the majority of teaching staff are under full-time contracts, 82.5 per cent of teachers overall across OECD countries. In Italy, Mexico and Turkey all teachers are employed full-time, and in Finland and Spain the proportion of teachers employed part-time is less than 10 per cent. At the other end of the scale are the Flemish Community of Belgium, Germany and Sweden, where between 32 and 41 per cent of all teachers are employed part-time. Among women, the incidence of part-time teaching is much more common than among men (Table B7.2).

Women generally outnumber men as teachers at the lower levels of education...

In all countries except Turkey, women outnumber men at the early childhood, primary and lower secondary levels of education. Among teachers of early childhood programmes, the percentage of female teachers exceeds 90 per cent in nearly all OECD countries. At the primary level, women also form the clear majority of teachers in all except one country.

... but women are generally under-represented in the better paid teaching jobs at the higher levels of education.

At the upper secondary level, the percentage of full-time teachers who are female ranges from 25 per cent or less in Germany, Japan and Korea to between 50 and 65 per cent in Canada, Hungary, Italy and the United States. At the tertiary level male teachers make up the majority in all countries for which such data are available. At this level, the proportion of female full-time teachers ranges from between less than a quarter in Austria, Germany and Japan to 35 per cent or above in Hungary and New Zealand.

In general, the education sector is a more important source of employment for women than for men. In Italy and Hungary more than 9 per cent of all employed women work in education.

Definitions

Data refer to the school year 94/95 and are based on the UOE data collection on education statistics, administered in 1996 (for details see Annex 3).

This indicator shows the number of full-time and part-time teaching staff, non-teaching staff and all educational personnel as percentages of the total employed population in each country. The figures include staff employed in primary, secondary and tertiary education in both public and private schools and other institutions. Teachers are defined as persons whose professional activity involves the transmitting of knowledge, attitudes and skills that are stipulated in a formal curriculum to students enrolled in a formal educational institution (see also the Glossary). Non-teaching staff includes two categories: *i*) other pedagogical staff such as principals, supervisors, counsellors, psychologists, librarians, etc.; and *ii*) support staff such as clerical personnel, building and maintenance personnel, food service workers, etc. The stipulation of full-time employment is generally based on "statutory hours", or "normal or statutory working hours" (as opposed to actual or total working time or actual teaching time). Part-time employment (see column 4 in Table B7.1) generally refers to persons who have been employed to perform less than 90 per cent of the number of statutory working hours required of a full-time employee.

The figures on the number of employed persons are taken from OECD
Labour Force Statistics. The total employed population includes civilian
employment plus armed forces. Those persons aged 15 years and older are
considered to be employed when they are either employed or self-employed
for at least one hour during a specific brief period, either one week or one
day.

Table B7.1 **Staff employed in public and private education as a percentage of the total employed population (based on head counts) (1995)**

	Teaching staff						
	Primary and secondary education	Tertiary education	All levels of education combined (including early childhood education)	Percentage of part-time teachers for all levels of education combined	Educational, administrative or professional support personnel and other support staff	All education personnel	Student enrolments as a percentage of the employed population
North America							
Canada	2.1	1.3	3.5	28.8	0.7	4.2	53.1
Mexico	3.0	0.5	3.8	a	1.5	5.3	81.4
United States	2.3	0.7	3.2	17.0	4.0	7.2	54.0
Pacific Area							
Australia	m	m	m	m	m	m	63.6
Japan	1.8	0.6	2.7	20.8	0.7	3.4	40.1
Korea	1.7	0.5	2.3	11.0	0.7	3.0	61.1
New Zealand	2.3	0.6	3.5	20.5	2.4	5.9	65.2
European Union							
Austria	3.2	0.7	4.2	m	m	m	44.0
Belgium (Flemish)	4.1	0.7	5.3	32.5	1.1	6.4	56.3
Denmark	3.2	0.4	4.3	27.0	2.8	7.1	44.0
Finland	x	x	4.0	5.7	1.9	5.9	54.7
France	3.1	0.6	4.2	12.8	x	4.2	65.7
Germany	2.1	0.8	3.5	40.5	m	m	45.6
Greece	2.8	0.4	3.4	m	0.2	3.6	51.8
Ireland	3.4	0.7	4.5	15.6	m	m	79.8
Italy	3.8	0.4	4.8	a	1.1	5.9	55.5
Luxembourg	m	m	m	m	m	m	m
Netherlands	m	m	m	m	m	m	m
Portugal	m	m	m	m	m	m	m
Spain	3.6	0.7	4.7	9.5	m	m	79.2
Sweden	3.5	0.7	4.6	36.9	m	m	49.5
United Kingdom	2.8	0.3	3.2	24.2	m	m	54.5
Other OECD countries							
Czech Republic	m	m	m	m	m	m	44.4
Hungary	4.2	0.5	5.7	11.6	2.8	8.6	59.8
Iceland	m	m	m	m	m	m	50.4
Norway	m	m	m	m	m	m	m
Poland	m	m	m	m	m	m	m
Switzerland	m	m	m	m	m	m	m
Turkey	2.2	0.2	2.4	a	m	m	62.0
Country mean	**2.9**	**0.6**	**3.9**	**17.5**	**1.7**	**5.4**	**57.2**
Other non-OECD countries							
Russian Federation	m	m	m	3.6	m	m	m

Source: OECD Database. See Annex 3 for notes.

Table B7.2 **Percentage of women among teaching staff by level of education (1995)**

	Full-time teaching staff			Part-time teaching staff		
	Primary and lower secondary education	Upper secondary education	Tertiary education	Primary and lower secondary education	Upper secondary education	Tertiary education
North America						
Canada	x	65	31	x	87	35
Mexico	m	m	m	a	a	a
United States	78	50	33	79	58	47
Pacific Area						
Australia	m	m	m	m	m	m
Japan	51	24	19	49	42	24
Korea	56	25	27	a	55	15
New Zealand	69	48	35	88	67	52
European Union						
Austria	72	49	23	m	m	27
Belgium (Flemish)	67	44	31	86	71	38
Denmark	58	45	30	60	45	31
Finland	68	m	m	80	m	m
France	m	m	31	m	m	31
Germany	52	24	22	85	61	35
Greece	58	46	33	m	m	m
Ireland	m	m	25	m	m	37
Italy	84	55	32	a	a	a
Luxembourg	m	m	m	m	m	m
Netherlands	m	m	m	m	m	m
Portugal	m	m	m	m	m	m
Spain	66	48	32	a	48	32
Sweden	73	42	m	70	53	m
United Kingdom	70	m	25	86	m	48
Other OECD countries						
Czech Republic	m	m	m	m	m	m
Hungary	84	55	36	84	52	m
Iceland	m	m	m	m	m	m
Norway	58	32	m	81	59	m
Poland	m	m	m	m	m	m
Switzerland	41	m	m	74	m	m
Turkey	43	40	33	a	a	a
Country mean	**64**	**43**	**29**	**77**	**58**	**35**

Source: OECD Database. See Annex 3 for notes.

Indicator B8: Ratio of students to teaching staff

Policy context

This indicator shows the ratio of students to teaching staff at the different levels of education.

Although schools in many countries are making greater use of computers and other educational technology, teachers are still the most important resource in student instruction. The ratio of students to teaching staff is therefore an important indicator of the resources countries devote to education. Because of the difficulty of constructing direct measures of educational quality, indicators on the quantity of school inputs are often used as substitutes to measure educational quality.

As countries face increasing constraints on education budgets, many are considering trade-offs in their investment decisions. Smaller student/teaching staff ratios may need to be weighed against higher salaries for teachers and larger class sizes, greater investment in instructional technology, or greater use of teacher aides and paraprofessionals, whose salaries are often considerably lower than those of teachers. Moreover, as larger numbers of children arrive at school with special educational needs, greater use of specialised personnel and support services may limit the resources available for reductions in student/teaching staff ratios.

Evidence and explanations

Early childhood through upper secondary education

In Korea the ratio of students to teaching staff in public primary schools (31.7) is about three times as large as in Norway (9.5).

Student/teaching staff ratios in primary and secondary education vary widely between countries. In public primary education, student/teaching staff ratios range from 31.7 in Korea to 9.5 in Norway. The range in public secondary education is slightly narrower, extending from 23.7 in Korea and Turkey to 6.9 in the Flemish Community of Belgium.

On average across OECD countries, student/teaching staff ratios in public early childhood education are slightly lower than the corresponding ratios in primary education – 18.0 for early childhood compared with 18.2 for primary. However, in 13 of the 20 countries reporting ratios for both levels, student/ teaching staff ratios are lower at primary than early childhood level. Early childhood student/teaching staff ratios are below 15:1 in the Czech Republic, Denmark, Hungary, Italy, Japan and New Zealand, and above 20:1 in Canada, France, Germany, Ireland, Korea, Mexico, the United Kingdom and the United States. Part of this variation may be due to differences in the organisation of early childhood education between countries. Within countries, early childhood education often includes several rather different types of institutions. A few countries such as Denmark and Italy have low student/teaching staff ratios in both early childhood education and primary education; and countries such as the United States have relatively high ratios at both levels. But the pattern for other countries is less consistent.

◆   Chart B8.1.   *Ratio of students to teaching staff by level of education (full-time equivalents) (1995)*

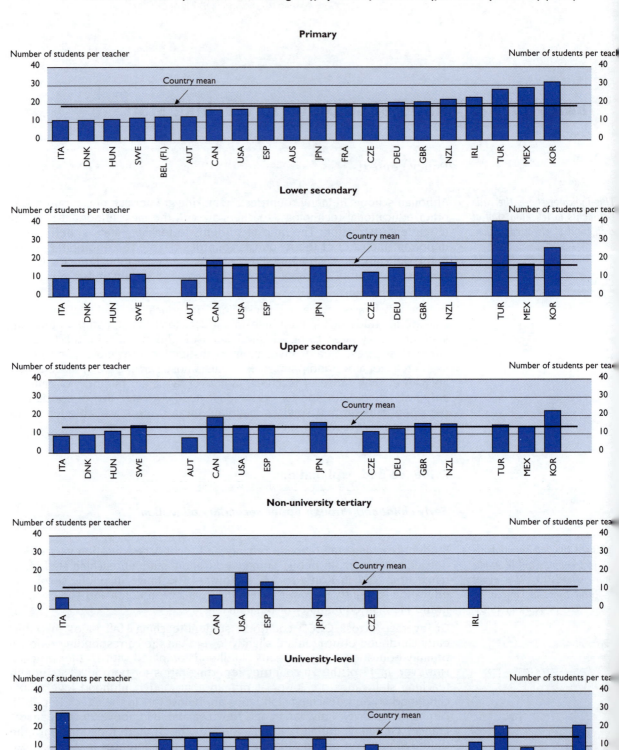

Source: OECD.

◆ Chart B8.2. *Ratio of students to teaching staff in early childhood and secondary education relative to the student/staff ratio at the primary level (times 100) (1995)*

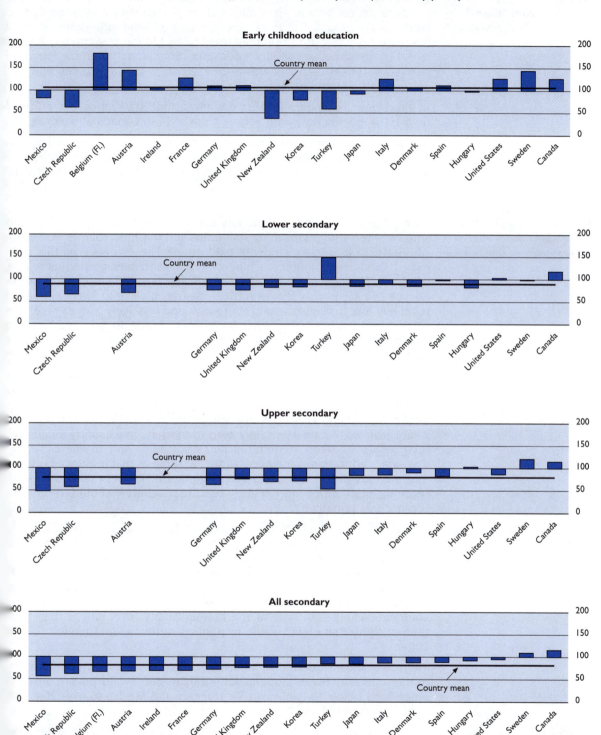

ries are ranked in ascending order of the student/teaching staff ratio at the secondary level relative to that at the primary level.

: OECD.

Student access to teachers improves from the primary to the secondary level of education.

Average student/teaching staff ratios in public schools in OECD countri tend to be higher in primary than in secondary education, that is, as the le of education rises there are more teachers in comparison with the number students enrolled. On average across countries, student/teaching staff rat decrease from 18.2 at the primary level to 16.2 in lower secondary educati and 13.5 in upper secondary education. Similar patterns are found wh public and private schools are taken together. Canada, Sweden and Turl are the only notable exceptions to this trend.

At the upper secondary level, student/teaching staff ratios range from l than 10 in Austria, Italy and Norway to over 19 in Canada and Korea.

Although student/teaching staff ratios differ in primary and secondary edu tion, countries' positions on this indicator tend to be similar at both level few countries, such as Italy and Norway, have low student/teaching staff rat at both the primary and secondary levels, while Korea, Mexico and Turl have high ratios at both levels.

Some countries compensate for low teacher salaries with low student/teaching staff ratios.

Another point to consider in primary and secondary education is the relati ship between student/teaching staff ratios and teachers' salaries. Are teach who have to face more students paid more? The evidence on this poin mixed. Examining student/teaching staff ratios and average starting salarie teachers with minimum training (see Indicator D1), there appear to be tra offs of this type in a few countries. Austria, Italy and Sweden have b relatively low student/teaching staff ratios and relatively low average star salaries for teachers. Germany, in contrast, tends to pay teachers hig starting salaries, but the trade-off is a relatively high student/teaching s ratio.

An analysis of trade-offs between student/teaching staff ratios and teach salaries must also consider a few other points. First, the salary measure u in this assessment only measures average starting salaries for teachers minimum training. This does not reflect the distribution of teachers on salary scale or the average salary paid to teachers in a country. Similarly, relationship between student/teaching staff ratios and teachers' salarie secondary education is not necessarily the same as that in primary educat Assessments of the trade-offs that countries make between lower stud teaching staff ratios and higher teachers' salaries should therefore regarded as tentative.

In general, student/teaching staff ratios at the university level tend to be similar to those in upper secondary education, but there is wide variation between countries.

At the university level, student/teaching staff ratios are, on average, simil those found in upper secondary education. The average student/teac staff ratio in public and private universities for all OECD countries is compared with 14.9 in public and private upper secondary schools. At non-university tertiary level, the student/teaching staff ratios are not uni across countries. For example, in public institutions in Italy and Japan, student/teaching staff ratio at the non-university level is less than half ratio at the tertiary level, while in public institutions in Turkey it is 5 t larger.

There is also considerable variability between countries in student/staff r at the university level. Student/staff ratios in public and private univers range from below 10:1 in Australia, Hungary and Mexico to over 20:1 in Spain, Switzerland and Turkey.

Many factors contribute to these differences.

A broad range of factors need to be considered to interpret difference student/teaching staff ratios at the tertiary level, including institutional s tures, typical class or lecture size, the number of classes that a ty "teacher" teaches per term, the degree of "hands on" training and the c tion of studies. In addition, better definitions of "teachers" and better co of full-time-equivalent students and teachers may be required to pro comparable ratios of teacher resources in tertiary education.

The student/teaching staff ratio not an indicator of class size.

It must be emphasised that the ratio of students to teaching staff does not translate directly into class size (which can be found in Chapter D). The fact that one country has a lower ratio of students to teaching staff than another does not necessarily imply that classes are smaller in the first country or that students in the first country receive more instruction. The relationship between student/teaching staff ratio and both average class size and the amount of instruction per student is complicated, for example, by differences between countries in the length of the school year, the number of hours that a student attends class each day, the length of a teacher's working day, the number of classes or students for which a teacher is responsible, the division of the teacher's time between teaching and other duties, the grouping of students within classes and the practice of team teaching.

Definitions

Data refer to the school year 94/95 and are based on the UOE data collection on education statistics, administered in 1996 (for details see Annex 3).

This indicator shows the ratio of students to teaching staff and is obtained by dividing the number of full-time-equivalent students at a given level of education by the number of full-time-equivalent "teachers" at that same level and for that same type of institution. The definition of "teachers" is sometimes not entirely consistent across countries. For public primary education, the Flemish Community of Belgium, Canada, Finland, Spain, Sweden, Switzerland and the United States include only classroom and other teachers as "teachers" in the staff data. Several other countries, including Austria, France, Germany, Ireland, Italy, Mexico, the Netherlands and the United Kingdom also include headteachers or school principals as "teachers", although in some cases these individuals may also have some teaching duties. Other countries also include professional support staff such as guidance counsellors and school psychologists in their "teacher" counts. Similar classifications apply in public secondary education as well, with the following exceptions. France reports only classroom and other teachers as "teachers", Finland includes headmasters as "teachers", and Ireland and Italy include some other professional support staff as "teachers."

Staff reported as "teachers" in early childhood education are generally similar to those reported in primary education. However, the situation in tertiary education is somewhat different. A larger number of countries, including Australia, Canada, France, Ireland, the Netherlands, New Zealand, Spain, Switzerland, the United Kingdom and the United States, appear to report only classroom teachers as "teachers", but a clear definition of a "teacher" in tertiary education has not been well established in international data collections. Future work on definitions of "teachers" and other staff in tertiary education may help to clarify this definition.

Table B8.1 **Ratio of students to teaching staff by level of education
(calculations based on full-time equivalents) (1995)**

	Public education							Public and private education					
	Early childhood education	Primary education	Lower secondary education	Upper secondary education	All secondary education	Non-university level	University level	Early childhood education	Primary education	Lower secondary education	Upper secondary education	All secondary education	Non-university level
North America													
Canada	21.4	17.0	19.5	19.3	19.4	14.5	17.3	21.1	16.7	19.7	19.2	19.4	7.6
Mexico	24.5	28.8	19.1	16.1	18.1	x	9.6	23.9	28.7	17.5	14.0	16.2	x
United States	21.5	17.2	17.9	15.0	16.5	20.4	14.4	21.5	17.1	17.6	14.7	16.2	19.4
Pacific Area													
Australia	m	17.9	m	m	m	x	5.7	m	18.1	m	m	m	x
Japan	13.9	19.5	16.7	15.5	16.1	4.1	8.5	18.1	19.5	16.6	16.4	16.5	11.4
Korea	20.8	31.7	26.0	19.9	23.7	m	m	25.1	31.8	26.6	22.7	24.6	m
New Zealand	8.9	22.7	18.6	15.0	16.9	m	m	8.4	22.3	18.4	15.6	17.1	m
European Union													
Austria	17.9	12.8	9.0	8.3	8.7	m	14.5	18.6	12.9	9.0	8.2	8.7	m
Belgium (Flemish)	19.0	13.0	x	x	6.9	x	12.4	23.3	12.8	x	x	8.5	x
Denmark	11.7	11.3	9.4	10.1	9.8	m	m	11.7	11.1	9.4	9.9	9.7	m
Finland	m	m	m	m	m	m	m	m	m	m	m	m	m
France	24.6	19.4	x	x	13.1	x	19.0	24.8	19.5	x	x	13.6	x
Germany	22.5	20.7	15.8	13.3	15.0	m	m	22.7	20.7	15.8	13.0	14.9	m
Greece	m	m	m	m	m	m	m	m	m	m	m	m	m
Ireland	24.8	23.6	x	x	16.2	9.9	13.5	24.6	23.4	x	x	16.0	12.1
Italy	12.3	10.6	10.0	9.7	9.9	6.2	29.1	13.8	11.0	9.9	9.3	9.6	6.3
Luxembourg	m	m	m	m	m	m	m	m	m	m	m	m	m
Netherlands	m	m	m	m	m	m	m	m	m	m	m	m	m
Portugal	m	m	m	m	m	m	m	m	m	m	m	m	m
Spain	19.1	16.4	16.5	13.6	14.5	14.1	21.3	19.8	17.8	17.5	14.8	15.7	14.7
Sweden	17.7	12.3	12.2	14.9	13.6	m	m	17.7	12.3	12.2	14.8	13.5	m
United Kingdom	23.2	21.9	16.7	13.1	14.9	a	a	23.2	21.0	16.0	15.9	15.9	x
Other OECD countries													
Czech Republic	12.0	19.6	13.0	10.2	11.4	5.7	10.9	12.3	19.7	13.1	11.5	12.2	9.9
Hungary	11.3	11.6	9.5	11.9	10.6	a	8.0	11.3	11.6	9.5	11.9	10.7	a
Iceland	m	m	m	m	m	11.5	7.7	m	m	m	m	m	m
Norway	m	9.5	9.4	8.2	8.7	m	10.1	m	m	m	m	m	m
Poland	m	m	m	m	m	m	m	m	m	m	m	m	m
Switzerland	18.1	15.7	12.3	m	m	m	21.5	m	m	m	m	m	m
Turkey	15.5	27.9	40.3	15.4	23.7	109.5	21.5	16.3	27.7	41.2	14.9	23.3	m
Country mean	**18.0**	**18.2**	**16.2**	**13.5**	**14.4**	**21.8**	**14.4**	**18.9**	**18.8**	**16.9**	**14.2**	**14.9**	**11.6**

Source: OECD Database. See Annex 3 for notes.

Chapter C

ACCESS TO EDUCATION, PARTICIPATION AND PROGRESSION

A well-educated population has become a defining characteristic of a modern society. Education is seen a mechanism for instilling democratic values, as well as the means for developing the productive and cial capacity of the individual. As modern manufacturing and service industries demand a labour force pable of adjusting to new technologies and making informed decisions, educated and highly skilled rkers are increasingly viewed as one of the most important economic inputs.

In this context, societies have an interest in both providing a wide range of educational opportunities for ldren and adults and ensuring broad access to these opportunities. Early childhood programmes prepare ung children socially and academically for entry into primary education; primary and secondary education ovide a foundation of basic skills that prepare young people to become productive members of society; d tertiary education provides a range of opportunities for individuals to gain advanced knowledge and lls, either immediately after initial schooling or later in life. In addition, many employers either encourage, even assist, workers to upgrade or reorient their skills in order to meet the demands of changing hnologies.

Information on enrolment rates at various levels of education and on the expected duration of schooling provide a picture of the structure of different education systems, as well as of access to educational portunities in those systems. Trends in the enrolments in the various levels of education and types of cational institutions are also an indicator of how the supply and demand of educational resources are anced in different countries.

Indicator C1 provides a broad comparison of enrolment rates in school-based education and training in h public and private educational institutions, and compares the expected duration of schooling for 5 to year-olds among countries. This information not only provides an overall picture of the size of education tems, but also serves as background information for the interpretation of Indicators B1, B2 and B8 that l with national resources invested in education. The remaining indicators in this chapter provide more ail on access, participation and progression at the different levels of education.

Both early childhood education and initial programmes in primary schooling are important aspects of a tegy aimed at ensuring that all students start school ready to learn. **Indicator C2** describes the participa- of very young children in early childhood and primary programmes and examines the average duration ducation for children up to the age of six.

A range of factors, including an increased risk of unemployment and other forms of exclusion for young ple with insufficient education, have strengthened the incentive for young people to stay enrolled ond the end of compulsory schooling. Patterns of participation towards the end of compulsory education beyond are examined in **Indicator C3**. This indicator also examines the age boundaries in the transition secondary to tertiary education, and compares the relative size of enrolments in general education and h school-based and combined school and work-based vocational education at the upper secondary level e various countries.

Beyond the end of upper secondary education, a number of options exist for further education. One nue is relatively short vocationally orientated programmes below university degree level. Another is ersity-level education, an option being taken by an ever increasing proportion of school-leavers. Still r options are enterprise-based and labour market training programmes adapted to individual and labour ket needs. Completion of tertiary education programmes is generally associated with better access to loyment (see Indicator E2) and higher earnings (see Indicator E4). The rate at which a country's popula- enters university-level tertiary education – as examined in **Indicator C4** – is a measure, in part, of the ee to which high-level skills are being acquired by the population. High tertiary entry rates help to ensure the development and maintenance of a highly educated population and labour force. **Indicator** examines patterns of participation in both non-university and university-level tertiary education for vario age groups between the ages of 18 and 29.

One way for students to expand their knowledge of other cultures and societies is to attend institutio of higher education in countries other than their own. International student mobility involves costs a benefits to students and institutions, in both the sending and host countries. While the direct short-te monetary costs and benefits of this mobility are more easily measured, the long-term social and econom benefits to students, institutions and countries are more difficult to quantify. Measures of the number students studying in other countries, however, provide some idea of the extent of this phenomenon and t degree to which it is changing over time. **Indicator C6** shows the mobility of students between countrie:

There is ample evidence that more secondary and tertiary education for young people improves th individual economic and social opportunities. There is also growing evidence, albeit less direct, of a pay for whole societies from increasing the educational attainment of the population. But as rapidly chang technology and globalisation transform the pattern of demand for skilled labour throughout the world, rais the proportion of young people who participate in upper secondary or higher education can only be part the solution, for two reasons. First, an inflow of better-educated young people will only very gradually char the overall educational level of the existing workforce. Secondly, educational attainment is only one comp nent of human capital accumulation. Knowledge and skills continue to be created throughout people's liv through experiences in families, communities and business, as well as within formal educational settir There is a growing demand in the workplace and elsewhere for individuals who are good at using a interpreting knowledge flexibly, and for groups that can work together effectively. These abilities can pa be acquired through education, but must also be developed in the settings where they will be us Strategies for developing lifelong learning opportunities must therefore look beyond mainstream educatio institutions, to ensure optimal investment in human capital. **Indicator C7** presents data on participatior job-related continuing education and training, that is, participation in education beyond the formal sch system.

Indicator C1: Participation in formal education

Policy context

his indicator shows enrolment rates at the different levels of education and the expected duration of schooling.

A well-educated population is critical for the current and future economic, intellectual and social development of a country. Societies therefore have an interest in providing a wide variety of educational opportunities for both children and adults and ensuring broad access to learning opportunities. Early childhood programmes prepare children for primary education; primary and secondary education provide a foundation of basic skills that prepare young people to become productive members of society; and tertiary education provides a range of options for individuals to gain advanced knowledge and skills either immediately following school or later in life.

Information on enrolment rates at various levels of education and the expected duration of schooling can provide a picture of the structure of different education systems, as well as of access to educational opportunities in those systems. Trends in the pattern of enrolments across levels of education and types of educational institutions are also an indicator of how the supply and demand of educational resources are balanced in different countries.

Evidence and explanations

Overall participation in education

In most OECD countries, rtually all 5 to 14 year-olds are enrolled in education.

Enrolment rates are influenced both by the relative number of persons participating in education and by the duration of studies. In more than half of OECD countries the number of persons enrolled in formal education who are aged 5 years or above exceeds 60 per cent of the population aged 5 to 29 years (see Table C1.1a). In most OECD countries, virtually all 5 to 14 year-olds are enrolled in education (see Table C1.2).

ountries differ widely in the ation of universal education.

In the majority of OECD countries, universal enrolment starts between the ages of 5 and 6 years, although in Belgium, France, the Netherlands, New Zealand and Spain 97 per cent or more of 4 year-olds are already enrolled in either early childhood or primary education programmes (see Table C2.1). Countries differ greatly in the years for which enrolment in formal education is universal. For example, the age band in which at least 95 per cent of students are enrolled spans 13 or more years in Belgium, France, the Netherlands and New Zealand. In contrast, Portugal, Mexico and Turkey have enrolment rates exceeding 90 per cent for a period of eight or fewer years.

How countries differ in enrolment rates in early childhood programmes and in enrolment rates towards the end of compulsory schooling and beyond is shown in detail in indicators C2, C3 and C5.

◆   Chart CI.I.   ***Number of students enrolled per 100 persons in the population age 5 to 29, by age group (based on head counts) (1995)***

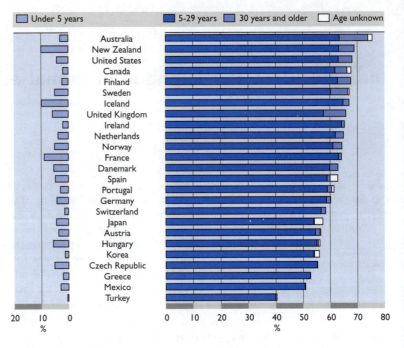

Source: OECD.

A third of 15-29 year-olds are enrolled, with variation between countries largely explained by differences in tertiary enrolments.

Participation rates in education beyond the age of 14 vary much more t[...] they do at early ages – from less than 20 per cent in the population aged 1[...] 29 in Mexico and Turkey to 40 per cent and over in Australia, Denm[...] France, Finland, the Netherlands and Norway (see Table C1.2).

The variation in enrolment rates between countries is largely explained[...] differences in enrolments at the tertiary level: from 3 tertiary education [...] dents per 100 persons in the population aged 5 to 29 years in Mexico to 1[...] more in Australia, Canada and the United States (see Table C1.1a).

In some countries, particularly in Australia, Sweden and the United Kingd[...] a significant portion of the population aged 30 to 39 years is enrolle[...] formal education (see Table C1.2).

Participation rates for full-time students have increased over the last two decades...

Across countries for which comparable data are available, the numbe[...] students enrolled full-time as a percentage of the population aged 5 to [...] years has increased, on average, from 51 to 55 per cent over the last dec[...] In Finland the increase has been even greater, from 53 to 64 per c[...] bringing Finland now to the highest overall level of full-time enrolment in [...] OECD. Canada, New Zealand, the United Kingdom and the United St[...] have also seen substantial increases (around 6 percentage points or mor[...] their enrolment of 5 to 29 year-olds (see Table C1.t).

In compulsory education, enrolments have tended to follow the declin[...] birth rates. However, the decline in the overall number of students enr[...] at the lower levels of education has been outweighed by sharp increase[...] post-compulsory enrolments.

. and the number of full-time tertiary students enrolled per 100 persons in the population aged 5-29 has doubled over the last two decades.

The number of full-time students as a percentage of the population aged 5 to 29 years who are enrolled in tertiary education has, on average, increased by more than 50 per cent over the last decade and doubled over the last two decades. This trend is continuing, with an increase in full-time tertiary enrolment rates of about a quarter, on average, over the last five years. The rates of increase have, however, differed between countries. While Austria, Germany, Switzerland and the United States have seen comparably modest increases in full-time tertiary enrolments over the last decade, increases in Finland, Norway and Spain have been substantial.

Note that, in order to provide comparable data over time, Table C1.t covers only full-time enrolments while the remaining tables in this indicator extend to both part-time and full-time participation.

School expectancy

In 21 out of 25 countries, a 5 year-old child can expect to attend school for between 14.5 and 16.5 years.

Another way of looking at participation in education is to estimate the number of years of education a 5 year-old child might expect to receive up to the age of 29, given current enrolment rates by age (see Chart C1.2). This varies from just over 9 years in Turkey to around 17 years in Belgium and the Netherlands. Typically, school expectancy is in the range of 14 to 16 years.

School expectancy has increased since the mid-1980s, in many countries by more than a year.

School expectancy has increased in recent years in all countries for which data are available. The increase since 1985 has exceeded more than one year in many countries and in the Nordic countries reached almost two years. Longer duration of schooling is one factor that contributes to the observed rise in enrolment rates over recent decades.

Participation by level of education

Typically, more than half of all students enrolled are at the primary and lower secondary levels.

In all countries, the majority of participants are enrolled in the lower levels of education – typically the compulsory or pre-compulsory phases. Variations between countries in enrolment rates at the lower levels are largely determined by the proportion of the population who are in the relevant age

◆ Chart C1.2. **Expected years of schooling for a 5 year-old child (based on head counts) (1995)**

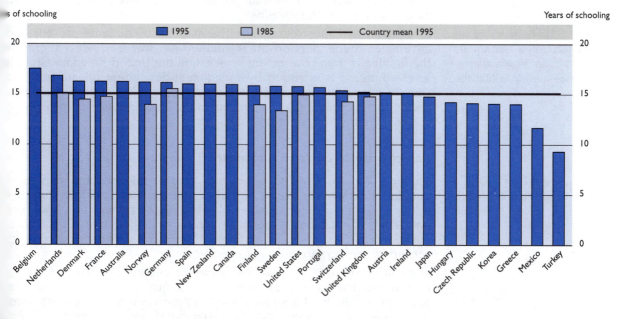

bracket, as well as by the variable lengths of primary and lower seconda programmes (between 8 and 10 years).

On average, the number of students enrolled in upper secondary educati corresponds to 14 per cent of the population aged 5 to 29 years. Mexico is the lower end of the scale, with upper secondary enrolment of 5 per cent o to 29 year-olds. In contrast, upper secondary enrolment exceeds 20 per ce in Belgium, Spain and the United Kingdom (see Table C1.1a).

At the tertiary level enrolment rates range from 3 to 17 per cent of 5-29 year-olds.

The participation rates in tertiary education vary between countries from 3 17 per cent. While in Australia, Canada, and the United States 14 per cent more of all 5 to 29 year-olds are enrolled in a tertiary programme, the p centage is 5 per cent and below in the Czech Republic, Hungary, Mexico a Turkey. A detailed profile of participation at the tertiary level is provided indicator C6.

Participation by type of institution

In most countries public schools compete with private institutions...

Most countries provide education through a range of different types of insti tions. Some of the institutions are controlled and managed directly by public education authority or agency or are controlled by a body who members are appointed by a public authority (these are referred to as *pu institutions in this indicator). Other institutions are controlled and manag by a non-governmental organisation (*e.g.* a Church, a Trade Union or a bu ness enterprise) (these institutions are referred to as *private* institutions in t indicator). In other cases, the management of schools is shared betwe public and private bodies.

... but private schools depend on governments for funding in most countries.

In most countries, the basic educational services of private institutions pri rily depend on funding from government sources (these institutions referred to as *government-dependent private* institutions in this indicator).

On average, one out of six students is enrolled in a private institution.

In most countries, public institutions compete with private providers of e cational services. On average, the enrolments in private institutions co spond to 10 per cent of the population aged 5 to 29, or 15 per cent of students. Private institution participation rates range from around 1 per c of all students in Ireland, the Russian Federation and Turkey to 35 per cen more of all students in Belgium, Korea and the United Kingdom and ab 75 per cent in the Netherlands.

In Belgium and the Netherlands a majority are enrolled in government-dependent private institutions.

In Belgium and the Netherlands the majority of students are enrolled government-dependent private institutions (*i.e.*, where 50 per cent or more the funding is from government sources). In the United Kingdom all terti level education is provided by government-dependent private institutio Only in Korea, Portugal and the United States is the independent priv sector (*i.e.* where less than 50 per cent of the funding comes from governm sources) a fairly important provider.

Participation by mode of enrolment

In about a third of OECD countries, part-time enrolments are significant.

Students may be enrolled either part time or full-time and they may enrolled continuously over a period of time or interrupt their studies periods of work or other activities. Whereas at the primary and lower se dary levels of education students are typically enrolled full-time and cont ously, alternative modes of enrolment are more prominent at the up secondary and tertiary levels of education.

In about a third of OECD countries, part-time enrolments account for a sig cant proportion. In Australia more than a quarter of all students att part-time and in the United Kingdom this proportion is almost a fifth. Alte tive modes of enrolment can be a significant way of opening up ter education to a wider target group. Part-time and evening courses, as we

◆ Chart C1.3. *Distribution of students aged 5 and over (based on head counts),*
by type of institution and by mode of enrolment (1995)

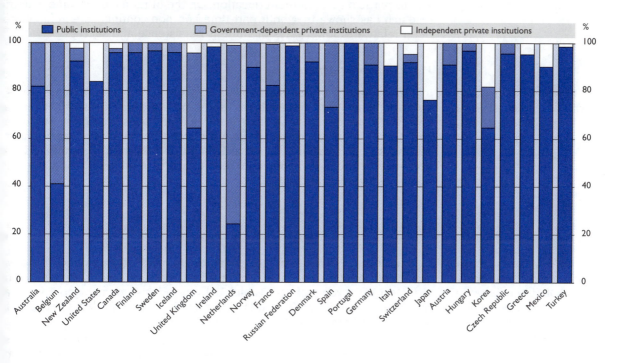

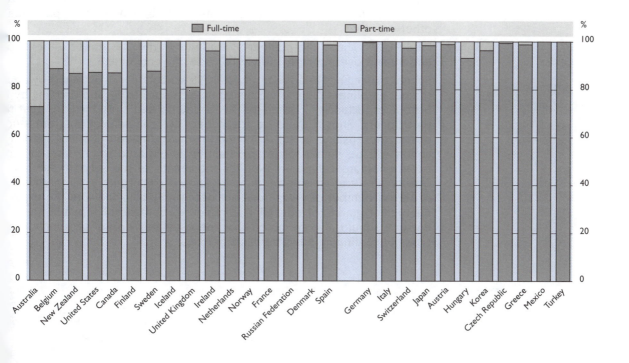

...ries are ranked in descending order of number of students enrolled.

...e: OECD.

long distance learning through video and computer connections, may of students who have already completed or left initial education an attracti way to participate in further education. On the other hand, in some countri research has shown that both part-time and non-continuous enrolment ha been related to lower rates of student persistence and success.

Participation by gender

In most OECD countries gender differences in enrolment rates are small.

In the majority of countries women can expect to receive more years education than men although the differences are usually small. There a however, countries with sizeable gender differences. In Korea, Switzerla and Turkey men can expect to stay between one and two years longer education than women whereas in Finland and Sweden the expected du tion of enrolment for women exceeds that of men by 12 and 8 mon respectively (see Table C1.2).

Definitions

Data refer to the school year 1994/95 and are based on the UOE data collection on education statistics, administered in 1996 (for details see Annex 3).

This indicator shows the number of students of all ages enrolled at the ea childhood, primary, secondary and tertiary levels of education per 100 in viduals 5 to 29 years of age. Table C1.1a includes students aged 5 years a older (even older than 29 years). The participation of students younger th 5 years is examined in Table C1.1b and indicator C2.

Figures are based on head counts, that is, they do not distinguish betwe full-time and part-time participants. The last two columns of Table C1.1a sh the number of students enrolled by mode of enrolment. A standardi distinction between full-time and part-time participants is very difficult si many countries do not recognise the concept of part-time study, althougl practice at least some of their students would be classified as part-time other countries.

Table C1.1b shows the number of students in the age-groups under 5, 5 and 30 and over, per 100 individuals 5 to 29 years of age.

School expectancy relative to the 1994/95 school year is obtained by adc the net enrolment rates for each year of age from 5 to 29, and dividing by School expectancy is based on head counts and thus includes part-ti participants. Should there be a tendency to lengthen (or shorten) stuc during the ensuing years, the actual average duration of schooling for cohort will be higher (or lower). Caution is required when data on sch expectancy are compared. Neither the length of the school year nor quality of education is necessarily the same in each country. Furthermore, expected number of years does not necessarily coincide with the expec number of grades of education completed, because of repeating and entry. It should also be noted that the estimates do not account for m types of continuing education and training.

Table C1.1a **Number of students aged 5 and over enrolled in public and private education per 100 persons in the population aged 5 to 29 (based on head counts), by level of education, by type of institution, by mode of enrolment (1995)**

	Enrolments in public and private education						Enrolments by type of institution				Enrolments by mode of enrolment	
	Early childhood education	Primary and lower secondary education	Upper secondary education	Tertiary education	Undefined	All levels of education combined	Public institutions	Government-dependent private institutions	Independent private institutions	Unknown type of institution	Full-time	Part-time
North America												
Canada	3.0	35.6	11.9	17.3	n	67.8	65.0	1.2	1.6	n	58.8	9.0
Mexico	3.5	39.7	4.8	2.9	n	50.8	45.9	a	4.9	n	50.8	n
United States	4.6	38.1	10.1	15.3	n	68.2	57.2	a	11.0	n	59.2	9.0
Pacific Area												
Australia	0.7	44.5	15.9	14.5	n	75.6	59.0	13.0	n	3.5	54.8	20.8
Japan	3.0	31.8	12.4	9.4	0.9	57.4	38.6	a	12.0	6.8	56.4	1.0
Korea	1.4	32.2	11.2	11.2	n	56.1	36.3	9.6	10.2	n	54.0	2.1
New Zealand	0.1	41.0	15.7	12.1	n	69.0	63.7	3.7	1.6	n	59.6	9.4
European Union												
Austria	4.4	28.6	14.9	8.7	n	56.6	51.5	5.1	x	n	55.9	0.7
Belgium	3.9	34.3	20.8	10.8	n	69.8	28.6	41.2	m	m	61.7	8.1
Denmark	6.7	32.6	13.6	10.1	n	62.9	58.0	5.0	a	n	62.9	a
Finland	3.6	36.0	15.6	12.6	n	67.7	64.9	2.8	a	n	67.7	n
France	3.8	37.5	12.5	10.3	n	64.2	52.8	11.0	0.3	n	64.2	n
Germany	4.6	35.2	11.7	8.5	0.2	60.2	54.8	5.5	x	n	60.0	0.3
Greece	1.7	x	x	8.2	a	52.7	50.3	a	2.4	n	52.0	0.7
Ireland	5.6	39.2	12.1	8.1	0.3	65.3	64.2	x	1.1	n	62.7	2.7
Italy	8.5	25.5	15.4	9.6	a	59.0	53.2	a	5.6	0.2	59.0	n
Luxembourg	8.1	31.4	9.5	m	n	48.9	m	2.3	m	m	m	m
Netherlands	3.7	37.7	14.0	9.6	n	65.0	15.9	48.5	0.6	n	60.1	4.9
Portugal	2.2	38.5	12.4	8.3	n	61.5	48.8	m	m	m	m	m
Spain	2.9	28.8	20.6	10.6	n	62.9	46.0	16.9	x	n	60.6	1.0
Sweden	6.3	35.0	17.0	8.8	n	67.1	63.8	2.2	0.1	1.1	58.7	8.4
United Kingdom	n	33.8	22.9	9.2	n	65.9	42.4	20.7	2.8	n	53.2	12.7
Other OECD countries												
Czech Republic	4.2	29.6	16.8	4.8	n	55.4	53.0	2.4	a	n	55.0	0.4
Hungary	5.6	28.8	17.1	4.8	n	56.3	54.5	1.8	a	n	52.3	3.9
Iceland	3.4	40.4	16.2	7.0	n	67.0	60.7	2.6	n	3.7	64.5	m
Norway	6.5	31.8	14.5	11.7	n	64.4	57.9	6.5	x	n	59.3	5.1
Poland	m	m	m	m	m	m	m	m	m	m	m	m
Switzerland	5.7	34.1	11.7	6.6	0.3	58.4	53.8	2.0	2.7	n	56.8	1.6
Turkey	0.4	29.5	6.6	3.8	n	40.4	39.8	a	0.5	n	40.4	n
Country mean	**3.9**	**34.5**	**14.0**	**9.4**	**0.1**	**61.3**	**51.1**	**7.5**	**2.7**	**0.7**	**57.7**	**4.1**
Other non-OECD countries												
Russian Federation	11.9	35.8	7.6	8.5	n	63.8	63.0	a	0.8	n	59.8	3.9

...nts aged 4 and under are excluded, students aged 30 and over are included.

...e: OECD Database. See Annex 3 for notes.

Table C1.1b **Total number of students enrolled per 100 persons in the population aged 5 to 29, by age group (based on head counts) (1995)**

	Enrolments in public and private education				
	overall	under 5	aged 5 -29	30 and over	unknown age
North America					
Canada	69.7	1.9	61.9	4.4	1.5
Mexico	53.7	2.8	50.7	0.1	n
United States	72.4	4.2	63.1	5.1	n
Pacific Area					
Australia	78.6	3.0	63.5	10.6	1.6
Japan	61.8	4.4	54.0	0.2	3.2
Korea	57.3	1.3	54.0	0.2	1.9
New Zealand	78.9	9.9	63.3	5.6	n
European Union					
Austria	60.2	3.6	54.6	1.7	0.3
Belgium	79.0	9.3	x	x	0.2
Denmark	68.3	5.3	60.0	2.9	n
Finland	70.0	2.3	62.9	4.9	n
France	72.9	8.8	63.2	1.0	n
Germany	64.5	4.2	58.8	1.5	n
Greece	54.7	2.0	52.6	0.1	n
Ireland	67.3	2.0	64.3	1.1	n
Italy	59.0	x	x	x	x
Luxembourg	48.9	x	x	x	x
Netherlands	68.7	3.7	62.0	3.0	n
Portugal	64.4	2.9	59.0	1.6	0.8
Spain	67.6	4.7	59.0	1.1	2.8
Sweden	72.0	4.9	60.3	6.3	0.6
United Kingdom	71.6	5.7	57.7	8.1	n
Other OECD countries					
Czech Republic	60.4	5.0	55.3	0.1	n
Hungary	61.8	5.5	55.1	0.5	0.6
Iceland	76.8	9.8	64.8	2.2	n
Norway	69.4	5.0	61.1	3.3	n
Poland	m	m	m	m	m
Switzerland	59.8	1.4	56.8	1.6	n
Turkey	40.4	0.1	39.8	0.5	n
Country mean	**65.4**	**4.4**	**58.3**	**2.7**	**0.5**
Other non-OECD countries					
Russian Federation	63.8	x	x	x	x

Source: OECD Database. See Annex 3 for notes.

Table C1.2 **Enrolment rates and expected years of schooling for a five-year old child by gender, in public and private institutions (based on head counts) (1995)**

	Students aged 5-14 as a percentage of the population aged 5-14	Students aged 15-29 as a percentage of the population aged 15-29	Students aged 30-39 as a percentage of the population aged 30-39	Years of school expectancy for a 5 year-old child			
				Men + Women		Men	Women
				1985	1995	1995	1995
North America							
Canada	99.7	38.3	5.3	m	16.0	16.0	16.0
Mexico	92.7	17.5	0.5	m	11.7	m	m
United States	101.9	36.6	6.5	15.0	15.8	15.7	16.0
Pacific Area							
Australia	99.3	41.2	12.8	m	16.3	m	m
Japan	101.3	29.2	0.3	m	14.8	m	m
Korea	89.5	33.5	0.6	m	14.1	14.7	13.5
New Zealand	101.8	38.2	7.4	m	16.0	16.1	16.0
European Union							
Austria	98.6	30.8	2.6	m	15.2	15.4	14.8
Belgium	99.6	m	m	m	17.6	17.6	17.9
Denmark	97.4	40.9	4.5	14.5	16.3	16.2	16.5
Finland	88.9	45.9	6.7	14.0	15.9	15.4	16.4
France	100.1	40.0	2.3	14.8	16.3	16.1	16.5
Germany	95.9	37.9	2.8	15.6	16.2	16.4	16.0
Greece	96.7	28.9	0.1	m	14.0	14.2	13.8
Ireland	100.0	38.6	m	m	15.2	15.0	15.3
Italy	m	m	m	m	m	m	m
Luxembourg	m	m	m	m	m	m	m
Netherlands	99.3	41.5	4.3	15.2	16.9	17.3	16.5
Portugal	103.1	36.4	3.2	m	15.7	15.5	16.0
Spain	104.0	37.4	2.1	m	16.1	15.8	16.3
Sweden	94.7	39.3	8.3	13.4	15.8	15.5	16.2
United Kingdom	98.9	32.5	8.7	14.8	15.3	15.1	15.5
Other OECD countries							
Czech Republic	99.3	30.5	0.2	m	14.1	14.1	14.2
Hungary	99.8	30.4	1.3	m	14.2	m	m
Iceland	m	m	3.7	m	m	m	m
Norway	95.1	41.6	4.8	14.0	16.2	16.2	16.3
Poland	m	m	m	m	m	m	m
Switzerland	97.5	33.5	3.2	14.3	15.4	16.0	14.9
Turkey	71.8	15.5	1.5	m	9.3	10.3	8.3
Country mean	**97.1**	**34.8**	**3.9**	**14.6**	**15.2**	**15.5**	**15.4**
Other non-OECD countries							
Russian Federation	m	m	m	m	m	m	m

Source: OECD Database. See Annex 3 for notes.

Table C1.t **Number of full-time students enrolled in public and private institutions per 100 persons in the population aged 5 to 29 (1975-95)**

	All levels of education combined (except early childhood education)				Upper secondary education				Tertiary education			
	1975	1985	1990	1995	1975	1985	1990	1995	1975	1985	1990	1995
North America												
Canada	54.5	52.7	55.6	58.6	12.5	10.6	10.9	11.9	6.7	8.6	9.3	11.2
Mexico	m	m	49.1	47.4	m	m	4.6	4.8	m	m	2.7	2.9
United States	55.6	50.2	52.6	57.0	7.3	10.3	9.7	10.1	6.6	7.4	8.2	8.7
Pacific Area												
Australia	m	m	m	54.1	6.9	6.5	m	6.4	4.5	m	m	6.4
Japan	47.6	m	57.1	53.4	9.7	12.0	13.5	12.0	4.3	m	7.1	8.7
Korea	m	52.1	52.4	52.6	10.2	10.1	11.0	11.0	m	6.0	7.2	9.4
New Zealand	55.1	50.9	53.5	59.6	6.6	7.5	9.5	11.6	2.5	3.0	4.8	7.0
European Union												
Austria	53.0	48.9	49.0	51.5	13.4	16.3	15.0	14.3	2.9	6.5	8.3	8.6
Denmark	53.2	55.6	55.2	56.3	7.4	12.1	12.8	13.6	6.1	6.8	8.2	10.1
Finland	49.2	53.2	58.3	64.1	9.4	13.2	13.2	15.6	5.0	7.3	9.8	12.6
France	51.3	55.1	57.1	60.4	8.7	9.6	12.0	12.5	4.9	6.4	7.7	10.3
Germany	57.2	53.0	49.6	55.4	11.0	15.2	13.0	11.6	4.4	7.1	8.2	8.2
Greece	m	m	m	50.4	6.8	m	m	10.9	3.4	m	m	8.2
Ireland	51.1	52.4	55.9	57.0	6.1	8.5	10.1	11.1	2.4	3.3	4.4	6.4
Italy	50.8	48.4	48.9	50.5	10.0	11.8	15.5	15.4	4.6	5.5	6.6	9.6
Netherlands	51.0	52.3	51.1	56.5	5.1	8.7	9.3	12.2	4.9	5.5	6.5	7.2
Spain	m	53.9	56.4	57.7	9.0	12.4	15.7	18.3	3.7	5.4	7.5	10.6
Sweden	m	52.2	49.8	52.4	7.4	11.1	10.4	12.5	5.6	6.5	6.7	6.4
United Kingdom	m	48.5	47.1	56.4	11.2	12.7	11.7	13.5	2.5	2.9	3.4	5.8
Other OECD countries												
Norway	m	52.7	53.6	55.7	m	12.7	15.1	14.4	m	4.7	7.6	9.1
Switzerland	41.2	49.4	48.0	51.1	3.2	13.9	13.2	11.5	m	4.0	4.7	5.1
Turkey	36.1	37.7	38.8	40.0	3.3	3.8	4.6	6.6	1.5	1.6	2.4	3.8

Source: OECD Database. See Annex 3 for notes.

Indicator C2:   Participation by young children

Policy context

It is widely recognised that the early years of education play an important role in a child's future, because they shape attitudes toward learning and develop basic social skills.

Both early childhood education and initial programmes in primary schooling are important aspects of a strategy aimed at ensuring that all students start school ready to learn. Involving students from disadvantaged backgrounds and their parents in early childhood programmes may provide them with valuable experiences that will help them to start primary school better prepared.

Research also indicates that progress through school is associated with the cognitive abilities obtained at young ages. At what age should early childhood education begin? What factors and conditions can make early intervention programmes successful? The data presented in this indicator provide a basic profile of participation in early childhood programmes.

Evidence and explanations

Participation by young children in education – even in the pre-compulsory years – is becoming increasingly important in OECD countries, and in a few countries it is virtually universal from age 3 (in Belgium and France) or 4 (in the Netherlands, New Zealand and Spain).

One measure that is useful for examining participation by young children is the average number of years a child can expect to be enrolled in either pre-primary or primary programmes before he or she reaches the age of 7.

On average across countries, children can expect almost 3 years of education before they reach the age of 7 of which, on average, 2.1 years are provided in early childhood programmes and 0.9 years are provided in primary programmes (See Table C2.2). In three countries (Belgium, France and New Zealand) young children receive more than 4 years of education before they reach the age of 7 years.

A long expected duration of early childhood education does not, however, necessarily imply that access to early childhood education is universal. In a number of countries, relatively few children participating for a long time appear to account for the long expected durations.

Overall, rates of participation increase with each succeeding year of age. Three countries, Belgium, France and New Zealand, report already significant participation rates for children under the age of 3. At age 3, 11 out of 26 countries report enrolment rates of over 50 per cent and in Belgium and France education at this age is nearly universal (See Table C2.1). On the other hand, in Canada, Ireland, the Netherlands and Turkey, enrolment rates at the age of

◆ Chart C2.1. *Expected number of years of early childhood and primary education for children aged up to 6 years (based on head counts) (1995)*

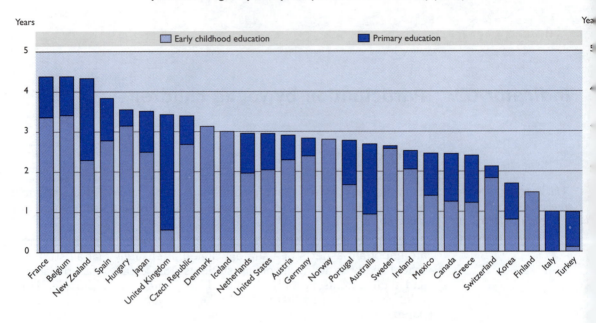

Source: OECD.

3 are below 1 per cent (but in the data for Ireland many privately owned schools are not included).

At ages 4 and 5, enrolment rates rise sharply in almost all countries. At age of 5, in all except three countries, participation rates exceed 50 per and in 14 out of 25 countries more than 90 per cent of 5 year-olds enrolled.

Education is virtually universal at the age of 6, except in Finland, Germany and Turkey.

At age 6, participation in early childhood and primary education is ne universal (90 per cent or more) in all but three countries (Finland, Germ and Turkey). In Finland school-based education starts for almost half of students after the age of 6.

In some countries early childhood education is typically part-time.

Participation in early childhood education does not necessarily mean time enrolment. Five countries report that over 50 per cent of the child enrolled in early childhood education attend part-time, and in Can New Zealand and the United Kingdom over 80 per cent of young children enrolled part-time.

The transition from early childhood education to the primary level takes place at age 6 in most countries.

The transition from early childhood education to primary education ta place around the age of 6 in 14 out of 25 countries (see Table C2.1). Howe in Australia, Canada, Greece, New Zealand and the United Kingdom pri schools are common providers at earlier ages. In the United Kingdom, 80 per cent of 4 year-olds are enrolled in primary schools. In five count Austria, the Czech Republic, Germany, Hungary and Ireland, primary sc starts between the ages of six and seven and in the Nordic countries pri schooling starts at the age of seven.

In practice, there is not a clear boundary between the type of educa offered in early childhood and primary programmes at these ages. The tinction is more relevant within a country than between countries, espe if the two programmes take place in different types of institutions or funded or staffed differently. Typically, the national distinction is bet

◆ Chart C2.2. **Net enrolment rates by single years of age (3 to 6) in early childhood and primary education (based on head counts) (1995)**

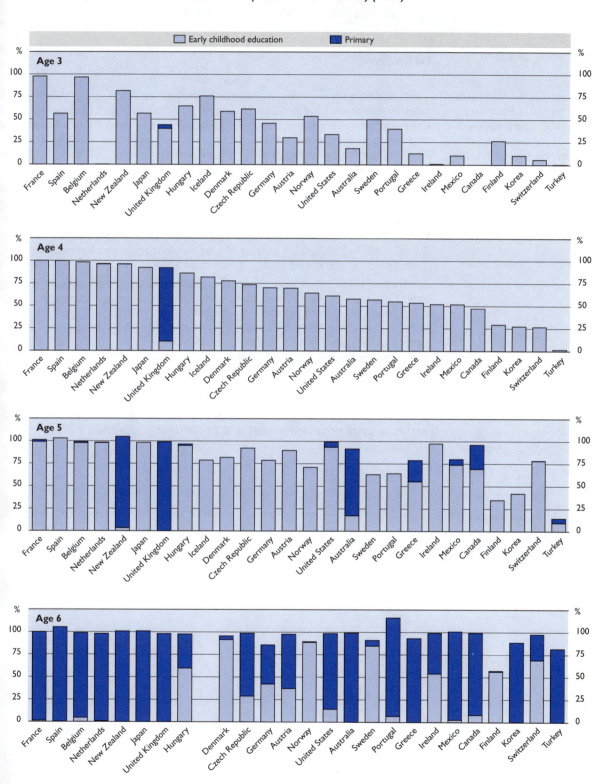

ries are ranked in decreasing order of net enrolment rates at age 4.

e: OECD.

pre-compulsory and compulsory schooling. Primary programmes are genera those offered to children in their first years of compulsory schooling (even some participants are below compulsory school age).

Definitions

Data refer to the school year 1994/95 and are based on the UOE data collection on education statistics, administered in 1996 (for details see Annex 3).

This indicator shows the number of children enrolled in early childhood a primary programmes from age 3 to age 6 as a percentage of the population the respective age. Early childhood programmes cover all forms of organis and sustained school-based and centre-based activities designed to fos learning and the emotional and social development of children.

For this indicator, all children enrolled are counted equally to reflect t number of children participating in early childhood education, regardless the number of daily hours for which they participate in programmes.

The average duration of early childhood education, primary education, a both levels combined – received by children up to and including the age 6 years – is calculated by adding the net enrolment rates for each single from age 0 to age 6 and dividing the total by 100.

Enrolment rates for young children are affected by differences in report practices, namely by the extent to which child-care programmes that mai offer custodial care have been included in the statistics. Especially for very youngest children, for whom the natural pace of development limits pedagogical possibilities, the distinction between early childhood educat and organised child care is difficult to operationalise in an internation consistent way. Countries also differ widely in their approaches to e childhood education. Some approaches focus on experiential education wh others emphasise skill development, academic development, the visual or a particular religious faith. In addition, there is great variation in the and quality of private day care and pre-school education.

Table C2.1 **Net enrolment rates by single year of age (3 to 6) in public and private early childhood and primary education (based on head counts) (1995)**

	Age 3			Age 4			Age 5			Age 6		
	Early childhood education	Primary	All levels of education combined	Early childhood education	Primary	All levels of education combined	Early childhood education	Primary	All levels of education combined	Early childhood education	Primary	All levels of education combined
North America												
Canada	n	n	n	48	n	48	70	27	97	8	92	100
Mexico	10	a	10	52	a	52	74	6	81	3	99	102
United States	34	n	34	62	n	62	94	6	100	15	85	100
Pacific Area												
Australia	18	n	18	58	n	58	17	75	92	n	100	100
Japan	58	a	58	93	a	93	99	a	99	a	102	102
Korea	10	n	10	28	n	28	42	n	42	n	90	90
New Zealand	83	n	83	97	n	97	3	102	106	n	102	102
European Union												
Austria	30	n	30	71	n	71	90	n	90	38	61	99
Belgium	98	n	98	100	n	100	98	1	100	5	95	100
Denmark	60	n	60	79	n	79	82	n	82	93	4	97
Finland	27	n	27	29	n	29	35	n	35	57	1	58
France	100	n	100	101	n	101	100	2	102	1	100	101
Germany	47	n	47	71	n	71	79	n	79	43	44	87
Greece	13	n	13	54	n	54	56	24	79	n	94	94
Ireland	1	n	1	53	n	53	98	n	98	54	46	100
Italy	m	a	m	m	a	m	m	m	m	m	m	m
Luxembourg	m	m	m	m	m	m	m	m	m	m	m	m
Netherlands	n	n	n	97	n	98	99	1	99	1	98	99
Portugal	40	n	40	56	n	56	65	n	65	7	111	118
Spain	57	n	57	101	n	101	104	n	104	n	107	107
Sweden	51	n	51	58	n	58	63	n	63	86	7	92
United Kingdom	41	4	45	11	83	93	n	100	100	n	99	99
Other OECD countries												
Czech Republic	63	n	63	75	n	75	93	n	93	29	71	100
Hungary	66	n	66	87	n	87	96	2	97	60	39	99
Iceland	77	n	77	83	n	83	79	m	m	1	m	m
Norway	54	n	54	65	n	65	71	n	71	90	1	91
Poland	m	m	m	m	m	m	m	m	m	m	m	m
Switzerland	6	n	6	27	n	27	79	n	79	70	29	99
Turkey	n	n	n	2	n	2	9	5	14	n	83	83
Country mean	**40**	**n**	**40**	**64**	**3**	**67**	**69**	**14**	**83**	**25**	**70**	**97**
Other non-OECD countries												
Russian Federation	m	n	m	m	n	m	m	n	m	m	n	m

Source: OECD Database. See Annex 3 for notes.

Table C2.2 **Expected number of years of early childhood and primary education for children aged up to 6 years in public and private institutions (based on head counts) (1995)**

	Early childhood education		Primary education		Early childhood and primary education
	Typical starting age	Expected number of years	Typical starting age	Expected number of years	Expected number of years
North America					
Canada	4	1.3	6	1.2	2.4
Mexico	3	1.4	6	1.1	2.5
United States	3	2.0	6	0.9	3.0
Pacific Area					
Australia	m	0.9	m	1.8	2.7
Japan	3	2.5	6	1.0	3.5
Korea	5	0.8	6	0.9	1.7
New Zealand	2	2.3	5	2.0	4.3
European Union					
Austria	3	2.3	6	0.6	2.9
Belgium	2.5	3.4	6	1.0	4.4
Denmark	3	3.1	7	n	3.1
Finland	3 to 6	1.5	7	n	1.5
France	2	3.4	6	1.0	4.4
Germany	3	2.4	6	0.4	2.8
Greece	4	1.2	6	1.2	2.4
Ireland	4 to 5	2.1	6 to 7	0.5	2.5
Italy	3	x	6	1.0	1.0
Luxembourg	m	m	m	m	m
Netherlands	4	2.0	6	1.0	3.0
Portugal	3	1.7	6	1.1	2.8
Spain	2	2.8	6	1.1	3.8
Sweden	3	2.6	6 to 7	0.1	2.6
United Kingdom	3	0.6	4	2.9	3.4
Other OECD countries					
Czech Republic	3	2.7	6	0.7	3.4
Hungary	3	3.2	6	0.4	3.6
Iceland	2	3.0	6	m	3.0
Norway	3	2.8	7	n	2.8
Poland	3	m	7	m	m
Switzerland	4 to 5	1.8	6 to 7	0.3	2.1
Turkey	3	0.1	6	0.9	1.0
Country mean	**3**	**2.1**	**6**	**0.9**	**2.8**
Other non-OECD countries					
Russian Federation	3	m	6	n	m

Source: OECD Database. See Annex 3 for notes.

Indicator C3: **Participation in education towards the end of compulsory schooling and beyond**

Policy context

This indicator shows net enrolment rates at the secondary and tertiary levels of education.

A number of factors, including an increased risk of unemployment and other forms of exclusion for young people with insufficient education, influence the decision to stay enrolled beyond the end of compulsory schooling. In many countries, the transition from education to employment has become a longer and more complex process, providing the opportunity, or the necessity, for students to combine learning and work in order to develop marketable skills. Recent years have also seen the dissolving of traditional age boundaries in the transition from secondary to tertiary education, with the transition now occurring largely in the age range from 15 to 24 years. These changes provide an opportunity for countries to explore new organisational frameworks for learning outside as well as inside the classroom.

Evidence and explanations

Participation towards the end of compulsory schooling and beyond

Although enrolment in compulsory education is universal in most countries, the age at which compulsory education ends ranges from 14 to 18 years.

Compulsory schooling ends in OECD countries between the ages of 14 and 18 – in most countries at age 15 or 16.

Until the end of compulsory schooling, virtually all young people are enrolled in school: in almost all countries enrolment rates at the age at which compulsory schooling ends exceed 90 per cent. Exceptions to this pattern are Mexico and Turkey, where enrolment rates are around 50 per cent at the end of compulsory schooling – at ages which are relatively young compared with other countries.

In a half of all OECD countries, enrolment in education remains close to universal beyond the end of compulsory schooling. Australia, Japan and Korea have participation rates of over 90 per cent even three years after the end of compulsory schooling (ages 15, 15 and 14 respectively).

Cross-national comparisons based on the enrolment rates for the year in which compulsory schooling ends – which is marked in bold in Table C3.1 – have to be interpreted with some caution since these ages vary widely by country. For example, enrolment rates for Portuguese 13 year-olds are compared with enrolment rates for 17 year-old Belgians and the motives for early leaving by each are likely to differ considerably.

In 17 out of 27 countries, over 90 per cent of all 16 year-olds participate in education.

Enrolment rates by age group allow a comparison of enrolment rates that is independent of the standards which countries set for the length of compulsory schooling. In 17 out of 27 countries, more than 90 per cent of 16 year-olds are enrolled in school and in only four countries does participation at this age fall below 80 per cent.

◆ Chart C3.1. **Net enrolment rates by single year of age and by level of education (1995)**

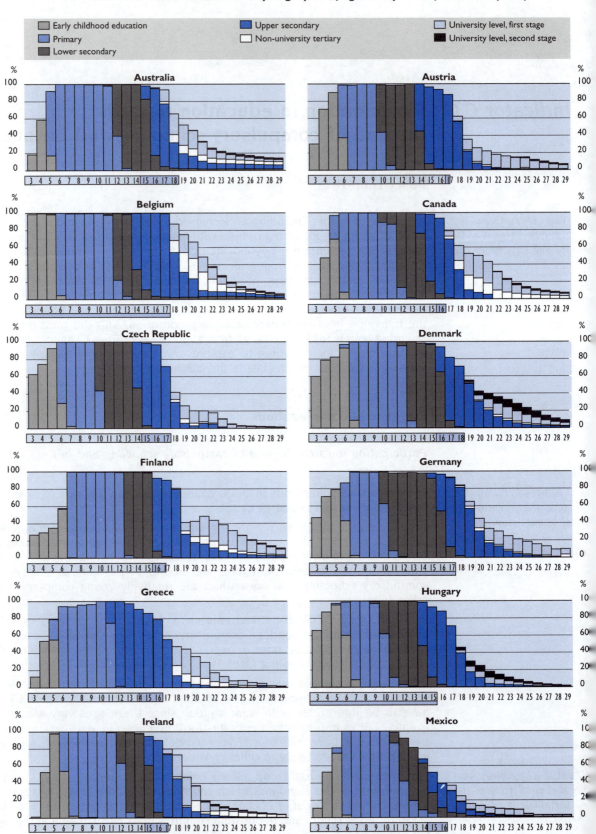

◆ Chart C3.1. *(cont.)* **Net enrolment rates by single year of age and by level of education (1995)**

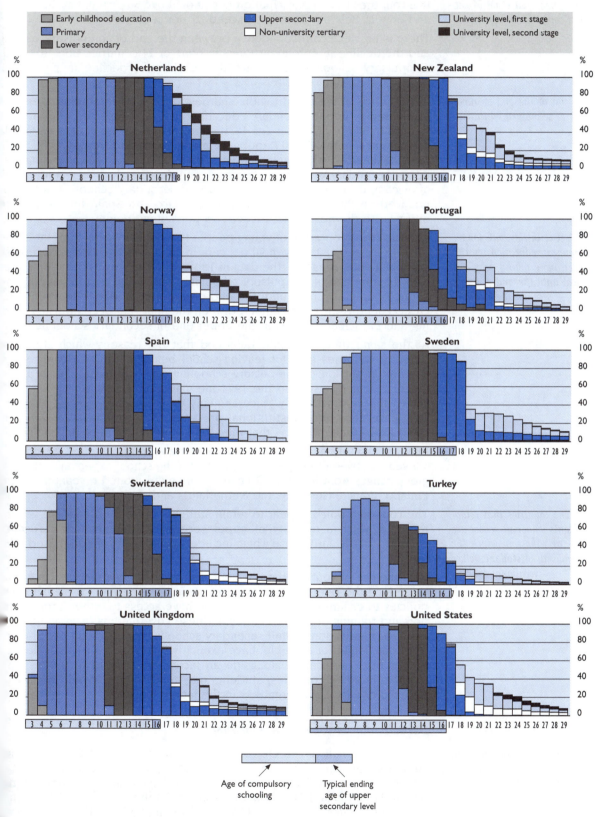

Age of compulsory schooling

Typical ending age of upper secondary level

The sharpest decline in participation occurs not at the end of compulsory schooling...

After the age of 16, enrolment rates begin to decline in most countries. On five countries have a participation rate at or above 50 per cent at the age of and only in Belgium does this exceed 65 per cent.

There is no close correspondence between the end of compulsory schooli and the decline in enrolment rates. In none of 24 countries does the end compulsory schooling coincide with the sharpest decline in participati rates.

... but at the end of upper secondary education.

In two-thirds of the countries the sharpest decline in enrolment rates occu at the end of upper secondary education. In Sweden, participation rates f from 88 to 35 per cent after age 18, the typical ending age of upper second programmes. In the Czech Republic, Finland, Korea and Norway, participati rates decline by 30 percentage points or more after the typical ending age upper secondary education. In other countries the decline in participati after compulsory schooling or even upper secondary schooling is less p nounced: in Belgium, the Netherlands, Mexico and Spain the decline fro one year to the next never exceeds 15 percentage points.

Yet countries with longer compulsory education tend to keep more young people at school until the end of upper secondary education.

Although the proportion of young people remaining in school until the age 17 or 18 exceeds 80 or even 90 per cent in some countries where compuls schooling ends at age 16, the data in Table C3.1 show that education syste with a higher age of compulsory schooling tend to succeed in keeping m young people at school until the end of upper secondary education. Wit OECD countries, the correlation between the final year of compulsory scho ing and participation rates at the upper end of secondary schooling is 0.

At the same time, it should be noted that the reasons which students different countries give for leaving school before getting a degree sugg that the extension of compulsory schooling can only have a limited eff recent research based on the 1994 International Adult Literacy Survey shown that approximately twice as many drop-outs cite reasons over wh they have no control (institutional pressures, economic need or family r sons) as do those who say that they left school out of personal choice.

In about two-thirds of the countries, young people stay enrolled for more t 4.5 years between the ages of 15 and 24 but the school expectancy of this group ranges from less than 2 years in Turkey to around 6 years in Belgi Finland, France, Germany, the Netherlands and Norway.

The countries that retain students longer in school are also those in which the majority of students follow vocational courses.

The countries which appear to retain students longer in school are gener those in which a majority of upper secondary students follow vocatic courses – particularly those which include a component of work-based edu tion.

With the rise of youth unemployment, a number of governments have sou to prolong the period of schooling by developing "youth" or "qualificati policies to ensure that all young people have access to either further edu tion and training or a job. As a result, these governments have accepted resource implications of full secondary schooling for all young people. Sc countries, Japan for example, have explicitly recognised a popular desire further broad education alongside an increased demand for more spe training. In some countries, students may tend to stay longer in educa because of a lack of alternatives in the labour market.

Participation in vocational education

In most countries, the majority of upper secondary students attend vocational programmes.

In more than half of the OECD countries, the majority of upper second students attend vocational or apprenticeship programmes. In countries dual-system apprenticeship programmes (such as Austria, Belgium, Germ the Netherlands and Switzerland), as well as in the Czech Republic, Hun and Italy, around 70 per cent or more of upper secondary students enrolled in vocational programmes. Among countries of the European Un

◆ Chart C3.2. ***Distribution of enrolled students in upper secondary education by type of programme (1995)***

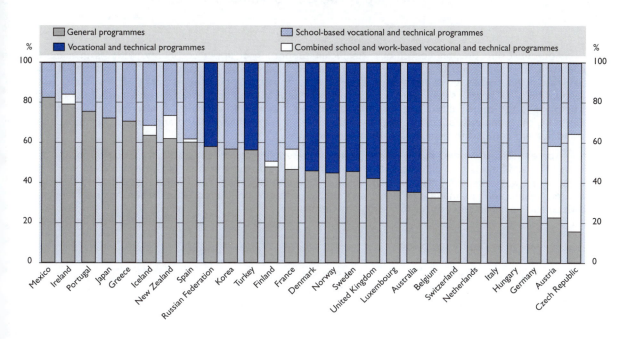

source: OECD.

only Greece, Ireland, Portugal and Spain have a minority of upper secondary students enrolled in vocational or apprenticeship programmes (see Table C3.2).

In most countries, vocational education is school-based, although in the Czech Republic, Germany and Switzerland programmes that have both school-based and work-based elements are the most common form of vocational education and training.

Women in upper secondary education are generally less likely to be in vocational programmes than men. In some countries the differences are substantial.

In some countries a significant proportion of young persons opt for a second upper secondary programme rather than entry into tertiary education.

Seven European countries for which data are available offer students who have completed upper secondary education the opportunity to re-enrol and pursue additional qualifications. In four of these countries, a significant proportion of upper secondary graduates opt for such programmes rather than for entry into tertiary education. Virtually all of these students pursue vocational or apprenticeship programmes.

The transition to tertiary education

The transition from upper secondary to tertiary education occurs at different ages in different countries.

Table C3.3 shows net rates of participation in secondary, non-university tertiary and university (or equivalent) education by single year of age. The transition from secondary education to tertiary education occurs at different ages in different countries. At age 17 more than 90 per cent of the students are still enrolled in secondary education in all but three countries, Australia, Canada and Mexico. At age 19 about half of the countries have more students in tertiary education than in secondary education and by age 20 only five countries (Denmark, Germany, Iceland, the Netherlands and Switzerland) have more students in secondary education than in tertiary education. However,

Apprenticeship in the United States and Germany

Apprenticeship programmes enrol a significant proportion of upper secondary students in many OECD countries. Apprenticeship is a method of teaching job-related skills through hands-on, work-based training. Skills are developed as the apprentice observes, assists, and is taught by one or more skilled workers, assuming responsibility for progressively more challenging tasks until all the necessary skills are mastered. Although the workplace is the principal location for training, related theoretical instruction is also part of the curriculum. Typically, the standards for completing an apprenticeship are explicitly stated and apprentices meeting those standards are certified to practice a particular occupation.

Apprenticeship systems in the United States and Germany are in many ways the polar opposites of each other. The similarities and differences between apprenticeship programmes in these two countries highlight many of the ways in which these programmes vary between countries. The United Kingdom and Canada have apprenticeship systems that are in many ways similar to that in the United States, while Austria, Denmark and Switzerland have systems similar to the one in Germany.

Apprenticeship in the United States

Apprenticeship programmes in the United States operate primarily as training for young adults (typically in their late 20s), providing upgrading and retraining for those who are already employed. Apprenticeship programmes can be sponsored by employers, employers' associations, or jointly by employers and unions. Apprenticeship programmes are not closely linked with school-based vocational and technical education.

In general, apprenticeship is not widely used as a training strategy. Two-thirds of all US apprentices are in 20 of the 830 apprenticeable occupations; and of those 20 occupations, all but three are in the construction and metal trades. Three-quarters of apprenticeships in the United States are concentrated in the unionised sector of commercial-industrial construction and in the maintenance departments of major manufacturers. Apprenticeship leads to formal, official credentials – a Certificate of Completion and journeyperson status. Little public money is spent on apprenticeships in the United States, especially in comparison with school-based training in public community colleges or post-secondary vocational-technical institutes.

Apprenticeship in Germany

Unlike the United States, apprenticeship is the predominant form of upper secondary education in Germany – enrolling between one-half and two-thirds of the youth population between the ages of 16 and 18. While apprenticeship programmes in the US are mostly confined to two industrial sectors, approximately 370 occupations in Germany have apprentices.

The objectives of apprenticeship programmes in Germany are: a full professional qualification, through training in practical and technical skills and through theoretical instruction; an enhancement of general knowledge; the promotion of the student's personality and his or her sense of responsibility; a basis for modular technical and general education and for continuing education and training. The organisational frame of these programmes involves: compulsory schooling in educational institutions of the public or private domain; a compulsory apprenticeship contract with the employer; supervision of the work-based component and inspection of the school-based component by public authorities and specially trained and certified authorities in companies. A typical apprenticeship in Germany lasts three years, mixing on-the-job training and school attendance, at a ratio of about 3 to 2. Employment in many apprenticeable occupations is effectively limited to those holding apprenticeship completion certificates.

The German states (*Länder*) pay for apprentices' schooling. Employers pay apprentices' wages and the costs of their on-the-job training. Apprentices' earnings are typically half those of what skilled workers earn in the same occupation. A large firm might spend as much as US$10 000 to 15 000 per year on each apprentice. These firms employ full-time trainers and provide on-site classrooms, shops and laboratories. Smaller firms often offer less thorough training. As the greatest proportion of the cost of apprenticeship is born by employers, private employers are, in effect, directly subsidising the society's cost for educating its youth.

Source: S.F. Hamilton and R. Glover, "Economics of Apprenticeship", in T. Husén, T.N. Postlethwaite (eds.), *International Encyclopedia of Education*, Vol. I, Pergamon, 1994.

some countries classify certain types of programmes as upper secondary which are similar in content to programmes classified as tertiary in other countries. Differences between countries in how education programmes are organised will clearly affect the relative proportion of students of a particular age enrolled at a particular level.

In many countries the transition process to university-level education continues up to the age of 25 and over.

Expanding youth education policies have, in many countries, increased pressure for greater access to tertiary education. Thus far, this pressure has more than compensated for demographic downturns which until recently led to predictions of stable or declining demand from school leavers in several countries, including Australia and Japan. In some countries, there are now signs of a levelling off in the demand for tertiary education, but the overall trend remains upward.

Definitions

Data refer to the school year 94/95 and are based on the UOE data collection on education statistics, administered in 1996 (for details see Annex 3).

Net enrolment rates in Table C3.1 are calculated by dividing the number of students of a particular age group enrolled in all levels of education by the number of persons in the population in that age group (times 100). Figures in bold in Table C3.1 indicate enrolment in full-time compulsory schooling; figures in italic indicate part-time compulsory schooling. Net enrolment rates in Table C3.3 are calculated by dividing the number of students of a particular age group enrolled in a specific level of education by the number of persons in the population in that age group (times 100).

These figures are based on head counts, that is, they do not distinguish between full-time and part-time study. A standardised distinction between full-time and part-time participants is very difficult since many countries do not recognise the concept of part-time study, although in practice at least some of their students would be classified as part-time by other countries. Note that in some countries part-time education is not completely covered by the reported data.

Table C3.2 shows the distribution of students within general, vocational and technical programmes by type of programme and gender. The last four columns give the net enrolment rates for first and second educational programmes. The enrolment rates are calculated by dividing the number of students in a particular programme enrolled by the number of persons at the theoretical age served by that programme (times 100).

Vocational and technical programmes include both school-based programmes and combined school and work-based programmes that are explicitly deemed to be parts of the education system. Entirely work-based education and training of which no formal education authority has oversight is not taken into account.

Table C3.1 **Total participation (net enrolment in all levels of education) for ages 15 to 24 in public and private institutions (based on head counts) (1995)**

	Ending age of compulsory schooling	Typical ending age of upper secondary education	Net enrolment rates by single year of age (in %)									
			15	16	17	18	19	20	21	22	23	2
North America												
Canada	16	17	**98**	94	79	62	53	57	38	32	24	
Mexico	15	17	52	39	37	25	15	14	12	10	9	
United States	17	17	**98**	**90**	79	56	42	35	35	25	23	
Pacific Area												
Australia	15	19	98	96	94	66	53	47	34	26	22	
Japan	15	17	101	97	94	m	m	m	m	m	m	
Korea	14	17	93	95	90	54	42	36	31	23	18	
New Zealand	16	17	**97**	100	77	57	48	45	51	26	19	
European Union												
Austria	17	17-18	**97**	**94**	88	62	36	26	22	18	16	
Belgium	18	17-19	*103*	*103*	*100*	87	75	67	49	38	28	
Denmark	16	19-20	**98**	94	82	72	55	42	40	36	33	
Finland	16	17-18	**99**	93	90	81	41	43	49	44	39	
France	16	17-19	**98**	96	93	84	70	56	42	31	21	
Germany	18	18	**99**	**97**	**94**	84	65	45	34	41	20	
Greece	14.5	16-18	86	79	56	48	45	36	29	17	13	
Ireland	15	17-18	96	91	81	73	47	37	20	15	13	
Italy	14	18	m	m	m	m	m	m	m	m	m	
Luxembourg	15	17-19	80	81	78	70	m	m	m	m	m	
Netherlands	18	18-19	**99**	**98**	**93**	83	70	60	48	38	30	
Portugal	14	17	88	73	73	55	45	44	47	25	22	
Spain	16	15-17	**94**	83	75	63	53	50	40	34	25	
Sweden	16	18	**96**	97	96	88	35	31	31	30	28	
United Kingdom	16	17	**98**	87	75	54	45	39	33	22	17	
Other OECD countries												
Czech Republic	15	17-19	99	97	72	42	26	20	20	18	11	
Hungary	16	15-17	**93**	88	71	46	30	25	18	15	12	
Iceland	m	19	m	89	77	65	64	43	38	37	33	
Norway	16	18	**100**	95	90	83	49	43	41	38	34	
Poland	15	17-19	m	m	m	m	m	m	m	m	m	
Switzerland	15	17-19	98	87	84	77	57	34	25	21	19	
Turkey	14	17-18	48	40	26	17	17	12	11	10	8	
Country mean	**16**	**17-18**	**93**	**88**	**79**	**64**	**47**	**39**	**33**	**27**	**21**	

Figures in bold indicate ages at which schooling is compulsory.
Figures in italics indicate ages at which schooling is compulsory at least part-time.
Source: OECD Database. See Annex 3 for notes.

Table C3.2 **Percentage of upper secondary students enrolled in public and private general and vocational education. Enrolment rates at typical ages (based on head counts) (1995)**

| | Men and women | | | | Women | | Enrolment rate at typical age | | | |
| | All programmes | | | | All programmes | | First educational programmes | | Second and further educational programmes | |
	General programmes	Vocational and technical programmes	of which: school-based	of which: combined school and work-based	General programmes	Vocational and technical programmes	General programmes	Vocational and technical programmes	General programmes	Vocational and technical programmes
North America										
Canada	m	m	m	m	m	m	m	m	a	a
Mexico	83	17	17	a	81	19	31	7	a	a
United States	m	m	m	m	m	m	88	x	a	a
Pacific Area										
Australia	35	65	x	x	38	62	m	m	m	m
Japan	72	28	28	a	75	25	73	28	a	a
Korea	57	43	43	n	53	47	54	41	a	a
New Zealand	62	38	26	12	67	33	86	80	a	a
European Union										
Austria	23	77	42	36	25	75	25	65	a	4
Belgium	32	68	65	3	35	65	44	62	n	n
Denmark	46	54	x	x	52	48	36	44	2	2
Finland	48	52	49	3	51	49	m	m	m	m
France	47	53	43	10	53	47	52	36	n	n
Germany	23	77	24	53	27	73	26	67	1	21
Greece	71	29	29	a	87	13	38	16	a	a
Ireland	79	21	16	5	79	21	52	7	a	14
Italy	28	72	72	a	31	69	23	54	a	12
Luxembourg	36	64	x	x	41	59	m	m	m	m
Netherlands	30	70	47	23	34	66	m	m	m	m
Portugal	76	24	24	a	79	21	m	m	m	m
Spain	60	40	38	2	61	39	74	31	a	22
Sweden	44	53	x	x	49	48	69	82	m	m
United Kingdom	42	58	x	x	38	62	68	94	a	a
Other OECD countries										
Czech Republic	16	84	36	49	19	81	9	47	a	6
Hungary	27	73	46	27	33	67	26	68	a	a
Iceland	64	36	31	5	74	26	m	m	m	m
Norway	45	55	x	x	53	47	60	74	a	a
Poland	m	m	m	m	m	m	m	m	m	m
Switzerland	31	69	9	61	39	61	6	16	a	a
Turkey	56	44	44	x	61	39	11	13	a	a
Country mean	**47**	**53**	**37**	**17**	**51**	**49**	**45**	**47**	**n**	**4**
Other non-OECD countries										
Russian Federation	58	42	x	x	x	x	56	27	a	a

Source: OECD Database. See Annex 3 for notes.

Table C3.3 **Transition characteristics at each year of age from 17 to 20: net enrolment rates by level of education in public and private institutions (based on head counts) (1995)**

	Age 17			Age 18			Age 19			Age 20		
	Secondary education	Non-university tertiary education	University-level education	Secondary education	Non-university tertiary education	University-level education	Secondary education	Non-university tertiary education	University-level education	Secondary education	Non-university tertiary education	University-level education
North America												
Canada	69	4	6	34	11	17	10	17	25	m	17	2(
Mexico	31	x	6	18	x	7	8	x	7	5	x	ε
United States	75	1	2	22	14	19	4	17	21	2	11	23
Pacific Area												
Australia	77	3	14	32	10	24	20	10	24	17	8	2
Japan	94	a	a	2	m	m	1	m	m	m	m	m
Korea	90	n	n	23	13	18	3	16	23	n	13	2
New Zealand	74	1	1	33	6	18	17	7	24	13	6	2(
European Union												
Austria	88	n	n	56	1	6	22	2	12	8	2	1(
Belgium	99	n	1	54	14	19	31	23	21	20	27	1
Denmark	82	n	n	71	n	n	52	n	3	31	1	1
Finland	90	n	n	80	1	n	28	4	10	18	7	1
France	91	m	m	60	m	m	34	m	m	15	m	n
Germany	93	1	n	82	2	1	57	3	6	31	4	1
Greece	56	n	n	14	12	22	6	10	29	4	9	2
Ireland	74	x	6	46	x	27	12	x	35	7	x	3
Italy	m	m	m	m	m	m	m	m	m	m	m	r
Luxembourg	78	m	m	70	m	m	54	m	m	33	m	r
Netherlands	91	a	2	69	a	13	47	a	23	32	a	2
Portugal	71	n	1	45	2	8	27	4	13	21	6	1
Spain	75	n	n	43	n	19	26	1	26	20	1	2
Sweden	96	x	n	87	x	1	24	x	11	12	x	1
United Kingdom	73	1	1	31	4	18	15	6	24	10	5	2
Other OECD countries												
Czech Republic	72	n	n	30	3	8	6	5	15	3	3	1
Hungary	71	a	n	39	a	7	17	a	13	11	a	1
Iceland	77	n	n	65	n	n	63	n	1	33	1	1
Norway	90	n	n	83	n	n	33	9	7	19	12	1
Poland	m	m	m	m	m	m	m	m	m	m	m	
Switzerland	82	n	n	75	1	n	52	1	3	23	3	
Turkey	23	1	2	10	2	5	6	3	8	n	3	
Country mean	**77**	**1**	**2**	**47**	**4**	**11**	**25**	**6**	**16**	**15**	**7**	

Source: OECD Database. See Annex 3 for notes.

Indicator C4: Rates of entry into university-level tertiary education

Policy context

This indicator estimates the percentage of today's school-leavers who will enter university-level education ~~ng~~ the course of their lives, given current conditions.

The size of entrance rates ~~cts~~ both the accessibility of university-level tertiary ~~ducation~~ and the perceived ~~e~~ of attending programmes at this level.

Tertiary education is associated with better access to employment (see Indicator E2) and higher earnings (see Indicator E4). The rate at which a country's population enters university-level tertiary education is a measure, in part, of the degree to which high-level skills are being acquired by the population. High university-level tertiary entry rates help to ensure the development and maintenance of a highly educated population and labour force.

As students' awareness of the economic and social benefits of university-level tertiary education has increased, so has entry into tertiary education. Continued growth in participation in tertiary education, accompanied by a widening diversity in the backgrounds and interests of those aspiring to university-level studies, requires new provision to cater for demand. Challenges facing universities and equivalent institutions will therefore not only be to meet demand with an expansion of places, but also to adapt programmes, teaching and learning to match the diverse set of needs that clients bring with them.

Evidence and explanations

Overall entry rates

First-time entry rates to ~~ersity~~-level education vary ~~idely~~ between countries. In OECD countries they are 39 per cent or more...

~~hereas~~ in Switzerland it is 15 per cent.

This indicator estimates the percentage of today's school-leavers who will enter university-level education during the course of their lives, assuming current university-level enrolment rates. In Iceland, New Zealand and the United Kingdom these are 39 per cent or more, and in Canada and the United States they reach around 50 per cent – with a considerable number of students in these two countries entering part-time programmes.

In contrast, the estimated first-time university entry rate for Switzerland is 15 per cent, although this is balanced to some degree by high participation in advanced upper secondary programmes and non-university tertiary programmes (which are not accounted for in this indicator).

Age of entrants

~~e~~ age of first-time entrants ~~~~ university-level education ~~ies~~ widely both within and between countries.

~~some~~ countries university-level education tends immediately to follow the ~~pletion~~ of upper secondary schooling...

The age profile of first-time entrants to university-level studies varies considerably between countries, with students entering university-level education at different stages of their lives.

Traditionally, university-level education has tended immediately to follow the completion of upper secondary schooling. In a number of countries this is still the case. In France and Ireland, for example, more than 80 per cent of all first-time entrants are aged 20 years or younger (see Chart C4.3). A similar age profile can be observed in Greece, New Zealand and the United States.

◆ Chart C4.1. **Net entry rates for university-level education, by age group (1995)**

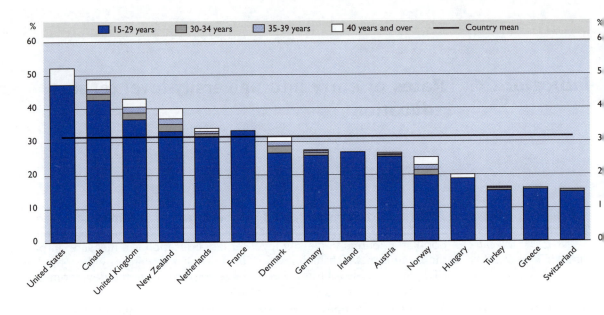

Source: OECD.

... whereas in others a prolonged transition has involved more flexible interspersion of study and work and a delayed entry to university.

In other countries, the transition has been prolonged by more flexible i
spersion of study and work, often combining part-time study, distance l
ing or "sandwich" courses. In these countries, first time entrants to the un
sity-level are typically older and show a much wider range of entry age
Denmark, Norway and Sweden, for example, more than half of students e
university-level education for the first time after the age of 22, and less
20 per cent of first-time entrants are younger than 20 years of age.

In Denmark, New Zealand, Norway and Sweden more than 20 per cent of first-time entrants to the university level are 28 years of age or older.

The proportion of older first-time entrants to university-level program
may, among other factors, indicate the flexibility of these programmes
their suitability for non-traditional students. In some countries a signif
proportion of new entrants are much older than the typical age of ent
Denmark, New Zealand, Norway and Sweden more than 20 per cent of
time entrants are 28 years of age or older. On the other hand in Fr
Greece and Ireland fewer than 5 per cent of first-time entrants are older
25 years of age.

It should be noted that this indicator only shows first-time entry to unive
level education. In some countries, most notably Canada and New Zeala
large number of people who have pursued tertiary studies in the pas
enter tertiary education at a later stage in their lives.

The reasons why adults in some countries participate so much less than in others are complex.

The reasons why adults in some countries are so much less likely than o
to participate in university-level education are complex, reflecting differe
in the educational structure, selectivity and exclusivity of university-
education and traditions. The extensive provision of vocational educatio
apprenticeships in Continental European countries has traditionally prov
a solid vocationally-based preparation for work and is likely to
reduced the perceived need to enrol in formal tertiary-level studies at a
date.

◆   Chart C4.2.   *New entrants and graduates at the university level by year of age as a percentage of the population (1995)*

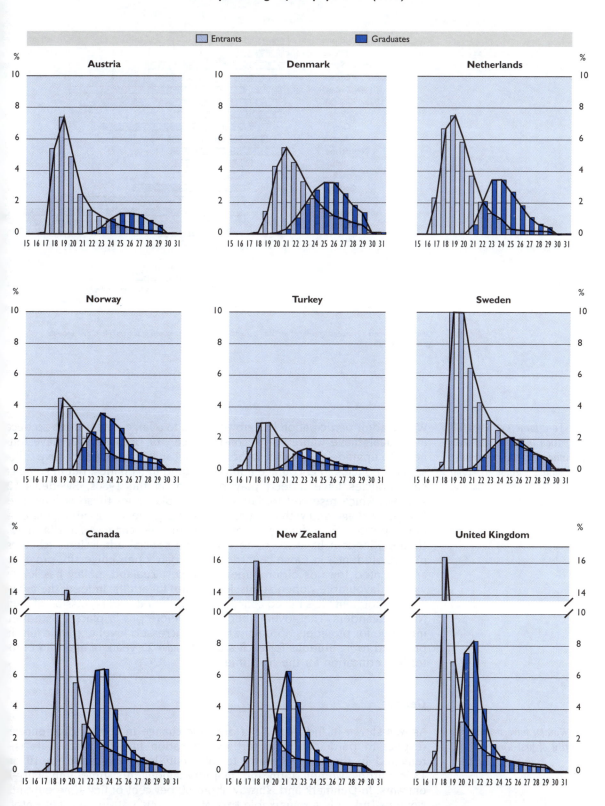

◆   Chart C4.3.   ***Age distribution of university-level***
new entrants (1995)

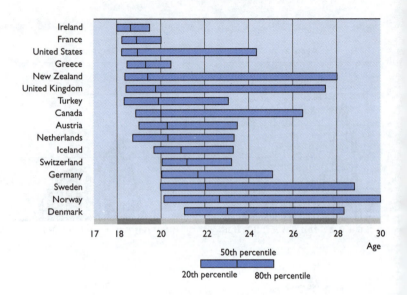

Countries are ranked in ascending order of the 50th percentile of the age distribution of university-level new entrants.
Source: OECD.

To a large extent, adult participation in university-level programmes has grown because individuals wanted a second chance.

Where adult participation has grown, it has to a large extent done so beca individuals have wanted a "second chance", or because they have felt need to upgrade their skills, rather than because governments have follo specific policies to encourage adults to attend universities. But in some ca such policies have indeed played a role: in the 1980s, Sweden's "2 scheme, which reserved tertiary education places for those at least twe five years of age and with four years of work experience, assured greater a participation than had previously been the case. Australia and United Kingdom have for some years had special admissions schemes mature students; in these countries and Japan, open university program are oriented towards older students. In New Zealand, policy has long vided a favourable, "open admissions" route for adults. Indeed, the grow adult enrolments has raised concerns about the rates of admission of you New Zealanders. The government has therefore put in place a "study-ri incentive for providers, through which an increased level of public fundir provided to institutions for each student *under* 22 years of age who enro tertiary education for the first time.

Gender

Women have become the majority of first-time entrants in most countries.

As was shown in Indicator A2, a dramatic change in gender differences respect to participation in tertiary education has occurred. This is reflected in the rates of entry to university-level education. In 10 o 13 countries women form the majority among first-time university-l entrants. In Denmark and Norway about 60 per cent of first-time entrant women. Turkey is a remarkable exception to this pattern, the net entry for men being almost twice as high as that for women.

The growth in women's entry rates has been stimulated by high upper secondary completion rates.

The growth in women's participation in university-level education has been stimulated by high upper-secondary school completion rates (see Indicator G1), particularly from general streams, which are more likely to lead to tertiary education. Indeed, in all but two of the 21 countries for which data are available, women are more likely than men to graduate from general upper secondary education; the exceptions being Korea and Turkey (Table G1.1).

But the gender balance varies widely in different fields of study.

While women have made important strides towards closing the gap in educational attainment between men and women, significant gender differences in women's participation in different fields of study still persist (see Indicator G3). The programmes least likely to enrol women are those in the natural sciences and industrial and engineering fields; women are more likely to enrol in fields related to the health professions, education and the social and behavioural sciences.

Definitions

Data refer to the school year 1994/95 and are based on the UOE data collection on education statistics, administered in 1996 (for details see Annex 3).

New (*i.e.* first-time) entrants are persons enrolling at the university level of education for the first time. Students who complete university-level non-degree programmes and transfer to degree programmes are not regarded as first-time entrants; nor are persons returning to university-level education after an absence. Foreign students who enrol in a country's education system for the first time in a post-graduate programme are considered first-time entrants. The definition of first-time entrants may differ between countries (for details refer to Annex 3).

Table C4.1 shows the sum of net entry rates for all students (times 100). The net entry rate is obtained by dividing the number of first-time entrants to the university level in a specified age group by the total population for the corresponding age group. The sum of net entry rates is calculated by adding the net entry rates for each single age from age 15 and over and dividing the total by 100. The result represents the proportion of persons of a synthetic age cohort who enter the tertiary level of education, irrespective of changes in the population sizes and differences between countries in the typical entry age. Table C4.1 shows also the 20th, 50th and 80th percentiles of the age distribution of first-time entrants, *i.e.* the ages below which are 20 per cent, 50 per cent and 80 per cent of first-time entrants.

Whereas Table C4.1 includes all first-time entrants, irrespective of their age, Table C4.2 shows the cumulative net entry rates for the age groups 15-29, 15-34, 15-39, and 15 and over. First-time entrants whose age is unknown have been included in the age group 40 years and older.

Not all countries can report the distinction between students entering a university-level tertiary programme for the first time and those transferring between the different tertiary levels of education or those repeating or re-entering a level after a time of absence. Even countries reporting first-time entrants cannot always exclude all forms of double counting.

Table C4.1 **Net entry rates for university-level education by gender and mode of participation, and age distribution of university-level new entrants (1995)**

	Net entry rates				Age at:		
	M+F	Male	Female	Full-time only	20th percentile[1]	50th percentile[1]	80th percentile[1]
North America							
Canada	48	41	56	37	18.9	20.0	26.5
Mexico	m	m	m	m	m	m	m
United States	52	45	59	42	18.3	19.0	24.4
Pacific Area							
Australia	m	m	m	m	m	m	m
Japan	m	m	m	m	m	m	m
Korea	m	m	m	m	m	m	m
New Zealand	40	34	46	28	18.4	19.4	28.0
European Union							
Austria	26	25	28	26	19.1	20.3	23.5
Belgium	m	m	m	m	m	m	m
Denmark	31	25	39	31	21.1	23.1	28.3
Finland	m	m	m	m	m	m	m
France	33	x	x	x	18.3	18.9	20.0
Germany	27	28	26	27	20.1	21.7	25.1
Greece	16	x	x	x	18.5	19.4	20.5
Ireland	27	27	28	27	18.0	18.6	19.4
Italy	m	m	m	m	m	m	m
Luxembourg	m	m	m	m	m	m	m
Netherlands	34	32	36	28	18.8	20.4	23.3
Portugal	m	m	m	m	m	m	m
Spain	m	m	m	m	m	m	m
Sweden	m	m	m	m	20.1	22.1	28.8
United Kingdom	43	42	44	38	18.5	19.8	27.5
Other OECD countries							
Czech Republic	m	m	m	m	m	m	m
Hungary	20	18	21	12	m	m	m
Iceland	39	x	x	39	19.8	21.0	23.3
Norway	25	20	30	22	20.2	22.7	>29
Poland	m	m	m	m	m	m	m
Switzerland	15	17	14	15	20.1	21.2	23.2
Turkey	16	21	11	16	18.4	19.9	23.1
Country mean	**31**	**29**	**34**	**28**	**19.2**	**20.5**	**24.3**

1. 20 / 50 / 80 per cent of new entrants are below this age.

Source: OECD Database. See Annex 3 for notes.

Table C4.2   **Net entry rates for university-level education (1995)**

	Net entry rates by age group			
	15-29	15-34	15-39	15 and over
North America				
Canada	43	44	46	49
Mexico	m	m	m	m
United States	47	x	x	52
Pacific Area				
Australia	m	m	m	m
Japan	m	m	m	m
Korea	m	m	m	m
New Zealand	33	35	37	40
European Union				
Austria	25	26	26	26
Belgium	m	m	m	m
Denmark	26	29	30	31
Finland	m	m	m	m
France	33	33	33	33
Germany	26	27	27	27
Greece	15	x	x	16
Ireland	27	27	x	27
Italy	m	m	m	m
Luxembourg	m	m	m	m
Netherlands	32	32	33	34
Portugal	m	m	m	m
Spain	m	m	m	m
Sweden	m	m	m	m
United Kingdom	37	39	40	43
Other OECD countries				
Czech Republic	m	m	m	m
Hungary	19	x	x	20
Iceland	m	m	m	m
Norway	20	21	23	25
Poland	m	m	m	m
Switzerland	15	15	15	15
Turkey	15	16	16	16
Country mean	**27**	**29**	**30**	**30**

Source: OECD Database. See Annex 3 for notes.

Indicator C5: **Participation in tertiary education**

Policy context

This indicator shows the percentage of persons in different age groups who participate in tertiary education. It also shows the number of years a person aged 17 can expect to spend in tertiary education.

OECD economies are more strongly dependent on the production, distribution and use of knowledge and skills than ever before. Output and employment are expanding fastest in high-technology industries, as well as in knowledge-intensive service sectors. It is highly skilled labour that is in greatest demand in OECD countries (see also Indicators E1, E2 and E4). At the same time, greater participation at the tertiary level of education, where unit costs tend to be significantly higher (see Indicator B4), puts an additional financial burden on public authorities and households.

Major shifts in policy and structural reforms have occurred in tertiary education in OECD Member countries, notably:

- continued pressure for expansion of student participation at the tertiary level;
- growing diversity among those seeking access to tertiary education and expanding needs and expectations of students, families, employers and the community;
- growing concern over quality and purposes;
- the emerging scenario of lifelong learning;
- competing demands for scarce public resources;
- challenges and opportunities presented by information and communication technologies; and
- attention to equity for previously under-represented groups.

Evidence and explanations

Overall level of participation

A growing minority participates in tertiary education: 21 per cent of 18-21 year-olds and 16 per cent of 22-25 year-olds.

Traditionally, tertiary education has educated an elite group of young people to higher levels immediately after they complete secondary schooling. Today it provides opportunities for learning to a much larger section of the young and adult population, on average for around 21 per cent of 18-21 year-olds, 16 per cent of 22-25 year-olds and still for around 7 per cent of persons in their late 20s (see Table C5.2b).

The proportion of 17 to 34 year-olds enrolled in tertiary education ranges from less than 6 per cent in Mexico and Turkey to 14 per cent or more in Australia, Canada, Finland and the United States (see Table C5.2a).

On average, a 17 year-old can expect about two years of tertiary education.

Today, a 17 year-old in Australia, Canada and the United States can expect to participate for three years or more in tertiary education, and in the majority of other countries for at least two years (see Table C5.1).

The enrolment rates in the different age bands reflect both the total number of individuals participating in tertiary education and the typical duration

◆ Chart C5.1. **Net enrolment in tertiary education for persons 17 to 34 years of age, by tertiary level and gender (1995)**

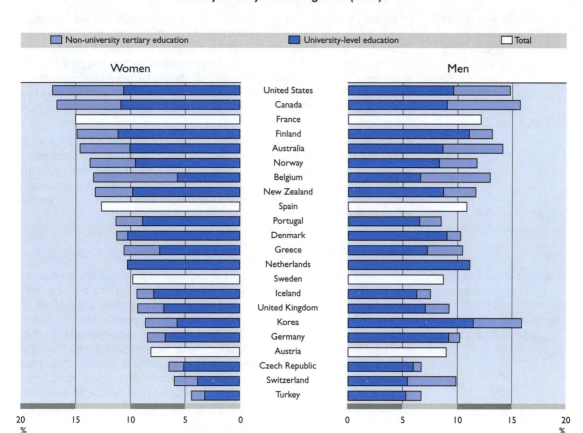

☐ Non-university tertiary education   ☐ University-level education   ☐ Total

Women   Men

United States
Canada
France
Finland
Australia
Norway
Belgium
New Zealand
Spain
Portugal
Denmark
Greece
Netherlands
Sweden
Iceland
United Kingdom
Korea
Germany
Austria
Czech Republic
Switzerland
Turkey

Countries are ranked in descending order of the total net enrolment rate for women.
Source: OECD.

tertiary programmes. Longer duration of studies (see also Indicator B4) tends to increase the stock of enrolments, and thus the level of resources required, all other things being equal. This also explains, in part, why some countries that report high tertiary enrolment rates still show comparatively low graduation rates (see Indicator G2).

...pansion has been driven by ...and from a wider and more diverse group of people...

The expansion in tertiary enrolments has been driven primarily by demand from a wider and more diverse group of secondary completers, as a result of social and economic developments common to all OECD countries. A system that caters for an increasingly heterogeneous group of students must work not only to develop its diversity, but also to ensure that students are in practice offered a range of choices that they can match to their needs.

... and in response, a wider range of tertiary learning opportunities has been developed.

In response to increased participation and to new kinds of demands from individuals, economies and society at large, a wide range of tertiary learning opportunities has been developed. Diversification has taken a number of forms both within and outside the formal tertiary education sector. It has included a blurring of the distinctiveness of programmes between sectors, better articulation between different courses, the networking of institutions, "franchise" arrangements and distance learning options. One indicator of diversity is the introduction and further development of "non-university" institutions that serve to broaden the types of programme available to lear ers in the first years of tertiary education.

In some countries, around half of all tertiary students are enrolled outside universities.

In some countries, around half of all tertiary students are enrolled outsi universities, while in other countries the proportion is negligible. Programm offered by non-university institutions often give greater emphasis to appli learning and, especially, links to employment. In some cases they have be seen as a tertiary-level extension of technical and professional second education. Austria, the Czech Republic, Finland, Italy and Mexico have und taken or are contemplating reforms aimed at developing new institutions a programmes of this type.

Evidence from surveys of earnings, employment and educational attainme indicates that the expansion of tertiary education has enabled individuals reduce their chances of being unemployed and to raise their earnings sign cantly. However, what is not clear is the extent to which increased access tertiary education – particularly at the university level – has contributed increased output or reduced unemployment overall.

Gender differences

On average about half of all 17-34 year-old tertiary students are women, although in some countries large gender differences do persist.

Over the last decade a clear trend towards higher tertiary participation ra among women has been observed and current entry rates (see Indicator show that this trend is continuing. Today, on average, about half of all 17 34 year-old tertiary students are women. In seven countries, women forr clear majority, with about 57 per cent of female students in Iceland a Portugal and 55 per cent in France, New Zealand, Norway, Sweden and United States. In countries in which the majority of students are men, gen differences tend to be considerable. In three countries, Korea, Switzerla and Turkey, the proportion of female students is below 40 per cent.

Gender differences tend to be higher in advanced tertiary programmes.

Gender differences tend to be higher in advanced tertiary programmes four out of five countries men form the majority of enrolments in secon higher degree programmes, and in the Czech Republic and Korea less tha third of the students enrolled in second stage university-level programr are women.

Men are more likely to participate in longer tertiary programmes and take slightly longer for their studies.

As indicators C4 and G3 show, both entry and graduation rates have a c predominance of women. The picture appears more balanced in the en ment rates, shown here. Several factors may contribute to this discrepancy particular, men are more likely to participate in programmes with a lor duration and/or take slightly longer for their tertiary studies.

Definitions

Data refer to the academic year 1994/95 and are based on the UOE data collection on education statistics, administered in 1996 (for details see Annex 3).

Tables C5.2a and C5.2b show the net enrolment rates at the tertiary leve education for students in the age groups 17 to 34 years, 18 to 21 years, 2 25 years and 26 to 29 years. Net enrolment rates are calculated by divic the number of tertiary education students in a specified age group by total population in that age group (times 100).

Table C5.1 shows the expected number of years for which persons a 17 years will on average be enrolled in tertiary education. It is calculate the sum of net enrolment rates for persons aged 17 years and over (divi by 100). The index is a function of both the number of persons participatir tertiary education and the duration of tertiary studies. Since it also inclu persons who have never participated in tertiary education, it cannot be ir preted as the average number of years an individual student needs to c plete tertiary education.

The figures are based on head counts, that is, they do not distinguish between full-time and part-time participants. A standardised distinction between full-time and part-time participants at the tertiary level is very difficult since many countries do not recognise the concept of part-time study, although in practice at least some of their students would be classified as part-time by other countries.

Table C5.1 **Expected years of tertiary education for all persons aged 17 (based on head counts) (1995)**

	Non-university tertiary education (ISCED 5)			University-level education first stage (ISCED 6)			All tertiary education (ISCED 5,6 and 7)		
	M + W	Men	Women	M + W	Men	Women	M + W	Men	Women
North America									
Canada	1.6	1.6	1.5	1.9	1.7	2.2	3.7	3.5	3.9
Mexico	x	x	x	0.8	x	x	0.8	x	x
United States	1.2	1.1	1.4	1.7	1.5	1.8	3.3	3.0	3.6
Pacific Area									
Australia	1.1	1.2	1.0	1.6	1.4	1.7	3.0	3.0	3.1
Japan	m	m	m	m	m	m	m	m	m
Korea	0.7	0.8	0.5	1.8	2.3	1.3	2.6	3.3	1.9
New Zealand	0.7	0.6	0.7	1.6	x	x	2.5	2.3	2.7
European Union									
Austria	0.2	x	x	1.5	1.6	1.5	1.8	1.8	1.8
Belgium	1.3	1.1	1.4	1.1	1.2	1.0	2.5	2.4	2.6
Denmark	0.2	0.2	0.2	1.0	0.8	1.2	2.1	2.0	2.2
Finland	0.6	0.4	0.8	2.1	2.0	2.1	2.8	2.6	3.1
France	x	x	x	x	x	x	2.5	2.2	2.8
Germany	0.3	0.2	0.3	1.6	1.8	1.4	1.8	1.9	1.7
Greece	0.6	0.6	0.6	1.3	1.3	1.3	1.9	1.9	1.9
Ireland	0.8	0.8	0.7	1.2	1.2	1.2	2.1	2.1	2.1
Italy	m	m	m	m	m	m	m	m	m
Luxembourg	m	m	m	m	m	m	m	m	m
Netherlands	a	a	a	1.2	1.2	1.2	2.1	2.2	2.0
Portugal	0.4	0.4	0.4	1.3	1.1	1.5	1.8	1.5	2.0
Spain	n	n	n	2.2	2.0	2.3	2.3	2.2	2.5
Sweden	x	x	x	1.7	1.6	1.9	1.8	1.7	2.0
United Kingdom	0.5	0.5	0.5	1.2	1.2	1.2	2.0	1.9	2.0
Other OECD countries									
Czech Republic	0.2	0.1	0.2	0.8	0.9	0.8	1.1	1.1	1.0
Hungary	a	a	a	0.6	0.5	0.6	1.1	1.0	1.1
Iceland	0.3	0.2	0.3	1.3	1.2	1.5	1.6	1.4	1.8
Norway	0.7	0.7	0.8	1.0	0.8	1.2	2.4	2.2	2.6
Poland	m	m	m	m	m	m	m	m	m
Switzerland	0.6	0.8	0.4	0.7	0.8	0.6	1.4	1.8	1.1
Turkey	0.3	0.3	0.2	0.7	0.9	0.5	1.0	1.2	0.8
Country mean	**0.5**	**0.6**	**0.6**	**1.3**	**1.3**	**1.4**	**2.1**	**2.1**	**2.2**

Source: OECD Database. See Annex 3 for notes.

Table C5.2a **Net enrolment in public and private tertiary education for persons 17 to 34 years of age, by tertiary level and gender (based on head counts) (1995)**

	Ages 17-34								
	Non-university tertiary education			University-level education			Total		
	M + W	Men	Women	M + W	Men	Women	M + W	Men	Women
North America									
Canada	6.3	6.8	5.9	9.9	9.0	10.9	16.3	15.8	16.8
Mexico	x	x	x	4.6	x	x	4.6	x	x
United States	5.9	5.2	6.5	10.1	9.6	10.6	16.0	14.8	17.2
Pacific Area									
Australia	5.0	5.5	4.6	9.4	8.6	10.1	14.4	14.2	14.7
Japan	m	m	m	m	m	m	m	m	m
Korea	3.7	4.5	2.9	8.7	11.5	5.7	12.4	16.0	8.6
New Zealand	3.2	3.0	3.4	9.3	8.7	9.8	12.5	11.7	13.2
European Union									
Austria	0.5	x	x	8.6	9.0	8.1	9.0	x	x
Belgium	7.1	6.4	7.7	6.2	6.6	5.7	13.2	13.1	13.4
Denmark	1.1	1.2	1.0	9.6	9.0	10.3	10.8	10.3	11.3
Finland	2.9	2.1	3.8	11.1	11.1	11.2	14.0	13.2	14.9
France	x	x	x	x	x	x	13.6	12.2	15.1
Germany	1.3	1.0	1.6	8.0	9.2	6.8	9.3	10.2	8.4
Greece	3.2	3.2	3.3	7.3	7.3	7.3	10.5	10.5	10.6
Ireland	m	m	m	m	m	m	m	m	m
Italy	m	m	m	m	m	m	m	m	m
Luxembourg	m	m	m	m	m	m	m	m	m
Netherlands	a	a	a	10.7	11.2	10.3	10.7	11.2	10.3
Portugal	2.2	2.0	2.4	7.7	6.5	8.9	9.9	8.5	11.3
Spain	0.2	0.2	0.2	11.5	10.6	12.5	11.7	10.8	12.7
Sweden	x	x	x	9.2	8.7	9.8	9.2	8.7	9.8
United Kingdom	2.3	2.2	2.4	7.0	7.1	6.9	9.3	9.2	9.3
Other OECD countries									
Czech Republic	1.0	0.7	1.4	5.5	6.0	5.1	6.6	6.7	6.4
Hungary	a	a	a	m	m	m	m	m	m
Iceland	1.4	1.3	1.6	7.0	6.3	7.8	8.5	7.5	9.4
Norway	3.8	3.5	4.2	8.9	8.3	9.6	12.8	11.8	13.7
Poland	m	m	m	m	m	m	m	m	m
Switzerland	3.3	4.5	2.1	4.6	5.4	3.8	7.9	9.9	5.9
Turkey	1.3	1.4	1.2	4.2	5.3	3.2	5.6	6.7	4.4
Country mean	**2.7**	**2.7**	**2.8**	**8.2**	**8.3**	**8.3**	**10.8**	**11.1**	**11.3**

Source: OECD Database. See Annex 3 for notes.

Table C5.2b **Net enrolment in public and private tertiary education for persons 18 to 21, 22 to 25 and 26 to 29 years of age, by type of tertiary education (based on head counts) (1995)**

	Ages 18-21			Ages 22-25			Ages 26-29		
	Non-university tertiary education	University-level education	Total	Non-university tertiary education	University-level education	Total	Non-university tertiary education	University-level education	Total
North America									
Canada	14.5	23.4	37.9	7.3	14.4	21.7	3.9	5.3	9.2
Mexico	x	0.9	0.9	x	0.5	0.5	x	2.3	2.7
United States	12.8	21.9	34.7	6.6	14.1	20.7	3.9	6.6	10.5
Pacific Area									
Australia	8.7	21.1	29.8	5.4	8.7	14.1	4.0	4.9	8.9
Japan	m	m	m	m	m	m	m	m	m
Korea	12.6	21.5	34.1	3.6	12.8	16.3	0.5	2.9	3.4
New Zealand	5.9	22.7	28.6	3.3	10.0	13.3	2.5	4.8	7.2
European Union									
Austria	1.6	12.6	14.2	0.9	14.1	15.0	x	8.5	8.5
Belgium	21.6	19.1	40.7	8.1	8.5	16.5	1.9	1.7	3.6
Denmark	1.0	7.9	8.9	2.3	20.3	22.6	1.1	10.0	11.2
Finland	5.2	12.3	17.5	5.6	21.8	27.4	1.8	11.2	12.9
France	x	x	34.2	x	x	17.7	x	x	4.6
Germany	2.7	7.9	10.6	1.7	15.3	17.0	1.9	9.5	11.4
Greece	9.7	23.2	32.9	3.8	6.8	10.6	1.0	2.2	3.2
Ireland	x	x	27.2	x	x	15.5	m	m	m
Italy	m	m	m	m	m	m	m	m	m
Luxembourg	m	m	m	m	m	m	m	m	m
Netherlands	a	23.2	23.2	a	18.7	18.7	a	5.6	5.6
Portugal	4.6	13.3	17.9	3.2	12.5	15.7	1.1	4.8	5.9
Spain	0.7	24.9	25.6	0.2	17.3	17.5	n	5.5	5.7
Sweden	x	13.0	13.0	x	16.6	16.6	x	7.5	7.7
United Kingdom	4.9	20.9	25.8	2.5	6.8	9.3	1.6	3.2	4.4
Other OECD countries									
Czech Republic	3.4	12.5	15.9	0.5	7.5	8.0	n	2.1	2.
Hungary	a	11.9	11.9	a	7.9	7.9	a	2.3	2.
Iceland	0.9	7.0	7.9	3.3	17.0	20.3	1.4	5.5	6.
Norway	8.0	9.5	17.5	5.6	17.9	23.6	2.3	7.7	10.
Poland	m	m	m	m	m	m	m	m	m
Switzerland	2.4	5.2	7.7	5.9	8.8	14.7	3.4	3.9	7.
Turkey	2.4	7.7	10.1	1.4	6.0	7.4	0.8	2.6	3.
Country mean	**5.9**	**14.9**	**21.1**	**3.4**	**12.4**	**15.5**	**1.7**	**5.2**	**6.**

Source: OECD Database. See Annex 3 for notes.

Table C5.3 **Percentage of female students in the non-university tertiary and university-level education (1995)**

	Ages 18-21			Ages 22-25			Ages 26-29		
	Non-university tertiary education	University-level education First Stage	University-level education Second Stage	Non-university tertiary education	University-level education First Stage	University-level education Second Stage	Non-university tertiary education	University-level education First Stage	University-level education Second Stage
North America									
Canada	48.3	56.9	51.1	41.2	51.7	49.3	42.8	52.5	42.9
Mexico	m	m	m	m	m	m	m	m	m
United States	52.3	55.0	30.5	50.4	49.5	50.9	62.4	48.6	55.1
Pacific Area									
Australia	49.7	55.4	66.5	43.6	48.5	54.7	41.1	51.0	48.9
Japan	m	m	m	m	m	m	m	m	m
Korea	43.3	41.9	a	20.8	19.9	45.4	24.3	10.3	26.9
New Zealand	54.5	54.6	53.4	53.4	50.4	48.5	52.1	54.6	46.4
European Union									
Austria	m	53.9	25.0	m	45.8	47.5	m	42.8	38.4
Belgium	60.0	47.6	69.5	45.3	42.9	48.5	41.7	36.6	32.7
Denmark	48.7	58.9	41.3	42.2	61.3	44.9	44.7	53.4	45.8
Finland	69.8	53.7	a	58.0	48.7	46.8	58.7	47.1	40.8
France	m	m	m	m	m	m	m	m	m
Germany	85.5	56.5	a	47.4	40.7	m	45.5	34.5	m
Greece	49.7	49.2	a	50.5	51.8	m	53.9	47.8	m
Ireland	55.3	49.9	55.7	45.2	49.2	46.3	m	m	m
Italy	m	m	m	m	m	m	m	m	m
Luxembourg	m	m	m	m	m	m	m	m	m
Netherlands	a	54.4	47.0	a	43.3	45.4	a	42.6	38.9
Portugal	60.1	60.1	38.1	53.8	57.1	57.8	43.4	53.0	59.5
Spain	48.6	57.2	a	54.8	50.9	m	m	45.6	m
Sweden	a	57.6	a	a	50.4	40.0	a	48.2	31.9
United Kingdom	46.9	50.9	50.1	54.0	43.7	46.2	56.8	46.4	43.9
Other OECD countries									
Czech Republic	64.8	42.9	a	56.3	48.3	26.5	7.7	61.0	27.0
Hungary	a	54.4	54.4	a	49.7	49.7	a	48.3	48.3
Iceland	51.7	48.6	a	57.4	56.7	48.6	50.2	53.0	47.4
Norway	58.1	60.8	48.8	50.3	55.6	45.6	47.9	52.5	42.6
Poland	m	m	m	m	m	m	m	m	m
Switzerland	45.2	47.1	53.8	29.4	40.2	46.6	26.1	39.0	29.4
Turkey	43.0	40.8	33.8	44.0	32.0	40.9	48.9	30.7	34.2
Country mean	**54.5**	**52.5**	**47.9**	**47.3**	**47.3**	**46.5**	**44.0**	**45.4**	**41.1**

Source: OECD Database. See Annex 3 for notes.

Indicator C6: Foreign students in tertiary education

Policy context

This indicator shows the mobility of students between countries.

The international, or cross-cultural, dimension of higher education is receiv more and more attention. The general trend towards free movement of ca tal, goods and people between countries, coupled with changes in openn of labour markets, has increased the demand for new kinds of skills a knowledge in OECD countries. Governments are increasingly looking higher education to play a role in broadening the horizons of students a allowing them to develop a deeper understanding of the languages, cultu and business methods found elsewhere in the world.

One way for students to expand their knowledge of other cultures and so ties is to attend institutions of higher education in countries other than th own. International student mobility involves costs and benefits to stude and institutions, in both the sending and host countries. While the di short-term monetary costs and benefits of this mobility are more easily m sured, the long-term social and economic benefits to students, instituti and countries are more difficult to quantify. Measures of the numbe students studying in other countries, however, provide some idea of extent of this phenomenon and the degree to which it is changing over tir

It is worth noting that besides student flows across borders, other issues, s as curriculum internationalisation and international electronic delivery highly flexible programmes aimed at satisfying specialised needs, are relevant to capturing the internationalisation of higher education. Today see cross-border mobility in the provision of education, in addition to mobility of participants. It will be important in the future to develop way quantify and measure these other components of the internationalisatio education.

Evidence and explanations

Proportion of foreign students studying in OECD countries, by host coun

More than eight out of ten foreign students study in seven OECD countries.

A relatively small number of OECD countries enrol the vast majority of for students. The United States is the largest receiving country of foreign dents (in absolute figures) with 34 per cent of the total, followed by Fr. (13 per cent), Germany and the United Kingdom (12 per cent each), Aust (7 per cent), Canada and Japan (4 per cent each) (see Chart C6.1 and co totals in Table C6.5). These seven receiving countries account for ni 85 per cent of all foreign students studying in OECD countries.

For the purpose of this indicator, a foreign student is someone who is r citizen in the country in which he or she is studying. In most countries, i not been possible to distinguish foreign students who are resident ir country as a result of a prior migration (by themselves or with their par

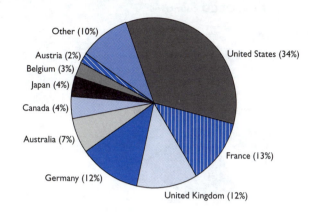

◆ Chart C6.1. **Distribution of foreign students in OECD countries, by host country (1995)**

Source: OECD.

from those who come to the country expressly for the purpose of pursuing their education.

A common language is an important factor in selecting a country in which to study.

An important factor in selecting a country in which to study abroad is likely to be the availability of a common language. The dominance of Australia, Canada, the United Kingdom and the United States in the receipt of foreign students is, to a large extent, attributable to the fact that English is both the medium of instruction in these countries and the language that students intending to study abroad are most likely to know. Many institutions in non-English-speaking countries provide courses in English to attract students from abroad. Some studies show, however, that the language question is less important to student mobility at the postgraduate level than at the undergraduate level.

Although Germany ranks highly as a destination for foreign students studying in OECD countries, the actual number of non-resident students (or students who attended upper secondary education in another country) registered in German higher education institutions is likely to be lower because of a significant number of "domestic foreigners," consisting mainly of children of "guest workers" who, although having grown up in Germany, are considered "foreign" for the purposes of this indicator. A quarter of all foreign students in Germany have ethnic origins in Turkey, Greece, and Italy.

Proportion of foreign students studying in OECD countries by sending countries

Just over half of foreign students in OECD countries from non-OECD countries.

The number of foreign students has been growing, world-wide, since at least the 1960s. By 1995, 1.3 million foreign students were enrolled in OECD countries. Of all foreign students studying in OECD countries, 44 per cent were from OECD countries and 56 per cent from non-OECD countries.

...nese and Koreans comprise ...argest proportion of foreign students from OECD countries...

Among all foreign students studying in OECD countries, Japanese and Koreans comprise the largest proportion of students from other OECD countries (each representing about 5 per cent of all foreign students), followed by Germans (3.6 per cent), Greeks (3.2 per cent), Turks, French and Italians (as can be derived from the row-totals in Table C6.5). Together, these countries

◆   Chart C6.2.   ***Distribution of foreign students in OECD countries by country of origin (1995)***

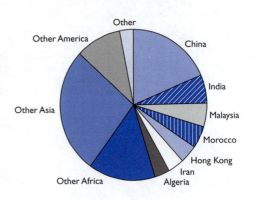

From OECD countries

From non-OECD countries

The areas of the charts represent the proportions of foreign students from OECD countries and non-OECD countries in OECD countries.
Source: OECD.

account for more than 25 per cent of all foreign students in OECD count
and for more than 50 per cent of the foreign students originating in OE
countries.

... while students from China and Southeast Asia make up the largest proportion of foreign students from non-OECD countries.

China represents 11.1 per cent of all foreign students studying in OE
countries, followed by India with 3.5 per cent. Southeast Asian countries
also very active in student exchange with OECD countries, 9 per cent of
foreign students originating from Hong Kong, Indonesia, Malaysia, Singap
and Thailand. The importance of international trade, finance and econo
issues are likely to be an important factor underlying student mobility in
different regions. For example, regional economic integration thro
organisations and treaties such as the EU, NAFTA, ASEAN and APEC may
influence international student mobility. National governments in the As
Pacific region such as Australia, Japan and New Zealand have initiated p
cies for their higher education institutions to attract foreign students.

Asia is the largest (46 per cent), and Europe (30 per cent) is the second largest source of foreign students.

The largest number of foreign students enrolled in OECD countries are f
Asia (46 per cent). With 30 per cent, Europe is the second largest world re
as a source of foreign students.

Foreign students as a proportion of the total enrolment

Another way to look at the size of student mobility in tertiary education
examine both the number of tertiary students that a particular cou
receives from other countries and the number of students that a cou
sends abroad, relative to the size of tertiary enrolments. These are meas
of the intensity of international exchange for each country, as a host as we
a sending country.

The percentage of foreign students enrolled in OECD countries ranges from below 1 to around 11 per cent.

With regard to the proportion of foreign students in total tertiary enrolm
Austria and Switzerland are the largest receivers, with a proportion of fo
students of around 11 per cent of their tertiary enrolment, followed
Belgium and the United Kingdom (see row "Total, all countries
Table C6.1).

◆ Chart C6.3. *Percentage of tertiary students enrolled who are not citizens of the country of study (1995)*

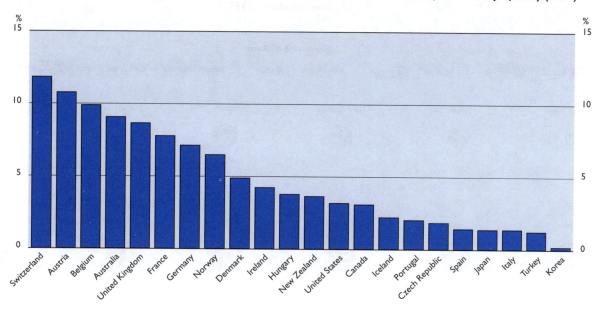

Countries are ranked in descending order of the percentage of foreign students enrolled.
Source: OECD.

The proportions of foreign students enrolled in first stage university-level programmes are even higher (see column 7 in Table C6.4). In Switzerland every fifth student at this level is a foreign student. In Australia, more than 13 per cent of all first-time university graduates are non-nationals (see last column in Table C6.4).

By contrast, the proportion of foreign students is very small in Korea and also in Italy, Japan, Spain and Turkey. These countries report a proportion of foreign students of less than 1.5 per cent (see Table C6.1).

It is also possible to estimate the extent to which students leave their country and study abroad. The ratio of the number of students studying abroad (in other OECD countries) to total enrolment in the home country (see Table C6.2) can be considered an indicator both of the flexibility of students and the structure of educational programmes in their home country (particularly when students study abroad for an academic term or two) as well as of the attractiveness of the education system in other countries.

This measure only covers students leaving their country to study in other OECD countries which report data. In other words, this measure does not cover students who study abroad in non-OECD countries or non-reporting OECD countries and thus is likely to underestimate the proportion of students who study abroad. It is also likely to underestimate the proportion of students who have some educational experience abroad because it is calculated on a full-year basis. For example, 53 per cent of the students from the United States who are studying abroad leave the country for half a year or less and only 14 per cent stay in the host country for a full academic year. These caveats aside, this measure provides some idea of the degree to which students in OECD countries study abroad.

◆ Chart C6.4. **Ratio of tertiary students studying in other OECD countries to total tertiary enrolment in home countries (1995)**

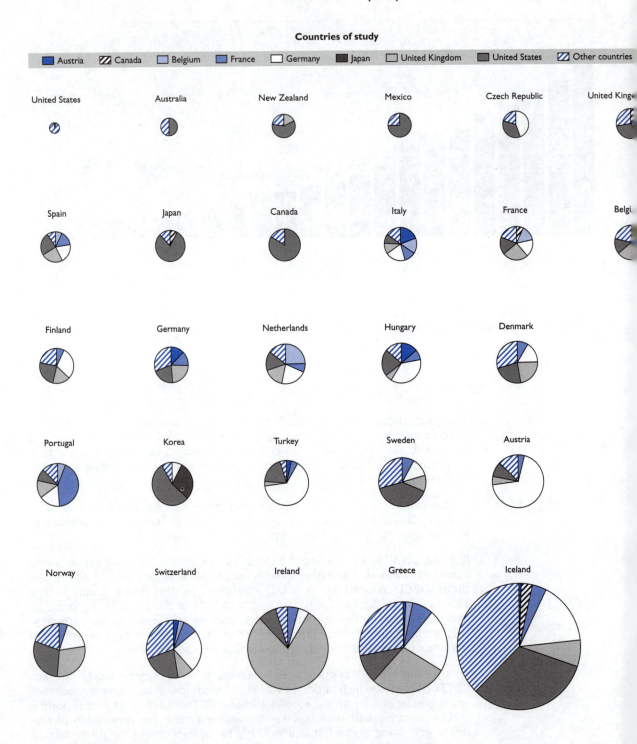

Countries of study

Austria | Canada | Belgium | France | Germany | Japan | United Kingdom | United States | Other countries

* The areas of the pie-charts represent the ratios of tertiary students abroad to the total tertiary enrolment in the home countries.

Countries are ranked by the percentage of total tertiary enrolment studying abroad.

Source: OECD.

Greece, Iceland and Ireland have a large proportion of students studying abroad while Australia, the Russian Federation and the United States have relatively few.

The ratio of students studying abroad in other OECD countries to total enrolment in the home country varies widely between countries. Typically, the proportion of these students amounts to 1 to 3 per cent of the total enrolment in their home countries (see row-totals in Table C6.2). The OECD countries with the largest proportions of students studying abroad are Greece, Iceland, and Ireland (with 10 per cent or more of tertiary enrolment in the country of origin). The countries with the smallest proportions (less than 0.5 per cent of tertiary enrolment) are Australia, the Russian Federation and the United States.

In many countries, students choose between very few destinations. More than 80 per cent of Canadian, Irish, Japanese, Korean, Mexican, and Turkish students studying abroad can be found in one or two other OECD countries (see Table C6.5).

Number of incoming and outgoing foreign students

Various "push" and "pull" factors may explain patterns of student mobility.

The patterns of student mobility can be attributed to a variety of "push" and "pull" factors, such as language barriers, the academic reputation of particular institutions or programmes, the flexibility of home programmes with respect to counting time spent abroad toward degree requirements, the limitations of higher education provision in the home country, restrictive policies of university admission at home, etc.

These patterns also reflect geographical and historical links between countries, future job opportunities, cultural aspirations and government policies to facilitate credit transfer between home and host institutions. The trans-

◆ Chart C6.5. **Net inflow of foreign students relative to tertiary enrolment (1995)**

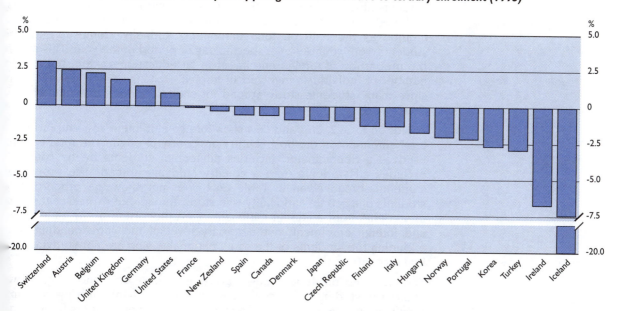

net inflow is calculated as the number of foreign students coming into a country minus the number of students from the particular country studying abroad. A ative figure indicates that there are more students studying abroad than foreign students coming into the country.
mple: There are more foreign students coming to Austria than Austrian students studying abroad. The difference between Austrian students studying abroad and foreign dents in Austria is 2.5% of the total tertiary enrolment in Austria.
ce: OECD.

parency and flexibility of courses and requirements for degrees also count the choice of institutions.

Relative numbers of incoming and outgoing students illustrate the relati strength of some of the "push" and "pull" factors noted above. For examp insufficient provision of university places explains at least some of the h level of outflow of students from Greece, particularly for male students.

The United States has the largest net inflow of students in absolute terms...

Most imbalances in student flows can be attributed to a single (negativ bilateral imbalance between the United States and all other countries between the United Kingdom and all other countries except Canada and t United States. The United States accepts over 120 000 students more than t total number of American students studying abroad. Relative to the size the American tertiary educational system, this represents about 1 per cent the total tertiary enrolment (see column 3 in Table C6.4).

... while the largest relative net inflows are in Austria, Belgium and Switzerland.

Although much smaller in absolute numbers, the net inflow of students Austria, Belgium and Switzerland, relative to tertiary enrolment in these co tries, is much greater, between 2.3 and 3.1 per cent. Iceland has by far largest relative net outflow of students, roughly equivalent to 22 per cen total tertiary enrolment.

Definitions

Data refer to the academic year 1994/95 and are based on the UOE data collection on education statistics, administered in 1996 (for details see Annex 3).

Students are classified as foreign students if they do not hold the citizens of the country for which the data are collected. The data were collec through the host countries, not through the sending countries, and there relate to incoming students to a particular country, rather than to stude from that country going abroad. Students studying in countries which did report to the OECD are not included in this indicator. As a consequence statements on students studying abroad underestimate the real numbe students abroad, since non-OECD countries and non-reporting countries excluded. The number of foreign students is obtained following the s method as the data on total enrolment. Normally, domestic and for students were counted on a specific day or period of the year. This meas the proportion of foreign enrolment in an education system, but the ac number of individuals involved in foreign exchange might be much hig since many students study abroad for shorter periods than the whole demic year.

Tables C6.1, C6.2, C6.3 and C6.4 show foreign enrolment as a proportion o total enrolment in the host country or country of origin. The total enrolm used as a denominator, includes all foreign students in the country excludes all students from a country studying abroad. The proportio students abroad given in Table C6.2 does not show the proportion o students of a certain nationality who study abroad, but expresses the nur of students from a certain nationality as a proportion of the total dom and foreign enrolment in the tertiary level of the corresponding cou excluding the students of the same nationality who are not studying in home country.

The balances of student flows, given in Tables C6.3 and C6.4, show number of students from country A (country of origin) studying in coun (destination, country of study) minus the number of students from coun studying in country A. A negative figure indicates a net inflow of students country B and a positive number indicates a net outflow from country *A*

The total balance of inflow and outflow, as presented in Table C6.4, is b only on those countries which reported foreign enrolments themselves. means that the sum of incoming students counts only students from reporting countries and ignores students from other countries, in order to ensure the full comparability with the outflow, which is based on other reporting countries' data.

Bilateral comparisons of the data on foreign students should be undertaken with caution, since some countries differ in the definition of foreign students (see Annex 3).

Table C6.1 **Number of foreign students enrolled in tertiary education as a percentage of the students in the country of destination (based on head counts) (1995)**

Countries of origin	Austria	Belgium	Canada	Czech Republic	Denmark	Finland	France	Germany	Hungary	Iceland	Ireland	Italy	Japan	Korea	New Zealand	Norway	Portugal	Spain	Switzerland	Turkey	United Kingdom	United States
North America																						
Canada	0.02	0.03	n	n	0.03	0.02	0.05	0.02	0.02	0.04	0.05	0.01	n	n	0.02	0.05	0.06	n	0.10		0.09	0.16
Mexico	0.02	0.01	0.04	n	0.01	n	0.03	0.01	n	0.04	n	0.03	n	n	0.01	0.01	0.01	n	0.04		0.03	0.06
United States	0.21	0.06	0.21	0.01	0.14	0.09	0.14	0.21	0.11	0.26	0.67	0.03	0.03	0.01	0.11	0.36	0.07	0.03	0.25		0.34	a
Pacific Area																						
Australia	0.01	n	0.02	n	0.02	0.01	n	0.01	n	0.01	0.02	0.01	0.01	n	0.19	0.02	0.01	n	0.03		0.04	0.02
Japan	0.12	0.02	0.25	n	0.01	0.03	0.06	0.07	0.01	n	0.04	0.01	a	0.02	0.14	0.02	0.02	n	0.06		0.15	0.32
Korea	0.16	0.01	0.08	n	n	n	0.08	0.22	n	n	n	0.02	0.45	a	0.05	0.30	n	0.01	0.02		0.04	0.24
New Zealand	n	n	0.01	n	0.01	n	n	n	n	n	n	n	n	n	a	0.01	n	n	n		0.01	0.01
European Union																						
Austria	a	0.01	n	n	0.02	0.01	0.02	0.31	0.01	0.03	0.01	0.01	n	n	n	0.02	n	0.03	0.34		0.03	0.01
Belgium	0.02	a	0.01	n	0.01	0.01	0.08	0.05	n	n	0.03	0.01	n	n	n	0.01	0.01	0.04	0.16		0.08	0.01
Denmark	0.03	0.02	n	n	a	0.02	0.02	0.03	n	0.45	0.03	n	n	n	0.01	0.38	n	0.01	0.05		0.06	0.01
Finland	0.05	0.01	0.01	n	0.03	a	0.01	0.05	0.01	0.07	0.01	n	n	n	n	0.10	n	0.01	0.05		0.03	0.01
France	0.12	1.46	0.14	n	0.05	0.02	a	0.27	0.01	0.03	0.24	0.03	n	n	0.01	0.08	0.08	0.19	1.11		0.49	0.04
Germany	2.22	0.19	0.04	0.02	0.32	0.11	0.26	a	0.30	0.20	0.37	0.07	0.01	0.07	0.07	0.25	0.07	0.16	3.08	0.01	0.52	0.06
Greece	0.16	0.26	0.01	0.24	0.01	0.01	0.14	0.38	0.57	n	0.03	0.39	n	n	n	0.02	n	0.01	0.16	0.09	0.57	0.03
Ireland	0.02	0.02	0.01	n	0.02	0.03	0.03	0.03	n	0.07	a	n	a	n	n	0.01	0.01	0.02	0.03	x	0.54	0.01
Italy	2.46	1.25	0.01	n	0.03	0.03	0.16	0.27	n	n	0.07	a	n	n	0.01	0.02	0.02	0.12	1.49	a	0.17	0.02
Luxembourg	0.13	0.46	n	n	n	n	0.05	0.06	0.01	n	0.01	n	n	n	0.01	n	n	0.05	0.14	n	0.02	0.02
Netherlands	0.04	0.84	0.01	n	0.05	0.01	0.04	0.12	0.01	n	0.04	0.01	n	0.01	0.01	0.08	n	0.05	0.16	n	0.11	0.01
Portugal	0.02	0.14	0.01	n	0.01	n	0.17	0.06	n	n	0.01	n	n	n	n	0.02	a	0.04	0.11	n	0.06	0.06
Spain	0.08	0.44	0.01	n	0.04	0.01	0.16	0.20	n	0.09	0.15	0.01	n	n	n	0.03	0.07	a	0.60	n	0.27	0.04
Sweden	0.08	0.02	0.01	n	0.17	0.18	0.03	0.05	0.06	0.18	0.04	0.01	n	n	0.01	0.46	0.03	0.01	0.11	n	0.05	0.02

Countries of destination

Countries of destination

Countries of origin	Austria	Belgium	Canada	Czech Republic	Denmark	Finland	France	Germany	Hungary	Iceland	Ireland	Italy	Japan	Korea	New Zealand	Norway	Portugal	Spain	Switzerland	Turkey	United Kingdom	United States
Other OECD countries																						
Czech Republic	0.04	0.01	n	a	n	n	n	0.04	0.03	n	n	n	n	n	n	n	n	n	0.04	n	n	n
Hungary	0.24	0.02	n	0.02	0.01	0.04	0.02	0.07	a	n	0.01	n	n	n	n	0.01	n	n	0.08	n	0.01	0.01
Iceland	n	n	n	n	0.24	0.02	n	0.01	n	a	n	n	n	n	n	0.10	n	n	n	n	0.01	n
Norway	0.03	0.01	0.01	n	0.44	0.02	0.02	0.06	0.06	0.19	0.01	n	n	n	n	a	a	0.01	0.08	n	0.12	0.01
Poland	0.23	0.04	0.01	0.05	0.08	0.04	0.06	0.22	0.05	0.04	n	0.01	n	n	n	0.13	0.13	n	0.16	n	0.02	0.01
Switzerland	0.10	0.03	0.01	n	0.03	0.01	0.03	0.08	0.01	0.03	0.01	0.08	n	n	n	0.03	0.03	0.03	a	a	0.04	0.01
Turkey	0.54	0.25	0.01	n	0.10	0.02	0.08	1.06	0.03	n	n	n	n	n	n	0.07	0.07	n	0.17	a	0.07	0.05
Other non-OECD countries																						
Russian Federation	0.07	0.02	n	0.03	0.01	0.12	0.04	0.13	0.08	0.01	0.01	n	n	n	n	0.02	0.02	n	0.13	0.03	0.02	0.03
Total: OECD and non-OECD countries																						
Total: Africa	0.43	3.10	0.45	0.25	0.09	0.25	3.42	0.62	0.20	0.01	0.16	0.14	0.01	n	0.06	n	0.63	0.15	0.88	0.06	0.47	0.15
Total: Asia	2.02	0.83	1.60	0.39	0.79	0.62	0.90	2.73	0.76	0.08	0.55	0.23	1.26	0.04	1.99	2.28	0.01	0.06	0.96	0.69	2.38	2.05
Total: Europe	7.76	5.46	0.47	0.88	1.87	0.93	1.72	3.23	2.63	1.67	2.79	0.83	0.03	n	0.19	2.28	0.39	0.88	9.00	0.26	3.29	0.45
Total: North America	0.28	0.13	0.38	0.03	0.18	0.13	0.25	0.28	0.14	0.34	0.73	0.05	0.04	0.02	0.15	0.44	0.13	0.10	0.44	n	0.53	0.35
Total: Oceania	0.02	n	0.03	n	0.02	0.01	0.01	0.01	n	n	0.03	0.03	0.01	0.01	0.84	0.02	0.01	n	0.03	n	0.06	0.03
Total: South America	0.14	0.22	0.08	0.02	0.06	0.03	0.18	0.18	0.02	0.04	0.01	0.06	0.02	0.01	0.02	0.18	0.45	0.21	0.50	n	0.08	0.15
Not specified	0.11	0.19	0.06	0.01	1.88	0.04	1.50	0.12	n	n	n	0.13	n	0.02	0.34	0.85	0.04	n	0.01	0.25	1.86	n
Total: All countries	10.76	9.92	3.07	1.59	4.90	2.01	7.98	7.17	3.76	2.15	4.26	0.13	1.37	0.09	3.59	6.45	2.04	1.40	11.82	1.25	8.66	3.17

The table shows the share of students in each country that have Citizenship of another country.
Example. Reading the first column: 0.02 per cent of Austrian tertiary students are Canadian citizens, 0.21 per cent of Austrian students are US citizens, etc.
Reading the first row: 0.02 per cent of Austrian tertiary students are Canadian citizens, 0.03 per cent of Belgian tertiary students are Canadian citizens, etc.
Source: OECD Database. See Annex 3 for notes.

Table C6.2 **Number of students enrolled in other countries in tertiary education as a percentage of students enrolled in tertiary education** *in the country of origin* **(head counts) (1995)**

Countries of origin	Countries of destination																						
	Austria	Belgium	Canada	Czech Republic	Denmark	Finland	France	Germany	Hungary	Iceland	Ireland	Italy	Japan	Korea	New Zealand	Norway	Portugal	Spain	Switzerland	Turkey	United Kingdom	United States	Total
North America																							
Canada	n	n	a	n	n	n	0.06	0.03	n	n	n	0.01	0.01	n	n	0.01	0.01	n	0.01	n	0.10	1.28	1.53
Mexico	n	0.01	0.06	n	n	n	0.04	0.02	n	n	n	n	0.01	n	n	n	n	0.04	n	n	0.04	0.63	0.85
United States	n	n	0.03	n	n	n	0.02	0.03	n	n	0.01	n	0.01	n	n	n	n	n	n	n	0.04	a	0.16
Pacific Area																							
Australia	n	n	0.03	n	n	n	0.01	0.02	n	n	n	0.01	0.03	n	0.03	n	n	n	n	n	0.07	0.23	0.46
Japan	0.01	n	0.12	n	n	n	0.03	0.04	n	n	n	n	a	0.01	0.01	n	n	n	n	n	0.07	1.16	1.45
Korea	0.02	n	0.06	n	n	n	0.07	0.22	n	n	n	0.01	0.80	a	a	0.02	n	n	n	n	0.04	1.51	2.76
New Zealand	n	n	0.07	n	0.01	n	0.01	0.03	n	n	n	n	0.04	n	a	0.01	n	n	n	n	0.15	0.49	0.82
European Union																							
Austria	a	0.01	0.02	n	0.01	0.01	0.17	2.86	0.01	n	0.01	0.04	0.01	n	n	0.01	n	0.17	0.21	n	0.21	0.38	4.15
Belgium	0.02	a	0.03	n	n	n	0.45	0.28	n	n	0.01	0.05	0.01	n	n	0.01	0.01	0.18	0.07	n	0.43	0.26	1.80
Denmark	0.04	0.03	0.05	n	a	0.02	0.23	0.42	0.01	0.02	0.02	0.03	0.02	n	n	0.39	n	0.11	0.04	n	0.59	0.60	2.62
Finland	0.06	0.02	0.05	n	0.03	a	0.13	0.55	0.01	n	0.01	0.03	0.01	n	n	0.09	n	0.05	0.03	n	0.31	0.45	1.84
France	0.01	0.25	0.12	n	n	n	a	0.28	n	n	0.01	0.03	0.01	n	0.01	0.01	0.03	0.14	0.08	n	0.43	0.28	1.68
Germany	0.24	0.03	0.03	n	0.03	0.01	0.25	a	0.02	n	0.02	0.06	n	n	n	0.02	0.01	0.11	0.21	0.01	0.44	0.40	1.91
Greece	0.12	0.31	0.07	0.15	0.01	0.01	0.95	2.78	0.33	n	0.01	2.38	n	n	n	0.01	n	0.06	0.08	0.36	3.50	1.25	12.36
Ireland	0.04	0.06	0.08	n	0.02	0.01	0.45	0.45	n	n	a	0.01	0.01	n	n	0.01	n	0.22	0.04	x	8.07	0.75	10.20
Italy	0.32	0.25	0.01	n	n	n	0.19	0.33	n	n	a	a	0.01	n	n	0.01	n	0.10	0.12	n	0.17	0.15	1.66
Luxembourg	m	m	m	n	n	n	0.17	m	m	n	m	m	m	n	n	m	m	0.14	0.05	0.01	0.40	m	m
Netherlands	0.02	0.59	0.03	n	0.02	n	0.17	0.51	n	n	0.01	0.02	0.01	n	n	0.03	n	0.14	0.05	0.01	0.36	0.37	2.38
Portugal	0.01	0.17	0.05	n	0.01	n	1.16	0.44	n	n	n	0.01	n	n	n	0.01	a	0.18	0.05	n	0.33	0.25	2.72
Spain	0.01	0.10	0.01	n	n	n	0.21	0.28	0.01	n	0.01	0.04	n	n	n	n	0.01	a	0.06	n	0.38	0.34	1.38
Sweden	0.07	0.03	0.09	n	0.12	0.09	0.29	0.44	0.04	a	0.02	0.04	0.01	n	0.01	0.33	0.33	0.09	0.07	n	0.38	1.40	3.53
United Kingdom	0.01	0.02	0.11	n	0.02	0.09	0.23	0.19	n	0.01	0.11	0.02	0.01	n	0.01	0.03	n	0.11	0.02	0.01	a	0.43	1.33
Other OECD countries																							
Czech Republic	0.06	0.01	0.01	a	n	n	n	0.47	0.03	n	n	n	0.01	n	n	n	n	n	0.04	0.01	0.05	0.37	1.05
Hungary	0.34	0.04	0.05	0.02	0.01	0.03	0.20	0.87	a	n	n	0.04	0.02	n	n	0.01	n	0.01	0.07	n	0.13	0.52	2.39
Iceland	0.15	0.09	0.70	n	5.42	0.28	0.89	3.83	0.07	a	0.01	0.31	0.08	n	n	2.37	n	0.09	0.08	0.09	1.62	7.69	23.81
Norway	0.04	0.02	0.06	m	0.43	m	0.23	0.74	0.06	0.01	0.01	0.03	m	m	m	a	n	0.06	0.07	m	1.21	1.23	4.22
Poland	m	m	m	m	m	m	m	m	m	m	m	m	m	m	m	m	m	m	m	m	m	m	m
Switzerland	0.16	0.08	0.15	n	0.03	0.01	0.41	1.19	0.01	n	0.01	1.00	0.01	n	n	0.04	0.01	0.31	a	0.02	0.46	1.10	4.98
Turkey	0.11	0.07	0.01	n	0.01	n	0.15	1.94	0.01	n	n	n	n	n	n	0.01	n	n	0.02	a	0.10	0.57	3.01
Other non-OECD countries																							
Russian Federation	n	n	n	n	n	n	0.02	0.06	n	n	n	n	n	n	n	n	n	n	n	n	0.01	0.11	0.22

The table shows the share of students from each country that are studying in other countries.
Example: Reading the first column: 0.01 per cent of Japanese tertiary students study in Austria, 0.02 per cent of Korean students study in Austria, etc.
Reading the first row: 0.01 per cent of Canadian students study in Belgium, 0.06 per cent of Canadian students study in France, etc.
* University students only.
Source: OECD Database. See Annex 3 for notes.

Countries of destination

Countries of origin	Austria	Belgium	Canada	Czech Republic	Denmark	Finland	France	Germany	Hungary	Iceland	Ireland	Italy	Japan	Korea	New Zealand	Norway	Portugal	Spain	Switzerland	Turkey	United Kingdom	United States
North America																						
Canada	m	n	a	-1	-1	m	-79	m	-15	-3	-2	6	-247	-74	-5	-1	1	-5	-4	-8	-13	1 065
Mexico	m	m	m	m	m	m	m	m	m	m	m	m	m	m	m	m	m	m	m	m	m	m
United States	-3	-5	-133	-4	-6	m	-20	-29	-5	-4	-1	-16	-309	-233	-4	-11	-4	-33	-9	-47	-11	a
Pacific Area																						
Australia	m	m	m	m	m	m	m	m	m	m	m	m	m	m	m	m	m	m	m	m	m	m
Japan	6	1	112	n	n	m	28	34	m	n	1	2	a	-445	4	1	n	n	2	-1	63	1 126
Korea	17	2	59	n	n	m	72	213	n	n	n	15	784	a	n	23	-2	4	1	n	35	1 495
New Zealand	2	n	52	n	n	m	5	-38	n	n	2	2	-100	n	a	2	-2	1	-1	-1	77	375
European Union																						
Austria	a	-12	-3	-42	-18	m	43	637	-235	-4	-13	-2 425	-103	-162	-1	-18	-13	93	116	-533	106	171
Belgium	8	a	2	-5	-12	m	-1 010	98	-18	-2	-7	-1 201	-9	-10	n	-2	-136	-258	34	-247	336	195
Denmark	25	25	14	1	a	m	182	98	-14	-216	3	-5	3	n	n	-48	-9	79	15	-98	400	466
Finland	-5	m	x	x	m	a	a	m	m	m	m	a	m	m	m	m	m	a	m	m	m	140
France	-69	-16	12	-37	-15	m	a	26	-16	-3	-12	-135	-52	-77	m	-13	-143	-18	50	-84	228	140
Germany	m	m	m	m	m	m	-25	a	-46	-12	-4	-214	-62	-220	3	-39	-52	-83	130	-1 048	278	189
Greece	m	m	m	m	m	m	m	m	m	m	m	-52	m	m	m	m	m	63	m	m	m	m
Ireland	26	21	35	2	-4	m	206	79	-5	-1	a	a	-25	-2	-3	2	-5	88	41	1	6 396	82
Italy	317	236	-6	n	1	m	156	257	-4	-1	4	a	-5	-18	n	-1	2	m	21	x	152	124
Luxembourg	m	m	m	m	m	m	m	m	m	m	m	m	m	m	m	m	m	m	m	m	m	m
Netherlands	10	159	m	m	m	m	m	375	m	n	m	m	m	1	1	7	a	114	51	n	m	m
Portugal	-14	60	-5	1	5	m	983	m	-1	n	2	-9	6	-5	1	-3	a	a	51	a	343	177
Spain	m	m	6	n	-9	a	24	117	-1	n	m	-103	-1	a	a	m	-22	a	29	n	199	311
Sweden	-14	m	m	m	m	m	m	m	m	m	m	m	m	m	m	m	m	m	m	n	m	m
United Kingdom	-14	-65	12	-3	-37	m	-260	-330	-12	-6	-428	-150	-135	-43	-7	-89	-57	-167	-22	-57	a	85
Other OECD countries																						
Czech Republic	55	9	10	a	-1	m	x	443	7	n	-1	42	-1	9	n	-1	-2	-2	36	10	27	358
Hungary	323	38	25	-8	14	m	189	577	a	-3	4	42	10	n	n	-45	2	11	63	-26	128	407
Iceland	122	95	664	n	4 970	m	867	3 629	68	a	14	284	81	n	n	2 180	a	54	54	95	1 544	7 434
Norway	24	5	8	1	47	m	151	484	44	a	-1	7	-14	-296	-2	a	-13	29	39	-65	934	871
Poland	m	m	m	m	m	-38	m	m	-73	-93	-18	7	-48	-20	-2	-45	-103	-294	a	-65	269	m
Switzerland	-183	-81	51	-44	-18	m	-701	-1 893	4	-3	x	-494	m	m	1	-45	-103	21	a	-165	269	846
Turkey	106	74	12	-1	14	m	147	1 925	m	-1	x	-2	3	1	n	10	n	n	21	a	a	570

The table shows the number of tertiary students from country A (country of origin) studying in country B (destination, country of study) minus the number of students from country B studying in country A. A negative figure indicates a net-inflow of students from country B and a positive number indicates a net-outflow from country A.

Example: Reading the third row: The United States receives more students from any OECD country than it sends students to this country. The difference between inflow and outflow of tertiary students from Austria amounts to 3 students for every 100 000 tertiary students in the United States.

Reading the eighth row, last column: Austria sends more students to the United States than it receives. The difference amounts to 171 students for every 100 000 tertiary students in Austria.

Source: OECD Database. See Annex 3 for notes.

Table C6.4 **Exchange of students within the OECD-countries as a percentage of the total enrolment.**
Foreign students enrolled as a percentage of all students. Foreign graduates as a percentage of all graduates. Tertiary education (1995)

	Exchange of students within OECD-countries[1]			Foreign enrolment				Foreign Graduates
	All levels of tertiary education			All levels of tertiary education			First University degree (ISCED6)	First University degree (ISCED6)
	Students from other OECD-Countries relative to tertiary enrolment	Students studying in other OECD-Countries relative to tertiary enrolment	Net outflow of foreign students relative to tertiary enrolment	M + W	% Men	% Women	M + W	M + W
North America								
Canada	0.9	1.5	0.6	3.1	55.9	44.1	2.1	2.7
Mexico	m	0.9	m	m	m	m	m	m
United States	1.1	0.2	-0.9	3.2	m	m	m	m
Pacific Area								
Australia	m	0.5	m	9.0	52.6	47.4	12.5	13.3
Japan	0.5	1.4	0.9	1.4	59.9	40.1	1.3	m
Korea	n	2.8	2.7	0.1	57.0	43.0	0.1	m
New Zealand	0.5	0.8	0.3	3.6	52.5	47.5	3.9	4.2
European Union								
Austria	6.6	4.1	-2.5	10.8	55.0	45.0	11.2	m
Belgium	4.1	1.8	-2.3	9.9	m	m	m	m
Denmark	1.7	2.6	0.9	4.9	48.9	51.1	4.2	m
Finland	0.5	1.8	1.3	m	m	m	m	m
France	1.6	1.7	0.1	7.8	m	m	x	m
Germany	3.3	1.9	-1.4	7.2	57.4	42.6	7.6	m
Greece	m	12.4	m	m	m	m	m	m
Ireland	3.4	10.2	6.8	4.3	49.0	51.0	m	m
Italy	0.3	1.7	1.3	1.3	52.1	40.4	1.3	m
Luxembourg	m	41.2	m	m	m	m	m	m
Netherlands	m	2.4	m	m	m	m	m	m
Portugal	0.5	2.7	2.2	2.0	48.3	51.7	2.1	m
Spain	0.8	1.4	0.6	1.4	50.3	49.7	1.5	m
Sweden	m	3.5	m	m	m	m	m	m
United Kingdom	3.2	1.3	-1.8	8.7	57.6	42.4	6.9	m
Other OECD countries								
Czech Republic	0.1	1.1	1.0	1.8	68.5	31.5	2.0	0.9
Hungary	0.6	2.4	1.8	3.8	m	m	7.3	3.7
Iceland	1.5	23.8	22.3	2.2	30.6	69.4	2.2	m
Norway	2.1	4.2	2.1	6.5	51.4	48.6	5.4	4.2
Poland	m	1.3	m	m	m	m	m	m
Switzerland	8.0	5.0	-3.1	11.8	72.5	27.5	19.7	m
Turkey	n	3.0	3.0	1.3	m	m	1.8	m
Country mean	~	~	~	4.8	54.1	45.5	5.2	~
Other non-OECD countries								
Russian Federation	m	0.2	m	m	m	m	m	m

Example: Reading the first column: Foreign tertiary students from other OECD countries (which report foreign students) represent 8 per cent of all tertiary students in Switzerland.
Reading the second column: 5 per cent of all Swiss tertiary students study in other OECD countries (which report foreign students).
Column 3 represents the difference between Column 1 and Column 2.
Reading the seventh column: 19.7 per cent of all students participating in first university degree programmes in Switzerland are foreign students.
1 Only those OECD countries which report the inflow into their system are included in the sum.

Countries of destination

Countries of origin	Austria	Australia	Belgium	Canada	Czech Republic	Denmark	Finland	France	Germany	Hungary	Iceland	Ireland	Italy	Japan	Korea	New Zealand	Norway	Portugal	Spain	Switzerland	Turkey	United Kingdom	United States	Total
North America																								
Canada	58	x	98	a	8	59	28	1 035	463	40	3	57	252	131	47	35	90	171	54	150	11	1 713	22 747	27 250
Mexico	55	x	36	783	2	12	4	605	277	n	3	3	n	98	4	14	15	1	509	53	n	598	9 003	12 075
United States	486	x	213	3 742	13	230	117	2 945	4 512	193	19	809	480	1 164	328	183	616	206	384	376	17	6 243	a	23 276
Pacific Area																								
Australia	34	x	8	290	2	27	9	86	209	2	1	22	115	248	21	317	32	18	33	39	19	674	2 247	4 453
Japan	271	x	55	4 530	n	22	41	1 219	1 599	16	n	45	146	a	350	234	37	1	54	92	7	2 673	45 276	56 668
Korea	380	x	36	1 360	2	m	n	1 601	4 799	n	n	3	323	17 788	a	84	512	n	80	31	n	784	33 599	61 382
New Zealand	3	x	2	120	n	10	2	19	53	n	n	5	4	70	n	a	10	n	2	5	n	238	798	1 341
European Union																								
Austria	a	x	30	51	3	29	13	392	6 686	20	2	16	93	31	2	n	35	5	402	501	9	497	887	9 704
Belgium	58	x	a	106	2	11	7	1 577	1 002	6	n	42	185	22	2	2	25	26	632	239	n	1 505	900	6 349
Denmark	71	x	54	83	1	a	28	389	710	2	33	32	45	27	n	10	663	2	195	70	n	1 003	1 022	4 440
Finland	126	x	32	102	2	58	a	275	1 126	17	5	18	63	25	1	4	175	4	108	70	10	630	924	3 775
France	291	x	5 137	x	x	80	28	a	5 872	12	2	297	575	131	5	10	130	537	2 895	1 649	145	8 936	5 843	32 433
Germany	5 195	x	655	722	42	544	135	5 332	a	503	15	445	1 282	270	51	116	436	204	2 458	4 560	1 056	9 518	8 592	41 220
Greece	369	x	928	198	430	20	12	2 806	8 231	967	n	38	7 046	14	2	12	27	3	177	239	x	10 374	3 699	36 638
Ireland	47	x	67	99	2	2	8	547	541	2	n	a	18	15	n	1	15	3	263	44	n	9 799	934	12 407
Italy	5 767	x	4 421	148	2	54	32	3 372	5 890	5	2	81	a	57	n	1	41	60	1 767	2 211	20	3 107	2 704	29 742
Luxembourg	298	x	1 605	3	n	1	1	1 048	1 193	13	n	10	37	1	n	1	1	11	17	203	2	273	65	4 782
Netherlands	91	x	2 949	153	1	80	16	841	2 564	14	n	43	106	39	n	18	138	21	698	243	74	2 009	1 847	11 945
Portugal	36	x	504	156	4	17	13	3 492	1 330	n	7	10	33	20	2	3	26	a	545	163	3	1 090	739	8 175
Spain	184	x	1 542	142	4	61	13	3 263	4 241	n	7	187	189	44	2	3	54	203	a	890	3	4 983	5 126	21 142
Sweden	178	x	69	232	9	289	229	708	1 079	103	13	53	104	30	6	11	803	8	216	166	6	943	3 432	8 687
United Kingdom	248	x	321	1 938	45	324	58	4 217	3 535	11	6	2 034	392	218	2	111	479	59	1 948	287	142	a	7 786	24 161
Other OECD countries																								
Czech Republic	102	x	18	26	a	n	3	3	835	46	n	n	1	16	n	n	4	1	n	66	18	94	654	1 884
Hungary	570	x	71	82	33	25	53	334	1 485	a	n	8	76	33	n	n	25	4	23	123	5	229	885	4 064
Iceland	11	x	7	52	1	400	21	66	283	2	a	1	23	6	n	n	175	n	7	6	n	120	568	1 758
Norway	77	x	33	104	5	745	28	392	1 274	101	14	13	53	12	n	7	a	4	104	120	1	2 094	2 123	7 304
Poland	531	x	153	133	98	134	46	1 331	4 659	89	3	5	232	43	1	1	220	3	48	235	3	409	1 593	9 969
Switzerland	230	x	119	225	1	44	13	611	1 756	15	2	18	479	21	7	7	53	11	454	a	2	686	1 630	7 378
Turkey	1 255	x	870	151	1	166	21	1 734	22 747	49	n	3	392	37	7	1	113	n	4	247	a	1 183	6 716	35 305
Other non-OECD countries																								
Russian Federation	164	x	65	n	57	12	157	891	2 727	138	1	9	n	122	9	n	26	n	n	196	408	302	4 832	10 116

Table C6.5 **Number of foreign students in OECD-Countries (absolute numbers) (1995)** (continued)

Countries of origin	Countries of destination																							
	Austria	Australia	Belgium	Canada	Czech Republic	Denmark	Finland	France	Germany	Hungary	Iceland	Ireland	Italy	Japan	Korea	New Zealand	Norway	Portugal	Spain	Switzerland	Turkey	United Kingdom	United States	Total
Total: OECD and non-OECD countries																								
Africa	1 014	x	10 927	8 096	445	155	317	70 788	13 292	343	1	200	2 495	442	30	96	1 093	3 057	2 215	1 303	648	8 446	20 724	146 127
Asia	4 738	x	2 911	28 452	703	1 344	789	18 624	58 945	1 300	6	663	4 098	49 277	914	3 262	3 536	36	871	1 418	8 096	43 158	292 325	525 466
Europe	18 151	x	19 237	8 387	1 576	3 176	1 195	35 591	69 665	4 477	123	3 383	14 797	1 329	91	306	3 948	1 174	13 415	13 340	3 033	59 569	64 485	340 448
North America	662	x	453	6 811	57	311	160	5 256	5 929	243	25	882	815	1 442	379	242	761	382	1 539	650	30	9 568	49 603	86 200
Oceania	38	x	10	446	2	37	11	129	279	2	1	38	467	345	21	1 379	43	18	42	46	19	1 014	4 327	8 714
South America	319	x	760	1 371	41	95	40	3 826	3 851	29	3	7	1 002	663	121	37	313	1 353	3 275	746	2	1 439	21 030	40 323
Not specified	253	87 247	668	1 149	12	3 195	54	31 136	2 575	n	n	4	69	13	427	561	1 464	120	46	14	2 891	33 783	105	165 786
All countries	25 175	87 247	34 966	54 712	2 836	8 313	2 566	165 350	154 536	6 394	159	5 177	23 743	53 511	1 983	5 883	11 158	6 140	21 403	17 517	14 719	156 977	452 599	1 313 064

Example: Reading column-wise: In Austria, there are 58 Canadian students, 55 Mexican students, 486 students from the United States, etc.
Reading row-wise: 58 Canadian tertiary students study in Austria, 98 in Belgium, 8 in the Czech Republic, etc.
Source: OECD Database. See Annex 3 for notes.

Indicator C7: # Patterns of participation in continuing education and training for the adult labour force

Policy context

This indicator shows the percentage of employed and nemployed persons who have participated in job-related or career-related continuing education and training.

Increases in access and quality in initial education can only result in increases in the average skill level of the labour force in the very long run. As a skilled labour force is a prerequisite for success in today's global economy, the education and training of current workers is likely to be the most effective means of maintaining and upgrading the skills of the current labour force. Continuing education and training may also be an effective mechanism for combating unemployment, as potential workers can develop skills that make them more attractive to employers. In the face of changing technologies, work methodologies and markets, policy-makers in many countries are encouraging enterprises to invest more in training, as well as promoting more general work-related training and informal learning by adults.

also provides an indication of e average number of courses aken and average amount of time spent on job-related education over a 12-month period.

Disparities in skills are also a potential source of earnings inequality. Governments trying to narrow disparities in wealth may be interested in increasing access to continuing education and training. Continuing education and training also allows individuals an opportunity to repair and/or complement previously received education and training and allows employers to maintain a productive work force.

The percentage of workers participating in job-related continuing education and training and the extent of their training is one indicator of the extent of the investment in increasing the skills of the employed workforce.

Evidence and explanations

Patterns of participation in continuing education and training

Over a 12-month period, veen 28 and 45 per cent of rkers in 6 OECD countries participated in job-related continuing education and training (CET).

For the six OECD countries for which data are available, participation rates in job-related continuing education and training (CET) among employed adults over a 12-month period ranged from 28 per cent in Canada to 45 per cent in Finland (see Table C7.1a). Participation rates in Germany, Switzerland and the United States were between 33 and around 35 per cent. In Sweden, participation rates were higher (42 per cent), even though participation was measured over a 6-month period.

As would be expected, participation rates were much lower in countries measuring the participation in CET over a 4-week period. The participation rate was, however, as high as 15 per cent in Denmark over that short period and 12 per cent in the United Kingdom.

◆   Chart C7.1.   ***Percentage of the employed population 25 to 64 years of age who have participated in job-related or career-related continuing education and training over a 12-month period, by highest level of educational attainmen***

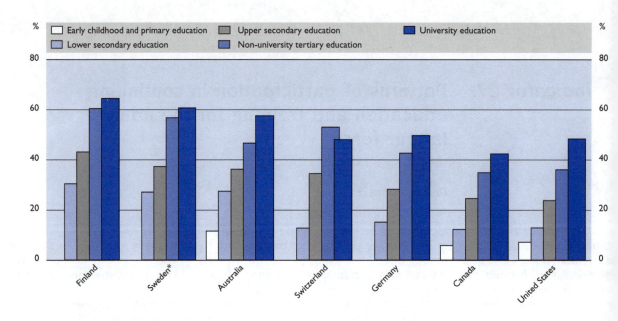

*The reference period for Sweden is 6 months.
Source: OECD.

Employed adults are generally more likely than unemployed adults to participate in job-related or career-related CET.

The degree of participation in job-related or career-related CET is in gen smaller among the unemployed than among the employed (see Table C7. In the United States the rate was more than twice as high for employed ad as for unemployed adults. Only in Belgium and Denmark were participa rates slightly higher for the unemployed. Caution must, however, be e cised when interpreting the data for the unemployed, as the participa rates for unemployed adults are subject to greater sampling error becaus small sample sizes.

Participation in job-related CET is closely linked to the previous level of education.

Participation rates in job-related or career-related continuing education training rise with the level of educational attainment of labour force par pants. Those with the highest formal qualifications – whether they employed or not – are most likely to receive such training. In all countries which data are available, those with university degrees are at least twice likely (and often much more) to participate in job-related training as th with only primary or lower secondary qualifications. Of the countries repor data with a 12-month reference period, each additional level of educa adds, on average, about 10 per cent to the proportion who receive trair However, there are a few exceptions to this general observation Switzerland, those who have attained university-level education are slig less likely to receive training than those who have obtained a non-unive tertiary qualification.

Skill differences that result from different levels of initial education are amplified by subsequent training decisions by employers and employ Current patterns of participation in job-related or career-related contin education and training may therefore detract from rather than enhance e ings equality.

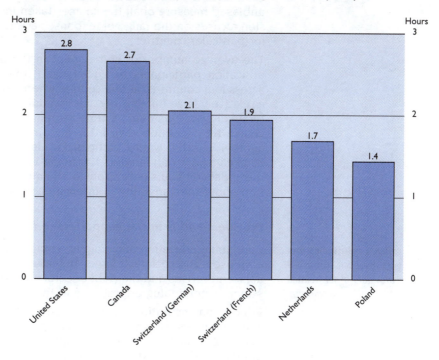

◆ Chart C7.2. *Average number of adult education courses taken over a 12-month period by adults aged 16 to 65 (1994)*

Full-time students younger than 26 excluded.
Source: International Adult Literacy Survey.

CET participation rates are generally similar for men and women.

Intensity of participation should also be considered when participation in adult education is compared across countries.

In most countries, CET participation rates are similar for men and women, both in general and at each level of education. There are a few exceptions, however. Among employed university graduates in Sweden and the United States, women are more likely than men to participate in CET (see Table C7.1a).

The impact of adult education is not only determined by the incidence of participation, but also by the intensity of participation. Participation in itself is a rather crude measure, because it can relate either to a single course or several courses and the duration of participation can range from a one-day seminar to a one-year part-time university course. Chart C7.2 shows the average number of courses, both those that are job-related or career-related and those that are for personal interest, taken by adult education participants aged 16 to 65 years in Canada, the Netherlands, Poland, Switzerland and the United States. These data are from the 1994 International Adult Literacy Survey (IALS) and exclude full-time students aged 16 to 25.

There are significant differences in the average number of courses taken in the five countries. Respondents in Canada and the United States took more courses (on average 2.7 and 2.8, respectively) than those in the other three countries participating in the survey. The smallest number of courses were taken in Poland (1.4).

While the number of courses taken is one component of the degree of involvement in adult education and training, the typical duration of a course is a second component. The analysis that follows is based on the characteristics of the first course mentioned by participants in adult education and training in IALS. The characteristics of the first course are utilised as an indicator of the variability in duration, providers, sources of financial support and modes of participation in adult education and job-related training acro countries. As the first course mentioned by IALS respondents may not be unbiased measure of all the courses taken in a particular country, the disc sion focuses on the range of responses across countries and not on estima for particular countries.

The average number of hours spent in the first course mentioned by ad education participants in IALS ranged from about 120 hours to 240 ho across four countries. In one country where IALS respondents indicated tak a relatively large number of courses, adult education participants also sper relatively large amount of time (around 240 hours, on average) in the f course they mentioned in IALS. In contrast, adult education participants another country, where participants also took a relatively large number courses, spent only around 120 hours in their first course mentioned. Wh these data on hours only apply to a single course, they provide some inforn tion about the variability in intensity across countries.

Providers and financial supporters of job-related training

Educational institutions and employers are each important providers of job-related training.

Continuing education and training entails a payoff to individuals, sponsor employers and society at large. An important policy issue is what role indiv uals, enterprises and the public sector each should play in supporting par pation in continuing education and training.

Educational institutions, including universities and further education colleg and employers (*i.e.* the "parent" company), are the primary providers of j related education and training programmes in four countries that participa in IALS. These providers each accounted for around a quarter or more of number of providers listed by IALS respondents for the first adult educat activity mentioned in their interview (each respondent was allowed to in cate multiple providers). Commercial providers are also involved in the pr sion of job-related training.

Employers are an important financial supporter of career or job-related training.

Financial support – for example from employers or governments – can k major stimulus for participation in career or job-related training. In four cc tries that participated in IALS, employers were an important financial s porter of this type of training, followed by financing directly by the particip or their family. However, a surprisingly high amount of job-related trair attracts no financial support from employers. In two countries participatin IALS, approximately 10 per cent of all adults participated in some form of related training over the previous 12 months without any financial sup from their employers.

Traditional media, such as classroom instruction and reading materials, remain an important component of career or job-related training.

As technology advances, it is possible both to standardise instruction an reduce costs by making use of educational software, radio or televi broadcasting, and audio or video cassettes. Although these types of m are being utilised to some degree in four countries participating in IALS, so-called "traditional" media of classroom instruction and reading mate are in each country by far the most frequently indicated media in the course mentioned. On-the-job training and audio/video cassettes, tape disks follow with similar percentages. A "modern" medium such as ed tional software is, in general, in a modest fifth position in the distributic responses.

Reasons for non-participation in adult education and training

In general, situational rather than institutional barriers are given as reasons for non-participation in desired career or job-related training.

Policy-makers interested in increasing participation in adult education training need to understand the barriers that current non-participants ceive to exist. In IALS, respondents were asked if there was any trainir education that they wanted to take for career or job-related reasons, bu not. Each respondent was allowed to give multiple reasons. The reasor not taking this training, and the distribution of all responses, can be grouped into two broad categories:

- situational barriers (those arising from one's situation in life – *e.g.* lack of time because of work, family responsibilities, etc.); and
- institutional barriers (practices and procedures that hinder participation – *e.g.* fees, lack of evening courses, entrance requirements, range of courses, etc.).

In general, situational barriers, rather than institutional barriers, are given as reasons for not participating in desired training. Among situational barriers, a general lack of time was given most often as a reason for not taking training they wanted to take. It was less common to refer to a specific situation such as being "too busy at work" or "family responsibilities". It was relatively uncommon for "lack of employer support" to be offered as a reason for not taking training that they wanted to take.

Among institutional barriers, financial reasons (too expensive/no money) was by far the most prevalent. Health and language problems, which are regarded dispositional barriers, were seldom brought up.

It is difficult to interpret the implications of these findings for increasing participation in adult education and training. Lack of time, which appears as the dominant barrier, is a vague concept. Time is not an endless resource and people have to make choices regarding how they want to spend their spare time. For some people, however, mentioning "lack of time" may be a statement of the value they ascribe to current adult education and training provision, as well as the expected outcome of engaging in such a learning activity.

Definitions

Data in Tables C7.1a and b are derived from National Labour Force Surveys (for details see Annex 3).

Continuing education and training for adults refers, in principle, to all job-related and career-related education and training organised, financed or sponsored by authorities, provided by employers or self-financed. The *job-related* and *career-*related continuing education and training captured in Table C7.1 refers to all organised, systematic education and training activities in which people take part in order to obtain knowledge and/or learn new skills for a current or a future job, to increase earnings, improve job and/or career opportunities in current or other fields, and generally to improve their opportunities for advancement and promotion. Continuing education and training for adults does not include military training or full-time studies at the tertiary level as defined by ISCED.

Data in Chart C7.2 and the discussion that follows are based on the International Adult Literacy Survey (IALS), which was undertaken by Statistics Canada and OECD at the end of 1994.

Chart C7.2 shows the average number of courses taken by adult education participants over a 12-month period by adults aged 16 to 65 in the 1994 International Adult Literacy Survey (IALS) in the preceding year, where full-time students younger than 26 are excluded.

The question which defines adult education in IALS is the following: during the past 12 months, did you receive any training or education including courses, private lessons, correspondence courses, workshops, on-the-job training, apprenticeship training, arts, crafts, recreation courses or any other training or education? What was the main reason you took this training or education: was it for career or job-related purposes, personal interest, or other? The characteristics of the first course mentioned by respondents were used in the discussion in this indicator. For the discussion on providers, financial contributors and media of instruction, the responses for the first adult education course mentioned were included if the main reason for taking the training or education was for career or job-related purposes. (*i.e.* courses taken for personal interest or other reasons were excluded). As questions

relating to the provider, financial source, and medium of instruction allow
for multiple responses, the responses (not the participants) were used as t
units of analysis in these comparisons. This was also the case for the discu
sion of reasons for non-participation, where respondents were allowed
choose multiple reasons for not participating in desired education or trainir

See Annex 3 for details on the questions that were asked as part of t
International Adult Literacy Survey.

Table C7.1a   **Percentage of the employed population 25 to 64 years of age that participated in job-related or career-related continuing education and training**

	Year	Gender	Early childhood and primary education	Lower secondary education	Upper secondary education	Non-university tertiary	University education	All levels of education
During the 12-month period preceding the survey								
Australia	1995	M+W	12	28	36	47	58	38
		Men	17	28	36	46	58	38
		Women	5	28	38	49	58	38
Canada	1993	M+W	6	12	25	35	43	28
		Men	6	13	22	36	40	27
		Women	5	11	28	34	47	30
Finland	1995	M+W	m	31	44	61	65	45
		Men	m	30	43	63	65	45
		Women	m	31	44	59	63	45
Germany	1994	M+W	m	15	28	43	50	33
		Men	m	m	29	44	50	35
		Women	m	14	28	40	50	31
Switzerland	1996	M+W	x	13	35	53	48	35
		Men	x	12	35	54	49	38
		Women	x	13	34	51	46	31
United States	1995	M+W	7	13	24	36	49	34
		Men	8	11	21	34	45	31
		Women	6	15	27	38	54	36
During the 6-month period preceding the survey								
Sweden	1996	M+W	m	27	37	57	61	42
		Men	m	28	35	56	56	39
		Women	m	27	40	58	67	44
During the 4-week period preceding the survey								
Austria	1995	M+W	m	3	8	13	14	8
		Men	m	4	9	14	13	8
		Women	m	2	7	13	15	7
Belgium	1994	M+W	1	1	2	4	6	3
		Men	1	1	3	5	6	3
		Women	0.5	1	2	3	6	2
Denmark	1995	M+W	x	5	14	18	24	15
		Men	x	4	12	15	22	13
		Women	x	6	17	21	26	17
Ireland	1994	M+W	1	2	5	7	8	4
		Men	1	2	4	6	8	3
		Women	1	3	6	8	9	6
Italy	1995	M+W	0.3	0.5	2	m	3	1
		Men	0.3	1	2	m	3	1
		Women	0.1	0.4	3	m	3	1
Luxembourg	1996	M+W	(n)	1	2	m	2	1
		Men	m	1	2	m	3	1
		Women	(1)	2	(1)	m	(1)	1
Spain	1995	M+W	0.4	1	7	4	9	3
		Men	0.3	1	6	3	7	2
		Women	1	2	8	6	11	5
United Kingdom	1995	M+W	m	4	10	22	23	12
		Men	m	3	9	19	22	11
		Women	m	4	12	25	24	13

Estimates on small samples are in brackets.
Source: OECD Database. See Annex 3 for notes.

Table C7.1b **Percentage of the unemployed population 25 to 64 years of age that participated in job-related or career-related continuing education and training**

	Year	Early childhood and primary education	Lower secondary education	Upper secondary education	Non-university tertiary	University education	All levels of education
During the 12-month period preceding the survey							
Australia	1995	8	20	23	34	51	24
Canada	1993	6	6	15	24	30	16
Germany	1995	28	13	21	23	24	20
Switzerland	1996	x	m	22	m	m	20
United States	1995	6	10	11	17	24	14
During the 4-week period preceding the survey							
Belgium	1994	m	m	m	m	m	5
Denmark	1995	m	15	15	25	15	16
Italy	1995	m	1	2	m	4	1
Ireland	1995	0.4	1	4	8	9	2
Luxembourg	1995	m	(1)	(3)	m	m	(1)
United Kingdom	1995	m	3	7	18	16	7

Source: OECD Database. See Annex 3 for notes.

Chapter D

THE LEARNING ENVIRONMENT
AND THE ORGANISATION OF SCHOOLS

The indicators in the preceding chapters have focused on financial and human resources devoted to education as well as on participation in and access to education. Some of these indicators, such as Indicator on expenditure per student or Indicator B8 on student/teaching staff ratios, are sometimes also used as a proxy for the quality of education.

But what can be said directly about the quality and efficiency of schools? Are schools providing a safe and supportive environment that allows students to devote their energies to learning? Are schools effectively organised and managed? Does the way in which instruction is organised and delivered reflect national goals and intentions and live up to best practices? Are schools attracting qualified people with enthusiasm, creativity and commitment into teaching and supporting them with competitive salaries and sustained professional development?

Because of the diverse and complex nature of activities within schools, many of these aspects are not as easily captured as enrolments or expenditure. It is particularly difficult to monitor the work of teachers, since most of it takes place behind closed doors, outputs are intangible and often visible only over the long term, and measurement is highly problematic. In addition, teachers' contracts are long-term and difficult to modify on an individual basis.

However, a certain number of national, school and classroom-level characteristics can be assessed, using data reported by those involved in the schooling process or data drawn from policy statements and guidelines. At the national level, such characteristics may include the distribution of decision-making authority across administrative levels or the salaries and working conditions of teachers, including the teaching load and the hours of work. At the school level, aspects such as the time allocated to different parts of the curriculum, the ways in which student progress is monitored, and the ways in which students are allocated to classes or groups, can be assessed.

Indicators D1, D3, D4 and D6 look at important aspects of teachers' working conditions. Ongoing debates about teachers' salaries, professional status and instructional time spark interest in the amount of time teachers spend working, the number of classes they teach per day, and the number of students in each class.

Indicator D1 compares teachers' salaries and pay scales. Observed differences in this indicator between countries with comparable standards of economic development raise questions about recruitment and retention policy, and the status of the teaching profession.

A teacher's working day does not end when classes are over. Time for school-related activities outside the formal school day can contribute substantially to the workload of teachers. **Indicator D3** shows the average number of hours 8th-grade mathematics teachers report spending on various school-related activities outside the formal school day during the school week. **Indicators D4 and D6** look at class sizes, student/teaching staff ratios and in-school management.

Indicator D2 describes the demographic composition and the years of teaching experience of mathematics teachers at the 8th-grade level. Teacher demography is becoming a major concern in many OECD countries, particularly in the context of recent and future trends in student numbers (see Indicator A1). The recruitment of new teachers will therefore be an important issue for many OECD countries over the coming decade, particularly in mathematics and the sciences. With seniority as an important criterion in teacher pay scales, the age distribution of teachers also has a significant impact on educational budgets. On the other hand, years of teaching experience can be considered one aspect of the quality of teaching.

Indicator D5 looks at what happens inside the classroom. It shows the use of different forms classroom organisation in 8th-grade mathematics classes. Although classroom organisation is to a large exte the responsibility of individual teachers, school management and higher administrative decisions can bo directly and indirectly influence it.

Finally, **Indicator D7** takes a student's perspective and looks at the amount of time 8th-grade studen spend after school studying or doing homework in mathematics, science or other school subjects. Homewc is an important tool that teachers use to help students review and practice what they have learned, to tea children to work independently and to encourage children to develop good habits and attitudes, such self-discipline and responsibility.

*

*   *

Indicator D1 draws on the 1997 OECD-INES survey on teachers and curriculum and refers to the sch year 1994/95.

Indicators D2 to D5 and D7 draw on the Third International Mathematics and Science Study (IEA/TIMS an international comparison of performance in mathematics and science tests that was conducted during t school year 1994/95 by the International Association for the Evaluation of Educational Achievement (IEA). IE TIMSS administered a background questionnaire to teachers to gather information on, among other thin their backgrounds, how they spend their teaching-related time (both in and out of class) and the instructio approaches they use in their classrooms. Because the sampling for the questionnaires was based participating students, the responses to the mathematics teachers' questionnaire do not necessar represent all of the 8th-grade mathematics teachers in each country. Rather, they represent teachers of t representative samples of students assessed in the study. It is important to note that in the indicat related to the Third International Mathematics and Science Study, the student is always the unit of analy: even when information from the teachers' questionnaires is being reported, which makes it possible describe the instruction received by representative samples of students.

Data for Indicator D6 are based on the OECD-INES survey on primary schools conducted in the sch year 1995/96. Figures on teaching hours per year are taken from the 1996 edition of *Education at a Glance* refer to the school year 1993/94. They are based on the 1995 OECD-INES survey on teachers and curriculum.

Indicator D1:

Statutory salaries of teachers in public primary and secondary schools

Policy context

This indicator shows the starting, mid-career and maximum statutory salaries of teachers in public primary and secondary education (in equivalent US dollars based on PPP's).

Teachers are the final and most important link in the delivery of education and are the interface through which the objectives of education systems are mediated. Ensuring that there will be enough skilled teachers to educate all children is an important policy concern in all OECD countries. Key determinants of the supply of teachers are the salaries and working conditions of teachers and the costs incurred by individuals in becoming teachers, relative to salaries and costs for other occupations. Incentives such as the creation of new career paths, the institution of merit pay schemes and the establishment of more attractive salary structures also affect the appeal of the teaching profession.

While salary is one of the malleable rewards of the teaching profession, the pressure to improve the quality of education and to expand access to education is under increasing fiscal constraints. In this context, the remuneration of teachers represents the most important component of educational spending (see Indicator B5).

Evidence and explanations

Statutory teachers' salaries differ widely: lower secondary starting salaries range from US$5 400 to more than US$37 000.

Annual statutory starting salaries of public school teachers at the primary level range from below US$15 000 in the Czech Republic, Greece, New Zealand and Sweden to above US$26 000 in Germany and Switzerland. The pattern at the lower and upper secondary level is similar although levels of lower secondary salaries are, on average, about US$1 000 per year higher than at the primary level. The size of the difference ranges from 0 to US$5 540, with differences of over US$2 000 in five countries. The level of teachers' salaries in general upper secondary education is higher than that in vocational upper secondary education in 6 countries: the size of the difference ranges in all reporting countries from 0 to US$5 330.

Salaries of teachers after 15 years of experience are generally above per capita GDP in both primary and secondary education.

Comparing teachers' salaries with per capita GDP provides some indication of the economic status of the teaching profession in a country. In Korea and Spain the starting salary of primary and secondary teachers is more than 1.7 times the per capita GDP, which suggests that the teaching profession in those countries has a comparatively high standing. Starting salaries are lowest relative to per capita GDP in the Czech Republic and Norway. After 15 years of experience, statutory salaries are above per capita GDP in most countries. Only in the Czech Republic and Norway do maximum salaries of teachers remain below per capita GDP, except for Norway at the general upper

◆ Chart D1.1. *Annual statutory teachers' salaries in public institutions at the primary and upper secondary levels (general and vocational programmes) (1995)*

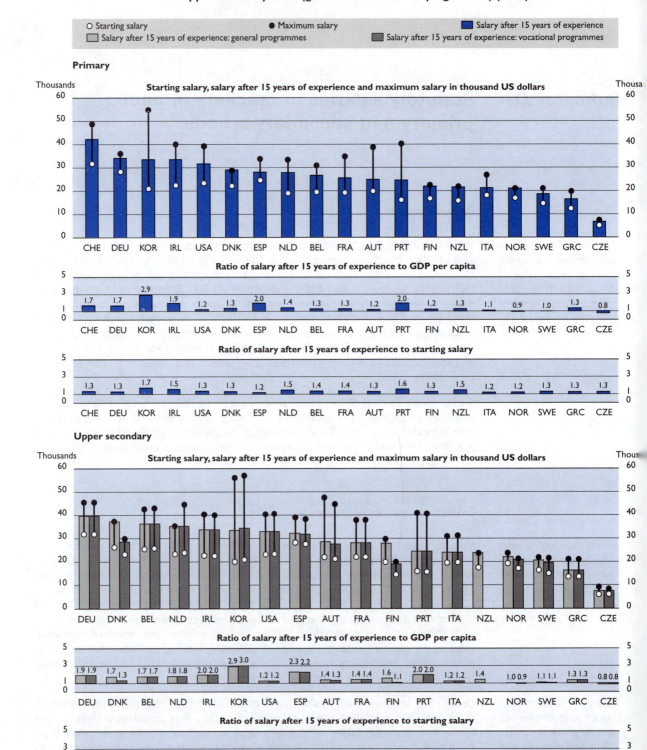

Countries are ranked in descending order of salary after 15 years of experience.
Source: OECD.

secondary level. In Norway, however, most starting teachers have more than the minimum required level of training and are therefore paid higher than the minimum statutory salary.

In most countries teachers are well paid relative to average earnings.

Chart D1.2 compares the statutory salaries of primary and upper secondary teachers with the 10th, 50th and 90th percentile of the overall distribution of gross annual earnings of full-time wage and salary workers for selected countries. Because data on average earnings are different in kind from data on statutory salaries, comparisons should be made with caution. Nevertheless, average earnings can provide a useful benchmark for teachers' salaries. While primary teachers in Austria, Finland, France, the Netherlands, Switzerland and the United States fare relatively well when compared with other full-time wage and salary workers, teachers in Sweden are paid comparatively low compensation. The general pattern is similar at the secondary level but, overall, teachers at this level appear to have more competitive salaries. Note, however, that in countries where levels of education are lower, teachers are often among the most educated workers and are therefore being compared with persons with lower average formal qualifications. Conversely, in countries with more highly-educated workers, teachers tend to fare worse. In interpreting this indicator, other aspects of working conditions of teachers need to be taken into account, such as the teaching load and the total working time of teachers compared with that of other professions.

Primary teachers in Austria, Finland, France, the Netherlands, Switzerland and the United States fare relatively well when compared with other full-time wage and salary workers, but teachers in Sweden are paid comparatively low compensation.

◆ Chart D1.2. **Level of teachers' salaries after 15 years of experience and gross average earnings of full-time employees (1995)**

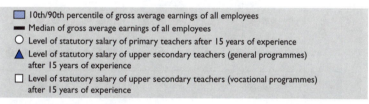

- 10th/90th percentile of gross average earnings of all employees
- Median of gross average earnings of all employees
- ○ Level of statutory salary of primary teachers after 15 years of experience
- ▲ Level of statutory salary of upper secondary teachers (general programmes) after 15 years of experience
- □ Level of statutory salary of upper secondary teachers (vocational programmes) after 15 years of experience

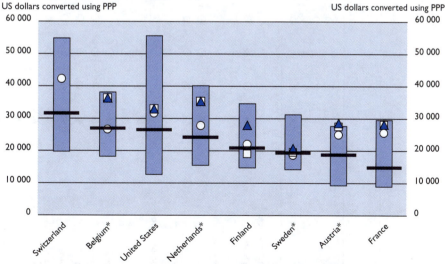

* 10th/90th percentile of gross average earnings of all employees are for 1994.
Countries are ranked in descending order of the median of gross average earnings of all employees.
Source: OECD.

◆ Chart D1.3. **Criteria applied for salary increments in teachers' salaries in public institutions (1995)**

Legend: ○ Never ◐ Sometimes ● Always

	Primary education					Lower secondary education					Upper secondary education, general					Upper secondary education, vocational				
	Seniority	Performance	Training	Qualifications	Other	Seniority	Performance	Training	Qualifications	Other	Seniority	Performance	Training	Qualifications	Other	Seniority	Performance	Training	Qualifications	Other
North America																				
United States	●	○	◐	●	○	●	○	◐	●	○	●	○	◐	●	○	●	○	◐	●	○
Pacific Area																				
Korea	●	◐	○	◐	○	●	◐	○	◐	○	●	◐	○	◐	○	●	◐	○	◐	○
New Zealand	○	●	○	●	○	○	●	○	●	●	○	○	●	●	●	○	○	●	●	●
European Union																				
Austria	●	◐	◐	○	○	●	◐	◐	◐	○	●	◐	◐	○	○	●	◐	◐	○	○
Belgium	●	○	○	○	○	●	◐	○	◐	○	●	◐	○	◐	○	●	○	◐	◐	○
Denmark	●	○	○	○	◐	●	○	○	○	○	●	◐	○	○	○	●	○	○	○	○
Finland	●	○	◐	◐	●	●	◐	◐	○	●	●	●	◐	◐	○	●	●	○	○	●
France	●	●	○	●	●	●	●	◐	●	●	●	●	○	◐	○	●	◐	◐	●	○
Germany	●	◐	◐	●	○	●	○	○	○	○	●	◐	○	○	○	●	◐	◐	○	○
Greece	●	○	○	○	○	●	○	○	○	○	●	○	○	○	○	●	○	○	○	○
Ireland	●	○	◐	○	○	●	○	○	●	○	●	○	○	●	○	●	○	○	○	○
Italy	●	○	○	○	○	●	○	○	○	○	●	○	○	○	○	●	○	○	○	○
Netherlands	●	○	●	○	●	●	○	●	○	●	●	○	●	○	●	●	○	●	○	●
Portugal	●	●	●	○	●	●	○	◐	○	●	●	○	◐	◐	●	●	◐	●	○	●
Spain	●	○	○	○	○	●	○	○	○	○	●	○	○	○	○	●	○	○	○	○
Sweden	●	○	○	○	○	●	○	○	○	○	●	○	○	○	○	●	○	○	○	○
Other OECD countries																				
Czech Republic	●	◐	○	◐	●	●	◐	○	◐	●	●	◐	○	◐	●	●	◐	○	◐	●
Norway	●	○	○	●	○	●	○	○	●	○	●	○	○	●	○	●	○	○	●	○
Switzerland	●	○	○	○	○	●	○	○	○	○	●	○	○	○	○	●	○	○	○	○

y scales differ widely but in many countries statutory laries increase by one-third to one-half over a period of 15 years of service.

Differences between minimum and maximum salaries of primary and lower secondary teachers are largest in Korea and Portugal and smallest in Norway. At the upper secondary level the differences are largest in Korea and Portugal and smallest in Norway and Sweden.

Whereas an upper secondary teacher in Germany, Norway or Spain can expect to earn 1.2 times his or her starting salary after 15 years of service, in Korea the salary level will have almost doubled over this period. In Denmark, Norway and New Zealand teachers have almost reached their maximum salary after 15 years of experience.

e number of years taken to progress from minimum to imum salary varies from 8 to over 40 years.

The number of years it takes teachers to progress from their minimum to their maximum salary varies from 8 to over 40 years, the average being 27 years for primary and 26/28 years for secondary education. In Italy, Korea and Spain (primary and lower secondary levels only) it takes 40, 41 and 42 years respectively for teachers to attain their maximum salary.

In some countries teachers may receive additional bonuses in addition to their gross salaries. Substantial additional bonuses are paid in the Czech Republic, Finland and the United States (about 20 per cent).

Seniority is a universal erion for salary increments. Performance, training and lifications are other criteria that some countries apply.

Almost all countries report "seniority" as a criterion that is universally applied for salary increments (see Chart D1.3). In France, New Zealand and in Portugal at the primary level, "performance" is a second criterion. "In-service training" (*e.g.* in Spain) and "qualifications" (*e.g.* in Greece and the United States) are also criteria for salary increments.

While teachers are usually aid according to a uniform scale, the financial ractiveness of teaching will ry according to the field of specialisation.

The supply of teachers is influenced not only by salaries and working conditions, but also by the quality of alternative career opportunities available to potential teachers. One way to evaluate teachers' salaries and working conditions is to see how they compare with the alternatives available to potential teachers. In most countries, teachers are paid according to a uniform scale in which salaries depend on the amount of formal education and the number of years of teaching experience but not, for example, on the field of subject specialisation. Since tertiary graduates trained in certain fields such as the sciences can earn more in business and industry than graduates from the liberal arts, the financial attractiveness of teaching will vary according to the field.

A decomposition of teachers' salaries

How do structural characteristics of education systems, such as teachers' alary levels, class sizes and aching hours translate into eaching costs per student?

Decisions made by ministries regarding education budgets represent trade-offs between a number of inter-related factors. With respect to the actual teaching process, these factors include the level of the teacher's salary, the size of the class, the designated number of teaching hours and the intended instruction time planned for students. How do these structural characteristics of education systems translate into higher or lower teaching costs per student? How much does it cost an education system, for example, to have a teaching force that teaches relatively fewer hours per year than in other countries, all other characteristics of the education system remaining unchanged? Or by how much do higher statutory salary levels increase costs per student? Chart D1.4 sheds light on this through a decomposition of statutory teachers' salary costs per student at the lower secondary level of education into three components: *i)* those due to the level of the statutory salary, *ii)* those due to the number of teaching hours per year and *iii)* those due to the teaching time per student per year ("intended hours of instruction per class divided by the number of students per class"). A fourth effect ("two or more of the other factors jointly considered") summarises the overall results when any two or more of the preceding three factors are changed simultaneously. Rather than average salary levels, which are affected by the

The case of Germany illustrates how to read the chart: High statutory salaries in Germany add US$624 per student to education costs compared with the average for the countries shown. Because of larger class sizes, instruction time per student is below-average and this lowers outlay per student significantly, by about US$741. The level of teaching hours in Germany tends to add approximately US$28 per student to teaching costs because more teachers are needed for a given number of students. Finally, US$247 of total statutory salary costs per student are not accounted for by considering independently the effect of the three factors.

◆   Chart DI.4.   **Contributions of various factors to increasing/decreasing statutory teachers' salary cost per student enrolled relative to the country-average (lower secondary level) (1995)**

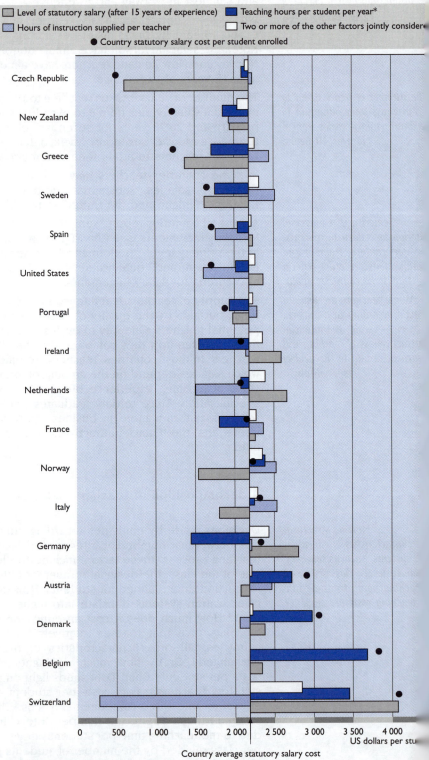

□ Level of statutory salary (after 15 years of experience)   ■ Teaching hours per student per year*
□ Hours of instruction supplied per teacher   □ Two or more of the other factors jointly considered
● Country statutory salary cost per student enrolled

Country average statutory salary cost

US dollars per student

* Intended hours of instruction per class divided by the number of students per class.
Countries are ranked in ascending order of country statutory salary costs per student enrolled.
Source: OECD.

age distribution of teachers, statutory salaries after fifteen years of experience have been used as the basis for examining the consequences for teaching costs of various features of national education systems (for details see Annex 3).

Low teaching hours and small class sizes in some countries add significantly to average costs per student.

In Austria, Italy and Norway annual teaching hours are relatively low (around 650 hours or less); as a result more teachers are required to cover the teaching workload. This adds significantly to salary outlays per student (between an additional US$280 and US$350 per student as shown in Column 3 of Table D1.2). Comparatively small classes add to this effect. Potentially at least, a significant instructional effort is being devoted to students in these countries (see Column H in Table D1.3), at an additional cost of between US$65 per student in Italy and US$538 in Austria (Column 4 of Table D1.2).

Very small class sizes in Belgium lead to high additional instructional costs per student, despite a number of teaching hours that is slightly below the average.

In some countries, costs for h salaries are offset by large class sizes.

In Germany, Ireland and the Netherlands, statutory salaries tend to be higher but class sizes are also significantly larger, which results in lower levels of teaching time per student. The additional costs attributable to higher salaries, ranging from an equivalent US$411 per student in Ireland to US$624 in Germany, are generally more than offset by the reduction in salary costs resulting from lower teaching time per student.

In Switzerland, on the other hand, high salaries coincide with comparatively small class sizes, leading to the highest statutory salary costs per student enrolled among OECD countries for which data are available.

costs per student are reduced countries with high teaching hours.

At the lower secondary level in the Netherlands, Spain, Switzerland and the United States teaching hours are much higher than average (between 900 and 1 050 hours per year). The effect is to reduce costs per student by between an equivalent US$423 in Spain and US$1 906 in Switzerland.

In the Netherlands, Spain and the United States relatively large class sizes translate into less teaching time per student, further reducing costs by US$103 in the Netherlands, US$141 in Spain and US$166 in the United States. In Switzerland teaching hours are also high but classes are comparatively small, resulting in an additional cost of more than US$1 270 per student.

This analysis is developed further in the volume *Education Policy Analysis.*

Definitions

Data on statutory salaries are from the 1997 OECD-INES survey on teachers and curriculum and refer to the school year 1994/95. They are reported in accordance with formal policies for public institutions.

The starting salaries reported refer to the average scheduled gross salary per year for a full-time teacher with the minimum level of training necessary to be fully qualified at the beginning of his or her teaching career. Reported salaries are defined as the wages received (total sum of money paid by the employer for the labour supplied), excluding the employer's contribution to social security and pension funding. Bonuses that constitute a regular part of the salary such as a 13th month, or holiday or regional bonuses, are included in the figures. Additional bonuses, for example remuneration for teachers in educational priority areas, for participating in school improvement projects or special activities, or for exceptional performance, are excluded from the reported gross salaries but reported separately in Table D1.1. The percentage of additional bonus is the average of two ratios: *i)* the maximum bonus during the initial year of service to the minimum statutory salary; and *ii)* the maximum bonus at the top of the pay scale to the maximum statutory salary.

Salaries after 15 years of experience refer to the scheduled salary per year of a full-time classroom teacher with the minimum level of training necessary to be fully qualified and with 15 years of experience. The maximum salaries reported refer to the scheduled maximum salary (top of the salary scale) p year of a full-time classroom teacher with the minimum level of training to fully qualified for his or her job.

Data on gross average earnings for wage and salary workers are taken from the OECD Earnings Distribution Database.

Data on gross average earnings for wage and salary workers generally refer overall wages and other remuneration paid in cash in the reference ye before deduction of income tax and social security contributions (for defi tions and sources see OECD, 1996 *Employment Outlook*).

Purchasing power parity (PPP) exchange rates used pertain to GDP and are from the OECD National Accounts Database (see Annex 2).

Intended instruction time refers to the number of hours per year wh students in the age group 12 to 14 years are supposed to receive (for defi tions see 1996 edition of *Education at a Glance*). Data on intended instructi time and teaching time are from the 1995 OECD-INES survey on teachers a curriculum and refer to the school year 1993/94. The "class size" is a theore cally constructed figure: it is estimated as the student/teaching-staff ra multiplied by the intended student instruction time and divided by statutory average number of teaching hours. This measure is equivalent weighting each class by the number of hours for which it meets over the ye The calculation formulas are explained in Annex 3.

Table D1.1a **Annual statutory teachers' salaries in public institutions at the primary level of education in equivalent US dollars converted using PPPs (1995)**

	Starting salary / minimum training	Salary after 15 years' experience / minimum training	Salary at top of scale / minimum training	Ratio of starting salary to GDP per capita	Ratio of salary after 15 years' experience to GDP per capita	Ratio of salary after 15 years' experience to starting salary	Years from starting to top salary	Percentage additional bonus *	Salary after 15 years' experience per teaching hour	Salary after 15 years' experience per student enrolled
North America										
United States	23 430	31 630	39 280	0.9	1.2	1.3	m	18	33	1 844
Pacific Area										
Korea	19 630	33 490	56 000	1.7	2.9	1.7	41	m	m	1 058
New Zealand	14 780	21 570	21 590	0.9	1.3	1.5	8	20	27	950
European Union										
Austria	19 470	24 950	39 240	0.9	1.2	1.3	34	n	35	1 951
Belgium	19 590	26 600	31 650	0.9	1.3	1.4	27	m	32	2 015
Denmark	22 490	28 990	28 990	1.0	1.3	1.3	14	1	39	2 576
Finland	16 980	21 980	22 480	1.0	1.2	1.3	20	16	m	m
France	18 910	25 540	35 360	0.9	1.3	1.4	32	12	28	1 316
Germany	26 820	34 070	36 790	1.3	1.7	1.3	22	n	45	1 644
Greece	13 120	16 420	20 700	1.1	1.3	1.3	32	12	24	805
Ireland	21 650	33 470	39 610	1.3	1.9	1.5	24	5	37	1 419
Italy	17 630	21 280	27 000	0.9	1.1	1.2	40	m	28	2 005
Netherlands	19 010	27 780	34 010	1.0	1.4	1.5	25	n	28	1 240
Portugal	15 690	24 560	40 810	1.3	2.0	1.6	29	5	30	2 030
Spain	23 890	28 020	33 830	1.7	2.0	1.2	42	n	31	1 710
Sweden	14 550	18 660	21 670	0.8	1.0	1.3	23	n	30	1 518
Other OECD countries										
Czech Republic	5 370	6 810	7 950	0.6	0.8	1.3	27	20	10	348
Norway	17 260	21 120	21 390	0.8	0.9	1.2	14	n	31	2 223
Switzerland	31 550	42 210	48 590	1.3	1.7	1.3	23	n	39	2 689
Country mean	**19 140**	**25 910**	**32 230**	**1.1**	**1.4**	**1.4**	**27**	**7**	**31**	**1 630**

Czech Republic: year of reference 1994.

* Percentage additional bonus is an average of two ratios: maximum bonus applicable to starting salary and maximum bonus applicable to salary at top of scale.

Source: OECD database. See Annex 3 for notes.

Table D1.1b **Annual statutory teachers' salaries in public institutions at the lower secondary level of education, in equivalent US dollars converted using PPPs (1995)**

	Starting salary / minimum training	Salary after 15 years' experience / minimum training	Salary at top of scale / minimum training	Ratio of starting salary to GDP per capita	Ratio of salary after 15 years' experience to GDP per capita	Ratio of salary after 15 years' experience to starting salary	Years from starting to top salary	Percentage additional bonus *	Salary after 15 years' experience per teaching hour	Salary after 15 years' experience
North America										
United States	22 930	30 460	40 470	0.9	1.2	1.3	m	23	32	1 7
Pacific Area										
Korea	19 720	33 580	56 090	1.7	2.9	1.7	41	m	m	1 2
New Zealand	15 780	22 750	22 750	0.9	1.4	1.4	8	11	26	1 2
European Union										
Austria	20 140	26 200	41 960	1.0	1.3	1.3	34	n	40	2 9
Belgium	20 040	28 360	34 640	1.0	1.4	1.4	27	m	39	3 8
Denmark	22 490	28 990	28 990	1.0	1.3	1.3	14	1	39	3 0
Finland	19 150	26 640	27 970	1.1	1.5	1.4	20	15	m	
France	21 580	28 210	38 190	1.1	1.4	1.3	32	12	43	2 1
Germany	29 450	37 060	40 800	1.4	1.8	1.3	21	n	52	2 5
Greece	13 120	16 420	20 700	1.1	1.3	1.4	32	17	29	1 2
Ireland	22 720	33 840	39 980	1.3	2.0	1.5	23	5	46	2
Italy	19 130	23 360	29 980	1.0	1.2	1.2	40	m	38	2
Netherlands	23 090	35 340	35 340	1.2	1.8	1.5	25	n	37	2
Portugal	15 690	24 560	40 810	1.3	2.0	1.6	29	10	36	1
Spain	23 890	28 020	33 830	1.7	2.0	1.2	42	n	31	1
Sweden	16 200	20 310	21 670	0.9	1.1	1.3	20	n	35	1
Other OECD countries										
Czech Republic	5 370	6 810	7 950	0.6	0.8	1.3	27	20	10	
Norway	17 260	21 120	21 390	0.8	0.9	1.2	14	n	35	2
Switzerland	37 090	50 400	56 880	1.5	2.0	1.4	21	n	48	4
Country mean	**20 260**	**27 660**	**33 990**	**1.1**	**1.5**	**1.4**	**26**	**7**	**36**	**2**

Czech Republic: year of reference 1994.

* Percentage additional bonus is an average of two ratios: maximum bonus applicable to starting salary and maximum bonus applicable to salary at scale.

Source: OECD database. See Annex 3 for notes.

Table D1.1c **Annual statutory teachers' salaries in public institutions at the upper secondary level of education, general programmes, in equivalent US dollars converted using PPPs (1995)**

	Starting salary / minimum training	Salary after 15 years' experience / minimum training	Salary at top of scale / minimum training	Ratio of starting salary to GDP per capita	Ratio of salary after 15 years' experience to GDP per capita	Ratio of salary after 15 years' experience to starting salary	Years from starting to top salary	Percentage additional bonus *	Salary after 15 years' experience per teaching hour	Salary after 15 years' experience per student enrolled
North America										
United States	23 160	33 020	40 470	0.9	1.2	1.4	m	27	35	2 199
Pacific Area										
Korea	19 720	33 580	56 090	1.7	2.9	1.7	41	m	m	1 691
New Zealand	16 910	23 920	23 920	1.0	1.4	1.4	8	3	25	1 593
European Union										
Austria	21 400	28 680	47 130	1.0	1.4	1.3	34	n	47	3 459
Belgium	24 790	36 350	43 750	1.2	1.7	1.5	25	m	55	4 912
Denmark	26 090	37 330	37 330	1.2	1.7	1.4	14	n	78	3 714
Finland	19 810	27 970	29 800	1.1	1.6	1.4	20	20	m	m
France	21 580	28 210	38 190	1.1	1.4	1.3	32	12	43	2 152
Germany	31 860	39 690	45 320	1.6	1.9	1.2	20	n	61	2 981
Greece	13 120	16 420	20 700	1.1	1.3	1.4	32	17	29	1 324
Ireland	22 720	33 840	39 980	1.3	2.0	1.5	24	5	46	2 091
Italy	19 130	24 090	31 390	1.0	1.2	1.3	40	m	39	2 471
Netherlands	23 090	35 340	35 340	1.2	1.8	1.5	25	n	37	2 142
Portugal	15 690	24 560	40 810	1.3	2.0	1.6	29	10	40	1 889
Spain	27 710	32 290	38 770	1.9	2.3	1.2	39	n	51	2 376
Sweden	16 200	20 760	21 770	0.9	1.1	1.3	20	n	39	1 395
Other OECD countries										
Czech Republic	5 960	7 550	8 820	0.7	0.8	1.3	27	25	12	739
Norway	18 700	22 160	23 740	0.8	1.0	1.2	16	n	47	2 699
Switzerland	m	m	m	m	m	m	m	m	m	m
Country mean	**20 430**	**28 280**	**34 930**	**1.2**	**1.6**	**1.4**	**26**	**8**	**43**	**2 343**

Republic: year of reference 1994.

centage additional bonus is an average of two ratios: maximum bonus applicable to starting salary and maximum bonus applicable to salary at top of le.

e: OECD database. See Annex 3 for notes.

Table D1.1d **Annual statutory teachers' salaries in public institutions at the upper secondary level of education, vocational programmes, in equivalent US dollars converted using PPPs (1995)**

	Starting salary / minimum training	Salary after 15 years' experience / minimum training	Salary at top of scale / minimum training	Ratio of starting salary to GDP per capita	Ratio of salary after 15 years' experience to GDP per capita	Ratio of salary after 15 years' experience to starting salary	Years from starting to top salary	Percentage additional bonus *	Salary after 15 years' experience per teaching hour	Salary after 15 years' experience
North America										
United States	23 160	33 020	40 470	0.9	1.2	1.4	m	27	m	2 1
Pacific Area										
Korea	20 340	34 470	57 150	1.8	3.0	1.7	41	m	m	1 7
New Zealand	m	m	m	m	m	m	m	m	m	
European Union										
Austria	20 880	27 630	44 930	1.0	1.3	1.3	34	n	44	3 3
Belgium	24 790	36 350	43 750	1.2	1.7	1.5	25	m	55	
Denmark	23 190	28 640	29 680	1.1	1.3	1.2	17	5	38	2 8
Finland	14 480	19 150	20 140	0.8	1.1	1.3	20	24	m	
France	21 580	28 210	38 190	1.1	1.4	1.3	32	12	43	2 1
Germany	31 860	39 690	45 320	1.6	1.9	1.2	20	n	60	2 9
Greece	13 120	16 420	20 700	1.1	1.3	1.4	32	17	29	
Ireland	22 720	33 840	39 980	1.3	2.0	1.5	24	5	46	2 0
Italy	19 130	24 090	31 390	1.0	1.2	1.3	40	m	39	2 4
Netherlands	23 090	35 340	44 890	1.2	1.8	1.5	m	n	m	
Portugal	15 690	24 560	40 810	1.3	2.0	1.6	29	10	40	
Spain	26 890	31 890	38 210	1.9	2.2	1.2	39	n	51	2 2
Sweden	15 300	19 660	21 670	0.8	1.1	1.3	20	n	32	1 2
Other OECD countries										
Czech Republic	5 960	7 550	8 820	0.7	0.8	1.3	27	21	12	
Norway	17 260	21 030	21 350	0.8	0.9	1.2	14	n	36	
Switzerland	m	m	m	m	m	m	m	m	m	
Country mean	**19 810**	**27 150**	**34 270**	**1.1**	**1.6**	**1.4**	**28**	**15**	**40**	**2**

Czech Republic: year of reference 1994.
* Percentage additional bonus: average of two ratios: maximum bonus applicable to starting salary and maximum bonus applicable to salary at top of
Source: OECD database. See Annex 3 for notes.

Table D1.2 **Contributions of various factors to increasing/decreasing statutory teachers' salary cost at 15 years' experience per student enrolled relative to the country-average (lower secondary level) (1995)**

	Country average statutory salary cost per student enrolled	Incremental or decremental effect of specified factor (in US dollars per student converted using PPPs)				Country statutory salary cost per student enrolled
		Level of statutory salary (after 15 years of experience)	Hours of instruction supplied per teacher	Intended hours of instruction per class divided by the number of students per class	Two or more of the other factors jointly considered	
	1	2	3	4	5	1+2+3+4+5
North America						
United States	2 184	183	− 576	− 166	80	1 706
Pacific Area						
New Zealand	2 184	− 239	− 252	− 327	− 143	1 224
European Union						
Austria	2 184	− 110	283	538	28	2 922
Belgium	2 184	158	4	1 500	− 13	3 832
Denmark	2 184	192	− 125	794	39	3 083
France	2 184	78	181	− 379	89	2 152
Germany	2 184	624	28	− 741	247	2 342
Greece	2 184	− 810	260	− 474	75	1 235
Ireland	2 184	411	− 41	− 636	174	2 091
Italy	2 184	− 381	351	65	107	2 326
Netherlands	2 184	482	− 677	− 103	205	2 091
Portugal	2 184	− 202	104	− 247	50	1 889
Spain	2 184	50	− 423	− 141	33	1 702
Sweden	2 184	− 562	333	− 430	133	1 658
Other OECD countries						
Czech Republic	2 184	−1 569	46	− 90	− 47	524
Norway	2 184	− 645	342	199	167	2 246
Switzerland	2 184	1 887	−1 906	1 271	662	4 098

Source: OECD database. See Annex 3 for notes and calculation formulas.

Table D1.3 **Working conditions of teachers and instructional characteristics, lower secondary level (1995)**

	Statutory salary after 15 years of experience (US dollars)	Instruction supplied per teacher in hours per year (teaching time)	Intended student instruction time in hours per year	Student / teaching staff ratio	Statutory salary per teaching hour (US dollars)	Total (statutory) salary cost of teachers per student enrolled (US dollars)	Class size estimated by C*D/B	Intended annual hours of instruction per class divided by the number of students per class
	A	B	C	D	E	F	G	H
					A/B	A/D	C*D/B	B/D=C/G
North America								
United States	30 460	964	980	18	32	1 706	18	54
Pacific Area								
Korea	33 580	m	m	26	m	1 293	m	m
New Zealand	22 750	869	918	19	26	1 224	20	47
European Union								
Austria	26 200	651	1 084	9	40	2 922	15	7?
Belgium	28 360	720	987	7	39	3 832	10	9?
Denmark	28 990	750	890	9	39	3 083	11	8
Finland	26 640	m	851	m	m	m	m	m
France	28 210	660	954	13	43	2 152	19	5
Germany	37 060	712	950	16	52	2 342	21	4
Greece	16 420	569	927	13	29	1 235	22	4
Ireland	33 840	735	935	16	46	2 091	21	4
Italy	23 360	612	1 020	10	38	2 326	17	6
Netherlands	35 340	954	1 067	17	37	2 091	19	5
Portugal	24 560	681	949	13	36	1 889	18	5
Spain	28 020	900	900	16	31	1 702	16	5
Sweden	20 310	576	828	12	35	1 658	18	4
Other OECD countries								
Czech Republic	6 810	657	m	13	10	524	m	5
Norway	21 120	611	823	9	35	2 246	13	6
Switzerland	50 400	1 056	m	12	48	4 098	m	8
Country mean	**27 496**	**746**	**941**	**14**	**36**	**2 134**	**17**	**5**
Mean excluding Finland and Korea	27 189	746	947	13	36	2 184	17	5

Source: OECD database. See Annex 3 for notes and calculation formulas.

Indicator D2: **Eighth-grade mathematics teachers' reports on their age, gender and teaching experience**

Policy context

This indicator describes the demographic composition and the years of teaching experience of mathematics teachers at the 8th-grade level.

The demography of teachers is becoming a major concern in many OECD countries, particularly in the context of recent and future trends in student numbers (see Indicator A1). The recruitment of new teachers will therefore be an important issue for many OECD countries over the coming decade, particularly in mathematics and the sciences. With seniority as an important criterion in teachers' pay scales, the age distribution of teachers has a significant impact on educational budgets, but years of teaching experience can be considered one aspect of the quality of teaching.

Evidence and explanations

Age

In 20 out of 25 countries the majority of 8th-grade students are taught by mathematics teachers aged 40 years or older.

If teachers were entering the teaching force at a constant rate, devoting their careers to the classroom and then retiring, one might expect roughly equivalent percentages of students taught by teachers in their 20s, 30s, 40s and 50s. However, this does not appear to hold for most countries, where the majority of 8th-grade students are taught mathematics by teachers aged 40 years or older (see Table D2.1). In Germany, mathematics teachers of about half of the students reported their age as 50 years or older. Teachers in the French Community of Belgium, the Czech Republic, Denmark, France, Norway, Spain and Sweden share the highly-skewed age profile of their German colleagues: in all eight countries more than two-thirds of the mathematics teachers reported an age of 40 years or over. On the other hand, Portugal seems to have a comparatively young teaching force, 45 per cent of Portuguese students having mathematics teachers aged younger than 30 years, and 80 per cent having teachers younger than 40.

In many countries, 8th-grade mathematics teachers are markedly older than other physics, mathematics, engineering, life-science and health professionals.

The age structure of 8th-grade mathematics teachers broadly reflects the age structure of lower secondary education teachers shown in the 1995 edition of *Education at a Glance*, but it is worth noting that the age profile of 8th-grade mathematics teachers shown by this indicator is very different from the age profile of other physics, mathematics, engineering, life-science and health professionals. For nine of the ten countries for which corresponding data are available, the 8th-grade mathematics teachers are older than their colleagues in related fields. In Germany, 50 per cent of the professionals in the

◆ Chart D2.1. ***Distribution of 8th-grade students by age of their mathematics teache***
(1995)

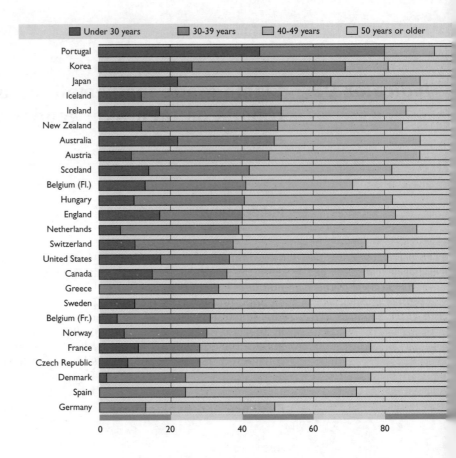

Countries are ranked in descending order of the percentage of students with mathematics teachers under 40 years of age.
Source: IEA.

above-mentioned fields are younger than 40 years of age whereas only 13
cent of 8th-grade mathematics teachers are younger than 40. In Belgi
Denmark, France and Spain the difference in the percentage of pers
below 40 years between the two groups still exceeds 25 percentage poi

Some countries may face
difficulties in recruiting
sufficient numbers of qualified
teachers.

Trends in birth rates and cohort sizes (see Indicator A1) have long-t
effects on the supply of teachers by influencing both the number of po
tial teachers and the likelihood that individuals who do prepare to t
will find teaching positions. The data suggest that some countries
face difficulties in recruiting sufficient numbers of qualified mathem
teachers at this level of education. In the United States, student num
are rising steeply and the post-war baby boom has created a heavy con
tration of older teachers. The more even age structure of teacher
Austria and the fact that the youth population is more stable over
in Austria and France make shortages of teachers less likely in t
countries.

Gender

Men generally outnumber women as mathematics teachers in 8th grade.

In just 7 out of 25 countries for which data are available, approximately equal percentages of 8th-grade students are taught by male and female mathematics teachers (see Table D2.1). On average, the gender gap is 10 per cent favouring males, and in nine countries it is 25 per cent or larger. In Denmark, Germany, Greece, Japan, the Netherlands, Norway, Sweden and Switzerland about one-third or fewer 8th-grade mathematics students are taught by female teachers. The countries that do not follow the predominant pattern and have more women than men teaching mathematics to 8th-grade students are the Flemish Community of Belgium, the Czech Republic, Hungary, Ireland, Portugal and the United States, with the Czech Republic and Hungary reporting percentages of over 80 per cent of women mathematics teachers.

The gender profile of 8th-grade mathematics teachers appears to be quite different from the gender profile of primary and lower secondary teachers in all subject domains shown in Table B7.2. In most countries the majority of teachers at primary and lower secondary levels are women.

Experience

out 70 per cent of 8th-grade students are taught by teachers with more than ten years' experience.

Not surprisingly, differences in teachers' ages are paralleled by differences in experience (see Table D2.2). On average across countries, about 70 per cent of 8th-grade students are taught by teachers who have more than ten years' experience. At least half of the students have mathematics teachers with more than 20 years' experience in the French Community of Belgium, the Czech Republic, France and Spain.

a average, teachers of 16 per cent of 8th-grade students reported five or less years of experience.

Countries with younger mathematics teaching forces will have more students taught by less experienced teachers. In particular this is the case for Japan (44 per cent are taught by teachers with no more than 10 years' experience), Korea (57 per cent), New Zealand (45 per cent) and Portugal (67 per cent). In Portugal 51 per cent of students are taught by teachers with no more than 5 years' experience, in Korea it is 28 per cent and in the United States 25 per cent.

The data show a positive elationship between teachers' years of experience and the mathematics achievement of students.

In many countries, the data show a positive relationship between teachers' years of experience and the mathematics achievement of their students (see Chart D2.2), although relatively large standard errors need to be taken into account when interpreting this relationship. In addition, the absence of such a relationship in these data does not mean that teachers' experience has no influence on student achievement. In some countries students are taught by different mathematics teachers in different years and courses, so that the influence of any single teacher at any point in time would not necessarily show up in the data.

Definitions

)ata are based on the Third ernational Mathematics and Science Study (TIMSS) undertaken by the rnational Association for the Evaluation of Educational hievement (IEA) during the school year 1994/95.

The target population of TIMSS refers to students at the higher of the two grade levels in which most 13 year-olds are enrolled and which, by convention, is referred to as the "8th" grade, since in most countries it refers to the eighth year of formal schooling. The mean achievement represents the national average TIMSS mathematics achievement score of 8th-grade students. The sampling of teachers was based on participating students.

For a country where teacher responses are available for 70 to 84 per cent of the students, an "r" is included next to the data. Where teacher responses are available for 50 to 69 per cent of the students, an "s" is included next to the

◆ Chart D2.2. *Distribution of 8th-grade students by years of teaching experience of their mathematics teachers (1995)*

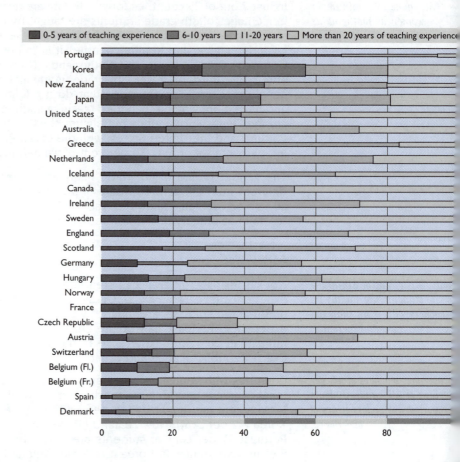

The width of the bars is proportional to the mean achievement score of the students taught by teachers with different levels of teaching experience (see Table D2.2).

Countries are ranked in descending order of the percentage of students with teachers with 10 years of experience or less.

Source: IEA.

data. Otherwise teacher responses are available for more than 84 per cent of the students. Values in brackets present standard errors of sampling. Because results are rounded to the nearest whole number, some totals may appear inconsistent. Countries marked with an asterisk did not satisfy one or more TIMSS guidelines for sample participation rates, age/grade specification or classroom sampling procedures. The reporting of data on a sub-national level for some countries is based on data availability from the IEA and does not represent a policy decision by the OECD.

Comparisons between the ages of teachers in TIMSS and the ages of other professionals are based on the 1995 European Labour Force Survey. These include all occupations in ISCO categories 21 and 22. Figures for the Flemish and French Communities of Belgium for this survey refer to Belgium as a whole.

Table D2.1 **Eighth-grade mathematics teachers' reports on their age and gender (in terms of the percentage of students in each category) (1995)**

		Under 30 years		30-39 years		40-49 years		50 years or older		Male		Female		Percentage of physics, mathematics, engineering, life-science and health professionals 40 years or older
North America														
Canada		15	(2.4)	21	(3.1)	39	(3.9)	26	(3.2)	62	(4.3)	38	(4.3)	
United States		17	(3.0)	19	(3.2)	44	(4.4)	19	(2.9)	35	(4.0)	65	(4.0)	
Pacific Area														
Australia*		22	(2.6)	27	(3.2)	41	(3.3)	10	(1.9)	56	(3.3)	44	(3.3)	
Japan		22	(3.2)	43	(3.7)	25	(3.5)	10	(2.5)	72	(3.8)	28	(3.8)	
Korea		26	(3.7)	43	(4.4)	12	(3.2)	19	(3.0)	55	(3.9)	45	(3.9)	
New Zealand		12	(2.5)	38	(4.2)	35	(3.8)	15	(3.3)	58	(4.1)	42	(4.1)	
European Union														
Austria*	r	9	(2.6)	38	(3.8)	42	(4.6)	10	(2.7)	52	(4.4)	48	(4.4)	
Belgium														
(Flemish Community)		13	(3.1)	28	(4.2)	30	(4.2)	29	(4.9)	34	(4.3)	66	(4.3)	31
(French Community)*	s	5	(2.3)	26	(5.0)	46	(6.0)	23	(5.1)	49	(5.5)	51	(5.5)	31
Denmark*		2	(1.4)	22	(4.0)	52	(4.7)	24	(4.0)	65	(4.5)	35	(4.5)	50
France		11	(2.7)	17	(3.7)	48	(5.0)	24	(3.8)	57	(4.5)	43	(4.5)	46
Germany*	s	n	(0.0)	13	(3.5)	36	(5.2)	51	(5.3)	67	(4.9)	33	(4.9)	50
Greece*		n	(0.4)	33	(4.4)	54	(4.2)	12	(4.2)	70	(3.8)	30	(3.8)	50
Ireland		17	(3.6)	34	(4.3)	35	(4.1)	14	(3.1)	42	(4.0)	58	(4.0)	34
Netherlands*		6	(2.5)	33	(5.2)	50	(5.2)	11	(2.9)	78	(4.1)	22	(4.1)	39
Portugal		45	(4.5)	35	(4.1)	14	(2.2)	6	(2.2)	32	(3.8)	68	(3.8)	46
Spain		n	(0.4)	24	(3.6)	48	(4.3)	28	(3.7)	63	(4.1)	37	(4.1)	42
Sweden		10	(2.2)	22	(3.5)	27	(3.2)	41	(4.3)	67	(3.3)	33	(3.3)	
United Kingdom														
England	s	17	(2.5)	23	(3.1)	43	(2.8)	17	(2.4)	55	(3.6)	45	(3.6)	
Scotland*		14	(3.3)	28	(4.4)	40	(4.9)	18	(3.2)	55	(4.6)	45	(4.6)	
Other OECD countries														
Czech Republic		8	(2.4)	20	(3.6)	41	(4.7)	31	(4.8)	18	(3.2)	82	(3.2)	
Hungary		10	(2.5)	31	(4.4)	42	(4.4)	18	(3.1)	13	(3.1)	87	(3.1)	
Iceland	r	12	(4.9)	39	(7.0)	29	(6.0)	20	(6.9)	61	(5.6)	39	(5.6)	
Norway		7	(2.1)	23	(3.8)	39	(4.1)	31	(3.5)	68	(3.9)	32	(3.9)	
Switzerland		10	(3.5)	27	(3.9)	37	(4.4)	25	(3.9)	87	(2.3)	13	(2.3)	
Country mean		**12**		**28**		**38**		**21**		**55**		**45**		

...countries did not satisfy one or more TIMSS sampling guidelines.
...andard errors appear in parentheses.
...ce: International Association for the Evaluation of Educational Achievement (IEA). See 'Definitions' in the text and notes in Annex 3.

Table D2.2 **Eighth-grade mathematics teachers' reports on the number of years of their teaching experience (in terms of the percentage of students in each category) and corresponding average mathematics achievement of students (1995)**

		0-5 years		6-10 years		11-20 years		more than 20 years	
		Percentage of students	Mean achievement	Percentage of students	Mean achievement	Percentage of students	Mean achievement	Percentage of students	Mean achievement
North America									
Canada		17 (2.6)	527 (6.7)	15 (2.9)	527 (5.0)	22 (3.6)	526 (7.6)	46 (3.8)	528 (3.8)
United States		25 (3.4)	484 (6.3)	14 (2.7)	488 (9.8)	25 (3.2)	501 (7.3)	36 (3.3)	513 (7.5)
Pacific Area									
Australia*		18 (2.3)	517 (8.5)	19 (2.6)	528 (11.6)	35 (2.7)	540 (8.5)	28 (2.6)	533 (8.5)
Japan		19 (3.3)	606 (5.0)	25 (3.5)	607 (4.3)	36 (3.8)	598 (3.5)	19 (2.9)	614 (4.0)
Korea		28 (3.5)	610 (4.7)	29 (3.9)	622 (5.6)	23 (3.7)	597 (5.6)	20 (3.1)	606 (5.5)
New Zealand		17 (3.1)	497 (7.5)	28 (4.0)	515 (7.9)	34 (4.1)	517 (9.2)	20 (3.4)	487 (9.4)
European Union									
Austria*	r	7 (2.3)	516 (19.7)	13 (2.5)	546 (9.5)	51 (4.0)	554 (6.7)	28 (3.6)	549 (8.8)
Belgium (Flemish Community)		10 (2.8)	556 (17.9)	9 (2.2)	590 (14.5)	32 (4.8)	554 (13.4)	49 (4.9)	575 (10.6)
Belgium (French Community)*	s	8 (3.2)	536 (12.3)	8 (2.3)	528 (13.8)	31 (5.2)	558 (7.0)	54 (4.8)	543 (6.4)
Denmark*		4 (1.9)	487 (2.6)	4 (2.0)	493 (14.4)	47 (4.9)	504 (3.3)	45 (4.8)	508 (4.4)
France		11 (2.5)	539 (8.1)	11 (3.1)	529 (10.2)	26 (4.6)	540 (8.8)	52 (4.3)	538 (5.4)
Germany*	s	10 (2.2)	534 (14.5)	14 (4.3)	471 (12.1)	32 (5.1)	521 (10.6)	44 (5.5)	516 (9.3)
Greece*		16 (3.1)	464 (7.2)	20 (3.4)	469 (5.3)	47 (4.3)	490 (3.5)	17 (4.4)	503 (11.9)
Ireland		13 (3.0)	513 (16.3)	18 (3.5)	512 (12.5)	42 (4.5)	535 (8.4)	28 (4.5)	523 (10.0)
Netherlands*		13 (3.6)	530 (19.5)	21 (3.6)	525 (10.2)	42 (5.3)	548 (17.8)	24 (4.0)	556 (9.3)
Portugal		51 (4.7)	449 (3.0)	16 (3.1)	447 (5.4)	27 (3.9)	462 (4.3)	6 (2.3)	477 (8.6)
Spain		3 (0.8)	472 (17.7)	8 (2.4)	487 (7.6)	39 (4.3)	488 (3.8)	50 (4.3)	488 (3.1)
Sweden		16 (2.4)	529 (7.1)	15 (2.8)	512 (9.5)	26 (3.1)	518 (6.2)	44 (4.1)	520 (4.4)
United Kingdom									
England	s	19 (2.5)	522 (10.8)	11 (2.1)	518 (13.5)	39 (3.5)	512 (8.1)	31 (3.0)	515 (11.3)
Scotland*		17 (3.4)	483 (9.2)	12 (3.2)	484 (14.3)	42 (4.4)	496 (8.5)	29 (4.3)	507 (12.3)
Other OECD countries									
Czech Republic		12 (3.1)	566 (17.7)	9 (1.9)	538 (8.6)	17 (4.1)	584 (11.4)	62 (4.7)	562 (5.7)
Hungary		13 (2.9)	530 (12.7)	10 (2.8)	510 (7.4)	38 (4.1)	537 (5.6)	38 (4.1)	547 (5.2)
Iceland	r	19 (5.1)	478 (5.3)	14 (3.8)	480 (8.5)	33 (7.1)	492 (7.3)	35 (7.7)	496 (10.6)
Norway		12 (2.7)	499 (10.7)	10 (2.5)	500 (6.1)	35 (4.0)	508 (4.0)	43 (4.6)	503 (3.4)
Switzerland		14 (3.3)	540 (10.1)	6 (1.8)	545 (19.0)	37 (4.6)	549 (8.4)	42 (4.9)	548 (7.4)
Country mean		**16**	**519**	**14**	**519**	**34**	**529**	**36**	**530**

* Countries did not satisfy one or more TIMSS sampling guidelines.
( ) Standard errors appear in parentheses.
Source: International Association for the Evaluation of Educational Achievement (IEA). See 'Definitions' in the text and notes in Annex 3.

Indicator D3: Eighth-grade mathematics teachers' reports on various school-related activities outside the formal school day

Policy context

This indicator shows the average number of hours 8th-grade mathematics teachers spend on various school-related activities outside the formal school day during the school week.

A teacher's working day does not end when classes are over. Time for school-related activities outside the formal school day can contribute substantially to the workload of teachers. Comparative information about the nature of school-related activities outside the formal school day can provide additional insight into the working conditions of teachers and can serve as useful benchmarks for school monitoring and school improvement.

Evidence and explanations

The average time 8th-grade mathematics teachers spend on school-related activities outside the school day ranges from hours a week in Ireland to 17.1 hours in Hungary.

The total time 8th-grade mathematics teachers report spending on average on school-related activities outside the formal school day ranges from around 10 hours a week in Greece, Ireland and Scotland to 15 hours or more in Germany, Hungary, Switzerland and the United States. Teachers in these four countries have, in addition, an above-average teaching load (see Indicator P33 in the 1996 edition of *Education at a Glance*). The average over OECD countries is 13 hours.

Eighth-grade mathematics teachers report that lesson planning, grading tests and grading student work are the most time-consuming activities.

Across countries the priority assigned to the various school-related activities outside the formal school day (according to the average number of hours spent on them) is as follows: *i)* planning lessons (3.0 hours); *ii)* preparing or grading tests (2.6); *iii)* reading and grading student work (1.9); *iv)* administrative tasks (1.7); *v)* professional reading and development (1.2); *vi)* meeting students outside classroom time (1.1); *vii)* keeping students' records up to date (0.9) and *viii)* meeting parents (0.6). In Germany and Hungary, for example, grading tests, grading student work and lesson planning averaged over 9 hours per week.

Definitions

Data are based on the Third International Mathematics and Science Study (TIMSS) undertaken by the International Association for the Evaluation of Educational Achievement (IEA) (see also Indicator D2).

The target population of TIMSS refers to students at the higher of the two grade levels in which most 13 year-olds are enrolled and which, by convention, is referred to as the "8th" grade. Table D3.1 shows the average number of hours 8th-grade mathematics teachers report spending on various school-related activities outside the formal school day during the school week. Data are weighted by the number of students in each category.

For a country where teacher responses are available for 70 to 84 per cent of the students, an "r" is included next to the data. Where teacher responses are

◆   Chart D3.1.   ***Distribution of the time spent by 8th-grade mathematics teachers on various school-related activities outside the formal school day (1995)***

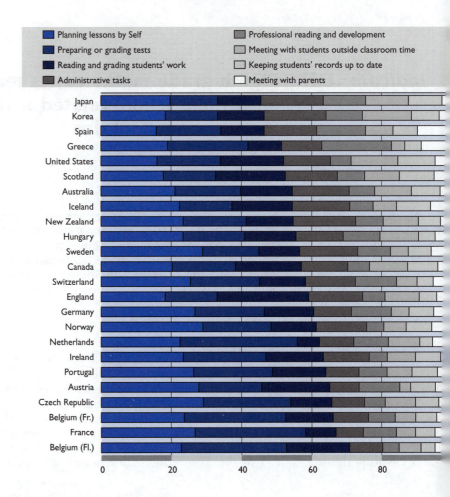

Countries are ranked in ascending order or the percentage of out-of-school time spent on planning lessons, preparing or grading tests and reading and grading student work.

Source : IEA.

available for 50 to 69 per cent of the students, an "s" is included next to data. Values in brackets present standard errors of sampling. Because res are rounded to the nearest whole number, some totals may appear incor tent. Countries marked with an asterisk did not satisfy one or more TI guidelines for sample participation rates, age/grade specification or classr sampling procedures.

Average hours are based on: no time = 0; less than 1 hour = 0.5; hours = 1.5; 3-4 hours = 3.5; more than 4 hours = 5.

Average number of hours spent on school-related activities outside the formal school day during the school week, (weighted by the number of students in each category, 1995)

	Preparing or grading tests	Reading and grading student work	Planning lessons by Self	Meeting with students outside classroom time	Meeting with parents	Professional reading and development	Keeping students' records up to date	Administrative tasks	Total
North America									
Canada	2.3 (0.1)	2.4 (0.2)	2.6 (0.1)	1.4 (0.1)	0.5 (0.0)	0.8 (0.1)	1.1 (0.0)	1.7 (0.1)	12.8 (0.2)
United States	2.7 (0.1)	r 2.7 (0.2)	2.4 (0.1)	2.0 (0.1)	0.7 (0.0)	0.9 (0.1)	1.6 (0.1)	2.0 (0.1)	15.0 (0.3)
Pacific Area									
Australia*	2.3 (0.1)	1.8 (0.1)	2.6 (0.1)	1.3 (0.1)	0.4 (0.0)	0.9 (0.1)	1.0 (0.1)	2.0 (0.1)	12.3 (0.3)
Japan	2.0 (0.1)	1.8 (0.1)	2.9 (0.1)	1.8 (0.1)	0.4 (0.0)	1.8 (0.1)	1.4 (0.1)	2.6 (0.2)	14.7 (0.3)
Korea	1.7 (0.1)	1.5 (0.1)	2.1 (0.1)	1.6 (0.1)	0.4 (0.0)	1.2 (0.1)	0.9 (0.1)	2.0 (0.1)	11.4 (0.3)
New Zealand	2.3 (0.1)	1.7 (0.1)	3.0 (0.1)	1.3 (0.1)	0.4 (0.0)	1.0 (0.1)	0.8 (0.0)	2.3 (0.1)	12.8 (0.2)
European Union									
Austria*	r 2.3 (0.1)	r 2.5 (0.1)	r 3.6 (0.1)	r 0.4 (0.1)	r 0.6 (0.0)	r 1.5 (0.1)	r 0.9 (0.1)	r 1.1 (0.1)	12.9 (0.3)
Belgium (Flemish Community)	s 3.8 (0.1)	s 2.3 (0.1)	2.9 (0.2)	0.8 (0.1)	0.6 (0.1)	0.6 (0.1)	0.5 (0.0)	1.2 (0.1)	12.7 (0.3)
Belgium (French Community)*	s 3.4 (0.2)	s 1.6 (0.1)	s 2.8 (0.2)	s 0.7 (0.1)	s 0.5 (0.1)	s 0.9 (0.1)	s 0.7 (0.1)	s 1.2 (0.1)	11.8 (0.4)
Denmark*	m m	r m m	m	m	m	m	m	m	m
France	4.0 (0.1)	r 1.1 (0.1)	3.4 (0.2)	0.7 (0.1)	0.6 (0.0)	r 1.2 (0.1)	0.7 (0.0)	1.0 (0.1)	12.7 (0.3)
Germany*	s 3.1 (0.1)	s 2.2 (0.2)	s 4.2 (0.1)	s 0.8 (0.1)	s 0.8 (0.1)	s 1.8 (0.2)	s 1.1 (0.1)	s 1.7 (0.1)	15.7 (0.4)
Greece*	2.4 (0.1)	1.0 (0.1)	2.0 (0.2)	0.4 (0.1)	0.9 (0.1)	2.1 (0.1)	0.5 (0.1)	1.2 (0.1)	10.5 (0.3)
Ireland	2.3 (0.1)	1.6 (0.1)	2.3 (0.1)	0.8 (0.1)	0.3 (0.0)	0.5 (0.1)	0.7 (0.0)	1.3 (0.1)	9.8 (0.2)
Netherlands*	3.7 (0.2)	0.7 (0.1)	2.5 (0.2)	1.0 (0.1)	0.6 (0.0)	1.1 (0.1)	0.4 (0.0)	1.1 (0.1)	11.1 (0.3)
Portugal	2.8 (0.1)	1.9 (0.1)	3.3 (0.1)	0.9 (0.1)	0.5 (0.1)	1.0 (0.1)	0.9 (0.1)	1.2 (0.1)	12.5 (7.0)
Spain	2.1 (0.1)	1.4 (0.1)	1.8 (0.1)	0.9 (0.1)	1.1 (0.0)	1.6 (0.1)	0.8 (0.0)	1.7 (0.1)	11.4 (0.2)
Sweden	2.2 (0.1)	1.6 (0.1)	4.0 (0.1)	0.7 (0.0)	0.8 (0.0)	1.3 (0.1)	0.9 (0.0)	2.3 (0.1)	13.8 (0.2)
United Kingdom									
England	s 2.1 (0.1)	s 3.7 (0.1)	s 2.6 (0.1)	s 1.4 (0.1)	s 0.6 (0.0)	s 0.9 (0.1)	s 0.7 (0.1)	s 2.2 (0.1)	14.2 (0.3)
Scotland*	1.5 (0.1)	r 2.0 (0.1)	1.8 (0.1)	1.0 (0.1)	0.5 (0.1)	0.8 (0.1)	1.0 (0.1)	1.5 (0.1)	10.1 (7.0)
Other OECD countries									
Czech Republic	3.4 (0.1)	1.6 (0.1)	4.0 (0.1)	1.2 (0.1)	0.5 (0.0)	0.8 (0.1)	0.9 (0.1)	1.3 (0.1)	13.7 (0.3)
Hungary	3.0 (0.1)	2.5 (0.1)	4.0 (0.1)	1.9 (0.1)	0.8 (0.1)	1.8 (0.1)	0.8 (0.1)	2.3 (0.1)	17.1 (0.3)
Iceland	r 2.0 (0.2)	r 2.3 (0.3)	3.0 (0.2)	0.9 (0.1)	0.8 (0.1)	0.9 (0.1)	1.3 (0.2)	2.2 (0.2)	13.4 (0.5)
Norway	2.4 (0.1)	1.6 (0.1)	3.6 (0.1)	0.8 (0.1)	0.7 (0.0)	0.6 (0.1)	0.9 (0.1)	1.8 (0.1)	12.4 (0.3)
Switzerland	3.0 (0.1)	r 2.0 (0.1)	3.9 (0.1)	0.9 (0.1)	0.8 (0.1)	1.8 (0.1)	0.7 (0.0)	2.2 (0.1)	15.3 (0.3)
Country mean	**2.6**	**1.9**	**3.0**	**1.1**	**0.6**	**1.2**	**0.9**	**1.7**	**12.9**

* Countries did not satisfy one or more TIMSS sampling guidelines.
( ) Standard errors appear in parentheses.
Source: International Association for the Evaluation of Educational Achievement (IEA). See 'Definitions' in the text and notes in Annex 3.

Indicator D4: Fourth and 8th-grade mathematics teachers' reports on average size of mathematics classes

Policy context

This indicator shows 4th and 8th-grade mathematics teachers' reports on average mathematics class sizes.

Class size is a measure of the average number of students a teacher s? during a school period. Smaller class sizes are valued because they may al? students to receive more individual attention from their teachers and red? the burden of managing large numbers of students and their work. At? same time, smaller classes are more expensive. There are potential trade-? between smaller classes on the one hand and the instruction time that can? devoted to each student, the teaching load for teachers and student/teach? staff ratios on the other. Because of the predominance of teacher cost? educational expenditure, class size alone can dominate cost patte? Other things being equal, reducing the class size will increase the costs? student.

Significant reductions in class size have sometimes been shown to be rela? to gains in achievement but there is no conclusive evidence that redu? class sizes is always the best policy option for improving the achievemen? students and the utilisation of educational resources.

Evidence and explanations

Mathematics classes at 4th and 8th grade levels generally have between 21 and 30 students.

In most OECD countries the majority of 8th-grade students are in mather? ics classes of between 21 and 30 students, and at least three-quarter? students are in classes of 30 or fewer students. Only in Japan and Korea is? percentage significantly lower (3 and 4 per cent). At the 4th-grade level, t? are in general comparatively more students in classes of 20 students or ? and comparatively fewer in classes of between 21 and 30 students.

The data reveal large variations from country to country.

In Austria and Norway, 50 per cent or more of 4th-grade students ar? classes with fewer than 20 students. In England, Ireland and New Zeala? higher proportion of students in the 4th grade than in the 8th grade ar? classes of more than 30 students.

According to teachers, in the Flemish Community of Belgium, Denmark? Switzerland about 50 per cent of 8th-grade students are in classes of 2? fewer students. Relatively small mathematics classes are also found in? French Community of Belgium, Hungary, Iceland and Sweden, where? third or more of 8th-grade students are in classes of 20 or fewer student? the other end of the spectrum, 93 per cent of 8th-grade students in Kore?

◆   Chart D4.1.   ***Distribution of 8th-grade students by size of their mathematics classes (1995)***

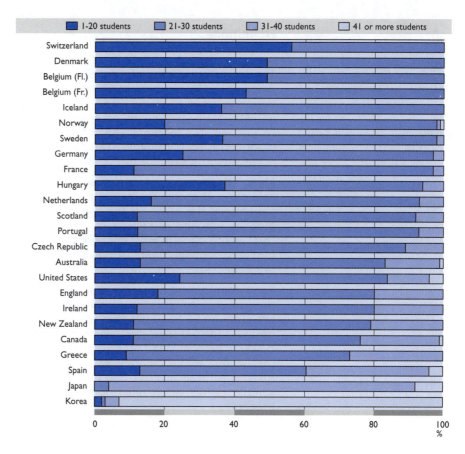

Countries are ranked in descending order of the percentage of students in classes with 30 students or less.

Source: IEA.

in mathematics classes with more than 40 students, and in Japan 96 per cent of students are in classes with more than 30 students.

re is no simple relationship between class size and mathematics achievement.

The relationship between class size and student achievement is complex. Significant reductions in class size have sometimes been shown to be related to gains in achievement, but research indicates that the main effect of smaller classes often relates to gains in teacher attitudes and instructional behaviours. The TIMSS data confirm the complexity of this issue. Across countries, the two highest performing countries in mathematics at the 8th-grade level – Japan and Korea – are those with the largest mathematics classes. After-school programmes and the educational culture at large may play an important role in these countries. On the other hand, high-achieving countries such as the Flemish Community of Belgium and Switzerland have on average small class sizes. Several countries show little or no relationship between achievement and class size, often because students are mostly all in classes of similar size. In other countries, those students with higher achievement appear to be in larger classes. Larger classes in some countries may represent the more usual situation for mathematics teaching, with smaller classes used primarily for students needing remedial help or for those in le advanced tracks.

Definitions

Data are based on the Third International Mathematics and Science Study (TIMSS) undertaken by the International Association for the Evaluation of Educational Achievement (IEA) (see also Indicator D2).

The target population of TIMSS refers to students at the higher of the t grade levels in which most 13 year-olds are enrolled and which, by conve tion, is referred to as the "8th" grade. The table shows the percentage of and 8th-grade students in mathematics classes of different sizes, as report by mathematics teachers. The data are reported in terms of the percentage students in each category. The table also shows the average mathemat achievement scores for the students in the corresponding categories.

Mean achievement refers to the national average of the TIMSS mathemat achievement score. The target populations studied in this indicator refer students at the higher of the two grade levels in which most 9 and 13 ye olds are enrolled and which, by convention, are referred to as the "4th" "8th" grade since in most countries they refer to the fourth and eighth yea formal schooling. Figures from TIMSS are based on data self-reported teachers.

For a country where teacher responses are available for 70 to 84 per cen the students, an "r" is included next to the data. Where teacher responses available for 50 to 69 per cent of the students, an "s" is included next to data. A tilde (~) indicates insufficient data to report achievement. Value brackets present standard errors of sampling. Because results are rounded the nearest whole number, some totals may appear inconsistent. Count marked with an asterisk did not satisfy one or more TIMSS guidelines sample participation rates, age/grade specification or classroom samp procedures.

and average mathematics achievement scores for 8th-grade students in the corresponding categories (1995)

	4th	8th	1-20 students — 4th grade % of students	1-20 — 8th grade % of students	1-20 — 8th grade Mean achievement	21-30 students — 4th grade % of students	21-30 — 8th grade % of students	21-30 — 8th grade Mean achievement	31-40 students — 4th grade % of students	31-40 — 8th grade % of students	31-40 — 8th grade Mean achievement	41 or more students — 4th grade % of students	41 or more — 8th grade % of students	41 or more — 8th grade Mean achievement
North America														
Canada		r	18 (2.4)	11 (2.1)	524 (10.3)	75 (2.7)	65 (4.0)	527 (3.4)	6 (1.3)	23 (3.6)	534 (11.7)	n (0.2)	1 (0.5)	~ ~
United States	r	s	23 (3.6)	24 (3.0)	504 (9.6)	67 (3.8)	59 (3.9)	507 (5.7)	9 (1.7)	12 (2.2)	506 (17.0)	1 (0.5)	4 (1.8)	490 (22.3)
Pacific Area														
Australia*	r	r	17 (3.1)	13 (2.4)	497 (14.6)	64 (4.8)	71 (3.3)	528 (5.4)	19 (4.7)	16 (2.6)	583 (9.7)	1 (0.0)	1 (0.5)	~ ~
Japan			3 (0.8)	n (0.2)	~ ~	29 (3.5)	4 (1.4)	598 (8.5)	67 (3.6)	88 (3.6)	600 (22.0)	1 (1.1)	8 (1.5)	667 (10.1)
Korea			2 (1.0)	2 (1.2)	~ ~	6 (1.6)	1 (1.0)	~ ~	24 (3.6)	4 (1.5)	562 (6.6)	69 (3.5)	93 (2.0)	611 (2.6)
New Zealand			13 (2.6)	11 (2.2)	460 (6.8)	37 (4.3)	68 (3.8)	508 (5.8)	50 (4.5)	21 (3.1)	536 (9.0)	n (0.0)	n (0.0)	~ ~
European Union														
Austria*			50 (5.0)	m	m	50 (5.0)	m	m	n (0.0)	m	~	n (0.0)	m	m
Belgium (Flemish Community)		s	m	49 (3.6)	552 (8.2)	m	51 (3.6)	596 (4.4)	m	n (0.0)	~	m	n (0.0)	~
Belgium (French Community)*		r	m	43 (5.3)	535 (6.2)	m	57 (5.3)	551 (6.1)	m	n (0.0)	~	m	n (0.0)	~
Denmark*		r	m	49 (4.8)	504 (3.8)	m	51 (4.8)	506 (3.7)	m	n (0.0)	~	m	n (0.0)	~
France			m	11 (2.6)	512 (8.8)	m	86 (2.9)	543 (3.9)	m	3 (1.8)	519 (8.7)	m	n (0.0)	~
Germany*		s	m	25 (4.4)	493 (15.6)	m	72 (4.5)	522 (5.6)	m	3 (1.8)	558 (40.8)	m	n (0.0)	~
Greece*			45 (3.9)	9 (2.3)	462 (9.7)	53 (4.0)	64 (4.4)	489 (3.3)	2 (1.1)	27 (3.9)	481 (7.2)	n (0.0)	n (0.0)	~
Ireland		r	27 (2.8)	12 (2.7)	454 (8.5)	33 (4.3)	68 (4.5)	526 (6.7)	41 (4.7)	20 (3.9)	575 (9.5)	n (0.0)	n (0.0)	~
Netherlands*			29 (4.0)	16 (4.7)	467 (21.0)	52 (5.5)	77 (5.6)	549 (6.5)	19 (4.4)	7 (3.6)	631 (18.1)	n (0.0)	n (0.0)	~
Portugal			39 (3.8)	12 (2.8)	440 (4.4)	60 (3.7)	80 (3.7)	456 (3.1)	1 (0.6)	7 (2.6)	469 (12.1)	n (0.0)	n (0.0)	~
Spain		r	m	13 (2.8)	470 (5.9)	m	48 (4.0)	484 (4.5)	m	36 (4.2)	497 (4.6)	m	4 (1.7)	476 (10.9)
Sweden	r	r	m	36 (3.9)	492 (5.8)	m	61 (4.0)	534 (3.9)	m	2 (1.2)	~	m	n (0.0)	~
United Kingdom														
England	s		9 (2.7)	18 (3.1)	482 (12.2)	56 (4.8)	62 (3.7)	511 (5.9)	35 (4.8)	20 (3.4)	554 (7.9)	n (0.0)	n (0.0)	~
Scotland*	r		15 (2.3)	12 (2.8)	455 (11.6)	70 (3.5)	80 (3.8)	496 (6.9)	14 (3.3)	8 (2.7)	543 (18.4)	1 (1.0)	n (0.0)	~
Other OECD countries														
Czech Republic			32 (3.6)	13 (3.3)	534 (6.2)	65 (3.7)	77 (5.3)	564 (6.2)	3 (1.4)	11 (4.5)	591 (13.7)	n (0.0)	n (0.0)	~
Hungary			38 (3.4)	37 (4.0)	528 (5.2)	58 (3.5)	57 (4.1)	541 (4.9)	4 (1.7)	6 (2.2)	551 (17.8)	n (0.0)	n (0.0)	~
Iceland	r		46 (5.0)	36 (5.9)	478 (4.8)	54 (5.0)	64 (5.9)	497 (7.1)	n (0.0)	n (0.0)	~	n (0.0)	n (0.0)	~
Norway	r		59 (4.4)	20 (3.5)	499 (6.2)	41 (4.4)	79 (3.7)	510 (2.9)	n (0.0)	1 (0.5)	~	n (0.0)	1 (0.8)	~
Switzerland	s		m	56 (4.5)	543 (8.1)	m	44 (4.5)	565 (6.6)	m	n (0.0)	~	m	n (0.0)	~
Country mean			27	22	495	51	60	526	17	13	546	4	5	561

* Countries did not satisfy one or more TIMSS sampling guidelines.
( ) Standard errors appear in parentheses.
Source: International Association for the Evaluation of Educational Achievement (IEA). See 'Definitions' in the text and notes in Annex 3.

Indicator D5: Eighth-grade mathematics teachers' reports about classroom organisation during mathematics lessons

Policy context

This indicator shows the use of different forms of classroom organisation in 8th-grade mathematics classes.

Although classroom organisation is to a large extent the responsibility individual teachers, school management and higher administrative decisi can directly and indirectly influence it. Whole class teaching, independ work by students and students working together in small groups are imp tant aspects of classroom organisation. A snapshot of the various ways which classrooms are organised can aid understanding of how teachers c municate with students, and can serve as a baseline for monitoring acceptance of these methods.

Evidence and explanations

Both whole-class and independent work are standard features of mathematics teaching.

Teachers can adopt a variety of approaches to classroom organisation. Wh class instruction can be very efficient, because it requires less time on m agement functions and provides more time for developing concepts. Te ers can make presentations, conduct discussions or demonstrate proced and applications to all students simultaneously. Both whole-class and ir pendent work have been standard features of mathematics teaching. dents can also benefit from the type of co-operative learning that occurs the effective use of small groups. Because they can help each other, stud in groups can often handle challenging situations beyond their indivi capabilities.

Whole-class teaching is one of the most common forms of classroom organisation in mathematics at the 8th-grade level.

Table D5.1 shows the relative emphasis on individual, small group and wh class work reported by mathematics teachers. Because learning may enhanced when the teacher guides and monitors individual and small-gr activities, the frequency of lessons using each of these organisati approaches is shown both with and without the assistance of the teache general, teachers report that students working together with the tea teaching the whole class is a frequently used instructional approach. In countries, approximately 50 per cent or more of 8th-grade students are ta this way during most lessons or every lesson. In contrast, students wor together as a class but with students responding to each other appears t a much less common approach, used for fewer than a third of the student a frequent basis in almost all countries.

Guided independent work was also reported as a commonly used approach in many countries.

Equally as popular as having students working together as a class with teacher teaching the whole-class is the practice of having students individually with assistance from the teacher. Working in pairs or small gr is reported as an infrequently used approach, and when such an approa indicated, it is more often with than without the assistance of the teach

◆ Chart D5.1. ***Classroom organisation during mathematics lessons, 8th grade (1995)***
Percentage of students whose teachers report using each organisational approach "most or every lesson"

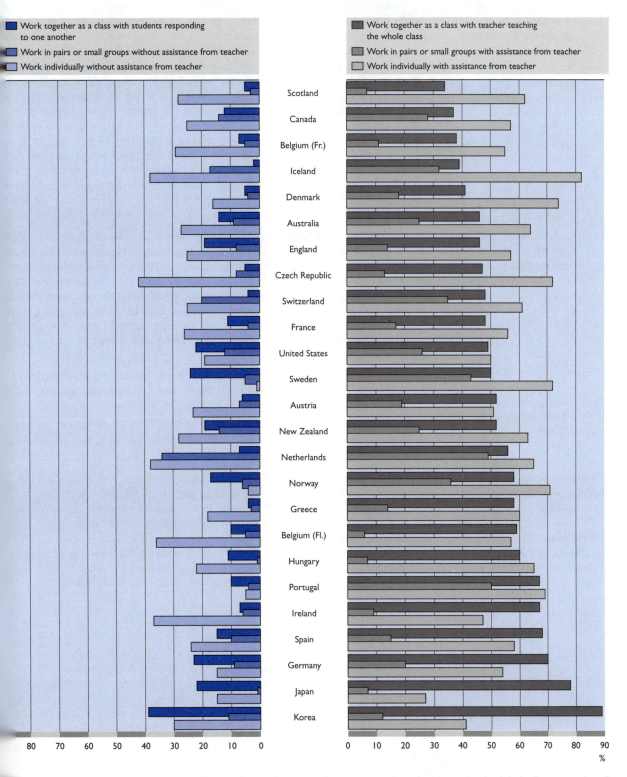

...tries are ranked in ascending order of the percentage of students whose teachers report working together as a class with teacher teaching the whole class "most or every lesson".

...e: IEA.

Unassisted individual work and assisted work in pairs or small groups are less common.

general, having students work without the assistance of the teacher, eith individually or in groups, is not common in most countries.

In Germany, Ireland, Japan, Korea and Spain, whole-class teaching is the mo common approach, with more than two-thirds of students having teachers w report using this approach in most lessons or every lesson. Working indivic ally with assistance from the teacher is reported for 70 per cent or more students in the Czech Republic, Denmark, Iceland, Norway and Sweden, a is employed in most lessons or every lesson for the majority of students in countries except Ireland, Japan and Korea. The other types of classro organisational approaches are in general less common, with rather large va tions between countries. Working together as a class with students respon ing to one another varies from 2 per cent in Iceland to 39 per cent in Kor Working individually without assistance from the teacher varies from 1 cent in Sweden to 42 per cent in the Czech Republic. Working in pairs or sm groups with assistance from the teacher varies from 6 per cent for the Flem Community of Belgium to 50 per cent for Portugal, and without assistar from 1 per cent in Japan and Hungary and 34 per cent in the Netherland

Whole-class teaching, independent learning and group work can each be effective in different circumstances.

The effectiveness of these rather broadly defined types of classroom orga sation is difficult to assess. Whole-class teaching, for example, can be v efficient under certain circumstances. Constructivists' notions about learn and instruction tend to emphasise the importance of independent learn and of students learning together in small group settings, on condition t students are well supported. Group work can also be seen as having a p tive influence on the social and affective development of students. Group is sometimes considered an effective strategy for adapting instruction individual needs.

Note that the row totals add up to more than 100 per cent because more t one form of classroom organisation is often used during one lesson.

Definitions

Data are based on the Third International Mathematics and Science Study (TIMSS) undertaken by the International Association for the Evaluation of Educational Achievement (IEA) (see also Indicator D2).

The target population of TIMSS refers to students at the higher of the grade levels in which most 13 year-olds are enrolled and which, by conv tion, is referred to as the "8th" grade. For a country where teacher respor are available for 70 to 84 per cent of the students, an "r" is included nex the data. Where teacher responses are available for 50 to 69 per cent of students, an "s" is included next to the data. Countries marked with asterisk did not satisfy one or more TIMSS guidelines for sample participa rates, age/grade specification or classroom sampling procedures.

Table D5.1 **Teachers' reports about classroom organisation during mathematics lessons, 8th grade, percentage of students whose teachers report using each organisational approach "most or every lesson" (1995)**

	Work together as a class with students responding to one another		Work together as a class with teacher teaching the whole class		Work individually with assistance from teacher		Work individually without assistance from teacher		Work in pairs or small groups with assistance from teacher		Work in pairs or small groups without assistance from teacher
North America											
Canada	r	12		37		57	r	25	r	28	r	14
United States	r	22	r	49	r	50	r	19	r	26	r	12
Pacific Area											
Australia*	r	14	r	46	r	64	r	27	r	25	r	9
Japan		22		78		27		15		7		1
Korea		39		89		41		30		12		11
New Zealand		19		52		63		28		25		14
European Union											
Austria*	r	6	r	52	r	51	r	23	r	19	r	7
Belgium											
(Flemish Community)		10		59		57		36		6		5
(French Community)*	s	7	s	38	s	55	s	29	s	11	s	5
Denmark*		5		41		74		16		18		4
France		11		48		56		26		17		4
Germany*	s	23	s	70	s	54	s	15	s	20	s	9
Greece*		4		58		60		18		14		3
Ireland	r	7		67		47		37	r	9	r	6
Netherlands*		7		56		65		38		49		34
Portugal		10		67		69		5		50		4
Spain	r	15	r	68	r	58	r	24	r	15	r	10
Sweden	r	24	r	50	r	72	r	1	r	43	r	5
United Kingdom											
England	s	19	s	46	s	57	s	25	s	14	s	8
Scotland*	r	5	r	34	r	62	r	28	r	7	r	3
Other OECD countries											
Czech Republic		5		47		72		42		13		8
Hungary		11		60		65		22		7		1
Iceland	r	2	r	39	r	82	r	38	r	32	r	17
Norway	r	17	r	58	r	71	s	4	r	36	s	6
Switzerland	s	4	s	48	s	61	s	25	s	35	s	20
Country mean		**13**		**54**		**60**		**24**		**22**		**9**

countries did not satisfy one or more TIMSS sampling guidelines.
ce: International Association for the Evaluation of Educational Achievement (IEA). See 'Definitions' in the text and notes in Annex 3.

Indicator D6: **Class size and school-level student/staff ratio in primary schools**

Policy context

This indicator provides a measure of class size, student/ teaching staff ratios and in-school management in primary schools.

The organisation and management of schools influences class sizes and s dent/staff ratios, as well as decisions at the macro-level of education syste The school-level ratio of students to teaching staff is an indicator of teaching resources that are invested per student.

From the perspective of the student, both class size and instructional ti determine the amount of access to learning. From the perspective of tea ers, class sizes and instructional time (teaching hours) have an impact on tl workload.

The relationship between the student/staff ratio on the one hand and class size on the other is determined by a range of educational policy choi relating to the number of hours that students attend class each day, length of a teacher's working day, the number of classes or students for wl a teacher is responsible and the division of the teacher's time betwe teaching and other duties. The policy debate on the reduction of class si as a means to improve the quality of education needs to be seen in context of these inter-related factors.

In the ongoing debate on increased school autonomy, new financial respo bilities for schools and educational leadership, school management can l factor of critical importance.

Evidence and explanations

School-level student/teaching staff ratios range from 10 students per teacher in Italy to 24 in Ireland.

Italy, Norway and Portugal report the smallest student/teaching staff ratio students in primary schools, with less than 15 students for each full-t equivalent teacher, whereas France, Ireland and the Netherlands report ra of 20 : 1 or higher. When class size is considered, most reporting countrie in the range between 15 and 20 students for each class, but in Netherlands there are on average almost 25 students per primary class. F the perspective of the workload of teachers, those working in the Netherla have relatively large classes and, in addition, have to teach relatively hours. Teachers in Greece, Norway and Portugal have a lighter bur (smaller classes and fewer teaching hours). In Sweden the number of teac hours is relatively low. As a result, despite a relatively small student/teac staff ratio (15), class sizes are comparatively large (21).

The figures for the school-based student/teaching staff ratio tend to be hi than the system-level student/teaching staff ratio reported by Indicato The differences are accounted for by teaching resources that are not alloc to schools as well as by a stricter definition of classroom teacher full-equivalents for the school-based computations.

Class sizes range from 15 students per class in Portugal to 25 in the Netherlands.

The results also show that countries differ significantly with respect to the average class size per school. In some countries, there are large within-country differences of class sizes implied. The interquartile range of class sizes is about three times as large in Finland and Spain as in Belgium and Italy (see Chart D6.1).

The student/teaching staff ratio not a direct indicator of class size as teachers may, for example, also provide support work.

The student/teaching staff ratio affects class sizes but it does not determine them. The ratio of students to teaching staff can be seen as the number of students per class (class size) divided by the number of teachers per class, and the number of teachers per class can be considered equivalent to the number of weekly lessons per class divided by the number of weekly lessons per teacher. For example, a number of teachers may be used to provide support work rather than smaller classes. Such support work makes a teacher's job easier. Subject teachers are also used in primary education (*e.g.* for foreign languages), and these do not have their own classes.

Differences in student/teaching staff ratios and class sizes can help to explain some of the differences in pay between countries.

Within a given teaching structure, more generous staffing will mean smaller classes. Poorer staffing levels can make teaching more demanding, and sometimes more frustrating. Potentially, large classes could offset the advantages of high pay in teacher's preferences, and small classes could help to compensate for lower pay. In fact, differences in student/teaching staff ratios and class sizes help to explain some of the differences in pay between OECD countries that were shown in Indicator D1.

Investment in school management is important but costs money.

In the ongoing debate on increased school autonomy, new financial responsibilities for schools and educational leadership, investment by countries in school management is an important factor. However, there are costs associated with school management. While a relatively high degree of in-school management can be considered conducive to teaching and learning, a high headteaching/teaching staff ratio can indicate a high proportion of human

◆　Chart D6.1. ***Mean and interquartile ranges of class sizes in primary education (1996)***

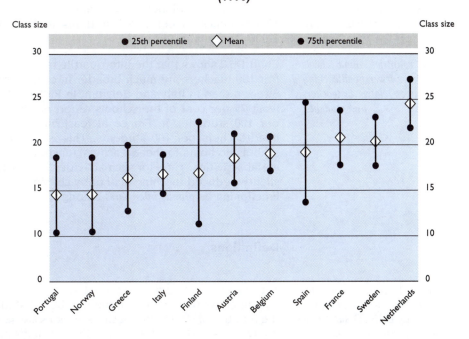

Source: OECD.

◆   Chart D6.2.   *Median and interquartile ranges of school-level headteaching/teachi* **staff ratios in primary education (1996)**

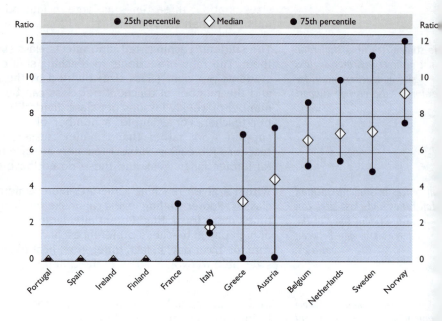

Source: OECD.

resources that are not actively involved in the schools' primary role of tea ing.

Countries differ in the number of headteachers relative to the number of classroom teachers and students in primary schools.

While there are 12 full-time equivalent headteachers per 100 teachers Norwegian primary schools, there is only one 1 headteacher per 100 teach in Portugal. In relation to the number of students, the range is betw 12 headteachers per 1 000 students in Norway and 0.6 headteachers 1 000 students in Portugal.

In some countries, small schools often have fewer headteaching resources relative to teachers and students.

Chart D6.2 shows that the interquartile ranges for the number of headteach per 100 teachers are much broader in countries such as Austria, Greece, Sweden than in Italy and Belgium. In Finland, Ireland, Portugal and Spair least 75 per cent of the schools report no full-time equivalent headteach per 100 students. In France at least 50 per cent of the schools report headteachers per 100 students. This is the result of the fact that in sr schools no hours for headteachers' functions are formally attributed to ma gerial activities. Time for such activities is allocated by giving headteache slightly reduced teaching load or by considering them an integral part of t functioning as *primus inter pares* among teachers.

Definitions

Data on teachers, schools and students are based on the OECD-INES survey on primary schools conducted in the school year 1995/96.

The school-level student/teaching staff ratio as presented in this indicate computed as the average of the number of students *in each school* divided the number of classroom teachers *in each school* (expressed in terms of full-t equivalents). This differs from the student/teaching staff ratio preser in Indicator B8, which is obtained by dividing the total number of

Figures on teaching hours per year are taken from the 1996 edition of Education at a Glance and refer to the school year 1993/94. They are based on the 1995 OECD-INES survey on teachers and the curriculum.

time-equivalent students at a given level of education by the total number of full-time-equivalent teachers at that same level of education.

Class size is computed as the average per country of the total number of students per school divided by the total number of classes per school.

Indicator D6 also shows country averages of the total full-time equivalent of non-teaching headteachers and deputy headteachers per school, relative to *i*) the number of full-time equivalent classroom teachers, and *ii*) the total number of students per school.

Table D6.1 **Class size, student/teaching staff ratio, number of teaching hours per year, headteaching/teaching staff ratio and headteaching staff/student ratio in primary schools (1996)**

	Class size	Student/ teaching staff ratio	Teaching hours per year (1994)	Headteaching/ teaching staff ratio * 100	Headteaching staff/ student ratio * 1 000
Austria	18.8	15.7	709	4.3	2.7
Belgium	19.4	16.5	832	7.3	4.1
Finland	17.3	16.1	m	2.4	1.6
France	20.6	20.2	923	1.7	0.8
Greece	16.5	15.2	696	4.2	2.7
Ireland	m	24.0	915	2.1	0.8
Italy	17.0	10.0	748	2.0	2.2
Netherlands	24.6	23.6	1000	8.0	3.8
Norway	15.1	10.5	686	11.9	12.4
Portugal	14.5	13.4	828	1.0	0.6
Spain	20.0	17.6	900	1.4	1.0
Sweden	20.6	15.3	624	9.4	6.1

Source: OECD database.

Indicator D7: Eighth-grade mathematics students' reports on how they spend their daily out-of-school study time

Policy context

This indicator shows the amount of time 8th-grade students spend after school studying or doing homework in mathematics, science or other school subjects.

Even though time in school is a dominant factor in the life of school-ag children, young people spend much more of their time outside school. H much of this out-of-school time is spent on learning – for example, in study or doing homework? Homework is an important tool that teachers use encourage students to review and practise what they have learned, to te children to work independently and to encourage children to develop gc habits and attitudes, such as self-discipline and responsibility.

Evidence and explanations

On average across OECD countries, 8th-grade students report spending 2.5 hours on studying or doing homework each day.

In more than two-thirds of the countries, the most common response fr 8th-graders about the amount of homework done is an average of 2 to 3 ho per day. Eighth-graders in the Flemish and French Communities of Belgi Greece, Hungary, Portugal and Spain report spending the most time homework, 3 or more hours per day. Students in Australia, the Cz Republic, Denmark, Germany and Scotland report spending the least amc of time per day on homework, 2 hours or less per day.

More than half the time for homework is devoted to mathematics and science.

The average time 8th-grade students spend each day studying mathema after school ranges in OECD countries from half an hour (Denmark) to hour and 10 minutes (Greece and Spain). Eighth-graders in the Cz Republic, Denmark, Germany, the Netherlands and Scotland are at the lo end of the range, reporting an average of less than 40 minutes per day. Th in Belgium (both the French and the Flemish Communities), Greece, Port and Spain are at the top end, reporting 1 hour or more of mathema homework per day. On average, students in nearly all countries report spe ing slightly less time per day studying science: science homework each takes on average between 20 minutes in Denmark and an hour and 10 r utes in Greece, while studying in other school subjects takes between ha hour in Denmark and 2 hours in Greece. Except in Ireland, studying mathematics and science takes up more than half the total time devote studying and homework after school, and usually substantially more.

In many countries, the highest student achievement is associated with a moderate amount of homework per day.

The relationship between the amount of homework and student achievem in mathematics is curvilinear in many countries, with the highest achievem being associated with a moderate amount of homework per day (one to t hours). This pattern suggests that, compared with their higher achiever

◆ Chart D7.1. *Average daily hours of out-of-school study time of 8th-grade mathematics students (1995)*

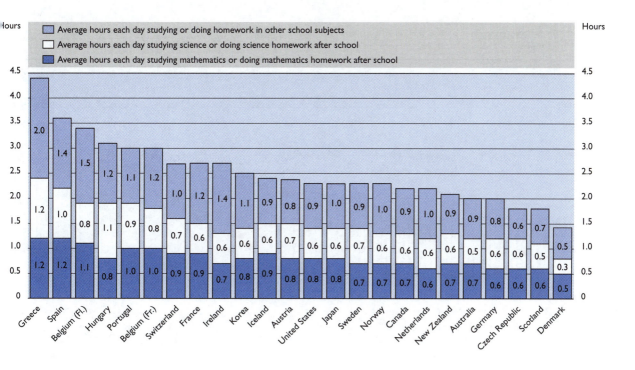

Countries are ranked in descending order by the total number of hours of out-of-school study time.

Source: IEA.

counterparts, students who perform less well may do less homework, because they do not do it or because their teachers do not assign it, or more homework, because they need to spend the extra time to keep up academically.

Definitions

Data are based on the Third International Mathematics and Science Study (TIMSS) undertaken by the International Association for the Evaluation of Educational Achievement (IEA) (see also Indicator D2).

Table D7.1 shows the average number of hours 8th-grade mathematics students spend each day on studying or doing homework in mathematics, science and other subjects (according to the students' reports).

The target population studied in this indicator refers to students at the higher of the two grade levels in which most 13 year-olds are enrolled and which, by convention, is referred to as the "8th" grade. The mean achievement represents the national average TIMSS mathematics achievement score of 8th-grade students.

Values in brackets present standard errors of sampling. Because results are rounded to the nearest whole number, some totals may appear inconsistent. A tilde (~) indicates insufficient data to report achievement. Countries marked with an asterisk did not satisfy one or more TIMSS guidelines for sample participation rates, age/grade specification or classroom sampling procedures. The reporting of data on a sub-national level for some countries

◆   Chart D7.2.   ***Mean mathematics achievement scores of 8th-grade mathematics students with different hour***
of out-of-school study time (1995)

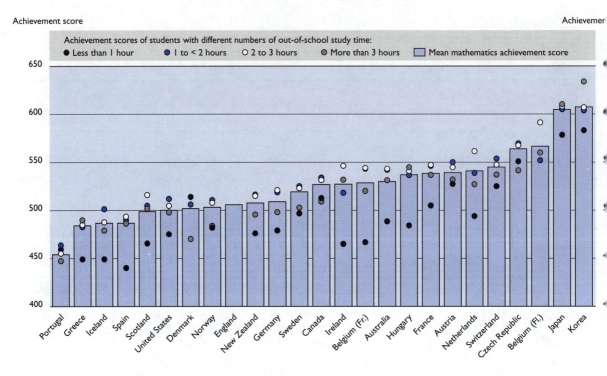

Countries are ranked in ascending order of the mean mathematics achievement score.

Source: IEA.

is based on data availability from the IEA and does not represent a p
decision by the OECD.

Average hours are based on: no time = 0; less than 1 hour = 0.5;
hours = 1.5; 3-5 hours = 4; more than 5 hours = 7. Table D7.2 refers to the
of time reported spent studying or doing homework in mathematics, sci
and other subjects.

Table D7.1   **Eighth-grade mathematics students' reports on how they spend their daily out-of-school study time (1995)**

	Average hours each day studying mathematics or doing mathematics homework after school	Average hours each day studying science or doing science homework after school	Average hours each day studying or doing homework in other school subjects	Total hours each day on average
North America				
Canada	0.7 (0.02)	0.6 (0.02)	0.9 (0.03)	2.2 (0.07)
United States	0.8 (0.02)	0.6 (0.01)	0.9 (0.02)	2.3 (0.04)
Pacific Area				
Australia*	0.7 (0.02)	0.5 (0.01)	0.9 (0.02)	2.0 (0.04)
Japan	0.8 (0.01)	0.6 (0.01)	1.0 (0.02)	2.3 (0.04)
Korea	0.8 (0.02)	0.6 (0.02)	1.1 (0.02)	2.5 (0.05)
New Zealand	0.7 (0.02)	0.6 (0.01)	0.9 (0.02)	2.1 (0.05)
European Union				
Austria*	0.8 (0.02)	0.7 (0.03)	0.8 (0.02)	2.4 (0.07)
Belgium				
(Flemish Community)	1.1 (0.03)	0.8 (0.02)	1.5 (0.03)	3.4 (0.07)
(French Community)*	1.0 (0.02)	0.8 (0.02)	1.2 (0.03)	3.0 (0.07)
Denmark*	0.5 (0.02)	0.3 (0.02)	0.5 (0.02)	1.4 (0.05)
France	0.9 (0.02)	0.6 (0.01)	1.2 (0.03)	2.7 (0.05)
Germany*	0.6 (0.02)	0.6 (0.02)	0.8 (0.02)	2.0 (0.05)
Greece*	1.2 (0.03)	1.2 (0.03)	2.0 (0.05)	4.4 (0.08)
Ireland	0.7 (0.02)	0.6 (0.01)	1.4 (0.03)	2.7 (0.05)
Netherlands*	0.6 (0.01)	0.6 (0.01)	1.0 (0.03)	2.2 (0.04)
Portugal	1.0 (0.02)	0.9 (0.02)	1.1 (0.02)	3.0 (0.05)
Spain	1.2 (0.02)	1.0 (0.02)	1.4 (0.03)	3.6 (0.06)
Sweden	0.7 (0.01)	0.7 (0.01)	0.9 (0.02)	2.3 (0.04)
United Kingdom				
England	m m	m m	m m	m m
Scotland*	0.6 (0.02)	0.5 (0.01)	0.7 (0.02)	1.8 (0.04)
Other OECD countries				
Czech Republic	0.6 (0.02)	0.6 (0.02)	0.6 (0.02)	1.8 (0.05)
Hungary	0.8 (0.02)	1.1 (0.02)	1.2 (0.03)	3.1 (0.06)
Iceland	0.9 (0.03)	0.6 (0.03)	0.9 (0.03)	2.4 (0.07)
Norway	0.7 (0.02)	0.6 (0.01)	1.0 (0.02)	2.3 (0.04)
Switzerland	0.9 (0.02)	0.7 (0.01)	1.0 (0.02)	2.7 (0.04)
Country mean	**0.8**	**0.7**	**1.0**	**2.5**

*Countries did not satisfy one or more TIMSS sampling guidelines.

Standard errors appear in parentheses.

Source: International Association for the Evaluation of Educational Achievement (IEA). See 'Definitions' in the text and notes in Annex 3.

Table D7.2 **Eighth-grade mathematics students' reports on total amount of daily out-of-school study time and corresponding average mathematics achievement (1995)**

	Less than 1 hour		1 to < 2 hours		2 to 3 hours		More than 3 hours	
	Percentage of students	Mean achievement	Percentage of students	Mean achievement	Percentage of students	Mean achievement	Percentage of students	Mean achievement
North America								
Canada	14 (1.2)	514 (5.6)	47 (1.1)	538 (2.8)	18 (0.7)	534 (3.7)	21 (1.1)	511 (3.6)
United States	17 (1.1)	471 (7.2)	42 (0.9)	514 (4.2)	17 (0.7)	507 (5.5)	24 (0.8)	498 (5.9)
Pacific Area								
Australia*	15 (0.9)	486 (5.7)	46 (1.0)	541 (4.4)	22 (0.6)	543 (5.2)	17 (0.7)	532 (4.8)
Japan	13 (0.8)	578 (5.3)	39 (0.8)	607 (2.6)	20 (0.6)	609 (4.0)	28 (1.0)	612 (2.7)
Korea	15 (0.9)	582 (4.9)	32 (1.1)	604 (3.5)	25 (0.8)	607 (4.0)	29 (1.2)	628 (4.3)
New Zealand	12 (0.9)	472 (5.6)	51 (1.2)	519 (4.7)	21 (1.0)	518 (6.1)	17 (0.9)	495 (5.6)
European Union								
Austria*	9 (0.8)	524 (6.7)	46 (1.3)	551 (4.1)	21 (0.9)	544 (4.5)	24 (1.2)	528 (5.3)
Belgium (Flemish Community)	2 (0.4)	~	25 (1.3)	552 (8.9)	28 (1.1)	592 (5.9)	45 (1.6)	560 (4.6)
(French Community)*	7 (0.8)	466 (7.4)	32 (1.0)	543 (4.6)	21 (1.3)	544 (5.5)	40 (1.5)	519 (4.5)
Denmark*	39 (1.6)	517 (4.4)	39 (1.4)	508 (3.8)	13 (0.8)	479 (4.1)	9 (0.7)	468 (6.9)
France	8 (0.7)	505 (8.0)	33 (1.2)	545 (3.6)	28 (1.0)	547 (4.5)	31 (1.2)	537 (3.7)
Germany*	14 (1.1)	476 (6.7)	51 (1.2)	521 (4.3)	18 (1.0)	524 (7.0)	17 (0.9)	498 (5.0)
Greece*	6 (0.6)	450 (7.4)	14 (0.7)	483 (5.2)	21 (0.7)	485 (3.9)	59 (1.2)	491 (3.3)
Ireland	5 (0.6)	465 (8.8)	29 (1.0)	517 (5.3)	40 (1.1)	547 (5.5)	26 (1.2)	533 (5.7)
Netherlands*	3 (0.9)	492(16.2)	54 (1.7)	539 (9.0)	27 (1.7)	562 (7.0)	16 (0.8)	524 (6.0)
Portugal	3 (0.3)	458 (8.1)	41 (1.1)	463 (3.1)	18 (0.7)	455 (3.3)	38 (1.2)	448 (3.0)
Spain	3 (0.4)	443 (5.5)	26 (1.0)	490 (3.1)	18 (0.9)	495 (3.3)	53 (1.3)	487 (2.4)
Sweden	7 (0.6)	496 (6.9)	55 (1.2)	528 (3.1)	17 (0.8)	525 (4.3)	21 (0.9)	503 (4.2)
United Kingdom								
England	m m	m m	m m	m m	m m	m m	m m	m m
Scotland*	17 (1.4)	461 (4.8)	54 (1.2)	506 (5.7)	17 (1.0)	517 (8.6)	12 (0.8)	503 (7.4)
Other OECD countries								
Czech Republic	13 (1.1)	551 (7.1)	57 (1.1)	571 (5.1)	17 (0.9)	568 (8.2)	13 (0.8)	542 (7.6)
Hungary	4 (0.4)	483(11.3)	33 (1.1)	536 (5.0)	22 (0.9)	541 (5.2)	41 (1.3)	545 (3.7)
Iceland	5 (1.0)	450(12.0)	46 (1.7)	501 (5.1)	25 (1.3)	489 (5.4)	23 (1.4)	477 (7.3)
Norway	6 (0.5)	481 (6.8)	50 (1.2)	514 (2.9)	24 (0.9)	510 (3.6)	21 (0.9)	483 (3.6)
Switzerland	4 (0.3)	523 (7.9)	44 (1.2)	556 (3.4)	19 (0.8)	548 (5.1)	33 (1.1)	536 (4.0)
Country mean	**10**	**493**	**41**	**531**	**22**	**533**	**27**	**519**

* Countries did not satisfy one or more TIMSS sampling guidelines.
( ) Standard errors appear in parentheses.
Source: International Association for the Evaluation of Educational Achievement (IEA). See 'Definitions' in the text and notes in Annex 3.

Chapter E

SOCIAL AND LABOUR MARKET OUTCOMES OF EDUCATION

Education and work are intimately connected, with education having two obvious effects on economic productivity. First, education can contribute to the development of knowledge, which translates into technological improvements and aggregate productivity gains. Second, education can increase the skills and knowledge of individual workers, allowing them to better accomplish particular tasks and more easily adapt to changing job requirements. In a free labour market, the success of an education system manifests itself among other things through the success of the individual in finding and holding a job, as well as in the level of wages that employers are willing to pay for the skills the individual holds.

The returns to education are not purely financial, however. Increased personal satisfaction, social position, civic participation and better health are all possible outcomes of education. While some educational returns accrue to the individual, others benefit society as a whole. Returns related to the economy, specifically to the labour market, include better job opportunities and jobs that are less sensitive to general economic conditions. Returns for the individual include higher relative earnings and greater opportunities to participate in training provided by employers.

This chapter examines labour market outcomes of education for the working-age population as a whole and for various demographic sub-groups.

Indicators E1 and **E2** provide the general background for this chapter, presenting first data on the rates of labour force participation by level of educational attainment and then employment and unemployment rates by level of educational attainment. As levels of skill tend to rise with levels of education, the costs of not working also rise. If labour markets are flexible enough to make use of the increasing skill levels of workers, higher levels of labour force participation should be associated with higher levels of education. **Indicator E1** shows that, with only a few exceptions, the labour force participation rates of both men and women in OECD countries rise with increasing educational attainment. To the extent that educational attainment is an indicator of skill, it acts as a signal to employers of the potential knowledge, capacities and work place performance of candidates for employment. **Indicator E2** shows that, in general, higher educational attainment tends to increase the likelihood of employment and to reduce the risk of unemployment.

Young people are the principal source of new skills in our societies, and **Indicator E3** shows how they perform in the labour market at various ages according to their educational attainment level. **Indicator E6** shows that despite the reductions in the size of the youth cohort observed in many countries over the past decade, the transition period remains difficult, even for the university-educated in some countries.

No examination of the outcomes of education would be complete without a look at earnings, which represent both the most obvious return on the investment in education and the incentive that ensures economies a steady supply of highly educated workers. **Indicator E4** shows the earnings of workers (both men and women) at various attainment levels, relative to those of persons with upper secondary attainment, as well as age-earnings profiles for these groups. This indicator shows that education and earnings from employment tend to be positively associated, whatever the type of socio-economic system or the level of economic development.

Finally, **Indicator E5** provides a cross-country comparison of the internal rates of return for different levels of education. The internal rate of return is a form of cost-benefit analysis, taking into account potential lifetime benefits from investing in a particular level of education relative to the costs of that investment. Although internal rates of return omit certain aspects of the social return to education (*e.g.*, increased tax revenues, reduced social security costs, lower crime rates, etc.), comparisons of these rates of return can provide valuable information about the incentives for investing in education in different countries.

Although the results shown in these indicators are influenced by many factors not directly related educational attainment (for example fiscal and monetary policies, the state of the business cycle, employment policies and labour market rigidities), the relative values of the indicators for different levels educational attainment provide valuable information on the importance which societies and economi attribute to increased levels of attainment.

Indicator E1: Labour force participation by level of educational attainment

Policy context

...is indicator shows the labour ...ce participation rate by level ...f educational attainment and gender.

OECD economies and labour markets are becoming increasingly dependent on a stable supply of well-educated workers to further their economic development and to maintain their competitiveness. As levels of skill tend to rise with levels of education, the costs of not working also rise. If labour markets are flexible enough to make use of the increasing skill levels of individuals, higher levels of labour force participation should be associated with higher levels of education. As populations in OECD countries age, higher levels of labour force participation can lower dependency ratios and help to alleviate the burden of financing public pensions.

Evidence and explanations

...st of the variation in labour force participation between ...ountries is accounted for by ...fferences in the participation of women.

Overall participation rates for the population aged 25 to 64 range from 63 to 91 per cent across OECD countries, with Belgium, Greece, Ireland, Italy, Luxembourg, Spain and Turkey showing rates under 70 per cent and the Czech Republic, the Nordic countries and Switzerland rates of 80 per cent or more. Among men, the dispersion is relatively narrow, ranging from 81 per cent participation rates in Belgium and Italy to 93 per cent in Korea and Sweden and 95 per cent in Switzerland and Turkey. The level of labour force participation among women is much more diverse across countries, with a low rate of 33 per cent in Turkey, rates of under 50 per cent in Greece, Ireland, Italy, Luxembourg and Spain, and rates of 75 per cent or more in the Czech Republic and the Nordic countries. It is evident from this that the participation of women largely determines the variability in overall participation rates across countries.

...i only a few exceptions, the ...our force participation rates ...f both men and women rise with increasing educational attainment.

Although overall labour force participation rates vary substantially between countries, there is a strong relationship between the level of educational attainment and labour force participation rates in almost all countries. The difference between the labour force participation rates of university graduates and those with less than an upper secondary credential range from 10 percentage points or less in Korea, Sweden and Turkey to around 35 percentage points in Belgium, Germany and Italy (see Table E1.1a). Notable exceptions to this general pattern are found in Turkey for men and in Korea for women, where persons with less than upper secondary attainment have higher participation rates than university graduates. These exceptions may be related to the continuing high incidence of subsistence agriculture in these countries and can be expected to disappear as their economies undergo further development (see Table E1.1b).

◆ Chart EI.Ia. **Labour force participation rate by level of educational attainment for the population 25 to 64 years of age (1995)**

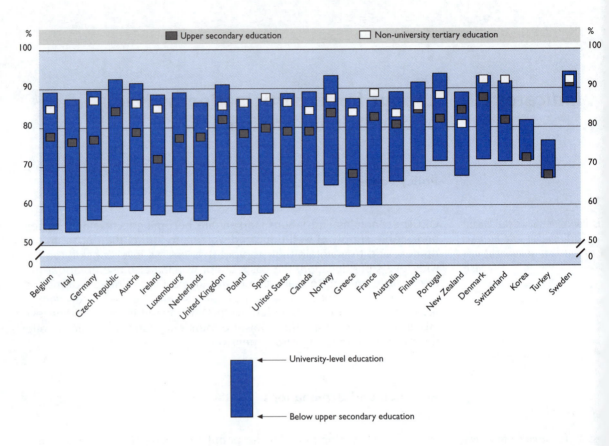

Countries are ranked in descending order of the difference between labour force participation rates for university-level attainment and for below upper secondary attainment.
Source: OECD.

On average, participation rates for men who have earned a university-level degree are 14 percentage points higher than for men with less than upper secondary education.

Participation rates of men at lower attainment levels (less than upper se
dary) are lowest in Poland, which is the only country where rates for men
less than upper secondary fall below 70 per cent. At the other end of
spectrum, participation rates for male university graduates exceed 90 per
everywhere except Turkey (84 per cent). In all countries there are only s
differences between participation rates of men with upper secondary at'
ment and those of men who have completed the university level. Differe
in participation rates between men with less than upper secondary and t
with upper secondary, on the other hand, average 10 percentage points. ˙
are small, however, in countries such as Greece, Korea, Portugal and Tu
where agriculture is still a major sector of activity in employment terms
also in Sweden and Switzerland, which are the only countries where parti
tion rates of men are over 90 per cent at all attainment levels.

For women, the educational background has a much stronger impact on labour force participation rates than for men.

By contrast, labour force participation rates of women show ma
differences not only as one moves from less than upper secondary to u
secondary (19 percentage points on average) but also from upper secor
to university (14 percentage points), with the exceptions of Denmark, Fin
France, Korea, New Zealand and Sweden, where participation rates of wc
with upper secondary approach those of women with university attainm

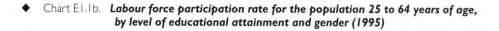

◆   Chart E1.1b.   **Labour force participation rate for the population 25 to 64 years of age, by level of educational attainment and gender (1995)**

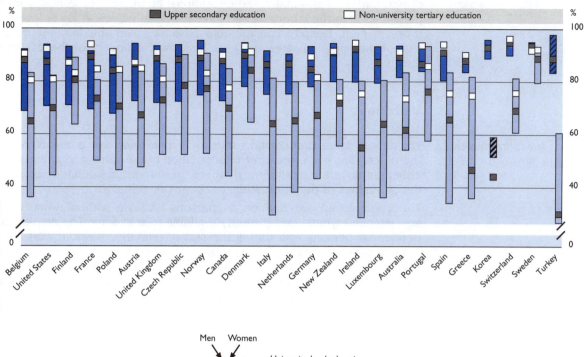

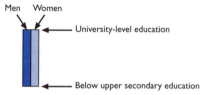

Korea and Turkey labour force participation rates are higher for below upper secondary than university-level education. This is indicated by dashes in the chart.
tries are ranked in descending order of the difference for men between labour force participation rates for university-level attainment and for below upper secondary attainment.
e: OECD.

gender gap in participation
ates among persons who did
t complete upper secondary
cation is, on average, three
times as large as among
university graduates.

Participation rates of women with less than upper secondary attainment are particularly low, averaging 50 per cent over all countries and exceeding 60 per cent only in Denmark, Finland, Korea, Sweden and Switzerland. Rates for women with university attainment exceed 80 per cent everywhere except in Korea and Turkey, but remain, on average, ten percentage points below those for men. Although a gender gap in labour force participation remains among those with the highest levels of educational attainment, the gap is much narrower than among those with lower levels of educational attainment. In general, with each additional attainment level the difference between the participation of men and that of women decreases by 10 percentage points: from about 30 percentage points at less than upper secondary and 20 at upper secondary to 10 at tertiary level.

e earnings tend to increase
ith educational attainment,
incentives are greater for
persons with a better
educational background.

The patterns observed here reflect a number of underlying causes. Since earnings tend to increase with educational attainment (see Indicator E4), the monetary incentive to participate is greater for persons at higher attainment levels.

243

Restructuring in many countries has reduced job opportunities for unskilled workers.

In addition, industrial restructuring in many countries has reduced job oppor-tunities for unskilled workers, a significant number of whom have left the labour market through early retirement schemes or because limited job opportunities exist. Finally, the educational attainment of women and their participation in the labour market have historically been at lower levels than those of men. Despite considerable advances over the last few decades, current participation rates continue to show the impact of these historical factors.

Definitions

Data are derived from national labour force surveys (for details see Annex 3).

The labour force participation rate for a particular age group is equal to the percentage of persons in the population of the same age group who are either employed or unemployed, where these terms are defined according to the guidelines of the International Labour Office (ILO).

The unemployed are defined as persons who are without work, actively seeking employment and currently available to start work. The employed are defined as persons who during the survey reference week: *i*) work for pay (employees) or profit (self-employed and unpaid family workers) for at least one hour or *ii*) have a job but are temporarily not at work (due to injury, illness, holiday or vacation, strike or lock-out, educational or training leave, maternity or parental leave, etc.) and have a formal attachment to their job.

Table E1.1a   **Rates of labour force participation by level of educational attainment for the population 25 to 64 years of age (1995)**

	Early childhood, primary and lower secondary education	Upper secondary education	Non-university tertiary education	University-level education	All levels of education
North America					
Canada	61	79	84	89	78
United States	60	79	86	89	79
Pacific Area					
Australia	66	81	84	89	75
Korea	72	72	x	82	74
New Zealand	68	85	81	89	77
European Union					
Austria	59	79	86	91	74
Belgium	55	78	85	89	69
Denmark	72	88	92	93	82
Finland	69	85	85	92	80
France	60	83	89	87	77
Germany	57	77	87	90	75
Greece	60	68	84	87	67
Ireland	58	72	85	88	67
Italy	54	76	x	87	63
Luxembourg	59	77	x	89	66
Netherlands	57	78	a	86	71
Portugal	72	82	88	94	75
Spain	58	80	88	87	66
Sweden	86	91	92	94	91
United Kingdom	62	82	86	91	79
Other OECD countries					
Czech Republic	60	84	x	93	81
Norway	65	84	88	93	82
Poland	58	79	86	87	74
Switzerland	71	82	92	92	82
Turkey	67	68	x	77	68
Country mean	**63**	**80**	**87**	**89**	**75**

Source: OECD Database. See Annex 3 for notes.

Table E1.1*b*   **Rates of labour force participation by level of educational attainment for the population 25 to 64 years of age, by gender (1995)**

	Gender	Early childhood, primary and lower secondary education	Upper secondary education	Non-university tertiary education	University-level education	All levels of education
North America						
Canada	Men	74	88	90	93	86
	Women	47	71	78	85	70
United States	Men	72	88	92	94	88
	Women	47	71	82	83	71
Pacific Area						
Australia	Men	82	90	91	94	88
	Women	56	64	75	84	63
Korea	Men	89	93	x	96	93
	Women	61	47	x	54	55
New Zealand	Men	81	92	92	94	88
	Women	58	73	75	81	67
European Union						
Austria	Men	74	87	88	94	85
	Women	50	69	85	86	63
Belgium	Men	70	88	91	92	81
	Women	39	66	81	84	57
Denmark	Men	79	90	93	95	87
	Women	66	85	91	91	78
Finland	Men	72	88	87	93	83
	Women	65	81	84	89	77
France	Men	71	90	94	92	85
	Women	53	75	85	81	68
Germany	Men	79	85	90	93	86
	Women	46	69	82	83	65
Greece	Men	84	88	90	91	87
	Women	39	49	76	82	48
Ireland	Men	81	93	95	94	86
	Women	32	57	76	81	49
Italy	Men	76	87	x	92	81
	Women	33	66	x	82	45
Luxembourg	Men	80	88	x	93	84
	Women	39	66	x	81	47
Netherlands	Men	76	87	a	91	84
	Women	41	67	a	81	58
Portugal	Men	85	87	94	94	86
	Women	60	77	86	93	65
Spain	Men	81	91	94	91	84
	Women	37	67	77	84	47
Sweden	Men	91	94	92	95	93
	Women	80	89	92	93	88
United Kingdom	Men	73	89	91	93	87
	Women	55	74	82	87	70
Other OECD countries						
Czech Republic	Men	74	89	x	94	88
	Women	55	79	x	90	75
Norway	Men	76	89	91	95	88
	Women	55	78	84	91	77
Poland	Men	69	85	91	90	82
	Women	49	72	85	85	67
Switzerland	Men	90	95	96	96	95
	Women	63	71	77	82	70
Turkey	Men	98	89	x	84	95
	Women	30	33	x	62	33
Country mean	**Men**	**79**	**89**	**92**	**93**	**87**
	Women	**50**	**69**	**82**	**83**	**63**

Source: OECD Database. See Annex 3 for notes.

Indicator E2: **Employment, unemployment and education**

Policy context

This indicator shows the employment/population ratios and unemployment rates by level of educational attainment, age group and gender.

To the extent that educational attainment is an indicator of skill, it acts as a signal to employers of the potential knowledge, capacities and work place performance of candidates for employment. Employment prospects of persons at various educational attainment levels will depend both on the requirements of labour markets and on the supply of workers at the various attainment levels. Ensuring that workers have sufficient skills for available jobs is a matter of significant policy interest in all countries.

Evidence and explanations

There is a strong link between education and employment whatever the unemployment rate or the rate of job creation.

In all countries, whatever the unemployment rate or the rate of job creation, the proportion of persons employed increases with the level of educational attainment. Thus, in terms of employment, the pay-off to both men and women from more education is beyond question. Even in countries where women generally participate less in the labour market than in other countries (see Indicator E1), those with tertiary level education have a likelihood of being employed similar to that of their counterparts with similar educational qualifications in other countries (between 80 and 90 per cent of all women aged 30 to 44 in most OECD countries). This is not the case, however, for women with only upper secondary education. While the gap in the employment/population ratios between women holding a university qualification and women holding only an upper secondary qualification is, on average, 14 per cent in OECD countries, the gap is even wider in countries with low overall levels of female labour force participation.

The likelihood of finding employment once in the labour market is higher for workers with higher levels of education.

Labour force participation rates are higher and unemployment rates are lower for more highly educated persons. As relative earnings are higher for the more highly educated (Indicator E4), the incentive for highly educated people to participate in the labour market is greater. Employers also use an individual's level of educational attainment as a screening device or tool that predicts the individual's future productivity. Thus the likelihood of finding employment once in the labour market is higher for workers with higher levels of education.

What distinguishes countries from one another is the ability of their economies to provide employment opportunities for those with low educational attainment.

The proportion of persons 25 to 64 years of age who are employed varies from about 53 per cent in Spain and 57 per cent in Italy to 79 per cent or above in the Czech Republic, Norway, Sweden and Switzerland – a range across OECD countries of almost 30 percentage points. For tertiary graduates, employment to population ratios are generally between 85 and 90 per cent, with the exception of Spain and Turkey where they are about 75 per cent, and France, Greece, Italy, Korea and the Netherlands where they are close to 80 per cent. The variation in the proportion of persons employed varies more across countries for lower attainment levels, from 65 per cent or less for persons with upper secondary education in Greece, Spain and Turkey to 80 per cent or

◆ Chart E2.1a. ***Unemployment rates by level of educational attainment for the population 25 to 64 years of age (1995)***

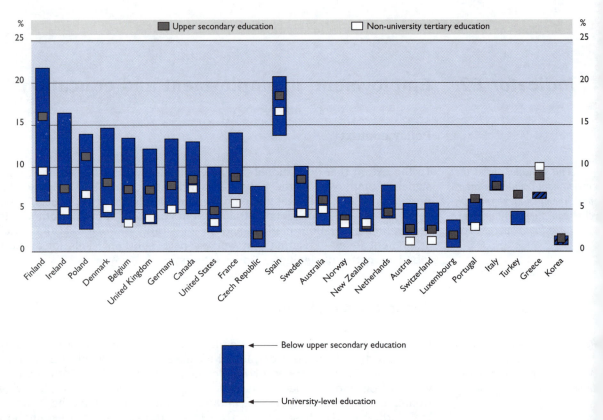

For Greece and Korea unemployment rates are higher for university-level education than for below upper secondary education. This is indicated by dashes in the cha
Countries are ranked in descending order of the difference between unemployment rates for below upper secondary attainment and unemployment rates for university-level attainm

Source: OECD.

above in the Czech Republic, Denmark, New Zealand, Norway, Sweden a Switzerland. There is further divergence across countries for persons with I than upper secondary attainment, with the proportion of persons emplo ranging from less than 50 per cent in some countries more than 70 per cer others.

Patterns of unemployment by level of educational attainment tend to mirror these results.

Patterns of unemployment by level of educational attainment tend to mi these results, with much less variation in unemployment rates across co tries at higher educational attainment levels than at lower ones. In all co tries except Spain, where the unemployment rate for persons with univer attainment is particularly high (13.8 per cent) and France, Greece and I where it is around to 7 per cent, unemployment rates for persons in category are less than 5 per cent. On the other hand, among persons with I than upper secondary education, unemployment rates range from 1 per c in Korea to over 20 per cent in Finland and Spain.

Difficult labour market conditions affect particularly those with low levels of education except in countries where agriculture is still an

The large variation between countries in unemployment rates observe low attainment levels is the consequence of a number of factors. In so countries (especially Finland and Spain), the high unemployment rate these levels reflect generally difficult labour market conditions that par larly affect individuals with low levels of education. Unemployment r

◆ Chart E2.1b. ***Unemployment rates for the population 30 to 44 years of age, by level of educational attainment and gender (1995)***

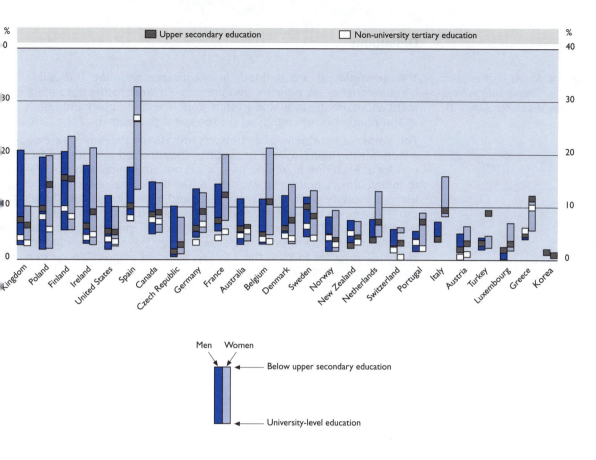

◻ Upper secondary education ◻ Non-university tertiary education

Men Women

← Below upper secondary education

← University-level education

area the unemployment rate is higher for university-level education than for below upper secondary.
ies are ranked in descending order of the difference for men between unemployment rates for below upper secondary attainment and unemployment rates for university-level
ment.
: OECD.

important sector. among those without an upper secondary qualification are also relatively high in some countries where labour markets are less regulated (Canada, the United Kingdom and the United States), although not in others (Australia and New Zealand). On the other hand, in countries where agriculture is still an important sector in employment terms (Greece, Korea, Portugal and Turkey), unemployment rates tend to be low. Finally, where overall labour market conditions are particularly favourable (Austria, the Czech Republic, Luxembourg, Norway and Switzerland), jobs appear to be available for workers with low as well as high levels of education.

increasing unemployment nd continuing upskilling of , the position of those with educational attainment has ne increasingly vulnerable. Since persons with less than upper secondary education still comprise a substantial proportion of the working-age population and of the labour force in most countries (see Indicator A2), an economy's ability to provide jobs for adult persons at this level has a significant effect on the overall unemployment rate. Over the 1989 to 1994 period, in a climate of generally increasing unemployment and continuing upskilling of jobs, the position of this group relative to that of the rest of the labour force has, with some exceptions (Germany, Ireland, the Netherlands and Norway), deteriorated in many reporting countries, and most notably in Canada, Denmark, Finland, Spa Sweden, the United Kingdom and the United States.

Definitions

Data are derived from national labour force surveys (for details see Annex 3).

The unemployed are defined, in accordance with the ILO guidelines labour statistics, as persons who are without work, actively seeking emplc ment and currently available to start work. The unemployment rate is defin as the number of unemployed persons as a percentage of the labour forc

The employed are defined as persons who during the survey reference wee i) work for pay (employees) or profit (self-employed and unpaid family wo ers) for at least one hour or ii) have a job but are temporarily not at work (d to injury, illness, holiday or vacation, strike or lock-out, educational or train leave, maternity or parental leave, etc.) and have a formal attachment to th job. The employment/population ratio is defined as the number of employ persons divided by the corresponding overall number of persons in population. Persons less than 25 years of age have been excluded from statistics, in order to base the analysis as much as possible on persons v have completed their initial education.

Table E2.1*a* **Employment/population ratios and unemployment rates for 25-64 year-olds by level of educational attainment**
(1995)

	Employment/population ratios					Unemployment rates				
	Below upper secondary education	Upper secondary education	Non-university tertiary education	University-level education	All levels of education	Below upper secondary education	Upper secondary education	Non-university tertiary education	University-level education	All levels of education
North America										
Canada	53	72	78	85	71	13.0	8.6	7.5	4.6	8.3
Mexico	m	m	m	m	m	m	m	m	m	m
United States	54	75	83	87	76	10.0	5.0	3.6	2.5	4.7
Pacific Area										
Australia	61	76	79	86	71	8.5	6.2	5.1	3.3	6.6
Japan	m	m	m	m	m	m	m	m	m	m
Korea	71	71	x	80	73	1.0	1.6	x	2.0	1.4
New Zealand	63	82	78	87	74	6.7	3.3	3.6	2.6	4.5
European Union										
Austria	56	77	85	89	71	5.7	2.9	1.4	2.1	3.5
Belgium	47	72	82	86	63	13.4	7.5	3.5	3.6	8.5
Denmark	61	80	87	89	74	14.6	8.3	5.3	4.3	10.0
Finland	54	71	77	86	67	21.6	16.1	9.7	6.2	15.8
France	52	75	84	81	69	14.0	8.9	5.9	7.0	9.7
Germany	49	71	83	85	69	13.3	7.9	5.2	4.7	8.1
Greece	56	62	75	81	62	6.3	9.0	10.1	7.1	7.4
Ireland	49	67	81	85	60	16.4	7.6	5.0	3.4	10.7
Italy	49	70	x	81	57	9.1	7.9	x	7.3	8.5
Luxembourg	57	76	x	88	64	3.8	2.1	x	0.6	3.0
Netherlands	52	74	a	83	67	7.9	4.8	a	4.1	5.6
Portugal	67	77	86	91	70	6.2	6.4	3.1	3.3	5.8
Spain	46	65	73	75	53	20.6	18.5	16.6	13.8	19.0
Sweden	78	84	88	90	83	10.1	8.7	4.8	4.2	7.8
United Kingdom	54	76	82	88	73	12.2	7.4	4.1	3.5	7.4
Other OECD countries										
Czech Republic	56	82	x	92	79	7.7	2.1	x	0.7	2.7
Hungary	m	m	m	m	m	m	m	m	m	m
Iceland	m	m	m	m	m	m	m	m	m	m
Norway	61	80	85	92	79	6.5	4.0	3.4	1.7	3.9
Poland	50	70	80	85	66	13.9	11.4	6.9	2.8	10.7
Switzerland	67	80	91	89	80	5.8	2.8	1.5	2.6	3.0
Turkey	64	63	x	74	65	4.8	6.9	x	3.3	5.0
Country mean	**57**	**74**	**82**	**85**	**70**	**10.1**	**7.0**	**5.6**	**4.0**	**7.3**

Source: OECD Database. See Annex 3 for notes.

Table E2.1*b* **Employment/population ratios and unemployment rates for 30-44 year-olds by level of educational attainment and gender (1995)**

	Gender	Employment/population ratios					Unemployment rates				
		Below upper secondary education	Upper secondary education	Non-university tertiary education	University-level education	All levels of education	Below upper secondary education	Upper secondary education	Non-university tertiary education	University-level education	All levels
North America											
Canada	Men	72	85	87	91	84	14.6	8.5	7.5	4.9	8
	Women	51	70	77	82	71	14.5	8.9	7.2	5.2	8
United States	Men	69	87	91	95	87	12.0	5.4	3.8	1.9	5
	Women	49	72	82	81	73	10.0	5.2	3.4	2.6	4
Pacific Area											
Australia	Men	80	89	92	93	87	11.5	5.9	4.5	2.9	7
	Women	60	66	76	83	66	6.6	6.1	5.4	3.6	5
Korea	Men	93	96	x	96	95	1.8	1.5	x	1.5	1
	Women	67	49	x	49	56	0.6	1.0	x	0.9	0
New Zealand	Men	80	93	91	92	88	7.4	2.7	5.0	2.9	4
	Women	60	69	74	77	67	7.3	4.2	3.4	3.8	5
European Union											
Austria	Men	86	95	95	95	94	5.0	2.0	0.6	1.9	2
	Women	63	75	89	88	73	6.4	3.2	1.1	2.7	3
Belgium	Men	81	92	95	94	88	11.5	4.8	3.9	3.0	7
	Women	48	70	87	83	66	21.1	11.0	3.4	4.8	11
Denmark	Men	76	89	92	93	84	12.1	6.0	4.6	4.4	8
	Women	69	84	91	93	79	14.2	7.5	4.0	3.1	9
Finland	Men	71	80	88	92	80	20.3	15.4	9.6	5.6	14
	Women	62	73	82	86	73	23.2	15.2	8.1	5.7	14
France	Men	79	90	94	92	89	14.2	7.4	4.1	5.5	8
	Women	53	71	84	79	69	19.8	12.2	5.3	7.5	12
Germany	Men	83	91	96	94	91	13.3	5.9	3.3	4.2	
	Women	56	70	83	82	69	12.6	9.1	6.7	5.2	
Greece	Men	91	94	93	95	93	4.9	4.9	5.6	4.0	
	Women	44	51	73	86	54	11.9	11.6	9.9	5.7	10
Ireland	Men	73	90	94	93	82	17.7	6.3	4.2	3.1	1
	Women	31	55	75	81	50	21.1	9.0	4.8	2.8	10
Italy	Men	87	92	x	93	90	7.2	4.0	x	4.0	
	Women	38	66	x	81	52	15.8	9.4	x	8.3	1
Luxembourg	Men	94	96	x	98	95	2.2	1.9	x	0.2	
	Women	48	69	x	79	55	6.9	3.1	x	1.8	
Netherlands	Men	83	93	a	94	90	7.7	3.8	a	3.3	
	Women	47	66	a	81	63	12.9	7.2	a	4.4	
Portugal	Men	89	94	96	96	91	5.4	3.4	3.3	1.7	
	Women	67	80	94	95	73	8.9	7.2	2.2	2.0	
Spain	Men	77	87	90	91	82	17.4	10.1	7.9	7.3	1
	Women	33	51	55	77	43	32.6	26.6	26.7	13.3	2
Sweden	Men	82	85	90	92	86	11.8	10.0	6.4	4.4	
	Women	70	83	90	89	83	13.1	8.3	4.1	4.6	
United Kingdom	Men	66	88	93	96	86	20.6	7.5	4.1	2.8	
	Women	51	70	84	84	69	10.0	6.5	3.1	3.3	
Other OECD countries											
Czech Republic	Men	80	96	x	98	95	10.1	1.5	x	0.6	
	Women	78	89	x	95	87	8.0	2.8	x	1.1	
Norway	Men	77	89	92	96	89	8.1	4.2	4.2	1.7	
	Women	59	79	84	90	79	9.3	3.7	2.9	1.7	
Poland	Men	70	84	88	97	83	19.3	9.6	8.1	1.9	
	Women	59	70	86	92	72	19.6	14.1	5.7	2.1	
Switzerland	Men	90	96	98	96	96	5.8	2.1	1.9	1.6	
	Women	69	69	73	78	70	6.1	3.2	0.4	5.2	
Turkey	Men	102	93	x	91	99	4.2	3.2	x	2.0	
	Women	31	33	x	67	33	4.5	9.7	x	2.3	
Country mean	**Men**	**81**	**91**	**92**	**94**	**89**	**10.7**	**5.5**	**4.9**	**3.1**	
	Women	**55**	**68**	**81**	**82**	**66**	**12.7**	**8.2**	**5.7**	**4.2**	

Source: OECD Database. See Annex 3 for notes.

Indicator E3: Youth unemployment and education

Policy context

This indicator shows ~employment rates for young ~rsons by level of educational attainment.

Young people represent the most important source of new skills in our societies. In most OECD countries, education policy has focused on encouraging young people to complete upper secondary education. With the continuing upskilling of jobs, persons with low levels of educational attainment are at a distinct disadvantage in the labour market. Even with increasing educational attainment, unemployment among young people in many countries is high. This is a waste of human resources and can be a risk factor socially for both the individual and society at large.

Evidence and explanations

Young people cannot ~mpensate for low educational attainment through work ~erience and skills learned on the job.

In many countries, when young people enter the labour market after completing their education, it is under less than favourable conditions. Although they may be more educated on average than workers in older age groups, they may have little experience of working or even of looking for work. The wages they are paid will often be lower than those of existing workers with comparable education and employers may need to invest in job-related training for them before their productivity levels can rise to those of other workers. Adaptation to working life may take time and may involve a certain amount of job-shopping before stable and/or attractive long-term employment is found. Because of seniority provisions in collective bargaining agreements in many countries, young workers may also be the first to be laid off if firms are undergoing economic difficulties. All of these factors mean that the period of entry into the labour market may be somewhat uncertain and turbulent.

~employment rates of young ~ple are substantially higher ~an those of workers in older age groups in all OECD countries.

Across OECD countries, unemployment rates among 20 to 24 year-olds with less than upper secondary education are, on average, about 22 per cent. Unemployment rates for this age group are under 10 per cent only in Austria, Korea and Luxembourg and are 30 per cent or above in Poland, Spain, Sweden and the United Kingdom and even 40 per cent in Finland and France.

~ problem of unemployment ~ng young people who have completed upper secondary ~cation is persistent through successive age cohorts.

The problem of unemployment among young people with less than an upper secondary education is a persistent one: for 25 to 29 year-olds, it still averages 17 per cent across countries and exceeds 25 per cent in Finland, France, Poland, Spain and the United Kingdom. Since upper secondary attainment has become the norm in most OECD countries, many young persons with less education than this can expect to encounter employment problems throughout their working lives.

The chances for upper ~dary graduates increase in ~y countries as one looks at successive age cohorts.

Although the situation for 20-24 year-old upper secondary completers is only somewhat better (a 16 per cent unemployment rate on average), unemployment of upper secondary graduates shows a marked improvement with age. Among 25-29 year-olds, the unemployment rate for persons with an upper secondary diploma is 10 per cent, and among 30-44 year-olds it is 7 per cent, scarcely different from the 7 per cent rate for persons 25-64 years old with

253

◆ Chart E3.1. ***Youth unemployment rate by level of educational attainment (1995)***

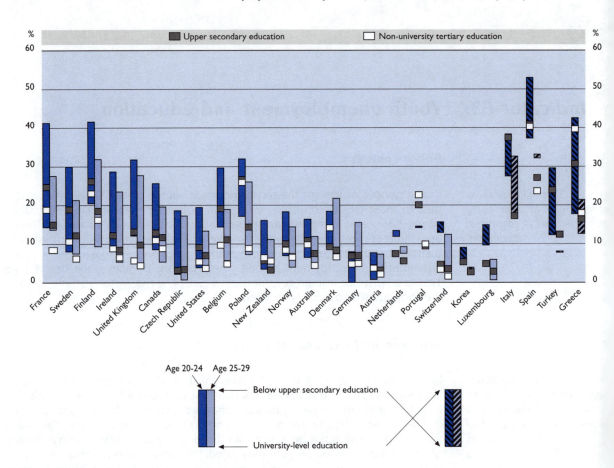

For some countries the unemployment rate is higher for university-level education than for below upper secondary. This is indicated by dashes in the chart.
Countries are ranked in descending order of the difference between unemployment rates of 20 to 24 year-olds for below upper secondary and university-level attainment.
Source: OECD.

Job prospects for 25-29 year-olds with a university qualification are much more favourable in most countries.

only an upper secondary level of education (see Table E2.1a). In a numbe[r of] countries, however, the risk of unemployment among 25 to 29 year-olds [with] only an upper secondary diploma remains high, despite the fact that mos[t of] them have been in the labour market for at least five years. In Spain, [the] unemployment rate for this group is 27 per cent and in Finland, Fra[nce,] Greece and Italy it is between 15 and 20 per cent. Thus even at level[s of] educational attainment which have become more or less a norm in O[ECD] countries, youth employment prospects remain difficult in some countri[es.]

In contrast, job prospects for 25-29 year-olds with a university qualifica[tion] are much more favourable in most countries, with unemployment rates b[elow] 8 per cent in 19 out of 25 OECD countries. Unemployment rates am[ong] university graduates in this age group remain high in a small group of c[oun]tries, however, exceeding 10 per cent in France, Greece and Portugal [and] even 30 per cent in Italy and Spain. In all of these countries except Fra[nce,] the unemployment rate of university graduates aged 25-29 meets or exce[eds] that of upper secondary graduates. The demand for highly skilled labo[ur in] these countries is clearly insufficient to absorb all of the graduates w[hich] education systems are producing.

he unemployment situation of young people is closely linked) general economic conditions.

In general, the unemployment situation of young people aged 25-29, particularly those having less than tertiary education, is closely linked to general economic conditions. In countries where the unemployment rate for the age group 25-64 is high, so generally are the rates for young people aged 25-29 with an upper secondary diploma. Although higher levels of educational attainment can improve employment prospects, further reductions in youth unemployment will probably depend mainly on more general improvements in the health of a country's economy.

Definitions

ata are derived from national our force surveys (for details see Annex 3).

The unemployment rate is calculated as the number of persons unemployed as a percentage of the labour force, where the terms "unemployment" and "labour force" are defined according to the guidelines of the ILO (see Definitions of Indicator E2). The unemployment rate for a particular age group is based on the proportion of persons in the labour force unemployed for that age group.

Table E3.1 **Youth unemployment rates by level of educational attainment and age group (1995)**

	Below upper secondary education			Upper secondary education			Non-university tertiary education		University-level education		All levels of education		
	Age 15-19	Age 20-24	Age 25-29	Age 15-19	Age 20-24	Age 25-29	Age 20-24	Age 25-29	Age 20-24	Age 25-29	Age 15-19	Age 20-24	
North America													
Canada	21.3	25.6	19.5	14.6	12.9	11.7	10.9	8.8	8.6	5.4	18.2	13.7	1C
Mexico	m	m	m	m	m	m	m	m	m	m	m	m	
United States	20.4	19.4	13.3	10.2	9.1	7.0	5.4	3.7	3.9	3.0	16.9	9.5	
Pacific Area													
Australia	23.0	16.4	11.9	17.4	10.9	7.5	9.8	4.4	6.5	4.7	21.0	12.0	
Japan	m	m	m	m	m	m	m	m	m	m	m	m	
Korea	8.9	4.5	2.7	7.6	5.3	2.6	x	x	9.0	3.8	7.9	5.9	
New Zealand	17.7	16.1	11.1	10.8	5.6	3.2	6.4	5.5	3.5	2.9	15.7	8.1	
European Union													
Austria	6.4	7.6	7.2	4.9	3.9	3.1	3.6	2.1	0.8	3.6	5.9	4.5	
Belgium	22.9	29.7	18.9	27.3	19.2	11.1	9.7	4.8	14.5	5.7	25.3	20.0	1
Denmark	3.3	18.4	21.7	7.4	9.3	8.3	14.2	6.6	9.9	7.7	3.7	12.9	
Finland	30.6	41.6	32.0	38.9	26.2	18.5	23.1	16.2	20.6	9.4	33.6	29.1	
France	25.3	41.3	27.6	23.2	24.8	15.0	18.9	8.4	14.4	13.8	24.4	26.1	
Germany	5.6	12.5	15.5	7.5	6.8	6.9	4.7	4.9	m	5.1	7.2	8.1	
Greece	25.7	17.8	12.6	50.4	30.9	16.4	39.8	18.1	42.6	21.4	35.2	28.4	1
Ireland	35.2	28.7	23.5	21.6	12.2	8.4	8.8	6.4	9.0	5.4	28.2	16.0	1
Italy	34.6	27.6	16.6	47.8	37.6	17.3	x	x	38.5	32.7	37.7	32.6	1
Luxembourg	15.0	9.6	5.9	18.8	4.8	2.8	x	x	14.9	0.6	15.2	9.1	
Netherlands	19.0	13.4	9.2	15.0	7.4	5.5	a	a	12.0	7.6	18.2	9.9	
Portugal	16.1	14.2	8.9	34.2	20.1	9.8	22.7	9.9	14.5	10.3	17.2	15.6	
Spain	49.6	37.4	32.3	54.3	41.0	27.2	40.4	23.7	53.1	33.2	50.6	39.8	3
Sweden	19.6	30.0	21.3	24.2	18.9	12.2	10.6	6.1	8.1	7.5	20.9	19.2	
United Kingdom	28.1	31.8	27.8	14.9	13.2	9.8	5.6	4.4	12.2	3.7	17.3	14.2	
Other OECD countries													
Czech Republic	24.8	18.6	17.2	9.0	3.1	3.4	x	x	2.2	0.7	13.0	4.0	
Hungary	m	m	m	m	m	m	m	m	m	m	m	m	
Iceland	m	m	m	m	m	m	m	m	m	m	m	m	
Norway	16.9	18.3	14.4	14.4	10.0	6.8	8.3	6.5	7.0	4.0	15.8	10.3	
Poland	30.6	32.0	26.1	50.8	26.7	14.4	26.0	8.8	17.2	7.4	44.2	27.1	
Switzerland	18.0	x	x	x	4.6	3.5	x	1.6	x	4.2	16.0	5.8	
Turkey	10.9	12.3	8.0	32.9	23.9	12.4	x	x	29.7	7.8	13.8	16.1	
Country mean	**21.2**	**21.9**	**16.9**	**23.3**	**15.5**	**9.8**	**14.9**	**7.9**	**15.3**	**8.5**	**20.9**	**15.9**	

Source: OECD Database. See Annex 3 for notes.

Indicator E4: Education and earnings from employment

Policy context

This indicator shows relative earnings for different levels of educational attainment, measured as mean earnings of persons at a given level of educational attainment divided by the mean earnings of persons with upper secondary school attainment. Age-earnings profiles are also presented.

Increased global competition and technological innovation have increased the skill requirements in many sectors of modern economies. One way in which markets supply incentives for workers to develop and maintain appropriate levels of skills is through wage differentials, in particular through the enhanced earnings accorded to persons completing additional education. The pursuit of higher levels of education can also be viewed as an investment in human capital. Human capital is the stock of skills that individuals maintain or develop, typically through education or training, and then offer in return for earnings in the labour market. The higher earnings that result from increases in human capital represent the return on that investment and the premium paid to enhanced skills and/or to higher productivity. Earnings differentials are a measure of the current financial incentives in a particular country for an individual to invest in further education. Earnings differentials by level of educational attainment may also reflect differences in the supply of educational programmes at different levels or the barriers in access to those programmes.

Evidence and explanations

Education and earnings for men and women

Education and earnings are positively linked, whatever the type of socio-economic system or the level of economic development.

The economic benefit of completing tertiary education can be seen by comparing the ratio of the mean annual earnings of those who attended and graduated from tertiary education with the mean annual earnings of upper secondary graduates. The earnings disadvantage from not completing upper secondary education is apparent from a similar comparison. Variations in relative earnings (before taxes) between countries reflect a number of factors, including skill demands in the workforce, minimum wage legislation, the strength of unions, the coverage of collective bargaining agreements, the supply of workers at the various educational attainment levels, the range of work experience of workers with high and low educational attainment, the distribution of employment across occupations and the relative incidence of part-time and part-year work among workers with varying levels of educational attainment.

University-level graduates earn significantly more than upper secondary graduates in all countries.

The data in Table E4.1a and Table E4.1b show a strong positive relationship between educational attainment and earnings. University-level graduates earn significantly more than upper secondary graduates in all countries.

Upper secondary education is a break-point for many countries beyond which additional education attracts a particularly high premium.

Earnings differentials between university tertiary and upper secondary education are generally more pronounced than those between upper secondary and below, suggesting that upper secondary education is a break-point for many countries beyond which additional education attracts a particularly high premium. Among countries reporting gross earnings, the earnings premium

◆   Chart E4.1.   *Mean annual earnings of persons 30 to 44 years of age at different levels of educational attainment as a percentage of mean annual earnings at the upper secondary level by gender, and mean annual earnings of women 30 to 44 years of age as a percentage of mean annual earnings of men at the same age by level of educational attainment (1995)*

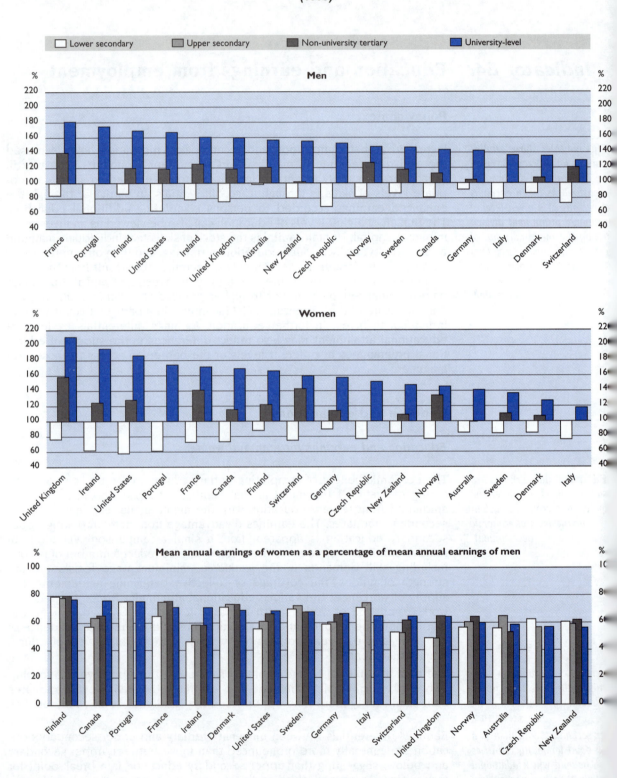

Source: OECD.

for university-level education ranges from about 40 per cent for men aged 25-64 in Denmark and Switzerland to 80 per cent or more in Finland, France and Portugal.

For women, the range in the premium on university-level education is even wider, extending from 20 to 95 per cent across countries.

For women in the same age range, the premium ranges from 20 per cent in Italy to 95 per cent in the United Kingdom. University education enhances earnings relative to secondary-level education more for women than for men in Canada, Ireland, the Netherlands, Norway, Switzerland, the United Kingdom and the United States, whereas the reverse is true for the remaining countries.

Non-university tertiary education in all countries yields a considerably smaller earnings advantage than university education. The advantage of non-university tertiary education over upper secondary education is typically 10 to 30 per cent among both men and women aged 25-64, although in the United Kingdom the earnings advantage at this level is over 50 per cent for women.

Earnings of people with less than upper secondary education tend to be 60-90 per cent of those of upper secondary graduates.

Earnings of men and women with less than upper secondary attainment tend to be between 60 and 90 per cent of those of persons who have completed upper secondary education. In general, men with lower levels of education fare slightly better than women relative to upper secondary completers of the same gender.

The earnings data shown in this indicator differ between countries in a number of ways that may render some country-to-country comparisons of relative earnings problematic. Caution should therefore be exercised in interpreting the results. In particular, for countries reporting annual earnings, differences in the incidence of part-year work among persons with different levels of educational attainment will have an effect on relative earnings that is not reflected in the data for countries reporting weekly or monthly earnings (see Definitions below).

Education and gender disparity in earnings

Women still earn less than men with similar levels of educational attainment.

While both men and women with upper secondary or tertiary attainment have substantial earnings advantages compared with those who do not complete upper secondary education, earnings differentials between men and women with the same level of educational attainment remain significant.

When all levels of education are taken together, women's earnings at age 30 to 44 range from about one-half of those of men in the Netherlands, Switzerland and the United Kingdom to over 70 per cent of those of men in Denmark, Finland, France, Italy, Portugal and Sweden (see Table E4.2). In a number of countries, but especially in Canada, Ireland, the Netherlands, Switzerland, the United Kingdom and the United States, earnings differentials between men and women narrow with increasing levels of educational attainment. In a number of other countries, however, including the Czech Republic, Italy and New Zealand, the reverse relationship tends to be true, that is, earnings differences between men and women tend to increase with educational attainment. Thus, although higher educational attainment levels are generally associated with higher earnings for both men and women, they do not seem to contribute systematically to reductions in gender inequality in earnings.

Occupational choices, time ~t in the labour market and ~e higher incidence of part-work may explain some of the differences in salaries between men and women.

Some of the differences in earnings between men and women may be explained by differences in career and occupational choices between men and women (see Indicators G3 and G4), differences in the amount of time men and women spend in the labour market (see Indicator E1) and the relatively higher incidence of part-time work among women. Variations in these effects between countries are reflected in the tables.

There may be movement towards greater earnings equality between men and women among younger workers.

Earnings data by age, however, suggest that there may be movement towar greater earnings equality between men and women at comparable levels educational attainment. In 10 of the 15 countries for which data are availabl the ratio of female to male earnings at the university level is between 1 a 16 percentage points higher for 30 to 44 year-olds than for 55 to 64 year-ol (see Table E4.2). Similar patterns apply at other levels of educational attai ment. The relative improvement in women's earnings may be the result o combination of supply and demand factors. Employment has been declini in the relatively male-intensive manufacturing sector, while the more fema intensive service sector has expanded. At the same time, women's marl skills and labour force experience have increased substantially (see Indi tor A2).

Education, earnings and age

Age is a third important variable in the relationship between education and earnings.

Age is a third important variable in the relationship between education a earnings. Chart E4.2 shows how the structure of earnings is distributed acr levels of education for different age groups. The chart is constructed fr cross-sectional rather than longitudinal data and therefore does *not* repres the true patterns of earnings of any real cohort of individuals over th lifetime. The patterns shown here for this "fictive cohort", however, are fa robust to changes over time in the level of educational development, institutional setting and the cyclical situation of the respective economie

Relative earnings are higher for persons with higher levels of attainment at each age level.

The relative earnings are typically higher for persons with higher levels educational attainment at each age level. An exception to this occurs 25-29 year-olds in Australia and Germany, for whom the non-university te ary level of education offers an earnings advantage comparable to the univ sity tertiary level. In Switzerland the age-earnings profiles for the non-uni sity and university levels start to diverge only after the age of 35. Th patterns reflect the high standing of non-university tertiary-level qualif tions in these countries. In Italy relative earnings of university graduate the age group 25-29 years are actually below those of upper secondary gra ates of the same age. However, young university graduates in Italy h particularly high unemployment rates (see Indicator E3) and their lat market involvement is still limited.

Earnings increase with age at a decreasing rate up to a maximum.

In most countries, age-earnings profiles are convex (see Chart E4.2). Earni increase with age at a decreasing rate up to a maximum (usually between ages of 45 and 55) and then flatten or even decline. This pattern holds n visibly at the higher levels of education.

The increase in earnings with age is steeper for persons with higher levels of education.

In most countries, the slope of the profile is steeper for higher level education. Before the earnings peak is reached, the mean earnings of pers with higher levels of education increase faster than those of persons lower levels of education. Thus while average earnings vary significantl educational level for all age groups, the relationship is stronger for older groups. There are some notable exceptions to this pattern, however.

The maximum level of earnings is reached later for persons with higher levels of education.

The maximum level of earnings tends to be reached at a later age for pe with a higher level of education.

Earnings differentials tend to increase with the level of education. At given age, the gap between earnings of tertiary and upper secondary ed tion graduates is generally more pronounced than that between upper se dary and lower secondary completers.

Several factors can help to explain these patterns:

- The positive relationship between educational attainment and e ings may reflect the impact of education and training on the produ ity of individuals or, to some extent, the premium paid to tra labour.

◆ Chart E4.2. **Relative age/earnings profiles of persons with income from employment (upper secondary level, 30 to 34 years of age = 100), by level of educational attainment (1995)**

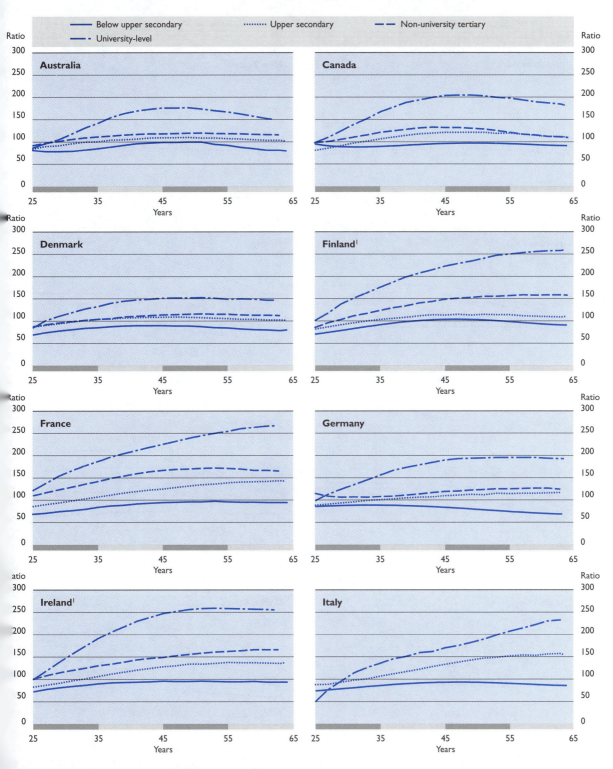

Ireland, Netherlands: 1993 data; Finland, Portugal: 1994 data.

...ngs profiles have been smoothed over age ranges.

...e: OECD.

261

◆ Chart E4.2 *(cont.)* **Relative age/earnings profiles of persons with income from employment (upper secondary level, 30 to 34 years of age = 100), by level of educational attainment (1995)**

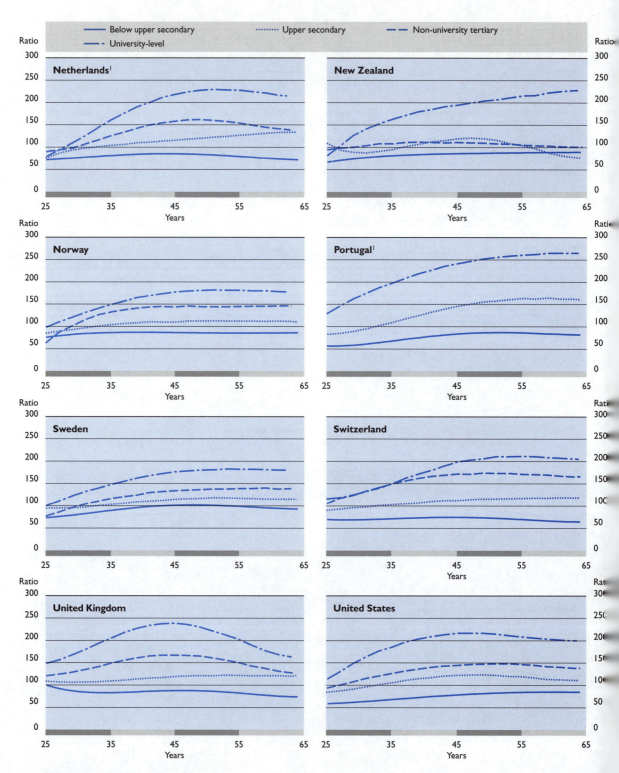

1.   Ireland, Netherlands: 1993 data; Finland, Portugal: 1994 data.

Earnings profiles have been smoothed over age ranges.

Source: OECD.

- Earnings tend to increase with age because age is a proxy for the work experience and knowledge acquired beyond the period of initial education and training. This additional human capital can be acquired through formal training, incidental learning or training on the job. Factors such as seniority, collective bargaining and other institutional arrangements, of course, also influence salaries (see Indicator D1). Over time, human capital tends to depreciate, very much like physical capital. For example, some skills and knowledge can become obsolete as a result of technological change. Human capital, unless renewed, can lose market value over time which, in turn, will be reflected in lower earnings. A person's human capital will increase only as long as his or her gross investment in human capital is greater than the depreciation. In addition, the later in life investment in education or training occurs, the shorter will be the period over which it can yield returns. As people age they may therefore invest less in acquiring additional human capital. These factors, taken together, may account for the concave shape of the profiles.
- Several factors may cause the peak in the earnings profile to occur later in life for more educated people. First, knowledge-based skills associated with higher education may be subject to less depreciation over time. Second, continuing education and training tend to be more common among the highly educated (see Indicator C7). Experience and continued educational investment, not age, are the variables which increase the stock of human capital after the period of initial education. The employment career of more educated people also tends to start later.

The relationship between earnings and educational attainment should be interpreted with some caution. Earnings differences among persons with different levels of educational attainment cannot all be attributed to education. The observation that, on average, university graduates earn more than upper secondary graduates should not lead to the conclusion that going to university necessarily yields higher income for any one person. Other factors, such as innate ability, social background, gender and occupation can also affect earnings. Why educated workers are more likely to get good jobs and how much they produce when they get these jobs are also influenced by a host of other factors relating to how labour markets operate and how work is organised. These factors may be as important in the determination of the earnings of individual workers, the profitability of firms and economy-wide productivity levels as are the levels of educational attainment of the workforce.

Definitions

ta are derived from national our force surveys (for details see Annex 3).

Relative earnings from employment are defined as the mean earnings (income from work before taxes) of persons at a given level of educational attainment divided by the mean earnings of persons with upper secondary school attainment. This ratio is then multiplied by 100. The estimates are restricted to persons with income from employment during the reference period.

Earnings data in Tables E4.1 and E4.2 are annual earnings for most countries. However, for France, Spain and Switzerland earnings data are monthly. Earnings for Italy are after taxes. Data cover only earnings of employees in France. In Spain, persons who work less than fifteen hours per week are excluded.

The observed differences in relative earnings across countries therefore reflect not only differences in wage rates, but also differences in coverage, in the number of weeks worked per year and in hours worked per week. To the extent that lower levels of educational attainment are associated with fewer hours of work (in particular with part-time work) and with less stable employment (a greater likelihood of temporary employment or more susceptibility to unemployment over the course of a year), the relative earnings figures shown for the higher education levels in the tables and chart will be magnified over and above what would be observed from an examination of relative rates of pay. The observed differences in relative earnings of men and women within a country can also be affected by some of these factors.

The age earnings profiles have been constructed by dividing mean earnings for persons in different age groups and at different levels of education by mean earnings of those 30-34 year-olds for whom upper secondary education was the highest completed level of education.

Table E4.1a **Relative earnings of persons aged 25-64 with income from employment
(upper secondary education = 100) by level of educational attainment and gender (1995)**

	Below upper secondary education			Non-university tertiary education			University-level education		
	M + W	Men	Women	M + W	Men	Women	M + W	Men	Women
North America									
Canada	87	84	75	110	108	113	156	148	163
United States	68	67	62	119	118	126	174	167	176
Pacific Area									
Australia	89	105	87	111	118	105	142	161	139
New Zealand	82	82	79	106	98	102	165	163	146
European Union									
Denmark	83	86	85	104	108	110	133	139	130
Finland	93	91	93	126	127	126	187	190	174
France	80	86	78	128	132	137	175	183	168
Germany	78	88	82	111	107	116	163	158	154
Ireland*	85	77	62	123	121	123	183	171	187
Italy	77	74	74	x	x	x	134	142	120
Netherlands	77	85	68	124	126	131	162	153	158
Portugal	68	66	67	x	x	x	183	180	174
Sweden	89	88	87	109	111	112	151	154	144
United Kingdom	75	73	73	132	114	151	179	153	195
Other OECD countries									
Czech Republic	66	72	75	x	x	x	158	154	149
Norway	82	84	77	123	125	124	149	149	150
Switzerland	67	75	70	145	124	134	157	141	156
Country mean	**79**	**81**	**76**	**119**	**117**	**122**	**162**	**159**	**158**

*1993 data.
Source: OECD Database. See Annex 3 for notes.

Table E4.1*b* **Relative earnings of persons aged 30-44 with income from employment
(upper secondary education = 100) by level of educational attainment and gender (1995)**

	Below upper secondary education			Non-university tertiary education			University-level education		
	M + W	Men	Women	M + W	Men	Women	M + W	Men	Wom
North America									
Canada	84	82	m	112	110	114	157	150	16
United States	65	63	59	119	120	127	177	170	18
Pacific Area									
Australia	86	101	86	109	118	102	145	163	14
New Zealand	85	82	84	112	102	108	173	163	14
European Union									
Denmark	84	87	86	101	107	108	131	138	12
Finland	91	89	91	121	121	123	175	175	16
France	79	86	73	132	138	139	174	180	17
Germany	87	90	88	107	105	114	159	148	16
Ireland*	84	78	61	122	122	123	183	169	19
Italy	80	79	76	x	x	x	129	139	12
Netherlands	78	83	71	122	121	134	159	148	16
Portugal	64	62	63	x	x	x	180	176	17
Sweden	89	88	86	113	119	111	147	152	13
United Kingdom	77	77	76	137	115	159	190	162	21
Other OECD countries									
Czech Republic	66	71	77	x	x	x	162	154	1
Norway	83	81	80	129	129	131	147	153	1
Switzerland	69	74	76	145	122	145	148	132	1
Country mean	**79**	**81**	**77**	**120**	**118**	**124**	**161**	**157**	**1**

1993 data.
Source: OECD Database. See Annex 3 for notes.

Table E4.2   **Mean annual earnings of women as a percentage of mean annual earnings of men 30 to 44 and 55 to 64 years of age, by level of educational attainment (1995)**

	Below upper secondary education		Upper secondary education		Non-university tertiary education		University-level education		All levels of education	
	Age 30-44	Age 55-64	Age 30-44	Age 55-64	Age 30-44	Age 55-64	Age 30-44	Age 55-64	Age 30-44	Age 55-64
North America										
Canada	57	55	64	52	65	66	76	60	67	56
United States	56	50	61	57	67	59	69	57	65	53
Pacific Area										
Australia	56	55	65	88	53	63	58	68	59	61
New Zealand	61	57	59	83	63	75	53	110	57	72
European Union										
Denmark	71	69	73	68	73	71	69	62	72	65
Finland	79	80	78	77	80	85	77	70	78	73
France	65	72	75	63	76	65	71	67	75	62
Germany	59	53	60	54	66	81	67	52	60	50
Ireland*	46	m	58	m	58	m	71	m	62	m
Italy	71	73	74	63	x	x	65	53	74	65
Netherlands	44	33	51	39	56	73	55	68	51	43
Portugal	75	74	76	69	x	x	75	66	76	72
Sweden	70	68	72	67	68	68	68	66	71	67
United Kingdom	49	45	49	47	65	66	64	69	52	50
Other OECD countries										
Czech Republic	62	47	57	66	x	x	57	60	54	57
Norway	57	m	60	m	64	m	60	m	62	m
Switzerland	53	42	52	49	62	58	64	64	52	44
Country mean	**61**	**58**	**64**	**63**	**65**	**69**	**66**	**66**	**64**	**59**

* 1993 data.

Source: OECD Database. See Annex 3 for notes.

Indicator E5: Internal rates of return at different levels of education

Policy context

This indicator shows the internal rates of return across levels of education, calculated by comparing additional earnings over a working lifetime with the additional cost of completing education at those levels.

Education is an investment that can help foster economic growth, contrib to personal and social development and reduce social inequality. Like investment, it involves both costs and returns. A cost-benefit analysis help assess whether the potential benefits individuals receive from attend a particular educational programme are worth the costs. Similarly, soci must ask whether the benefits it will receive from allocating public funds education are worth as much as the benefits that would be derived fr alternative uses of these funds.

Evidence and explanations

Indicator E4 shows the earnings advantage from completing higher levels of education but not the costs involved.

Indicator E4 showed the earnings advantage of completing upper second and tertiary education. Although these data give some indication of returns to education across countries, they do not take into account relative costs. From an investment standpoint, however, it is necessar consider the costs involved in completing a particular level of educatio simple rate of return from completing an additional level of education ca estimated by comparing additional lifetime earnings for those attainir particular level of education with the additional costs of completing level.

From an individual's point of view, costs correspond to tuition, student living costs and forgone earnings. Social costs include public investment in education.

From the individual's point of view, costs correspond to direct costs of tui (*e.g.* fees), educational materials, student living costs and forgone earning students. Social costs include all of these private costs as well as those d costs incurred by public authorities in providing education. If the total so cost of completing a particular level of education is taken into account, a of return can be estimated by comparing additional lifetime earnings with additional cost of completing that level. This is a hybrid between an ind ual and social rate of return, since it compares individual benefits with s costs. But it does give some indication whether investment in educatio worthwhile for an individual, given the structure of the labour market particular country.

A rate of return of 10 per cent on an investment may be treated as a "th old" rate above which rates of return may be viewed as "socially profita compared with alternative investments in physical or financial capital. B this threshold, there is less certainty about the return on an investme education due to the omission of some other socially desirable "spill-d effects that can also result from increasing the aggregate level of educati a society (*e.g.*, increases in productivity, reduction in inequality, lower c rates, etc.).

◆   Chart E5.1. **Internal rates of return at different levels of education by gender (1995)**

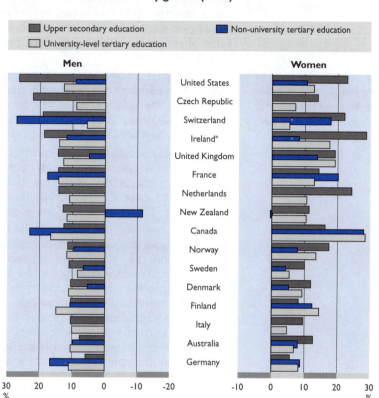

■ Upper secondary education   ■ Non-university tertiary education
□ University-level tertiary education

Men   Women

United States
Czech Republic
Switzerland
Ireland*
United Kingdom
France
Netherlands
New Zealand
Canada
Norway
Sweden
Denmark
Finland
Italy
Australia
Germany

30 20 10 0 -10 -20   -10 0 10 20 30
%   %

* Ireland: 1994 data.
Countries are ranked in descending order of the internal rates of return for men at the upper secondary level of education.
Source: OECD.

The rate of return for upper secondary education is generally high.

Estimates of internal rates of return shown in Table E5.1 indicate that rates of return for completing upper secondary education (relative to lower secondary education) are generally high (above 10 per cent in 11 out of 16 countries) for both men and women. For men, upper secondary rates of return range from 10 per cent or below in Australia, Denmark, Finland, Germany and Italy to above 20 per cent in the Czech Republic and the United States. Upper secondary rates of return for women range from 10 per cent or below in Finland, Germany, Italy and Sweden to 29 per cent in Ireland.

While rates of return at the upper secondary level are calculated by comparing the additional costs and benefits for completing upper secondary with stopping at the lower secondary level, tertiary rates of return are an attempt to measure the value of completing a tertiary qualification as opposed to stopping after upper secondary education. At the tertiary level, internal rates of return are slightly lower, on average, than rates of return at the upper secondary level. In three countries, however, internal rates of return for both men and women are greater at the university level than at the upper secondary level (in Canada, Finland and Germany). At the university level, rates of return for men range from 10 per cent or below in Australia, the Czech Republic, Italy, Sweden and Switzerland to 15 per cent or above in Canada and Finland. For women, university-level rates of return range from 5 per cent in Italy, Sweden and Switzerland to 19 per cent in the United Kindgdom and 29 per cent in Canada.

On average across OECD countries, rates of return at the upper secondary a▪ non-university tertiary levels are slightly higher for women than for me Cross-country variability in rates of return is greater for women than for men the upper secondary and university levels, however, and more countries ha rates of return for women below 10 per cent at the tertiary level than is t case for men.

The rate of return is lower for tertiary education, despite the high earnings advantage of tertiary education.

Even though earnings at the tertiary level relative to upper secondary a higher than earnings at upper secondary level relative to the lower second level, after the relative costs of education (including forgone earnings) a taken into account rates of return at the upper secondary level compare least as favourably as those at the tertiary level.

This indicator needs to be interpreted with caution, however. Although the internal rates of return provide an overall picture of the incentive structure investing in education, they lack both the information and the precisi necessary to base policy decisions regarding investment in education them alone. There are several reasons for this:

- The measure of returns is limited to additional gross earnings a takes no account of broader social or economic effects. If other form: income (*e.g.*, state transfers) and other social costs (*e.g.*, unemploym support) were fully accounted for, it is possible that the advantage completing upper secondary education would be greater.
- The effects of various underlying assumptions in arriving at the e mates of rates of return may be open to question. For example, i not certain that lifetime earnings across different age-groups at (point in time are a reliable guide to the likely future earnings profil a cohort of persons graduating at a particular level of education toc
- Inter-country differences in rates of return may be affected by inst tional and non-market influences on the distribution of earnings · some European countries, for example, the more compressed w structure may be less attributable to a more equitable distribution human capital than to the fact that as a result of institutional fac there is less flexibility in relative earnings than elsewhere.
- Estimates of the rates of return are based on average earnings costs. No account is taken of the distribution or within-cou differences in returns for a particular level of education. For exam▪ the payoff of different kinds of schooling or different fields of st may be different and may also differentially benefit different so groups and individuals, even at the same level of education.
- The estimates focus solely on the financial gains from education▪ those in employment. They take no account of the fact that n educational attainment is likely to be associated with a lower ris unemployment.

Apart from these considerations, it is also debated to what extent earn differences associated with different levels of education reflect not only effects of education but also other, unmeasured variables correlated additional schooling. For example some portions of the earnings benefits be returns to innate ability differences between those individuals ta more or less schooling.

The analysis of the returns to human capital investment is taken furthe *Education Policy Analysis*.

Definitions

Data are derived from national labour force surveys (for details see Annex 3).

The rate of return to investment in education is a measure of the future economic payoff to an individual of increasing the amount of educ undertaken. The rate of return to each level of education is calculate finding the rate of discount that would equate the present value of the costs of completing a level of education to the present value of increased earnings associated with completing that level of education. These calculations are based on the creation of the lifetime earnings profiles of persons who attain different levels of education (see Chart E4.2).

The earnings benefit of completing each higher level of education for each age from graduation at that level to age 65 is calculated as the difference between the average earnings of workers with successive levels of education. The average earnings of persons who completed the university level of education were compared to those who stopped at the upper secondary level of education rather than at the non-university tertiary level of education, because in most countries the choice of attending the university level or of following another path is made at the end of upper secondary education. The added costs of completing each higher level of education are calculated for each level of education as the sum of the direct costs and forgone earnings. The direct costs are estimated from data on average annual expenditure per student (see Indicator B4). For some countries, these cover only public expenditure. It is assumed that these average annual expenditures were incurred for each year the student was enrolled at that level of education. The costs were applied at the ages at which a person would be expected to be enrolled in each level of education, which varies across countries (see Annex 1). The forgone earnings of students who continue to the next higher level of education are estimated as the average earnings of persons who did not continue minus the average earnings of students at that level of education.

For definitions relating to the data on earnings refer to Indicator E4.

Table E5.1 **Internal rates of return at different levels of education by gender (1995)**

	Men			Women		
	Upper secondary education	Non-university tertiary education	University-level tertiary education	Upper secondary education	Non-university tertiary education	University-level tertiary education
North America						
Canada	13	23	17	16	28	29
United States	26	9	13	23	11	13
Pacific Area						
Australia	8	10	10	13	8	7
New Zealand	13	−12	12	11	−1	10
European Union						
Denmark	10	5	11	12	5	9
Finland	10	11	15	8	12	14
France	14	18	14	14	20	13
Germany	6	17	11	6	9	8
Ireland*	19	12	14	29	8	17
Italy	10	m	10	10	m	5
Netherlands	14	m	11	24	m	11
Sweden	11	7	8	10	4	5
United Kingdom	14	5	13	19	14	19
Other OECD countries						
Czech Republic	22	m	9	14	m	7
Norway	11	9	12	17	8	13
Switzerland	19	27	6	22	18	5
Country mean	**14**	**11**	**11**	**15**	**11**	**12**

* Data refer to 1994.
Source: OECD Database. See Annex 3 for notes.

Indicator E6: Unemployment rates of persons leaving education

Policy context

This indicator shows the employment rates of persons one and five years after completing a particular level of education.

The transition from school to work is a critical period for young people. This is the point at which the knowledge and skills imparted to them by modern education systems come up against the actual skill requirements of labour markets and enterprises. The extent to which school or university learning translates into work-place skills and performance, and the work habits acquired at this stage, have a significant effect on social integration and future labour force activity and earnings. Since young workers represent the future production potential of economies, societies have an interest in ensuring that the transition occurs reasonably smoothly.

Evidence and explanations

The handicap of low educational attainment makes itself felt quickly in the labour market, with exceedingly high unemployment rates one year and even five years after leaving school.

With about 90 per cent of an age cohort entering upper secondary education in many OECD countries (see Indicators C1, G1), leavers from lower secondary education constitute a highly vulnerable group. They have lower rates of participation in the labour force and significantly higher rates of unemployment than leavers from upper secondary education. Labour markets in OECD countries discriminate strongly on the basis of educational attainment at entry into the labour force (see Chart E6.1). As a result, there are few opportunities for those with lower levels of education to overcome deficiencies in formal qualifications through on-the-job training or the accumulation of work experience.

Even after five years, leavers from the lower secondary level of education have higher unemployment rates than the average for the total labour force after one year.

This situation improves as one moves up the attainment ladder...

This situation improves as one moves up the attainment ladder. However, in some countries leavers from upper secondary education also show relatively high rates of unemployment upon leaving school. In Finland, Poland and Spain, the unemployment rates for this group are above 35 per cent after one year and remain at 20 per cent and more (in Spain over 30 per cent) after five years.

...with highly educated young people often showing lower unemployment after one year than less educated people after five years.

Highly educated young people are in general more fully integrated into the labour force one year after leaving school than are their less educated counterparts after five years.

In many countries, in particular the Czech Republic, Germany, Sweden, Switzerland and the United States, university graduates rapidly move into jobs and show relatively low unemployment rates one year after completion of education. In Sweden and Switzerland the unemployment rate of university graduates one year after completion is only slightly higher than the unemployment rate of all people having a university degree, and in Germany the

◆ Chart E6.1. **Unemployment rates of persons having completed their education
at various levels of attainment (1995)**

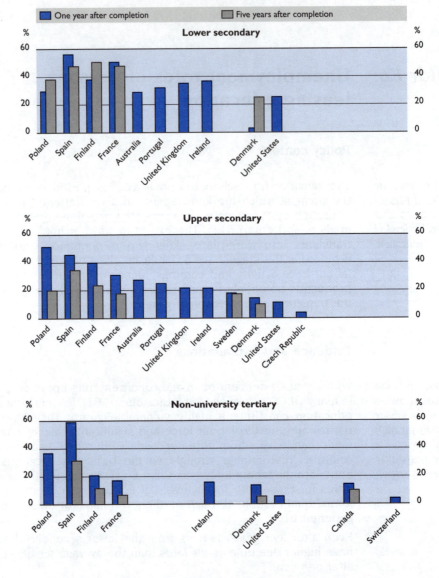

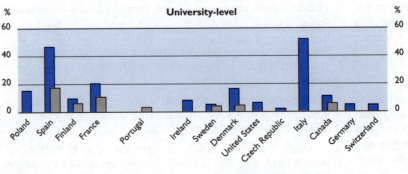

Countries are ranked in descending order of the unemployment rates at the upper secondary level.

Source: OECD.

unemployment rate is the same in both groups (see Indicator E2).

However, in Italy and Spain, almost one-half of even university graduates in the labour force have still not found work one year after leaving university. Labour demand in these countries is simply not able quickly to absorb the number of university graduates leaving the education system each year.

To a certain extent, the difficult transition from school to work may be viewed as a "frictional" phenomenon that reflects inefficiencies in the matching of youth qualifications and job requirements, and a lack of correspondence between the knowledge and skills imparted by education systems and the needs of labour markets. On the other hand this might be an indication that the economy in some countries shows a lack of flexibility and interest in investing in young people and trusts too much in the employment of experienced workers. However, education systems are not designed purely to generate a steady supply of productive workers, but have larger societal aims, which include, for example, the formation of an informed citizenry capable of participating intelligently in public and social life. For many persons who leave school with low attainment, both of these aims may be threatened. Indeed, the inability to find gainful employment may result in social marginalisation that persists throughout life.

Definitions

ta are derived from national labour force surveys (for details see Annex 3).

This indicator shows the unemployment rates of persons who at the beginning of a given year were not enrolled in full-time education or training and who in the course of the preceding year had completed education at a particular level of the education system.

"Leavers" from a particular level of the education system are defined here as persons who: *i*) at the beginning of a given year (whether the school year or the calendar year) were not enrolled in full-time education or training; and *ii*) in the course of the preceding year had completed education at a particular level of the education system.

For some countries (Denmark, Ireland and the United States), the data include persons who may not have actually completed their education in the preceding year ("drop-outs"). Sources for the data may be administrative (Denmark and Finland) or sample surveys (all other countries). Sample surveys include Labour Force Surveys (France and the United States), special graduate or school leavers' surveys (Australia, Canada, Ireland, Sweden, Switzerland and the United Kingdom) and general purpose panel surveys (Spain).

Table E6.1 **Unemployment rates of persons having completed their education at various levels of attainment, by gender**

	Year	Gender	Lower secondary education	Upper secondary education	Non-university tertiary education	University-level education
One year after completion						
Australia	1995	M + W	28	27	m	m
		Men	28	25	m	m
		Women	28	29	m	m
Canada	1992	M + W	m	m	14	11
		Men	m	m	16	10
		Women	m	m	12	11
Czech Republic	1995	M + W	n	4	m	2
		Men	m	m	m	m
		Women	m	m	m	m
Denmark	1995	M + W	3	14	13	16
		Men	2	11	14	18
		Women	4	17	13	14
Finland	1995	M + W	37	39	20	9
		Men	39	48	21	9
		Women	35	32	20	9
France	1995	M + W	50	31	17	20
		Men	37	20	12	15
		Women	70	44	21	27
Germany	1994	M + W	m	m	m	5
		Men	m	m	m	5
		Women	m	m	m	4
Ireland	1995	M + W	36	21	15	8
		Men	32	20	16	7
		Women	m	22	15	8
Italy	1993	M + W	m	m	m	52
		Men	m	m	m	49
		Women	m	m	m	54
Poland	1994	M + W	29	51	36	15
		Men	23	46	50	14
		Women	44	55	32	16
Portugal	1994	M + W	32	25	m	m
		Men	23	19	m	m
		Women	40	28	m	m
Spain	1994	M + W	55	45	58	46
		Men	34	40	64	51
		Women	79	51	51	43
Sweden	1994	M + W	m	17	m	5
		Men	m	21	m	7
		Women	m	14	m	4
Switzerland	1995	M + W	m	m	4	4
		Men	m	m	4	4
		Women	m	m	3	4
United Kingdom	1994	M + W	34	21	m	m
		Men	m	m	m	m
		Women	m	m	m	m
United States	1995	M + W	25	11	5	6
		Men	27	12	8	6
		Women	22	10	4	6
Five years after completion						
Canada	1995	M + W	m	m	9	6
		Men	m	m	11	6
		Women	m	m	9	6
Denmark	1995	M + W	25	10	5	4
		Men	21	8	5	5
		Women	30	11	5	4
Finland	1995	M + W	50	23	11	6
		Men	51	25	12	5
		Women	47	21	10	6
France	1995	M + W	47	17	6	10
		Men	48	13	8	7
		Women	45	22	5	14
Poland	1994	M + W	38	20	m	m
		Men	32	17	m	m
		Women	44	22	m	m
Portugal	1991	M + W	m	m	m	3
		Men	m	m	m	3
		Women	m	m	m	3
Spain	1994	M + W	47	34	31	17
		Men	39	21	13	29
		Women	56	49	56	10
Sweden	1996	M + W	m	17	m	4
		Men	m	16	m	3
		Women	m	18	m	4

Source: OECD Database. See Annex 3 for notes.

Chapter F

STUDENT ACHIEVEMENT

How well are our schools performing? Do they provide young people with the skills and knowledge they I need to enter the labour market and to become lifelong learners who analyse, reason and communicate eir ideas effectively? Parents, students, the general public and those responsible for running education stems all want to know how well the population is being educated. The most common way of assessing ucational outcomes at the student, institution and system levels is to measure the relative performance of dents within each country. A school whose students get good marks, perform well in examinations or gain mission to the best universities is considered to have performed well.

There has recently been a growing demand for indicators on student performance for three main sons: to make education more accountable; to provide a tool for school improvement, especially where ferent schools or programmes with similar inputs achieve varying results; and to allow standards to be nitored centrally under conditions of devolved administration and extended partnership with employers I workers. Indicators on student performance can communicate meaningful standards to which school tems, schools, teachers and students can aspire. These standards can provide direction for schools' tructional efforts and for students' learning and insight on curriculum strengths and weaknesses. Coupled h appropriate incentives, assessments can motivate students to learn better, teachers to teach better and ools to be more educationally effective.

Such considerations have led to a shift in public and governmental concern, away from the mere control ·r the resources and content of education towards a focus on outcomes. At the same time, advances in cational measurement have made it possible to collect and report aggregated performance data in ways t make them a useful tool for evaluating the quality, equity and effectiveness of education and training.

This chapter focuses on indicators of student performance in mathematics and science. These subjects y a crucial role in equipping young people to meet the responsibilities of adult life in the public and ate spheres, and they are of particular importance in modern economies, which increasingly depend on ntific discoveries and technological innovation. In most countries, the attention given to mathematics is ond only to the emphasis given to instruction in the national language, and many countries consider hematics and science among the most important instructional content domains for schools. The emphasis mathematics and science in national curricula reflects, in part, a widespread interest in identifying and paring young people to play a leadership role in the research and development activities that underpin dern economies, and a wider need for adults to have the capacity to understand and be able to talk about ntific, technological and environmental issues.

Four of the indicators focus on the performance of primary students and contrast the achievement of iary students with the achievement of students at the lower secondary level. A fifth indicator reviews the ience of socio-economic factors at the lower secondary level, and a sixth indicator relates the attitudes of lents towards mathematics to their achievement.

The indicators draw on the Third International Mathematics and Science Study (IEA/TIMSS), an interna- al comparison of performance in mathematics and science tests that was conducted during the school 1994/95 by the International Association for the Evaluation of Educational Achievement (IEA) and largely 1sored by the governments of the participating countries.

Indicator F1 shows policy-makers whether the average student achievement in their country is signifi- ly better or worse than that in other countries. Differences between countries in average mathematics science achievement need to be interpreted against the background of curricular emphases, and student udes and perceptions. Achievement is also influenced by school resources and processes and the ·room environment, including the quality of teaching, the resources available for students to use in the classroom and the nature of the teaching methods used. Finally, test results are clearly affected in importa ways by the social context outside school, including the educational and economic resources supporti learning at home. The availability and content of the mass media (television and the popular press) may al have an influence.

Mean achievement is an important quality index for classrooms, schools and education systems a whole. However, overall means can mask significant disparities. It is therefore instructive to compare not o the average performance of countries but also how well the highest and lowest achievers in a country perfo in relation to international standards. This is shown by **Indicator F2**, which examines the relative standing different parts of the achievement distribution in 4th grade. This indicator can also be interpreted a measure of equity. Teachers, schools and education systems as a whole must cope with the variation achievement that exists within classes, within schools, and within the country. Such variation may be result of disparities in resources and in the socio-economic background of students and schools as well a curricular differences and the way in which instruction is organised and delivered.

Taken together, Indicators F1 and F2 provide a measure of the cumulative yield of formal and infor education in which children participate, typically from birth to the end of the 4th grade.

Indicator F3 examines gender differences in mathematics and science achievement in the 4th 8th grades. It provides an indication of the extent to which a gender gap is observable before students er their adolescence and the key middle years of their school careers.

Indicator F4 examines progress in achievement from the 4th to the 8th grade in the sampled populati (Indicator F4 is based on data comparing the performance of 4th and 8th-grade students tested in 1994/9 is not based on data following the same students over time.) This indicator, more than the first two, isola the effects of formal schooling, since the effects of family and other social resources are captured at leas part in 4th-grade achievement. Thus, the difference in average achievement between the 4th and 8th gra may be viewed largely (although not entirely) as a function of the curriculum and the school.

Indicator F5 focuses on the mathematics and science achievement of students in the 8th grade relation to the social context. First it examines the achievement of students by their parents' highest leve educational attainment. Research has demonstrated that a student's educational achievement is associa with the parents' educational attainment. Secondly it reviews the performance of students from lingui minorities and the variation of their performance across countries. The linguistic handicap experienced these students is often compounded by socio-economic handicaps. Both handicaps are highly related to students' achievement. These and other aspects of the students' social context have to be taken into acc in order to plan education in a way that minimises disparities.

Students' perceptions about the value of learning mathematics and science may be considered as l inputs to and outcomes of the educational process, since their attitudes towards these subjects can related to educational achievement in ways that reinforce higher or lower performance. **Indicator F6** revi the attitudes of students towards mathematics and relates these to mathematics achievement.

Like any sample survey results, the IEA/TIMSS data reported in this chapter are subject to error, w must be taken into account when comparisons are made. For this reason, the standard errors of estimates reported together with the data. It is important to review the possible sources of the errors that are pres and to reflect on how they constrain the data analysis and the interpretation of observed differe between countries.

The effect of sampling error is to set a lower limit on the size of the observed differences which statistically significant. By adding ± 2 standard errors to the reported means, the reader can obta reasonable estimate of the error margins (i.e., a 95 per cent confidence interval).

The IEA/TIMSS results are based on different combinations of test items being administered to respondent – introducing an additional source of error to the estimates, which should be considered.

Finally, subtle differences in design, implementation or patterns of non-coverage or non-response have introduced non-sampling errors into the IEA/TIMSS study that can lead to overestimation or under mation of the true size of population differences. The extent to which non-sampling sources of erro present in the data and bias the results cannot be readily determined. Annex 3 reports non-response and the population coverage of the survey results.

Indicator F1: Student achievement in mathematics and science at the 4th-grade level

Policy context

This indicator shows the average achievement of students in mathematics and science at the 4th grade of primary education across countries.

For many countries, international comparisons of student achievement have become an essential tool for assessing the performance of education systems and the adequacy of students' preparation for an increasingly global economy. Beyond providing international benchmarks, such indicators also serve as measures of accountability that inform key stakeholders in education, such as taxpayers, employers, educators, parents and students.

Proficiency in mathematics and science is an important outcome of education. In an increasingly technological world, the ability of workers to solve complex scientific problems and to use advanced mathematical skills are crucial components of countries' abilities to compete in the global marketplace. Early success in mathematics and science is important, both because a firm foundation in basic principles is necessary before more complex materials can be mastered and because early success can keep young people interested in these fields.

Evidence and explanations

Indicator F1 shows policy-makers whether the average student achievement in their country is significantly better or worse than that in other countries. Together with Indicator F2, it provides a measure of the comparative yield of education systems in mathematics and science at the primary level.

Variation in achievement between countries is substantial, with the average Japanese and Korean 4th-graders outperforming the average Portuguese 8th-graders in mathematics.

In mathematics, Japanese and Korean 4th-graders score significantly higher than those in all other participating countries (597 and 611 score points respectively, see Chart F1.1). In fact, the average mathematics achievement of 4th-grade students in Japan and Korea is higher than the average achievement of students in Portugal at the 8th-grade level and higher than the 25 per cent of 8th-graders with the lowest performances in almost half of the OECD countries. The remaining countries can be classified into five groups: the Czech Republic and the Netherlands, with means of 567 and 577; Australia, Austria, Hungary, Ireland and the United States, with scores somewhat above the OECD average; Canada and Scotland, with scores just below the OECD average; England, Greece, New Zealand and Norway, with scores around 500; and Iceland and Portugal, with scores of 474 and 475.

Variation in student achievement is somewhat narrower in science, but it is still considerable.

Korea, with a mean score of 597, scores significantly higher in science than all other participating countries (see Chart F1.2). Japan, with a mean score of 574, scores higher than all remaining countries (although differences between Austria, Japan and the United States are not statistically significant). Australia, Austria, Canada, the Czech Republic, England, the Netherlands and the United States form a cluster of countries with scores ranging from 565 to 549. Hungary, Ireland, New Zealand, Norway and Scotland have scores just below

◆ Chart F1.1. **Multiple comparisons of overall student achievement in mathematics, 4th grade (1995)**

	Mean achievement of row country significantly lower than column country
▼	Mean achievement of row country significantly lower than column country
●	No statistically significant difference between row and column countries
▲	Mean achievement of row country significantly higher than column country

	Mean	Standard error	Average age	Korea	Japan	Netherlands*	Czech Republic	Austria*	Ireland	Hungary*	Australia*	United States	Canada	Scotland	England**	Norway	New Zealand	Greece	Portugal	Iceland
Korea	611	(2.1)	10.3		▲	▲	▲	▲	▲	▲	▲	▲	▲	▲	▲	▲	▲	▲	▲	▲
Japan	597	(2.1)	10.4	▼		▲	▲	▲	▲	▲	▲	▲	▲	▲	▲	▲	▲	▲	▲	▲
Netherlands*	577	(3.4)	10.3	▼	▼		●	▲	▲	▲	▲	▲	▲	▲	▲	▲	▲	▲	▲	▲
Czech Republic	567	(3.3)	10.4	▼	▼	●		●	▲	▲	▲	▲	▲	▲	▲	▲	▲	▲	▲	▲
Austria*	559	(3.1)	10.5	▼	▼	▼	●		●	●	●	▲	▲	▲	▲	▲	▲	▲	▲	▲
Ireland	550	(3.4)	10.3	▼	▼	▼	▼	●		●	●	●	▲	▲	▲	▲	▲	▲	▲	▲
Hungary*	548	(3.7)	10.4	▼	▼	▼	▼	●	●		●	●	▲	▲	▲	▲	▲	▲	▲	▲
Australia*	546	(3.1)	10.2	▼	▼	▼	▼	●	●	●		●	▲	▲	▲	▲	▲	▲	▲	▲
United States	545	(3.0)	10.2	▼	▼	▼	▼	▼	●	●	●		●	▲	▲	▲	▲	▲	▲	▲
Canada	532	(3.3)	10.0	▼	▼	▼	▼	▼	▼	▼	▼	●		●	▲	▲	▲	▲	▲	▲
Scotland	520	(3.9)	9.7	▼	▼	▼	▼	▼	▼	▼	▼	▼	●		●	▲	▲	▲	▲	▲
England**	513	(3.2)	10.0	▼	▼	▼	▼	▼	▼	▼	▼	▼	▼	●		●	●	▲	▲	▲
Norway	502	(3.0)	9.9	▼	▼	▼	▼	▼	▼	▼	▼	▼	▼	▼	●		●	●	▲	▲
New Zealand	499	(4.3)	10.0	▼	▼	▼	▼	▼	▼	▼	▼	▼	▼	▼	●	●		●	▲	▲
Greece	492	(4.4)	9.6	▼	▼	▼	▼	▼	▼	▼	▼	▼	▼	▼	▼	●	●		●	▲
Portugal	475	(3.5)	10.4	▼	▼	▼	▼	▼	▼	▼	▼	▼	▼	▼	▼	▼	▼	●		●
Iceland	474	(2.7)	9.6	▼	▼	▼	▼	▼	▼	▼	▼	▼	▼	▼	▼	▼	▼	▼	●	

Read across the row to compare a country's mean achievement with the countries listed in the columns of the chart. For example, mean achievement for the United States is significantly lower than that for Korea, not significantly different from that for Australia, and significantly higher than that for Portugal.

Countries are ranked by descending order of mean achievement.

* Countries did not meet TIMSS sampling requirement.

** Countries met TIMSS sampling requirement only partially.

Source: International Association for the Evaluation of Educational Achievement (IEA). See Annex 3 for notes.

◆ Chart F1.2. *Multiple comparisons of overall student achievement in science, 4th grade (1995)*

▼ Mean achievement of row country significantly lower than column country

● No statistically significant difference between row and column countries

▲ Mean achievement of row country significantly higher than column country

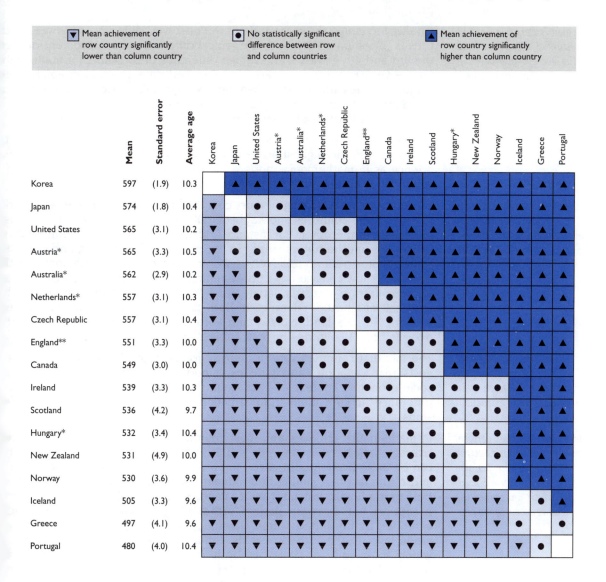

Read across the row to compare a country's mean achievement with the countries listed in the columns of the chart. For example, mean achievement for the United States is significantly lower than that for Korea, not significantly different from that for Australia, and significantly higher than that for Portugal.

...ries are ranked by descending order of mean achievement.

...ountries did not meet TIMSS sampling requirements.

...ountries met TIMSS sampling requirements only partially.

...e: International Association for the Evaluation of Educational Achievement (IEA). See Annex 3 for notes.

the OECD average, and Greece, Iceland and Portugal have scores rangin▮ from 505 to 480.

Achievement differences remain substantial when compared with the average gap between children a year apart in age.

One way to gauge the magnitude of the observed differences between cou▮ tries is to compare them with the typical difference in achievement betwee▮ the 3rd and 4th grades – an average difference of 65 points for mathemati▮ for the OECD countries tested. The observed differences in scores betwee▮ some countries are greater than the average difference between 3rd a▮ 4th grades, which suggests that between-country variation in mathemati▮ achievement is of considerable educational and practical importance.

In science, the pattern is similar but not identical. The gap between t▮ countries with the highest achievement and the remainder is not as large▮ science as in mathematics, nor are the differences between a large group▮ countries of middle rank as great.

Some countries differ in their relative standing in mathematics and science...

While the relative ranking of most countries is similar in mathematics and▮ science, some countries show substantially higher performance in one dis▮ pline than in the other. For instance, Hungary and Ireland perform relativ▮ better in mathematics than in science, whereas England and t▮ United States perform relatively better in science than in mathematics. Oth▮ countries show consistency between mathematics and science achieveme▮ Three countries – Austria, Japan and Korea – score significantly higher th▮ over half of all other countries in both disciplines. Five countries – Gree▮ Iceland, New Zealand, Norway and Portugal – score significantly lower th▮ over half of all countries in both subject areas.

... which suggests that variation can in part be explained by differences in curriculum and instruction.

The fact that countries vary in their performance in the two disciplines s▮ gests that variation cannot be explained entirely by the demographic▮ socio-economic context of each country but may reflect, at least in p▮ differences in curriculum and instruction, which are amenable to policy d▮ sions.

Most countries that perform well in mathematics at the 4th-grade level also perform well at the 8th-grade level, which underlines the importance of early success.

In mathematics achievement, most countries maintain nearly the same r▮ tive standing between the 4th and 8th-grade levels (see Chart F1.3), wh▮ can be an indication both of the importance of success in early school ye▮ and of the fact that similar determinants of student success are operating▮ both grade levels. Ireland, New Zealand, Scotland and the United States▮ exceptions to the general pattern, with the largest change in relative stand▮ exhibited in the United States. US students fall from the 9th rank at the ▮ grade level to the 13th rank at the 8th-grade level (among the 17 count▮ which took part in TIMSS at both grade levels). On the other ha▮ New Zealand rises in rank by 4 places from the 14th to the 10th position▮

In science there is generally less consistency between performance of 4th and 8th-graders.

In science, countries also maintain similar relative standings in the 4th ▮ 8th grades, but there is generally less consistency. Two countries show l▮ improvements in their relative standing in science between 4th ▮ 8th grades: the Czech Republic and Hungary. Czech students rise f▮ 7th rank at the 4th grade to 1st rank at the 8th grade (among the 17 count▮ participating in both grade levels) and Hungarians rise from 12th to 6th r▮ On the other hand, US students fall in science from 3rd to 10th rank.

The results reflect many factors, including values and aspirations of education systems.

Although comparing the relative standing of countries can be informative▮ useful, it is important to realise that results reflect many factors, including▮ values and aspirations of particular education systems. Moreover, each c▮ try may place varying levels of importance on different discipline▮ different points in students' school careers. Because these achievem▮ results come from young children, some additional notes of caution are ▮ ranted: first, different countries start formal schooling at different ages. ▮ "first grade" occurs at age 5 in some countries, at age 6 in others, and at a▮ in yet others. Secondly, the average age of students tested varied some▮ across countries.

◆ Chart F1.3. **Mathematics performance in 4th and 8th grades compared
with international averages (1995)**

■ Significantly higher than international average	□ Not significantly different from international average	▨ Significantly lower than international average

Fourth grade		
Country	Mean score	Standard error
Korea	611	(2.1)
Japan	597	(2.1)
Netherlands*	577	(3.4)
Czech Republic	567	(3.3)
Austria*	559	(3.1)
Ireland	550	(3.4)
Hungary*	548	(3.7)
Australia*	546	(3.1)
United States	545	(3.0)
Canada	532	(3.3)
Scotland	520	(3.9)
England**	513	(3.2)
Norway	502	(3.0)
New Zealand	499	(4.3)
Greece	492	(4.4)
Portugal	475	(3.5)
Iceland	474	(2.7)

International average = 537

Eighth grade		
Country	Mean score	Standard error
Korea	607	(2.4)
Japan	605	(1.9)
Czech Republic	564	(4.9)
Netherlands*	541	(6.7)
Austria*	539	(3.0)
Hungary	537	(3.2)
Australia*	530	(4.0)
Ireland	527	(5.1)
Canada	527	(2.4)
New Zealand	508	(4.5)
England**	506	(2.6)
Norway	503	(2.2)
United States**	500	(4.6)
Scotland*	498	(5.5)
Iceland	487	(4.5)
Greece*	484	(3.1)
Portugal	454	(2.5)

International average = 526

untries did not meet TIMSS sampling requirements.
untries met TIMSS sampling requirements only partially.
: IEA.

*wledge of the determinants
of successful student
performance enables policy-
makers to make informed
choices about priorities for the
future.*

Examining the relative performance of countries leads to the more pertinent question of what influences student performance. What factors explain the patterns of performance in different countries, and are they amenable to policy intervention? Knowledge of the determinants of successful student performance enables policy-makers to make informed choices about priorities for the future. Success may be associated, for example, with student attitudes and perceptions, with teachers' instructional practices or with curricular emphases. Future editions of this publication will attempt to explore the factors that can contribute to high standards of performance in school.

*riation in mathematics and
cience achievement between
untries cannot be explained
one in terms of financial or
staff resource levels.*

The fact that there appears to be neither a strong nor a consistent relationship at the national level between the level of resources (see Indicators B1, B4 and B7) and student outcomes provides further evidence that variation between countries cannot be explained alone in terms of financial or staff resource levels and that the search for improvement in school performance must extend to factors that lie beyond material inputs.

◆ Chart FI.4. **Science performance in 4th and 8th grades compared with international averages (1995)**

■ Significantly higher than international average	□ Not significantly different from international average	□ Significantly lower than international average

Fourth grade				**Eighth grade**		
Country	Mean score	Standard error		Country	Mean score	Standard error
Korea	597	(1.9)		Czech Republic	574	(4.3)
Japan	574	(1.8)		Japan	571	(1.6)
United States	565	(3.1)		Korea	565	(1.9)
Austria*	565	(3.3)		Netherlands*	560	(5.0)
Australia*	562	(2.9)		Austria*	558	(3.7)
Netherlands*	557	(3.1)		Hungary	554	(2.8)
Czech Republic	557	(3.1)		England**	552	(3.3)
England**	551	(3.3)		Australia*	545	(3.9)
Canada	549	(3.0)		Ireland	538	(4.5)
Ireland	539	(3.3)		United States**	534	(4.7)
Scotland	536	(4.2)		Canada	531	(2.6)
Hungary*	532	(3.4)		Norway	527	(1.9)
New Zealand	531	(4.9)		New Zealand	526	(4.4)
Norway	530	(3.6)		Scotland**	517	(5.1)
Iceland	505	(3.3)		Greece*	497	(2.2)
Greece	497	(4.1)		Iceland	494	(4.0)
Portugal	480	(4.0)		Portugal	480	(2.3)

International average = 543   International average = 537

* Countries did not meet TIMSS sampling requirements.
** Countries met TIMSS sampling requirements only partially.
Source: IEA.

Definitions

The achievement scores are based on tests administered as part of the Third International Mathematics and Science Study (IEA/TIMSS), undertaken by the International Association for the Evaluation of Educational Achievement (IEA) during the school year 1994/95.

The data are subject to sampling error, which sets a lower limit on the si observed differences that can be considered statistically significant. N scores are therefore reported together with their standard errors. The c indicate whether the differences between pairs of countries are statisti significant or not. The statistical tests used to compare country means conducted using the Bonferroni adjustment for multiple comparisons a 5 per cent significance level. (To maintain consistency with results rep by IEA/TIMSS, the Bonferroni adjustment was based on the full set of c tries participating in the IEA/TIMSS, and not just OECD countries.)

The target population studied in this indicator refers to students in the u grade of the two grade levels in which most 9 year-olds are enrolled. Con

tionally, this grade is referred to as the "4th" grade, since in most countries it refers to the fourth year of formal schooling (see also column 4 in Table F4.1). Countries marked with an asterisk (*) met the IEA/TIMSS sampling standards only partially, and countries marked with two asterisks (**) did not meet the IEA/TIMSS sampling standards. For further details see Annex 3. For the results on the achievement of 8th-graders refer to the 1996 edition of *Education at a Glance*.

The reporting of data on a sub-national level for some countries is based on data availability from the IEA and does not represent a policy decision by the OECD.

Indicator F2: Student differences in mathematics and science achievement at the 4th-grade level

Policy context

Indicator F2 provides insight into how each country's highest and lowest achievers perform in relation to their counterparts in other countries.

The demand for highly skilled labour in modern economies cannot be sat fied by a small intellectual elite but requires excellence throughout t education system. Both parents and the wider public have become aware the gravity of the phenomenon of under-achievement and the fact t school-leavers who lack basic skills face poor labour market prospects.

The performance of a country's best students in mathematics and scier may have implications for the part that country will play in the pool fr which tomorrow's mathematicians and scientists will be drawn. Similarly high proportion of students at the lower end of the scale may give rise concern that a significant proportion of tomorrow's taxpayers and voters ᵥ not have the understanding of the basic mathematical and scientific conce needed for the informed judgements which they will be called upon to mak

The indicator also illustrates variation and disparities of student achievement within countries.

A general aim of most OECD countries is not only to reach a high level performance, but also to minimise disparities within the country. If the g between low and high achievers is found to be equivalent to several year schooling, the "weaker students" may be at risk of being unable to particip fully in the economy and society.

Finally, a comparison of the distribution of achievement between the 4th ᵢ 8th-grade levels can provide some insight into the extent to which educat systems and societies moderate or reinforce early educational disparitie

Evidence and explanations

Mean achievement can mask significant variation within classrooms, schools or education systems.

Mean achievement scores are typically used to assess the quality of schc and education systems. However, mean achievement does not provide a picture and can mask significant variation within an individual classro school or education system.

Countries vary considerably in the achievement of their low-performing students.

In many countries, a sizeable number of students fall behind in performa and may face difficulties in following the programmes of study set out in curriculum.

Less than 5 per cent of 4th-graders in Iceland and Portugal reach the average level of mathematics performance in Korea.

There is a wide variation in achievement of the top-performing 4th-gr students across countries. Less than 5 per cent of 4th-graders in Iceland Portugal reach the average level of mathematics performance of their Kor counterparts. More than 40 per cent of Japanese and Korean students s above the collective OECD 75th percentile in mathematics and a quarte them score higher than nearly all students in Greece, Iceland, New Zeal Norway and Portugal. On the other hand, less than 10 per cent of the stud in Greece, Iceland, New Zealand, Norway and Portugal score above the O 75th percentile in mathematics.

◆ Chart F2.1 ***Distribution of mathematics achievement scores, 4th grade (1995)***

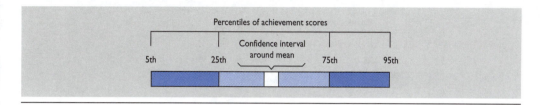

Percentiles of achievement scores

Confidence interval around mean

5th 25th 75th 95th

Country standing with respect to interquartile range

	Rank order 4th grade	Rank order 8th grade
Iceland	1	2
Norway	2	3
Korea	2	17
Netherlands*	4	7
Austria*	5	13
Portugal	6	1
Japan	7	15
Canada	8	4
United States	9	9
Ireland	9	12
England**	11	9
Czech Republic	11	14
Greece	13	6
Hungary*	14	11
New Zealand	15	7
Scotland	16	5
Australia*	17	16

200 300 400 500 600 700 800
Achievement score

…es are ranked in ascending order of interquartile range of mathematics achievement scores.

…ntries did not meet TIMSS sampling requirements.

…ntries met TIMSS sampling requirements only partially.

IEA.

◆ Chart F2.2. **Distribution of science achievement scores, 4th grade (1995)**

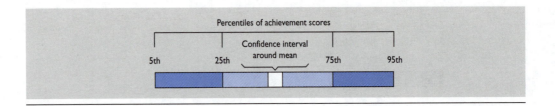

	Country standing with respect to interquartile range	
	Rank order 4th grade	Rank order 8th grade
Netherlands*	1	3
Korea	2	10
Japan	3	5
Greece	4	6
Austria*	5	10
Czech Republic	6	8
Hungary*	6	6
Portugal	6	1
Ireland	9	13
Canada	10	8
Norway	11	4
Iceland	12	2
Australia*	13	17
Scotland	14	12
England**	14	15
New Zealand	16	14
United States	17	16

Achievement score (x-axis: 200 300 400 500 600 700 800 900)

Countries are ranked in ascending order of interquartile range of science achievement scores.

* Countries did not meet TIMSS sampling requirements.

** Countries met TIMSS sampling requirements only partially.

Source: IEA.

There is also substantial variation within each country...

The interquartile range – the difference between scores at the 75th and 25th percentiles – varies between countries in both mathematics and science, although the variation is wider in science.

...and in many countries the interquartile range of achievement is twice as wide as the average gap between children one year apart.

The differences between the 25th and 75th percentiles of student performance in mathematics in half of the countries is about twice the average progress in achievement that students at that level accomplish over a school year – a significant challenge for schools and teachers. In mathematics, the interquartile range is narrowest in Iceland, at 95 scale points, and widest in Australia, at 122 points – nearly twice the typical progress in achievement that students accomplish between the 3rd and 4th grade. In science, the interquartile range extends from 88 points in the Netherlands to 128 points in the United States.

Countries usually show similar patterns of disparities in mathematics and science but there are notable exceptions.

There exists a moderate correlation ($r = 0.54$) between countries' interquartile ranges in mathematics and science at the 4th-grade level. Some countries, such as Austria, Korea and the Netherlands, have interquartile ranges in both subjects that are narrow relative to those of other countries. Other countries, such as Australia, England, New Zealand and Scotland, have relatively wide interquartile ranges in both subjects. Yet other countries, such as the Czech Republic, Greece, Hungary, Iceland and Norway, have a relatively wide interquartile range in one subject along with a relatively narrow interquartile range in the other. Such variation in disparities between subject matter domains may reflect differences in curriculum and instruction, which are amenable to policy decisions.

Education systems must address the challenge of disparities in achievement that exist within classes, within schools and within the country.

Teachers, schools and education systems must address the variation in achievement that exists within classes, within schools and within the country as a whole. Such variation can result from disparities in resources and in the socio-economic background of students and schools as well as from curricular differences and the way in which instruction is organised and delivered. Some education systems deal with this variation explicitly by forming homogeneous student groups through selection either within or between classes and schools, while others leave it as an individual challenge for teachers and students.

Some countries with similar levels of average performance show a different extent of disparities in achievement...

It is notable that countries with similar levels of average performance show a considerable variation in disparities of student achievement. For example, New Zealand and Norway show the same average level of mathematics performance, but the 25th percentile in New Zealand is 14 score points below the 25th percentile in Norway, indicating that the weaker performers in New Zealand have markedly lower scores than their counterparts in Norway. At the other end of the scale, the stronger performers in New Zealand score higher than the stronger performers in Norway.

...which indicates that a wide range of achievement is not a necessary condition for a system to attain a high level of overall performance.

Comparing the range of achievement within a country with its average performance thus shows that a wide range of achievement is not a necessary condition for a system to attain a high level of overall performance. Some countries with high levels of achievement, such as Austria, Japan, Korea and the Netherlands, show a narrow distribution of mathematics performance, with below-average interquartile ranges. This indicates that wide disparities are not a necessary condition for high average achievement.

Generally, countries with a low interquartile range also show a narrow distribution among the lowest achievers.

Examining the range from the 25th percentile to the 5th percentile gives an indication of the relative performance of the students with very low achievement, who are at risk of failing. Does the range of achievement become wider at the bottom end of the distribution? Generally, countries such as Korea or the Netherlands with a narrow interquartile range show also a narrow distribution at the bottom end of the achievement distribution as well.

Some countries with comparatively low disparities in mathematics achievement at the 4th-grade level show wide disparities at the 8th-grade level...

A comparison of the disparities in achievement between the 4th and 8 grade levels (see also Indicator R7 in the 1996 edition of *Education at a Glan* provides some insight into the extent to which education systems and soc ties moderate or reinforce educational disparities.

One can gauge the change in variation in achievement "over time" by co paring the relative ranks of countries' interquartile ranges in mathematics a science achievement at the 4th grade with those at the 8th grade. While so countries exhibiting relatively wide variation in mathematics achievement the 4th grade also exhibit relatively wide variation in the 8th grade, so countries with low variation in the 4th grade have – relative to other countr – high variation in the 8th grade.

Korea, which has one of the narrowest interquartile ranges at the 4th-gra level, shows the widest disparity at the 8th grade. Similarly, Austria mov from the 5th position at the 4th grade to the 13th position at the 8th-gra level (among the 17 countries which took part in TIMSS at both grade leve

... but some countries contain the growth in disparities better than others.

Scotland shows the second highest disparities in mathematics achievemen the 4th-grade level, but at the 8th-grade level there are only four count with lower disparities. Similarly, Greece moves from the 14th position at 4th grade to the 6th position at the 8th grade, albeit with comparatively overall performance at both levels. Iceland and Norway show some of narrowest interquartile ranges in mathematics achievement at both gr levels.

In science, the relative standing of countries in interquartile ranking at both 4th and 8th grades is more consistent than in mathematics.

In science, the relative standing of countries in the 4th and 8th grades is m consistent. Most countries showing relatively high variation in 4th-grade ence achievement (*e.g.*, Australia, England, New Zealand, Scotland and United States) maintain it in the 8th grade, while countries showing relati low variation in 4th-grade achievement (*e.g.*, Japan and the Netherlands) show relatively low variation in the 8th grade.

It must be noted, however, that two different groups of students are being compared.

The comparison of interquartile ranges between the 4th and 8th grades o not make use of 4th-grade and 8th-grade achievement scores for a si cohort of students. Instead, two different groups of students – one at 4th grade and the other at the 8th grade – have been tested at the same ti

Definitions

Data are based on tests administered as part of the Third International Mathematics and Science Study (IEA/TIMSS), undertaken by the International Association for the Evaluation of Educational Achievement (IEA) during the school year 1994/95.

Tables F2.1 and F2.2 show the achievement scores of students at the 25th, 75th, and 95th percentiles of the *national* mathematics score dist tions. The 5th percentile, for example, refers to the achievement score b which 5 per cent of the population score.

Tables F2.3 and F2.4 show the percentage of students from each country reach the 50th, 75th, and 90th percentiles of the *collective* OECD distrib These percentiles are based on all OECD Member countries which pa pated in the study at the 4th-grade level; each country is weighted in calculations according to the size of its student population. Thus, the achi ment scores of countries with large student populations, such as Japan the United States, have more weight on the resulting OECD percentiles do the achievement scores of countries with relatively small student po tions, such as Iceland and Scotland.

The target population studied in this indicator refers to students in the u grade of the two grade levels in which most 9 year-olds are enrolled further details on the target population and sampling standards see In tor F1 and Annex 3. For the results on the achievement of 8th-graders re the 1996 edition of *Education at a Glance*.

Strictly speaking, an interquartile range calculated on the 4th-grade scale cannot be directly compared with an interquartile range calculated on the 8th-grade scale. Direct comparisons could not be made since the two populations were not represented on the same scale. Thus, while it is meaningful to compare country ranks between grades, it is not appropriate to compare the numerical values of interquartile ranges between the 4th and 8th grades.

Table F2.1 **Distribution of mathematics achievement scores, 4th grade (1995)**

	Mean	5th percentile[1]	25th percentile[1]	75th percentile[1]	95th percentile[1]	Interquartile range[2]
North America						
Canada	532	394	477	588	670	111
United States	545	398	488	603	682	115
Pacific Area						
Australia*	546	394	486	608	696	122
Japan	597	458	545	653	726	108
Korea	611	489	565	661	727	96
New Zealand	499	350	440	560	641	120
European Union						
Austria*	559	420	508	613	687	105
Greece	492	341	435	553	637	118
Ireland	550	401	495	610	687	115
Netherlands*	577	462	528	625	690	97
Portugal	475	340	424	531	605	107
United Kingdom						
England**	513	366	452	569	672	117
Scotland	520	373	460	581	667	121
Other OECD countries						
Czech Republic	567	427	509	626	711	117
Hungary*	548	404	488	607	695	119
Iceland	474	359	424	519	595	95
Norway	502	376	454	550	623	96
Country mean	**537**	**399**	**483**	**593**	**671**	**110**

 * Countries did not meet TIMSS sampling requirements.
** Countries met TIMSS sampling requirements only partially.
1. 5 (or 25 or 75 or 95) per cent of students score below this point.
2. Difference between the 75th and 25th percentiles.

Source: International Association for the Evaluation of Educational Achievement (IEA). See Annex 3 for notes.

Table F2.2 **Distribution of science achievement scores, 4th grade (1995)**

	Mean	5th percentile[1]	25th percentile[1]	75th percentile[1]	95th percentile[1]	Interquartile range[2]
North America						
Canada	549	409	493	607	691	114
United States	565	397	505	633	711	128
Pacific Area						
Australia*	562	403	502	626	707	124
Japan	574	453	527	624	687	97
Korea	597	481	554	643	704	89
New Zealand	531	364	471	598	683	127
European Union						
Austria*	565	429	513	619	692	106
Greece	497	354	448	552	627	104
Ireland	539	388	487	596	674	109
Netherlands*	557	448	514	602	661	88
Portugal	480	331	427	535	610	108
United Kingdom						
England**	551	388	489	615	708	126
Scotland	536	376	472	598	687	126
Other OECD countries						
Czech Republic	557	425	502	610	689	108
Hungary*	532	396	478	586	660	108
Iceland	505	360	447	564	632	117
Norway	530	387	476	592	663	116
Country mean	**543**	**400**	**489**	**600**	**674**	**111**

Countries did not meet TIMSS sampling requirements.
Countries met TIMSS sampling requirements only partially.
(or 25 or 75 or 95) per cent of students score below this point.
Difference between the 75th and 25th percentiles.
Source: International Association for the Evaluation of Educational Achievement (IEA). See Annex 3 for notes.

Table F2.3 **Percentage of students scoring above the 50th, 75th, and 90th percentiles of the collective OECD achievement distribution in mathematics, 4th grade (1995)**

	Percentage above OECD 50th percentile	Standard error	Percentage above OECD 75th percentile	Standard error	Percentage above OECD 90th percentile	Standard error
North America						
Canada	37.7	(1.6)	15.5	(1.3)	5.0	(0.6)
United States	44.8	(1.5)	19.8	(1.2)	6.9	(0.8)
Pacific Area						
Australia*	44.5	(1.5)	22.1	(1.0)	9.6	(0.7)
Japan	69.8	(1.0)	40.7	(1.2)	18.2	(0.8)
Korea	77.8	(1.0)	47.5	(1.3)	21.9	(1.1)
New Zealand	25.7	(1.6)	8.3	(1.0)	2.8	(0.6)
European Union						
Austria*	51.0	(1.6)	23.4	(1.5)	8.2	(1.0)
Greece	23.4	(1.5)	7.7	(0.8)	2.2	(0.4)
Ireland	47.0	(1.8)	21.6	(1.3)	7.7	(0.6)
Netherlands*	60.9	(1.9)	28.3	(1.7)	9.8	(0.9)
Portugal	14.9	(1.0)	3.4	(0.4)	0.4	(0.1)
United Kingdom						
England**	28.9	(1.4)	13.1	(1.1)	5.5	(0.7)
Scotland	33.6	(1.8)	14.3	(1.4)	4.7	(0.7)
Other OECD countries						
Czech Republic	53.6	(1.5)	28.9	(1.5)	11.6	(1.1)
Hungary*	45.6	(1.9)	21.3	(1.5)	8.9	(0.9)
Iceland	12.7	(1.2)	2.8	(0.6)	0.5	(0.1)
Norway	21.9	(1.3)	6.1	(0.7)	1.2	(0.4)
Country mean	**41.4**		**19.4**		**7.5**	

* Countries did not meet TIMSS sampling requirements.
** Countries met TIMSS sampling requirements only partially.

Source: International Association for the Evaluation of Educational Achievement (IEA). See Annex 3 for notes.

Table F2.4 **Percentage of students scoring above the 50th, 75th, and 90th percentiles of the collective OECD achievement distribution in science, 4th grade (1995)**

	Percentage above OECD 50th percentile	Standard error	Percentage above OECD 75th percentile	Standard error	Percentage above OECD 90th percentile	Standard error
North America						
Canada	41.6	(1.7)	18.4	(1.3)	7.6	(0.7)
United States	51.6	(1.5)	27.8	(1.3)	12.2	(0.8)
Pacific Area						
Australia*	49.6	(1.3)	25.6	(1.0)	10.7	(0.6)
Japan	54.0	(1.1)	24.5	(0.8)	7.7	(0.5)
Korea	67.5	(1.1)	35.1	(1.2)	12.3	(0.7)
New Zealand	35.9	(1.8)	16.1	(1.2)	6.6	(0.8)
European Union						
Austria*	49.1	(1.6)	22.9	(1.3)	8.0	(0.9)
Greece	18.7	(1.2)	5.2	(0.6)	0.9	(0.2)
Ireland	36.6	(1.6)	15.1	(1.0)	5.2	(0.5)
Netherlands*	42.8	(1.9)	15.4	(1.0)	3.0	(0.4)
Portugal	14.0	(1.1)	3.2	(0.5)	0.7	(0.2)
United Kingdom						
England**	43.9	(1.4)	21.6	(1.2)	10.6	(0.8)
Scotland	37.4	(1.8)	16.7	(1.1)	6.9	(0.7)
Other OECD countries						
Czech Republic	43.8	(1.6)	19.8	(1.4)	8.3	(0.8)
Hungary*	33.2	(1.7)	11.7	(1.0)	3.6	(0.4)
Iceland	22.9	(1.1)	6.5	(0.7)	1.7	(0.4)
Norway	34.1	(1.5)	12.8	(1.1)	3.7	(0.5)
Country mean	**39.7**		**17.4**		**6.3**	

* Countries did not meet TIMSS sampling requirements.
** Countries met TIMSS sampling requirements only partially.

Source: International Association for the Evaluation of Educational Achievement (IEA). See Annex 3 for notes.

Indicator F3: Gender differences in mathematics and science at the 4th and 8th-grade levels

Policy context

This indicator compares the mathematics and science achievement of boys and girls.

Reducing educational disparities between young men and women is important policy objective, particularly since gender disparities at an ea age tend to grow during the school years and may ultimately affect furth education, training and career opportunities. Many factors contribute to achievement of girls in mathematics and science: encouragement from p ents, interactions between teachers and students, curriculum content a delivery, self-concept and attitudes towards mathematics and educatio resources available at home.

Evidence and explanations

In comparison with other factors influencing student achievement, gender differences in mathematics achievement are relatively low.

Gender disparities in mathematics at the 4th-grade level tend to be smal moderate (see Chart F3.1). On average, boys score 4 points higher than g on a scale for which a standard deviation is about 100 points. In the majo of countries, boys do score higher, with differences ranging from 1 poin Iceland to 15 points in Korea and the Netherlands. However, the differenc achievement is statistically significant only for Japan, Korea and Netherlands. In three countries (Greece, Ireland and New Zealand) girls sc higher than boys, by up to 10 points, but none of these differences is stat cally significant. In Scotland, there is no difference between the aver scores of boys and those of girls.

Gender differences in science achievement are more pronounced, favouring boys in about half of the countries in a statistically significant way...

In science, the gap in achievement between the genders is larger. On aver, boys score 11 points higher than girls in science. Boys score higher in all one country, with differences ranging from 3 points in Portugal to 26 point the Netherlands. For 9 countries, the difference in achievement betw boys and girls is statistically significant (Australia, Austria, the Czech Repu Hungary, Iceland, Japan, Korea, the Netherlands and the United States New Zealand, the gap favours girls (by 8 points), but the difference is significant.

... but girls in some countries with high achievement perform better than boys in other countries.

In some countries which achieve high scores but show significant gender g in achievement, female students have higher average scores than both l and girls in other countries. For instance, in mathematics, girls in Japan, K and the Netherlands (with 8, 15 and 15 points of gender differences, res tively) outscore boys, on average, in all other countries. The Czech Repu combines high mathematics achievement and low gender disparity, perfe ing in the top quarter of countries in achievement, with a below-ave gender gap. In science, the picture is similar but less pronounced. In Ko

◆   Chart F3.1.   **Difference in mean mathematics achievement scores between boys and girls,
4th grade (1995)**

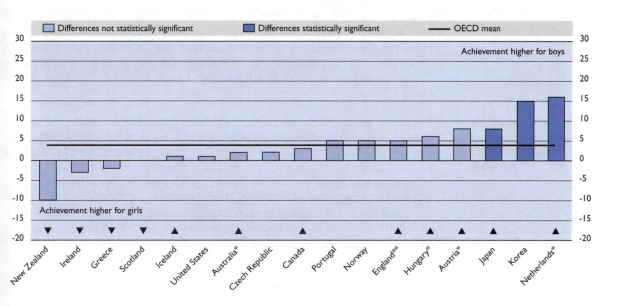

◆   Chart F3.2.   **Difference in mean science achievement scores between boys and girls,
4th grade (1995)**

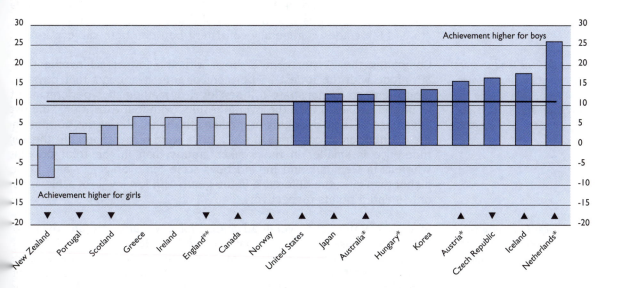

riangles at the bottom of the charts indicate where the relative standing of a country with respect to gender differences differs between 4th and 8th graders by
  than three positions.
e relative standing of the country improves over the four grade years, *i.e.* gender differences among 8th-graders are comparatively smaller.
e relative standing of the country declines over the four grade years, *i.e.* gender differences among 8th-graders are comparatively larger.

untries did not meet TIMSS sampling requirements.
untries met TIMSS sampling requirements only partially.

:   IEA.

where boys score an average of 14 points higher than girls in science, gi
outscore students in all other countries.

In general, countries that show large differences between boys and girls
one subject also tend to show a large gender gap in the other subje
However, several countries with a gender gap in mathematics below t
OECD average have gender gaps in science that are above the OECD avera;
These countries include Australia, the Czech Republic, Iceland and t
United States.

In some countries gender differences rise significantly between the 4th and 8th grades...

Are these gender differences predictive for 8th-graders? While the indica
cannot answer this question directly, a comparison of the gender gap at bc
the 4th and 8th grades (see Indicator R10 in the 1996 edition of *Education c
Glance*) can provide some insight. In some countries, the advantage favour
boys increases from the 4th to the 8th grade, relative to other countries,
both mathematics and science. For example, in science, Portugal a
Scotland have much larger gender gaps favouring boys in the 8th grade th
in the 4th grade. In New Zealand, an advantage for girls at the 4th-grade le
in mathematics and a small advantage in science turns into a signific
advantage for boys in both subjects at the 8th-grade level. Greece ;
Ireland (in mathematics) also exhibit substantial changes in their relat
standing with respect to gender differences between the 4th and 8th grac

... while others succeed in reducing the gender gap between the 4th and 8th grades.

However, there are other countries which successfully contain this tender
In Australia and Canada 4th-grade boys are at an advantage in mathemat
whereas in the 8th grade this tendency is reversed. Also, the Netherla
changes its relative standing considerably in favour of girls over the I
grades. In science, changes in rank order towards smaller gender gaps can
most clearly observed in Australia, Austria, Iceland, Japan, the Netherla
and the United States. The direction of change in gender gaps between
4th and 8th grades is generally consistent between both subject areas.

Although boys tend to score higher than girls on average, the pattern differs among the lowest performing boys and girls.

Comparing the 25 per cent of boys with the lowest achievement in
8th grade with the lowest 25 per cent of girls, it appears that boys in
group tend to demonstrate a lower level of mathematics performance t
would be expected from the overall results. With four exceptions, the ove
advantage of boys over girls in mathematics is smaller at the bottom en
the distribution. In countries in which boys score higher than girls, the ger
difference is smaller in the weaker groups than in the total populat
Whereas in Denmark and Ireland boys score, on average, 17 and 14 po
higher than girls, the difference in the group with low levels of achieveme
only 9 and 5 points respectively.

Boys appear to be at greater risk of low achievement than girls in some countries.

In some countries the overall advantage for boys turns into an advantage
girls in the weaker groups. In Japan the gender difference overall favours l
by 9 score points, whereas girls score higher than boys among the 25 per <
with the lowest achievement by 10 score points. In Australia and the Fler
Community of Belgium, where girls perform better overall, the differenc
slightly larger among the weaker boys and girls. The trend in science, in w
in general boys are also favoured, is very similar.

This tendency is reflected in other school subjects as well.

It is noteworthy that these patterns are mirrored in reading achievemen
measured by the 1991 IEA Reading Literacy Survey (see the 1992 editic
Education at a Glance). Fourteen-year old girls generally perform better in r
ing than 14-year old boys. Among the 25 per cent of boys with the lo
achievement and the 25 per cent of girls with the lowest achievement,
gender difference is wider.

Definitions

Data on mathematics and science achievement are based on tests administered as part of the Third International Mathematics and Science Study (IEA/TIMSS), undertaken by the IEA during the school year 1994/95.

Tables F3.1 and F3.2 show the average difference in mathematics and science achievement scores between boys and girls in the fourth year of schooling, together with an indication of whether these differences are statistically significant at the 5 per cent level. (The results are based on simple t-tests, not adjusted for the number of participating countries.)

Table F3.3 shows gender differences in the groups of boys and girls with the lowest achievement which are based on a comparison of the mathematics and science scores of the total TIMSS population with the mathematics and science scores of the weaker boys and girls. The group of the boys with the lowest achievement are defined as the 25 per cent of boys with the lowest scores. The girls with the lowest achievement are the 25 per cent of girls with the lowest scores.

The mathematics and science achievement scores for this comparison are based on IEA/TIMSS data. The target populations studied in this indicator refer to students in the upper grades of the two grade levels in which most 9 and 13 year-olds are enrolled. For further details on the target population and sampling standards see Indicator F1 and Annex 3.

e reading achievement scores e based on the results of the ternational Reading Literacy udy undertaken by the IEA during the school year 1990/91.

The reading achievement scores are based on the results of the International Reading Literacy Study undertaken by the IEA in October 1990 and April 1991. The data were collected in the grade level containing the majority of all 14 year-olds. Table F3.3 reports the results for narrative reading; the results for explanatory reading and documentary reading that are not shown here reveal a similar pattern.

Table F3.1 **Mean mathematics achievement by gender in 4th grade (1995)**

	Boys		Girls		Differences in means[1]	Standard err
	Mean	Standard error	Mean	Standard error		
North America						
Canada	534	(3.4)	531	(3.9)	**3b**	(5.1)
United States	545	(3.1)	544	(3.3)	**2b**	(4.5)
Pacific Area						
Australia*	547	(3.5)	545	(3.7)	**2b**	(5.1)
Korea	618	(2.5)	603	(2.6)	**15b**	(3.6)
Japan	601	(2.5)	593	(2.2)	**8b**	(3.3)
New Zealand	494	(5.7)	504	(4.3)	**10g**	(7.1)
European Union						
Austria*	563	(3.6)	555	(3.6)	**8b**	(5.1)
Greece	491	(5.0)	493	(4.5)	**2g**	(6.8)
Ireland	548	(3.9)	551	(4.3)	**3g**	(5.8)
Netherlands*	585	(3.8)	569	(3.4)	**15b**	(5.1)
Portugal	478	(3.8)	473	(3.7)	**4b**	(5.3)
United Kingdom						
England**	515	(3.4)	510	(4.4)	**5b**	(5.5)
Scotland	520	(4.3)	520	(3.8)	**0**	(5.8)
Other OECD countries						
Czech Republic	568	(3.4)	566	(3.6)	**3b**	(5.0)
Hungary*	552	(4.2)	546	(3.9)	**5b**	(5.8)
Iceland	474	(3.3)	473	(3.0)	**1b**	(4.5)
Norway	504	(3.5)	499	(3.6)	**5b**	(5.0)
Country mean	**538**		**534**		**4b**	

* Countries did not meet TIMSS sampling requirements.
** Countries met TIMSS sampling requirements only partially.
1. b means boys score higher.
  g means girls score higher.
Source: International Association for the Evaluation of Educational Achievement (IEA). See Annex 3 for notes.

Table F3.2 **Mean science achievement by gender in 4th grade (1995)**

	Boys		Girls		Differences in means[1]	Standard error
	Mean	Standard error	Mean	Standard error		
North America						
Canada	553	(3.7)	545	(3.2)	**8b**	(4.9)
United States	571	(3.3)	560	(3.3)	**12b**	(4.6)
Pacific Area						
Australia*	569	(3.3)	556	(3.2)	**13b**	(4.6)
Korea	604	(2.2)	590	(2.5)	**14b**	(3.3)
Japan	580	(2.0)	567	(2.0)	**14b**	(2.9)
New Zealand	527	(6.1)	535	(4.8)	**8g**	(7.7)
European Union						
Austria*	572	(3.9)	556	(3.7)	**15b**	(5.3)
Greece	501	(4.5)	494	(4.3)	**7b**	(6.2)
Ireland	543	(3.5)	536	(4.5)	**7b**	(5.7)
Netherlands*	570	(3.6)	544	(3.5)	**26b**	(5.0)
Portugal	481	(4.5)	478	(4.2)	**3b**	(6.2)
United Kingdom						
England**	555	(4.0)	548	(3.4)	**7b**	(5.3)
Scotland	538	(4.5)	533	(4.3)	**4b**	(6.2)
Other OECD countries						
Czech Republic	565	(3.4)	548	(3.6)	**17b**	(5.0)
Hungary*	539	(3.8)	525	(3.9)	**14b**	(5.4)
Iceland	514	(4.3)	496	(3.3)	**18b**	(5.4)
Norway	534	(4.7)	526	(3.7)	**8b**	(5.9)
Country mean	**548**		**537**		**11b**	

Countries did not meet TIMSS sampling requirements.
Countries met TIMSS sampling requirements only partially.
means boys score higher.
means girls score higher.
Source: International Association for the Evaluation of Educational Achievement (IEA). See Annex 3 for notes.

Table F3.3 **Mean mathematics, science and expository reading achievement for the 25 per cent of boys and girls with the lowest achievement in 8th grade (1995)**

| | Mathematics achievement scores | | | | | | Science achievement scores | | | | | | Expository reading achievement scores | | | | | |
| | Low achieving 25 per cent | | | Total | | | Low achieving 25 per cent | | | Total | | | Low achieving 25 per cent | | | Total | | |
	Boys	Girls	Difference in means[1]	Boys	Girls	Difference in means[1]	Boys	Girls	Difference in means[1]	Boys	Girls	Difference in means[1]	Boys	Girls	Difference in means[1]	Boys	Girls	Difference in means[1]
North America																		
Canada	413	418	5g	527	530	4g	409	401	8b	538	526	12b	396	417	21g	513	524	10g
United States **	378	382	4g	502	498	4b	386	388	2g	539	530	9b	410	429	19g	536	546	10g
Pacific Area																		
Australia *	407	417	10g	528	533	5g	413	418	5g	551	541	9b	m	m	m	m	m	m
Japan	467	477	10g	609	600	9b	459	451	8b	579	562	17b	m	m	m	m	m	m
Korea	476	459	17b	615	598	17b	455	436	19b	576	552	25b	m	m	m	m	m	m
New Zealand	399	396	3b	513	503	9b	407	395	12b	538	513	25b	416	422	6g	536	537	1g
European Union																		
Austria *	434	428	6b	544	536	8b	453	429	24b	566	549	18b	m	m	m	m	m	m
Belgium																		
(Flemish Community)**	460	467	7g	564	567	4g	464	451	14b	558	543	15b	379	392	12g	477	480	3g
(French Community)*	424	425	1g	530	524	6b	373	367	6b	479	463	16b	407	424	17g	524	525	1g
Denmark *	403	394	9b	512	495	17b	381	356	25b	495	464	31b	443	477	34g	538	546	8g
Finland	m	m	m	m	m	m	m	m	m	m	m	m	448	453	5g	549	546	3b
France	452	442	10b	542	536	6b	412	396	16b	506	490	16b	415	417	2g	523	523	1b
Germany *	404	396	7b	512	509	3b	414	395	19b	542	524	18b	416	421	5g	510	507	2b
Greece *	379	375	4b	490	478	12b	399	387	12b	505	489	16b	392	414	22g	498	517	19g
Ireland	417	411	5b	536	521	14b	424	419	5b	545	532	13b	418	434	16g	518	531	14g
Italy	m	m	m	m	m	m	m	m	m	m	m	m	413	414	1g	503	504	1g
Netherlands *	439	433	6b	545	537	8b	467	453	14b	570	550	21b	438	431	7b	527	521	7b
Portugal	384	372	11b	460	449	11b	401	376	25b	491	469	22b	402	408	6g	495	496	2g
Spain	402	397	5b	492	483	10b	431	413	18b	526	508	18b	m	m	m	m	m	m
Sweden	414	408	6b	520	518	2b	428	415	14b	543	528	15b	427	444	17g	531	536	6g
United Kingdom																		
England**	390	392	2g	509	505	4b	428	411	17b	563	543	20b	m	m	m	m	m	m
Scotland*	400	389	11b	507	490	17b	403	388	15b	529	507	22b	m	m	m	m	m	m
Other OECD countries																		
Czech Republic	448	442	6b	569	558	11b	474	453	21b	586	562	24b	425	446	21g	531	540	10g
Hungary	425	423	2b	539	538	0	454	432	22b	564	545	19b	428	451	24g	545	553	8g
Iceland	388	395	7g	489	486	3b	393	389	4b	502	485	16b	424	439	14g	523	523	1g
Norway	399	401	2g	505	501	4b	418	417	1b	534	521	13b	423	438	15g	528	522	6b
Switzerland **	440	442	2g	548	544	5b	416	410	6b	529	515	15b	m	m	m	m	m	m
Country mean	418	415	2b	519	513	7b	423	410	13b	538	520	18b	418	430	12g	521	524	4g
Other non-OECD countries																		
Russian Federation	409	423	14g	535	536	1g	419	413	7b	544	533	11b	m	m	m	m	m	m

* Countries did not meet TIMSS sampling requirements.

** Countries met TIMSS sampling requirements only partially.

The 25 per cent of boys and girls with the lowest achievement is not identical to the 25 per cent of lowest achievers overall.

1. b means boys score higher.

Indicator F4: Differences in mathematics and science achievement between two grade levels

Policy context

Using a synthetic cohort, this indicator approximates the gains in mathematics and science achievement between the 4th and 8th grades.

Measuring the level of achievement of students is important in evaluating the performance of education systems. However, it is not only important to examine absolute achievement but also the progress in achievement from grade to grade. A related issue is whether countries with poorer performance at the lower grade are catching up or whether the achievement gap is widening between countries.

Evidence and explanations

This indicator provides an approximation of the progress in mathematics and science achievement accomplished between the 4th and 8th grades. The results are based on a synthetic cohort and do not show the progress of a specific group of students. They rather show the difference in achievement between two different groups of students at the same point in time. Some of the differences that are observed could be due to changes in curricular emphases and instruction that have occurred at different grade levels.

Some of the countries showing a comparatively low performance at the 4th-grade level catch up at the 8th grade...

Iceland, Japan and New Zealand demonstrate the largest improvement in mathematics achievement whereas the Czech Republic, Hungary and Portugal show the largest improvement in science achievement. Iceland, New Zealand and Norway, whose 4th-graders perform particularly poorly in mathematics, are among the countries with the highest gains over the four grade years. The situation is similar for Greece and Portugal with respect to science performance.

... but there are some high-performing countries which can extend their advantage...

There are also countries with high performance in mathematics at the 4th-grade level which succeed in extending their advantage through particularly high gains over the four grade years, in particular Japan and Korea.

...and there are countries that perform well at the 4th-grade level but fall behind at the 8th grade.

At the other end of the spectrum are countries, such as the United States, which perform well at the 4th-grade level but which fall considerably behind at the 8th-grade level.

In science, there appears to be a more consistent relationship between 4th-grade achievement and the difference between 4th and 8th-grade scores. The five top-scoring countries in 4th-grade science achievement – Australia, Austria, Japan, Korea and the United States – are all in the bottom half of countries as ranked by improvement in science achievement between the 4th and 8th grades. It may be that some countries scoring relatively low in 4th-grade science achievement begin teaching science later, but then catch up with other countries in their curricular coverage of science by the 8th grade.

◆ Chart F4.1. *Mean mathematics achievement of students in 4th and 8th grades (1995)*

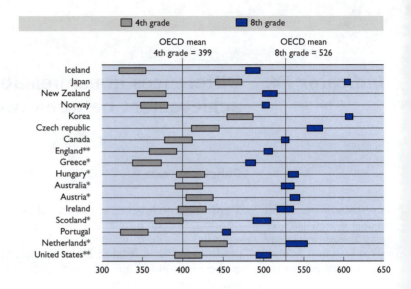

The width of the symbols indicates the confidence interval for the mean (95%).
Countries are ranked in descending order of difference in means between 4th and 8th grades.

* Countries did not meet TIMSS sampling requirements.
** Countries met TIMSS sampling requirements only partially.
Source: IEA.

Some countries show much more improvement in one subject area than in the other. Variation in the curriculum may offer some explanation.

Some countries, such as the Czech Republic, show consistent strong impro ment in both mathematics and science achievement while others s smaller improvement, such as the United States. Yet other countries, suc Korea or Portugal, show high growth in one subject area and low growth in other. Variation in the curriculum may offer some explanation for this. Perl mathematics is taught at an earlier stage than science, so that there app to be a greater gain in science achievement over time. Indeed, some grade students may not yet have been exposed to any science topics at

Definitions

Data are based on tests administered as part of the Third International Mathematics and Science Study (IEA/TIMSS), undertaken by the International Association for the Evaluation of Educational Achievement (IEA) during the school year 1994/95.

This indicator presents the mean scores and estimated mean scores of dents in mathematics and science achievement on the 8th-grade scale in target populations.

The target populations studied in this indicator refer to students in the u grades of the two grade levels in which most 9 and 13 year-olds are enro For further details on the target population and sampling standards Indicator F1 and Annex 3.

Fourth-grade average achievement scores and their standard errors for country are adjusted to fit the 8th-grade achievement scale.

Fifteen of the items in mathematics (15 per cent) and 18 in science (1 cent) were included in the tests for both Population 1 (9 year-olds in grad and 4) and Population 2 (13 year-olds in grades 7 and 8). The differen performance between the populations on these items was used to esti

◆ Chart F4.2. ***Mean science achievement of students in 4th and 8th grades (1995)***

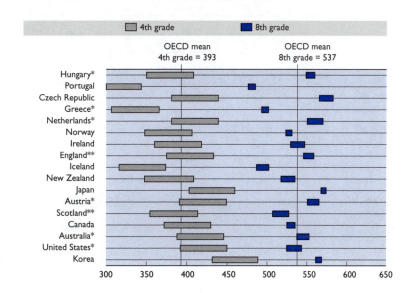

The width of the symbols indicates the confidence interval for the mean (95%).
Countries are ranked in descending order of difference in means between 4th and 8th grades.

* Countries did not meet TIMSS sampling requirements.
** Countries met TIMSS sampling requirements only partially.
Source: IEA.

the change between the 3rd and 4th grades on one hand and the 7th and 8th grades on the other.

The country means for the 4th grade transformed to the 7th and 8th-grade scale are shown in Tables F4.1 and F4.2. These estimates are based on all items administered to the 3rd and 4th-graders. Since there were relatively few items in common, the size of the link is approximate. The standard errors for the 4th grade incorporate an added component to account for the uncertainty of this approximation. Because the link is approximate, the achievement increases between the 4th grade and the 8th grade must be interpreted with caution.

Table F4.1 **Mean mathematics achievement for students in 4th and 8th grades (1995)**

	Fourth grade			Eighth grade			Differences in means	Standard error
	Mean	Standard error	Years of formal schooling	Mean	Standard error	Years of formal schooling		
North America								
Canada	395	(8.5)	4	527	(2.4)	8	133	(8.
United States[a]	407	(8.4)	4	500	(4.6)	8	93	(9
Pacific Area								
Australia[b, d]	408	(8.4)	4 or 5	530	(4.0)	8 or 9	121	(9
Japan	457	(8.1)	4	605	(1.9)	8	148	(8
Korea	471	(8.1)	4	607	(2.4)	8	137	(8
New Zealand	362	(8.9)	4.5-5.5	508	(4.5)	8.5-9.5	146	(10
European Union								
Austria[b, d]	421	(8.4)	4	539	(3.0)	8	119	(9
Greece[d]	356	(8.9)	4	484	(3.1)	8	128	(9
Ireland	412	(8.6)	4	527	(5.1)	8	116	(10
Netherlands[b, d]	438	(8.5)	4	541	(6.7)	8	103	(10
Portugal	340	(8.6)	4	454	(2.5)	8	115	(8
United Kingdom								
England[a, c]	376	(8.5)	5	506	(2.6)	9	130	(8
Scotland[d]	383	(8.7)	5	498	(5.5)	9	115	(10
Other OECD countries								
Czech Republic	428	(8.5)	4	564	(4.9)	8	135	(9
Hungary[b]	410	(8.7)	4	537	(3.2)	8	127	(9
Iceland	338	(8.3)	4	487	(4.5)	8	149	(9
Norway	365	(8.4)	3	503	(2.2)	7	138	(8
Country mean	**399**			**526**			**127**	

a) Countries met TIMSS sampling requirements only partially, 8th grade.
b) Countries did not meet TIMSS sampling requirements, 4th grade.
c) Countries met TIMSS sampling requirements only partially, 4th grade.
d) Countries did not meet TIMSS sampling requirements, 8th grade.

Source: International Association for the Evaluation of Educational Achievement (IEA). See Annex 3 for notes.

Table F4.2   **Mean science achievement for students in 4th and 8th grades (1995)**

	Fourth grade			Eighth grade			Differences in means	Standard error
	Mean	Standard error	Years of formal schooling	Mean	Standard error	Years of formal schooling		
North America								
Canada	401	(14.4)	4	531	(2.6)	8	130	(14.6)
United States[a]	421	(14.4)	4	534	(4.7)	8	113	(15.2)
Pacific Area								
Australia[b, d]	417	(14.4)	4 or 5	545	(3.9)	8 or 9	127	(14.9)
Japan	431	(14.1)	4	571	(1.6)	8	140	(14.2)
Korea	460	(14.1)	4	565	(1.9)	8	105	(14.2)
New Zealand	378	(15.2)	4.5-5.5	526	(4.4)	8.5-9.5	147	(15.8)
European Union								
Austria[b, d]	420	(14.5)	4	558	(3.7)	8	138	(14.9)
Greece[d]	336	(14.8)	4	497	(2.2)	8	161	(15.0)
Ireland	389	(14.5)	4	538	(4.5)	8	149	(15.2)
Netherlands[b, d]	410	(14.4)	4	560	(5.0)	8	150	(15.2)
Portugal	314	(14.8)	4	480	(2.3)	8	165	(14.9)
United Kingdom								
England[a, c]	404	(14.5)	5	552	(3.3)	9	149	(14.9)
Scotland[d]	384	(14.8)	5	517	(5.1)	9	133	(15.7)
Other OECD countries								
Czech Republic	410	(14.4)	4	574	(4.3)	8	164	(15.0)
Hungary[b]	379	(14.5)	4	554	(2.8)	8	175	(14.8)
Iceland	345	(14.5)	4	494	(4.0)	8	148	(15.0)
Norway	377	(14.6)	3	527	(1.9)	7	150	(14.7)
Country mean	**393**			**537**			**144**	

countries met TIMSS sampling requirements only partially, 8th grade.
countries did not meet TIMSS sampling requirements, 4th grade.
countries met TIMSS sampling requirements only partially, 4th grade.
countries did not meet TIMSS sampling requirements, 8th grade.

ce: International Association for the Evaluation of Educational Achievement (IEA). See Annex 3 for notes.

Indicator F5: The social context and student achievement at the 8th-grade level

Policy context

This indicator shows the relationship between achievement and levels of parental education; it also compares differences in achievement between students from different language backgrounds.

Children come from a variety of family, socio-economic and cultural ba grounds. As a result, schools are faced with unique challenges as they str to provide equal opportunities to all students. The learning environment schools can be enhanced by what students with a variety of backgrounds a interests bring with them; however, heterogeneity of student ability lev and differences in school preparedness also increase the challenges scho face in meeting the needs of students from diverse social backgrounds.

Indicators on the characteristics of students most likely to fail can help edu tors and policy-makers to identify the problems. At the same time, by sh ing that in some countries these tendencies are less marked than in oth these indicators can also give support to policy incentives designed to fos equity.

Evidence and explanations

In all countries, higher levels of parental education are associated with higher levels of student achievement.

Parental education continues to be an important source of disparities student achievement, notwithstanding the considerable efforts underta by OECD countries to guarantee equal educational opportunities for all.

On average, children whose parents completed upper secondary education are about a year ahead of others in mathematics performance...

On average across OECD countries, the gap in mathematics achievem between students who reported that their parents had not completed up secondary education and their peers for whom at least one of the parents completed upper secondary education amounts to 28 score points – ab the same level as the difference between the average 7th-grader and average 8th-grader.

... and for children whose parents have a university degree, the difference is more than twice as large.

The average gap between children whose parents completed the univer level and children whose parents did not complete upper secondary ed tion is more than twice as large – 58 score points.

Substantial differences between countries in the extent to which such background factors affect student achievement show that these disparities are not inevitable.

However, substantial differences in the relationship between parental ed tion and mathematics student achievement across countries show that th disparities are not inevitable, and give cause to believe that policy inter tions might help to reduce them.

In Canada, for example, a country whose students score close to the O average in mathematics, children whose parents have not completed u secondary education score higher than the average of several other O countries. In contrast, in some countries with high mean scores, children disadvantaged backgrounds have worse prospects than students in c countries with lower overall averages. In Canada and Spain, for example difference in mathematics achievement between students whose par

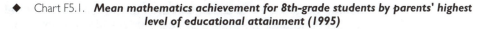

◆ Chart F5.1. **Mean mathematics achievement for 8th-grade students by parents' highest level of educational attainment (1995)**

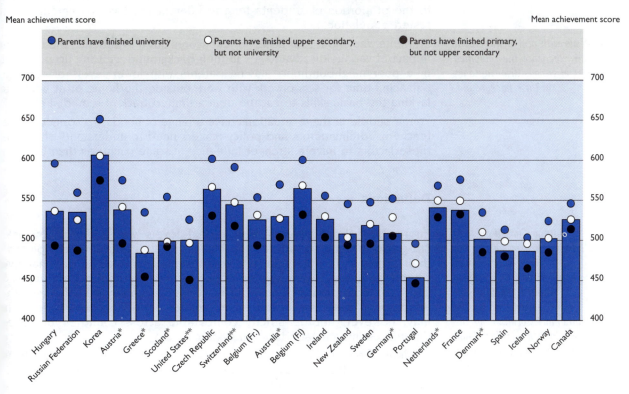

The bar indicates the mean achievement among all students. The three symbols indicate the mean mathematics achievement of students with different levels of parental education.

Countries are ranked in descending order of the differential in mean mathematics achievement scores of students whose parents completed the highest and lowest levels of education specified.

* Countries did not meet TIMSS sampling requirements.
** Countries met TIMSS sampling requirements only partially.

Source: IEA.

A similar relationship can be observed when the achievement of students from a different linguistic background is compared with the average.

In most countries, students from a different linguistic background tend to be at a significantly higher risk of being low achievers.

highest level of educational attainment is university and students whose parents' highest level of educational attainment is primary school is 34 and 38 scale points, respectively (see Table F5.1). For Hungary and the Russian Federation, the same scale score difference is 102 and 81 points, respectively.

Education systems in many OECD countries are confronted with the specific problem of students whose mother tongue is different from the language of instruction. The linguistic handicap experienced by these students is often compounded by other socio-economic handicaps.

On average across countries, 28 per cent of all 8th-grade students from a linguistic background different from the language of instruction score in the bottom 15 per cent in mathematics. However, in some education systems, there seems to be less risk of poor achievement for linguistic minorities. In the Netherlands the proportion of students from a different language background with low achievement is only slightly larger than that of students who reported that they normally speak the language of the test. On the other

hand, the gap is twice as large in the French Community of Belgium, Scotlan
Switzerland and the United States. This result does not appear to be relate
to the proportion of students from a different language background in t
tested population.

Students with poor achievement often experience the combined impact of various disadvantages in their background.

Students who show poor achievement scores often experience the combine
impact of various disadvantages in their background: growing up poor, livi
in a poor neighbourhood, having parents with lower levels of educatic
balancing time for schoolwork with work outside the home or at home, a
lacking the basic skills to escape from a limited track of remedial classes.

Young people in these situations have a range of needs. To cope with the
teachers, administrators and policy-makers need to understand what caus
these factors to have a stronger influence in some countries than in othe

Definitions

Data are based on tests administered as part of the Third International Mathematics and Science Study (IEA/TIMSS), undertaken by the International Association for the Evaluation of Educational Achievement (IEA) during the school year 1994/95.

Information about parents' educational levels was gathered by ask
8th-grade students to indicate the highest level of education completed
their fathers and mothers. Results are presented for three educational leve
completed university; completed upper secondary school but not univers
and completed primary school but not upper secondary school. These th
educational levels are based on internationally defined categories, wh
may, however, not be strictly comparable across countries because
differences in national education systems.

Students from a different language background are those students v
reported that they "always" or "almost always" speak a language at ho
other than the language of the test. They are not necessarily immigrants,
may also belong to linguistic minorities. The composition of the groups v
different language backgrounds may differ substantially between countr
For the purpose of this indicator, low achievers are defined as the 15 per c
of the tested population with the lowest scores in mathematics.

The target population studied in this indicator refers to students in the up
grade of the two grade levels in which most 13 year-olds are enrolled.
further details on the target population and sampling standards see Ind
tor F1 and Annex 3. For the results on the achievement of 8th-graders refe
the 1996 edition of *Education at a Glance*.

Percentage of students from a different linguistic background who scored below the 15th percentile in mathematics (1995)

| | Mathematics achievement by parents' highest level of educational attainment (1995) | | | | | | | | Percentage of students from a different linguistic background who are low achievers (below the 15th percentile)[1] |
| | Finished university | | Finished upper secondary school, but not university | | Finished primary school, but not upper secondary school | | Do not know | | |
	Mean	Standard error	Mean	Standard error	Mean	Standard error	Mean	Standard error	
North America									
Canada	544	(3.4)	526	(2.9)	510	(5.1)	504	(4.2)	35.1
United States**	527	(5.9)	494	(4.0)	455	(4.8)	489	(8.5)	34.5
Pacific Area									
Australia*	572	(4.4)	528	(4.4)	510	(3.6)	494	(4.9)	25.9
Japan	m	m	m	m	m	m	m	m	m
Korea	654	(5.1)	607	(2.8)	575	(4.2)	573	(9.3)	+
New Zealand	543	(6.0)	504	(4.4)	491	(5.7)	494	(5.4)	32.3
European Union									
Austria*	574	(7.2)	547	(3.7)	496	(7.4)	513	(6.1)	30.4
Belgium									
(Flemish Community)**	599	(6.0)	572	(5.3)	538	(10.3)	548	(5.9)	22.9
(French Community)*	557	(3.9)	537	(3.9)	491	(6.2)	501	(7.4)	29.6
Denmark*	528	(5.5)	512	(3.5)	488	(8.0)	498	(4.0)	35.3
France	576	(5.8)	549	(3.6)	530	(4.1)	529	(3.8)	+
Germany*	553	(8.5)	526	(5.0)	504	(4.2)	488	(6.7)	30.8
Greece*	537	(6.3)	492	(4.5)	462	(2.9)	457	(8.1)	+
Ireland	564	(7.6)	535	(4.7)	510	(5.7)	499	(6.6)	+
Netherlands*	570	(10.6)	549	(7.7)	524	(9.2)	522	(7.8)	18.5
Portugal	494	(4.6)	473	(4.0)	447	(2.1)	452	(5.8)	+
Spain	517	(3.6)	502	(3.3)	479	(2.3)	478	(3.5)	16.7
Sweden	544	(3.9)	524	(3.4)	494	(4.6)	511	(3.4)	31.9
United Kingdom									
England**	m	m	m	m	m	m	m	m	+
Scotland*	559	(8.4)	499	(5.3)	485	(5.5)	487	(5.6)	35.2
Other OECD Countries									
Czech Republic	604	(7.5)	571	(4.9)	532	(4.1)	516	(7.8)	+
Hungary	594	(4.9)	539	(3.2)	492	(6.0)	m	m	+
Iceland	505	(7.0)	495	(4.7)	467	(6.8)	472	(6.5)	+
Norway	524	(4.5)	505	(3.1)	487	(4.6)	495	(3.2)	34.2
Switzerland**	588	(5.4)	552	(2.6)	520	(5.1)	534	(4.7)	31.5
Country mean	**557**		**527**		**499**		**502**		**28.0**
Other non-OECD countries									
Russian Federation	565	(4.9)	526	(6.4)	484	(8.0)	519	(10.8)	+

* Countries did not meet TIMSS sampling requirements.
** Countries met TIMSS sampling requirements only partially.
1. Countries marked with + show results according to the international trend, but the number of students from a different linguistic background in the low achieving 15% is too small to report qualitative results.
Source: International Association for the Evaluation of Educational Achievement (IEA). See Annex 3 for notes.

Indicator F6: **Fourth and 8th-grade students' attitudes towards mathematics**

Policy context

This indicator shows 4th and 8th-grade students' overall attitudes towards mathematics and their corresponding mean mathematics achievement.

Students' perceptions of the value of learning mathematics and science m be considered as both inputs to and outcomes of the educational proce since their attitudes towards these subjects can be related to educatio achievement in ways that reinforce higher or lower performance. Stude who do well in mathematics and science generally have more positive at tudes towards those subjects, and those who have more positive attitud tend to be more likely to specialise in those subjects and to perform bett

Evidence and explanations

This indicator shows the percentage of 4th and 8th-grade students in f categories of a composite scale of students' attitudes towards mathematic also shows the average mathematics achievement scores for the students the corresponding categories.

Fourth and 8th-grade students generally have positive attitudes towards mathematics.

In all countries, the majority of students report positive or strongly posit attitudes towards mathematics at both the 4th and 8th-grade levels. Very students (usually 5 per cent or less) consistently have strongly negat opinions about all aspects of the subject.

Across countries it is not those with highest mean achievement scores that have the most positive attitudes towards mathematics...

Interestingly, in the countries with the highest performance, Japan and Ko the lowest percentage of students report a positive or strongly positive a tude towards mathematics: just over 50 per cent. The highest positive a tudes towards mathematics are reported by students in Denmark a England, where more than 80 per cent of students have a positive or stro positive attitude towards mathematics.

... but within countries those with more positive attitudes demonstrate higher average levels of mathematics achievement.

Within countries students with positive attitudes perform better on aver than those with negative attitudes. The positive relationship between a tudes and achievement is in general less pronounced at the 4th-grade le than it is at the 8th-grade level.

Attitudes are generally more positive in 4th grade than in 8th grade.

On the whole there is a higher percentage of students with positive attitu towards mathematics at the 4th-grade level than among 8th-graders. W the average percentage of students with positive or strongly positive a tudes ranges from 68 to 94 per cent across countries at the 4th-grade leve ranges from 51 to 83 per cent at the 8th-grade level.

Eighth-grade girls generally have lower perceptions than boys about how well they usually do in mathematics.

Data from IEA/TIMSS (not shown in this indicator) also indicate that ac countries, 8th-grade girls generally have lower perceptions than boys ab how well they usually do in mathematics. Boys were more likely than gir report that they usually did well in mathematics in England, France, Germ and Japan. In IEA/TIMSS, 8th-grade students were also asked how much

◆ Chart F6.1a. **Mean mathematics achievement scores of 4th-grade students and their attitudes towards mathematics (1995)**

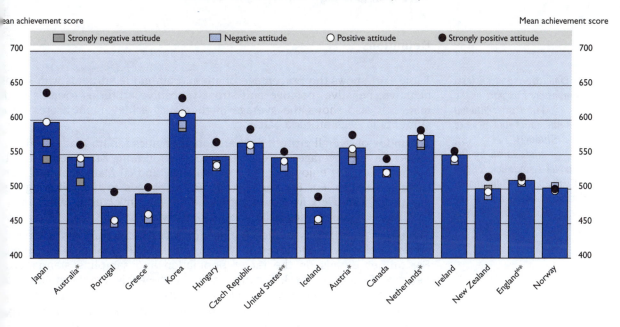

◆ Chart F6.1b. **Mean mathematics achievement scores of 8th-grade students and their attitudes towards mathematics (1995)**

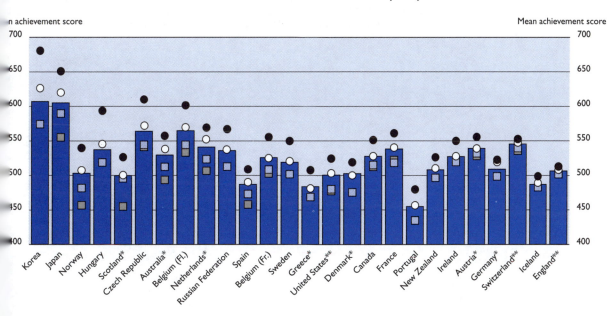

The bar indicates the mean achievement among all students. The four symbols indicate the mean achievement of students with different attitudes towards mathematics.

...ries are ranked in descending order of the difference in mathematics achievement scores between students with strongly positive and strongly negative attitudes.

...untries did not meet TIMSS sampling requirements.
...untries met TIMSS sampling requirements only partially.

...: IEA.

liked or disliked science. In England and Japan, boys reported liking scien more than girls did.

Definitions

Data are based on tests administered as part of the Third International Mathematics and Science Study (IEA/TIMSS), undertaken by the International Association for the Evaluation of Educational Achievement (IEA) during the school year 1994/95.

Table F6.1 shows the percentage of 4th and 8th-grade students with stron negative, negative, positive and strongly positive attitudes towards matl matics. It also shows the average mathematics achievement scores for t students in each attitude category.

The index of overall attitudes towards mathematics for 4th-grade students based on the average of responses to the following statements: *i*) I I mathematics; *ii*) I enjoy learning mathematics; and *iii*) Mathematics is bor (reversed scale). For 8th-grade students, responses to the following sta ments are also used: *iv*) Would you like a job that involved using mathem ics?; and *v*) Mathematics is important to everyone's life.

The target populations studied in this indicator refer to students in the up; grades of the two grade levels in which most 9 and 13 year-olds are enroll For further details on the target population and sampling standards ; Indicator F1 and Annex 3. For the results on the achievement of 8th-grad refer to the 1996 edition of *Education at a Glance*.

Countries marked with an asterisk did not satisfy one or more IEA/TIN guidelines for sample participation rates, age/grade specification or classrc sampling procedures. The reporting of data on a sub-national level for sc countries is based on data availability from the IEA and does not represe policy decision by the OECD.

Standard errors of sampling are included in Annex 3. A tilde (~) indic; insufficient data to report data. Because results are rounded to the nea whole number, some totals may appear inconsistent.

	Fourth grade								Eighth grade							
	Strongly negative		Negative		Positive		Strongly positive		Strongly negative		Negative		Positive		Strongly positive	
	% students	Mean achievement	% students	Mean achievement	% students	Mean achievement	% students	Mean achievement	% students	Mean achievement	% students	Mean achievement	% students	Mean achievement	% students	Mean achievement
North America																
Canada	3	522	10	522	41	524	46	544	3	510	23	512	58	528	16	554
United States [a]	5	527	14	527	37	542	44	556	4	481	26	483	55	503	15	526
Pacific Area																
Australia [b, d]	5	513	14	531	44	543	37	567	4	492	32	514	55	540	9	561
Japan	3	547	22	570	56	598	18	636	4	558	44	592	48	619	3	649
Korea	4	588	24	591	43	610	29	633	2	~	48	581	46	630	5	680
New Zealand	5	498	15	479	41	493	40	515	2	~	23	491	60	511	15	530
European Union																
Austria [b, d]	6	548	19	537	36	559	39	574	4	527	38	535	47	542	12	560
Belgium (Flemish Community) [a]	m	m	m	m	m	m	m	m	4	535	33	547	52	572	11	604
(French Community) [d]	m	m	m	m	m	m	m	m	3	507	28	514	53	526	15	558
Denmark [d]	m	m	m	m	m	m	m	m	1	~	16	479	57	502	26	523
France	m	m	m	m	m	m	m	m	3	520	27	518	54	543	16	564
Germany [d]	m	m	m	m	m	m	m	m	5	498	38	498	43	518	13	521
Greece [d]	1	~	5	463	28	471	66	509	2	~	21	467	57	482	20	512
Ireland	5	542	15	542	39	546	41	560	2	~	26	515	59	530	13	551
Netherlands [b, d]	8	569	24	570	41	581	27	590	4	506	40	526	50	554	6	570
Portugal	1	~	7	448	42	457	51	498	2	~	24	436	58	456	16	480
Spain	m	m	m	m	m	m	m	m	3	459	33	474	52	491	13	513
Sweden	m	m	m	m	m	m	m	m	2	~	33	503	55	523	10	553
United Kingdom England [a, c]	m	m	m	m	m	m	m	m	1	~	17	497	64	509	18	514
Scotland [d]	5	510	13	505	32	509	50	518	7	458	19	493	57	498	17	529
Other OECD countries																
Czech Republic	2	~	16	553	55	565	26	583	3	543	39	544	52	574	6	613
Hungary [b]	4	538	17	536	49	538	30	577	2	~	38	518	53	547	7	592
Iceland	3	459	7	459	31	461	59	487	2	456	24	478	59	489	14	499
Norway	5	507	17	509	39	503	40	504	3	~	30	481	55	511	12	538
Switzerland [a]	m	m	m	m	m	m	m	m	3	532	28	540	53	549	16	554
Country mean	4	528	15	521	41	531	40	553	3	505	30	509	54	530	13	554
Other non-OECD countries																
Russian Federation	m	m	m	m	m	m	m	m	1	~	24	512	63	538	12	570

a) Countries met TIMSS sampling requirements only partially, 8th grade.
b) Countries did not meet TIMSS sampling requirements, 4th grade.
c) Countries met TIMSS sampling requirements only partially, 4th grade.
d) Countries did not meet TIMSS sampling requirements, 8th grade.
Source: International Association for the Evaluation of Educational Achievement (IEA). See Annex 3 for notes.

Chapter G

GRADUATE OUTPUT OF EDUCATIONAL INSTITUTIONS

This chapter examines the output of educational institutions, specifically the number of graduates at the per secondary and tertiary levels of education relative to the sizes of the populations at their typical duation ages. Unlike measures of educational attainment (Indicator A2), which relate to the stock of owledge and skills in the population, graduation rates measure the current output of education systems. ferences between countries in graduation rates reflect differences in both enrolment and persistence rates oss educational programmes – programmes that vary in structure and content both within and between ucation systems.

The award of a degree or other type of qualification marks the formal culmination of an investment in ucation or training activities. The level, type, and field of a particular educational qualification earned can ve as useful information to employers, signalling that the recipient has gained occupationally relevant lls and knowledge. One way to measure the productive capacity of education systems is to examine their put of educational qualifications. Graduation rates, approximated here by a ratio of the number of duates at a particular level to the population at the typical age of graduation, are one indicator of the gree to which education systems are producing individuals with various types of skills. Although measures oth quality (Chapter F) and cost (Chapter B) are also critical factors evaluating educational productivity, duation rates do allow us to compare the output of education systems.

Comparisons of graduation rates between countries are difficult, however, because education pro-mmes vary widely – both within and between countries – in duration, intensity, and level of theoretical or lied content. One country can have higher graduation rates than another simply because the programmes of shorter duration or a lower level of difficulty. Some of these differences in educational programme cture are represented in the categories used to present data in the following indicators, while others are e difficult to quantify. Even with these qualifications, international comparisons of graduation rates can vide an important insight into the degree to which education systems are preparing individuals for entry the labour force at different levels.

Indicator G1 is a measure of the output of new graduates at the upper secondary level. Although e countries legally allow students to leave the education system at the end of lower secondary educa-, the completion of upper secondary education has become the minimally desirable credential in most D countries. An upper secondary credential is necessary not only to secure employment and participa-in labour markets with rising skill requirements (see also Indicators E2 and E3), but also to serve as a s for subsequent learning later in life. Low upper secondary graduation rates may therefore signal lems for the future.

The remaining indicators in this chapter focus on the output of new graduates at the tertiary level of cation. Tertiary graduation rates, of which **Indicator G2** provides a measure, are influenced by the and for higher skills in the labour market, as well as the supply (*i.e.*, the availability) of tertiary education rammes. Tertiary graduation rates are also influenced by the typical duration of programmes, the level of culty, the graduation requirements, and the way in which degree and qualification structures are nised within countries, particularly at the university level of education (see Annex 3 for a description of ertiary degrees and qualifications awarded in different countries). Countries which have more exit points their university (or equivalent) tertiary programmes can offer more transition points into the labour et. A greater number of transition points allows students to leave the higher education system at rent knowledge or skill levels, depending on the current demand for these skills in the labour market, as their own aptitudes and interests.

Technological innovation affects the industrial, occupational and skill requirements of the labour forc New growth industries tend to be those involved in the creation, processing and distribution of informati and knowledge. **Indicators G3** and **G4** examine two different aspects of the particular fields that studer study at the tertiary level. The distribution of tertiary graduates by field of study (Indicator G3) measur which fields students are most likely to study in different countries. The relative popularity of a particu field is likely to be driven, at least in part, by the job opportunities for graduates with skills in that field, well as by relative earnings across different occupations and industries. In addition, field concentration m also be influenced by the method by which students choose, or are assigned, their field of study. H example, entrance examination scores can be used to screen students for entry into the most popular fie of study, such as medicine or law. Education systems may differ in the degree to which the distribution students between fields of study is managed or controlled. Differences in field of study may also refl differences in the degree to which students in a particular country perceive that field to be person; interesting or gratifying.

While Indicator G3 examines the relative emphasis on particular fields of study within education s tems, Indicator G4 measures the absolute emphasis on science-related fields. In this indicator, the numbe science graduates at university level is weighted by the size of the respective labour force; this make: possible to compare countries' raw outputs of university-level science graduates. Differences between co tries in the supply of high-level qualifications in science-related fields are likely to be influenced by relative rewards in the labour market for different fields, as well as the degree to which the market dri field selection in a particular country.

Indicator G1: Completion of upper secondary education

Policy context

This indicator shows the number of upper secondary graduates relative to the size of the population at the typical age of upper secondary completion.

Completing an upper secondary education has become the minimum requirement for entering labour markets with rising skill demands. Education at this level also serves as the foundation for higher (post-secondary) learning and training opportunities. Many countries do legally allow students to leave the education system at the end of lower secondary education but people who do so tend to face poor labour market opportunities (see Indicators E2 to E4).

Although high upper secondary completion rates do not guarantee that those finishing compulsory education have acquired the necessary foundation skills to enter the labour market, the upper secondary graduation rate is one indicator of the size of the "qualification deficiency" among early school-leavers across countries. Limited measures of the skills of graduates are also available. Cross-country comparisons of the literacy level of recent upper secondary school completers is one measure of the skills output of education systems up to the upper secondary level.

Evidence and explanations

Overall rates of upper secondary completion

The percentage of students completing a first upper secondary programme ranges from below 40 per cent in two countries to 85 per cent and above in ten countries.

Upper secondary graduation rates are estimated as the number of upper secondary graduates per 100 persons at the age at which students typically complete upper secondary education (see Annex 1). In all but two countries, upper secondary graduation rates exceed 64 (Chart G1.1). In 10 of the 23 countries for which data are available, the graduation rates are at or above 85 per cent and in the Flemish Community of Belgium, Finland, Ireland, Japan, New Zealand, and Norway they exceed 90 per cent. The lowest upper secondary graduation rates are in Mexico (26 per cent) and Turkey (37 per cent).

A comparison of the level of educational attainment across age groups (see Indicator A2) indicates that there has been a marked increase in the percentage of persons who complete upper secondary education. However, while upper secondary completion has firmly become the norm, it is one from which a significant minority continues to be left out.

Increasing upper secondary completion rates appear to be pushing the expansion of tertiary education.

The increase in rates of upper secondary completion tends to lead to higher participation in tertiary education independently of policies adopted for that sector. Once the entry qualifications to tertiary education are attained, it is hard to resist the consequent demand for tertiary studies – particularly in countries that give a specific entitlement to further study to those who complete secondary schooling. In countries such as Australia, Denmark and France, policies to increase the proportion of the age cohort completing upper secondary education have succeeded not only in achieving that objec-

◆ Chart GI.I. *Ratio of upper secondary graduates to population at typical age of graduation,
by type of programme (1995) (first educational programmes)*

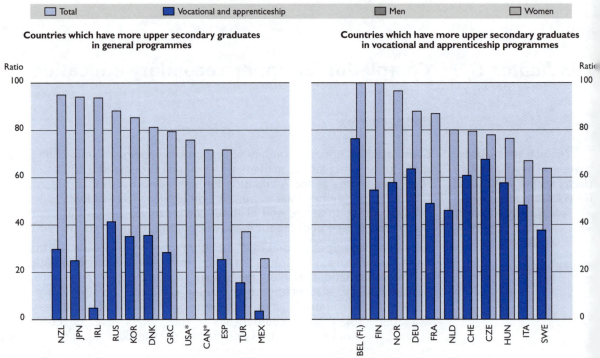

Countries are ranked in descending order of ratio of upper secondary graduates to population at typical age of graduation.

* Data by type of programme are not available.

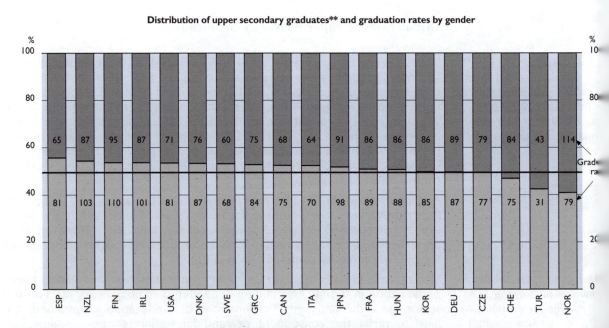

** Distribution of upper secondary graduates is calculated as the graduation rate of women as a percentage of the sum of graduation rates for men and women
example a percentage lower than 50% means that there are more men graduates than women, regardless of graduation rates.

Countries are ranked in descending order of the proportion of female graduates.

Source: OECD.

tive but have also led directly to a sharp rise in the numbers entering tertiary education institutions and programmes.

Gender differences in completion rates

Gender disparities in upper secondary graduation rates have been successfully eliminated in almost all countries.

In 14 of the 20 countries reporting upper secondary graduation rates for first programmes by gender, graduation rates for women exceed those of men (see Chart G1.1), in the Flemish Community of Belgium, Denmark, Finland, Ireland, New Zealand, Spain, and the United States by over 10 percentage points. In Norway, Switzerland and Turkey, however, male graduates outnumber female graduates by around 10 percentage points or more. The situation is quite different from the attainment levels in the total adult population, in which women are often under-represented among persons with attainments at the upper secondary level or higher because of a large gender gap in older age groups (see Indicator A2, Table A2.3).

Female graduation rates may be higher than those for males in many countries because there remain more opportunities for men to perform manual or unskilled labour. Relatively high unemployment rates or relatively low earnings for those having attained less than upper secondary education suggest, however, that both female and male non-graduates are likely to be economically at risk.

Upper secondary graduates by field of study

The relative emphasis on vocational and general education varies between countries at the upper secondary level.

The breakdown between general education and vocational/technical education differs widely between countries. Of the 21 countries which split their data into these two programme types, 10 reported that the majority of first programme graduates complete general programmes and 11 reported that they complete vocational or apprenticeship programmes. In Ireland, Japan, Mexico, and New Zealand the proportion of general graduates is more than double the proportion of vocational and technical graduates, while the opposite is true in the Flemish Community of Belgium, the Czech Republic, Germany, Hungary, Italy and Switzerland. These differences must be interpreted with caution, however, since the classification of programmes as general and vocational is not entirely consistent across countries.

In some countries, many upper secondary graduates re-enrol and pursue a second upper secondary qualification.

Nine countries – the Czech Republic, Denmark, Finland, France, Germany, Ireland, Italy, the Netherlands, and Spain – reported counts for persons who had re-enrolled in an upper secondary education programme and graduated a second (or subsequent) time. Graduation from a second upper secondary programme was most common in Finland, Germany and Ireland, where more than 19 per cent of the population at the typical graduation age complete a second upper secondary programme. In other countries, however, graduates from programmes that may be similar in content to these secondary programmes are counted as tertiary graduates.

Upper secondary graduation and adult literacy skills

High upper secondary completion rates do not necessarily translate into a large stock of highly skilled graduates.

Although higher levels of educational attainment are usually associated with higher skill levels, high upper secondary completion rates do not necessarily translate into highly skilled graduates. As economies become more complex, even jobs that were once considered "low-skilled" require higher levels of skills than before. The International Adult Literacy Survey (IALS) provides one important cross-national measure of key skills: namely a measure of functional literacy.

This survey showed that there is a strong association between the possession of adequate levels of literacy (IALS Literacy Level 3 and above) and the completion of upper secondary education.

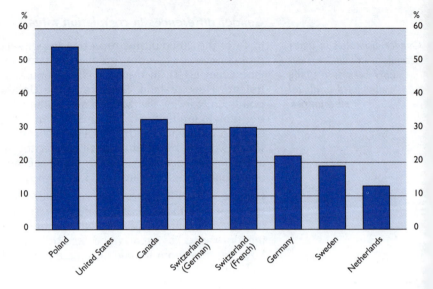

◆ Chart G1.2. **Percentage of 16 to 29 year-old upper secondary completers perform** at level 2 or below on IALS (document scale) (1994)

Source: International Adult Literacy Survey (OECD and Statistics Canada, 1995).

In the 7 countries participating in IALS in 1994, a significant proportion of young adults who have completed upper secondary education do not have adequate literacy skills.

However, data presented in Chart G1.2 also show that even among up secondary completers in these 7 countries, a significant proportion of yo persons have not attained adequate levels of literacy. Among 16 to 29 y olds with only an upper secondary qualification, the percentage that score level 2 or below on the documents portion of the assessment ranges around 20 per cent or below in Germany (21 per cent), the Netherla (13 per cent) and Sweden (19 per cent) to nearly 50 per cent or above in United States (48 per cent) and Poland (55 per cent).

The generally high percentage of upper secondary graduates at or below level of literacy is a cause for concern. Completing an upper secondary ed tion in each of these countries does not guarantee a level of skill associ with positive economic and social outcomes.

Definitions

Data are based on the UOE data collection on education statistics, administered in 1996 (for details see Annex 3). Data on literacy levels are based on tests administered as part of the International Adult Literacy Survey undertaken by Statistics Canada and the OECD in 1994 (for details see the 1996 edition of Education at a Glance).

Upper secondary graduates are persons who successfully complete the year of upper secondary education. In some countries, successful comple requires a final examination; in others it does not. In some countries, stud may enrol in and complete additional programmes at the same lev education after initial completion. For this indicator, graduation rate: therefore separated into first and second (or further) upper secondary grammes. Each country has identified a theoretical age (or average of age which graduation typically occurs (see Annex 1). Graduation rates obtained by dividing the number of first-time or second-time upper se dary graduates by the population at the typical graduation age. Cou with differentiated upper secondary institutions have, in most cases, rep the numbers of graduates by the type of institution attended, rather tha type of educational programme pursued. A few countries with upper se dary institutions offering multiple types of programmes have reported the qualifications obtained by graduating students by programme type (general or vocational).

Graduation rates may be overestimated in some countries.

Note that in some countries graduation rates may be overestimated because some graduates may be counted more than once if they complete multiple programmes at the same level.

Table G1.1 **Ratio of upper secondary graduates to population at typical age of graduation (times 100) by type of programme (1995)**

First educational programmes

	Total			General			Vocational and apprenticeship		
	M + W	Men	Women	M + W	Men	Women	M + W	Men	Women
North America									
Canada	72	68	75	72	68	75	x	x	x
Mexico	26	x	x	22	x	x	4	x	x
United States	76	71	81	76	71	81	x	x	x
Pacific Area									
Australia	m	m	m	65	59	71	m	m	m
Japan	94	91	98	69	66	73	25	25	25
Korea	85	86	85	50	54	46	35	32	39
New Zealand	95	87	103	65	61	70	30	26	34
European Union									
Austria	m	m	m	m	m	m	m	m	m
Belgium (Flemish Community)	110	95	117	33	29	38	76	70	82
Denmark	81	76	87	46	38	54	36	38	33
Finland	102	95	110	47	39	55	55	55	54
France	87	86	89	38	32	44	49	53	45
Germany	88	89	87	24	22	27	64	67	60
Greece	80	75	84	51	43	59	28	32	25
Ireland	94	87	101	89	83	96	5	5	5
Italy	67	64	70	18	15	20	48	48	49
Luxembourg	m	m	m	m	m	m	m	m	m
Netherlands	80	x	x	32	x	x	46	x	x
Portugal	m	m	m	m	m	m	m	m	m
Spain	73	69	81	46	40	52	26	24	29
Sweden	64	60	68	25	18	34	38	42	33
United Kingdom	m	m	m	m	m	m	m	m	m
Other OECD countries									
Czech Republic	78	79	77	10	8	13	68	71	64
Hungary	76	86	88	17	17	27	58	66	59
Iceland	m	m	m	m	m	m	m	m	m
Norway	106	123	88	44	38	50	62	85	38
Poland	m	m	m	m	m	m	m	m	m
Switzerland	79	84	75	19	16	21	61	68	54
Turkey	37	43	31	22	24	20	16	19	12
Country mean	**80**	**80**	**85**	**43**	**40**	**49**	**41**	**46**	**41**
Other non-OECD countries									
Russian Federation	88	m	m	47	m	m	41	m	m

Source: OECD Database. See Annex 3 for notes.

Table G1.2 **Ratio of upper secondary graduates to population at typical age of graduation (times 100) by type of programme (1995)**

Second or further programmes only

	Total			General			Vocational and apprenticeship		
	M + W	Men	Women	M + W	Men	Women	M + W	Men	Women
North America									
Canada	a	a	a	a	a	a	a	a	a
Mexico	a	a	a	a	a	a	a	a	a
United States	a	a	a	a	a	a	a	a	a
Pacific Area									
Australia	a	a	a	a	a	a	a	a	a
Japan	a	a	a	a	a	a	a	a	a
Korea	a	a	a	a	a	a	a	a	a
New Zealand	a	a	a	a	a	a	a	a	a
European Union									
Austria	a	a	a	a	a	a	a	a	a
Belgium (Flemish Community)	a	a	a	a	a	a	a	a	a
Denmark	13	11	15	4	3	4	9	8	11
Finland	36	22	52	2	1	4	34	21	48
France	12	13	12	a	a	a	12	13	12
Germany	19	19	19	1	1	1	18	19	18
Greece	a	a	a	a	a	a	a	a	a
Ireland	21	13	30	a	a	a	21	13	30
Italy	10	8	12	a	a	a	10	8	12
Luxembourg	m	m	m	m	m	m	m	m	m
Netherlands	6	x	x	2	x	x	4	x	x
Portugal	m	m	m	m	m	m	m	m	m
Spain	14	13	15	a	a	a	14	13	15
Sweden	a	a	a	a	a	a	a	a	a
United Kingdom	a	a	a	a	a	a	a	a	a
Other OECD countries									
Czech Republic	5	6	4	a	a	a	5	6	4
Hungary	x	x	x	x	x	x	x	x	x
Iceland	m	m	m	m	m	m	m	m	m
Norway	a	a	a	a	a	a	a	a	a
Poland	m	m	m	m	m	m	m	m	m
Switzerland	a	a	a	a	a	a	a	a	a
Turkey	a	a	a	a	a	a	a	a	a
Country mean	**6**	**5**	**7**	**n**	**n**	**n**	**5**	**4**	**6**
Other non-OECD countries									
Russian Federation	a	a	a	a	a	a	a	a	a

Source: OECD Database. See Annex 3 for notes.

Indicator G2: **Graduates at the tertiary level**

Policy context

This indicator shows the number of tertiary graduates as a percentage of the population at the typical age of graduation. For some countries it also shows net graduation rates.

Unlike measures of educational attainment, which relate to the stock knowledge and skills in the population, tertiary graduation rates are an in cator of the current production rate of higher-level knowledge by e country's education system. Countries with high graduation rates at the te ary level are the most likely to be building or maintaining a highly skill labour force. The age at which students graduate and become available the labour market is a factor of importance as well.

Evidence and explanations

Tertiary programmes vary both within and between countries in duration, intensity and degree of theoretical and applied content.

Comparisons of tertiary qualifications between countries are difficult becau education programmes vary widely in duration, intensity and degree of th retical and applied content. Nevertheless, international comparisons of gr uation rates can provide an insight into the potential flow of persons w higher qualifications into the labour force. For the purpose of this indica tertiary qualifications are divided into those equivalent and those equivalent to a university-level qualification. The indicator distinguish between five categories of qualifications: those that are equivalent to *i*) a n university tertiary qualification; *ii*) a first university qualification from a p gramme with a theoretical duration typically equal to or less than 4 years; *i* first university qualification of a theoretical duration typically longer tł 4 years; *iv*) a second university qualification at the Master's level; and *v*) advanced research degree at the doctorate level. Although the te "equivalent" is used to guide data reporting for these categories, these (tinctions remain dependent to some degree on national definitions of edu tional qualifications and on historical distinctions between the types of p grammes that are, and are not, offered in traditional universities.

Overall completion rates at the tertiary level

A growing minority completes tertiary education.

Traditionally, tertiary education has educated an elite group of young peo to higher levels immediately after they complete secondary schooling. Too it provides opportunities for learning to a much larger section of the yc and adult population. On average across OECD countries, 12 per cent typical age cohort complete a short university-level programme, 8 per ce long first programme, 4 per cent complete a second university-level ŗ gramme and 1 per cent a programme leading to an advanced rese degree. Graduation rates for non-university level programmes range f above 20 in seven countries to below 3 in two countries.

The duration of first university-level programmes ranges from 3 to over 5 years.

Tertiary graduation rates are influenced by the supply of, and deg of access to, tertiary programmes, as well as the demand for higher skil the labour market. Educational research has shown that access to hiç

◆ Chart G2.1. *Ratio of university-level graduates to population at typical age of graduation (times 100) by type of programme (1995)*

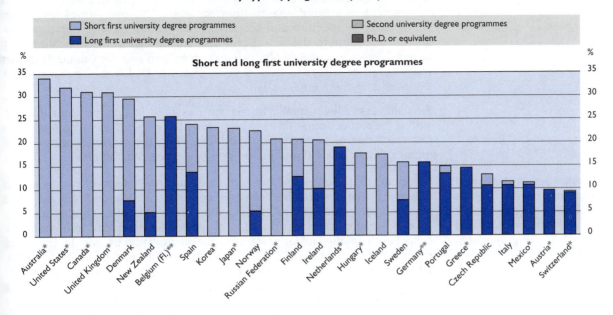

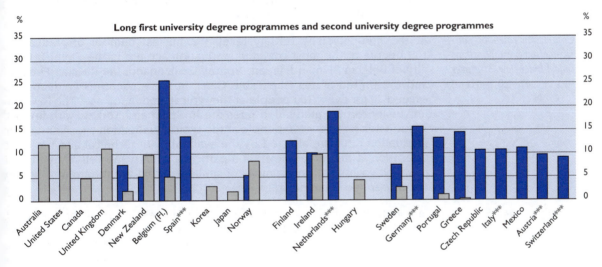

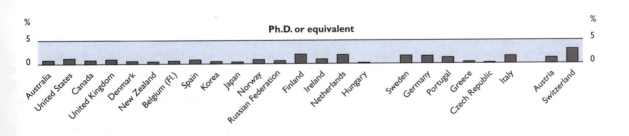

* Short and long first degree programmes combined.
* Short first university degree programmes not applicable.
* Second university degree programmes not applicable.

...ntries are ranked in descending order of ratio of tertiary graduates in long and short first university degree programmes to population at typical age of graduation.

...rce: OECD.

education is also influenced by the social background of students. Graduati
rates also appear to be affected by the way in which the degree and qualifi
tion structures are organised within countries. University-level programm
vary greatly in structure and scope between countries. The duration of p
grammes leading to the award of a first university-level qualification rang
from 3 years (*e.g.*, the Bachelor's degree in Ireland and the United Kingdom
most fields of study) to over 5 years (*e.g.* the D*iplom* in Germany and t
Doctorandus in the Netherlands).

First university-level qualifications are classified in this indicator into the
with a theoretical duration typically equal to or less than 4 years (short f
university degree programmes) and those with a theoretical duration typica
greater than 4 years (long first university degree programmes).

Education systems that award short university-level degrees have higher completion rates in first university-level programmes.

It appears that countries whose tertiary education systems offer only long f
university-level programmes have, in general, significantly lower overall u
versity-level graduation rates than those that also offer shorter universi
level programmes. Longer duration of studies tends to lead to higher terti
costs, both in the actual costs of tertiary programmes and in the forgo
earnings of students who delay entry into the full-time labour market. Wh
such differences in university-level graduation rates are interpreted, the c
tent of the educational programmes, the labour market opportunities th
offer, and the graduation rates and educational content of non-univers
tertiary programmes and upper secondary programmes need to be cons
ered as well.

Completion rates for non-university tertiary qualifications range from below 3 to over 20 per cent.

At the non-university tertiary level, the highest number of graduates
100 people at the most common graduation age are in the Flemish Comm
nity of Belgium, Finland, Japan, Norway, Switzerland, the Russian Federati
and the United States (see Table G2.1). In these countries graduation ra
exceed 20 for every 100 people at the typical graduation age. The lowest n
university tertiary graduation rates are in Spain and Turkey, with fewer th
3 graduates for every 100 people at the typical graduation age. Non-univer
graduation rates are affected by the availability of technical and professio
education at the tertiary level in a particular country, as well as by the ext
to which vocational programmes of similar content are (or are not) offerec
the upper secondary level.

Completion rates for short university degree programmes average 12 per cent...

In countries that offer short first university degrees, such as the Bachelor'
the United States, graduation rates average around 12 per cent acr
OECD countries (see Chart G2.1). In Denmark, Japan, Korea, New Zeala
and the Russian Federation more than 20 per cent of persons at the theor
cal age obtain such a degree and in Australia, Canada, the United Kingd
and the United States, more than 30 per cent do. The median age of comp
tion of these programmes is between 22 and 27.

... and 8 per cent for long university programmes.

For long first university degree programmes, such as the German D*iplom* or
Italian *Laurea*, which are often equivalent in total duration and academic le
to second university degrees in countries such as Australia or
United States, graduation rates average 8 per cent across countries. Grac
tion rates for long first university-level programmes in the Flemish Com
nity of Belgium, Germany and the Netherlands are higher than the gradua
rates from second university-level programmes in Australia and the Un
States, the two countries with the highest second university degree grac
tion rates. Graduation rates for long first university-level programmes
between 10 and 14 per cent in Austria, the Czech Republic, Finland, Gre
Ireland, Italy, Mexico, Portugal and Spain. Students completing these
grammes are generally older than those completing short first unive
degrees, especially in countries which award both types of degrees.

Completion rates for second university degrees range from less than 1 per cent to 12 per cent.

Graduation rates for second university degrees, such as the Master's in the United States, range from less than 1 per cent in Greece and Turkey to 12 per cent in Australia and the United States, with an OECD average of 3.6 per cent. On average, about 1 per cent of the typical age cohort obtain an advanced research degree such as a Ph.D. In Finland and the Netherlands it is around 2 per cent, in Switzerland 3.1 per cent.

Table G2.2 presents net university-level graduation rates for 15 countries for which such data are available. These net rates provide a more accurate estimate for first-time graduation rates than the gross rates presented in Table G2.1, which were obtained by dividing the total graduate output by the population at the typical age of graduation. For these 15 countries, the gross rates appear to be reasonable approximations of the net rate. Countries unable to produce net rates may, however, be unable to provide unduplicated counts of graduates. Rates for these countries may be slightly overestimated, due to double counting of graduates at the same level of education.

Gender differences in tertiary completion

First university degree graduation rates for women meet or exceed those for men in most countries...

Although the first university degree graduation rates for women meet or exceed those for men in most OECD countries, men are still more likely than women to attain more advanced degrees. Graduation rates from first university-level programmes (short and long) are higher among women than among men in most countries. Only in Germany, Japan, Korea, Switzerland and Turkey are graduation rates among women significantly lower than those among men. In Sweden, women are more likely than men to complete short programmes and less likely to complete long ones. The opposite is true in Finland.

but men are still more likely than women to earn more advanced degrees.

For second university degrees, graduation rates for women are slightly below those for men in most countries. In Japan and Korea, however, women earn less than half as many second university degrees as men. With respect to advanced research degrees such as a Ph.D., women in OECD countries are typically half as likely as men to earn them.

The age distribution of tertiary graduates

The typical age for completing tertiary degrees varies between countries, especially between those awarding short and long university degrees.

Students complete tertiary education at different stages of their lives. Age profiles of tertiary graduates differ widely between countries. Table G2.3 indicates, for countries for which this information is available, the 25th, 50th and 75th percentiles of the age distributions of tertiary-level graduates. Of the 16 countries for which the age distribution of first university degree graduates is available, Austria, Denmark, Finland, Iceland and Italy reported about 75 per cent or more of all university-level graduates as aged 25 years or older. The typical university-level graduation age (*i.e.*, assuming continuous, full-time study, see Annex 1) ranges from around 21 years in Australia, the Czech Republic, Hungary, Ireland, New Zealand, Portugal, the Russian Federation, Spain and the United Kingdom (short university-level programmes) to around 26 years or more in Denmark, Finland, Germany, Switzerland and Turkey (long university-level programmes).

Differences in national degree and qualification structures

Tertiary completion rates appear to be influenced by the national degree and qualification structure.

Annex 3 lists the types of university-level and non-university qualifications awarded in 20 OECD countries, using data which countries provided through the OECD Taxonomy Survey of National Educational Programmes. This table highlights some of the variability in the national qualification structure at the tertiary level. Several patterns emerge from a comparison between national

◆ Chart G2.2. ***Distribution of tertiary graduation rates by gender (1995)***

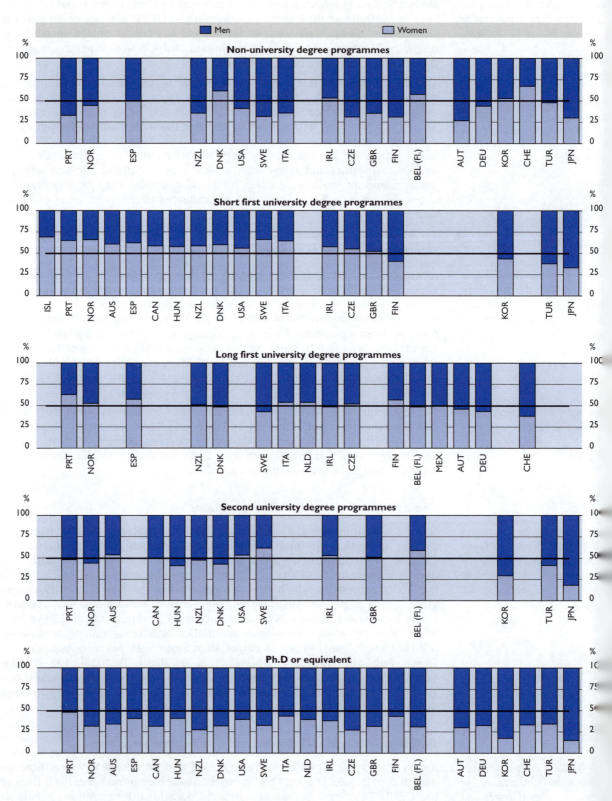

Countries are ranked in descending order of the proportion of female graduates in short and long first university degree programmes combined.

Source: OECD.

qualification structures and the tertiary graduation rates presented in Table G2.1. First, non-university tertiary graduation rates appear to be greatly affected by the availability of occupationally specific education and training at the upper secondary level. Secondly, graduation rates for the first university degree (or equivalent) seem to be influenced by the typical duration of these programmes, as well as by the requirements for earning the qualification.

Non-university tertiary completion rates are affected by the degree to which technical and vocational training is available at the secondary level.

The level or age group at which vocational and technical education programmes are primarily targeted in a particular country will affect that country's non-university tertiary graduation rate. The 29 countries in Annex 3 can be divided into three broad categories reflecting the levels at which they primarily offer technical and vocational education: *i*) those offering technical and vocational qualifications largely at the upper secondary level; *ii*) those offering this level of training mainly at the tertiary level; and *iii*) those offering qualifications at both levels. The Czech Republic and Hungary are examples of countries in the first category. In these countries, students can enrol in specialised trade or vocational schools as early as age 14 and complete their upper secondary education with a specific occupational qualification. The non-university tertiary graduation rates for these countries are low or non-existent. Countries in the second category (*e.g.* Canada and the United States) offer a rather general programme at the secondary level which allows for relatively minor vocational specialisation. Most occupationally specific education and training in these countries is undertaken after the completion of upper secondary education and, as a result, non-university tertiary graduation rates are relatively high. Countries in the third category offer a variety of vocational and technical programmes which span the upper secondary and tertiary levels of education (*e.g.* Australia, Finland, Germany, New Zealand and the United Kingdom). In these countries, only advanced technical qualifications are awarded at the tertiary level (*e.g.* the *Meister* qualification in Germany and the Higher National Diploma in the United Kingdom) and the non-university graduation rates are lower than in the second, but higher than in the first, category.

University-level completion rates are affected by the typical duration, graduation requirements, and variety of credentials offered.

Graduation rates for first university-level qualifications are affected by the typical duration, graduation requirements, and variety of credentials offered at the tertiary level. In general, countries which do not offer short first university-level programmes have lower first university degree graduation rates than countries which offer short first university degree programmes as well. For example, the first university degree graduation rate in Germany is 16, about half of the first university degree graduation rates in Australia (34), the United Kingdom (31) and the United States (32). While the typical duration of a first university degree in the latter three countries is 4 years or less, the typical duration of a first university degree programme in Germany is 4 to 7 years (4 to 5 for a *Fachhochschule* D*iplom* and 5 to 7 for a university D*iplom*). If the academic level and total duration of a first university degree in Germany are compared with similar qualifications in other countries (*e.g.*, a US Master's degree), however, the gap in high-level qualifications between these countries becomes much smaller. Nonetheless, countries which have more exit points from their university (or equivalent) tertiary programmes offer more transition points into the labour market, allowing students to leave the higher education system at different knowledge or skill levels, depending on the current demand for these skills in the labour market, as well their own aptitude and interest.

Data are based on the UOE data collection on education statistics, administered in 1996 (for details see Annex 3).

Definitions

Tertiary graduates are people who obtain a university-level or non-univers qualification or equivalent in the specified reference year. The indica distinguishes between five categories of qualifications: those that a equivalent to *i*) a non-university tertiary qualification; *ii*) a first univers qualification from a programme with a theoretical duration typically equal or less than 4 years; *iii*) a first university qualification of a theoretical durati typically longer than 4 years; *iv*) a second university qualification at t Master's level; and *v*) an advanced research degree at the doctorate level. some countries, these distinctions are not always clear and data are available for the requested categories. In such cases, graduates have be assigned by the country to the most appropriate category. In many countr the duration of studies also varies significantly between fields of study. some countries, the non-university tertiary level includes some programn that in other countries may be classified at the upper secondary level.

For each tertiary category, countries identify the age at which graduat typically occurs. Graduates themselves, however, may be of any age. estimate graduation rates, the number of graduates is divided by the pop tion at the typical graduation age (see Annex 1). In many countries, definir typical age at graduation is difficult because graduates are dispersed ove wide range of ages. As a result, a more accurate indicator is a net graduat rate. This rate, which represents the sum of age-specific graduation rate presented in Table G2.2 for countries which were able to provide informat on graduates by single year of age. The net graduation rate can be in preted as the percentage of people within a virtual age cohort who obta tertiary qualification, this being independent of changes in the popula sizes or the typical graduation age.

Tertiary education graduates generally do not include graduates from grammes offered by private business institutions operating for profit.

	Non-university tertiary programmes (A)			Short first university degree programmes (e.g. U.S. Bachelor's) (B)			Long first university degree programmes (e.g. German Diplom or Italian Laurea) (C)			Second university degree programmes (e.g. U.S. Master's) (D)			Ph.D or equivalent (E)		
	M + W	Men	Women	M + W	Men	Women	M + W	Men	Women	M + W	Men	Women	M + W	Men	Women
North America															
Canada	m	m	m	31	26	36	x	x	x	4.9	5.0	4.8	0.8	1.1	0.5
Mexico	x	x	x	x	x	x	11	11	11	x	x	x	x	x	x
United States	22	18	26	32	29	36	x	x	x	12.0	11.2	12.8	1.2	1.4	0.9
Pacific Area															
Australia	m	m	m	34	27	41	x	x	x	12.1	11.2	13.0	0.8	1.1	0.5
Japan	29	17	40	23	31	15	x	x	x	1.9	3.1	0.7	0.4	0.7	0.1
Korea	16	17	15	23	26	20	x	x	x	3.0	4.2	1.8	0.5	0.8	0.2
New Zealand	17	12	22	21	17	24	5	5	5	9.8	10.3	9.3	0.5	0.7	0.3
European Union															
Austria	5	3	7	x	x	x	10	10	9	a	a	a	1.2	1.7	0.7
Belgium (Flemish Community)	28	23	32	a	a	a	26	27	25	5.2	4.9	5.5	0.7	0.9	0.4
Denmark	8	10	6	21	17	25	8	8	7	2.1	2.4	1.8	0.6	0.8	0.4
Finland	22	14	31	8	10	6	13	11	14	m	x	x	2.0	2.2	1.7
France	m	m	m	m	m	m	m	m	m	m	m	m	m	m	m
Germany	12	11	14	a	a	a	16	18	14	a	a	a	1.6	2.1	1.0
Greece	5	x	x	x	x	x	14	x	x	0.3	x	x	0.4	m	x
Ireland	14	15	13	10	9	12	10	10	10	9.8	9.2	10.3	1.0	1.2	0.7
Italy	7	5	9	1	1	1	11	10	12	a	a	a	1.6	1.8	1.4
Luxembourg	m	m	m	m	x	m	m	m	m	m	m	m	m	m	m
Netherlands	a	a	a	x	x	x	19	18	20	a	m	a	1.9	2.2	1.5
Portugal	6	4	8	2	1	2	13	10	17	1.2	1.3	1.2	1.2	1.3	1.2
Spain	2	2	2	10	8	13	14	12	16	x	x	x	0.9	1.0	0.7
Sweden	9	6	13	8	6	11	8	9	6	2.8	2.2	3.5	1.7	2.3	1.1
United Kingdom	17	12	22	31	30	32	x	x	x	11.2	11.0	11.4	0.9	1.3	0.6
Other OECD countries															
Czech Republic	6	4	8	2	2	3	11	10	11	x	x	x	0.2	0.3	0.1
Hungary	a	a	a	18	15	20	x	x	x	4.3	5.1	3.5	0.2	0.2	0.1
Iceland	m	m	m	17	11	24	m	m	m	m	m	m	m	m	m
Norway	48	42	53	17	12	23	5	5	6	8.4	9.4	7.4	0.9	1.2	0.5
Poland	m	m	m	m	m	m	m	m	m	m	m	m	m	m	m
Switzerland	23	31	15	x	x	x	9	11	7	a	a	a	3.1	4.1	2.0
Turkey	3	3	3	8	10	6	x	x	x	0.6	0.7	0.5	0.2	0.3	0.1
Country mean	**13**	**11**	**15**	**12**	**11**	**13**	**8**	**7**	**8**	**3.6**	**3.6**	**3.5**	**1.0**	**1.2**	**0.7**
Other non-OECD countries															
Russian Federation	26	x	x	21	x	x	x	x	x	a	a	a	0.7	0.7	0.6

Source: OECD Database. See Annex 3 for notes.

Table G2.2 **Net graduation rates in university-level education by type of programme (1995)**

	Short first university degree programmes (e.g. U.S. Bachelor's) (B)			Long first university degree programmes (e.g. German Diplom or Italian Laurea) (C)			Second university degree programmes (e.g. U.S. Master's) (D)			Ph.D or equivalent (E)		
	M + W	Men	Women	M + W	Men	Women	M + W	Men	Women	M + W	Men	Women
North America												
Canada	29	24	34	x	x	x	4.4	4.5	4.4	0.7	0.9	0.4
Mexico	m	m	m	m	m	m	m	m	m	m	m	m
United States	m	m	m	m	m	m	m	m	m	m	m	m
Pacific Area												
Australia	34	27	42	x	x	x	12.4	11.6	13.2	0.8	1.1	0.5
Japan	m	m	m	m	m	m	m	m	m	m	m	m
Korea	m	m	m	m	m	m	m	m	m	m	m	m
New Zealand	m	m	m	m	m	m	m	m	m	m	m	m
European Union												
Austria	x	x	x	9	9	8	a	a	a	1.2	1.6	0.7
Belgium (Flemish Community)	a	a	a	27	28	27	5.2	4.9	5.6	0.7	0.9	0.4
Denmark	21	17	25	7	8	7	2.1	2.4	1.8	0.6	0.8	0.4
Finland	7	8	6	12	10	14	x	x	x	1.9	2.2	1.7
France	m	m	m	m	m	m	m	m	m	m	m	m
Germany	a	a	a	m	m	m	a	a	a	m	m	m
Greece	m	m	m	m	m	m	m	m	m	m	m	m
Ireland	m	m	m	m	m	m	m	m	m	m	m	m
Italy	m	m	m	11	10	11	a	a	a	m	m	m
Luxembourg	m	m	m	m	m	m	m	m	m	m	m	m
Netherlands	x	x	x	20	19	22	10.2	10.6	9.7	1.8	2.2	1.4
Portugal	m	m	m	m	m	m	m	m	m	m	m	m
Spain	9	6	11	10	8	12	x	x	x	m	m	m
Sweden	8	5	11	7	8	6	2.8	2.2	3.5	1.8	2.4	1.2
United Kingdom	30	29	31	x	x	x	10.9	10.7	11.0	1.0	1.4	0.6
Other OECD countries												
Czech Republic	m	m	m	m	m	m	m	m	m	m	m	m
Hungary	18	16	21	x	x	x	m	m	m	m	m	m
Iceland	14	10	19	10	9	10	0.6	0.6	0.6	n	n	n
Norway	17	12	23	5	5	6	8.6	9.6	7.5	0.9	1.3	0.6
Poland	m	m	m	m	m	m	m	m	m	m	m	m
Switzerland	a	a	a	m	m	m	a	a	a	m	m	m
Turkey	7	9	5	x	x	x	0.6	0.7	0.5	0.2	0.3	0.2
Country mean	**12**	**10**	**14**	**8**	**8**	**8**	**3.6**	**3.6**	**3.6**	**1.0**	**1.3**	**0.7**

Source: OECD Database. See Annex 3 for notes.

Table G2.3 **Age distribution of tertiary-level graduates (1995)**

	Age at the 25th percentile	Median age	Age at the 75th percentile	Typical age (see Annex 1)	Range 25th-75th percentile and median age
Non-university tertiary programmes					20 25 30 35
Belgium (Flemish Community)	21.2	22.4	26.6	21-23	
Canada	23.4	31.2	41	21	
Denmark	23.8	25.8	29.1	23-24	
Finland	23.8	26.3	33.7	21-22	
New Zealand	21.1	24.5	34.6	21	
Norway	21.4	23.1	26.3	20-21	
Sweden	22.4	25.2	33.2	20-22	
Turkey	21.4	23.4	29.3	19	
United Kingdom	20.7	24.2	33.4	20	
Short first university degree programmes (e.g. U.S. Bachelor's)					
Australia	20.9	22.4	26.9	21	
Canada	22.8	23.9	26.5	22	
Denmark	24.8	26.7	29.9	25-27	
Finland	24.4	26.3	31.0	22-24	
Hungary	22.9	24.3	25.5	21-22	
Iceland	24.6	27.2	34.9	23	
New Zealand	21.3	22.5	25.9	21	
Norway	23.4	25.3	29.5	23	
Spain	22.4	24.0	26.6	21	
Sweden	24.0	26.2	30.1	22	
Turkey	22.8	24.1	26.1	a	
United Kingdom	21.0	22.0	24.9	21	
Long first university degree programmes (e.g. German Diplom or Italian Laurea)					
Austria	25.6	27.3	29.6	22-25	
Belgium (Flemish Community)	20.5	22.0	23.3	22-24	
Denmark	26.5	28.2	30.5	25-27	
Finland	26.1	27.6	29.9	25-26	
Ireland	24.7	26.0	28.0	25	
Italy	25.5	26.8	28.7	23	
Netherlands	23.8	25.3	28.0	23	
New Zealand	21.7	22.7	24.7	23	
Norway	23.8	25.2	27.5	24	
Spain	23.9	25.3	41	23	
Sweden	25.3	26.9	29.4	23-24	
Second university degree programmes (e.g. U.S. Master's)					
Australia	26.4	32.8	41	24	
Belgium (Flemish Community)	22.9	24.0	27.7	23-26	
Canada	26.4	30.1	37.2	24	
Denmark	26.8	29.4	33.5	26-27	
Ireland	27.3	34.1	39.2	25-28	
Netherlands	24.1	25.2	26.9	25	
New Zealand	23.4	28.4	37.7	23	
Norway	25.4	27.1	30.0	24-28	
Sweden	26.2	30.5	38.1	24-27	
Turkey	26.3	28.0	30.0	25-27	
United Kingdom	24.2	28.6	36.6	22	

Source: OECD Database. See Annex 3 for notes.

Indicator G3: Tertiary qualifications by field of study

Policy context

This indicator shows the distribution of university and non-university tertiary graduates over six broad categories of fields of study.

Changing opportunities within the job market may affect the fields whi students choose to study. In turn, the fields of study affect the demand courses and faculty, as well as the supply of new graduates in different field

The relative popularity of a particular field is likely to be driven by the j opportunities for graduates with skills in that field, as well as relative earnir across different occupations and industries. It may also be influenced by t relative level of tertiary completion rates. For example, countries whose ec cation systems have relatively high participation rates in tertiary educat may not be able to absorb the same proportion of students into a particu occupation as countries with lower participation rates.

Evidence and explanations

Overall completion by field of study

The humanities and the combined field of law and business are the most popular subjects at the university level.

The largest concentration of university-level qualifications awarded is in humanities in all countries providing data except the Flemish Communit Belgium, Italy, Japan, Spain and Switzerland, in which the largest concen tion is in law and business. However, patterns of student choices still d markedly between countries. The percentage of university-level qualificati awarded in the humanities ranges from about 25 per cent in the Flem Community of Belgium, Italy, Switzerland, and Japan to 56 per cent in Cana The percentage of students in science-related fields (medical science, nat science, mathematics and computer science, engineering and architect ranges from under 30 per cent in Canada, the Netherlands, Portugal, and United States to over 50 per cent in Finland and the Russian Federation

The distribution of qualifications awarded by field is driven by the rela popularity of these fields among students, the relative number of stude admitted to these fields in universities and equivalent institutions and degree structure of fields in a particular country. For example, in some cc tries degrees are typically earned at several different levels in the human (Bachelor's, Master's, and Ph.D.), while only one level of degree is typic the field of law (Juris Doctor or J.D.). Thus, the relative popularity of humanities compared with law in the United States may be overestim because a single individual in that field can earn multiple degrees.

The humanities, law and business, and medical science are popular at the non-university tertiary level.

At the non-university tertiary level, the humanities and the combined fie law and business have the largest concentration of graduates. The degre which students concentrate in particular fields at this level varies wi between countries, however. For example, the percentage of students major in the humanities at this level ranges from below 10 per cent in Finl

◆ Chart G3.1. ***Percentage distribution of subjects in which university-level degrees are awarded (1995)***

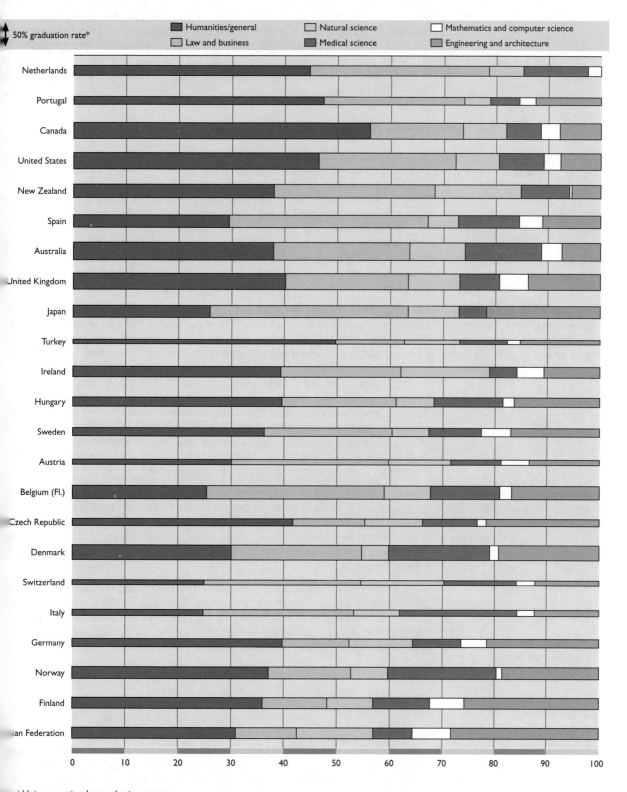

50% graduation rate*

Humanities/general · Natural science · Mathematics and computer science
Law and business · Medical science · Engineering and architecture

Netherlands, Portugal, Canada, United States, New Zealand, Spain, Australia, United Kingdom, Japan, Turkey, Ireland, Hungary, Sweden, Austria, Belgium (Fl.), Czech Republic, Denmark, Switzerland, Italy, Germany, Norway, Finland, ...an Federation

0 10 20 30 40 50 60 70 80 90 100

...idth is proportional to graduation rates.
...es are ranked in decreasing order of the proportion of university-level qualifications in humanities/general and law and business.

OECD.

337

Ireland and Turkey to over 60 per cent in Austria and Norway. Field conce tration at this level is heavily dependent on opportunities to study simi subject matter, or prepare for similar occupations, at the upper secondary university tertiary level. For example, if nurses in a particular country a primarily trained in non-university tertiary programmes, the proportion students graduating with qualifications in medical science would be higl than if nurses were primarily trained in upper secondary or university tertia level programmes.

Gender differences in study choices

Although women are more likely than men to earn first university degrees...

Indicator G2 and the analysis in the 1996 edition of *Education at a Glance* h shown that women have made important strides towards closing the gen gap in educational attainment. It is also important, however, to examine h women have progressed in specific areas that are important to domestic a international competitiveness. Research suggests that many factors cont ute to the attitudes, access and achievement of young women in mathema and science: encouragement from parents, preparation of mathematics a science teachers, interactions between teachers and students, curricul content, hands-on laboratory experience, self-concept, attitudes towa mathematics and resources available at home.

... women are far less likely than men to earn degrees in mathematics and computer science and in engineering and architecture.

One measure of gender disparity in fields of study is the percentage degrees or qualifications awarded in a particular field to women. Among OECD countries that provided data on the number of graduates by field gender, more university-level qualifications are awarded, on average women than men in the humanities and medical sciences (64 and 62 per c respectively). Gender parity is also approached in many countries in law business and in the natural sciences. In the fields of mathematics, comp science, engineering and architecture, however, women earn far fewer uni sity-level qualifications than men. The percentage of university-level degr in engineering and architecture that are awarded to women ranges from 7 cent or below in Japan, Korea, and Spain to 25 per cent or above in the C Republic, Denmark, New Zealand, Portugal, and Turkey.

Engineering and architecture are also uncommon fields for women at the non-university tertiary level.

As with women graduating from university-level programmes, engineering architecture are also uncommon for women at the non-university ter level. The percentage of non-university tertiary qualifications in enginee or architecture awarded to women ranges from 6 per cent in German 38 per cent or above in Austria, the Flemish Community of Belgium and Czech Republic.

At a time when technological innovation is becoming an increasingly im tant component of industries' ability to compete in the global marketp and when employment is growing in high-technology, science-based sec closing the gender gap can be an important policy objective to ensu sufficient supply of the required skills and knowledge.

Definitions

Data are based on the UOE data collection on education statistics, administered in 1996 (for details see Annex 3).

For this indicator, tertiary graduates who received their qualification i reference year were divided into categories based on their subject of sp isation. Graduates can be at each of the levels reported in Indicator G2 comparability of the results depends heavily on the extent to which cou were able to apply consistent subject definitions in accordance with I! (see Annex 3). There is still considerable variation between countries i way educational programmes are classified according to field of study.

◆ Chart G3.2. *Distribution of university-level qualifications in each field of study awarded to men and women (1995)*

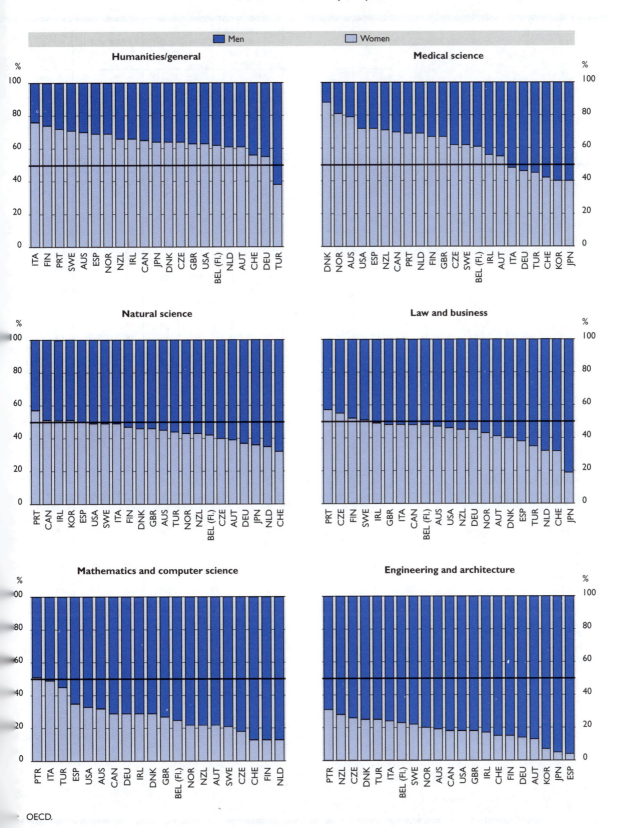

Table G3.1 **Percentage distribution of non-university tertiary and university-level qualifications between subject categories (1995)**

	Medical science		Natural science		Mathematics and computer science		Humanities / general		Law and business		Engineering and architecture	
	Non-university	University level	Non-university	University level	Non-university	University level	Non-university	University level	Non-university	University level	Non-university	University level
North America												
Canada	9	7	3	8	2	4	36	56	49	18	n	8
Mexico	m	m	m	m	m	m	m	m	m	m	m	m
United States	21	9	5	8	2	3	33	46	32	26	6	8
Pacific Area												
Australia	m	15	m	11	m	4	m	38	m	26	m	7
Japan	10	5	14	10	x	x	33	26	23	37	19	21
Korea	11	5	9	17	x	x	m	m	m	m	37	18
New Zealand	15	9	5	17	n	1	46	38	30	30	3	5
European Union												
Austria	16	10	n	12	1	5	61	30	12	30	10	13
Belgium (Flemish Community)	12	13	2	9	4	2	25	25	58	34	1	17
Denmark	4	19	6	5	n	2	39	30	38	25	14	19
Finland	52	11	10	9	5	7	7	36	7	12	19	26
France	m	m	m	m	m	m	m	m	m	m	m	m
Germany	33	9	6	12	1	5	27	40	10	13	23	21
Greece	m	m	m	m	m	m	m	m	m	m	m	m
Ireland	1	5	16	17	7	5	9	39	40	23	27	11
Italy	m	22	m	9	m	3	m	25	m	29	m	12
Luxembourg	m	m	m	m	m	m	m	m	m	m	m	m
Netherlands	a	12	a	7	a	2	a	45	a	34	a	x
Portugal	22	6	4	5	2	3	22	47	38	27	12	12
Spain	7	12	2	6	1	4	10	29	48	37	33	11
Sweden	36	10	2	7	2	6	36	36	9	24	15	17
United Kingdom	37	8	4	10	5	5	22	40	22	23	11	14
Other OECD countries												
Czech Republic	20	11	1	11	n	2	11	42	62	14	6	22
Hungary	a	13	a	7	a	2	a	40	a	22	a	16
Iceland	m	m	m	m	m	m	m	m	m	m	m	m
Norway	1	20	1	7	1	1	67	36	30	15	n	18
Poland	m	m	m	m	m	m	m	m	m	m	m	m
Switzerland	m	14	m	16	m	4	m	25	m	30	m	12
Turkey	36	9	5	10	2	2	7	50	23	13	28	15
Country mean	**17**	**11**	**5**	**10**	**2**	**3**	**26**	**37**	**28**	**24**	**13**	**15**
Other non-OECD countries												
Russian Federation	m	7	m	14	m	7	m	31	m	12	m	28

Source: OECD Database. See Annex 3 for notes.

Table G3.2 **Percentages of non-university tertiary and university-level qualifications in each subject category that are awarded to women (1995)**

	Medical science		Natural science		Mathematics and computer science		Humanities / general		Law and business		Engineering and architecture	
	Non-university	University level	Non-university	University level	Non-university	University level	Non-university	University level	Non-university	University level	Non-university	University level
North America												
Canada	67	70	31	51	42	29	60	65	36	48	n	18
Mexico	m	m	m	m	m	m	m	m	m	m	m	m
United States	82	72	62	49	50	33	56	63	53	46	12	18
Pacific Area												
Australia	m	79	m	45	m	32	m	70	m	47	m	19
Japan	85	40	96	36	x	x	86	64	63	19	18	5
Korea	73	40	75	51	x	x	m	m	m	m	22	7
New Zealand	91	71	38	43	44	22	72	66	53	45	15	28
European Union												
Austria	86	55	100	39	32	22	75	61	77	41	38	13
Belgium (Flemish Community)	82	61	46	42	22	25	71	62	48	48	52	23
Denmark	79	88	5	46	a	29	68	64	17	40	13	25
Finland	91	67	57	47	28	13	69	74	87	52	14	15
France	m	m	m	m	m	m	m	m	m	m	m	m
Germany	78	46	30	37	27	29	84	55	27	45	6	14
Greece	m	m	m	m	m	m	m	m	m	m	m	m
Ireland	84	56	55	51	37	29	56	66	63	49	9	17
Italy	m	48	m	49	m	49	m	76	m	48	m	24
Luxembourg	m	m	m	m	m	m	m	m	m	m	m	m
Netherlands	a	69	a	35	a	13	a	61	a	32	a	x
Portugal	82	69	49	57	41	51	86	72	64	57	26	31
Spain	67	72	37	50	1	35	88	69	54	38	18	4
Sweden	87	62	11	49	20	21	85	71	31	51	17	22
United Kingdom	90	67	44	46	26	27	63	63	57	48	13	18
Other OECD countries												
Czech Republic	89	62	66	40	a	18	59	64	65	55	38	26
Hungary	a	m	a	m	a	m	a	m	a	m	a	m
Iceland	m	m	m	m	m	m	m	m	m	m	m	m
Norway	87	81	46	43	33	22	59	69	47	43	20	20
Poland	m	m	m	m	m	m	m	m	m	m	m	m
Switzerland	m	42	m	32	m	13	m	56	m	32	m	15
Turkey	84	45	53	44	28	45	39	38	52	35	12	25
Country mean	**82**	**62**	**50**	**45**	**31**	**28**	**69**	**64**	**53**	**44**	**19**	**18**

Source: OECD Database. See Annex 3 for notes.

Indicator G4: Production of high-level science qualification relative to the size of the labour force

Policy context

This indicator shows the number of tertiary science graduates per 100 000 persons in the labour force.

Technological innovation has become an increasingly important compon of economic competitiveness and employment is growing in high-technolo science-based sectors ranging from computers to pharmaceuticals. While In cator G3 examines the relative emphasis on particular fields of study wit education systems, Indicator G4 is a measure of the absolute productio graduates in science-related fields. Weighing the number of science gra ates at university level by the size of the respective labour force make possible to compare countries' raw outputs of university-level science gra ates. Differences between countries in the supply of high-level qualificati in science-related fields are likely to be influenced by the relative reward the labour market for different fields, as well as the degree to which market drives field selection in a particular country.

◆   Chart G4.1.   *Number of science graduates per 100 000 persons in the labour force 25 to 34 years of age, by level of education (1995)*

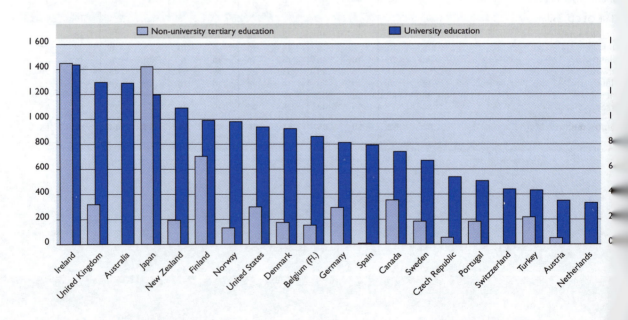

Source: OECD.

Evidence and explanations

The number of persons obtaining tertiary science-related qualifications relative to the size of the young labour force is an important indicator of the recent output of high-level skills and knowledge by different education systems. This indicator does not, however, provide information on the number of graduates actually employed in scientific fields or, more generally, those using their degree-related skills and knowledge in their employment. It therefore measures a potential supply of skills rather than their utilisation. Furthermore, some countries provide qualifications at the upper secondary level which are equivalent to tertiary qualifications in other countries and which are not taken into account in this indicator.

Output of non-university science qualifications relative to the size of the young labour force varies significantly between countries.

At the non-university tertiary level, the number of science graduates is comparatively high in Finland, Ireland, and Japan (more than 600 science graduates per 100 000 persons in the labour force 25 to 34 years of age), whereas it is comparatively low in Austria, the Czech Republic, Norway and Spain (less than 150 science graduates per 100 000 persons in the labour force) (see Chart G4.1).

Countries that award high numbers of non-university science qualifications also tend to award higher numbers of university-level science qualifications.

At the university tertiary level, the number of science graduates is comparatively high in Australia, Ireland, Japan, New Zealand, and the United Kingdom (more than 1 000 science graduates per 100 000 persons in the labour force) while it is low in Austria, the Netherlands, Switzerland and Turkey (less than 500 science graduates per 100 000 persons in the labour force). Taking all OECD countries together, the number of tertiary science graduates as a ratio of the labour force aged 25-34 is, on average, more than twice as high at university level (831 graduates per 100 000 persons) than at the non-university tertiary level of education (344 graduates per 100 000 persons). This corresponds roughly to the respective proportions of total enrolments at these levels of education (see Indicator C5).

Men remain far more likely than women to earn degrees or qualifications in science-related fields...

Indicator G3 demonstrated that men remain more likely than women to earn a university-level science qualification in the vast majority of OECD countries. In the natural sciences, women, on average across OECD countries, earn 45 per cent of university-level qualifications, while they earn only 28 per cent of the university-level degrees in mathematics and computer sciences and 18 per cent of the degrees at this level in engineering and architecture.

... and this gender gap is reflected in the respective young male and female labour markets.

Gender disparities in the completion of science degrees is also reflected in the composition of the skill pools available for entry into young male and female labour markets. Across OECD countries, the number of university-level science degrees awarded to males per 100 000 25 to 34 year-old males in the labour force is almost double the number of university-level science degrees awarded to females per 100 000 25 to 34 year-old females in the labour force – ranging from a ratio of 1.2 in New Zealand to 3.5 in Japan. Turkey is the only OECD country reporting more female science graduates relative to the size of the young female labour force than young male graduates relative to the size of the young male labour force. Although the labour force participation rate varies for young women between countries, and has changed dramatically in many countries over time, current gender disparities in high-level science degree production are likely to reproduce the relative skill disparities in male and female labour markets.

Definitions

Data are based on the UOE data collection on education statistics, administered in 1996 (for details see Annex 3).

This indicator shows the number of persons who obtained a tertiary level qualification in a science-related field per 100 000 persons in the labour force aged 25 to 34 during the reference years. It distinguishes between graduates at the university level of education and the non-university tertiary level.

◆ Chart G4.2. **Number of science graduates at university level per 100 000 persons in the labour force 25 to 34 years of age, by gender (1995)**

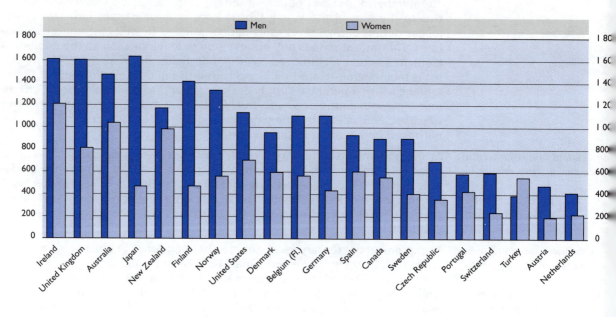

Source: OECD.

The indicator takes into account graduates from the following fields study: "Natural science" (ISCED 42), "Mathematics and computer scien (ISCED 46), "Engineering" (ISCED 54), "Architecture and town planni (ISCED 58), "Agriculture, forestry and fishery" (ISCED 62) and "Home econ ics (domestic science)" (ISCED 66).

As with Indicator G3, the results depend heavily on the extent to wh subject definitions and classifications are consistent between countries (also Annex 3). There is still considerable variation between countries in way educational programmes are classified according to field of study.

Table G4.1 **Number of science graduates per 100 000 persons in the labour force 25 to 34 years of age, by gender (1995)**

	Non-university tertiary education			University education		
	M+W	Men	Women	M+W	Men	Women
North America						
Canada	355	420	277	741	899	552
Mexico	m	m	m	m	m	m
United States	300	348	243	938	1 133	704
Pacific Area						
Australia	m	m	m	1 290	1 473	1 039
Japan	1 421	1 112	1 933	1 196	1 635	468
Korea	m	m	m	m	m	m
New Zealand	194	242	130	1 090	1 171	983
European Union						
Austria	50	57	42	350	477	193
Belgium (Flemish Community)	154	187	113	862	1 104	565
Denmark	176	290	41	924	954	596
Finland	705	920	440	991	1 413	471
France	m	m	m	m	m	m
Germany	293	459	78	813	1 105	434
Greece	m	m	m	m	m	m
Ireland	1 449	1 847	929	1 436	1 611	1 208
Italy	m	m	m	m	m	m
Luxembourg	m	m	m	m	m	m
Netherlands	a	a	a	332	416	222
Portugal	183	237	125	507	583	425
Spain	7	5	4	794	932	603
Sweden	185	288	67	670	902	405
United Kingdom	320	430	162	1 296	1 605	814
Other OECD countries						
Czech Republic	55	58	50	538	693	355
Hungary	m	m	m	m	m	m
Iceland	m	m	m	m	m	m
Norway	132	154	107	981	1 333	559
Poland	m	m	m	m	m	m
Switzerland	m	m	m	440	593	239
Turkey	218	242	151	432	390	551
Country mean	**344**	**405**	**272**	**831**	**1 021**	**569**

Science fields include natural science; mathematics and computer science; engineering, architecture and town planning; agriculture, forestry and fishery; and home economics (domestic science).

The ratio for male graduates is relative to the male labour force and the ratio for female graduates is relative to the female labour force.

Source: OECD Database. See Annex 3 for notes.

TYPICAL AGES AND REFERENCE YEARS

Table XI.1 shows the typical number of years of schooling that corresponds to each level of education. This number is obtained by converting the attainment levels into years of schooling on the basis of the theoretical cumulative duration of the respective levels of education. It should be noted that the estimates are based on the highest completed levels of education. In respect of individuals who have not completed the full typical duration for a given ISCED level, a certain length of time has been ascribed in relation to time spent at that level. For example, the cumulative duration for ISCED level 2 may be assumed to be 10 years instead of 9 years based on typical duration to the end of ISCED 2, to reflect the incidence of drop-out in the course of ISCED 3.

Table XI.1. **Typical cumulative years of schooling by level of education**

	Primary education	Lower secondary education	Upper secondary education	Non-university tertiary education	University-level education
Australia	7 or 8	11	13	15	16
Austria	4	9	13	15	19
Belgium	6	8	12	15	16
Canada	6	9	12	15	16
Czech Republic	4	8	12	15	17
Denmark	6	9	13	14	18
Finland	6	9	12	14	17
France	5	9	12	14	16
Germany	4	10	13	15	19
Greece	6	9	12	16	16
Hungary	4	8	12	14	17
Iceland	7	10	14	17	18
Ireland	8	11	14	16	17
Italy	5	8	13	15	19
Luxembourg	6	9	13	16	m*
Netherlands	6	10	12	a	17
New Zealand	6	11	13	15	16
Norway	6	9	12	14	16
Portugal	6	8	12	14	16
Spain	6	10	12	14	17
Sweden	6	9	12	14	16
Switzerland	6	9	13	16	19
Turkey	6	8	11	14	16
United Kingdom	7	10	14	16	17
United States	7	10	12	14	16

* In Luxembourg, only the first year of university studies can be taken. Afterwards, students have to continue their university studies in foreign countries.

Typical starting ages   The typical starting age is the typical age at the beginning of the first school/academ... year of the corresponding level and programme.

Table X1.2a   **Typical starting age, tertiary level of education**

	Non-university tertiary education (ISCED 5)	University-level education, first stage (ISCED 6)	University-level education, second stage (ISCED 7)
Australia	18	18	22
Austria	18-19	18-19	22-25
Belgium	18-19	18-19	22-24
Canada	18	18	22
Czech Republic	18-19	18-19	23-25
Denmark	21-22	19-23	19-26
Finland	19-20	19-20	21-23
France	18-19	18	21
Germany	19	19	26
Greece	18-19	18-19	22-24
Hungary	18	18-19	23-25
Iceland	20	20	24
Ireland	17-18	17-18	20-24
Italy	19	19	23
Japan	18	18	22
Korea	18	18	22
Luxembourg	19	19	a
Mexico	18	18	24
Netherlands	a	18	19
New Zealand	18	18	21
Norway	19	19	m
Poland	19	19-20	22-26
Portugal	18	18	22
Russian Federation	15-18	17-19	22-25
Spain	18	18	22-24
Sweden	19	19	22-24
Switzerland	19-25	20	26
Turkey	17	17	21
United Kingdom	18	18	21
United States	18	18	22

Typical graduation ages   The typical graduation age is the age at the end of the last school/academic year of ... corresponding level and programme when the degree is obtained. The typical ag... based on the assumption of full-time attendance in the regular education sys... without grade repetition. (Note that at some levels of education the term "gradua... age" may not translate literally and is used here purely as a convention).

Table X1.2b **Typical graduation age, upper secondary level, first educational programmes**

	All programmes	General programmes	Vocational and technical programmes	School-based vocational and technical programmes	Combined school and work-based vocational and technical programmes
Australia	19	18	20	20	20
Austria	17-19	18	17-19	17-19	18-19
Belgium	18-20	18	18-20	18-20	18-20
Canada	18	m	m	m	m
Czech Republic	18-19	18-19	18-19	18-19	17-19
Denmark	19-22	19-20	19-22	19-22	19-22
Finland	19	19	18-19	18-19	18-19
France	18-20	18	18-20	18-20	18-20
Germany	19	19	19	19	19
Greece	18-19	18-19	18-19	18-19	a
Hungary	17-18	18	17-18	18	17
Iceland	20	20	20	20	20
Ireland	17-18	17-18	17-18	17-18	17-18
Italy	17-19	19	17-19	17-19	a
Japan	18	18	18	18	a
Korea	18	18	18	18	18
Luxembourg	18-19	19	18-19	18-19	18-19
Mexico	18	18	18	18	a
Netherlands	18-19	18-19	19-20	19	18-21
New Zealand	18	18	18	18	a
Norway	19	19	19	19	19
Poland	18-20	19	18-20	18-20	18-20
Portugal	18	17	18	18	18
Russian Federation	18	17	18	18	a
Spain	16-18	17-18	16-18	16-18	18
Sweden	19	19	19	19	a
Switzerland	18-20	18-20	18-20	18-20	18-20
Turkey	17	17	17-19	17-19	17-18
United Kingdom	16-18	16-18	18	18	18
United States	18	m	m	m	m

Table X1.2c. **Typical graduation age, upper secondary level, second educational programmes**

	All programmes	General programmes	Vocational and technical programmes	School-based vocational and technical programmes	Combined school and work-based vocational and technical programmes
Austria	18-20	a	18-20	18-20	a
Czech Republic	21-23	a	21-23	21-23	21-23
Denmark	22-23	22-23	22-23	22-23	22-23
Finland	20-21	21	20-21	20-21	20-21
France	19-20	a	19-20	19-20	19-20
Germany	22	25	22	22	22
Hungary	19-21	20	20	21	19
Iceland	20	20	20	20	20
Ireland	18-19	a	18-19	18-19	18-19
Italy	19	a	19	19	a
Netherlands	19-20	19	20	20	20
Portugal	18	18	18	18	18
Spain	19	a	19	19	a

Note: Only countries which report second or further educational programmes at the upper secondary level are listed.

Table X1.2d **Typical graduation age, tertiary level of education**

	Non-university tertiary education (ISCED 5)	University-level education, first stage (ISCED 6)		University-level education, second stage (ISCED 7)	
	All programmes	Short programmes	Long programmes	Second programmes (e.g. U.S. Master's)	Ph.D. or equivalent
Australia	20	21	x	24	25
Austria	20-22	a	22-25	a	24-27
Belgium	21-23	a	22-24	23-26	26-30
Canada	21	22	x	24	27
Czech Republic	21-22	21-22	23-25	a	26-28
Denmark	23-24	25-27	25-27	26-27	29-35
Finland	21-22	22-24	25-26	25-26	29-30
France	20-21	a	22	a	26
Germany	21	a	26	a	29-31
Greece	20-22	a	22-24	23-24	25-27
Hungary	a	21-22	23-24	26-28	a
Iceland	23	23	25	25-28	29-35
Ireland	19-21	20-22	23-24	21-24	24-27
Italy	21	22	23	a	25
Japan	20	a	22	24	27
Korea	20	22	x	24	29
Luxembourg	21-22	a*	a*	a*	a*
Mexico	23	x	23	26	28
Netherlands	a	a	23	25	28
New Zealand	21	21	x	23	25
Norway	20-21	23	24	24-28	25-29
Poland	20-22	22-23	23-26	24-26	27-29
Portugal	21-22	21-22	22-24	24	26-27
Russian Federation	19-20	20-23	22-25	a	26
Spain	20	21	23	x	26-28
Sweden	20-22	22	23-24	24-27	26-29
Switzerland	23-29	a	26	a	31
Turkey	19	a	25-27	25-27	25-27
United Kingdom	20	21	x	22	26
United States	20	22	a	24	27

* In Luxembourg, only the first year of university studies can be taken. Afterwards, students have to con
their university studies in foreign countries.

◆ Table XI.3. **School years and financial years as used for the calculation of the indicators**

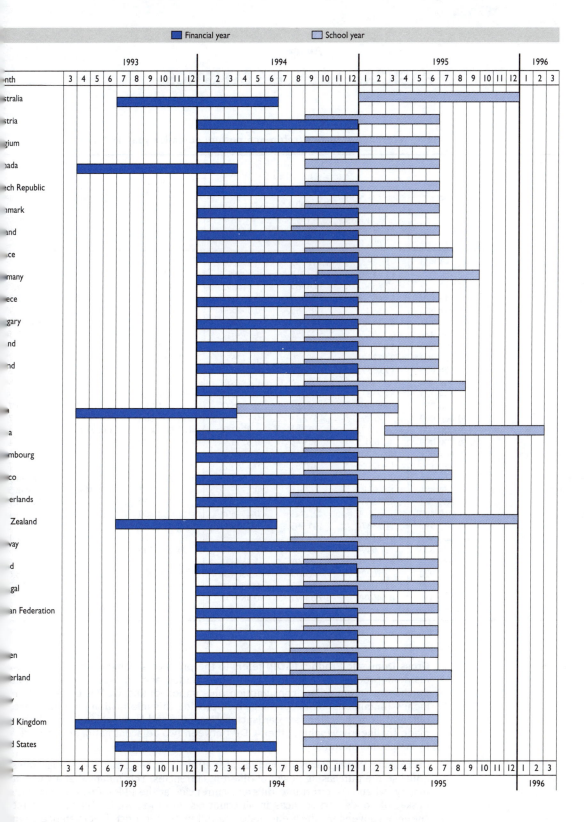

Annex 2

BASIC REFERENCE STATISTICS

Table X2.1   **Basic reference statistics (reference period: calendar year 1994)**

| | Gross Domestic Product (in millions of local money) | Exchange rates (basis: US dollar) | | | Total public expenditure (in millions of local money) | Adjustment factor | GDP per capita (in equivalent US dollars converted using PPPs |
		Purchasing Power Parity exchange rate	Unadjusted market exchange rate	Comparative price levels of GDP			
Australia	443 020	1.34821	1.419155	0.950009	17 189 090	1.006715	18515.73
Austria	2 262 917	13.94502	11.4218	1.220913	1 186 658	1	20205.97
Belgium	7 678 129	37.36062	33.4565	1.116692	4 304 222	1	20315.7
Canada	740 129	1.246578	1.36564	0.912816	363 553	1.005452	20297.7
Czech Republic	1 037 500	11.3	28.785	0.392566	462 922	1	8882.9
Denmark	928 597	8.725988	6.3606	1.371881	590 203	1	20445.2
Finland	509 924	6.158574	5.22351	1.179011	310 407	1	16273.40
France	7 389 654	6.635775	5.552	1.195204	4 022 211	1	19233.3
Germany	3 320 400	2.073371	1.62279	1.277658	1 649 310	1	19668.2
Greece	23 755 806	196.5893	242.603	0.810333	8 342 381	1	11590.2
Hungary	4 364 800	67.5	105.16	0.641879	1 430 300	1	6301.8
Iceland	434 525	84.21833	69.9444	1.204075	177 021	1	19323.9
Ireland	36 051	0.63966	0.66863	0.956672	14 985	1	15782.7
Italy	1 640 000 000	1536.391	1612.44	0.952836	893 000 000	1	18647.7
Japan	479 000 000	181.092	102.21	1.771764	167 000 000	1.002131	21170.4
Korea	306 000 000	661.5	803.45	0.823324	64 627 000	1	10405.1
Luxembourg	487 671	40.08204	33.4565	1.198034	m	1	30115.8
Mexico	1 420 159	1.952115	3.3751	0.578387	249 619	1	7821.7
Netherlands	612 980	2.128271	1.81999	1.169386	341 030	1	18724.3
New Zealand	84 481	1.506272	1.727518	0.871929	31 477	1.009488	15958.5
Norway	869 742	9.136664	7.05758	1.294589	453 019	1	21953.9
Poland	210 407	1.09	2.2723	0.479690	68 800	1	5008.1
Portugal	14 082 597	118.3374	165.993	0.712906	m	1	12018.1
Russian Federation	611 000 000	912.1001	m	m	m	1	45232.1
Spain	64 698 800	121.5498	133.958	0.907372	25 276 700	1	13595.9
Sweden	1 531 102	9.917516	7.71598	1.285322	1 069 905	1	17581.5
Switzerland	352 920	2.10205	1.3677	1.536924	129 300	1	23858.6
Turkey	3 870 000 000	12116.16	29608.7	0.409210	899 000 000	1	5270.7
United Kingdom	665 570	0.646799	0.653427	0.989857	300 025	1.014424	17621.7
United States	6 649 800	1	1	1	2 397 400	1.011397	25512.2

Explanations

Gross Domestic Product (GDP) refers to the producers' value of the gross output resident producers, including distributive trades and transport, less the valu purchasers' intermediate consumption plus import duties. GDP is expressed in money (in millions). For countries which provide this information for a reference different from the calendar year (such as Australia and New Zealand) adjustment made by linearly weighting their GDP between two adjacent national reference to match the calendar year.

Purchasing Power Parity exchange rates (PPP) are the currency exchange rates equalise the purchasing power of different currencies. This means that a given s money when converted into different currencies at the PPP rates, will buy the basket of goods and services in all countries. In other words, PPPs are the rat currency conversion which eliminate the differences in price levels among coun Thus, when expenditure on GDP for different countries is converted into a con currency by means of PPPs, it is, in effect, expressed at the same set of international prices so that comparisons between countries reflect only differences in the volume of goods and services purchased.

The **unadjusted exchange rates** are par or market exchange rates that have been averaged over the calendar year 1994. They have been calculated by the International Monetary Fund, and are published in *International Financial Statistics*.

The **comparative price level of GDP** is obtained by dividing the purchasing power parity exchange rate by the corresponding unadjusted exchange rate. This provides an indication of the relative price level in a country compared with the United States. For example, for Portugal the exchange rate to the U.S. dollar equals 118 while the market exchange rate is equal to 166. The price level of GDP for Portugal is therefore 71 per cent. This means that in Portugal the same basket of goods costs only 71 per cent of what it would cost in the United States.

Total public expenditure as used for the calculation of the education indicators corresponds to the sum of the following items (for details refer to "Accounts for General Government": Table 6, *National Accounts - Detailed Tables, Volume II*, OECD, Paris, 1995): Total public expenditure = Total current disbursements and net saving + (Capital: gross accumulation) Increase in stocks + (Capital: gross accumulation) Gross fixed capital formation + (Capital: gross accumulation) Purchases of land net + (Capital: gross accumulation) Purchases of intangible assets net + (Capital: gross accumulation) Capital transfers − (Capital: finance of gross accumulation) Net saving − (Capital: finance of gross accumulation) Capital transfers. Total public expenditure is expressed in local money (in millions).

The **adjustment factor** is used to shift the reference period for expenditure data from the national financial year to the calendar year 1994.

The **GDP per capita** is the Gross Domestic Product (in equivalent US dollars converted using PPPs) divided by the population.

OECD countries (unless otherwise specified below)
- OECD *National Accounts*, January 1997
- OECD Analytical Data Base, January 1997

Czech Republic
- GDP: *Short-term Economic Indicators, Central and Eastern Europe*, OECD/CCET, July 1995
- Total public expenditure: Statistical Yearbook of the Czech Republic
- Population: CESTAT Statistical Bulletin, 1996-2

Hungary
- Total public expenditure: CESTAT Statistical Bulletin, 1996-2

Ireland
- Total Public Expenditure: Department of Education, Statistics Section.

Korea
- PPP: Estimated figures provided by the World Bank

Mexico
- Total public expenditure: National Institute of Geographical and Computerised Statistics, Mexico

New Zealand
- Total public expenditure: Ministry of Education, Wellington

Norway
- Total public expenditure: The Royal Norwegian Ministry of Education, Research and Church Affairs, Oslo

urces

SOURCES, METHODS AND TECHNICAL NOTES

This annex provides notes on the coverage of the indicators as well as on methods, sources and interpretation of the indicators. It is organised by indicator. Only indicators requiring additio comment appear in this annex.

Indicator A2: | **Educational attainment of the adult population**

General notes

Notes on methodology

For the purposes of the projections the assumption of a constant level of educatio attainment for future "incoming" cohorts (25 to 29 year-olds) is subject to the c straint that the attainment of the "incoming" cohort should be at least as high as t of all age groups in 1995, including the 20 to 24 year-olds. Even with the additior the above constraint on the "incoming" cohort, it is likely that the attainment of t cohort is underprojected because of the significant acceleration in enrolment at upper secondary level in recent years, which still has to feed through to the age grc 25 to 29 years. Moreover, completion of upper secondary education is likely increase well into the next decade. Finally, no account is taken of accumulated edu tional attainment beyond the age of 29.

Notes on specific countries

Coverage

Turkey: Persons without educational qualifications (ISCED 0) are *not included*.

Notes on interpretation

Canada: ISCED 3 *includes* secondary school graduates and individuals with some p secondary education who have not received a certificate/diploma.

Czech Republic: Data for ISCED category 0/1 refer to persons with no school ed tion.

Denmark: Persons with unknown qualifications (around 5%) are included in ISCED egory 0/1/2.

Germany, New Zealand: Persons with unknown qualifications (Germany 7% New Zealand 3.5%) are redistributed to ISCED categories proportionally to the distribution of ISCED categories in the population with known qualifications.

Norway: Persons with unknown qualifications are included in ISCED category 0/1

Switzerland: Persons with unknown qualifications are redistributed to ISCED cat ries 2 (40%) and 3 (60%). Apprentices are defined as in full-time education and n the labour market.

Sources

Australia	Transition from Education to Work, May 1995
Austria	Microcensus, 1995
Belgium	Labour Force Survey
Canada	Labour Force Survey
Czech Republic	Labour Force Sample Survey
Denmark	The Register of Educational Attainment of the Population and the Register of Labour Force and Unemployment
Finland	Labour Force Survey
France	Labour Force Survey
Germany	Labour Force Survey
Greece	Labour Force Survey
Ireland	Labour Force Survey, 1995
Italy	Labour Force Survey, 1995
Korea	Annual report on the Economically Active Population Survey
Luxembourg	Labour Force Survey, 1996
Netherlands	Labour Force Sample Survey
Norway	Labour Force Survey
New Zealand	Household Labour Force Survey
Poland	Labour Force Survey
Portugal	Labour Force Survey
Spain	Labour Force Survey
Sweden	Labour Force Survey
Switzerland	Swiss Labour Force Survey
Turkey	Household Labour Force Survey
United Kingdom	Labour Force Survey
United States	Labour Force Survey

Indicator A3:

Expected number of years in employment, unemployment and outside the labour market between the ages 25 and 64 by level of educational attainment

See also notes on Indicator A2.

General notes

Notes on methodology

The labour force survey estimate for a particular characteristic (employment, unemployment and outside the labour market), expressed as a proportion of the total population, can be interpreted in two ways. The employment/population ratio can serve as an example. One interpretation of this ratio is the standard one, namely the proportion of persons employed in the total population (see Indicator E2). A second interpretation is that it represents the proportion of time for which an average person is employed over the reference period. Thus if the employment/population ratio for the population 25-64 is 0.70 for a given year, one can say that a typical person is employed on average for 70 per cent of the weeks during a year. The age interval 25-64 covers 40 years. If one assumes that current labour market conditions remain unchanged, an average person aged 25 can then expect to work 40 times 0.70 or 28 years between his/her 25th and 65th years.

This is of course not an actual observed phenomenon, but nonetheless provides a useful indicator of possible time spent in employment over the life cycle under current labour market conditions. In practice, if the sizes of age cohorts differ significantly, the indicator will be distorted, with more weight being applied to the employment situation of larger cohorts. It is thus preferable to carry out the calculation by individual age and to sum over all ages. For example, in a particular year, if the employment/population ratio of persons aged 40 were 50 per cent, then, on average, 40 year-olds would be employed for six months in that year. The total expected years in employment is simply the sum of these calculations for persons of all ages. For this indicator, given data availability, the calculation has been done using age groups. Employment for each five-year age band is multiplied by five. Thus the estimate for five-year age groups is as follows: expected time in employment = $\mathrm{Sum}(5*(E_i/P_i))$, where E_i and P_i are the estimates of the number of persons employed and the number of persons in the population of age group i, and the sum is over all five-year a groups in the interval 25-64.

Indicator B1:   **Educational expenditure relative to Gross Domestic Product**

General notes   *Notes on methodology*

- *Reference period*

Statistics on educational expenditure relate to the calendar year 1994. GDP consumer price deflators from the OECD National Accounts database are used to adjust the da on expenditure where the national financial year does not coincide with the calendar year. In order to make this adjustment, the data on educational finance multiplied by the ratio of GDP price levels between the calendar year for which d are published and those of the preceding calendar year, in proportion to the fract of the national financial year that overlaps with the previous calendar year. following two limitations of the use of such deflators should be recognised: *i)* adjustments relate to changes in the general (GDP) price level but not to the pr level for educational services. The assumption is made that educational costs measured in terms of national income forgone so that a GDP price index is justif (the alternative would be to express costs in terms of volume of resources spent education by means of a price index that is specific to the education sector). *ii)* allowance has been made for real growth in educational expenditure (increases excess of inflation or smaller increases) that might have taken place during the co sponding period of adjustment. It would only be possible to take real growth i account retrospectively. Nevertheless, the adjustment for inflation does eliminate significant source of non-comparability of expenditure figures.

For countries for which GDP is not reported for the calendar year, GDP is estimated w_{t-1} (GDP$_{t-1}$) + w_t (GDP$_t$) with w_t and w_{t-1} being the weights for the respec portions of the two calendar years.

- *Assumptions concerning the allocation of financial aid to students*

Indicators B1 and B2 distinguish between public financial aid to students an households that is attributable to household payments to educational institution educational services (*e.g.* tuition fees) and other public aid to students/househo (such as subsidies for student living costs). For countries which have not made distinction in their data submissions on educational finance, the following coeffici are used to estimate the proportion of public financial aid to households tha destined for educational institutions.

	Primary (ISCED 1)	Secondary (ISCED 2/3)	Tertiary (ISCED 5/6/7)	All leve of educat combine
Australia	0	0	0.45	0.2
Canada	0	0	0.828	0.82
Ireland	0	0	0.42	0.2
Mexico	0	0	0.0074	0.012
Netherlands	0	0.26	0.26	0.2
New Zealand	0.5	0.5	0.5	0
United Kingdom	0.5	0.5	0.5	0
United States	0.50725	0.50725	0.50725	0.507

- *Calculation of estimates in Chart B1.3*

The estimates in Chart B1.3(A) are calculated as follows: let B(*i*) be the percenta persons 5 to 29 years of age in the total population of country *i*, divided by average percentage of 5 to 29 year-olds in all OECD countries for which dat available. Let A(*i*) be the expenditure on educational institutions as a percenta GDP in country *i*. The expected difference for country *i* shown in Chart B1.3(A) is calculated as A(*i*)/B(*i*) − A(*i*).

Chart B1.3(C) and (D) show shifts in educational expenditure that would be expected if participation by children in a country's education were at the OECD average level. This is based on an estimate of the number of students at the primary and secondary level and at the tertiary level if enrolment rates were at the OECD average. The expected enrolment for country EE(i) is calculated as follows: let POP(i,k) be the population in country i at age k and AER(k,l) the OECD average enrolment rate at age k at level of education l. The expected enrolment is calculated as:

$$EE(i) = \sum_{k=5}^{29} POP(i,k)*AER(k,l).$$

The expected difference in expenditure for country I at level l, as shown in Charts B1.2(C) and (D), is calculated as A(i,l)*(EE(i,l)/RE(i,l))–A(i,l), with RE(i,l) representing the observed enrolment at level l at country i. The OECD average enrolment rate is calculated using data from countries for which enrolment data by single year of age are available.

Notes on specific countries

Coverage

Australia: Educational expenditure *excludes* payments to private vocational education and training institutions; open learning courses; and payments to two private universities. Private expenditure on early childhood education is now *included* (it was not included in the 1996 edition of *Education at a Glance*).

Austria: Local government expenditure on private schools is *excluded*. Private payments other than to educational institutions and payments of private entities other than households are *excluded*. Some expenditure such as on conservatories, out-of-school educational activities for young persons, seminars for administrators, instruction of civil servants, further education of teachers, and libraries and adult education, is no longer taken into account. Expenditure classified as "not allocated by level" *includes* the main non-tertiary level scholarships, schoolbooks and free travel arrangements for students, and expenditure on adult and special education.

Belgium: Research expenditure is *included* only if covered by funds provided by the Community authorities responsible for education. Research funds from other public and private sources are *excluded*.

Czech Republic: Public expenditure on upper secondary and tertiary education *includes* estimates of child allowances, meals, accommodation, and transport subsidies. In some cases, the allocation of expenditure by level of education is estimated on the basis of enrolments. Data from the Ministry of Defence and the Ministry of Internal Affairs are *not included*.

Canada: Funds from foreign sources are *excluded*.

Denmark: Expenditure on adult education programmes that are similar in content to programmes in the normal school system has been allocated to the corresponding level of education. Expenditure on other adult education programmes has been allocated to the upper secondary and tertiary levels of education. The allocation of expenditure on early childhood, primary and lower secondary education is estimated on the basis of the corresponding enrolments.

Finland: Expenditure on adult education programmes that are similar in content to programmes in the regular school system has been allocated to the corresponding level of education. Some additional expenditure connected with unemployment policy which was included in the 1996 edition is now *excluded*. Government transfers and payments to private entities, except financial aid to students, are *excluded*. Ancillary services are *included* as current expenditure other than compensation of staff. Funds from foreign sources are *not included*. Local government expenditure also contains private expenditure.

France: Expenditure "not allocated by level" *includes* expenditure on arts education. Expenditure on special education is now included in the respective ISCED levels. All separately identifiable R&D expenditure is *excluded*; however, compensation of university teaching staff (and other regular university staff) is *included*, a portion of which is attributable to research.

Germany: Expenditure on the following types of programmes/institutions is *not included* in total expenditure: colleges of nursing; agricultural training and research centres; training of trainee civil servants in public service; support payments for dependent children made to persons undergoing education/training; scholarships granted ▮ private institutions; purchases of commodities and educational services by hous holds. Payments by private households and other private entities to governmer dependent institutions are *excluded*. Almost all expenditure on research performed ▮ the higher education sector is *included*.

For the period 1970-92 the data refer to the former territory of the Federal Republic Germany. From 1975 onwards, the coverage of financial statistics has increased a substantial modifications have taken place steadily. Since 1985, university research included.

Greece: Private payments to independent private institutions are *excluded*. The institutions are completely privately funded and account for approx. 4 per cent of to enrolment in Greece.

Hungary: Expenditure "not allocated by level" *includes* educational services provic by independent institutions in the fields of educational and psychological counselli methodology and administration. Financial data for non-tertiary level education o *include* expenditure reported under educational budget categories, whereas data tertiary-level education *include* all expenditure by tertiary institutions, whatever ▮ budget category, *except* in the case of medical institutions of higher education. addition, expenditure on early childhood education *includes* meals, expenditure primary and lower secondary education *includes* student hostels and day-care schools and meals, and expenditure on upper secondary education *includes* me hostels, and expenditure on work places for apprentices. Expenditure on governme dependent institutions is *excluded*.

Iceland: Expenditure by private entities other than households and all capital exp diture by or on private institutions are *excluded*. Funds from foreign sources are a *excluded*. Central payments to private institutions are *not included* for primary and sec dary education. These payments are included in the total.

Ireland: Educational expenditure *includes* mainstream higher education research. C household expenditure on the running costs of schools is *included*. Household exper ture on school transport, schoolbooks and other educational materials is *exclu* Expenditure by private entities other than households is *only included* for tert education. Child benefits for students in tertiary education (who would not qualify benefit if they were not enrolled in full-time education) are *not included*. Such bene apply to less than 20 per cent of such students.

Italy: Expenditure "not allocated by level" *includes* expenditure from internatic sources as well as an estimate of expenditure by regional and local governments "educational assistance" (at ISCED levels 0 to 5). Expenditure on private institut. at all levels of education except university *only includes* expenditure by public sour Private expenditure on vocational training in higher education is not negligible.

Japan: Expenditure "not allocated by level" *includes* expenditure on special trair colleges, miscellaneous schools and educational administration. Expenditure research institutes attached to universities, inter-university research institutes grants-in-aid for scientific research from the Ministry of Education and Scienc *included*. Data for R&D personnel are expressed as the number of physical per (working mainly on R&D) rather than in terms of full-time equivalents (FTE). In co quence R&D personnel and labour cost data are overestimated by international s dards. Recent studies by the Japanese authorities suggest that 100 researchers in Higher Education sector correspond to about 60 FTEs and 100 researchers in Business Enterprise sector correspond to about 70 FTEs. In consequence expendi on research and development at the Higher Education sector (HERD) woulc reduced by about 25 per cent and expenditure on research and development in Business Enterprise sector (BERD) and other public institutions outside educ (GERD) by about 15 per cent each.

Korea: Expenditure "not allocated by level" *includes* expenditure by research i tutes, non-educational organisations supporting educational activities, teacher trai institutions and libraries, *but not* expenditure by central government or house expenditure on independent private institutions. For primary and lower secor education, expenditure by the central government is *excluded*. Central governr expenditure on primary and secondary schools affiliated to universities is includ tertiary-level expenditure. Compensation of "other educational, administrative, professional staff" in public institutions of early childhood education is *not inc*

Expenditure at the regional level of government on university-level education is *excluded*.

Netherlands: Expenditure on regional and local government is estimated from expenditure in 1993. Allocation to level is often based on numbers of pupils/students enrolled in the different levels, by age, or by some other key.

New Zealand: Expenditure "not allocated by level" *includes* policy advice, management of contracts/administration of payments, provision and support of the curriculum, ministerial servicing, payment of salaries and allowances, provision of information, provision of teaching/learning accommodation, provision of housing for teachers and caretakers, losses on sales of fixed assets, restructuring expenses, provision for retirement and long-service leave, and capital investment.

Norway: Expenditure on early childhood education in government-dependent institutions is *included* in expenditure on primary education.

Spain: Data differ from earlier editions, because contributions paid by employers for teaching staff in public institutions are now *included*. Public expenditure on education is still *underestimated* because contributions paid by employers for non-teaching staff are *not included*. Expenditure on research has been *partially included*. Some tertiary institutions have all R&D expenditure in their budgets; others have only general university funds and certain types of contracts. Expenditure by private entities other than households is *only included* for public tertiary education.

Payments to independent private institutions for tertiary education are *underestimated* because only payments by private entities to universities for R&D are *included*. Expenditure by private entities other than households on private institutions and scholarships is *underestimated*.

Sweden: Early childhood education at pre-schools and day-care centres from the age of three is *included*. Expenditure on the educational element is *estimated*. Expenditure on Folk High Schools and education run by the Labour Authority is *excluded*. Expenditure on all research performed in higher education institutions is *included*.

Switzerland: Funds from foreign sources for public institutions are *not included*.

Turkey: Foreign funds are *not included* for primary and secondary education. These payments are included in the total.

United Kingdom: Expenditure on research and development is *included*. (In the 1996 edition of *Education at a Glance* only general university funds and grants from the Department for Education and Employment were included). Funds originating in the public sector spent by households on tuition fees are *included*, *but not* amounts spent by households from their own resources. Expenditure relating to nursing and paramedical non-university tertiary programmes is *not included*.

United States: All research expenditure is *included*, *except* funds for major federal R&D centres administered by universities.

Notes on interpretation

Denmark: Expenditure on early childhood education is slightly *overestimated*.

Finland: Expenditure at universities refers to expenditure by educational institutions.

Mexico: Expenditure broken down by level of tertiary education cannot be compared with figures shown in the 1996 edition of *Education at a Glance*, because teacher training programmes were reclassified as university-level programmes.

Notes on methodology

Australia: Figures on expenditure by source are based on financial year data (July to June) provided by the Australian Bureau of Statistics. These data are supplemented with averaged calendar year data (provided by major educational organisations) to apportion total expenditure across ISCED levels and expenditure categories. The ISCED level data for the Technical and Further Education (TAFE) institutions are apportioned by expenditure item based on data supplied by the New South Wales TAFE and across ISCED levels according to student hours.

Australia, New Zealand and the United States report educational expenditure and national account data for the period July to June. For these countries, the "calculated" ratio of national GDP price levels adjusts the expenditure data to the calendar year.

GDP figures are adjusted by creating a weighted average for the two adjacent refe ence years.

Austria, **Belgium**, the **Czech Republic**, **Denmark**, **Finland**, **France**, **Germany**, **Hunga Ireland**, **Italy**, **Korea**, **Mexico**, the **Netherlands**, **Norway**, **Poland**, the **Russian Feder tion**, **Spain**, **Sweden**, **Switzerland** and **Turkey** report both educational expenditu and national account data by calendar year. No adjustment is therefore needed.

Canada, **Japan** and the **United Kingdom** report educational expenditure for t period April to March.

Finland: The distribution of expenditure by level of education in vocational a technical education institutions (ISCED levels 3, 5 and 6) is estimated on the basis enrolments at these levels.

Hungary: Government expenditure on public institutions is estimated by subtracti the income from the expenditure of public institutions. Private payments to pub institutions are taken as income of public institutions.

Mexico: The proportion of public financial aid to students that is attributable household payments to educational institutions is estimated and applies for fede public expenditure. Private expenditure on independent private institutions is es mated. Expenditure by local government on public institutions and the distribution regional and local government expenditure across ISCED levels are also estimated

Sources

1996 UNESCO/OECD/EUROSTAT (UOE) data collection on education statisti National sources are:

Australia: Department of Employment, Education, Training and Youth Affairs, Hig Education Division, Canberra; Australian Bureau of Statistics, "Expenditure on Edu tion Finance" collection; in the case of regional government expenditure, state gove ment data (for public institutions) and school data (for private institutions) were us "Collection of National Financial Data on Vocational Education and Training"; N South Wales Technical and Further Education, unpublished data.

Austria: Austrian Central Statistical Office, Vienna.

Belgium: Flemish Community: Ministry of the Flemish Community, Education Dep ment, Brussels; French Community: Ministry of the French Community, Educati Research and Training Department, Brussels; German Community: Ministry of German-speaking Community, Eupen.

Canada: Statistics Canada, Ottawa.

Czech Republic: Unpublished information from Ministry of Agriculture, Ministry Health, Ministry of Economic Affairs and Ministry of Education.

Denmark: Ministry of Education, Department of Economic Affairs, Copenhagen.

Finland: Statistics Finland, Helsinki.

France: Ministry of National Education, Higher Education and Research, Directorat Evaluation and Planning, Paris.

Germany: Federal Office of Statistics, Wiesbaden.

Greece: Ministry of National Education and Religious Affairs, Directorate of Inv ment Planning and Operational Research, Athens.

Hungary: Ministry of Culture and Education, Ministry of Finance, Central Statist Office, Budapest.

Iceland: National Economics Institute, Reykjavik.

Ireland: Department of Education, Statistics Section, Dublin.

Italy: National Institute of Statistics (ISTAT), Rome; Ministry of Public Education, St tical Service, Rome.

Japan: Ministry of Education, Science, Sports and Culture, Research and Stati Planning Division, Tokyo.

Korea: Korean Educational Development Institute, Educational Information Rese Centre, Seoul.

Mexico: Secretariat of Public Education.

Netherlands: Central Bureau for Statistics, Department for Statistics of Education, Voorburg; Ministry of Education and Science, Zoetermeer.

New Zealand: Ministry of Education, Wellington.

Norway: Statistical Central Office, Division for Population, Education and Regional Conditions, Kongsvinger; The Royal Norwegian Ministry of Education, Research and Church Affairs, Oslo.

Poland: Central Statistical Office, Republic of Poland, Warsaw.

Portugal: Ministry of Education, Office of Research and Planning, Department of Programming, Lisbon.

Russian Federation: Centre for Science Research and Statistics, Moscow.

Spain: National Institute of Statistics, Sub-directorate General of Social Research and Statistics, Madrid; Ministry of Education, Planning and Statistical Office, Madrid; Ministry of Labour, Madrid.

Sweden: Swedish National Agency for Education (*Skolverket*), Stockholm; Swedish National Agency for Higher Education (*Hogskoleverket*); Statistics Sweden, Örebro.

Switzerland: Federal Statistical Office, Berne.

Turkey: State Institute of Statistics, Ankara.

United Kingdom: Department for Education and Employment, Darlington.

United States: Department of Education, Office of Educational Research and Improvement, National Centre for Education Statistics, Washington, D.C.

Indicator B2:	## Public expenditure on education
	See also notes on Indicator B1.
General notes	*Notes on methodology*

• *Trend data*

For 1985 and 1990, possible inconsistencies with the 1994 data may arise because reporting practices changed in 1992. Since then the data include public subsidies which are not attributable to household payments for educational institutions.

• *Calculation of estimates in Chart B2.1 (bottom graph)*

The estimates in Chart B2.1 (bottom graph) are calculated as follows: let B(i) be the percentage of persons 5 to 29 years of age in the total population of country i, divided by the average percentage of 5 to 29 year-olds in all OECD countries for which data are available. Let A(i) be the expenditure on educational institutions as a percentage of total public expenditure in country i. The expected difference for country i shown in Chart B2.1 (bottom graph) is then calculated as A(i)/B(i) − A(i).

Notes on specific countries *Coverage*

Belgium: Public subsidies to the private sector *include* scholarships only.

Denmark: Trend data (Table B2.t): The 1985-92 figures do *not include* expenditure on adult education and *include only* expenditure on early childhood education at primary schools for 6 year-olds. The 1993 and 1994 figures *include* expenditure on all pre-primary education for children aged 3 and over (kindergartens, age-integrated institutions and pre-primary classes in primary schools) and include expenditure on adult education (open education, single-subject education qualifying for examination, adult vocational training programmes).

Germany: Trend data (Table B2.t): For the period 1985-92 data refer to the former territory of the Federal Republic of Germany.

Mexico: Public subsidies to the private sector from regional governments are included in direct expenditure on educational services. Public subsidies to the private sector from central government are included in the total. Trend data (Table B2.t): *Only includes* federal (central) public education expenditure.

Portugal: Figures on total public expenditure from OECD National Accounts are *not available* for 1994.

Sweden: Trend data (Table B2.t): The 1985-91 figures do *not include* expenditure on adult education and *include only* the (estimated) educational element of early child-

hood education for 6 year-olds. The 1992 figures *include* municipal adult education a
all expenditure on early childhood education (for children aged 3 and over). The 19
and 1994 figures include municipal adult education but only the (estimated) edu
tional element of expenditure on early childhood education (3 and over).

Sources

See Indicator B1.

Indicator B3:

Notes on specific countries

Public subsidies to households

Coverage

Data refer to the financial year 1994 for **Austria, Canada, Finland, Germany, Irela
Mexico, the Netherlands, Switzerland** and **the United States**. They refer to
financial year 1995 for **Belgium (Flemish Community), Denmark, Fran
New Zealand, Norway, Spain, Sweden** and the **United Kingdom**.

Australia: Tax reductions for tertiary education *include* upper secondary.

Czech Republic: Public subsidies shown in B3 *include* specific public subsidies
housing, meals and medical expenses. Those are not shown as subsidies in ind
tor B1. In B1 expenses for housing and meals are included in "Direct expenditures
educational institutions". Medical expenses are *not included* at all.

Denmark: In the UOE data collection, subsidies to households *include* the state edu
tion grant and loan scheme, provision for specially disadvantaged groups, educa
and training provision, and the education and training allowance (Indicator B2). Ind
tor B3 *only includes* expenditure on the state education grant and loan scheme.

Belgium (Flemish Community), Germany, United Kingdom: Data on upper second
education *include* lower secondary.

France: Subsidies per upper secondary student *include* lower secondary.

Germany: Allowances and tax reductions for tertiary education *include* upper sec
dary. Substantial categories of subsidies have *not* been *included* (*e.g.* household dec
tions from taxable income, price reductions on public transport, telecommunicati
public social and recreational institutions, reductions in contributions to non-pri
health insurance, imputed loss of contributions to the pension system during per
of study, child allowances contingent on student status for public employees, su
dies for medical treatment of children of civil servants contingent on student sta
excess housing subsidies contingent on student status, and prolonged pensions
orphans contingent on student status). Figures on tax reductions represent prel
nary estimates of child and education deductions on taxable income related to
sons aged 19 to 27 as well as deductions on taxable income related to students u
age 29 participating in vocational training and having completed military or alterna
service. Specific types of deductions on taxable income contingent on special circ
stances (*e.g.* low family income) are, however, *not included*.

Mexico: Scholarships/grants *include* payments for special subsidies.

Spain: Data refer to subsidies from the Ministry of Education (about 85 per cent o
total). Subsidies from other Ministries and from Regional Governments are *not inclu*

Sweden: Specific public subsidies refer to meals, transportation, medical exper
books and supplies supplied to students by schools. Specific subsidies also *in*
public expenditure on interest on public student loans.

United Kingdom: At the secondary level, scholarships/grants covering tuition
refer to local and central government awards to cover fees in institutes of Fu
Education (vocational programmes) and central government grants for parents to
tuition fees in independent schools (general programmes). At the tertiary level,
refer mainly to awards made by local education authorities to cover tuition fe
institutes of Higher Education. Scholarships/grants for general purposes are m
awarded by local education authorities. Loans at the secondary level refer to the
to central government of administering and providing interest subsidies for C
Development Loans, which allow persons to pursue typically vocational courses
the aim of furthering their careers. These loans are made by banks and are repa
at a preferential interest rate, subsidised by the Department for Education
Employment. Loans at the tertiary level are made by central government an

repayable by those students whose income reaches a particular threshold level after leaving tertiary education.

Notes on interpretation

Finland: The distribution of subsidies between upper secondary and tertiary level is estimated. About 10 per cent of subsidies are for adults who have not been enrolled during the last five years and who study for general interest, personal development or because they are unemployed. Because of a system revision in 1992, no public subsidy is paid for those students who took their first private loan in 1992 or later. The loan-related subsidies reported refer to interest subsidies for loans taken before 1992, so they are diminishing every year (to almost zero by the year 2000).

Norway: Loans and grants are intended to meet such expenses as housing, food and study materials. They are allocated according to an official cost of living estimate. An effort is being made to provide a higher proportion of the total financial support awarded in the form of grants. Loans are repaid over a maximum period of 20 years after graduation.

Switzerland: Public subsidies vary depending on the different cantons. Tuition fees are very low or non-existent. Family allowances contingent on student status exist only for families in the agricultural sector. Direct public subsidies specifically for housing, meals, transport etc. do not exist, but indirect subsidies are very common (such as reductions on public transport).

dicator B4:

Educational expenditure per student

See also notes on Indicator B1.

neral notes

Notes on methodology

• *Reference period*

Indicator B4 refers to the calendar year 1994. For countries for which the financial year and/or the school year does not match the calendar year, corresponding adjustments are made. The size of the overall adjustment is minimised by adjusting either the enrolment or the financial data, as appropriate, to accord with the calendar year. For countries in which the financial year closely matches the calendar year but for which the school year is different from the calendar year, the enrolment data are weighted to match the calendar year. For countries in which the school year closely matches the calendar year but in which the financial year is different from the calendar year, the enrolment data remain unchanged but the GDP price deflators mentioned under B1 are used to match the financial data to the calendar year. For countries in which neither the school year nor the financial year matches the calendar year, the enrolment data are weighted to match the financial year and afterwards the above-mentioned GDP price deflators are used to adjust the financial year data to accord with the calendar year.

• *Influence of R&D expenditure on tertiary education expenditure*

Comparisons of expenditure on tertiary education, especially per tertiary student, can be misleading because the figures for universities and other tertiary institutions include substantial expenditure on research. The research share of total tertiary spending varies between countries, partly because of differences in the proportion of total national research and development (R&D) performed by the higher education sector.

Another reason why research spending distorts comparison of expenditure per tertiary student is that research outlays have not been included to the same extent in the tertiary expenditure figures of all countries. For example, while some countries have excluded separately funded or separately budgeted research, others, such as Hungary and Sweden, have essentially included all research outlays by institutions of higher education in their tertiary expenditure statistics.

A comparison of expenditure per student including and excluding R&D for selected countries is shown in Annex 3 of the 1995 edition of *Education at a Glance*. The results shown there indicate that research spending accounts for a significant portion of total expenditure on tertiary education. They also show that there is wide variation in the estimated research share of total tertiary expenditure. For the handful of countries that were covered by this comparison, the subtraction of R&D expenditure from tertiary education expenditure reduced the estimated expenditure per student ▶ amounts ranging from 14 to 37 per cent.

It follows that international differences in spending per tertiary student shown in th indicator, and in spending on tertiary education as a percentage of GDP shown Indicator B1, partly reflect differences between countries in the research roles institutions of higher education. The spending differences do not necessarily refle differences in the amounts spent per student to support the teaching functions tertiary institutions.

• *Estimation of unit costs using the approximation formula*

The estimates of cumulative expenditure on education over the average duration tertiary studies were obtained by multiplying Indicator B4 by an estimate of t average duration of tertiary studies. Using the approximation formula, the latter es mate was approximated by the rate of turnover of the existing stock of enrolmen obtained through the ratio of flow data (entrants and leavers) to the correspondi numbers of students enrolled. The formula $D = (S_{t-1} + S_t)/(Z_t + A_t)$ was used for t calculation, where S_t is the number of students enrolled at the end of year t, S_{t-1} the number of students at the beginning of year t (approximated by the number students enrolled at the end of the preceding school year), Z_t is the number students who are in their first year of study in year t, and A_t is the number of leavers the school year t (approximated by $S_{t-1} + Z_t - S_t$). Full-time equivalents have be used to estimate enrolments. The number of entrants to full-time programmes ▶ been used to estimate the inflow. All participants are included, even those who ▼ eventually not obtain a degree.

The estimate is based on a number of simplifying assumptions: First, it is assum that transition ratios are constant over time. Secondly, expenditure for the curr reference year is assumed to be representative for the total duration of studies. OE trend data indicate that real expenditure per student is fairly constant.

• *Estimation of unit costs using the chain method*

The estimates of cumulative expenditure on education over the average duration tertiary studies are obtained by multiplying Indicator B4 by an estimate of the aver. duration of tertiary studies. Using the chain method, the duration of study is defir as the sum of the probabilities, for each year of study, that a student who has ente tertiary education will still be enrolled in that year of study. So the duration defined as:

$$D = \sum_{i=1}^{10} q_i,$$ where q_i is the probability that a student will reach the i-th year of stu

i.e., the proportion of individuals in the i-th year of study relative to those studyin the 1st year of study $i - 1$ years ago. With the chain method all conditional proba▶ ties are derived from data of two adjacent years, the reference year and the prec ing year. Given the number of students s in the year i of study for the year t and number of students in the year $i - 1$ of study for the year $t - 1$ the transition rates be calculated for each year of study as $a_{i,t} = s_{i,t}/s_{i-1,t-1}$. The transition rates give each year of study, the probability that a student from year $i - 1$ will continue stud▼ in year i of study. The product of all transition rates 1 to i, gives the probabi▶ for year i of study, that a student who started $i - 1$ years ago will still be enro in year i of study. Finally, the sum of all conditional probabilities gives an estimat the average duration of tertiary education. Expenditure for the current reference ▾ is assumed to be representative for the total duration of studies.

Notes on specific countries

Coverage

Austria, Czech Republic, Germany, Hungary, Italy, Norway, Portugal, Switzerl Turkey: Figures cover expenditure on public institutions *only*.

Belgium, Greece, United Kingdom: Figures cover expenditure on public and gov ment-dependent private institutions *only*.

Finland: Figures for the pre-primary level *include* day care and pre-school educatio well as meals provided for 3-6 year-olds in day-care centres, generally 8 to 10 ho day, five days a week. All funds outside the budget of central government excluded from the figures for the expenditure on universities at ISCED level 6.

Spain: For financial data, students in open universities have been considered part-time students. Financial data for private institutions at ISCED level 6 *only include* university institutions.

• *Estimation of the duration of tertiary education calculated using the chain method*

Canada: The 6th year of study *includes* the 7th, 8th, 9th and 10th year of study.

Germany: In general, non-university tertiary education has a duration of 2 years, but part-time courses take up to 4 years. No distinction is made between part-time and full-time studies at the university level.

Greece: The 5th year of study *includes* the 6th year and beyond.

Italy: For non-university education the maximum duration of study is only 4 years. Part-time is not applicable.

Korea: Maximum duration of non-university education is 3 years. The 6th and 8th years and beyond are *included* in the 7th year of study.

Russian Federation: Data on part-time enrolments are *not included*.

United Kingdom: The chain method has been amended slightly in order to be able to use the available UK data. Average durations have been calculated separately using the chain method described above, for each of the main types of course at tertiary level. To take account of the fact that many students go on to take a further course after their initial course, these figures have then been combined according to the numbers of students following each of the main pathways at tertiary level. The total average durations shown for university and all tertiary levels are therefore weighted averages of the individual average duration for each type of course. Coverage excludes those studying in further education institutions, though these account for less than 10 per cent of all students at the tertiary level.

Notes on interpretation

Denmark: Expenditure on early childhood education is slightly *overestimated*.

Korea: A new adjustment factor for part-time students in tertiary education has been used this year.

United Kingdom: Expenditure per student in pre-primary education is higher than in the 1996 edition of *Education at a Glance*. This is mainly due to the use of an improved method of separating nursery and primary expenditure into ISCED 0 and ISCED 1.

Notes on methodology

Denmark: Kindergartens, all receiving substantial public subsidies, are classified as public institutions.

Hungary: The separation of financial statistics for primary and lower secondary education is estimated from the numbers of students enrolled.

Sweden: Only children 3 years and older in early childhood education institutions are *included*. Expenditure on the educational element and total expenditure on the age group, are estimated. Expenditure on primary and lower secondary education (*grundskola*) is not available separately. The breakdown between these levels is estimated from teachers' salaries and the numbers of teaching periods. The breakdown of expenditure on special education at primary, lower and upper secondary levels, and on municipal adult education, is also estimated. Students in municipal adult education have been converted to full-time equivalents at primary, lower and upper secondary education according to the type of course they attend. Full-time equivalents for students in tertiary education have been calculated according to the registered course load (as a percentage of a full-time course load). In the last edition of *Education at a Glance*, data for this calculation were not available and all students were counted as full-time.

Switzerland: Expenditure per student is very high at university level. This is mainly due to the structure of the university system: a high number of universities in relation to the size of the country (due also to the coverage of three language regions), the small size of some universities, the wide range of provision at each university, and therefore the relatively low student/teaching staff ratios. Furthermore, teachers' salaries at university level are comparatively high, and university expenditure also *includes* expenditure on research and development.

Sources

See Indicator B1.

Indicator B5:

Educational expenditure by resource category

See also notes on Indicator B1.

General notes

Notes on methodology

Initial public spending includes both direct public expenditure on educational institions and transfers to the private sector. Initial private spending includes tuition feand other student or household payments to educational institutions, less the portiof such payments offset by public subsidies. The final public and private portions the percentages of education funds spent directly by public and private purchasers educational services. Final public spending includes direct public purchases of edutional resources and payments to educational institutions, but excludes transfers households and other private entities. Final private spending includes tuition feand other private payments to educational institutions (whether or not offset public subsidies). Direct household purchases of educational goods and services excluded from the main calculations of initial and final portions of expenditure.

Notes on specific countries

Coverage

Belgium, Finland, United Kingdom: Figures cover expenditure on public and govement-dependent private institutions *only*.

Czech Republic, Germany, Greece, Italy, Mexico, Norway, Portugal, Switzerla Figures cover expenditure on public institutions *only*.

Ireland, Korea, Sweden: Data on expenditure by resource category refer to expeture on public institutions *only* but the figures on average staff and teacher compertion per student have been estimated on the basis of expenditure per student in public and private institutions.

Germany: Average compensation per student is *underestimated* in this indicator. Spayments which are included in the calculation of indicator B4 cannot be broken dby resource category.

United States: Figures on primary and secondary education cover expenditure public institutions *only*.

Notes on methodology

Denmark: The breakdown of expenditure by category is estimated.

Sources

See Indicator B1.

Indicator B6:

Public funds by level of government

See also notes on Indicator B1.

General notes

Notes on methodology

See also notes on Indicator B5.

Table B6.2 shows the distribution of public expenditure across public and preducational institutions. Since this shows only the proportion of public funds speprivate institutions and does not include private funds, this table gives no indicon the total distribution of private and public educational expenditure.

Notes on specific countries

Coverage

United States: Transfers from regional to local governments for tertiary educatio*excluded*.

Notes on interpretation

Australia: The mechanism for funding universities has changed. Previously, univties were funded by the Commonwealth Government through transfer funds tState Governments, which would then pay grants to the universities. Since 199Commonwealth pays grants directly to universities.

United Kingdom: In 1993 a large number of upper secondary institutions (Sixth Form Colleges and Further education Colleges) transferred from the control of local government to a new central government agency, the Further Education Funding Council. These institutions, which used to be regarded as public institutions funded by local government, are now classed as government-dependent private institutions largely funded by central government. Most programmes in these institutions are at upper secondary level, but a small proportion are at the tertiary level.

Notes on methodology

Hungary: Regional governments (counties) and municipalities have been regarded as local government agencies because regional governments have no significant redistributive role: they provide services which are not provided by municipalities in the region.

Japan: Expenditure by prefectures and municipalities (regional and local funds) cannot be reported separately.

Sources

See Indicator B1.

Indicator B7: Staff employed in education

General notes

Coverage

The coverage of support staff is still uneven across countries. In some countries, such as the United States, "other support staff" includes bus drivers, custodians, clerical staff, district administrators and other non-professional staff who in many other countries, especially in Europe, are under the auspices of non-educational authorities and are not included. For the definition of a teacher for the purpose of this indicator, see the *Glossary*.

Notes on methodology

In a manner different from the 1996 and 1995 editions of *Education at a Glance*, data on the number of employed persons in education are divided by the number of persons employed, not by the number of persons in the total labour force. Differences between countries in this indicator are thus less affected by differences between countries in unemployment rates.

Calculations are based on head counts instead of full-time equivalents.

Notes on specific countries

Coverage

Australia: Teaching staff *includes* some principals, deputy principals and senior teachers who are mainly involved in administration. Teachers in tertiary non-university education are *excluded*.

Belgium (Flemish Community): Primary and lower secondary education *includes* only primary education; upper secondary education *includes* all secondary education. Data on staff *do not include* staff employed in the Royal Military School or those employed in the Protestant Theological Faculty.

Denmark: Teaching staff *includes* principals and deputy principals.

Finland: Data on support staff do *not include* staff in kindergartens.

Germany: Data on teachers of the work-based component of combined school and work-based programmes (dual system) are *not available*. Data on support staff are not available for all levels of education. These data are only available for university education.

Greece: Figures are *underestimated* because part-time teachers in early childhood and primary institutions are *not included*. Secondary part-time teachers in private institutions are also *excluded*.

Japan: Teaching staff *includes* principals and deputy principals.

Netherlands: Teaching staff *includes* principals and deputy principals.

Norway: Teaching staff *includes* principals and headteachers.

Spain: Teachers in adult education programmes at primary and secondary levels are *excluded*.

Sweden: For primary, lower and upper secondary education, not only teachers ordinary comprehensive schools are *included* (*grundskola* and *gymnasieskola*), but a teachers in municipal adult education and in special education for severely han capped and mentally retarded students. Figures for teachers broken down by level education are estimates. "Support staff" *only includes* support staff in public terti institutions.

Switzerland: For university-level education, only teachers paid from the regu budget are *included*, while those paid from external sources are *excluded* (200-300 p sons, 100-150 in full-time equivalents). Primary and lower secondary teaching s *includes only* public institutions.

United Kingdom: Teachers in independent upper secondary vocational education a nursing and paramedical establishments are *excluded*.

Notes on interpretation

Switzerland: Teachers at university level are not only involved in teaching, but als research activities and services, in the following estimated proportions: teach 40-45 per cent; research and development: 35-40 per cent; services and other act ties: 15-25 per cent.

Notes on methodology

Denmark: Most figures are estimates. Not all teachers in non-university education not all teachers doing research at the university level are covered.

France: The numbers of teachers in private institutions of tertiary education and independent private institutions of secondary education are estimates. A signific proportion of educational and support staff has been estimated.

New Zealand: In primary and secondary education, most schools cover more than level of education, so that exact numbers of teachers at each level are not kno These have been estimated according to the number of students.

Spain: The distribution by educational level of teachers who teach more than level of education is estimated.

Sources

See Indicator B1.

Indicator B8:

Ratio of students to teaching staff

See general notes on Indicator B7.

Notes on specific countries

Coverage

Denmark: Adult education is *excluded*.

Finland: Data on teachers cannot be classified by ISCED levels of education.

Iceland: Part-time students are *excluded* from the calculation. The number of part- students is negligible (less than 100).

Notes on interpretation

Germany: Data on full-time-equivalent teachers in tertiary education are not avai at the moment. In view of the large numbers of persons on the teaching st colleges of health at ISCED 5 who hold another main employment, as well as te rary lecturers at universities, calculation using a provisional FTE coefficient for time teachers would lead to significant distortions.

New Zealand: The decrease in the student/teaching staff ratio for early child education as compared to earlier editions is largely explained by the impr coverage of data on staff in Maori pre-schools. In addition, in previous editio *Education at a Glance* data on teaching staff included some non-teaching manage time.

Turkey: Open distance education is *included* in non-university education.

United Kingdom: Teachers and pupils in independent upper secondary vocat education and nursing and paramedical establishments are *excluded*.

Notes on methodology

Germany: Since data on teachers of the work-based component of combined school and work-based programmes are *not available*, full-time students in combined school and work-based programmes are counted as part-time students (with a conversion factor of 0.4) for the calculation of the teacher/student ratio.

Sources

See Indicator B1.

dicator C1:

eneral notes

Participation in formal education

Notes on methodology

Statistics which relate participation data to population data are published for the reference date that was used by national authorities for these statistics. The assumption is made that age references in the enrolment data refer to 1 January of the reference year. Population data are, where necessary, linearly interpolated to 1 January as the reference date (which for most countries is a good proxy for the mid-point of the school year) except for **Australia** and **Korea**, where 1 July is used as the reference date for both enrolments and population data.

The dates or periods at which students, educational staff and educational institutions were counted have not been provided to the Secretariat by all countries. Some countries collect these statistics through surveys or administrative records at the beginning of the school year while others collect them during the school year, and yet others at the end of the school year or at multiple points during the school year. It should be noted that differences in the reference dates between, for example, enrolment data and population data can lead to errors in the calculation (*e.g.* net enrolment rates exceeding 100 per cent) in cases where there is a significant decrease or increase over time in any of the variables involved. If the reference date for students' ages used in the enrolment data differs from the reference date for the population data (usually 1 January of the reference year), this can be a further source of error in enrolment rates.

Participation rates are based on head counts of enrolments and do not differentiate between full-time and part-time enrolments.

Participation rates shown in Table C1.1a are measured as the number of students aged 5 and over enrolled in public and private education per 100 persons in the population aged 5 to 29. The numerator of this rate includes students aged 5 years and older (even older than 29 years), but excludes students aged 4 and younger. In order to calculate this enrolment rate by institutional type, the number of students younger than 5 must be excluded. The number of students younger than 5 by type of institution is estimated using the proportions of enrolment in each type of institution for all students. In cases in which the proportion of types of institution for young students is significantly different from the total proportion, this estimate is slightly biased towards the types of institution which are more important in early childhood education. In the case of **Germany** the figure is corrected using the real proportion of students younger than 5.

es on specific countries

Coverage

Australia: Private vocational education and some government-funded 'Industry Training Institutions' for vocational education are *not included*. Students doing Open Learning Courses and two private universities are *excluded*. The vocational education and training sector recording system does not separately identify apprentices so that apprentices are counted as part-time students rather than full-time. Data on early childhood education are now *included* (they were not included in the 1996 edition of *Education at a Glance*).

Austria: Non-university level students aged 30 and older are counted as aged 25-29. They represent less than 5 per cent of students aged 30-39. The age distribution by single year of age is estimated for primary and secondary education on the basis of corresponding data for the school year 1992/93.

Austria, **Germany**, **Norway**, **Spain**: Figures for government-dependent private institu tions *also include* some independent private institutions.

Belgium: In the French Community the data concerning entrepreneurship trainin courses are estimated; these data are *not included* for the Flemish Community. Data f independent private institutions are *not available*. Since institutions of this type are n very numerous, data for all types of institution are only slightly underestimated.

Denmark: Kindergartens and "age-integrated" institutions are classified as pub institutions. Although one-third of these are nationally referred to as private institu tions, they are mainly publicly controlled and managed, and the fees paid by paren are the same. Adult education is *excluded*.

Germany: Students pursuing doctoral studies are not obliged to register at univers and it is not possible to estimate their number. Trend data: For the period 1985- data refer to the former territory of the Federal Republic of Germany.

Hungary: Disabled students have been *included* in the figures for the primary and low secondary level of education.

Iceland: Part-time students are *excluded* for upper secondary and tertiary education

Ireland: Government-dependent private schools are not reported separately fr public schools.

Mexico: Mexico has an adult education programme in which 3 million students enrolled. Part of this enrolment corresponds to adults who have attended liter courses (persons who are at least capable of reading and writing a brief, sim account of their daily lives), and the other 2.5 are students with previous school (persons who have attended any compulsory level and can attend a job train programme afterwards). This programme is not formal, because its content is differ to that of formal programmes. For this reason, adult education is *not included* in the t enrolment of 26 million.

Netherlands: Only educational programmes with a theoretical duration of more t 12 months are *included*.

Spain: Students in adult education programmes at primary and secondary level *excluded*.

Switzerland: Students aged 40 and older are included in the age group 30-39.

United Kingdom: Data on vocational programmes at upper secondary level in in pendent private institutions are *not available*. Their number is quite small but negligible.

Notes on interpretation

Germany: Most private institutions are government-dependent.

Japan: Net enrolment rates exceed 100 for some ages because there are diffe reference dates for school enrolment and demographic data. Data in Table C1. enrolment rates for 15 to 29 year-olds now *include* students at the tertiary leve education, while they were not included in the 1996 edition of *Education at a Glan*

Mexico: Net enrolment rates exceed 100 in some years because there are diffe reference dates for the school enrolment and the demographic data.

New Zealand: The 5-14 year-old participation rate is over 100 because of a ce undercount. Education in New Zealand is compulsory from 6 to 16 years of age, an 5 year-olds attend school or pre-school.

Spain: Net enrolment rates exceed 100 in some cases. The reason lies partly i nature of the population forecasts by the National Institute of Statistics, and partly possible over-reporting of enrolments by schools.

Notes on methodology

Czech Republic: All data on enrolments by age are estimates (with the exceptic children in early childhood education). The so-called "extraordinary students" (st ing only some courses) are classified as part-time students. Adult students are c fied as full-time students, since they follow the same curriculum and take the s examinations as other students.

Denmark: All ordinary formal education is classified as full-time education. The ber of students refers to the number of persons enrolled on 1 October.

Hungary: Age distribution data (by single age) are not available for tertiary education.

Japan: Figures broken down by age are estimates.

Mexico: Teacher training programmes are reclassified as programmes at the university tertiary level. Job-related training is classified as lower secondary education. Figures broken down by age are estimates for tertiary education.

Norway: Figures broken down by age are estimates for primary and lower secondary education. The figures for participation in upper secondary and tertiary education for the school year 1994/95 are not directly comparable with the previous figures because of a change in the registration method. Until 1993/94 all enrolments were counted, so that students enrolled twice were double-counted, but since 1994/95 multiply enrolled students have only been counted once.

United States: No distinction is made between full-time and part-time students in upper secondary education.

Sources

See Indicator B1.

dicator C2:

Participation by young children

See also notes on Indicator C1.

tes on specific countries

Coverage

Austria: Figures refer only to kindergartens and pre-primary classes in primary schools. Day-care centres are generally *excluded*.

Denmark: Early childhood education *includes* children above 3 years of age in kindergartens, "age-integrated institutions" and pre-primary classes in primary schools. Children in crèches (normally below 2 years of age) are *excluded*. Children in private day-care/child-minding institutions are also *excluded*.

Ireland: Not all pre-primary enrolments are included, because data are not collected from many privately owned pre-schools.

Spain: Children in day-care centres are *excluded*.

United Kingdom: At ages 2 to 4, early childhood education refers to public nursery schools and to nursery classes in public primary schools. Children in educational programmes such as play groups and day-care facilities are *excluded*: data are therefore *underestimated*.

Notes on interpretation

Czech Republic: There are no private kindergartens.

Ireland, Japan, Mexico, New Zealand: See also notes on Indicator C1.

United Kingdom: Ages are calculated at 31 August, but children are counted in the following mid-January, so some children are actually older than their measured age.

Notes on methodology

Denmark: Age groups for children in pre-primary classes in primary schools are estimated. A small number of children enrolled in both kindergartens and pre-primary classes in primary schools are classified as enrolled in primary school.

Japan, Norway: See notes on Indicator C1.

Sources

See Indicator B1.

icator C3:

Participation in education towards the end of compulsory schooling and beyond

See also notes on Indicator C1.

eral notes

Notes on methodology

Calculations are based on head counts instead of full-time enrolments.

Notes on specific countries

Coverage

Czech Republic, Denmark, Hungary, Norway: *See notes on* Indicator C1.

Ireland: Persons aged 13 and over enrolled in special schools are classified as "n
allocated by level".

Portugal: Distribution by age does *not include* enrolments for Madeira and Açores.

Spain: Students in adult education programmes at the secondary level are *exclud*
Distribution by age does *not include* 300 486 students in upper secondary educati
and 42 984 students in tertiary education.

Sweden: Adult students in primary and secondary education are not classified by a
National schools for adults and students in schools for the mentally retarded are
separated into general or vocational. Thus, general and vocational do not add up
the total number of students. In the 1996 edition of *Education at a Glance* the figu
added up to 100 per cent, because the proportion of students in schools for t
mentally retarded was ignored.

United Kingdom: In the UK it is not the case that general and vocational strea
begin at the same age or are of the same length. Therefore, in order to make the
figures more comparable with those of other countries, vocational programmes ha
been regarded as 4-year programmes beginning at age 14 (the first two years of wh
are general education). Enrolments in private institutions for vocational programm
in upper secondary education are *excluded*.

Notes on interpretation

Japan: See notes on Indicator C1.

Luxembourg: Net enrolment rates by single year of age are *underestimated* since t
only include those students who attend a public or publicly funded school
Luxembourg. Students who are residents of Luxembourg but attend either a
publicly funded school in Luxembourg or a school in a neighbouring country
excluded.

Mexico: Figures broken down by level of tertiary education cannot be compared
figures shown in the 1996 edition of *Education at a Glance*, because teacher trai
programmes were reclassified in 1995 as university-level programmes.

Sweden: The proportion of 18 year-old students has increased. Since 1995, all edu
tional programmes (both vocational and general) have lasted 3 years instead of

United Kingdom: Enrolment in vocational courses is inflated by large number
adults taking one or two courses at the upper secondary level who are much o
than the typical age. Participation rates are slightly under-reported because of the
of reliable estimates of the number of enrolments in independent private institut
at upper secondary level (vocational and technical programmes).

Notes on methodology

Austria: The age distribution by single year of age is estimated for secondary ed
tion on the basis of corresponding data for the school year 1992/93. For the unive
level the age distribution is derived from data about studies in the current yea
reference. The estimates for the non-university level are based on disparate sour

Czech Republic, Finland, Greece, Ireland: Figures broken down by single age
estimates.

Mexico: Figures broken down by single age for first-stage university-level educa
are estimates.

Japan, Mexico, United Kingdom: See notes on Indicator C1.

• *Notes on Chart C3.1*

Austria: Participation rates at upper secondary level for students aged over 2
estimates.

Belgium: The distribution by age is estimated for students aged over 28 in s
advancement education.

Canada: Participation rates at upper secondary level for students aged over 2
estimates.

Germany: Participation rates for upper secondary students aged over 22 are estimates.

Hungary: Participation rates for students aged over 26 are estimates.

Ireland: Participation rates for students aged over 25 are estimates.

New Zealand: Participation rates for secondary students aged over 21 are estimates.

Portugal: Participation rates at secondary level for students aged over 25 are estimates.

Sources

See Indicator B1.

dicator C4:	**Rates of entry to university-level tertiary education**
eneral notes	See also notes on Indicator C1.

• *Calculation of net entry rates*

The net entry rates given in table C4.1 represent the proportion of persons of a synthetic age cohort who enter university-level tertiary education. The net entry rates are defined as the sum of net entry rates for single ages. The total net entry rate is therefore the sum of the proportions of new entrants to the university level aged i to the total population aged i, at all ages. Since data by single year are only available for ages 15 to 29, the net entry rates for older students are estimated from data for 5-year age bands.

• *Calculation of age at the 25th, 50th and 75th percentiles*

The ages given for the 25th, 50th and 75th percentiles are linear approximations from data by single year of age. The *i*-th percentile is calculated as follows: let age k be the age for which less than i per cent of new entrants are younger than k years of age and more than i per cent are younger than $k + 1$. Let $P(<k)$ be the percentage of new entrants aged less than k and $P(k)$ the percentage of new entrants aged k, then the age at the *i*-th percentile is $k + (i - P(<k) / (P(k) - P(<k)))$.

tes on specific countries	*Coverage*

Austria: Data refer to all first year students.

Canada, France: New entrants who have had previous education at the non-university tertiary level are *not included*.

Denmark: Adult education is *not included*.

Germany: Part-time education is not applicable in university education.

Hungary: New entrants aged 26 to 29 are reported as aged 26; 14 per cent of new entrants are classified as age unknown.

Netherlands: New entrants who have had previous education at the second-stage university level are *not included*.

Ireland, United States: Data broken down by age group are not available for students aged 30 and older.

Sweden: Data refer to new entrants both at non-university and university level. All registration in each term is done for each single course, and therefore when the students start it is not possible to know whether they will continue to a full degree or just take one or more single subject courses.

Sources

See Indicator B1.

icator C5:	**Participation in tertiary education**
	See also notes on Indicator C1.
es on specific countries	*Coverage*

Austria: See notes on Indicator C3.

Germany: In university-level education, only data on students at ISCED level 6 are available. Nevertheless, enrolment at ISCED 7 is quite small and does not have much influence on the results. Part-time is not applicable in university-level education.

Denkmark: The first part of the diploma in economics was upgraded from non-unive sity level to university level in 1995.

Notes on interpretation

Japan: See notes on Indicator C1.

Notes on methodology

Czech Republic, **Hungary**, **Finland**: See notes on Indicator C1.

Sources

See Indicator B1.

Indicator C6:	**Foreign students in tertiary education**
General notes	*Notes on methodology*

Students are classified as foreign students if they do not have the citizenship of t country for which the data are collected. Countries unable to provide data or estima for non-nationals on the basis of their passports were requested to substitute d according to a related alternative criterion, *e.g.* the country of residence, the n national mother tongue or non-national parentage. (See Notes on specific countrie

The number of students studying abroad is obtained from the report of the countr of destination. Students studying in countries which did not report to the OECD not included in this indicator.

• *Total balance of inflow and outflow*

The total balance of inflow and outflow (Table C6.4) is based on all countries wh reported foreign students by country of origin. All foreign students coming f countries which did not report these data and non-OECD countries are exclud Consequently the inflow reported here is smaller than the total inflow of fore students, which is reported in column 4 of Table C6.4. The reporting countries Austria, Belgium, Canada, Czech Republic, Denmark, Finland, France, Germa Hungary, Iceland, Ireland, Italy, Japan, Korea, New Zealand, Norway, Portugal, Sp Switzerland, Turkey, United Kingdom, United States. Across these countries the t balance of inflow and outflow is in absolute figures zero, and full comparabilit ensured.

Notes on specific countries

Coverage

Canada: Only students who come to Canada for the purpose of study are counte foreign students. Students with foreign passports who have lived in Canada bef and persons who come to Canada and start studying but declare themselves immigrants, are not counted as foreign students.

Denmark: The number of foreign graduates and the distribution of foreign student countries of origin are estimated.

Finland: Data on foreign students refer to universities only.

Ireland: Foreign students are defined by domiciliary origin.

New Zealand: Most Australian students are not counted as foreign students.

Norway: Foreign students are defined by country of birth.

Poland: The proportion of foreign students in Poland given in Table C6.5 is base enrolment data for the academic year 1993/94.

Turkey: Only students who come to Turkey for the purpose of study are counte foreign students.

Sweden: Students who are not registered in the Swedish population register (m from other Nordic countries), are *not included*.

Switzerland: Some foreign students at non-university level tertiary education ar *included*. The total number of foreign students is *underestimated*.

United Kingdom: Foreign students are defined by home address.

Coverage

See Indicator B1.

Indicator C7: **Patterns of participation in continuing education and training for the adult labour force**

General notes **Chart C7.2 and the following discussion:**

Notes on methodology

Data are based on the International Adult Literacy Survey (IALS), which is a household-based survey conducted in 1994 by Statistics Canada. In general, household surveys tend to achieve somewhat lower response rates than do surveys conducted in schools. The structured group setting in which school-based surveys are conducted both encourages participation and facilitates the administration of questionnaires and tests. In household surveys, on the other hand, efforts to secure participation must be made individually for each sampled household, and the time, date, and location of administration must be negotiated. Although a response rate of 80 per cent or higher is desirable, it is not uncommon for well-designed and properly implemented household surveys to achieve final response rates as low as 60 per cent.

In IALS, each country was obliged to draw a probability sample that would be representative of the civilian, non-institutionalised population of 16-65 year-olds. In six countries, the survey was conducted in the national language (see table below); **Canada**'s respondents were given a choice of English or French; and in **Switzerland**, respondents drawn from French-speaking and German-speaking cantons were required to respond in those respective languages (Italian and Rhaeto-Romanic-speaking cantons were excluded).

Language of tests, sample coverage and sample yield were as follows:

	Language of test	Population covered (ages 16-65)	Sample yield (ages 16-65)
Canada	English	13 676 612	3 130
	French	4 773 648	1 370
Germany	German	53 826 289	2 062
Netherlands	Dutch	10 460 359	2 837
Poland	Polish	24 475 649	3 000
Sweden	Swedish	5 361 942	2 645
Switzerland	French	1 008 275	1 435
	German	3 144 912	1 393
United States	English	161 121 972	3 053

IALS data for **Germany** were not included in this indicator, since the main question on participation in adult education and training was phrased differently from the other countries. Data for **Sweden** are not included because the question on the reason for which respondents had participated in adult education had not been included in the questionnaire, so that it was not possible to distinguish those taking courses for job-related reasons from the rest.

The International Adult Literacy Survey consisted of three parts: a "Background Questionnaire" providing demographic information about respondents; a "Core Tasks" booklet screening out respondents with low levels of literacy; and a "Main Tasks" booklet containing the main literacy items.

Response rates for the Background Questionnaire were as follows:

	Response rate (%)
Canada	69
Germany	69
Netherlands	45
Poland	75
Sweden	60
Switzerland	55
United States	60

Data refer to adults between the ages of 16 and 65. Students younger than 26 we excluded from this analysis. For further information consult: *Literacy, Economy and So ety: Results from the first International Adult Literacy Survey*. Paris, OECD and Statisti Canada, 1995.

Data are based on the following questions in the Background Questionnaire of the International Adult Literacy Survey:

– During the past 12 months, that is, since August 1993, did you receive a training or education including courses, private lessons, corresponden courses, workshops, on-the-job training, apprenticeship training, arts, cra recreation courses or any other training or education?

– What was the main reason you took this training or education? Was it for: car or job-related purposes; personal interest; other.

• *Chart C7.2*

– In total, how many courses did you take in the past 12 months?

• *The discussion of the average number of hours spent in the first course*

For the first course mentioned by the respondent:

– For how many weeks did this training or education last?
– On average, how many days per week was it?
– On average, how many hours per day was it?

Total hours were calculated by multiplying the number of weeks times the numbe days per week by the number of hours per day.

• *The discussion of providers of career or job-related training*

– Was this training or education given by: a university or other higher educat establishment; a further education college; a commercial organisation example, a private training provider); a producer or supplier of equipmen non-profit organisation such as an employer association, voluntary organisat or a trade union; a parent company; other provider.

Responses are for the first course mentioned by the respondent. Respondents w allowed to indicate multiple providers. Each provider indicated is given equal wei

• *The discussion of financial supporters of career or job-related training*

– Was this training or education financially supported by: yourself or your fan an employer; the government; a union or professional organisation; other fees; don't know.

Responses are for the first course mentioned by the respondent. Respondents w allowed to indicate multiple financial supporters. Each one indicated is given ec weight.

• *The discussion of medium of instruction for career or job-related training*

– Was this training or education provided through: classroom instruct seminars or workshops; educational software; radio or TV broadcasting; au video cassettes, tapes or disks; reading materials; on-the-job training; o methods.

Responses are for the first course mentioned by the respondent. Respondents were allowed to indicate multiple media or forms of instruction. Each form indicated is given equal weight.

- *The discussion of reasons for non-participation*

    - Since August 1993, was there any training or education that you WANTED to take for career or job-related reasons but did not? Respondents indicating "yes" were asked:
    - What were the reasons you did not take this training or education? Too busy/ lack of time; too busy at work; course not offered; family responsibilities; too expensive/no money; lack of qualifications; lack of employer support; course offered at inconvenient time; language reasons; health reasons; other.

Respondents were allowed to indicate multiple reasons for not taking desired training or education. Each reason indicated is given equal weight.

tes on specific countries

Tables C7.1a and C7.1b:

Notes on interpretation

Australia: These data are based on a different survey to last year's data, so that the data are not fully comparable. The survey has a relatively small sample, so that the standard errors are higher than normal. Households are primary sampling units, but only one person per household was selected for the survey.

Finland: Job-related continuing education and training covers employees' participation (in the past 12 months) in any employer-sponsored training programmes which employees attend with full or reduced pay or against full or partial compensation (in money or in time off) for lost free time. Job-related education and training also includes self-employed persons' participation in professional training, which refers to all training related to some trade or profession and the costs of which are borne by the participating self-employed persons or by the respective professional organisations, etc.

In the Labour Force Survey, employed persons were asked whether they had studied at an educational institution during the previous four weeks. There was no question on part-time and full-time studies. The number of employees who participate in employer-sponsored training programmes and self-employed persons who participate in continued professional training covers all employed persons who have participated in training for not less than 6 hours in the past 12 months.

Germany: The definition refers to courses planned and held which are listed in the questionnaire ("narrow definition"). Part-time education at ISCED levels 5/6/7 for employed persons is *included* if classified as "Weiterbildung" (Further Training) but *not* in the case of "Ausbildung" (Apprenticeship).

Training for unemployed persons covers only courses that are sponsored by the Federal Labour Office.

Italy, Spain, Switzerland: Part-time enrolment in regular education at ISCED levels 5/6/7 is *not included*.

Sweden: Data on participation in training refer to 6 months. Only training paid for or sponsored by the employer is *included*.

United States: Part-time enrolment in regular education leading to credentials is classified as non job-related training (even if the person concerned described it as job-related). Non job-related training includes: 1) English as a second language, 2) basic skills, 3) ISCED 3 credential for dropouts (GED), 4) part-time enrolment in regular education leading to a credential, 5) personal, and 6) apprenticeship (small numbers). Persons can be in both the "job-related" category and the "non job-related" category. These two categories should not be added together.

Sources

Austria	Labour Force Survey
Canada	Adult Education and Training Survey
Czech Republic	Continuing Education and Training
Denmark	Labour Force Survey
Finland	Labour Force Survey
Germany	Report System for Further Training
Greece	Labour Force Survey
Italy	Labour Force Survey
Luxembourg	Labour Force Survey, 1996
Spain	Labour Force Survey
Sweden	Labour Force Survey supplement
Switzerland	Labour Force Survey, 1996
United Kingdom	Labour Force Survey
United States	National Household Education Survey, 1995 (Adult Education File)

Indicator D1:

Statutory salaries of teachers in public primary and secondary schools

General notes

Tables D1.2 and D1.3:

Statutory salary costs per student C can be expressed as the product of three fact
as follows:

$$C = W * T/S = W * (t * T/S) * (1/t),$$

where W is the statutory salary after 15 years of experience, T is the number of f
time equivalent teachers, S is the number of full-time equivalent students and t is
annual teaching time of a teacher. The term $t * (T/S)$ is what has been called in the
the teaching time per student per year, or intended hours of instruction per c
divided by the number of students per class.

The difference in statutory salary costs per student between a particular cou
(referred to as country A) and the mean over all countries (m) can be decompose
follows:

$$C_A - C_m = (W_A - W_m) * (t * T/S)_A * (1/t)_A$$
$$+ W_A * ((t * T/S)_A - (t * T/S)_m) * (1/t)_A$$
$$+ W_A * (t * T/S)_A * ((1/t)_A - (1/t)_m)$$
$$+ I$$

where I is the so-called "interaction" and represents the sum of a number of te
involving the product of two or more of the factor differences.

The four terms shown here are precisely the ones which figure in Table D1.2. The
term can be interpreted as the portion of the difference between statutory salary c
per student in country A and average statutory salary costs that is attributable to
difference between the statutory salary in country A and the average statutory sa
the second term the portion attributable to the difference between the inter
instruction time per class divided by the number of students per class in count
and the average value of this over all countries, and so on.

The salary at 15 years' experience per student enrolled is calculated by dividing
statutory teachers' salary by the ratio of students to teaching staff.

The ratio of students to teaching staff generally refers to public institutions at
lower secondary level in 1995 (see Indicator B8).

Data on intended instruction time for students are relative to 1994 and are base
Indicator P11 of the 1996 edition of *Education at a Glance*. Data on teaching time
relative to 1994 and are based on Indicator P33 of the 1996 edition of *Education*
Glance.

Notes on specific countries

Coverage

Czech Republic: year of reference 1994.

Belgium, Greece, the Netherlands and Portugal: The ratio of students to tea
staff is based on 1994 data.

Belgium, France, Ireland and Portugal: The ratio of students to teaching staff is relative to all secondary education.

Denmark: For lower secondary education, public, private and continuation schools are *included*. For upper secondary general programmes, gymnasium, higher preparatory examination and higher commercial or technical examination programmes are *included*. For upper secondary vocational programmes, vocational education and training programmes at vocational schools are *included*.

France: Data refer to school teachers for primary education and certified teachers for secondary education.

Germany: All data on salaries refer only to the former territory of the Federal Republic of Germany. Data refer to salaries of civil servants, although not all teachers have the status of civil servants.

In vocational programmes at the upper secondary level, the majority of those who teach theoretical subjects are university graduates ("higher service"). But there are also different kinds of teachers for practical instruction who are paid less ("upper service") and who have to teach more lessons per week than the others. Only salaries of teachers of theoretical instruction are reported.

The German system of payment in the public sector has a component which relates to family status. The gross salary reported refers to unmarried teachers, but in general gross salaries are higher because the majority of teachers are married and have children.

Greece: *Only* overtime compensation is *included* as an additional bonus. However, there are further possible occasional benefits such as those for marriage and children.

Italy: *Only* teachers in state institutions are *included*. Additional remuneration, though it exists, is *not included*. Data for the upper secondary level refer to the most common types of both general and vocational education.

Netherlands: The ratio of students to teaching staff refers to both public and private institutions.

Portugal: Data refer to teachers having attended a three-year higher education course and professional training (Teaching Career Statute).

Spain: Some bonuses do exist (for example, bonuses for teachers in grouped rural schools or assistant teachers), but these are *not included* because they only exist in some Autonomous Communities and not everywhere in Spain.

Sweden: For general programmes in upper secondary education, figures refer to teachers of general subjects in both general and vocational programmes.

Switzerland: At the lower secondary level, "Mittelschule" teachers are *not included*.

Notes on interpretation

Belgium: It is difficult to provide a unified figure for teachers' salaries in vocational education programmes at the upper secondary level, as salaries at this level largely depend on the qualifications required for a given subject.

Czech Republic: "Other" criteria for salary increments *include* additional functions and specific responsibilities.

Finland: "Other" criteria for salary increments *include* overtime.

France: "Other" criteria for salary increments *include* teaching in a *Zone d'Education Prioritaire* or "établissement sensible" (school in a sensitive environment). Sometimes specific criteria are used at the secondary level: 5 per cent of promotions are left to the principal 's discretion.

Germany: Teachers with special tasks or functions can be promoted to the next salary group in some cases so that their gross salary is higher, although this is not counted as a bonus. The starting salary is related to the actual age of the teacher at the time, so that the number of years taken to reach the top of the scale varies.

Greece: 90-93 per cent of teachers have the reported gross starting salary. There is also a small percentage of starting teachers who have a salary bonus because of qualifications in different fields of study (doctors, engineers, etc.).

Ireland: Salaries *include* an allowance for teachers with a basic degree. In secondary education, salaries also include an allowance for teachers with the Higher Diploma in Education.

In primary education, a full-time classroom teacher with 15 years' experience cou receive one of the following additional bonuses: Vice-Principal; Post of Responsibili A Level; Post of Responsibility B Level. At secondary level, a full-time classroo teacher with 15 years' experience could receive one of the following allowances: Pc of Responsibility A Level; Post of Responsibility B Level.

New Zealand: Additional bonuses *include* an isolation allowance (a widely variab allowance), a staffing incentive allowance for teachers in specific schools with a reco of staff shortages, and the normal school allowance. Primary school teachers a unlikely to be eligible for more than a couple of the above allowances and therefc the maximum may be misleading.

Additional remuneration to which teachers are entitled when they take on sen teaching positions at primary level or management responsibilities at upper secc dary level are *not included*. The associate teacher allowance for teachers who assist classroom training of student teachers is also not included. "Other" criteria for sal, increments include relevant prior work experience.

Portugal: "Other" criteria for salary increments *include* passing a specific examination mid-career.

Spain: Salaries of teachers in primary and secondary education are the same. A 15 years' experience, salaries rise by five *trienios*. A *trienio* is a small supplement wh is added for every 3 years of service (in both public and private institutions). teachers in public institutions, another supplement is added: two *sexenios*. A *sexenio* new supplement added after every 6 years provided that the teacher has comple 100 hours of in-service training in that period of 6 years. The *trienios* have a differ value at different ISCED levels (and vary between public and private institution while *sexenios* have the same value at all educational levels.

The retirement age is 65. In primary and lower secondary education, it is assumed t teachers can begin their professional career at age 21 and can accumulate a maxim of 14 *trienios* (42 years). At upper secondary level, the initial training requiremen higher. It is assumed that teachers can begin their professional career at age accumulating a maximum of 13 *trienios* (39 years). But until 1995 only a maximum c *sexenios* was granted to public school teachers.

"Other" criteria for salary increments *include* being headmaster, deputy head, se tary, head of studies, head of a department or seminar.

Notes on methodology

France: Starting salaries refer to the third level of the salary scale, to salarie 15 years of experience at the eighth level, and to salaries at the top of the scale at last level ("*hors-classe*"). Residence allowances are *included*.

For primary teachers, additional bonuses *include* a starting allowance, the *Zone d'Ec tion Prioritaire* allowance, and the allowance for headteachers with 5 grades (excep the beginning of their careers). For secondary teachers, they include the star allowance, the *Zone d'Education Prioritaire* allowance, and the main teacher allowa (ISOE, flexible amount).

Germany: For the school year 1994/95 it was necessary to calculate averages from tl different salary scales which were in force successively during that time. At the lc secondary level, there are at least three types of teachers with three different sa scales. The recorded salaries are weighted means, with roughly estimated weight- the three main types of teachers.

New Zealand: Salaries at lower secondary level are calculated as the averag primary and upper secondary level salaries.

Spain: Each Autonomous Community has the right to determine the salaries c teachers (in accordance with the general guidelines for teachers' salaries in National General Budget) since they pay them from their own budgets. The teac salaries reported for Spain are obtained by calculating the weighted average o salaries of teachers at different levels of education and at different points in professional careers in all the Autonomous Communities. The variation between t is, in many cases, quite substantial.

Switzerland: Salaries vary considerably by category of teacher and canton. The data represent a mean weighted by the number of teachers in each category and canton. The number of years from starting to top salary varies between cantons: from 11 to 40 years in primary education and from 10 to 40 years in lower secondary education. Data represent a mean weighted by the number of teachers in each canton.

Sources

Austria: Salaries Act.

Denmark: Collective agreements.

Finland: Teachers' Wage & Salary Agreement of Municipalities, and Wage Statistics of Finland, October 1994, TWSA 1991.

France: Statutory texts.

Germany: Laws, salary tables, decrees.

Greece: National legislation established in 1984 and 1988 (Decrees 150 5/84 and 1810/88).

Italy: National legislation: PPCM 21/7/1995, DPR 399/88.

Korea: The Presidential decree on Public Servant compensation and allowances.

New Zealand: Teacher Collective Employment Contracts.

Sweden: National agreements, 1 April 1992 (valid until 31.3.95).

Switzerland: Salary statistics 1 January 1994, Swiss Teachers' Umbrella Organisation (*Association faîtière des enseignantes et des enseignants suisses*).

United States: Schools and Staffing Survey 1993-94 (national sample postal inquiry), updated to 1994-95 on the basis of changes in salaries of public school teachers in NEA survey.

Indicator D2:

Eighth-grade mathematics teachers' reports on their age, gender and teaching experience

See notes on Indicators F1–F4.

Indicator D3:

Eighth-grade mathematics teachers' reports on various school-related activities outside the formal school day

General notes

See also notes on Indicators F1–F4.

Data are based on the following question in the teachers' questionnaires:

Approximately how many hours per week do you normally spend on each of the following activities outside the formal school day?
- preparing or grading student tests or exams;
- reading and grading other student work;
- planning lessons by yourself;
- meeting with students outside of classroom time (*e.g.*, tutoring, guidance);
- meeting with parents;
- professional reading and development activity (*e.g.*, seminars, conferences, etc.);
- keeping students' records up to date;
- administrative tasks including staff meetings (*e.g.*photocopying, displaying students' work).

Although no specific definition of the formal school day is provided, the formal school day is to be taken as the time teachers spend at school on teaching and on other scheduled or timetabled activities.

Indicator D4:

Fourth and 8th-grade mathematics teachers' reports on average size of mathematics classes

See notes on Indicators F1–F4.

Indicator D5:	**Eighth-grade mathematics teachers' reports about classroom organisatio during mathematics lessons**
General notes	See notes on Indicators F1–F4.

The relative priority given to particular forms of classroom organisation was determined on the basis of the following question:

In mathematics lessons, how often do students:
- work individually without assistance from the teacher;
- work individually with assistance from the teacher;
- work together as a class with the teacher teaching the whole class;
- work together as a class with students responding to one another;
- work in pairs or small groups without assistance from the teacher;
- work in pairs or small groups with assistance from the teacher.

Respondents were asked to indicate whether each classroom organisational approa occurred never, almost never, during some lessons, during most lessons or dur every lesson. Data are based on self-estimates by teachers and not on exter observations.

Indicator D7:	**Eighth-grade mathematics students' reports on how they spend their da out-of -school study time** See notes on Indicators F1–F4.
Indicators E1, E2 and E3:	**Rates of labour force participation by level of educational attainment; Employment, unemployment and education; and Youth unemployment and education** See Indicator A2.
Notes on specific countries	**Denmark:** There are many special programmes and restrictions on the receip unemployment benefit for young persons who leave school without having comple upper secondary education.
Indicator E4:	**Education and earnings from employment**
Notes on specific countries	*Notes on interpretation*

Italy: Data refer to income from work after taxes.

Data for ISCED 0/1 for age groups 15-24, 25-29 and 30-34 are not reliable.

Norway: The data for 45-54 years of age refer to 45-64 years of age.

United Kingdom: Data are not available for 15 year-olds. The data for 15-24 yea age refer to 16-24 years of age.

Sources

Canada	Survey of Consumer Finances
Czech Republic	Microcensus, 1992
Denmark	The Register of Personal Income and the Register of Educational Attain of the Population
Finland	The Register-based Employment Statistics
Germany	German Socio-Economic Panel (SOEP)
Ireland	European Community Household Panel Survey
Netherlands	Socio-Economic Panel
Norway	Registers of Salaries and Taxes, Labour Force Survey
New Zealand	Household Economic Survey
Portugal	Lists of Personnel
Sweden	The National Income Register
Switzerland	Swiss Labour Force Survey
United Kingdom	General Household Survey
United States	Current Population Survey, March 1995

dicator E5:   **Internal rates of return at different levels of education**

eneral notes   Notes on methodology

The rate of return that may be expected for an investment in an additional level of education is estimated by comparing the difference in earnings for each education level across different age groups at a single point in time relative to the additional costs, both direct and indirect, of completing the additional level of education. The estimate is obtained by finding the discount rate which equates the present value of the additional gross annual earnings (over the 16-64 age group) to the present value of additional costs (including expenditure per student and forgone earnings) from attaining a particular level of education rather than remaining at the next lowest level. Various assumptions are made concerning the estimation of forgone earnings of students, the earnings of persons aged 16-24 and the growth in earnings of different cohorts over a simulated period of 50 years. For further details, refer to Alsalam, N., Conley, R. (1995), "The rate of return to education: a proposal for an indicator", in *Education and Employment*, Centre for Educational Research and Innovation, OECD, Paris.

tes on specific countries   **New Zealand:** Rates of return for the tertiary level may be inflated relative to upper secondary. This is because private contributions to education are *not included* in New Zealand's expenditure data, and these are much higher for tertiary students than for upper secondary students.

dicator E6:   **Unemployment rates of persons leaving education**

tes on specific countries   *Notes on interpretation*

Australia: Data refer to successful leavers in upper secondary education, and to all leavers in lower secondary education.

Canada: Data for "one year after completion" refer to the situation 2 years after leaving.

Czech Republic: Data for "one year after completion" refer to the situation 8 months after leaving.

Denmark: Labour force status is measured as the main activity during the last week of November 1994 about 1 year and 3 months or 5 years and 3 months after leaving.

France: Apprenticeship is considered as initial vocational education/training. Thus, there are no school leavers enrolled in apprenticeship, in particular at ISCED level 2. Young persons are considered to be school leavers at the end of apprenticeship.

Ireland: Data for "one year after completion" of higher education refer to the situation 6-9 months after leaving.

Portugal: Data for "five years after completion" of higher education refer to the situation 1-6 years after leaving.

Sweden: Labour force status is measured as the main activity during a specified week. Data for "five years after completion" refer to the situation 3-4 years after leaving.

Switzerland: Data for ISCED level 5 refer only to the future "Fachhochschulen" (20 per cent of all leavers from ISCED 5). Data for ISCED level 6/7 refer to leavers from ISCED level 6 only.

United Kingdom: Only England and Wales are covered. Labour force status is based on the self-reported main activity. Data for "one year after completion" refer to the situation 9 months after leaving. All leavers with qualifications are classified as ISCED 3. Those leaving at age 16/17 without qualifications are classified as ISCED 2.

United States: Data for "one year after completion" refer to the situation 5 months after leaving. Both successful leavers and leavers without graduation/diploma are *included*.

Sources

Australia	Transition from Education to Work, May 1995 (LFS supplement)
Canada	1992 Graduates Survey, Follow-up of 1990 Graduates Survey
Czech Republic	School leavers – job seekers at Labour Offices
Denmark	*a)* Register of Educational Attainment of the Population
	b) Register of Labour Force and Unemployment
Finland	The data are based on the combined data files of the Regional Employment Statistics and the Register of Completed Education and Degrees
France	Labour Force Survey
Germany	Survey on Graduates, 1993
Ireland	School Leaver Survey, Higher Education Authority Survey, 1995
Poland	Professional life of School-leavers, LFS supplement
Sweden	Entry into the Labour Market
Switzerland	Survey of leavers, 1995
United Kingdom	Youth Cohort Study, 1994
United States	Current Population Survey, October, 1995

Indicators F1, F2, F3 and F4:

Student achievement in mathematics and science at the 4th-grade level Student differences in mathematics and science achievement at the 4th-grade level; Gender differences in mathematics and science at the 4th and 8th-grade levels; and Differences in mathematics and science achievement between two grade levels

General notes

Notes on methodology

The Third International Mathematics and Science Study (TIMSS) collected data mathematics and science achievement in 44 countries at five grade levels, though every country participated at every grade level. The data on which Indicators F1, and F3 are based concern achievement outcomes in the two adjacent grades in e country in which 9 year-olds are most likely to be enrolled (for the average age of students tested in each country, see Chart F1.1). For most countries, the two gra tested refer to the 3rd and 4th grades of formal schooling. By convention, these target grade levels are referred to as the "3rd" and "4th" grade in this editio *Education at a Glance*. The reporting of data on a subnational level for United Kingdom is based on data availability from the International Association the Evaluation of Educational Achievement (IEA) and does not represent a p decision by the OECD. The term "country" refers to all entities for which data reported as a convention.

The data on which table F3.3 is based concern achievement outcomes in the adjacent grades in each country in which 13 year-olds are most likely to be enro (for the average age of the students tested in each country, see Chart R6.1, *Educati a Glance* (1996)). For most countries, the two grades tested refer to the 7th and grades of formal schooling. By convention, these two target grade levels are referre as the "7th" and "8th" grade in this and the 1996 edition of *Education at a Glance*. reporting of data on a subnational level for Belgium and the United Kingdom is b on data availability from the International Association for the Evaluation of Ed tional Achievement (IEA) and does not represent a policy decision by the OECD. term "country" refers to all entities for which data are reported as a convention.

Indicator F4 uses data from both the 4th and the 8th grades but includes only t countries which participated in TIMSS at both those levels.

The TIMSS achievement tests in mathematics and science are based on curric frameworks developed to cover the diverse topics and approaches common in countries tested. The frameworks pertain to three aspects of teaching and learni mathematics and science: curriculum content, performance expectations (*e.g.*, rou procedures, reasoning skills, and non-routine problem-solving strategies), and spectives (*e.g.*, attitudes and beliefs about mathematics and science). For a des tion of the TIMSS frameworks, see D. F. Robitaille, W. H. Schmidt, S. Raize McKnight, E. Britton, and C. Nicol. *Curriculum Frameworks for Mathematics and Sc TIMSS Monograph Number 1.* Vancouver: Pacific Educational Press, 1993.

• *Scaling*

The tests in mathematics and science are scored using models based on item response theory. The scale scores in mathematics and science (*i.e.*, the combined grade 3 and 4 scores) are standardised to produce an overall mean of 500 and a standard deviation of 100 for grades 3 and 4 combined, with each of the participating countries in the TIMSS study weighted equally.

• *Sampling and response rates*

Multi-stage samples were drawn for each participating country. IEA established a set of standards to ensure that the samples obtained in all participating countries were of high quality. (See M. O. Martin and I. V. S. Mullis. *Third International Mathematics and Science Study: Quality Assurance in Data Collection*. Chestnut Hill, MA: Boston College, 1996.) The sample for a country was classified as fully meeting the IEA/TIMSS standards if it met four conditions:

1. the national sampling frame for the country (the "national desired population") included the full national population of students at the two grades tested;

2. no more than 10 per cent of sampled students were excluded from testing for special reasons (*i.e.*, due to special education status);

3. the response rate for schools exceeded 85 per cent (or the combined school and student response rate exceeded 75 per cent) prior to the inclusion of any replacement schools; and

4. the classroom and student samples within schools were selected using a procedure that guaranteed that all classrooms and students at the designated grades had a chance of being drawn.

Twelve of the countries included in F1, F2, F3 and F4 met all four of these conditions at the 4th-grade level. These countries are: Canada, the Czech Republic, Greece, Iceland, Ireland, Japan, Korea, New Zealand, Norway, Portugal, Scotland and the United States.

Ten of the countries included in F4 met all four of these conditions at the 8th-grade level. These countries are: Canada, the Czech Republic, Hungary, Iceland, Ireland, Japan, Korea, New Zealand, Norway, and Portugal.

Countries that did not meet the guidelines at one of the grade levels are marked with one asterisk or with two, depending on the criterion they failed to meet: countries that did not meet all four criteria, but achieved a school response rate of at least 50 per cent before including replacement schools, met criterion 3 after replacement schools were included in the sample, and met criterion 4, are marked with one asterisk. All other countries are marked with two asterisks.

• *Calculation of country means*

The country means appearing in Indicators F2, F3 and F4 are based on all OECD Member countries which participated in the survey at the pertinent grade level(s); with each country in the calculations given equal weight. For purposes of computing the OECD means at 4th grade (and also at 8th grade for indicators in which the two grades are compared), a weighted average of the scores for the United Kingdom (England) and the United Kingdom (Scotland) was calculated and the resulting average was treated as a single country. For purposes of computing the OECD means at the 8th-grade level for Indicator F3.3, a weighted average of the scores for Belgium (Flemish Community) and Belgium (French Community) were treated similarly.

• *Calculation of OECD percentiles*

The OECD percentiles appearing in Indicator F2 are based on all OECD Member countries which participated in the survey at the 4th-grade level; each country is weighted in the calculations according to the size of its student population. Thus, the achievement scores of countries with large student populations, such as the United States and Japan, have more weight in the resulting OECD percentiles than do the achievement scores of countries with relatively small student populations, such as Iceland and Scotland.

Notes on specific countries

Notes on methodology

• *Countries/systems partially meeting sampling guidelines*

England: Achieved required response rate of 75 per cent only after including replac ment schools; and more than 10 per cent of the students were excluded from sa pling.

• *Countries/systems not meeting sample guidelines*

Australia, Austria: Did not achieve required response rate of 75 per cent.

Hungary: Did not comply with the guidelines for sampling classrooms.

Netherlands: Did not achieve a 50 per cent school response rate before includ replacement schools; and did not achieve required response rate of 75 per cent a replacement.

• *School and student-level sample sizes and combined school and student-level response rates in two grades in which most 9 year-olds are enrolled*

	% of population covered	% of students excluded	Number of schools sampled	Number of students sampled	Response rate before replacing schools (%)	Respon rate after replaci school (%)
Australia	100	1.8	178	6 507	66	69
Austria	100	2.8	133	2 645	51	72
Canada	100	6.2	390	8 408	90	90
Czech Republic	100	4.1	188	3 268	91	94
England	100	12.1	127	3 126	63	88
Greece	100	5.4	174	3 053	93	93
Hungary	100	3.8	150	3 006	100	100
Iceland	100	6.2	144	1 809	95	95
Ireland	100	6.9	165	2 873	94	96
Japan	100	3.0	141	4 306	93	96
Korea	100	6.6	150	2 812	100	100
Netherlands	100	4.4	130	2 524	31	62
New Zealand	100	1.3	149	2 421	80	99
Norway	100	3.1	139	2 257	85	94
Portugal	100	7.3	143	2 853	95	95
Scotland	100	6.7	152	3 301	78	83
United States	100	4.7	182	7 296	85	85

Indicator F5:

The social context and student achievement at the 8th-grade level

See also notes on Indicators F1–F4, and notes to Indicators R6–R10 in *Education Glance* (1996), pp. 372–374.

General notes

Notes on methodology

The data on which Indicator F5 is based concern achievement outcomes in the adjacent grades in each country in which 13 year-olds are most likely to be enr (for the average age of the students tested in each country, see *Education at a G (1996), Charts R6.1 and R6.2). For most countries, the two grades tested refer to th and 8th grades of formal schooling. By convention, these two target grade level referred to as the "7th" and "8th" grade in this and the 1996 edition of *Education Glance.*

• *Parents' educational levels*

Information about parents' educational levels was gathered by asking 8th-grade dents to indicate the highest level of education completed by their parents. Re are presented at three educational levels: finished university; finished upper se dary school but not university; and finished primary school but not upper secon school. The second reporting category (finished upper secondary school bu university) is complicated because, in many countries, particularly in Europe, there are several upper secondary tracks leading to university or other tertiary institutions as well as vocational/apprenticeship programmes. In most countries, finishing upper secondary school means completion of 11 to 13 years of education. In some systems, however, general secondary education may be completed after 9 or 10 years, followed by 2 to 4 years of full or part-time vocational/apprenticeship training that may be either included as part of secondary education or considered post-secondary. All of the upper-secondary tracks and any upper-secondary or post-secondary vocational education programmes included as response options are combined in the second reporting category.

Some countries also differ in their interpretation of what is included in the category "finished university". For example, qualifications obtained from post-secondary technical institutes and other non-university institutions of higher education are considered equivalent to a university degree in some countries but not in others. Therefore, completion of a course at one of these institutions may have been included in either the "finished university" or the "finished upper secondary school but not university" category, depending on each country's own definitions.

Finally, the proportion of "do not know" responses from students when asked their parents' highest level of educational attainment is more than trivial (see following table). More than one-fifth of student respondents in nine countries do not know their parents' highest level of education. Moreover, the proportion varies between countries, ranging from just 3, 5, or 7 per cent in several countries to over 30 per cent in some others. Casual observation of the relative performance of the "do not know" students on the IEA/TIMSS would suggest that, in most cases, their performance is most similar to that of students whose parents have attained the lowest of the three available levels of education.

- *Students from a different linguistic background*

Table F5.1 presents the percentage of students from a different linguistic background who are low achievers (below the 15th percentile). Detailed results are presented only for those countries in which more than 5 per cent of all students and more than 10 per cent of the low achieving students are students from a different linguistic background. Countries that do not fit these criteria are marked with a +. All countries show the same trend: among the low achieving 15 per cent of students, more than 15 per cent are from a different linguistic background. Countries with small national sample sizes of students from a different linguistic background are included in the country mean.

Indicator F6: **Fourth and 8th-grade students' attitudes towards mathematics**

See also notes on Indicators F1–F4.

Standard errors:

	Fourth grade								Eighth grade							
	Strongly negative		Negative		Positive		Strongly positive		Strongly negative		Negative		Positive		Strongly positive	
	Percentage of students	Mean achievement	Percentage of students	Mean achievement	Percentage of students	Mean achievement	Percentage of students	Mean achievement	Percentage of students	Mean achievement	Percentage of students	Mean achievement	Percentage of students	Mean achievement	Percentage of students	Mean achievement
Australia	0.5	6.1	0.7	4.7	0.9	3.6	1.1	4.4	0.3	8.3	0.9	4.5	0.8	4.3	0.6	
Austria	0.7	5.8	1.0	4.7	1.2	3.9	1.5	4.5	0.5	11.1	1.1	4.1	0.9	3.5	0.9	
Belgium (Fl.)	m	m	m	m	m	m	m	m	0.5	10.7	1.1	5.2	1.2	6.4	0.9	
Belgium (Fr.)	m	m	m	m	m	m	m	m	0.5	10.0	1.3	5.4	1.4	4.0	0.9	
Canada	0.4	8.4	0.7	5.1	1.2	4.2	1.1	3.5	0.3	9.1	0.8	3.5	0.7	2.7	0.7	
Czech Republic	0.3	~	0.9	5.3	1.0	3.7	1.2	4.4	0.3	10.4	1.4	6.1	1.4	5.6	0.6	
Denmark	m	m	m	m	m	m	m	m	0.2	~	1.1	4.8	1.3	3.5	1.4	
England	0.5	7.3	0.8	6.2	1.1	4.3	1.5	3.9	0.3	~	1.0	5.9	1.1	3.0	1.0	
France	m	m	m	m	m	m	m	m	0.5	7.7	1.5	4.5	1.1	3.2	1.0	
Germany	m	m	m	m	m	m	m	m	0.5	8.0	1.4	5.2	1.1	5.3	0.8	
Greece	0.2	~	0.5	10.5	0.9	4.4	1.2	4.0	0.3	~	0.8	3.9	0.9	3.7	0.8	
Hungary	0.5	7.6	1.2	5.7	1.1	3.8	1.2	5.2	0.3	~	1.2	4.1	1.3	3.7	0.6	
Iceland	0.6	9.9	0.6	5.5	1.5	3.9	1.6	3.6	0.5	~	1.6	5.5	1.5	4.9	1.2	
Ireland	0.6	6.5	0.8	4.4	1.0	4.5	1.2	3.9	0.3	~	1.1	5.3	1.2	5.3	0.9	
Japan	0.3	6.8	0.9	3.3	1.0	2.3	0.8	3.8	0.4	7.1	1.2	2.7	1.3	2.0	0.2	
Korea	0.4	8.5	0.9	3.1	0.9	2.6	0.9	2.7	0.2	~	1.1	3.0	1.1	3.4	0.4	
Netherlands	0.8	6.9	1.1	4.3	1.4	4.3	1.2	4.1	0.5	14.7	1.9	9.1	1.8	6.2	0.8	
New Zealand	0.6	7.1	0.8	5.7	1.1	5.0	1.3	5.8	0.3	~	0.9	4.4	0.9	5.0	0.8	
Norway	0.6	7.8	1.2	5.0	1.3	3.4	1.7	3.5	0.3	8.3	0.9	2.9	0.8	2.7	0.7	
Portugal	0.1	~	0.6	7.2	1.2	4.2	1.4	3.3	0.3	~	1.2	3.0	1.0	2.5	1.1	
Scotland	m	m	m	m	m	m	m	m	0.6	6.4	0.9	5.3	1.0	6.0	1.0	
Spain	m	m	m	m	m	m	m	m	0.4	5.9	1.0	2.8	1.0	2.2	0.8	
Sweden	m	m	m	m	m	m	m	m	0.3	~	1.1	3.3	0.9	3.2	0.7	
Switzerland	m	m	m	m	m	m	m	m	0.3	9.2	1.1	4.1	1.2	3.0	0.6	
United States	0.4	7.4	0.7	4.0	1.1	3.9	1.5	3.5	0.3	7.5	0.9	5.0	1.0	4.8	0.7	

Indicator G1: **Completion of upper secondary education**

General notes

Notes on methodology

Statistics which relate data on enrolments to population statistics are publishec the reference date that was used by national authorities for these statistics. assumption is made that age references in the enrolment data refer to 1 January o reference year. Population data are, where necessary, linearly interpolated to 1 J ary as the reference date (which for most countries is a good proxy for the mid-poi the school year) except for **Australia** and **Korea** where 1 July is used as the refere date for both enrolments and population data.

Graduation rates from general and vocational programmes do not always exactly up to the total, largely because of differences in the underlying typical age graduation.

Typical graduation ages are shown in Annex 1.

University and non-university degrees and qualifications awarded at the tertiary level

gree or qualification	Entry requirement	Duration	Cumulative duration	Equivalent to a university degree	Notes	Programme is classified in this column of Table G2.1:
ofessional qualification ormalschule, nkenpflegeschule)	Diploma from secondary school	3 to 4	3 to 4		German-speaking Community of Belgium	A
ndidaat	Diploma from secondary school	2 to 3	2 to 3	Yes	Entrance examination for civil engineering, music and performing arts, nautical sciences.	N
entiaat	Kandidaat	2 to 3	4 to 5	Yes	Degree awarded by hogescholen (long cycle) and universiteiten.	C
enieur	Kandidaat	2 to 3	4 to 5	Yes	Degree awarded by hogescholen (industrieel ingenieur and handelsingenieur) and universiteiten (bio-ingenieur, burgerlijk ingenieur and handelsingenieur).	C
otheker	Kandidaat-apotheker	3	5	Yes		C
darts	Kandidaat-tandarts	3	5	Yes		C
renarts	Kandidaat-dierenarts	3	6	Yes		C
s	Kandidaat-arts	4	7	Yes		C
rtgezette opleidingen	Einddiploma 2de cyclus	min. 1	min. 5	Yes	These programmes include aggregatie-opleidingen, aanvullende en gespecialiseerde studies.	D
toraat	Einddiploma 2de cyclus	min. 2	min. 6	Yes	Is the highest degree of specialisation at the academic research level.	E

gium (French ommunity)

duat-Régendat fessional ification-short cycle)	12 years, diploma from secondary school or entrance examination	3 to 4	3 to 4			A*
didature	12 years, diploma from secondary school and entrance examination in the application of science	2 to 3	2 to 3	Yes		N*
nce	Candidature	2 to 3	4 to 6	Yes		C*
gation nseignement ndaire supérieur	Licence or equivalent diploma	2	6 to 8	Yes		B*
nieur	Candidature	3	5	Yes		C*
torat en médecine édecine véterinaire	Candidature en médecine et médecine véterinaire	4	7	Yes		C*
rise diplôme valents	Licence or equivalent diploma	1 to 2	5 to 8			D*
orat	Licence or equivalent diploma	1 to 6	5 to 13	Yes		E*
gation de eignement supérieur octorat spécial	Doctorat (or licence in some fields)	2+	7+	Yes		E*

da

oma	Secondary school certificate usually required.	1	1			A*
ficate	Secondary school certificate usually required.	2+	2+			A*
elor's degree eral or pass)	Secondary school diploma (12 years, 13 years in Quebec and Ontario)	3	3			B
elor's degree ours), baccalaureat	Secondary school diploma (12 years, 13 years in Quebec and Ontario)	4	4			B
professional degree	Secondary school diploma (12 years, 13 years in Quebec and Ontario)	5 to 7	5 to 7		Includes minimum two years undergraduate before entering 1st professional.	C*
er's degree, mâitrise	Bachelor's degree (honours)	1 or 2	5 or 6		Some require thesis but not all.	D
rate, doctorat	Master's degree	3 to 5	8 to 11		Requires thesis to be deposited in library of institution of study.	E

University and non-university degrees and qualifications awarded at the tertiary level *(cont.)*

Degree or qualification	Entry requirement	Duration	Cumulative duration	Equivalent to a university degree	Notes	Program is classi in thi column Table C
Czech Republic						
Absolutoruim	Maturitní vysvedcení (12 years, secondary-school leaving exam, entrance exam)	2, 3	2, 3			A
Bakalár (Bak.)	Maturitní vysvedcení (12 years, secondary-school leaving exam, entrance exam)	3	3	Yes	Equivalent to a Bachelor's.	B
Magister (Mgr.)	Maturitní vysvedcení (12 years, secondary-school leaving exam, entrance exam)	4 (5 typical)	4 (5 typical)	Yes	Equivalent to a Master's.	C/Γ
Inženýr (Ing.)	Maturitní vysvedcení (12 years, secondary-school leaving exam, entrance exam)	4 (5 typical)	4 (5 typical)	Yes	Equivalent to a Master's.	C/Γ
Doktor všeobecné medicíny (MUDR) or Doktor veterinarní medicíny (MVDr), Inženýr architekt (Ing. Arch)	Maturitní vysvedcení (12 years, secondary-school leaving exam, entrance exam)	6	6	Yes	Equivalent to a Master's.	▶
Doktor (PhD)	Magister and an entrance exam	3	8 to 9	Yes	Equivalent to a Ph.D.	▶
Denmark						
Videregående teknikeruddannelse (Short-term higher education)	Successful completion of upper secondary vocational education and training or general upper secondary qualification [Studentereksamen, HF-eksamen, HHX or HTX (Upper sec. school Leaving Exam, Higher Preparatory, Commercial or Technical Exam)] Min. 12 years	1 to 3	1 to 3		Certificate is usually a final qualification for technicians, but can also be used to enter a Bachelor of Science (Engineering) programme (diplomingeniør).	
Korte videregående uddannelser løvrigt (Short-term higher education)	General upper secondary qualification [Studentereksamen, HF-eksamen, HHX or HTX (Upper sec. school Leaving Exam, Higher Preparatory, Commercial or Technical Exam.)]	1 to 3	1 to 3		Certificate is usually a final qualification.	
Mellemlang videregående uddannelse (Medium-term higher education)	General upper secondary qualification (Studentereksamen, HF-eksamen, HHX or HTX)	3 to 4	3 to 4	Yes	Awarded by teacher training college, college of education, business school, school of social work, school of engineering, school of journalism. Equivalent to a Bachelor's.	
Bacheloruddannelse (Bachelor of Arts or Bachelor of Science)	General upper secondary qualification (Studentereksamen, HF-eksamen, HHX or HTX)	3	3	Yes	One area of specialisation. Awarded by university, business school or other equivalent school or institution.	
Kandidatuddannelse (Master's degree)	General upper secondary qualification (Studentereksamen, HF-eksamen, HHX or HTX)	5 to 6.5	5 to 6.5	Yes	One area of specialisation. Awarded by university, dental college, school of pharmacy, school of architecture or equivalent institutions. Equivalent to a Master's.	
Kandidatuddannelse (Master's degree)	Bacheloruddannelse	2	5	Yes	One area of specialisation. Awarded by university, business school or other equivalent school or institution. Equivalent to a Master's.	
Ph.D. (Doktor)	Kandidatuddannelse lang videregående uddannelse	3	8 to 9	Yes		
Finland						
Ammatilliset opistoasteen tutkinnot/ Vocational diplomas at the tertiary level	Lukio, ammatillinen koulu tai perukoulu/Matriculation examination, upper sec. vocational or lower sec. general	2 to 5	2 to 5		The old education system.	
Ammattikorkeakoulu-tutkinnot (AMK)/Polytechnics degrees	Ylioppilastutkinto tai keskisateen ammatillinen tutkinto/matriculation examination or upper second. voc. dipl.	3,5 to 4	3,5 to 4	Yes	Bachelor level degree (the new education system).	
Kandidaatin tutkinnot/Bachelor's degree	Ylioppilastutkinto tai ammatillinen opistoasteen tutkinto/Matriculation examination or voc. dipl. at the institute level or equiv.	3	3	Yes	The new degree structure.	

University and non-university degrees and qualifications awarded at the tertiary level *(cont.)*

gree or qualification	Entry requirement	Duration	Cumulative duration	Equivalent to a university degree	Notes	Programme is classified in this column of Table G2.1:
aisterin tutkinnot ja st./Master's or equivalent	Ylioppilastutkinto tai ammatillinen opistoasteen tutkinto tai kandidaatin tutkinto	5	5	Yes		C
aketiet. lis. tutkinto ja st./Licentiate in medicine	Ylioppilastutkinto tai ammatillinen opistoasteen tutkinto tai kandidaatin tutkinto	6	6	Yes		C
sensiaatin kinnot/Licentiate degrees	Master's degree	2	7	Yes	Advanced research qualification.	E
htorin tutkinnot/Doctorate	Licentiate or Master's degree	4	9 to 10	Yes		E
koistumistutkinnot	Licentiate (medicine, dentistry, veterinary medecine)	4 to 8	10 to 14		Post-graduate specialised training.	E
ance						
evet de technicien périeur (BTS)	Baccalauréat or Brevet de technicien	2	2		Holders of a BTS may, in certain circumstances, continue their studies at university or higher schools.	A*
lôme universitaire technologie (DUT)	Baccalauréat or equivalent	2	2		Short course in technology offered by a university institute of technology. Holders of a DUT may, in certain circumstances, continue their studies in a university programme.	A*
lôme écoles supérieures cialisées	Baccalauréat or equivalent	2 or 3	2 or 3		Final qualification.	A*
lôme d'études versitaires scientifiques et hniques (DEUST)	Baccalauréat or equivalent	2	2		Final qualification.	N*
lôme d'études versitaires générales UG)	Baccalauréat or equivalent	2	2		First cycle of a university programme.	N*
ence	DEUG or DUT	1	3	Yes		N*
îtrise	Licence	1	4	Yes		C*
lôme écoles supérieures cialisées	Baccalauréat or equivalent	5	5	Yes	Award often serves as a professional qualification.	C*
lôme (of a school in a ticular subject)	Baccalauréat or equivalent, entrance examination taken after 1 to 3 years of post-baccalauréat preparatory classes	3	5	Yes	Award often serves as a professional qualification.	C*
gistère	DEUG or DUT	3	5	Yes	University diploma, multi-disciplinary in content.	C*
lôme d'études érieures spécialisées SS)	Maîtrise	1	5	Yes	Professionally oriented final qualification awarded after a year of research work.	E*
lôme d'études rofondies (DEA)	Maîtrise	1	5	Yes	First year of a 3-year programme involving a high degree of specialisation and training in research.	E*
teur en chirurgie taire, Docteur en rmacie, Docteur en lecine	Baccalauréat or equivalent	5 to 8	5 to 8	Yes	Awarded at the end of professional training and the submission of a *thèse de doctorat d'exercice de la profession.*	C*
tificats d'études cialisées (CES)	Docteur en chirurgie dentaire ou pharmacie	1	6 or 7	Yes	Post-graduate specialised training.	E*
lôme d'études cialisées (DES)	Docteur en médecine	1	9	Yes	Post-graduate specialised training.	E*
torat	Diplôme d'études approfondies (DEA)	3	9	Yes	Awarded after the submission of a thesis based on original research.	E*
ilitation à diriger des erches	Doctorat	3	12	Yes	Diploma awarded to doctorat holders who have proved their ability to carry out original research of a high order and to supervise young researchers.	N*
many						
ster/Techniker, ification of Trade and nical Schools	Successful completion of vocational upper secondary (dual system)	1 to 4	1 to 4		Most programmes require prior work experience. 3 and 4-year programmes are mainly part-time.	A

University and non-university degrees and qualifications awarded at the tertiary level *(cont.)*

Degree or qualification	Entry requirement	Duration	Cumulative duration	Equivalent to a university degree	Notes	Program is classif in this column Table G
Qualification of Specialised Academies	Realschulabschluβ	2	2		Only in Bavaria. Mainly kindergarten teaching, business administration, translation.	A
Qualification of Vocational Academies	Hochschulreife	3	3			A
Qualification of Health Schools	Completion of lower secondary general + prior vocational training/experience + minimum age 18	1 to 3	1 to 3		Non-academic medical training. Duration varies by specialisation: 1 year: Auxiliary medical professions; 2 years: Medical assistants: 3 years: Nurses.	A
Diplom (Fachhochschule)	Fachhochschulreife	4 to 5	4 to 5	Yes	Practice-oriented programmes in science, engineering, economics, and some social sciences which may include supplementary practical semesters.	
Lehramtsprüfung	Hochschulreife	5 to 7	5 to 7	Yes	Teaching qualification, degree for teachers.	
Diplom (University) and similar degrees	Hochschulreife	5 to 7	5 to 7	Yes	Includes Magister, Staatsprüfung, Künstlerischer Abschluβ, Kirchlicher Abschluβ.	
Promotion	First university degree	2 to 3	7 to 10	Yes		
Greece						
Certification of Vocational Training	Apolytirion lykiou (Secondary-school leaving certificate)	0.5 to 2	0.5 to 2		Awarded by Institute of Vocational Training (IEK).	
Ptychio-TEI	Apolytirion lykiou (Secondary-school leaving certificate)	3.5 to 4	3.5 to 4		Awarded by Technological Education Institutions (TEI). Includes training practice. Can lead to a post-graduate specialisation, Master's and Doctorate.	
Ptychio	Apolytirion lykiou (Secondary-school leaving certificate)	4	4	Yes		
Ptychio (Veterinary, Eng.)	Apolytirion lykiou (Secondary-school leaving certificate)	5	5	Yes		
Ptychio (Medecine)	Apolytirion lykiou (Secondary-school leaving certificate)	6	6	Yes		
Metaptychiako Diploma Spoydon (Master's)	Ptychio	1	5	Yes		
Didactorico Diploma (Doctorate)	Metaptychiako Diploma Spoydon	3	8	Yes		
Hungary						
Technician or other vocational certificate	12 years, érettségi	1 to 3	1 to 3		Integrated in the education system.	N (
Non school-based vocational certificate	12 years, érettségi	1 to 3	1 to 3		Not integrated in the education system.	
Oklevél (College diploma)	12 years, érettségi	3 or 4	3 or 4		More practice-oriented than university studies.	
Specialisation diploma (college)	Oklevél (College diploma)	1	4 to 5		Special supplementary courses.	
Oklevél (University diploma)	12 years, érettségi	4 to 5	4 to 5	Yes		
Specialisation diploma (university)	Oklevél (University diploma)	2	6 to 7	Yes	Special supplementary courses.	
Doctorátus (Law, Dentistry, Veterinary Medicine)	12 years, érettségi	5	5	Yes		
Doctorátus (Medicine)	12 years, érettségi	6	6	Yes		
Doctor of Philosophy (Ph.D.)	Oklevél (University diploma)	3	7 to 9	Yes		
Ireland						
Certificate (NCEA or DIT)	13-14 years, school leaving certificate (*ardteistmeireacht*) examination	2	2			
Diploma (NCEA or DIT)	13-14 years, school leaving certificate (*ardteistmeireacht*) examination	3	3			
Bachelor's degree (pass)	*Ardteistmeireacht*	3 to 4	3 to 4	Yes		

University and non-university degrees and qualifications awarded at the tertiary level *(cont.)*

gree or qualification	Entry requirement	Duration	Cumulative duration	Equivalent to a university degree	Notes	Programme is classified in this column of Table G2.1:
chelor's degree (honours)	*Ardteistmeireacht*	4	4	Yes	Covers a wider field than the "pass degree" and may take a year longer (*e.g.* science).	B
chelor's degree rchitecture, veterinary dicine)	*Ardteistmeireacht*	5	5	Yes		C
chelor's degree (medicine)	*Ardteistmeireacht*	6	6	Yes		C
aduate Diploma, Higher ploma	Bachelor's degree	1	4 to 5	Yes		B
ster's degree (taught)	Bachelor's degree	1	4 to 5	Yes		D
ster's degree (research)	Bachelor's degree	2	5 to 6	Yes		D
ctorate	Master's degree	3 to 4	7 to 9	Yes	It is sometimes possible to pursue a Ph.D. without having a Master's degree.	E
ly						
ploma universitario urea breve)	Maturità	2 to 3	2 to 3	Yes		B
enza accademia di belle	Maturità	4	4			A
loma di laurea (art, law, ogy, philosophy)	Maturità	4	4	Yes		B
oma di laurea iculture, architecture, tistry, engineering, rinary med.)	Maturità	5	5	Yes		C
oma di laurea (Medicine)	Maturità	6	6	Yes		C
oma di specialista	Laurea	2 to 5	6 to 11	Yes		D*
torato di ricerca	Laurea	3	7 to 14	Yes		E
an						
akushi (Associate)	Upper secondary	2 to 3	2 to 3			A
shi (Bachelor's)	Upper secondary	4	4	Yes		B
shi (Bachelor's- icine, Veterinary icine, and Dentistry)	Upper secondary	6	6	Yes		C*
shi (Master's)	Gakushi (Bachelor's)	2	6	Yes		D
shi (Doctor)	Shushi (Master's)	3	9	Yes		E
ea						
ficates or licenses	Scholastic achievement examination for the college entrance, high-school academic record, and an essay test	2 to 3	2 to 3			A
elor's degree		4	4	Yes		B
elor's degree (medicine dentistry)		6	6	Yes		C
er's degree		2	6 to 8	Yes	Duration of 8 years in medicine and dentistry.	D
or's degree		3	9 to 11	Yes	Duration of 11 years in medicine and dentistry.	E
co						
ma	12 years, bachillerato	2	2		Professional qualification.	A*
ciatura	12 years, bachillerato	4 to 5	4 to 5	Yes		C
cialisacion	Licenciatura	0.5 to 1	5 to 6	Yes		D*
tría	Licenciatura	1 to 2	5 to 7	Yes	Sometimes a first degree in certain subjects, but usually a higher degree or a professional title.	D*
rado	Licenciatura or Maestría	3	8 to 10	Yes		E*

University and non-university degrees and qualifications awarded at the tertiary level *(cont.)*

Degree or qualification	Entry requirement	Duration	Cumulative duration	Equivalent to a university degree	Notes	Program is classif in this column Table G
Netherlands						
Baccalaureas	11 years plus HAVO diploma	4	4	Yes	Degrees in teacher training, technical and commercial fields, social work, community education, health care, arts awarded by hogescholen (HBOs). Equivalent to US Bachelor's degree.	B*
Ingenier (ing).	11 years plus HAVO diploma	4	4	Yes	Degrees in engineering/agriculture awarded by hogescholen (HBOs). Equivalent to US Bachelor's degree.	B*
Doctorandus (drs.)	12 years plus VWO diploma or 12 years plus HBO-propedeuse	5	5	Yes	Equivalent to US Master's degree.	C
Ingenieur (Ir.)	12 years plus VWO diploma or 12 years plus HBO-propedeuse	5	5	Yes	Degrees in engineering/agriculture. Equivalent to US Master's degree.	C
Meester in de rechten (Mr.)	12 years plus VWO diploma or 12 years plus HBO-propedeuse	5	5	Yes		C
Doctoraat	University or HBO degree	3	8	Yes		E
New Zealand						
Certificate	12 years, sixth-form level and 17 years of age	.25 to 3	.25 to 3			
Diploma	12 years, sixth-form certificate and 17 years of age	2 to 3	2 to 3			
Bachelor's degree	13 years, NZ university bursaries examination	3	3	Yes		
Bachelor's degree (honours)	Bachelor's degree	1	4	Yes		
Bachelor's degree	13 years, NZ university bursaries examination	4	4	Yes	May be awarded with "honours" depending on the performance of the student.	
Bachelor's degree	13 years, NZ university bursaries examination	5	5	Yes		
Bachelor's degree	13 years, NZ university bursaries examination	6	6	Yes		
Post-graduate Certificates and Diplomas	Bachelor's degree	1	4	Yes		
Master's degree	Bachelor's degree	1 to 4	5 to 8	Yes		
Master of philosophy	Bachelor's degree (honours)	1	5	Yes		
Doctor of philosophy	Master's degree	2	6 to 8+	Yes		
Higher doctorate	Doctor of philosophy				Normally awarded on the basis of published work – at least 5 years after the Ph.D.	
Norway						
Professional qualification or diploma	12 years, videregående skole, generell studiekompetanse (upper secondary final examination)	1 to 4	1 to 4			
Hogskole-kandidat (college graduate)	12 years, videregående skole, generell studiekompetanse (upper secondary final examination)	2 to 3	2 to 3			
Candidatus magisterii	12 years, videregående skole, generell studiekompetanse (upper secondary final examination)	3.5 to 4	3.5 to 4	Yes		
Candidatus (+ name of field)	Candidatus magisterii	2	5.5 to 6	Yes		
Doctor scientiarum	candidatus scientiarum	2	7.5 to 8	Yes	Requires one year of course-work and a thesis based on independent research or a selection of 2 to 3 interrelated research reports.	
Doctor (+ name of field)	Candidatus	3	8.5 to 9	Yes	Requires original research, course-work and a dissertation.	
Doctor pilosophiae				Yes		

University and non-university degrees and qualifications awarded at the tertiary level *(cont.)*

gree or qualification	Entry requirement	Duration	Cumulative duration	Equivalent to a university degree	Notes	Programme is classified in this column of Table G2.1:
oland						
cencjat	12 years (general) or 13 years (vocational), secondary-school leaving certificate (swiadectwo dojroalosci) and entrance examination	3	3	Yes		
ynier	swiadectwo dojroalosci	4	4	Yes		
agister	swiadectwo dojroalosci	5 to 6	5 to 6	Yes		
karz (stomatolog and eterynarii)	swiadectwo dojroalosci	5	5	Yes		
karz	swiadectwo dojroalosci	6	6	Yes		
oktorat	Magister degree			Yes	The candidate must present a thesis offering an original solution to a scientific problem and pass three examinations.	
ktor habilitowany	Doktorat			Yes	The candidate must present a thesis constituting a considerable contribution to the progress of knowledge in a given discipline.	
rtugal						
charel degree	12 years, prova de aferição (aptitude test), provas específicas (specific examination for desired field of study), fulfilled course prerequisites	3	3		Awarded by polytechnic institutions and at universities offering training courses for teachers of basic education.	A/B
loma do ciclo básico	Same as bacharel	3	3			B
loma de estudos eriores especializados	Bacharel degree	2	5	Yes	Corresponds to the licenciado for academic and professional purposes.	C
enciado	Bacharel degree	2	5	Yes	Awarded by polytechnics.	C
loma do ciclo especial	Diploma do ciclo básico	2	5	Yes		C
enciado	Same as bacharel	4 to 6	4 to 6	Yes		C
strado	Licenciado	2		Yes		D
toramento	Mestrado	3 to 6		Yes		E
egarão	Doutoramento			Yes	Requires the ability to undertake high-level research and special pedagogical competence. It is obtained after success in specific examinations.	N
sian Federation						
oma of incomplete er education	11 years secondary school or 12 years of secondary-professional education	2	2		Awarded to students who discontinue their studies after 2 years.	
cialist's certificate	11 years secondary school or 12 years of secondary-professional education	4	4	Yes	Upon completion of the course, the student is granted the title of specialist in a given specialty.	
helor's degree		4	4	Yes		
cialist extended-cation qualification	Specialist's certificate	1	5	Yes		
ter's degree	Bachelor's degree	2	6	Yes		
rnatura	Bachelor's degree in Medicine	1	7	Yes		
didat nauk	Master's degree	3	9	Yes	Requires public defence of an independently elaborated thesis and by final examinations.	
or nauk	Kandidat nauk	3	12	Yes	Requires defence of thesis offering new solutions to a major scientific/academic problem which is of substantial importance to the given field or discipline.	
n						
ico Superior	Bachillerato	2	2			A
omado	Bachillerato or vocational training	3	3	Yes	Vocationally oriented.	B
itecto Técnico, Ingenier ico	Bachillerato or vocational training	3	3	Yes	Vocationally oriented.	B
er Ciclo de Licenciatura, ería and Arquitectura	Bachillerato or vocational training	2 or 3	2 or 3	Yes	Academically oriented. Leads to award of a certificate that has a professional equivalence to Diplomado when working in the Public Admininistration.	N

University and non-university degrees and qualifications awarded at the tertiary level *(cont.)*

Degree or qualification	Entry requirement	Duration	Cumulative duration	Equivalent to a university degree	Notes	Programme is classified in this column Table G2
Licenciado and Ingeniero	Primer Ciclo de Licenciatura or Ingeniería. Diplomado or Ingeniero Técnico	2 or 3	4 or 5	Yes		
Arquitecto	Primer Ciclo de Arquitectura	2 or 3	5	Yes		
Licenciado Medicina	Primer Ciclo de Medicina	3	6	Yes		
Doctorado	Licenciado, Arquitecto, Ingeniero or university programmes lasting more than 4 years	2	6, 7, 8	Yes	Doctorado required from teaching staff holding univ. chairs and associate staff with permanent contracts.	
Post grado and Master	Licenciado, Arquitecto, Ingeniero	1 or 2	6 or 7			
Especialidades Sanitarias	Licenciado Medicina, Farmacia, Química, Biología, Psicología	3 or 4	8 to 10			
Sweden						
Högskoleexamen (diploma)	12 years, secondary-school leaving certificate or be 25 years of age and have 4 years of professional experience and a good reading knowledge of English	2 to 2.5	2 to 2.5	Some, see note	Some programmes longer than 3 years are classified as C/D. The 2-year engineering programme can be intermediate (though this is infrequent) and continued to a civil engineering degree.	A/B/C
Kandidatexamen (Bachelor's degree)	13 years, secondary-school leaving certificate or be 25 years of age and have 4 years of professional experience and a good reading knowledge of English	3 to 3.5	3 to 3.5	Yes		
Magisterexamen (Master's degree)	13 years, secondary-school leaving certificate or be 25 years of age and have 4 years of professional experience and a good reading knowledge of English	4 to 5.5	4 to 5.5	Yes	Counted as category D if earned after a first university degree.	C
Yrkesexamen (professional degrees)	13 years, secondary-school leaving certificate or be 25 years of age and have 4 years of professional experience and a good reading knowledge of English	1 to 5.5	1 to 5.5	Some, see note		A/B/C
Licenciatexamen	Degree of at least 3 years' duration	2 to 2.5	5 to 5.5	Yes	All degrees are reported as category E though persons who earn a Doctor's degree after a Licentiate degree will not be double-counted.	
Doktorsexamen	Degree of at least 3 years' duration	4	7	Yes		
Switzerland						
Fachausweis Brevet (or equivalent certificate)	13 ans; Certificat de capacité (ISCED 3); several years of vocational exp.	1 to 3	1 to 3		Frequently modular structure and studied while working; exams organised by professional associations; qualifications recognised by the Confederation.	
Fachdiplom/Diplôme Meister/Maître (or equivalent certificate)	13 ans; Certificat de capacité (ISCED 3) or Brevet (ISCED 5); several years of vocational exp.	1 to 3	1 to 4		Frequently modular structure and studied while working; exams organised by professional associations; qualifications recognised by the Confederation.	
Techniker TS/Technicien ET Diplom FS/Diplômes équivalents	13 ans; Certificat de capacité (ISCED 3) or equiv. attestation	2 to 3	2 to 3		ET = École technique.	
Diplom Höhere Fachschule/Diplôme École supérieure Ingenieurschule/École technique supérieure	13 ans; Certificat de capacité (ISCED 3) or vocational Maturité or equiv. attestation	3 to 4	3 to 4		From 1997, some Écoles supérieures (Höhere Fachschulen) will become specialised Hautes écoles (Fachhochschulen). Various post-graduate diplomas.	
Diplom Fachhochschule/Diplôme Haute école spécialisée	13 ans; vocational Maturité or Maturité + voc. training	3 to 4	3 to 4	Yes	First foundation of specialised Hautes écoles (Fachhochschulen) in 1997; first diplomas will be delivered in year 2000.	N
Lizentiat Universität/Licence Université	13 ans, Maturité	4 to 6/7	4 to 6/7	Yes	For licence and diplôme, thesis of 50-200 pages required.	

University and non-university degrees and qualifications awarded at the tertiary level *(cont.)*

gree or qualification	Entry requirement	Duration	Cumulative duration	Equivalent to a university degree	Notes	Programme is classified in this column of Table G2.1:
aatsexamen ledizin)/Diplôme fédéral édecine)					Several post-graduate diplomas.	
olom Hochschule/Diplôme ute École						
ktorat/Doctorat	Licence Université, Diplôme Haute École, Diplôme fédéral (médecine)	1 to 5	5 to 11	Yes		E
rkey						
lisans diplomasi ssociate's degree)	11-12, lise diplomasi and the university entrance exam	2	2		Awarded by 2-year vocational schools.	B
ans diplomasi (Bachelor's gree)	11-12, lise diplomasi and the university entrance exam	4	4	Yes		B/C*
ans diplomasi (dentistry d veterinary medeicine)	11-12, lise diplomasi and the university entrance exam	5	5	Yes		C*
ans diplomasi (medicine)	11-12, lise diplomasi and the university entrance exam	6	6	Yes		C*
sek lisans diplomasi ister's degree taught or earch)	Lisans diplomasi	2	6	Yes		E/D
atta yeterlik (proficiency in	Yüksek lisans diplomasi	3 to 5	9 to 11	Yes	Equivalent in fine arts of the Doktora, although instead of a thesis based on scholarly research, the candidate's works of art are evaluated by a jury.	E
a uzmanlik	Lisans diplomasi			Yes	Equivalent in medicine of Doktora in other fields.	E
tora (Doctorate)	Yüksek lisans diplomasi	2 to 4	8 to 10	Yes		
ted Kingdom						
er national certificate	13 years, GCE A level or equivalent	1	1		Advanced technical training.	A
er national diploma	13 years, GCE A level or equivalent	2	2		Advanced technical training.	A
elor's degree	13 years, GCE A level or equivalent	3	3	Yes	An honours degree is at a higher level than an ordinary or pass degree. May include a sandwich course which incorporates periods of industrial training or professional experience outside the university.	B
elor's Degree (MB, BDS, tc.)	13 years, GCE A level or equivalent	5 to 7	5 to 7	Yes	Medicine, Veterinary Medicine, and Dentistry.	B
graduate Diplomas and ficates (including PGCE)	Bachelor's degree	1	4	Yes		D
essional qualifications in us fields (accountancy, audit etc.)	Bachelor's degree	1 to 3	4 to 6	Yes	Training takes place "on the job", but certification usually involves taking an examination through a professional body.	D
er's degree (taught)	Bachelor's degree (honours)	1 to 2	4 to 5	Yes	Award based on a written examination requires a memoir or short thesis.	D
er's degree (research)	Bachelor's degree (honours)	1 to 2	4 to 5	Yes	Award based on research and presentation of a thesis.	D
orates	Bachelor's degree (honours)	2 to 4	7 to 9	Yes		E
d States						
secondary awards, cates, and diplomas	Typically 12 years, High school diploma or equivalent (not always required)	1 to 4	1 to 4		Certificate is usually a final qualification for technicians.	A
ciate of Arts or Associate ence Degree (A.A. or	Typically 12 years, High school diploma or equivalent (not always required)	2	2		Possible to receive credit for first 2 years of a Bachelor's degree programme.	A
elor of Arts or Bachelor of ce Degree (B.A. or B.S.)	12 years, High school diploma or equivalent	4	4	Yes	Two components: general education (humanities, social sciences, applied or natural sciences and fine arts) and an area of specialisation or major.	B
graduate certificates (e.g. ng Credential)	Bachelor's degree	1	5	Yes		N

University and non-university degrees and qualifications awarded at the tertiary level *(cont.)*

Degree or qualification	Entry requirement	Duration	Cumulative duration	Equivalent to a university degree	Notes	Programme is classified in this column Table G2
Master of Arts, Science, Fine Arts, etc. (M.A., M.S., M.F.A)	Bachelor's degree	1 to 2	5 to 6	Yes	Duration varies by field and institution.	D
Master of Business Administration, Public Administration, Public Health etc.	Bachelor's degree	1 to 2	5 to 6	Yes	Awarded for the completion of a professionally-oriented programme.	D
First professional degrees: Juris Doctorate (J.D. – Law), Pharm.D. (Pharmacy), Master of Divinity Degree	Bachelor's degree	3	7	Yes	Signifies both completion of the academic requirements for beginning practice in a given profession and a level of professional skill beyond that normally required for a Bachelor's degree.	D
First professional degrees: Doctor of Medicine (M.D.), Doctor of Dentistry (D.D.S), Doctor of Veterinary Medicine	Bachelor's degree	4	8	Yes		D
Doctorate of philosophy (Ph.D.)	Master's degree	3 to 5	9 to 11	Yes	If a Master's degree is not required, then duration of programme is longer.	E

Category in which programme is classified in Indicator G2:

A = Non-university tertiary programmes.

B = Short first university degree programmes.

C = Long first university degree programmes.

D = Second university degree programmes.

E = Ph.D. or equivalent.

N = Not included.

* Missing or included in another column in this year's data collection.

Notes on specific countries

Coverage

Denmark: Adult education is *excluded*.

Hungary: The number of upper secondary graduates *includes* all those in the last yea study. As a consequence, the number of graduates is *overestimated* because of dou counting of repeaters and inclusion of those students who fail.

Italy: Graduates of regional vocational programmes are *excluded* (they were include the 1996 edition of *Education at a Glance*).

Spain: Adult education graduates from vocational programmes are *included* for the time (they were not included in the 1996 edition of *Education at a Glance*).

Sweden: For graduates from vocational programmes, only the gymnasium is incl adult education is *excluded*.

Notes on interpretation

Belgium (Flemish Community): Graduation rates obtained are subject to bias for t reasons: *i)* presence of double counting, particularly for part-time programme diplomas in part-time programmes are awarded to students whose age is much hi than the typical age; and *iii)*many diplomas are awarded to students aged over 19 years.

Ireland: Students graduating from some vocational programmes receive only a ce cate of participation, not a formal qualification; however, there are changes unde in this regard. Students of first educational programmes at this level have us completed 12 years of education, and students in second educational progran have usually completed 14-15 years of education.

Norway: In contrast to the 1996 edition of *Education at a Glance*, apprenticeships are *included* in the data. The data for 1994/95 are more correct, but are not fully compa with the previous edition.

Sweden: The number of graduates has decreased. Since 1995, all educational programmes (both vocational and general) last for 3 years instead of 2. Because of this, 18 year-old students did not graduate in 1995 but stayed enrolled and graduated in the following year. This mainly affects vocational programmes.

Notes on methodology

Finland: For graduates from combined school and work-based programmes, the age distribution is estimated. Graduates from second educational programmes are *included* in first educational programmes. Their number is insignificant.

Germany: The reference date for the relative population data is the end of a school/academic year (mid-year). The population data for this reference date are calculated by linear interpolation of data at the end of the year.

Hungary: The number of upper-secondary graduates *includes* all those in the last year of study.

Switzerland: Figures for graduates from final programmes are estimated.

Sources

See Indicator B1.

dicator G2:

Graduates at the tertiary level

neral notes

Notes on methodology

The results are now shown for each type of tertiary programme: non-university tertiary education and university-level education, short programmes, long programmes, second programmes (*e.g.* US Master's), Ph.D. or equivalent programmes.

• *Calculation of the country mean for short and long university-level programmes*

Countries which included the graduates of short university-level programmes together with the graduates of long university-level programmes (*x*-code for short programmes) are counted as zero for the calculation of the country mean for short programmes. In a similar manner, the countries using an *x*-code for long programmes, caused by inclusion of long programmes in the category for short programmes, are counted as zero for the country average for long programmes. This is necessary to ensure that the country averages for short programmes and long programmes add up to the correct country average for all first stage university programmes. The country averages cannot be compared with figures shown in the 1996 edition of *Education at a Glance*.

• *Calculation of age at the 25th, 50th and 75th percentiles*

The ages given for the 25th, 50th and 75th percentiles are linear approximations from data by single year of age. The *i*-th percentile is calculated as follows: let age k be the age for which less than i per cent of new entrants are younger than k years of age and more than i per cent are younger than $k + 1$. Let $P(<k)$ be the percentage of new entrants aged less than k and $P(k)$ the percentage of new entrants aged k, then the age at the *i*-th percentile is $k + (i - P(<k) / (P(k) - P(<k)))$.

Typical graduation ages are shown in Annex 1.

es on specific countries

Coverage

Austria: Data for the non-university level correspond to the calendar year 1994.

Belgium (Flemish Community): Data on the age of graduates of non-university tertiary education only refer to school-based non-university higher education.

Canada, New Zealand, United Kingdom: At ISCED 6, graduates from long programmes are *included* in short programmes.

Denmark: Adult education is *excluded*.

Ireland: The following are *excluded*: full-time accountancy students who receive qualifications from professional associations; a significant number of part-time students in non-university tertiary education who receive professional qualifications from professional bodies (accountancy, marketing, secretarial); about 1 500 student nurses, who obtain a nursing qualification after completing 3-4 years of on-the-job training hospitals; and graduates from independent private colleges. Only first-time graduat« are *included* (unduplicated counts).

Italy: The age distribution used to estimate the net graduation rates for 1995 estimated from the age distribution of Italian graduates in 1993.

Portugal: Doctorates are *not included*: the graduation rate at ISCED 7 is therefo *underestimated.*

Spain: Master's or equivalent degrees at ISCED 7 are *included* in long programmes ISCED 6.

Sweden: Second degrees awarded at ISCED 6 are *included* in ISCED 7 as Master's equivalent (programmes of 3 to 5.5 years' duration).

Notes on interpretation

Canada: See notes on Indicator C5.

Czech Republic: A Bachelor's degree has been introduced. In some universities i« awarded after 3 years of study, which can be followed by a Master's degree (after additional 2 or 3 years). In others, the first degree is the Master's degree, typicɑ awarded after 5 years of study. Both types of Master's degrees are classified as a f degree for the purpose of this indicator (there is no distinction between the two typ neither in the length of study, nor in the amount of knowledge attained).

Denmark: There are no Bachelor's degrees in some fields of study (*e.g.* medicine ɑ law), so that the first university degree obtainable is the Master's degree. The r classifications of university graduates vary therefore according to subjects.

Greece: First-degree programmes in medicine last 6 years. Engineering studies ⊫ 5 years and lead to a diploma which is a first degree but equivalent to a Master's. Pc graduate studies do not set limits to starting or ending ages and their minim« duration is 2 years for the equivalent of a Master's and 3 years for the equivalent ɑ Ph.D.

Mexico: Figures broken down by level of tertiary education cannot be compared v figures shown in the 1996 edition of *Education at a Glance*, because teacher-trair programmes were reclassified in 1995 as university-level programmes.

Netherlands: Short first university degree programmes refer to Higher Professic Education (HBO). Long first university degree programmes refer to the normal university programmes leading to titles such as Drs., Mr. or Ir. (WO). In Table (graduates from short first university degree programmes are *included* with graduɑ from long programmes.

Norway: Some programmes at the non-university tertiary level of education one year, while others last two years.

Sweden: A number of supplementary courses, especially in the field of health c are no longer regarded as leading to separate qualifications. Therefore the numbe graduations has decreased compared with the 1996 edition of *Education at a Glanc*

United Kingdom: Because of a change in the data source, some qualifications ⊦ been reclassified from non-university to university level. The breakdown by leve tertiary education cannot be compared with figures shown in the 1996 editio *Education at a Glance*. The ages of graduates for the academic year 1994/95 ⱴ recorded at the start of the academic year (*i.e.* 31 August 1994). Since most of t⊦ students will have graduated in June/July 1995 the age at graduation is aroun« months older than the reported age.

Notes on methodology

Germany: See notes on Indicator G1.

Ireland: Figures on full-time and part-time graduates are estimates, based on from the first destination survey of full-time students only.

Sources

See Indicator B1.

ndicator G3: **Tertiary qualifications by field of study**

eneral notes

Notes on methodology

In accordance with ISCED the following classification of subject categories has been used:

Medical science" includes "Medical science and health-related" (ISC50)

Natural science" includes "Natural science" (ISC42), "Agriculture, forestry and fishery" (ISC62) and "Home economics (domestic science)" (ISC66).

Mathematics and Computer Science" is defined in accordance with ISC46.

Humanities" includes "Education, science and teacher training" (ISC14), "Fine and applied arts" (ISC18), "Humanities, religion and theology" (ISC20), "Social and behavioural science" (ISC30) and "Other fields of study" (ISC89).

Law and business" includes "Commercial and business administration" (ISC34), "Law" (ISC38), "Trade, craft and industrial programmes" (ISC52), "Transport and communications" (ISC70), "Service trades" (ISC78), and "Mass communication and documentation" (ISC84).

Engineering and architecture" includes "Engineering" (ISC54) and "Architecture and town planning" (ISC58).

tes on specific countries

Coverage

Austria: Data for the non-university level correspond to the calendar year 1994.

Denmark: Adult education is *excluded*.

France: "Mathematics and computer science" *includes* "Natural science". "Engineering and architecture" *includes* "Trade, craft and industrial programmes" and "Transport and communications". "Humanities" *includes* "Agriculture, forestry and fishery", "Home economics", "Service trades" and "Mass communication and documentation".

Hungary: "Natural science" *includes* "Mathematics and computer science". "Humanities" *includes* only "Law and business".

Ireland: Not only first-time graduates, but all graduations are *included* (unduplicated counts are not available).

Japan: "Natural science" and "Engineering and architecture" *include* "Mathematics and computer science". "Law and business" *includes* "Social and behavioural science". "Engineering and architecture" *includes* "Trade, craft and industrial programmes".

Korea: "Natural science" *includes* "Mathematics and computer science", "Humanities/General" *includes* "Law/Business".

Spain: "Engineering and architecture" *includes* "Trade, craft and industrial programmes".

Notes on interpretation

Belgium (Flemish Community), Canada, Japan, Korea, Netherlands, New Zealand, Norway, Spain, United States: The sum of all categories does not always equal 100 because the category "field of study unknown" (ISC99) is not taken into account in the calculations and is sometimes not negligible.

Canada: See notes on Indicator C5.

Czech Republic: The number of degrees in "Law and business" has increased significantly in recent years.

Denmark: Some programmes have been reclassified to different categories compared with the 1996 edition of *Education at a Glance*.

Spain, United Kingdom: See notes on Indicator G2.

Sources

See Indicator B1.

Indicator G4:	Production of high-level qualifications relative to the size of the labour force

General notes

Notes on methodology

The "Science" category takes into account the following fields of study: "Natural science" (ISC42), "Mathematics and computer science" (ISC46), "Engineering" (ISC5◄ "Architecture and town planning" (ISC58), "Agriculture, forestry and fishery" (ISC6 and "Home economics (domestic science)" (ISC66). Since the classification of t▶ fields of study has changed, the new results cannot be compared with the resul published in the 1995 edition of *Education at a Glance* and earlier editions.

Notes on specific countries

Coverage

Austria: Data for the non-university level correspond to the calendar year 1994. Da on non-university tertiary education are *underestimated*. Higher technical and vocatior schools are classified as upper secondary, although the qualifications are equal those of shorter non-university tertiary education programmes.

Japan, Spain: "Science" *includes* "Trade, craft and industrial programmes".

Notes on interpretation

United Kingdom: See notes on Indicator G2.

Sources

See Indicator B1.

GLOSSARY

NTINUING
UCATION AND
AINING FOR ADULTS

Continuing education and training for adults refers to all kinds of general and job-related education and training organised, financed or sponsored by authorities, provided by employers or self-financed. Job-related continuing education and training, as used in Indicator C7, refers to all organised, systematic education and training activities in which people take part in order to obtain knowledge and/or learn new skills for a current or a future job, to increase earnings* and to improve job and/or career opportunities in current or other fields.

RNINGS

Earnings from work

Earnings from work refer to annual money earnings, *i.e.* direct pay for work before taxes. Income from other sources, such as government aid programmes, interest on capital, etc., is not taken into account. Mean earnings are calculated on the basis of data for all people with income from work, including the self-employed.

Relative earnings from work

Relative earnings from work are defined as the mean annual earnings from work of individuals with a certain level of educational attainment* divided by the mean annual earnings from work of individuals whose highest level of education is the upper secondary level.

JCATIONAL
TAINMENT

Educational attainment is expressed by the highest completed level of education, defined according to the *International Standard Classification of Education**
(ISCED).

JCATIONAL COSTS

Educational costs represent the value of all resources used in the schooling process, whether reflected in school budgets and expenditures or not.

JCATIONAL
PENDITURE

Educational expenditure refers to the financial disbursements of educational institutions for the purchase of the various resources or inputs of the schooling process such as administrators, teachers, materials, equipment and facilities.

Current and capital

Current expenditure is expenditure on goods and services consumed within the current year, which needs to be made recurrently to sustain the production of educational services. Minor expenditure on items of equipment, below a certain cost threshold, are also reported as current spending. *Capital expenditure* represents the value of educational capital acquired or created during the year in question – that is, the amount of capital formation – regardless of whether the capital outlay was financed from current revenue or by borrowing. Capital expenditure includes outlays on construction, renovation, and major

repair of buildings and expenditure for new or replacement equipme
Although capital investment requires a large initial expenditure, the plant a
facilities have a lifetime that extends over many years.

Debt servicing expenditure

The stock of educational debt is the cumulative amount of funds borrowed
educational purposes by educational service providers or funding sour
and not yet repaid to the lenders. Such debt is usually incurred to finar
capital expenditure but may also be incurred, on occasion, to finance porti
of current expenditure. The term educational debt does not include ;
funds borrowed by students or households (student loans) to help finar
students' educational costs or living expenses. Expenditure on debt servic
consists of *i*) payment of interest on the amounts borrowed for educatio
purposes; and *ii*) repayment of loan principal. Neither component of exper
ture on debt servicing is included as capital or current expenditure.

Direct expenditure on educational institutions

Direct expenditure on educational institutions may take one of two forms: *i*) purcha
by the government agency itself of educational resources to be used
educational institutions (*e.g.* direct payments of teachers' salaries* b
central or regional education ministry); *ii*) payments by the governm
agency to educational institutions that have responsibility for purchas
educational resources themselves (*e.g.* a government appropriation or b
grant to a university, which the university then uses to compensate staff .
to buy other resources). Direct expenditure by a government agency does
include tuition payments received from students (or the families) enrolle
public schools under that agency's jurisdiction, even if the tuition payme
flow, in the first instance, to the government agency rather than to the ins
tion in question.

Financial aid to students

Financial aid to students comprises: *i*) *Government scholarships and other go*
ment grants to students or *households*. These include, in addition to scholars
and similar grants (fellowships, awards, bursaries, etc.), the following it
the value of special subsidies provided to students, either in cash or in k
such as free or reduced-price travel on public transport systems; and fa
allowances or child allowances *that are contingent on student status*. Any ben
provided to students or households in the form of tax reductions, tax su
dies, or other special tax provisions are not included; *ii*) *Student loans*, w
are reported on a gross basis – that is, without subtracting or netting
repayments or interest payments from the borrowers (students or ho
holds).

Intergovernmental transfers

Intergovernmental transfers are transfers of funds designated for education
one level of government to another. The restriction to funds earmarke
education is very important in order to avoid ambiguity about fun
sources. General-purpose intergovernmental transfers are not included
revenue sharing grants, general fiscal equalisation grants, or distributio
shared taxes from a national government to provinces, states, or *Länder*),
where such transfers provide the funds that regional or local authorities
on to finance education.

Public and private sources

Public expenditure refers to the spending of public authorities at all levels. Expenditure that is not directly related to education (*e.g.* culture, sports, youth activities, etc.) is, in principle, not included. Expenditure on education by other ministries or equivalent institutions, for example Health and Agriculture, is included.

Private expenditure refers to expenditure funded by private sources, *i.e.* households and other private entities. "*Households*" means students and their families. "*Other private entities*" include private business firms and non-profit organisations, including religious organisations, charitable organisations, and business and labour associations. Private expenditure comprises school fees; materials such as textbooks and teaching equipment; transport to school (if organised by the school); meals (if provided by the school); boarding fees; and expenditure by employers on initial vocational training*. Note that private educational institutions* are considered service providers, not funding sources.

Staff compensation

Expenditure on staff compensation includes gross salaries plus non-salary compensation (fringe benefits). *Gross salary* means the total salary earned by employees (including any bonuses, extra allowances, etc.) before subtracting any taxes or employee's contributions for pensions, social security, or other purposes. *Non-salary compensation* includes expenditure by employers or public authorities on retirement programmes, health care or health insurance, unemployment compensation, disability insurance, other forms of social insurance, non-cash supplements (*e.g.* free or subsidised housing), maternity benefits, free or subsidised child care, and such other fringe benefits as each country may provide. This expenditure does not include contributions made by the employees themselves, or deducted from their gross salaries.

Transfers and payments to other private entities

Government transfers and certain other payments (mainly subsidies) to other private entities (firms and non-profit organisations) can take diverse forms – for example, transfers to business or labour associations that provide adult education; subsidies to firms or labour organisations (or associations of such entities) that operate apprenticeship programmes; subsidies to non-profit organisations that provide student housing or student meals; and interest rate subsidies to private financial institutions that make student loans.

**UCATIONAL
STITUTIONS**

Educational institutions are defined as decision-making centres which provide educational services to individuals and/or other institutions. The definition is based on the point of view of management and control, which are normally carried out by a Director, Principal, or President and/or a Governing Board, (or similar titles such as Management Committee, etc.). In general, if a centre has a Director, Principal, or President and a Governing Board then it is classified as an institution. If it lacks these, however, and is controlled by an Instructional Educational Institution (see next paragraph), then it is not a separate institution but rather an off-campus centre of an institution. Where a centre is not managed by a Governing Board but is administered directly by a public education authority, the centre is classified as an institution in its own right.

Public and private institutions

Educational institutions are classified as either public or private according to whether a public agency or a private entity has the ultimate power to make decisions concerning the institution's affairs.

An institution is classified as *public* if it is: *i*) controlled and managed direct by a public education authority or agency; or *ii*) controlled and manage either by a government agency directly or by a governing body (Counc Committee, etc.), most of whose members are either appointed by a publ authority or elected by public franchise.

An institution is classified as *private* if it is controlled and managed by a no governmental organisation (*e.g.* a Church, a Trade Union or a business ente prise), or if its Governing Board consists mostly of members not selected by public agency.

In general, the question of who has the ultimate management control over institution is decided with reference to the power to determine the gener activity of the school and to appoint the officers managing the school. Th extent to which an institution receives its funding from public or priva sources does *not* determine the classification status of the institution.

A distinction is made between "government-dependent" and "independer private institutions on the basis of the degree of a private institution's depe dence on funding from government sources. A government-dependent p vate institution is one that receives more than 50 per cent of its core fundi from government agencies. An independent private institution is one th receives less than 50 per cent of its core funding from government agenci "Core funding" refers to the funds that support the basic educational servic of the institution. It does not include funds provided specifically for resear projects, payments for services purchased or contracted by private organi tions, or fees and subsidies received for ancillary services, such as lodgi and meals. Additionally, institutions should be classified as governme dependent if their teaching staff are paid by a government agency – eitl directly or through government.

EDUCATIONAL PERSONNEL: FULL-TIME, PART-TIME AND FULL-TIME EQUIVALENT

The classification of educational staff as "full-time" and "part-time" is bas on a concept of statutory working time (as opposed to actual or total work time or actual teaching time). Part-time employment refers to individuals w have been employed to perform less than the amount of statutory work hours required of a full-time employee. A teacher* who is employed for least 90 per cent of the normal or statutory number of hours of work of a f time teacher over the period of a complete school year is classified as a f time teacher for the reporting of head-count data. A teacher who is employ for less than 90 per cent of the normal or statutory number of hours of worl a full-time teacher over the period of a complete school year is classified part-time teacher. *Full-time equivalents* are generally calculated in person ye The unit for the measurement of full-time equivalents is full-time empl ment, *i.e.* a full-time teacher equals one FTE. The full-time equivalence part-time educational staff is then determined by calculating the ratic hours worked over the statutory hours worked by a full-time employee du the school year.

EDUCATIONAL RESEARCH AND DEVELOPMENT (R&D)

Educational R&D is systematic, original investigation or inquiry and associa developmental activities concerning: the social, cultural, economic and po cal context within which education systems operate; the purposes of edu tion; the processes of teaching, learning and personal development; the v of educators; the resources and organisational arrangements to support e cational work; the policies and strategies to achieve educational objecti and the social, cultural, political and economic outcomes of education.

The major categories of R&D personnel are researchers, technicians equivalent staff, and other support staff. Post-graduate students are cour as researchers, but reported separately within that category.

EDUCATIONAL SUPPORT PERSONNEL

Educational, administrative and professional staff covers non-teaching staff providing educational, administrative, and professional support to teachers and students. Examples are: principals, headteachers, supervisors, counsellors, librarians or educational media specialists, psychologists, curriculum developers, inspectors, and former teachers who no longer have active teaching duties. *Other support staff* covers personnel providing indirect support in areas such as: secretarial and clerical services, building and maintenance, security, transportation, catering, etc.

EMPLOYED POPULATION

The *employed population* is defined, in accordance with ILO guidelines, as all persons above a specific age who during a specified brief period, either one week or one day, were in paid employment or self-employment. It includes both those in civilian employment and those in the armed forces.

FIRST AND SECOND (OR FURTHER) EDUCATIONAL PROGRAMMES

A *first upper secondary programme* is any educational programme selected by a student in the ordinary cycle of upper secondary education that leads to a first qualification or certification at that level. A student is counted as enrolled in a *second (or further) upper secondary programme* if he or she has completed a normal or ordinary cycle of upper secondary education and has graduated from that sequence and then enrols in upper secondary education again, in order to pursue another upper secondary education programme. If the student then completes that programme (by obtaining the corresponding certification) he or she is considered a graduate of a second (or subsequent) upper secondary education programme. However, those students who enrol only in a partial programme, or repeaters who did not graduate from an ordinary cycle of upper secondary education but nevertheless repeat a cycle, are not counted as enrolled in a second or further educational programme.

GRADUATES

Graduates are those who were enrolled in the final year of a level of education and completed it successfully during the reference year. However, there are exceptions (especially at the university tertiary level of education) where graduation can also be recognised by the awarding of a certificate without the requirement that the participants are enrolled. *Completion* is defined by each country: in some countries, completion occurs as a result of passing an examination or a series of examinations. In other countries, completion occurs after a requisite number of course hours have been accumulated (although completion of some or all of the course hours may also involve examinations). *Success* is also defined by each country: in some countries it is associated with the obtaining of a degree, certificate, or diploma after a final examination; while in other countries, it is defined by the completion of programmes without a final examination.

GROSS DOMESTIC PRODUCT

Gross Domestic Product (GDP) refers to the producers' value of the gross outputs of resident producers, including distributive trades and transport, less the value of purchasers' intermediate consumption plus import duties. GDP is expressed in local money (in millions). Data for GDP are provided in Annex 2.

GROSS SALARY

Gross salary is the sum of wages (total sum of money that is paid by the employer for the labour supplied) minus employer's contributions for social security and pension (according to existing salary scales). Bonuses that constitute a regular part of the wages – such as a thirteenth month or a holiday or regional bonus – are included in the gross salary.

ISCED LEVELS OF EDUCATION

The levels of education used in this publication are defined with reference to the *International Standard Classification of Education* (ISCED). However, some further elaboration of the ISCED definitions has been undertaken to enhance international comparability.

Early childhood education (ISCED 0)

Early *childhood education* serves the dual purpose of giving the child daily car while the parents are at work and contributing to the child's social an intellectual development in keeping with the rules and guidelines of the pr primary curriculum. It covers all forms of organised and sustained centre based activities designed to foster learning, and emotional and social deve opment in children. The term *centre-based* distinguishes between activities institutional settings (such as primary schools, pre-schools, kindergarten day-care centres) and services provided in households or family settings. Th *standard starting age* at this level is *age* 3. Children aged 2 years or older ar however, also included in the statistics if they are enrolled in programm that are considered educational by the country concerned.

Primary level of education (ISCED 1)

Primary *education* usually begins at age 5, 6, or 7 and lasts for 4 to 6 years (th mode of the OECD countries is 6 years). Programmes at the primary level ge erally require no previous formal education. Coverage at the prima level corresponds to ISCED 1, except that an upper threshold is specified follows: in countries where basic education covers the entire compulsc school period (*i.e.* where there is no break in the system between primary ar lower secondary education) and where in such cases basic education lasts more than 6 years, only the first 6 years following early childhood educati are counted as primary education.

Lower secondary level of education (ISCED 2)

The core of *lower secondary education* continues the basic programmes of t primary level but usually in a more subject-oriented manner. This usua consists of 2 to 6 years of schooling (the mode of OECD countries is 3 year The common feature of lower secondary programmes is their entrar requirement, *i.e.* a minimum of primary education completed or demonst ble ability to benefit from participation in the programme. Coverage at t lower secondary level corresponds to ISCED 2, except that an upper thre old is specified as follows: in countries with no break in the system betwe lower secondary and upper secondary education and where lower second education lasts for more than 3 years, only the first 3 years following prim education are counted as lower secondary education. Lower secondary ec cation may either be *terminal* (*i.e.* preparing the students for entry directly i working life) or *preparatory* (*i.e.* preparing students for upper secondary edu tion).

Upper secondary level of education (ISCED 3)

Coverage at the *upper secondary level* corresponds to ISCED 3. This level usu consists of 2 to 5 years of schooling. Admission into educational programn at the upper secondary level requires the completion of the lower second level of education, or a combination of basic education and vocational exp ence that demonstrates an ability to handle the subject matter. Upper sec dary education may either be *terminal* (*i.e.* preparing the students for er directly into working life) or *preparatory* (*i.e.* preparing students for tert education).

Non-university tertiary level of education (ISCED 5)

The *non-university tertiary level* corresponds to ISCED 5. Programmes at level generally do not lead to the awarding of a university degree equivalent. A minimum condition of admission into a programme at level is usually the successful completion of a programme at the up secondary level. In some countries, evidence of the attainment of an equivalent level of knowledge, or the fulfilment of specific conditions (such as a combination of age and/or work experience) permits admission. In terms of subject matter, the core programmes at this level often tend to parallel those for which university degrees are granted. They are usually shorter, however, and more practical in orientation. Programmes of a level equivalent to this core vary widely in most countries and are provided through many organisations of very different types.

University tertiary level of education (ISCED 6 and 7)

This level of education refers to any programme classified as leading to a university degree or equivalent. Programmes at ISCED level 6 are intended for students who have successfully completed prerequisite programmes at the upper secondary level and who continue their education in a programme that generally leads to the award of a first university degree or a recognised equivalent qualification. University programmes at ISCED level 7 are intended for students who have completed a first university programme. Some countries do not distinguish, for purposes of international reporting, between ISCED levels 6 and 7.

EW ENTRANTS TO A :VEL OF EDUCATION

New entrants to a level of education are students who are entering any programme leading to a recognised qualification at this level of education for the first time, irrespective of whether students enter the programme at the beginning or at an advanced stage of the programme. Individuals who are returning to study at a level following a period of absence from studying at that same level are not considered new entrants. *New entrants to the tertiary level of education* are students who have never entered any tertiary level before. In particular, students who complete tertiary-level non-degree programmes (ISCED 5) and transfer to degree programmes (ISCED 6) are not considered new entrants. On the other hand, foreign students who enrol in a country's education system for the first time in a post-graduate programme are considered new entrants to the tertiary level. *Entrants to a level of education* are all students enrolled at that level who were not enrolled at that level during the previous reference period.

JRCHASING POWER IRITIES

Purchasing Power Parities (PPP) are the currency exchange rates that equalise the purchasing power of different currencies. This means that a given sum of money, when converted into different currencies at the PPP rates, will buy the same basket of goods and services in all countries. In other words, PPPs are the rates of currency conversion which eliminate the differences in price levels among countries. Thus, when expenditure on GDP for different countries is converted into a common currency by means of PPPs, it is, in effect, expressed at the same set of international prices so that comparisons between countries reflect only differences in the volume of goods and services purchased. The purchasing power parities used in this publication are given in Annex 2.

UDENTS

A *student* is defined as any individual participating in educational services covered by the data collection. The *number of students enrolled* refers to the number of individuals (head count) who are enrolled within the reference period and not necessarily to the number of registrations. Each student enrolled is counted only once.

UDENTS ENROLLED: LL-TIME, PART-TIME D FULL-TIME UIVALENT

Students are classified by their pattern of attendance, *i.e.*, full-time or part-time. The part-time/full-time classification is regarded as an *attribute of student participation* rather than as an attribute of the educational programmes or the provision of education in general. Four elements are used to decide whether a student is full-time or part-time: the units of measurement for course load; normal full-time course load, which is used as the criterion for establishing full-time participation; the student's actual course load; and the period of time over which the course loads are measured. In general, students enrolled in *primary and secondary level* educational programmes are considered to participate full-time if they attend school for at least 75 per cent of the school day or week (as locally defined) and would normally be expected to be in the programme for the entire academic year. Otherwise, they are considered part time. When determining full-time/part-time status, the work-based component in combined school and work-based programmes is included. At the *tertiary level*, an individual is considered full-time if he or she is taking a course load or educational programme considered to require at least 75 per cent of full-time commitment of time and resources. Additionally, it is expected that the student will remain in the programme for the entire year.

The *full-time equivalent* (FTE) *measure* attempts to standardise a student's actual load against the normal load. For the reduction of head-count data to FTE where data and norms on individual participation are available, course load measured as the product of the fraction of the normal course load for a full time student and the fraction of the school/academic year. [FTE = (actual course load/normal course load) × (actual duration of study during reference period/normal duration of study during reference period).] When actual course load information is not available, a full-time student is considered equal to one FTE.

STUDENT STOCK AND FLOW DATA

Stock data refer to the characteristics and attributes of a specified pool of students for the reference period under consideration. *Flow data* refer to individuals who join the pool at the beginning or during the reference period and to students who leave the pool during or at the end of the reference period. The *inflow* is the number of students who do not fulfil any of the conditions for inclusion in the stock data before the beginning of the reference period but gain at least one of them during this time. The *outflow* refers to the number of individuals who fulfil at least one of the conditions for inclusion in the stock as a group of students at the beginning of the reference period and who lose them all during or at the end of the reference period.

TEACHERS

A *teacher* is defined as a person whose professional activity involves the transmission of knowledge, attitudes and skills that are stipulated in a formal curriculum to students enrolled in an educational programme. The teacher category includes only personnel who participate directly in instructing students.

This definition does not depend on the qualification held by the teacher or on the delivery mechanism. It is based on three concepts: *activity*, thus excluding those without active teaching duties – although teachers temporarily not at work (*e.g.* for reasons of illness or injury, maternity or parental leave, holiday or vacation) are included; *profession*, thus excluding people who work occasionally or in a voluntary capacity in educational institutions;* and *educational programme*, thus excluding people who provide services other than formal instruction to students (*e.g.* supervisors, activity organisers, etc.), whether programme is established at the national or school level.

In vocational and technical education,* teachers of the "school element" of apprenticeships in a dual system are included in the definition, and trainers of the "in-company element" of a dual system are excluded.

Headteachers without teaching responsibilities are not defined as teachers but classified separately. Headteachers who do have teaching responsibilities are defined as (part-time) teachers, even if they only teach for 10 per cent of their time.

Former teachers, people who work occasionally or in a voluntary capacity in schools, people who provide services other than formal instruction, *e.g.*, supervisors or activity organisers, are also excluded.

TYPICAL AGES

Typical ages refer to the ages that normally correspond to the age at entry and ending of a cycle of education. These ages relate to the theoretical duration of a cycle assuming full-time attendance and no repetition of a year. The assumption is made that, at least in the ordinary education system, a student can proceed through the educational programme in a standard number of years, which is referred to as the theoretical duration of the programme. The *typical starting age* is the age at the *beginning* of the *first* school/academic year of the relevant level and programme. The *typical ending age* is the age at the *beginning* of the *last* school/academic year of the relevant level and programme. The *typical graduation age* is the age at the *end* of the *last* school/academic year of the relevant level and programme when the qualification is obtained. Using a transformation key that relates the levels of a school system to ISCED, the typical age range for each ISCED level can be derived.

TOTAL LABOUR FORCE

The *total labour force* or currently active population comprises all persons who fulfil the requirements for inclusion among the employed or the unemployed as defined in OECD *Labour Force Statistics*.

TOTAL POPULATION

The *total population* comprises all nationals present in or temporarily absent from the country and aliens permanently settled in the country. For further details, see OECD *Labour Force Statistics*.

UNEMPLOYED

The *unemployed* are defined, in accordance with the ILO guidelines on unemployment statistics, as persons who are without work, actively seeking employment and currently available to start work. The unemployment rate is defined as the number of unemployed persons as a percentage of the labour force.

VOCATIONAL AND TECHNICAL EDUCATION

Some indicators distinguish between "general and academic" and "vocational and technical" education. *Vocational and technical education* comprises educational programmes, generally offered by countries at the secondary and non-university tertiary level of education, that prepare participants for a specific trade or occupation or a range of trades and occupations within an industry or group of industries. Completion of a vocational or technical programme can result in direct entry into the labour force or prepare students for entry into technical and vocational tertiary programmes and institutions. Graduates of vocational schools often attend further educational programmes at the same or higher level.

School-based and combined school and work-based programmes

Some indicators divide vocational and technical programmes into school-based programmes and combined school and work-based programmes on the basis of the amount of training that is provided in school as opposed to training in the workplace. In *school-based* vocational and technical programmes, instruction takes place (either partly or exclusively) in educational institutions*. These include special training centres for vocational education run by public or private authorities or enterprise-based special training centres if these qualify as educational institutions. These programmes can have an on-the-job training component, *i.e.* a component of some practical experience in the workplace. In *combined school and work-based programmes*, instruction is shared between school and the workplace, although instruction may take place primarily in the workplace. Programmes are classified as combined school and work-based if less than 75 per cent of the curriculum is presented in the school environment or through distance education. Programmes that are more than 90 per cent work-based are excluded.

Contributors to this publication

any people have contributed to the development of this publication. The following lists the names of the
ountry representatives, policy-makers, researchers and experts who have actively taken part in the prepara-
ry work leading to the publication of this edition of *Education at a Glance – Indicators*. The OECD wishes to
ank them all for their valuable efforts.

INES Steering Group

r. Thomas ALEXANDER (OECD)
r. Karsten BRENNER (Germany)
r. Pat FORGIONE (United States)
r. Mark FREQUIN (Netherlands)
r. Walo HUTMACHER (Switzerland)
r. Arvo JÄPPINEN (Finland)

Mr. Ulf LUNDGREN (Sweden)
Mr. Graham REID (United Kingdom)
Mr. Kunio SATO (Japan)
Mr. Claude THÉLOT (France)
Mr. Alejandro TIANA FERRER (Spain)

National Co-ordinators

. Dan ANDERSSON (Sweden)
. John ASLEN (United Kingdom)
. Antonio AUGENTI (Italy)
. Birgitte BOVIN (Denmark)
. Karina BUTLAGINA (Russian Federation)
. Se Yeoung CHUN (Korea)
. Nicolaas DERSJANT (Netherlands)
. Antonio FAZENDEIRO (Portugal)
. José Luis GARRIDO (Spain)
. Heinz GILOMEN (Switzerland)
. Sean GLENNANE (Ireland)
. Hiroshi HIROSE (Japan)
. Douglas HODGKINSON (Canada)
. Anna IMRE (Hungary)
. Gregory KAFETZOPOULOS (Greece)
. Reijo LAUKKANEN (Finland)
. Jerome LEVY (Luxembourg)
. Dieter MAGERKURTH (Germany)

Ms. Dawn NELSON (United States)
Ms. Tatiana PALCHIKOVA (Russian Federation)
Mr. Friedrich PLANK (Austria)
Mr. Nicholas POLE (New Zealand)
Mr. Miroslav PROCHÁZKA (Czech Republic)
Mr. Johan RAAUM (Norway)
Mr. Jean-Claude ROUCLOUX (Belgium)
Mr. Ingo RUß (Germany)
Mr. Claude SAUVAGEOT (France)
Mr. Eamon STACK (Ireland)
Mr. Thorolfur THORLINDSSON (Iceland)
Mr. Alejandro TIANA (Spain)
Ms. Ann VAN DRIESSCHE (Belgium)
Mr. Victor VELAZQUEZ CASTANEDA (Mexico)
Mr. Paul VOLKER (Australia)
Mr. Ziya YEDIYILDIZ (Turkey)
Mr. Pavel ZELENÝ (Czech Republic)

Technical Group on Education Statistics and Indicators

Ruud ABELN (Netherlands)
Paul AMACHER (Switzerland)
Birgitta ANDRÉN (Sweden)
Antonio ARAUJO LOPES (Portugal)
Michele BARBATO (Italy)
Birgitte BOVIN (Denmark)

Ms. Ema LEANDRO (Portugal)
Mr. Yong-Kyun LEE (Korea)
Mr. Young-Chan LEE (Korea)
Ms. Elena LENSKAYA (Russian Federation)
Mr. Jerome LEVY (Luxembourg)
Ms. Marie LIDEUS (Sweden)

Mr. Fernando CELESTINO REY (Spain)
Mr. Vassilios CHARISMIADIS (Greece)
Mr. Se Yeoung CHUN (Korea)
Mr. Janos CSIRIK (Hungary)
Ms. Maria DE GRAÇA PACHECO (Portugal)
Mr. Eduardo DE LA FUENTE (Spain)
Ms. Gemma DE SANCTIS (Italy)
Ms. Mary DUNNE (Ireland)
Ms. Lena ERIKSSON (Sweden)
Mr. Timo ERTOLA (Finland)
Mr. Paul ESQUIEU (France)
Ms. Maia Ruth GOMES (Portugal)
Mr. Carlos GUTIERREZ HERNANDEZ (Mexico)
Ms. Katarzyna HANOWSKA (Poland)
Mr. Heikki HAVEN (Finland)
Mr. Walter HÖRNER (Germany)
Mr. Ho-Jin HWANG (Korea)
Mr. Jesus IBANEZ MILLA (Spain)
Mr. Mitsuo ISHII (Japan)
Mr. Per ISRAELSSON (Norway)
Ms. Michèle JACQUOT (France)
Ms. Nathalie JAUNIAUX (Belgium)
Ms. Vladimíra JELINKOVÁ (Czech Republic)
Mr. Steffen JENSEN (Denmark)
Mr. Tor JØRGENSEN (Norway)
Ms. Judit KÁDÁR-FÜLÖP (Hungary)
Mr. Gregory KAFETZOPOULOS (Greece)
Mr. Felix KOSCHIN (Czech Republic)
Mr. Hjalti KRISTGEIRSSON (Iceland)
Mr. Johan LASUY (Belgium)

Mr. Laszlo LIMBACHER (Hungary)
Mr. Douglas LYND (Canada)
Mr. Ian MAGUIRE (United Kingdom)
Mr. Robert MAHEU (Canada)
Ms. Maria MASTORAKI (Greece)
Ms. Aurea MICALI (Italy)
Ms. Inger MUNKHAMMAR (Sweden)
Mr. Andrzej OCHOCKI (Poland)
Mr. Friedrich ONDRASCH (Austria)
Mr. Cesar ORTIZ PEÑA (Mexico)
Mr. Wolfgang PAULI (Austria)
Mr. João PEREIRA DE MATOS (Portugal)
Mr. Nicholas POLE (New Zealand)
Mr. Stelios PSARAKIS (Greece)
Mr. Johan RAAUM (Norway)
Mr. Stanislaw RADKOWSKI (Poland)
Mr. Jean-Paul REEFF (Luxembourg)
Mr. Ron ROSS (New Zealand)
Mr. Ingo RUB (Germany)
Mr. Alexander SAVELIEV (Russian Federation)
Mr. Kazunari SAKAI (Japan)
Ms. Gülay SEVINE (Turkey)
Mr. Joel SHERMAN (United States)
Mr. Thomas SNYDER (United States)
Mr. Dave SORENSEN (United Kingdom)
Mr. Matti VÄISÄNEN (Finland)
Ms. Liselotte VAN DE PERRE (Belgium)
Mr. Max VAN HERPEN (Netherlands)
Mr. Paul VOLKER (Australia)
Mr. Jean-Pierre WITSCHARD (Switzerland)

Network A on Educational Outcomes

Lead Country: United States
Network Leader: Mr. Eugene OWEN

Ms. Gertrudes AMARO (Portugal)
Ms. Jean BRITTON (Canada)
Mr. Julian CRITCHLEY (United Kingdom)
Ms. Chiara CROCE (Italy)
Ms. Hara DAFERMOU (Greece)
Mr. Guillermo GIL (Spain)
Ms. Marit GRANHEIM (Norway)
Ms. Aletta GRISAY (Belgium)
Mr. Carlos GUTIERREZ (Mexico)
Ms. Judit KÁDÁR-FÜLÖP (Hungary)
Mr. Thomas KELLAGHAN (Ireland)
Mr. Kimmo LEIMU (Finland)
Ms. Jacqueline LEVASSEUR (France)

Mr. Sten PETTERSSON (Sweden)
Mr. Friedrich PLANK (Austria)
Mr. Niels PLISCHEWSKI (Denmark)
Mr. Dominique PORTANTE (Luxembourg)
Mr. Lucio PUSCI (Italy)
Ms. Rosemary RENWICK (New Zealand)
Mr. Michael RICHARDSON (United Kingdom)
Mr. Dieter SCHWEDT (Germany)
Mr. Arnold SPEE (Netherlands)
Ms. Jana STRAKOVÁ (Czech Republic)
Mr. Uri Peter TRIER (Switzerland)
Mr. Luc VAN DE POELE (Belgium)
Ms. Tzella VARNAVA-SKOURA (Greece)

Network B on Student Destinations

Lead country: Sweden
Network Leader: Mr. Allan NORDIN

Ms. Regina BARTH (Austria)
Ms. Gisèle BERLIE (Mexico)

Ms. Christine MAINGUET (Belgium)
Ms. Aurea MICALI (Italy)

Ms. Anna BORKOWSKY (Switzerland)
Ms. Birgitte BOVIN (Denmark)
Mr. Bertil BUCHT (Sweden)
Mr. Fernando CELESTINO REY (Spain)
Mr. Vassilios CHARISMIADIS (Greece)
Mr. Patrice DE BROUCKER (Canada)
Mr. Fayik DEMIRTAS (Turkey)
Mr. Laurent FREYSSON (EUROSTAT)
Mr. Sverre O. FRIIS-PETERSEN (Norway)
Mr. Michel-Henri GENSBITTEL (France)
Mr. Damian F. HANNAN (Ireland)
Mr. Olaf JOS (Sweden)
Ms. Eleni KECHRI (Greece)
Mr. Pavel KUCHAR (Czech Republic)
Mr. Young Chan LEE (Korea)
Mr. Jerome LEVY (Luxembourg)

Ms. Marion NORRIS (New Zealand)
Mr. Andrzej OCHOCKI (Poland)
Mr. Alf RASMUSSEN (Norway)
Ms. Aila REPO (Finland)
Mr. Erland RINGBORG (Sweden)
Ms. Emilia SAO PEDRO (Portugal)
Mr. Claude SAUVAGEOT (France)
Mr. Peter SCRIMGEOUR (United Kindgom)
Mr. Thorolfur THORLINDSSON (Iceland)
Ms. Éva TÓTH (Hungary)
Mr. Luc VAN DE POELE (Belgium)
Mr. Max VAN HERPEN (Netherlands)
Mr. Paul VOLKER (Australia)
Ms. Eveline VON GÄSSLER (Germany)
Mr. Ron F. WESSEL (Netherlands)
Ms. Shelagh WHITTLESTON (Australia)

Network C on School Features and Processes
Lead Country: The Netherlands
Network Leader: Mr. Jaap SCHEERENS

Ms. Bodhild BAASLAND (Norway)
Ms. Giovanna BARZANO (Italy)
Mr. Vassilios CHARISMIADIS (Greece)
Mr. Chris BRYANT (United Kingdom)
Mr. Ferry DE RIJCKE (Netherlands)
Mr. Philippe DELOOZ (Belgium)
Mr. Pol DUPONT (Belgium)
Mr. Jean-Claude EMIN (France)
Mr. Rainer FANKHAUSER (Austria)
Ms. Maria GAROFALO (Belgium)
Ms. Flora GIL TRAVER (Spain)
Mr. Steen HARBILD (Denmark)
Ms. Heidi HENKELS (Germany)
Mr. Sean HUNT (Ireland)

Ms. Anna IMRE (Hungary)
Mr. Arno LIBOTTON (Belgium)
Mr. Heikki LYYTINEN (Finland)
Ms. Marilyn McMILLEN (United States)
Mr. Ramon PAJARES BOX (Spain)
Mr. Nicholas POLE (New Zealand)
Mr. Walter SCHWAB (Eurostat)
Mr. Joel SHERMAN (United States)
Mr. Eugen STOCKER (Switzerland)
Ms. Jana ŠVECOVÁ (Czech Republic)
Mr. Alfons TEN BRUMMELHUIS (Netherlands)
Ms. Gonnie VAN AMELSVOORT (Netherlands)
Mr. Erik WALLIN (Sweden)
Mr. Ziya YEDIYILDIZ (Turkey)

Other experts and consultants for this publication

Nicolaas DERSJANT
Michael GARET
Trutz HAASE
Walter HÖRNER
Foad KAZEMZADEH
Douglas LYND

Mr. Jay MOSKOWITZ
Mr. Kenny PETERSSON
Mr. Ingo RUß
Mr. Joel SHERMAN
Mr. Alfons TEN BRUMMELHUIS
Ms. Gonnie VAN AMELSVOORT

OECD

Seiko ARAI
Giorgina BROWN
Michael BRUNEFORTH
Valérie CISSÉ
Catherine DUCHÊNE
Thomas HEALY
Georges LEMAÎTRE

Mr. Joseph LOUX
Ms. Marlène MOHIER
Ms. Carline PIETRASZEWSKI
Mr. Andreas SCHLEICHER
Mr. Thomas SMITH
Ms. Jean YIP

ALSO AVAILABLE

Literacy, Economy and Society
Results of the First International Adult Literacy Survey
(OECD and Statistics Canada) (1995)
ISBN 92-64-14655-5   FF 210   £26   US$40   DM 60

Employment Outlook (1997)
ISBN 92-64-15579-1   FF 250   £32   US$49   DM 73

Lifelong Learning for All (1996)
ISBN 92-64-14815-9   FF 255   £33   US$50   DM 74

Education at a Glance – Analysis (1996)
ISBN 92-64-15357-8   FF 50   £6   US$10   DM 15

Education at a Glance – OECD Indicators (1996)
ISBN 92-64-15356-X   FF 260   £34   US$50   DM 76

Education Policy Analysis (1997)
ISBN 92-64-15682-8   FF 50   £5   US$8   DM 15

Measuring What People Know: Human Capital
Accounting for the Knowledge Economy (1996)
ISBN 92-64-14778-0   FF 145   £20   US$29   DM 41

Literacy Skills for the Knowledge Society (1997)
ISBN 92-64-15624-0   FF 180   £23   US$35   DM 53

MAIN SALES OUTLETS OF OECD PUBLICATIONS
PRINCIPAUX POINTS DE VENTE DES PUBLICATIONS DE L'OCDE

AUSTRALIA – AUSTRALIE
D.A. Information Services
648 Whitehorse Road, P.O.B 163
Mitcham, Victoria 3132   Tel. (03) 9210.7777
                             Fax: (03) 9210.7788

AUSTRIA – AUTRICHE
Gerold & Co.
Graben 31
Wien I   Tel. (0222) 533.50.14
                             Fax: (0222) 512.47.31.29

BELGIUM – BELGIQUE
Jean De Lannoy
Avenue du Roi, Koningslaan 202
B-1060 Bruxelles   Tel. (02) 538.51.69/538.08.41
                             Fax: (02) 538.08.41

CANADA
Renouf Publishing Company Ltd.
5369 Canotek Road
Unit 1
Ottawa, Ont. K1J 9J3   Tel. (613) 745.2665
                             Fax: (613) 745.7660
Stores:
71 1/2 Sparks Street
Ottawa, Ont. K1P 5R1   Tel. (613) 238.8985
                             Fax: (613) 238.6041

12 Adelaide Street West
Toronto, QN M5H 1L6   Tel. (416) 363.3171
                             Fax: (416) 363.5963

Les Éditions La Liberté Inc.
3020 Chemin Sainte-Foy
Sainte-Foy, PQ G1X 3V6   Tel. (418) 658.3763
                             Fax: (418) 658.3763

Federal Publications Inc.
165 University Avenue, Suite 701
Toronto, ON M5H 3B8   Tel. (416) 860.1611
                             Fax: (416) 860.1608

Les Publications Fédérales
1185 Université
Montréal, QC H3B 3A7   Tel. (514) 954.1633
                             Fax: (514) 954.1635

CHINA – CHINE
Book Dept., China National Publications
Import and Export Corporation (CNPIEC)
16 Gongti E. Road, Chaoyang District
Beijing 100020   Tel. (10) 6506-6688 Ext. 8402
                             (10) 6506-3101

CHINESE TAIPEI – TAIPEI CHINOIS
Good Faith Worldwide Int'l. Co. Ltd.
9th Floor, No. 118, Sec. 2
Chung Hsiao E. Road
Taipei   Tel. (02) 391.7396/391.7397
                             Fax: (02) 394.9176

**CZECH REPUBLIC –
RÉPUBLIQUE TCHÈQUE**
National Information Centre
NIS – prodejna
Konviktská 5
Praha 1 – 113 57   Tel. (02) 24.23.09.07
                             Fax: (02) 24.22.94.33
E-mail: nkposp@dec.niz.cz
Internet: http://www.nis.cz

DENMARK – DANEMARK
Munksgaard Book and Subscription Service
35, Nørre Søgade, P.O. Box 2148
DK-1016 København K   Tel. (33) 12.85.70
                             Fax: (33) 12.93.87
J. H. Schultz Information A/S,
Herstedvang 12,
DK – 2620 Albertslund   Tel. 43 63 23 00
                             Fax: 43 63 19 69
Internet: s-info@inet.uni-c.dk

EGYPT – ÉGYPTE
The Middle East Observer
41 Sherif Street
Cairo   Tel. (2) 392.6919
                             Fax: (2) 360.6804

FINLAND – FINLANDE
Akateeminen Kirjakauppa
Keskuskatu 1, P.O. Box 128
00100 Helsinki

Subscription Services/Agence d'abonnements :
P.O. Box 23
00100 Helsinki   Tel. (358) 9.121.4403
                             Fax: (358) 9.121.4450

*FRANCE
OECD/OCDE
Mail Orders/Commandes par correspondance :
2, rue André-Pascal
75775 Paris Cedex 16   Tel. 33 (0)1.45.24.82.00
                         Fax: 33 (0)1.49.10.42.76
                         Telex: 640048 OCDE
Internet: Compte.PUBSINQ@oecd.org

Orders via Minitel, France only/
Commandes par Minitel, France exclusivement :
36 15 OCDE

OECD Bookshop/Librairie de l'OCDE :
33, rue Octave-Feuillet
75016 Paris   Tel. 33 (0)1.45.24.81.81
                         33 (0)1.45.24.81.67
Dawson
B.P. 40
91121 Palaiseau Cedex   Tel. 01.89.10.47.00
                             Fax: 01.64.54.83.26

Documentation Française
29, quai Voltaire
75007 Paris   Tel. 01.40.15.70.00

Economica
49, rue Héricart
75015 Paris   Tel. 01.45.78.12.92
                             Fax: 01.45.75.05.67

Gibert Jeune (Droit-Économie)
6, place Saint-Michel
75006 Paris   Tel. 01.43.25.91.19

Librairie du Commerce International
10, avenue d'Iéna
75016 Paris   Tel. 01.40.73.34.60

Librairie Dunod
Université Paris-Dauphine
Place du Maréchal-de-Lattre-de-Tassigny
75016 Paris   Tel. 01.44.05.40.13

Librairie Lavoisier
11, rue Lavoisier
75008 Paris   Tel. 01.42.65.39.95

Librairie des Sciences Politiques
30, rue Saint-Guillaume
75007 Paris   Tel. 01.45.48.36.02

P.U.F.
49, boulevard Saint-Michel
75005 Paris   Tel. 01.43.25.83.40

Librairie de l'Université
12a, rue Nazareth
13100 Aix-en-Provence   Tel. 04.42.26.18.08

Documentation Française
165, rue Garibaldi
69003 Lyon   Tel. 04.78.63.32.23

Librairie Decitre
29, place Bellecour
69002 Lyon   Tel. 04.72.40.54.54

Librairie Sauramps
Le Triangle
34967 Montpellier Cedex 2   Tel. 04.67.58.85.15
                             Fax: 04.67.58.27.36

A la Sorbonne Actual
23, rue de l'Hôtel-des-Postes
06000 Nice   Tel. 04.93.13.77.75
                             Fax: 04.93.80.75.69

GERMANY – ALLEMAGNE
OECD Bonn Centre
August-Bebel-Allee 6
D-53175 Bonn   Tel. (0228) 959.120
                         Fax: (0228) 959.12.17

GREECE – GRÈCE
Librairie Kauffmann
Stadiou 28
10564 Athens   Tel. (01) 32.55.321
                             Fax: (01) 32.30.320

HONG-KONG
Swindon Book Co. Ltd.
Astoria Bldg. 3F
34 Ashley Road, Tsimshatsui
Kowloon, Hong Kong   Tel. 2376.2062
                             Fax: 2376.0685

HUNGARY – HONGRIE
Euro Info Service
Margitsziget, Európa Ház
1138 Budapest   Tel. (1) 111.60.61
                             Fax: (1) 302.50.35
E-mail: euroinfo@mail.matav.hu
Internet: http://www.euroinfo.hu//index.html

ICELAND – ISLANDE
Mál og Menning
Laugavegi 18, Pósthólf 392
121 Reykjavik   Tel. (1) 552.4240
                             Fax: (1) 562.3523

INDIA – INDE
Oxford Book and Stationery Co.
Scindia House
New Delhi 110001   Tel. (11) 331.5896/5308
                             Fax: (11) 332.2639
E-mail: oxford.publ@axcess.net.in
17 Park Street
Calcutta 700016   Tel. 240832

INDONESIA – INDONÉSIE
Pdii-Lipi
P.O. Box 4298
Jakarta 12042   Tel. (21) 573.34.67
                             Fax: (21) 573.34.67

IRELAND – IRLANDE
Government Supplies Agency
Publications Section
4/5 Harcourt Road
Dublin 2   Tel. 661.31.11
                             Fax: 475.27.60

ISRAEL – ISRAËL
Praedicta
5 Shatner Street
P.O. Box 34030
Jerusalem 91430   Tel. (2) 652.84.90/1/2
                             Fax: (2) 652.84.93
R.O.Y. International
P.O. Box 13056
Tel Aviv 61130   Tel. (3) 546 1423
                             Fax: (3) 546 1442
E-mail: royil@netvision.net.il
Palestinian Authority/Middle East:
INDEX Information Services
P.O.B. 19502
Jerusalem   Tel. (2) 627.16.34
                             Fax: (2) 627.12.19

ITALY – ITALIE
Libreria Commissionaria Sansoni
Via Duca di Calabria, 1/1
50125 Firenze   Tel. (055) 64.54.15
                             Fax: (055) 64.12.57
E-mail: licosa@ftbcc.it
Via Bartolini 29
20155 Milano   Tel. (02) 36.50.83
Editrice e Libreria Herder
Piazza Montecitorio 120
00186 Roma   Tel. 679.46.28
                             Fax: 678.47.51
Libreria Hoepli
Via Hoepli 5
20121 Milano   Tel. (02) 86.54.46
                             Fax: (02) 805.28.86

Libreria Scientifica
Dott. Lucio de Biasio 'Aeiou'
Via Coronelli, 6
20146 Milano　　　　Tel. (02) 48.95.45.52
　　　　　　　　　　Fax: (02) 48.95.45.48

JAPAN – JAPON
OECD Tokyo Centre
Landic Akasaka Building
2-3-4 Akasaka, Minato-ku
Tokyo 107　　　　　Tel. (81.3) 3586.2016
　　　　　　　　　　Fax: (81.3) 3584.7929

KOREA – CORÉE
Kyobo Book Centre Co. Ltd.
P.O. Box 1658, Kwang Hwa Moon
Seoul　　　　　　　Tel. 730.78.91
　　　　　　　　　　Fax: 735.00.30

MALAYSIA – MALAISIE
University of Malaya Bookshop
University of Malaya
P.O. Box 1127, Jalan Pantai Baru
59700 Kuala Lumpur
Malaysia　　　　　Tel. 756.5000/756.5425
　　　　　　　　　　Fax: 756.3246

MEXICO – MEXIQUE
OECD Mexico Centre
Edificio INFOTEC
Av. San Fernando no. 37
Col. Toriello Guerra
Tlalpan C.P. 14050
Mexico D.F.　　　　Tel. (525) 528.10.38
　　　　　　　　　　Fax: (525) 606.13.07
E-mail: ocde@rtn.net.mx

NETHERLANDS – PAYS-BAS
SDU Uitgeverij Plantijnstraat
Externe Fondsen
Postbus 20014
2500 EA's-Gravenhage　Tel. (070) 37.89.880
Voor bestellingen:　　Fax: (070) 34.75.778

Subscription Agency/　　Agence d'abonnements :
SWETS & ZEITLINGER BV
Heereweg 347B
P.O. Box 830
2160 SZ Lisse　　　Tel. 252.435.111
　　　　　　　　　　Fax: 252.415.888

**NEW ZEALAND –
NOUVELLE-ZÉLANDE**
GPLegislation Services
P.O. Box 12418
Thorndon, Wellington　Tel. (04) 496.5655
　　　　　　　　　　Fax: (04) 496.5698

NORWAY – NORVÈGE
NIC INFO A/S
Ostensjoveien 18
P.O. Box 6512 Etterstad
0606 Oslo　　　　　Tel. (22) 97.45.00
　　　　　　　　　　Fax: (22) 97.45.45

PAKISTAN
Mirza Book Agency
65 Shahrah Quaid-E-Azam
Lahore 54000　　　Tel. (42) 735.36.01
　　　　　　　　　　Fax: (42) 576.37.14

PHILIPPINE – PHILIPPINES
International Booksource Center Inc.
Rm 179/920 Cityland 10 Condo Tower 2
HV dela Costa Ext cor Valero St.
Makati Metro Manila　Tel. (632) 817 9676
　　　　　　　　　　Fax: (632) 817 1741

POLAND – POLOGNE
Ars Polona
00-950 Warszawa
Krakowskie Prezdmiescie 7　Tel. (22) 264760
　　　　　　　　　　Fax: (22) 265334

PORTUGAL
Livraria Portugal
Rua do Carmo 70-74
Apart. 2681
1200 Lisboa　　　　Tel. (01) 347.49.82/5
　　　　　　　　　　Fax: (01) 347.02.64

SINGAPORE – SINGAPOUR
Ashgate Publishing
Asia Pacific Pte. Ltd
Golden Wheel Building, 04-03
41, Kallang Pudding Road
Singapore 349316　　Tel. 741.5166
　　　　　　　　　　Fax: 742.9356

SPAIN – ESPAGNE
Mundi-Prensa Libros S.A.
Castelló 37, Apartado 1223
Madrid 28001　　　Tel. (91) 431.33.99
　　　　　　　　　　Fax: (91) 575.39.98
E-mail: mundiprensa@tsai.es
Internet: http://www.mundiprensa.es

Mundi-Prensa Barcelona
Consell de Cent No. 391
08009 – Barcelona　　Tel. (93) 488.34.92
　　　　　　　　　　Fax: (93) 487.76.59

Libreria de la Generalitat
Palau Moja
Rambla dels Estudis, 118
08002 – Barcelona
　　　(Suscripciones) Tel. (93) 318.80.12
　　　(Publicaciones) Tel. (93) 302.67.23
　　　　　　　　　　Fax: (93) 412.18.54

SRI LANKA
Centre for Policy Research
c/o Colombo Agencies Ltd.
No. 300-304, Galle Road
Colombo 3　　　　Tel. (1) 574240, 573551-2
　　　　　　　　　　Fax: (1) 575394, 510711

SWEDEN – SUÈDE
CE Fritzes AB
S–106 47 Stockholm　Tel. (08) 690.90.90
　　　　　　　　　　Fax: (08) 20.50.21

For electronic publications only/
Publications électroniques seulement
STATISTICS SWEDEN
Informationsservice
S-115 81 Stockholm　Tel. 8 783 5066
　　　　　　　　　　Fax: 8 783 4045

Subscription Agency/Agence d'abonnements :
Wennergren-Williams Info AB
P.O. Box 1305
171 25 Solna　　　Tel. (08) 705.97.50
　　　　　　　　　　Fax: (08) 27.00.71

Liber distribution
Internatinal organizations
Fagerstagatan 21
S-163 52 Spanga

SWITZERLAND – SUISSE
Maditec S.A. (Books and Periodicals/Livres
et périodiques)
Chemin des Palettes 4
Case postale 266
1020 Renens VD 1　　Tel. (021) 635.08.65
　　　　　　　　　　Fax: (021) 635.07.80

Librairie Payot S.A.
4, place Pépinet
CP 3212
1002 Lausanne　　　Tel. (021) 320.25.11
　　　　　　　　　　Fax: (021) 320.25.14

Librairie Unilivres
6, rue de Candolle
1205 Genève　　　　Tel. (022) 320.26.23
　　　　　　　　　　Fax: (022) 329.73.18

Subscription Agency/Agence d'abonnements :
Dynapresse Marketing S.A.
38, avenue Vibert
1227 Carouge　　　Tel. (022) 308.08.70
　　　　　　　　　　Fax: (022) 308.07.99

See also – Voir aussi :
OECD Bonn Centre
August-Bebel-Allee 6
D-53175 Bonn (Germany)　Tel. (0228) 959.120
　　　　　　　　　　Fax: (0228) 959.12.17

THAILAND – THAÏLANDE
Suksit Siam Co. Ltd.
113, 115 Fuang Nakhon Rd.
Opp. Wat Rajbopith
Bangkok 10200　　　Tel. (662) 225.9531/2
　　　　　　　　　　Fax: (662) 222.5188

**TRINIDAD & TOBAGO, CARIBBEAN
TRINITÉ-ET-TOBAGO, CARAÏBES**
Systematics Studies Limited
9 Watts Street
Curepe
Trinidad & Tobago, W.I.　Tel. (1809) 645.3475
　　　　　　　　　　Fax: (1809) 662.5654
E-mail: tobe@trinidad.net

TUNISIA – TUNISIE
Grande Librairie Spécialisée
Fendri Ali
Avenue Haffouz Imm El-Intilaka
Bloc B 1 Sfax 3000　Tel. (216-4) 296 855
　　　　　　　　　　Fax: (216-4) 298.270

TURKEY – TURQUIE
Kültür Yayinlari Is-Türk Ltd.
Atatürk Bulvari No. 191/Kat 13
06684 Kavaklidere/Ankara
　　　　　Tel. (312) 428.11.40 Ext. 2458
　　　　　　　　　　Fax : (312) 417.24.90

Dolmabahce Cad. No. 29
Besiktas/Istanbul　　Tel. (212) 260 7188

UNITED KINGDOM – ROYAUME-UNI
The Stationery Office Ltd.
Postal orders only:
P.O. Box 276, London SW8 5DT
Gen. enquiries　　　Tel. (171) 873 0011
　　　　　　　　　　Fax: (171) 873 8463

The Stationery Office Ltd.
Postal orders only:
49 High Holborn, London WC1V 6HB
Branches at: Belfast, Birmingham, Bristol,
Edinburgh, Manchester

UNITED STATES – ÉTATS-UNIS
OECD Washington Center
2001 L Street N.W., Suite 650
Washington, D.C. 20036-4922 Tel. (202) 785.6323
　　　　　　　　　　Fax: (202) 785.0350
Internet: washcont@oecd.org

Subscriptions to OECD periodicals may also be
placed through main subscription agencies.

Les abonnements aux publications périodiques de
l'OCDE peuvent être souscrits auprès des
principales agences d'abonnement.

Orders and inquiries from countries where Distribu-
tors have not yet been appointed should be sent to:
OECD Publications, 2, rue André-Pascal, 75775
Paris Cedex 16, France.

Les commandes provenant de pays où l'OCDE n'a
pas encore désigné de distributeur peuvent être
adressées aux Éditions de l'OCDE, 2, rue André-
Pascal, 75775 Paris Cedex 16, France.

12-1996

OECD PUBLICATIONS, 2, rue André-Pascal, 75775 PARIS CEDEX 16
PRINTED IN FRANCE
(96 97 04 1) ISBN 92-64-15622-4 – No. 49637 1997